THE DEAD SEA SCROLLS

The Dead Sea Scrolls

A New Translation

Michael O. Wise,
Martin G. Abegg Jr.,
and Edward M. Cook

HarperSanFrancisco
A Division of HarperCollins*Publishers*

REVISED EDITION

ISBN-10: 0-06-076662-X
ISBN-13: 978-0-06-076662-7

To my wife, Cathy

M.O.W.

To my wife, Sue, and our girls, Stephanie and Jennifer

M.G.A.

To Elizabeth and Tristan

E.M.C.

Contents

I. Prolegomena

II. Texts

III. Indices

Preface

The authors of the book, on the completion of their work, are acutely conscious of being part of a larger academic enterprise, and wish to acknowledge their debt not only to each other, but also to the greater world of Dead Sea Scrolls scholarship. We of the new generation acknowledge the broad shoulders upon which we stand in the hope of furthering the understanding of these ancient texts. Although the names of the scholars of the first generation will become familiar as readers enter into the discussions that follow, let these take their proper places from the beginning: J. T. Milik, John Strugnell, John Allegro, and Andre Dupont-Sommer.

The authors also acknowledge their indebtedness to the academic fathers at whose feet they were introduced to the intricacies — and excitement — of Dead Sea Scrolls studies: Norman Golb, of the University of Chicago; Emanuel Tov, of the Hebrew University; Ben Zion Wacholder, of Hebrew Union College; Stanislav Segert, of UCLA; and the late William S. Lasor, of Fuller Theological Seminary. Their influence and example is evident on every page.

To our families we owe a great debt of gratitude. For the frequent occasions on which our labors were allowed to take precedence, we are thankful for their understanding. We are also mindful of their more concrete contributions. From the challenging questions ("So what?" — thanks, Jenny!) to the reading of chapters in the making (thanks, Cathy!), this work is richer.

To our editor at Harper San Francisco, Mark Chimsky, we offer our heartfelt gratitude for shepherding this book from its inception and for improving its every page. And to Ralph Fowler and Mimi Kusch for their respective design and production editing, we thank you for going above and beyond the call of duty.

The authors of this book complete their labors on the eve of the fiftieth anniversary of the discovery of the Dead Sea Scrolls. In the reckoning of one ancient Dead Sea Scrolls community, fifty years stood as a benchmark: the year of advancement from the strength of one's youth to the responsibilities of leadership. Yet in the history of scholarship, fifty years might not be enough time to publish an entire cache of manuscripts, much less produce definitive interpretations of them. This book, then, is more of a beginning of research on the scrolls than it is a completion. Many of the conclusions reached in the following pages will stand the test of time and become foundation stones for subsequent generations of students. Other affirmations — few, we hope — will be revised, overturned, and eventually forgotten. The field of Dead Sea Scrolls research is yet young, but therein lies its excitement. Out of that sense of excitement the authors offer this volume.

June 7, 1996.

Preface to the Revised Edition

Generations are a relative thing. In the Bible, a generation represents forty years; in twenty-first-century America, most people would probably put the number closer to twenty. In Dead Sea Scrolls research, a generation is more like ten years, so rapid is the life cycle, so compressed the span from young to old, from new to outdated. This revised edition of our translation therefore appears nearly a full generation after the first, and in that time much has happened of which we are keen to take account.

Perhaps the most obvious change in the years since the preparation of the first edition (1994 – 95) can be stated in a single word: publication. The "official" scholarly editions of virtually all the scrolls have now appeared. When we went to press in 1995, *Discoveries in the Judaean Desert,* vol. 10, was of recent appearance. Since then, all but one of the remaining volumes have finished their often extended gestation and come forth into the world: *Discoveries* now numbers thirty-nine volumes. Simple arithmetic will thus lead to two conclusions: first, everyone interested in the Bible and the biblical world, in Jesus and the New Testament, in Christianity and Judaism owes a large debt of gratitude to the many scholars who labored to produce those volumes, and most especially to the editor-in-chief of the project since the early 1990s, Emanuel Tov. We the authors owe that debt personally and especially, and so we say thank you.

Second, arithmetic (or, put precisely, subtraction) reveals that we as authors lacked official editions of many of the texts in this book when we produced the first edition. We made do as best we could. We used preliminary editions and photographs and this from here and that from there, and in particular the several fascicles of the work, edited by Martin Abegg Jr. and Ben Zion Wacholder, *A Preliminary Edition of the Unpublished Dead Sea Scrolls.* Nevertheless, we certainly did not possess anything like the riches of texts and tools that have appeared in the past ten-year generation, and it is that richness that calls forth this revised edition.

This edition continues the theme of arithmetic (or, put precisely, of addition). We have added numerous texts, partly because various critics suggested that we should, but mostly because our publisher has generously agreed that we could. Many of these appeared in some form in the German version of our book; others are making their debut. The intention in making these additions has been consistent with the intention of the first edition: completeness, so far as practical matters would allow. By "practical" we mean especially so far as the interest of general readers would dictate. Not every exiguous fragment of each fragmentary text appears in this book. But if in our judgment (and our editors'!) general readers would like to read it, or even just know it exists, it is here.

We have revised virtually every translation and every text introduction, often substantially. These revisions are an effort to take account of a generation's worth of change in the field of Dead Sea Scrolls research, and to give account as well. Some texts had to be pulled apart and reassembled as several works. In other cases seemingly separate works needed to be combined. In every such matter we have followed our own judgment, while naturally giving considerable weight to the published ideas and conclusions of many other scholars. An expanded Bibliography makes our deepest intellectual debts explicit. We have also responded to the suggestion of numerous users of the first edition to add page headers so as to alleviate troublesome navigation through the text.

Thus readers have a different and, we hope, better book than the first edition. Doubtless flaws of omission or commission remain despite our best efforts. We sincerely request that readers communicate to us about those flaws, so that a future edition may perhaps take advantage of those insights.

Michael O. Wise, Martin G. Abegg Jr., and Edward M. Cook
March 31, 2005

The Dead Sea Scrolls

I

Prolegomena

Introduction

Like Shangri-la, the term "Dead Sea Scrolls" has the power to evoke images and emotions even in those who have only a vague idea of what they are. The term is redolent of enigma, of intrigue, perhaps even of sacred mysteries; hovering in the background are images of caves, scrolls, barren deserts, and intense scholars hunched over tiny scraps of leather. A closer acquaintance with the scrolls does not dispel the air of mystery, because even when all the documents are read, translated, and explained, huge areas of uncertainty remain. Who wrote the scrolls, and when? What purpose did they serve, and what influence did they have? And what do they mean for us? Scholars still give different answers to all these questions.

We, the authors of this book, feel that the right answers are closer than ever. For decades, specialists have been able to study many of the scrolls, but not all of them. They reached conclusions that did not—could not—take into account all of the documents, many of which remained unavailable until recently.

Now all of the texts are available. Some of them support, and some undermine, cherished theories about the scrolls and their origins. Some of them suggest that long-discarded hypotheses may have been amazingly accurate. Others suggest new and subtle shadings of old interpretations. Most important, the scrolls, now that we can see all of them, testify to the astonishingly rich and fertile literary culture that gave birth to the foundational religious documents of Judaism and Christianity. We find here previously unknown stories about biblical figures such as Enoch, Abraham, and Noah—including a work explaining why God asked Abraham to sacrifice his only son, Isaac. A dozen writings that claim Moses as their author—yet are not a part of our Bibles—have come forth from the caves. Newly deciphered scrolls reveal ancient doctrines about angels, while others claim to be revelations by angels themselves, including the archangel Michael. Among the scrolls are never before seen psalms attributed to King David and to the leader of the conquest of the Holy Land, Joshua. The scrolls include extrabiblical prophecies by Ezekiel, Jeremiah, and Daniel. The last words of the patriarchs Joseph, Judah, Levi, Naphtali, and Amram, father of

Moses, are here among the scrolls. Still other writings pulse with the conviction that the end of the world is at hand and describe the rise of the Antichrist.

Yet the scrolls, like the Bible they often imitate, are more frequently honored than read. One reason for this neglect is the genuine difficulty of reading and translating texts that survive, many of them only in bits and pieces; another is that few of the published translations are intended for nonspecialists. This one is. In it we have aspired to be both responsible to the sources and understandable to the public.

Discovery and Publication

Archaeology is the study of *archaia,* "old things," but for a long time nobody knew that old things were interesting. The past, they thought, was pretty much the same as the present, and so in illuminated medieval Bibles King David is pictured in a medieval suit of armor. But people began to gain a sense of historical perspective during the Renaissance, and some things began to be valued *because* they were old. The wealthy began to collect antiquities: *archaia.* When Napoleon and his legions entered Egypt in the early nineteenth century, they opened up not only a new arena of cultural interchange, but a rich new source of *archaia.* The antiquities trade began in earnest at that time, along with colonialism, its sponsor, and a new science—archaeology.

Private collectors and professional archaeologists have always vied for the same antiquities. "That belongs in a museum!" is the cry of Indiana Jones and his professional colleagues as they struggle against mere collectors. Both parties, of course, are willing to pay for their antiquities under the right circumstances. An awareness of that fact led certain Bedouin tribesmen of the Taamireh tribe to preserve some old scrolls that they had found in the Judean desert in 1946 or 1947. They happened to enter a narrow cave, they said, and there they were, rolled up in stone jars. Could not someone be found to buy the manuscripts—old, dirty, and tattered as they were?

The original seven scrolls were early divided into two lots. One lot of four was purchased by the Syrian Orthodox archbishop of Jerusalem, Athanasius Samuel, the other lot of three by a scholar at the Hebrew University, E. Y. Sukenik. Samuel, wishing to authenticate the antiquity of his purchase through experts, eventually showed his texts to specialists at the American Schools of Oriental Research. They realized that Samuel's scrolls had been written at least two thousand years earlier, not the oldest *archaia* ever, but centuries older than the oldest manuscript ever discovered in the Holy Land. These excited scholars announced the discovery of the oldest known biblical manuscripts to the press on April 11, 1948, and Sukenik followed suit days later. The original seven scrolls are the *Charter of a Jewish Sectarian Association* (then called the *Manual of Discipline,* text 7 in the present collection), *Tales of the Patriarchs* (text 4), *Thanksgiving Hymns* (text 12), *A Commentary on Habakkuk* (text 2), the *War Scroll* (text 11), and two copies of the book of Isaiah.

Samuel took the scrolls to the United States and continued to try to sell them for years, without success. Potential buyers were aware that some scholars doubted the scrolls' authenticity and that questions lingered about the propriety of Samuel's removing the scrolls from their country of origin. Finally, in 1955, an agent of the young State of Israel paid Samuel $250,000 for his four scrolls, and the texts were reunited with Sukenik's three scrolls. Today they are the prize displays of the Shrine of the Book museum in Jerusalem.

But by 1955, no one really cared anymore whether Israel or the archbishop had the scrolls, because by then the industrious Bedouin had discovered nine more caves containing scrolls equally ancient. Another cave would turn up in 1956, for a total of eleven. The first astonishing discovery was succeeded by a steady stream, as the caves of Judea seemed eager to disgorge everything that had silently lain in their depths for millennia. These eleven caves, it should be noted, were all in the general vicinity of the Wadi Qumran, near the northwest end of the Dead Sea, and their treasures do not exhaust the total number of discoveries. Ancient writings were also found in caves near the Wadi Murabba'at and Nahal Hever, the Wadi Daliyeh, and in the ruins of Masada. Except for the Masada texts, the other discoveries came from times and milieux different from the Qumran texts. When people use the term "Dead Sea Scrolls," they sometimes mean all of these treasure troves, but more usually only the Qumran scrolls are meant. That will be our own usage in the pages that follow.

The total number of scrolls, when the books were intact, may have been as high as 1,000. Some have vanished without a trace, but scholars have identified the remains of about 900 separate scrolls. Their long centuries in the earth have reduced the vast majority of them to bits and pieces, mere scraps, some no larger than a fingernail. The fourth cave alone, where the biggest cache of manuscripts was unearthed, contained an estimated 15,000 fragments.

The great glut of material—a bonanza that far exceeded the wildest dreams of scholars—was not without its problems. The biggest was simply finding scholars equipped with enough knowledge and time to sort through the material. The government of Jordan—in whose territory, after 1948, the Qumran caves lay—allowed foreign scholars to form a team in the early 1950s to deal with all the incoming texts. These eight young men were to have the responsibility—and the privilege—of publishing everything.

The scrolls team began well, publishing its first volume of texts in 1955, *Discoveries in the Judaean Desert, Vol. 1: Qumran Cave 1* (abbreviated as *DJD* 1). This book contained additional fragments from the first cave the Bedouin had entered, pieces of documents that had turned up after the first seven scrolls were removed. "Work of this nature is of necessity slow," wrote G. L. Harding, director of the Jordanian Department of Antiquities, in the foreword. "It may well be a few years before the series can be completed." Harding could not have foreseen that forty years later the work would still not be complete. What explains the achingly slow pace of publication?

For one thing, the work required considerably more time than originally estimated. The first seven scrolls were all more or less intact (although some were in better repair than the others). The publishing program consisted of simply publishing photographs of the texts, which were (and still are) legible to anyone who can read ancient Hebrew. But undamaged scrolls like these turned out to be the exception. Most were fragmentary, and it required considerable painstaking work even to figure out which fragments originally belonged to the same scroll. That work necessarily had to be done before even preliminary translations and interpretations could be issued. (This work, by the way, still continues, and new "joins"—ways of connecting the fragments—are discovered from time to time. We propose a few ourselves in the pages that follow.)

The work of collecting and joining fragments, then, required much painstaking work and not a little ingenuity. The original team did this phase of its work well, but in hindsight it is clear that the task was too large and the team too small. The second volume of *DJD* came out in 1961, with texts from Murabba'at, and *DJD* 3 followed in 1962, containing all the texts from Caves 2, 3, 5, 6, 7, and 10, the so-called Minor Caves (for comparatively few scrolls were found in these caves). *DJD* 4 (1965) contained a single manuscript of the book of Psalms from Cave 11. Only with *DJD* 5 (1968) were several manuscripts from the "mother lode," Cave 4, issued.

At this point the already slowing pace of publication ground to a complete halt. As a result of the Six-Day War of June 1967, the Palestine Archaeological Museum, where the scroll fragments were stored, had become the property of the State of Israel. The members of the scrolls publication team—most of whom held decidedly pro-Arab convictions—were reluctant to continue under Israeli auspices, even after the authorities assured them they could continue their work without interference.

Eventually the Israelis and the team worked out an agreement, and the team published *DJD* 6, containing a number of minor texts, in 1977. By this time, however, the scholarly community was growing increasingly unhappy with the official scrolls team. The scrolls that had already been published had revolutionized study of the Bible, early Judaism, and early Christianity. The thought that hundreds of texts—more than half of what had been found—had never been seen outside a small circle of privileged editors was maddening, "the academic scandal of the century" in the words of Britain's Geza Vermes.

In fact, after a modus operandi had been reached with Israel, there was no good reason why the rest of the texts could not be published rapidly. The team had finished most of the initial work of reconstruction by 1960. But they had come to feel that a simple publication was no longer enough. The scrolls had become an entire subdiscipline of ancient history, and a "proper" publication now had to include vast analyses, large syntheses, and detailed assessments placing every fragment in its place in the history of Judaism, Christianity, and humankind. This was a daunting task for a large team; for a small team, it was simply impossible. And, although the team had slowly begun to increase its size—taking on a few Israeli members and select graduate students (those who studied with team members) in the 1980s—it still refused to allow other scholars access to the texts. In academia, of course, knowledge is power, and the scroll editors enjoyed theirs immensely.

Throughout the 1970s and 1980s, complaints about the slow pace of publication snowballed. Team members continued to publish individual texts from time to time, but control of the process always remained in their hands. Even when a text was published it seemed like noblesse oblige, and the perceived arrogance behind the slow pace of publication acted as a catalyst, goading "outsiders" to work at achieving unfettered access. New obstacles to publication had arisen as well: several members of the original team had died, and others were battling poor health.

Finally, in the early 1990s, the monopoly of the official team was broken, both from within and from without. In 1990, John Strugnell, head of the scrolls team since 1987, was forced to resign by the Israel Antiquities Authority for derogatory comments he made about Judaism. The Authority put Israeli scholars in charge of the project, and they began to invite more scholars to join the team, intending to speed up the pace of publication.

But outside forces played the decisive role. The official team had compiled a concordance—a comprehensive word list that also provides the context in which each word listed occurs—of all the words in the unreleased texts. Until now they had limited use of the concordance to themselves, but before Strugnell's departure he allowed certain academic libraries to receive copies of the concordance. Since the concordance listed each word along with one or two on either side of it, theoretically one might reconstruct not only entire lines, but entire scrolls.

A graduate student at Hebrew Union College in Cincinnati, Martin Abegg, with his adviser Ben Zion Wacholder, put the theory into practice. He carried out the reconstruction with the aid of a desktop computer, and the first volume of hitherto unreleased scrolls was published in September 1991. The publication was a bombshell, and it triggered another. Later that same month, the director of the Huntington Library in southern California, William Moffett, announced that the library had in its possession photographs of all of the unreleased Dead Sea Scrolls and that scholars would be allowed full access to them. These twin attacks on the monopoly of the scrolls team proved decisive. After initially threatening legal action, in November 1991 the new editor-in-chief of the official team, Emanuel Tov, announced that all scholars would have free and unconditional access to all the photographs of the Dead Sea Scrolls. This victory over scholarly secrecy and possessiveness made the book you hold in your hand possible.

How the Dead Sea Scrolls Were Written

What exactly are the Dead Sea Scrolls? The objects themselves are documents written with a carbon-based ink, usually on animal skins, although some are inscribed on papyrus. The scrolls were written right to left using no punctuation except for an occasional paragraph indentation—no periods, commas, quotation marks, or any of the other reader helps to which we are so accustomed. Indeed, in some cases there are not even spaces between words: the letters simply run together in a continuous stream. The codex, the early form of the book with pages bound on one side, had not yet been invented, so the "pages," or columns, were written consecutively on the scroll. To read them one slowly unrolled the scroll and then, to be polite, rerolled it, like rewinding a modern videotape. Not a few of the scrolls testify that the ancients failed to rewind as often as we do. The scrolls are written in several languages and half a dozen scripts, and though all are religious texts, within that category their contents are amazingly varied.

The Languages Used in the Scrolls

Prior to the discovery of the Dead Sea Scrolls, the dominant view of the Semitic languages of Palestine in this period was essentially as follows. Hebrew had died; it was no longer learned at mother's knee. It was known only by the educated classes, just as educated medieval Europeans knew Latin. Rabbinic Hebrew, the written language of the Mishnah, Tosephta, and other rabbinic literature of 200 C.E. and later, was considered a sort of scholarly invention—artificial, not the language of life put to the page. The spoken language of the Jews had in fact become Aramaic. Even in this tongue, literary production was thought to be meager. Accordingly, prominent scholars writing in the mid-1940s (on the eve of the scrolls' discovery) expressed doubts that the composition of a Semitic gospel was even possible. Edgar Goodspeed, for example, argued, "The gospel is Christianity's contribution to literature. It is the most potent type of religious literature ever devised. To credit such a creation to the most barren age of a never very productive tongue like Aramaic would seem the height of improbability. For in the days of Jesus the Jews of Palestine were not engaged in writing books. It is not too much to say that a Galilean or Jerusalem Jew of the time of Christ would regard writing a book in his native tongue with positive horror."*

The discovery of the scrolls swept these linguistic notions into the trash bin. Here were hundreds and hundreds of texts, tangible evidence of substantial literary productivity. Apart from copies of biblical books, about one out of six of the Dead Sea Scrolls is inscribed in Aramaic. Clearly the writing of an Aramaic Gospel was eminently possible. Yet the vast majority of the scrolls were Hebrew texts. Hebrew was manifestly the principal literary language for the Jews of this period. The new discoveries underlined the still living, breathing, even supple character of that language. A few texts pointed to the use of Hebrew for speech as well as writing. These works (for example, *A Sectarian Manifesto,* text 100) displayed a missing-link type of Hebrew, intermediate between the form of Hebrew used in the Bible and that used by the rabbis. Rabbinic Hebrew was shown to be no invention, but simply a development from ordinary spoken Hebrew of biblical times.

The scrolls have therefore proven that late Second Temple Jews used various dialects of Hebrew along with Aramaic. (These two languages are closely related—Aramaic is to Hebrew as French is to Italian.) For writing, however, they generally tried to imitate biblical Hebrew, an older form of the language. The situation would be analogous to our trying to write in the style of Elizabethan English. Not all the scroll writers could perform this feat equally well, so the "correctness" of the Hebrew varies considerably. Modern scholars actually appreciate the mistakes more than the deft performances, because the mistakes arise out of the writer's own language usage. The written form teaches us about the spoken.

A small minority of the scrolls was written in Greek. Their discovery has vouchsafed us a further glimpse into the linguistic complexity of first-century Jewish society. Hebrew, Aramaic, Greek: each was being used in particular

*Edgar Goodspeed, "The Original Language of the Gospels," in *Contemporary Thinking About Jesus: An Anthology,* ed. Thomas S. Kepler (New York: Abingdon-Cokesbury, 1944), 59.

situations of speech and writing. We are only just beginning to discover some of the rules for those uses, to bring to bear the more sophisticated perspectives of sociolinguistics. Since, as noted above, many of the Dead Sea Scrolls have but recently become known to a wide range of scholars, we are presently at an early stage of linguistic understanding.

Scripts Used for Writing the Scrolls

The script most commonly used to write these texts, whether Hebrew or Aramaic, has come to be called the *Jewish script*. Before the discovery of the scrolls, we knew relatively little about it. The Jewish script proves to be a development of an earlier script of the fourth and third centuries B.C.E., one that has been known to scholars since the nineteenth century. Perhaps surprisingly, that script had originally been used only for Aramaic, not for Hebrew. In the time of the scrolls it came to be used for Hebrew as well. Whereas Hebrew won the battle of the languages, when it came to script Aramaic was the victor. The scrolls reveal various forms of the Jewish script: beautiful, careful chancellery hands decorated with serifs, informal varieties, cursive and extremely cursive (i.e., illegible and extremely illegible!) types. From this script later developed the medieval scripts used to write Hebrew, and one descendant became that most often used in modern printed Hebrew Bibles and books.

Also surviving among a small group of the scrolls, however, is a developed form of the ancient Hebrew script that the Aramaic form had supplanted among the Jews. This script had been the standard in the days of David and Solomon and on down to the time of Jeremiah. In our period this form of writing, known as *Paleo-Hebrew,* was especially used for copies of the books of Moses (Genesis through Deuteronomy) and of Job. Presumably the scribes who chose it regarded those books as the oldest of the Hebrew Scriptures; Paleo-Hebrew was therefore most appropriate. The scrolls have shown, then, that the Jews of Jesus' day used scripts descended from both earlier Aramaic and earlier Hebrew scripts.

In addition, three different *cryptic,* or secret, *scripts* have emerged. Before the discovery of the scrolls, we had never seen these forms of writing. Although cryptic writing as a concept goes back as far as the third millennium B.C.E. in ancient Mesopotamia, these are the oldest forms associated with Hebrew ever discovered. The most important of these secret scripts has come to be called Cryptic Script A. Perhaps fifty scrolls use Cryptic Script A either entirely or for marginal notes (see especially the *Sage to the "Children of Dawn,"* text 65, and the *Phases of the Moon,* text 69).

As Edgar Allan Poe once noted in an essay, "A Few Words on Secret Writing": "Few persons can be made to believe that it is not quite an easy thing to invent a method of secret writing which shall baffle investigation. Yet it may be roundly asserted that human ingenuity cannot concoct a cipher which human ingenuity cannot resolve." Cryptic Script A, likewise, has yielded up its secrets to modern scholars, who have discovered that it is a simple substitution cipher—that is, each symbol of the cryptic alphabet corresponds to one symbol of the regular Hebrew alphabet.

Contents

As noted, all the scrolls, with a few minor exceptions, are Jewish religious texts. In a way, the fact that all the writings are religious is surprising. Why are there no copies of works on agriculture or animal husbandry—on secular, practical topics? The Jews in this period were an agricultural people. Wouldn't they want to read such secular books? Immediately, then, as we consider the contents of the scrolls, we begin to perceive an element of intentionality in their being gathered and hidden in the caves. This is not a random collection of "what there was"—not a chance sweeping from this bookshelf and that.

These religious writings are of two different kinds: the *biblical* and the *nonbiblical*. The *biblical* texts are copies of the Hebrew Bible (the religiously neutral term for the Christian Old Testament), forming about one-quarter of the total number of scrolls in the collection. The caches included a copy of every one of the books of the Jewish Bible, except, apparently, the book of Esther.

The "Dead Sea Bible" is the oldest group of Old Testament manuscripts ever found—at least a thousand years older than the traditional Hebrew texts from the early medieval period that have been the basis of all our modern Bible translations. In many cases, the scrolls have supported the traditional text of the Bible, but, in others, what they say in particular verses (their "readings") agrees with nontraditional versions like the Septuagint. (The Septuagint is the ancient translation of the Old Testament into Greek that was used among Egyptian Jews.) Sometimes the scrolls preserve readings we never knew existed.

At other times, the scrolls contain differences more profound than the readings of individual verses. They preserve "editions" of entire biblical books that differ from the traditional text. For example, two forms of the book of Jeremiah have emerged from the caves, one agreeing with that usually printed and translated in modern Bibles, the other about 15 percent shorter and with the contents in a different order. Several versions of the book of Psalms have likewise come to light. These versions differ strongly from one another, in particular from Psalm 90 onwards. Psalms 90–150 are arranged in different orders, and what is more, some of the manuscripts include additional, previously unknown, psalms. The content and form of the book of Psalms was manifestly in flux in the period when the scrolls were written. (To read some of these additional Psalms, attributed to David, turn to *Apocryphal Psalms,* text 17, and *Apocryphal Psalms of David,* text 151).*

In a similar vein, the discovery of the scrolls has uncovered the existence in this period of anthologies of biblical excerpts, of "rewritten Bibles," and of lost sources used, perhaps, by the writers of the biblical books. The first two of these categories were apparently methods of interpreting the Bible; in both, material was added to the biblical texts quoted. The additions were intended to give a particular spin to the biblical portions they were interpreting. Whether people understood these types of texts as less authoritative than the Bible itself is a legitimate question, given that the final contours of the Bible were not yet fixed. the *Healing of King Nabonidus* (text 47) is an example of a scroll manuscript that has preserved a source that may have inspired a biblical writer, in this case the author of Daniel. *Healing* is a more primitive version of a story about the Babylonian king Nebuchadnezzar that is familiar to modern readers from Daniel 4.

In short, the scrolls have proven that the Jews of Jesus's day knew and used more than one form of many biblical books, and it seems not to have disturbed them or driven them to resolve the differences. There was as yet no agreed-upon canon of the Bible. Which books would be included in the Bible and in what form or edition had not yet been decided. Doubtless different Jews and groups of Jews would have made different selections of authoritative books. Many of the Dead Sea Scrolls, though not a part of our Bible today, were certainly regarded as holy and authoritative by at least some Second Temple Jews. Only later, after 100 C.E., did a standard version of the Bible emerge.

The *nonbiblical* texts are, simply, copies of religious texts not found in the Bible. Based on our ignorance, these can be further subdivided into two categories. There are nonbiblical texts that were known before the discovery and others that were completely unknown until the scrolls were read.

The previously known nonbiblical texts are religious works like *Jubilees, 1 Enoch,* and the *Testaments of the Twelve Patriarchs.* Although Jews wrote them (or some early form of them) in Aramaic and Hebrew in ancient times, these writ-

*The biblical scrolls from Qumran have now been translated and published as *The Dead Sea Scrolls Bible: The Oldest Known Bible Translated for the First Time into English,* edited by Martin G. Abegg, Peter W. Flint, and Eugene Ulrich (HarperCollins, 1999).

ings did not survive in Jewish circles. They survived only among Christians, who adapted them and republished them as edifying literature, even sometimes adopting them as part of Holy Writ. Both *Jubilees* and *1 Enoch* survived, translated into the ancient language of Ethiopia, as components of the Old Testament of the Ethiopian church. The *Testaments* are extant only in Greek. Another example is Tobit. Translated into Greek in ancient times, it became a part of the Roman Catholic Old Testament canon. Until the Qumran finds, however, it was unknown in its original language. Copies in both Hebrew and Aramaic have turned up. These manuscripts in themselves would be enough to earn the title of Greatest Find of the Century.

But it is the texts that no one knew existed that give the Qumran collection its special quality, and they defy easy summary by their sheer variety and richness. They are the texts that are translated here, and the best way of finding out about them is just to read them. They include works of poetry and prose, and in them we find astrology, magic, and apocalyptic dreams of worldwide domination. There are biblical commentaries, descriptions of messiahs and Antichrists, stories about angels and giants; there is even a list of buried treasure—actual, not imaginary, treasure (*A List of Buried Treasure,* text 16). Yet even this part of the collection can be thought of as comprising two kinds of texts: the *sectarian* writings and the *nonsectarian* writings.

Such a division is much more controversial, and some scholars would rush to deny the validity of it. Yet even a rough-and-ready perusal of the materials shows that some texts presuppose a particular kind of organization and share a distinctive set of doctrines, a unique theological vocabulary, and a special perspective on history, things absent from other Qumran texts and other sorts of Judaism in general. Quite a few works advocate or presuppose an unorthodox calendar. Perhaps 40 percent of the nonbiblical Dead Sea Scrolls fall into this subgroup. These texts, it seems clear, were the central documents of the group or groups behind the Dead Sea Scrolls, and these are the ones we would designate as sectarian. Those to whom they belonged, who wrote most of them, called themselves the *Yahad,* a Hebrew word meaning "unity." This is the term we shall use for them throughout the book.

Of the many controversies surrounding the scrolls, probably the most lasting has been over the identification of the group responsible for the sectarian documents. This controversy continues as we write. It is quite rightly felt that if one could securely make such an identification, most of the other questions surrounding the scrolls and their nature would fall in line. Unfortunately, the identity of the sect has been, and remains, a knotty problem—although some of the newly available scrolls suggest new solutions.

The Origin of the Dead Sea Scrolls

It is not true that within a month after the discovery of the scrolls everyone thought Essenes wrote them, although in retrospect it may seem that way. The Essenes were one of the major groups among the Jews at the turn of the era. It is true that the initial press release in April 1948 mentioned them and both popular and academic studies of the first scrolls argued for Essene authorship. As the studies piled up, though, the "Essene hypothesis" did not have the field to itself.

Why did, and do, the Essenes look so attractive to those looking for the group behind the Dead Sea Scrolls? This question leads us in several directions.

First, it is important to understand the dating of the scrolls. Though a number of contracts and other nonliterary materials of uncertain provenience (probably not from Qumran) may have internal dates, none of the literary Dead Sea Scrolls is dated internally. Unlike medieval scribes, for example, their copyists did not use *colophons* (summarizing statements praising God and giving the date) to identify themselves. Relatively few works refer to identifiable historical events, and none of these writings was among the initial discoveries. The men who first saw the archbishop's scrolls guessed, on the basis of the letter shapes, that the scrolls were penned in the first century B.C.E., and almost all of the studies of the scroll writing since have confirmed that initial impression. In fact, the Qumran texts have so galvanized the science of paleography—the study of ancient writing and its evolution—that some proponents claim to be able to date a text within twenty-five years on that basis alone. Others (including the authors) are less confident, although few would argue with the broader view that paleography can date a text to within about a century. On that evidence, then, a few scrolls would date from the second century B.C.E., the vast majority from the first century B.C.E., and a smaller number from the first century C.E.

Beyond paleography, carbon-14 analysis provides another strand of evidence for dating. The carbon-14 atom, found in all life, decays to nitrogen-14 by releasing an electron—which produces the "tick" on a Geiger counter. Analysis of the extent of this decay can indicate a general date for objects made of organic material. In 1951, some of the linen scroll covers from Cave 1 were tested, and yielded a date between 60 B.C.E. and 20 C.E. Swiss scientists made additional tests in 1991, the technique having been refined in the interim to allow individual texts to be tested. Further tests, on different texts, were conducted in Arizona in 1994. All the Qumran texts tested fell between the parameters established by the broader view of paleography.

Finally, a few texts from Cave 4 actually refer to historical individuals by name. These references, though isolated, are of enormous importance, as will be seen below. For now, it is enough to state that the individuals so named are the Syrian king Demetrius Eukairos (r. 95–78 B.C.E.), King Alexander Jannaeus of Israel (r. 103–76), Queen Salome Alexandra of Israel (r. 76–67), King John Hyrcanus II (r. 63–40), and the Roman general Aemilius Scaurus (active in Israel 65–63). In addition, the *Commentary on Habakkuk* and the *Commentary on Nahum* make transparent references to the Roman invasion of Israel in 63 B.C.E. All of these individuals and events fall within the first century B.C.E., again broadly confirming the first centuries B.C.E. and C.E. as the time when the scrolls were put down in writing.

Artifacts found in or around the scroll caves also provide supporting evidence for dating the scrolls. Researchers found pottery in several caves, and pottery styles are the basis of most kinds of archaeological dating. Although dating by pottery types is subject to the same kinds of reservation as paleographical dating, archaeologists estimate that the Qumran pottery types are typical of the period 150 B.C.E.–100 C.E.

In short, there are good—indeed, overwhelming—reasons to locate those who wrote and copied the Dead Sea Scrolls in the Israel of the period ca. 200 B.C.E. to, say, 100 C.E. As it happens, we have only one comprehensive contemporary source for the history of Israel during that period: the writings of the Jewish historian Flavius Josephus. Josephus was a generation younger than the apostle Paul and spent the later years of his life under the patronage of the Flavian family in Rome writing about his own people. He wrote two books that tell us almost everything we know (or think we know) about Israel during that time: the *Jewish War* (abbreviated *War*), describing the Jewish revolt against the Romans from 66 to 73/74 C.E. and the events leading up to it, and the *Antiquities of the Jews* (abbreviated *Ant.*), a sweeping chronicle of Jewish history from creation to Josephus's own time.

In both books, Josephus describes what he calls three Jewish "schools of philosophy" that existed in his time: the Pharisees, the Sadducees, and the Essenes. It is what Josephus says about the Essenes that made the Essene hypothesis of the scrolls' origins so appealing. Particularly noteworthy in this respect is the correspondence between his description of the Essenes and the text we call the *Charter of a Jewish Sectarian Association* (text 7).

Some of the correspondences are as follows. Josephus says that "those entering the sect transfer their property to the order" (*War* 2.122); the *Charter* says that new members must give their property to the Overseer (6:19; see also 1:11–12; 5:1–2). Essenes emphasize the role of fate, or divine providence, in all things, unlike the Pharisees and Sadducees, who allow some scope for free will

(*Ant.* 13.171–173); the doctrine of predestination is common in the scrolls (see the *Charter* 2:13–4:26 for its most notable expression). The Essenes allow new members to join only after a period of one trial year, when the novice shows his aptitude for the Essene way of life, followed by two years as a probationary member with some privileges (*War* 2.137–138); according to the *Charter,* the would-be initiate must also pass a trial year as a member, and then a second year (note: not two *more* years) under probation (6:13–23) before becoming a full member.

There is also some striking agreement in details. For instance, Josephus mentions (and it says volumes about ancient mores that he considers it worth mentioning) that Essenes "avoid spitting in the midst of the group or on the right side" (*War* 2.147); the *Charter* also stipulates that "anyone who spits into the midst of a session of the general membership is to be punished" (7:13).

These data in themselves would naturally make anyone consider the Essenes as possibly the sect of the scrolls; but another description of the Essenes from an ancient travelogue clinched the matter for many. The Roman writer Pliny wrote in his *Natural History* that a sect called the Essenes lived "without women, sex, or money" by the shores of the Dead Sea, south of Jericho and north of En-gedi—an area corresponding to the region where the Dead Sea Scrolls were found. For many, that settled the matter: the Qumran group were Essenes. That view still prevails today, but it is facing new challenges.

The Standard Model

The Essene hypothesis is one leg of an influential three-legged theory about the Qumran texts that we shall call the Standard Model. There are two other legs to it, which will here be called the anti-Hasmonean hypothesis and the "mother house" hypothesis. The anti-Hasmonean hypothesis has to do with the historical origins of the Essene movement; the "mother house" hypothesis concerns the connection of the scrolls to the Khirbet Qumran ruins located near some of the caves. It will be convenient to consider each of the three legs in turn, starting with what we know about the Essenes.

Josephus goes into some detail about the beliefs and customs of the Essenes, but he says—and probably knew—nothing about their origin or how they came to have their beliefs. The scrolls, if they are of Essene origin, tell us more, although in veiled terms. The *Damascus Document* (text 1) and the commentaries, particularly the *Commentary on Habakkuk* (text 2), mention some of the prominent people and events involved in the founding of the group. Ordinarily such information would be of tremendous historical value. In the scrolls, however, there is a catch: most of the dramatis personae are named only under symbolic pseudonyms. Thus the apparent founder of the group is called only the Teacher of Righteousness; the prominent member of the group or groups opposing him is called the Man of the Lie (or sometimes the Spewer of Lies), who may be the leader of a sinister cabal called the Flattery-Seekers; and the sect's chief persecutor is designated only as the Wicked Priest. There is another ruler called the Lion of Wrath, and there is a menacing foreign power known as the Kittim.

A story can be pieced together from the various texts. The Teacher of Righteousness was a priest exceptionally gifted in religious insight; indeed, he had been granted special revelations from God about the true meaning of Scripture and the proper interpretation of the Law of Moses. Although he succeeded in gaining a following among other priests and righteous Jews, he was opposed by the Man of the Lie, who by his cunning rhetoric was able to dissuade many from submitting to the Teacher's precepts. The Flattery-Seekers also opposed the ministry of the Teacher. The Wicked Priest, however, initially seemed to be favorable to the Teacher; but "when he ruled in Israel" he showed himself to be irreligious, greedy, corrupt, and violent. He harried the Teacher and his followers, drove them into exile, and on at least one occasion made an attempt to have the Teacher killed—apparently without success. The Wicked Priest was threatened by Gentile powers and was captured and mistreated by them. There is no certain indication that the Teacher died a violent death, although that is possible.

The texts often combine elements of this story of the Teacher with imprecations on his and the group's enemies. In particular, the imminent coming of the rapacious "Kittim" is understood to be divine punishment on the nation for its rejection of the Teacher of Righteousness and his followers.

Scholars have ransacked the turbulent history of Israel in the second and first centuries B.C.E. to find scenarios that match the synopsis above. Very briefly, that history goes like this: after the Jews had thrown off the yoke of the Greek kings of Syria in 165 B.C.E., they were ruled by the priestly family of the Hasmoneans (also known as the Maccabees), leaders of the revolt. For slightly less than a century (152–63 B.C.E.), Judea was independent under Hasmonean rule, and even expanded its territory to something like its boundaries under David and Solomon. At the same time, however, the country was riven by religio-political factions, of which the two main ones were the Pharisees and the Sadducees.

The origins of both groups are obscure. Josephus first mentions them as existing, with the Essenes, during the reign of the early Hasmonean high priest Jonathan Maccabee (152–142 B.C.E., *Ant.* 13.171). It is certain that the Pharisees, largely a lay movement and the liberals of their day, generally opposed the Hasmoneans. The Sadducees, on the other hand, were composed primarily of priests and as the conservatives supported the Hasmoneans.

The Pharisees were distinguished in particular for their oral law, an unwritten adjunct to the Scriptures that claimed to provide the correct interpretation of Holy Writ. As Josephus wrote, "The Pharisees have imposed on the people many laws from the tradition of the fathers not written in the Law of Moses" (*Ant.* 13.297). These traditions of the fathers were the genius of the movement, for they spelled flexibility, enabling the Pharisees to adjust to new situations and to recast old laws as new circumstances required. Naturally, to the Sadducees and other non-Pharisaic groups among the Jews these same traditions were anathema. The Pharisees were nevertheless often able to impose their will because they were the group that enjoyed the most support among the general populace. They were the forebears of the rabbis, and rabbinic literature contains a fair number of laws and traditions that go back to the Pharisees. The Pharisees were also the group most often depicted in the Gospels as opposing Jesus and his interpretations of the Law, although in many respects Jesus stood close to their position. (Our strongest arguments are often within our own family.) Josephus further tells us that the Pharisees believed in resurrection and the existence of angels and spirits, whereas according to the New Testament (Acts 23:8) their principal competitors for power, the Sadducees, denied both.

Whether the Sadducees actually did deny these doctrines pure and simple, especially the existence of angels, is problematic. Angels appear in the books of Moses, after all, and every Jew embraced those writings. As a priestly party, the Sadducees may, however, have questioned the resurrection, since the ancient priestly doctrine of the afterlife—as found in the Hebrew Bible and in the apocryphal book of Sirach, for example—held that a shadowy existence in Sheol follows death. This ill-defined existence was much less desirable than earthly life. For the ancient priests true life after death consisted primarily in the continuation of one's name through children and grandchildren, and in leaving behind a "blessed memory." In any case, what is certain is that the Sadducees, whose primary support lay with the Jerusalem elite, denied the Pharisaic understanding of these matters. That denial was part conviction, part political necessity.

During the tenure of Alexander Jannaeus (103–76 B.C.E.) the Pharisees helped invite the Greek king of Syria, Demetrius III, to mount a military campaign against Alexander—for which they were severely punished when the revolt failed. Alexander later received very bad press from Josephus, who depicted him as a drunken, war-besotten monarch whose greatest pleasure, outside of drink and war, was consorting publicly with his many concubines. But as we shall see, not everyone among the Jews would have accepted Josephus's characterization, and the other side finds a voice among the scrolls.

Alexander and the Pharisees were for six years on opposite sides of a civil war among the Jews, and it was in this context that, desperate to remove Alexander, the Pharisees turned to the traditional Syrian Greek enemies of the Jews for help. Later, after Alexander's death, his widow, Salome Alexandra, came under Pharisaic influence and allowed them to suppress dissenting views. She was thus the antithesis of her husband. Whereas he had embraced, and been embraced by, the Sadducees and other priestly groups, she allied herself with the Pharisees. The reason for the switch was purely political. Knowing that she could not hope to appeal to both Sadducees and Pharisees, Salome (depicted by Josephus as a prudent and energetic queen, if a bit naive) simply calculated which group's support would most strengthen her own position.

After Salome's death (67 B.C.E.) yet another civil war broke out between her two sons, Hyrcanus II and Aristobulus II, partisans of the Pharisees and Sadducees, respectively. Thus the militant disputes between the principal religious factions among the Jews continued for yet another generation. Hyrcanus had already been the high priest while his mother reigned. Upon her death he simply assumed the royal mantle as well. But Hyrcanus was weak and had no real stomach for war or the other duties that monarchs of that period were expected to perform (at least, that's the way Josephus tells it). He abdicated the throne in favor of his much more ambitious brother, Aristobulus, but later, at the instigation of members of the Jerusalem elite, had second thoughts. War broke out between the brothers. The war ended only when the Romans invaded and added Judea to the list of Roman provinces in 63 B.C.E.

Qumran pseudonyms can be correlated with Judean history in two cases: the Kittim and the Wicked Priest. The Kittim, conquerors of nations, are pretty clearly the Romans; and the Wicked Priest, who was also a ruler of Israel, must have been one of the Hasmoneans. But which one? Rather than focus on the period from Alexander Jannaeus to the coming of the Romans, most proponents of the Standard Model look to an earlier time and favor early members of the family: either Jonathan Maccabee or his brother and successor, Simon (142–134 B.C.E.). Why?

One main reason is archaeological, and that leads us to the "mother house" hypothesis. The Standard Model stipulates that the Khirbet Qumran site (see below, on the archaeology of Khirbet Qumran) was the central headquarters of the Essene movement and the main dwelling place of the Teacher and his disciples after their rejection by the establishment. Proponents then proceed to read out a chronological framework for Essene history from the settlement history of the ruin. Since the site's history has been understood to begin around the middle of the second century B.C.E., the Wicked Priest must have been the Hasmonean then holding office—Jonathan or Simon.

That conclusion is then further buttressed by a certain reading of the *Damascus Document:*

> When in their treachery Israel abandoned Him, He turned away from Israel and from His sanctuary and gave them up to the sword; but when He remembered the covenant of the forefathers, He left a remnant to Israel and did not allow them to be totally destroyed, but in a time of wrath—three hundred and ninety years when He put them into the power of Nebuchadnezzar, king of Babylon—He took care of them and caused to grow from Israel and from Aaron a root of planting to inherit His land and to grow fat on the good produce of His soil. They considered their iniquity and they knew that they were guilty men, and had been like the blind and like those groping for the way twenty years. But God considered their deeds, that they had sought Him with a whole heart. So He raised up for them a Teacher of Righteousness to guide them in the way of His heart. (A 1:3–11)

The Standard Model understands this passage to be, in a nutshell, the history of the founding of the sect. The ambiguous statement about 390 years is interpreted so that the 390 years follow rather than precede (as is possible in the original Hebrew) the conquest of Nebuchadnezzar, which happened in 586 B.C.E. Subtraction yields the date 196, and an additional twenty years leads to 176 as the beginning of the Teacher's ministry. Since his activity could have lasted some thirty years, the Teacher and Jonathan Maccabee could easily have been contemporaries.

But what made Jonathan so wicked? There is no indication in Josephus or other sources that he was notably corrupt or violent. Here the model baldly asserts that Jonathan's great sin was precisely in accepting appointment as high priest of Israel under the auspices of the Syrian Greek king Alexander Balas in 152 B.C.E. The Hasmonean family, although of priestly stock, did not belong to the descendants of David's high priest Zadok, from whom alone many Jews thought the high priest could come. Of course, if this act was what made Jonathan wicked, then his successors to the high-priestly throne—in short, all the Hasmoneans—must likewise have been odious to the Essenes.

In turn, so the theory goes, their opposition to Hasmonean rule made the Essenes obnoxious to the government and to some other Jews, and they were hounded by Jonathan (or his successor, Simon) into exile in the Judean desert, where they built a settlement. There they remained for at least two centuries, isolated and insulated from the evil regime of the Hasmoneans, from the Roman successors to the Hasmoneans, and from the corrupt society of Judea, which had rejected the holy verities of the Teacher of Righteousness. During the Jewish revolt against the Romans in 66–73/74 C.E., they fell afoul of the Roman legions and their settlement was destroyed—but not before they were able to conceal a precious library in the nearby caves.

Such, in brief, is the understanding of the historical background of the Dead Sea sect that many scholars hold today. It would be pointless to deny the element of truth in the Standard Model, but is also fair to say that it has had much too easy a time of it in scholarly circles. There are significant gaps in this theory, and some of the new texts have the effect of spotlighting these gaps. Also, there are many weaknesses in the notion that the ruin was once the headquarters of the Essenes.

The Site of Khirbet Qumran

Khirbet Qumran lies on the northwest coast of the Dead Sea, within easy walking distance of Jericho and not difficult to reach from Jerusalem. (*khirbet* is the Arabic word for "ruin," and the name means "ruin of Qumran"; generally scholars use the shorthand reference "Qumran.") When the scrolls were discovered, their caves seemed to radiate north and south from this site, so early investigators thought it reasonable to suppose there might be some connection. Believing that an understanding of Khirbet Qumran could clarify the human situation behind the scrolls, they decided to excavate. The Department of Antiquities of Jordan, the Palestinian Archaeological Museum, and the École Archéologique Française de Jérusalem undertook joint campaigns beginning in 1951 and continuing through 1956. Unfortunately, Father Roland de Vaux, who led the excavations, never published the results scientifically. (Some have now appeared, and preparations to publish the rest are now ongoing, two generations later.) De Vaux did, however, publish a variety of preliminary reports, as did some of the others who had helped in the work. De Vaux also lectured widely on the findings, culminating in the Schweich Lectures of 1959, published as *Archaeology and the Dead Sea Scrolls.*

De Vaux distinguished four basic occupational levels (periods of habitation): one in the seventh century B.C.E., and, after a long hiatus, three others beginning about 135 B.C.E. and ending shortly after 70 C.E. The fourth and final period represented a few years of Roman occupation, so the two periods between 135 B.C.E. and 70 C.E. were the important ones in terms of the scrolls. De Vaux and other early proponents of the Standard Model linked these two periods to the sectarian scrolls. The group that had produced them was imagined to have lived on the site in those years. A layer of ash pointed to fiery destruction at the end of that time, the walls around the site being mined under in the fashion of Roman siege warfare. Iron arrowheads were also associated with this level. De Vaux argued that in 68 C.E., when their forces invested Jericho, the Romans had destroyed a resisting Qumran. De Vaux's view, therefore, was that a community lived in this abandoned region for a period of almost two centuries.

The excavators went on to equate Qumran with the Essene habitation on the shores of the Dead Sea described by Pliny. The findings of the excavations now fed into and became a crucial element of the Standard Model, bolstering the Essene hypothesis. Qumran, the theory held, had been the center of Essene activity, the "mother house" of the sect. To shore up this equation, de Vaux and others tended to push the resettling of the site in the Second Temple period back even earlier than 135 B.C.E. Archaeological findings offered no real support, but the move was necessary because they could hardly position Qumran as the center of the Essenes unless it had come into existence about when the Essenes had. As noted above, Josephus had written of the Essenes as existing before 135 B.C.E.

Estimating that between a hundred and fifty and two hundred people could inhabit the site itself, de Vaux and the members of his team theorized that numerous others must have lived in the nearby caves—not only in the ones where manuscripts were discovered, but also in the many others in the region where signs of habitation had turned up. Additional members of the community, they suggested, probably lived in huts and tents that they would have set up around Qumran. Common meals would have been held at the mother house, as shown by the hundreds of bowls and pitchers found in one of the rooms dubbed the "refectory." (Note the monastic terminology: the excavation team was led and dominated by Catholic priests. One cannot but suspect that in interpreting the excavation they peered down into the well of time and there beheld—themselves.)

The excavators were particularly excited about the discovery at Qumran of plastered tables. Here, they urged, were the very tables upon which the Dead Sea Scrolls had been inscribed, copied out by generation after generation of monkish scribes. The tables were found on the ground amidst rubble that had piled up with the collapse of a second-story room. The archaeologists reasoned that the tables had likewise fallen from that vanished room and named this room the *scriptorium*, "the room of the writing" (more monastic terminology). The unearthing of an elaborate waterwork system transversing the site led to the notion that these channels and pools served for elaborate Essene ablutions. All of these interpretations of the archaeological findings found their way into countless articles and books on the scrolls and, like other aspects of the Standard Model, were repeated so often that the mist of theory congealed and became solid fact.

In the past several years, however, a growing number of scholars have begun to question the nature of the connection between the scrolls and Khirbet

Qumran. The discoveries at the site were not, after all, *facts;* archaeology seldom yields those. What archaeology yields is not facts, but artifacts—which then have to be interpreted. Those interpretations, no matter how convincing they may seem, are not facts. Thus, Pauline Donceel-Voûte (one of those who has been responsible for full publication of the de Vaux excavations) argues that the principal evidence for the scriptorium—the plastered "tables"—points rather to a Roman-period *triclinium,* or dining room. The Romans did not sit down to eat, but instead reclined on cushioned couches. During the years of the Second Temple period, the Jews came to do likewise. She says the tables were actually couches. Suddenly the idea of the scriptorium no longer seemed self-evident, although it still continues to have its defenders.*

Before it could recover from this blow, the Standard Model's romantic image of sustained scribal activity at Qumran suffered yet another challenge with the release of all the scrolls in late 1991. Now that scholars could examine the totality of the manuscript evidence for themselves, a puzzling fact became evident: hundreds of different scribes appeared to have written the scrolls. Since each writer had a distinct handwriting, just as we do, it was possible to isolate individual scribes and determine which scrolls each had copied. Not only were hundreds of different scribes responsible for the texts, but very few seemed to have written more than one scroll. Only about a dozen "repeats" have been identified. Needless to say, this situation does not square very well with the theory-now-fact that Qumran scribes produced the scrolls at the site. If that theory were correct, what one would have expected to find is a limited number of hands, with many more texts traceable to each scribe. This is precisely what we do find at analogous sites, such as the ancient Jewish military colony at Elephantine, Egypt. Presumably a given scribe, laboring for a generation at Qumran, would have produced numerous manuscripts. At Elephantine, for example, which boasted a population some fifty times greater than that estimated for Qumran, one or two full-time scribes labored for each generation from about 500 to 400 B.C.E. Even allowing for the fact that some of the Qumran scrolls would have perished before being discovered in our century, release of the manuscripts has revealed a notably different profile. The logical inference is that most of the scrolls come from elsewhere. Indeed, once that much has been conceded, the burden shifts and it becomes necessary to prove that *any* of the scrolls were written at Qumran.

Other questions have arisen regarding the notion of Qumran as an Essene laura, or mother house. Recent investigation by Joseph Patrich and other Israeli

*Jodi Magness, *The Archaeology of Qumran and the Dead Sea Scrolls* (Grand Rapids: Eerdmans, 2002), 60–61.

archaeologists has uncovered no network of paths converging on the supposed communal center. Medieval monasteries always display such a network connecting the church and dining room to the dispersed cells. Moreover, Patrich has been unable to locate any traces of the hypothesized huts and tents, although in the case of desert archaeology such traces should still be evident. Ancient Bedouin temporary encampments in the desert are readily identifiable centuries later. Qumran was supposedly no mere temporary encampment, but a site occupied more or less continuously for two centuries. Yet there are no traces of any surrounding habitats. At most, then, about fifty people inhabited the site, only those who could fit within its walls. Consequently, most of the hundreds of communicants populating the picture drawn by de Vaux and the Standard Model have now been called into question.

Aerial photography has likewise revealed no paths linking the caves where the scrolls were discovered to the site of Qumran. The movement back and forth that would have produced a path evidently did not occur. Thus the caves could not have functioned as separate libraries or repositories to which sectarians would repair for reading and reflection.*

Nevertheless, still under the sway of the Standard Model, the archaeologists continued to attach the Essenes to the site, simply recalculating their existence there to a later date. Based on no particular evidence, they hypothesized that Herod the Great, put on the throne by the Romans, gave Qumran to the Essenes shortly after taking power from the Hasmoneans in 37 B.C.E. They apparently did not perceive how badly their reassessment of the site would cripple the Standard Model they invoked. By lowering the date of Essene occupation to 37 B.C.E., these investigators have kicked out the chronological underpinnings of the model's view of Essene beginnings. Qumran could hardly have been founded as the center of a breakaway new movement if that movement had already existed for a century. Nor could the Teacher of Righteousness have come here if it was a fortress under the control of the Hasmoneans, who, according to the model, were his bitterest enemies. In her recent full-scale treatment of the archaeology of Qumran, Jodi Magness, while not affirming Hasmonean construction, has agreed that the site was probably only founded later, between 100 and 50 B.C.E. Other respected archaeologists of Roman Palestine, such as Magen Broshi, have also adopted Magness's dating.

More and more, then, it is becoming clear that the archaeology of Qumran cannot bear the weight of a theory that it has too long been forced to sup-

*Patrich's conclusions have been disputed, but not conclusively refuted, by Magen Broshi and Hanan Eshel, "Residential Caves at Qumran," *Dead Sea Discoveries* 6 (1999), 328–48.

port. Even the strongest proponents of the Standard Model are beginning to admit as much. One former staunch adherent, Jonas Greenfield, conceded a few years ago, "The problem is we all bought de Vaux's version hook, line, and sinker." One can no longer reasonably argue for a strong connection between the site and the scrolls, though the two may have a weak connection; that is, though the site may have been used by the sect, it cannot have been their main location.*

Further Problems with the Standard Model

Not only is the connection of the ruin to the scrolls unsure, but the Essene hypothesis leg of the Standard Model is itself vulnerable to criticisms of one kind and another. As noted, the parallels between some of the scrolls, especially the *Charter,* and Josephus's description of the Essenes are striking. But the scrolls give no evidence of other notable characteristics of the Essenes. For instance, Josephus and Pliny and the Jewish philosopher Philo all describe the Essenes as celibate—indeed, it is perhaps their most arresting trait. But the scrolls contain no command to be celibate; on the contrary, numerous passages presuppose the opposite, that the group members will be married.

Philo also says that the Essenes pursued only peaceful occupations—and yet the *War Scroll* (text 11) gives detailed prescriptions for the conduct of a very real, though future, armed conflict against the powers of darkness.

Philo and Josephus also agree that the Essenes rejected slavery—and yet the *Damascus Document* has rules governing the treatment of slaves (11:12; 12:10–11). Another writing, called here *Ordinances* (text 19), further regulates slavery. Josephus mentions, among other things, the white garments of the Essenes—of which the scrolls say nothing.

If the classical sources describe the Essenes in ways that conflict or lack support from the contents of the scrolls, the opposite is also the case. The scrolls stress beliefs that Josephus and Philo say nothing about. The doctrine that God had commanded Israel to follow a 364-day solar calendar instead of a 354-day lunar calendar was a key tenet of the Qumran group. This peculiar calendar unifies the scrolls more than any other single sectarian element. Yet Josephus and Philo say nothing of the calendar. The scrolls strongly emphasize the role

*Edward Cook speculates that the Qumran site might have been used for purposes of ritual purification by the sectarians in Jerusalem; see his article "What Was Qumran? A Ritual Purification Center," *Biblical Archaeology Review* 22 (1996): 37–38, 48–51, 74–75.

of priests in the group leadership; but again, Josephus says not a word about priestly dominance, although he himself came from a priestly family and claims to have studied with the Essenes as a youth. Josephus also fails to mention the Teacher of Righteousness in his extensive descriptions of the Essenes.

There are ways to finesse all of these objections, and some of them are more or less convincing. For instance, Josephus, living so long after the Teacher, might not have heard of him, especially if, over the years, the Essenes had changed and were no longer so attached to the Teacher. Also, Josephus does allude to a sect of "marrying Essenes" (*War* 2.160–161)—and that could perhaps account for the lack of interest the scrolls show in celibacy. But the Essene hypothesis, however appealing, is hardly airtight.

A part of the difficulty may be in too ready acceptance of Josephus's over-simplifying division of the Jews into Pharisees, Sadducees, and Essenes. We know from other sources, both Jewish and early Christian, that there were more than three groups among Second Temple Jews. In fact, Josephus himself mentions others in passing or in detail, including Zealots and *sicarii,* and describes various movements that centered on charismatic leaders such as John of Gischala or Simon bar Giora. Trying to apply Josephus's three labels to a complex historical reality is like trying to use only the categories of "Catholic," "Protestant," and "Jew" to understand every shade of religious opinion in the United States in our own day. Which one was David Koresh, leader of the Branch Davidian group at Waco? Well, if forced, you would probably say "Protestant"—but such a label would prove singularly unhelpful for anyone studying Koresh and his followers. The same may well be true of the Teacher of Righteousness and his flock.

Finally, the idea that the Qumran group—Essenes or some other persuasion—originated in the second century B.C.E. out of opposition to the Hasmonean takeover of the high-priesthood is crumbling. The newly released scrolls offer this notion no support. In both old scrolls and new there are indeed many references to the corruption of Israel's rulers—to their rapacity, to their greed, to their complicity in the profanation of holy sites—but *not a single passage objects to the high priest's line of descent.* In fact, a close reading of Josephus will reveal that only the Pharisees ever objected to a Hasmonean as such holding the high-priesthood (*Ant.* 13.288–292).

In short, the Standard Model, while an elegant idea, has become less convincing, not more, as additional evidence has come forth from archaeology and the texts. The situation is reminiscent of Thomas Huxley, who in a very different context decried the great tragedy of "the slaying of a beautiful hypothesis by an ugly fact." Various ugly facts are now making themselves known, and many come from the new texts.

A New Proposal for Scroll Origins

Not only is there no evidence that the Dead Sea group objected to the Hasmonean pontificate as such, the newly available texts actually show the opposite: they held some of the Hasmoneans in high regard. One such writing is the so-called *In Praise of King Jonathan* (text 114), technically referred to as 4Q448. The difficult script on this scrap of leather has been brilliantly deciphered by Ada Yardeni. It is a poem in honor of a king of Israel known as Jonathan; the vital opening portion reads "For Jonathan the king" and goes on to say "and all the congregation of Your people Israel that is (dispersed) to the four winds of the heavens, let peace be on all of them and Your kingdom" (2:2–8). Yardeni and her colleagues, Hanan and Esther Eshel, believe that the text refers to the Hasmonean ruler Alexander Jannaeus (Hebrew name: Jonathan), who was the first Hasmonean officially to style himself as "king." If they are correct, as we believe they are, then *In Praise of King Jonathan* undermines the idea that the Teacher and his followers were on principle opposed to the Hasmoneans. Not only were they not opposed to them, they supported one of the most ill-famed of the family, for Alexander, as noted, was described by the historian Josephus as an extraordinary villain. (Proponents of the Standard Model have labored to explain *In Praise of King Jonathan*. Lawrence Schiffman, for example, can do no better than saying, "It may have happened that a text presenting an opposing view simply ended up there [in the collection]—an exceptional occurrence, but not impossible."* Indeed.)

At least one new text, then, has provided a big surprise. But as often with new discoveries, it has sent us back to the old texts with new eyes. One of the old texts, already published in the 1950s, is the *Commentary on Nahum*. The ancient Qumran group liked to pore over the ancient prophecies of the Hebrew Bible looking for foreshadowings of their own history. One result of this activity was a commentary on the prophet Nahum from Cave 4 (text 23); it was the first published scroll to refer to identifiable historical figures. One of them was Alexander Jannaeus, the "Lion of Wrath." Alexander, according to the writer, "used to hang men alive [. . . GAP. . .] in Israel in former times, for to anyone hanging alive on the tree, [the verse app]lies: 'Behold, I am against [you, says the LORD of Hosts']" (Frags. 3–4 1:7–9).

*Lawrence H. Schiffman, *Reclaiming the Dead Sea Scrolls* (Philadelphia: Jewish Publication Society, 1994), 240.

The crucial gap was initially filled in so as to yield "[*which had never been done*] in Israel in former times," expressing outrage at the act of crucifixion. But when another scroll, the *Temple Scroll* (text 155), was published in 1977, it became clear that, under certain circumstances, the scroll writers did approve of crucifixion: "If a man is a traitor against his people and gives them up to a foreign nation, so doing evil to his people, you are to hang him on a tree until dead" (64:7–8). It so happens that Alexander did crucify eight hundred men for the crime of siding with the Greek king Demetrius III and inviting him to invade Judea. With the publication of the *Temple Scroll,* it now seemed that the proper restoration of the gap was that suggested by Yigael Yadin: "The Lion of Wrath used to hang men alive, [*as it was done*] in Israel in former times."

Now, according to the *Commentary on Nahum,* some of those that the Lion of Wrath crucified were the Flattery-Seekers, and they are known in other historical sources as the Pharisees. We already knew that the Qumran sect hated the Pharisees, but it is now apparent that Alexander, the sworn enemy of the Pharisees during his reign, was a hero to the sect. The sect, in other words, heartily approved of Alexander's crucifying eight hundred Pharisaic rebels.

If the Teacher's group could side with Alexander Jannaeus, then clearly they need not have disapproved of any Hasmonean ruler on principle. This new chain of evidence makes it very unlikely that the group originated in a dispute concerning the high-priestly succession in the mid-second century B.C.E. Moreover, not only does this newly possible combination of evidence change our ideas about the origin of the sect; it suggests that they were fully involved in the internal politics of Israel in the first century B.C.E. They supported Alexander and opposed the Pharisees. One of the effects of the Standard Model was to distance the scroll writers geographically and ideologically from the Judean mainstream: they were insular monastic dropouts. But the new model suggested here brings the group back into the flow of history.

King Alexander, as we know from other sources, was himself sympathetic to the group known as Sadducees. What did the Qumran group think of the Sadducees?

Another newly published text sheds some light on that question. Although known to the tiny group of official scroll editors since the late 1950s, it was only in the 1980s that the existence of the work now called *Miqsat Maase ha-Torah* (MMT, for short), or the *Sectarian Manifesto* (text 100), was revealed. The *Manifesto* is a position paper of some kind and juxtaposes the views of three parties: a "we" group, a "you" individual who is a ruler, and a "they" group who are doing things in the Temple that the "we" group condemns. The "we" group further tries to persuade the "you" ruler to support them in this condemnation. Who are these three parties?

Certain scholars, most notably Schiffman of New York University, early recognized that the positions of the "we" group sometimes bore a striking resemblance to laws of the Sadducees described in rabbinic literature—so much so that Schiffman now leaps to redefine the Qumran sect as being itself Sadducees. We may prefer to look before we leap with him, but we can walk as far as the cliff's edge: if the "we" group are Sadducees (or a Sadducean subgroup or priestly sympathizers), then logically the opposing "they" group are Pharisees. The royal "you" to whom the text is addressed must be one of the Hasmonean rulers. The connections with rabbinic literature thus point to a tentative identification of the three parties, at least in general terms.

The social setting implicit in the *Manifesto* permits further deductions. Strugnell argues that the text was written against the background of the Sadducean loss of power over the Temple and the concomitant rise of Pharisaic control there: "[The *Manifesto*] was sent by a priestly faction that was later to evolve, under the influence of the Teacher of Righteousness, into the Qumran sect. Further, it was sent to keep the then High Priest of Israel faithful to those Sadducean priestly laws that were shared at that time by him and them."*

Yet the idea that Sadducees wrote the sectarian scrolls is vulnerable in some of the same ways that the theory connecting them to the Essenes is. The "Sadducean theory" does not easily square with important aspects of what we know about the Sadducees from other sources. According to Josephus, for example, the Sadducees of his day had no use for the doctrine of predestination. The New Testament further says that they did not believe in an afterlife or in angels (Acts 23:8). In contrast, we know from their writings that the authors of the sectarian scrolls strongly held all these convictions.

The evidence suggests, then, that the scrolls group resembled the Sadducees in some ways and the Essenes in others. Yet there are major obstacles to identifying the group straightforwardly as one or the other.

Apart from this problem of labeling the group, so far we can say the following. *In Praise of King Jonathan,* the *Commentary on Nahum,* and the *Manifesto,* taken together, seem to imply that the sect (whoever they were) took sides in the intra-Jewish political conflicts of the first century B.C.E. They favored Alexander over his opponents, the Pharisees, and favored Sadducean law over its opponents, also the Pharisees. The *Sectarian Manifesto* in particular seems to point to an era when the tide was turning away from Alexander's partisans—including the scroll writers—and in favor of his old enemies, the Pharisees. Josephus describes only one possible period of rising Pharisaic power in the Hasmonean period: the reign of Salome Alexandra, the widow of Alexander.

*J. Strugnell, "MMT: Second Thoughts on a Forthcoming Edition," in E. Ulrich and J. VanderKam, eds., *The Community of the Renewed Covenant* (Notre Dame, IN: University of Notre Dame Press, 1994), 72.

The *Commentary on Nahum* fits very well into this watershed era. Its author considers the activity of the Lion of Wrath to be past, while the "dominion of the Flattery-Seekers" is a tragic reality at the time he is writing. Since, as we have seen, the Lion was Alexander, the writer must have been living in the period after Alexander's death in the year 76 B.C.E. Salome Alexandra followed him in power, and she favored the Pharisees, granting them unprecedented sway over the internal affairs of the nation.

Josephus wrote of this turn of events with thinly veiled disapproval, and of Salome Alexandra's allowing it with outright disdain. The Pharisees, he noted,

> are a certain sect of the Jews that appear more religious than others, and seem to interpret the laws more accurately. Now [Salome] Alexandra hearkened to them to an extraordinary degree. . . . These Pharisees artfully insinuated themselves into her favour by little and little, and became themselves the real administrators of the public affairs: they banished and reduced whom they pleased; they bound and loosed men at their pleasure: and they had the enjoyment of the royal authority. . . . While [Salome Alexandra] governed other people, the Pharisees governed her.
> (*War* 1.110–112)

Another reason for focusing on the first century B.C.E. rather than the second rests in other newly published texts, collected here under the title *Fragmentary Historical Writings* (text 74). What gives these works special significance is their occasional mention of historical events in plain terms, without using the ciphers that commonly appear in the Qumran texts. Unfortunately, since the works are very fragmentary, mere phrases survive, but they are enough to tell us to what era they are referring. The phrases include "Shelamziyon secretly came," referring to Queen Salome Alexandra by her Hebrew name; "Hyrcanus rebelled against Aristobulus," referring to the sons of Salome and Alexander, Hyrcanus II and Aristobulus II; and "Aemilius killed," referring to the Roman general Aemilius Scaurus, who led the armies of Pompey into Judea in the 60s of the first century B.C.E.

As noted above, Salome reigned from 76 to 67 B.C.E., during which time her eldest son, Hyrcanus, was high priest. Aristobulus was king and high priest from 67 to 63 B.C.E., when the Romans arrived. A confused period ensued, with Roman dominion overlaying first civil war, then continuing general discord between Hyrcanus and Aristobulus and their followers. This confusion continued until 37 B.C.E. with the rise of Herod the Great. The *Fragmentary Historical Writings* seem to refer only to events in the first half of the first century B.C.E.—not to later events, and most particularly not to earlier ones. Conspicuous by their absence are any events of the second half of the previous century, when the Standard Model would locate the rise of the sectarians.

The prominence of the period 76–63 B.C.E. in the *Fragmentary Historical Writings* has not escaped the notice of adherents of the Standard Model, nor have they failed to see the implications. Forced to offer alternate explanations, they either fall silent or are reduced to a response something like Schiffman's: "These names designate heavenly bodies rather than actual people."* Schiffman offers no support for his proposal, and we have otherwise no reason to believe that heavenly bodies were known to the Jews of this period by human names.

Just as *In Praise of King Jonathan* sent us back to the *Commentary on Nahum* with a new perspective, so the *Fragmentary Historical Writings* send us back to another commentary with new appreciation, the *Commentary on Habakkuk* (text 2).

As noted earlier, the *Commentary on Habakkuk* was one of the first seven scrolls found in Cave 1. For over fifty years it has been the subject of intense scrutiny. The Qumran writer interpreted the biblical prophet's Chaldeans as the Kittim, "who are swift and mighty in war. . . . attacking and pillaging the cities of the land. . . . From far away they come, from the seacoasts, to eat up all the peoples like an insatiable vulture" (2:12–13; 3:1, 10–12). Scholars are agreed today that the term "Kittim" refers to the Romans, and that the advent of the Roman armies in the 60s of the first century B.C.E. led to the highly colored account of the commentary. There seems to be no good reason why the personalities of the commentary should be drastically separated in time from the Roman invasion, as required by the Standard Model. The Roman invasion is portrayed as a punishment for the sins of the Wicked Priest and the Man of the Lie. What makes most sense is that the Wicked Priest should have been active in the first decades of the first century B.C.E., and so also the Teacher of Righteousness.

If the Wicked Priest is from the first century B.C.E., there are only two candidates for the position: Hyrcanus II and Aristobulus II. Hyrcanus was supported by the Pharisees, Aristobulus by the Sadducees; hence, in view of the anti-Pharisaic cast of the scrolls, Hyrcanus II is the best suggestion for the Wicked Priest.

As for the Man of the Lie, it appears from a close reading of the sources that he was probably the head of the Pharisaic party. Rabbinic sources preserve the name of a prominent Pharisaic leader of the first century B.C.E., a man who was noted both for his violence and for his success in winning approval for his views: Shimeon ben Shetah. He may have been a brother or more distant kinsman of Salome Alexandra. Ben Shetah is known only from later rabbinic literature, but

*Schiffman, *Reclaiming the Dead Sea Scrolls,* 240.

the legends told of him there match up with what we know of Pharisaic power from Josephus. Shimeon was able and apparently willing to sentence people to death, and one story tells of his hanging eighty women in Ashkelon for witchcraft. From the Pharisaic perspective, the era was remembered as that of "Shimeon ben Shetah and Queen Salome," and it is said that during this golden age "wheat grew to the size of kidneys, barley to that of olive berries, lentils to that of gold denarii." Although it can be no more than a suggestion, it is interesting to speculate that the Man of the Lie may have been this proto-rabbinic figure. If he was, it would fit well with the idea that the Wicked Priest was Hyrcanus II. We are not the first to propose equating Ben Shetah with the Man of the Lie; F. F. Bruce argued the possibility as early as 1956. This is an example of what we meant when we spoke above of the newly released materials sometimes bringing us back to long-discarded hypotheses.

Finally, what of the Teacher of Righteousness? We know little about him, other than that the Wicked Priest persecuted him—an undertaking that would fit well, by the way, within the Pharisaic reign of terror described by Josephus during the reign of Salome Alexandra:

> [The Pharisees] became the real administrators of the public affairs; they banished and reduced whom they pleased; they bound and loosed men at their pleasure: and, to say all at once, they had the enjoyment of the royal authority. . . . Now she [Salome] was so superstitious as to comply with their desires, and accordingly they slew whom they pleased themselves.
> (*War* 1.111–113)

Josephus goes on to say that Aristobulus prevailed upon the queen to allow the enemies of the Pharisees to be banished from Jerusalem instead of executed, "so they were suffered to go unpunished, and were dispersed all over the country." And we are reminded that the Wicked Priest, according to the *Commentary on Habakkuk,* followed the Teacher to his "place of exile."

In short, we suggest a scenario markedly different from that of the Standard Model: the Teacher of Righteousness began his ministry late in the second or early in the first century B.C.E., perhaps during the reign of Alexander. After the Pharisees came to power under Salome, they persecuted the Teacher's group, which was sympathetic to the Sadducean establishment, eventually hounding the Teacher into exile. When Hyrcanus II became king, he renewed his efforts to destroy the Teacher and his group. The Roman intervention ended the Jewish civil war of Pharisee versus Sadducee, Hyrcanus versus Aristobulus. All of the verifiable historical references within the scrolls, and the apparent attitudes of the scroll writers to those references, fit this model exceedingly well. Of the approximately thirty-five identifiable references in the scrolls to people, processes, and events, virtually all of them fall in the first century B.C.E. This is not what one would expect if the Teacher and his group had existed fifty to seventy-five years before the dawn of that century. We should have historical references in texts identifiably inscribed in the second century, and we do not.

What, then, became of the Teacher and his group after this period? We have been using the Josephan categories of Pharisees, Sadducees, and Essenes as if these were distinct and different entities in the first century B.C.E., and indeed that is how Josephus presents them. But he was writing toward the end of the first century C.E., nearly two hundred years later, and the three parties he knew did not necessarily exist in the same form in the first century B.C.E. How much are today's Democrats and Republicans like the Whigs and Tories of two hundred years ago? In other words, the Qumran group may have been (or been part of) the ancestor movement of more than one group that existed in the first century C.E. We should consider a distinction seldom raised in research on the scrolls: those who write a text may have little or no direct connection with those who later read it. People may read a work because they find something attractive in it that was not necessarily foremost in the mind of the work's author. Sociologists refer to groups who adopt another's ideology as "carrier groups." Various carrier groups may well have been reading the scrolls in the century after the Teacher.

The Dead Sea Scrolls taken as a whole give evidence of a diverse movement, although not so diverse that it could accommodate just any point of view. This is a judgment supported both by the works we have called sectarian and by those that seem to be nonsectarian texts. This movement was clearly favorable to priests, inclined to support those rulers who submitted to priestly direction, and was violently averse to Pharisaism—perhaps because that ideology allowed lay teachers, the later rabbis, to revise traditional laws. The movement arose among the religious conservatives of its day, whereas the Pharisees were more liberal. In addition to supporting old legal positions against Pharisaic innovation, the Teacher's group held to a calendar that they claimed—and probably believed—was very old. This is the mind-set of conservatives. The Teacher's group supported conservative politicians such as Alexander Jannaeus and his son Aristobulus II, at the same time opposing those under liberal domination.

After the Romans came to power, the situation changed. The movement could no longer hope to influence the political course of events directly, although the priests could still attempt, by collaborating with the occupying powers, to control the religious practices of the people. We can guess that some in the movement did exactly that, while others were not willing to cooperate with the Romans. The uncooperative group still had two further choices to make: to seek the violent overthrow of Roman power or to wait quietly for the intervention of God. Some chose the latter option, and they may have been described by Josephus under the umbrella term "Essenes."

We know that many others chose the way of violence, and bands of Zealots and *sicarii* played a role in igniting the Jewish revolt in 66 C.E. Both these groups could have drawn inspiration from the primarily first-century B.C.E. texts now known as the Dead Sea Scrolls, for there they would have read of a group much like themselves, organized for holy war. That such freedom-fighting groups were reading these texts is more than speculation. The Dead Sea Scroll we have called *A List of Buried Treasure* (text 16) is a list of treasure trove from Herod's Temple, compiled as part of an effort to hide the gold, silver, and other valuables from the Romans, should the Temple fall. Logically, the compilers of the list must have been in control of the treasures they wanted to save. According to Josephus, it was freedom fighters and Zealots who seized the temple when the war broke out in 66, and they never relinquished control during the subsequent years of war against Rome and against other Jewish groups. Who but they could have drawn up this list? Thus, when it was found in Cave 3 among other Dead Sea Scrolls, we cannot but conclude that not only the *List,* but the other scrolls as well, may have been hidden by the same people.

Another clue to the identity of some first-century readers comes from the finds at Masada. The story of the Masada excavations is, wearily, much like that of the Qumran texts. In both cases, materials discovered in the late 1950s and early 1960s have only recently come to be fully available. The Masada finds present a profile similar to those of Qumran: various different handwritings, similar types of literary works (seventeen were found). The salient difference is that in the case of Masada we possess ancient eyewitness testimony as to who had collected these scrolls. Josephus was involved with the freedom fighters in the first stages of the war, and he gives us a name: the *sicarii*. This group, named for their penchant for using a *sica,* or short dagger, to assassinate collaborators with Rome, seized control of Masada at the time the war broke out. They made numerous forays against the Romans and collaborating Jews in the years that followed, and at the last, about to be overcome by Roman forces, they committed mass suicide.

Among the writings they left behind was a copy of the *Songs of the Sabbath Sacrifice.* This work also appears among the Dead Sea Scrolls, in fully nine copies (see text 101). Perhaps the most significant aspect of the *Songs* in the present connection is that it adheres to the 364-day calendar we have previously mentioned and that had been so important to the Teacher's followers more than a century earlier. This calendar was integral to what made the work so attractive for the *sicarii,* for it was an antiestablishment, conservative symbol as much in their own time as in the Teacher's. Indeed, for all the importance of the calendar to the scrolls, the only group of ancient Jews that followed it to whom the ancient sources give a name is the *sicarii,* the last defenders of Masada.

The Dead Sea Scrolls Today

We are immigrants from the past," writes Jack Miles in *God: A Biography.* For both Christians and Jews, Palestine in the first century C.E. is our homeland, our Old Country. We have immigrated from the world of the Dead Sea Scrolls, so it is only natural that, though they are two thousand years old, they still have much to say to us.

For Jews, the Qumran texts say, "Our family was larger than you knew." The watchword is *diversity.* Modern Judaism comes from Pharisaism, but in the first centuries B.C.E. and C.E. there were also other kinds of Judaism, and it was not obvious that the Pharisees would be the ones still standing at the end of the day. Understanding the world of the first century C.E. now means understanding the fact of diversity, and the scrolls have helped cultivate a sense of the historical complexity of the matrix of Judaism and of early Christianity. The scrolls teach, indirectly, a message the scroll writers themselves would have repudiated; that is, that there are different ways of being authentically Jewish. Any effort to "reclaim the scrolls for Judaism" must acknowledge that truth.

For Christians, the texts say, "You are more Jewish than you realized." There are many individual parallels between passages in the scrolls and the New Testament, and we point out some of these in the body of the book. But those connections are less important than certain broad views that the two groups of documents share: a pervasive dualism expressed as Light versus Darkness; the necessity of conversion; the idea that God's purposes are secrets revealed only to those who accept certain teachings; the high estimate placed on poverty—all are traits of early Christian belief that scholars used to attribute to the influence of Greco-Roman culture, not to Jewish background. Yet all are now attested in the scrolls. Early Christianity, we learn, was not a hybrid of Judaism and Hellenism—it was rooted in the native soil of Palestine.

For both Jews and Christians, the Dead Sea Scrolls group are the cousins we never knew we had; the scrolls themselves are lost letters from home. When they tell us about our forebears, they tell us about ourselves. Like all lost letters from home, they beckon to us, draw us irresistibly to hear their message. Like all letters from home, they are well worth reading.

A Dead Sea Scrolls Timeline

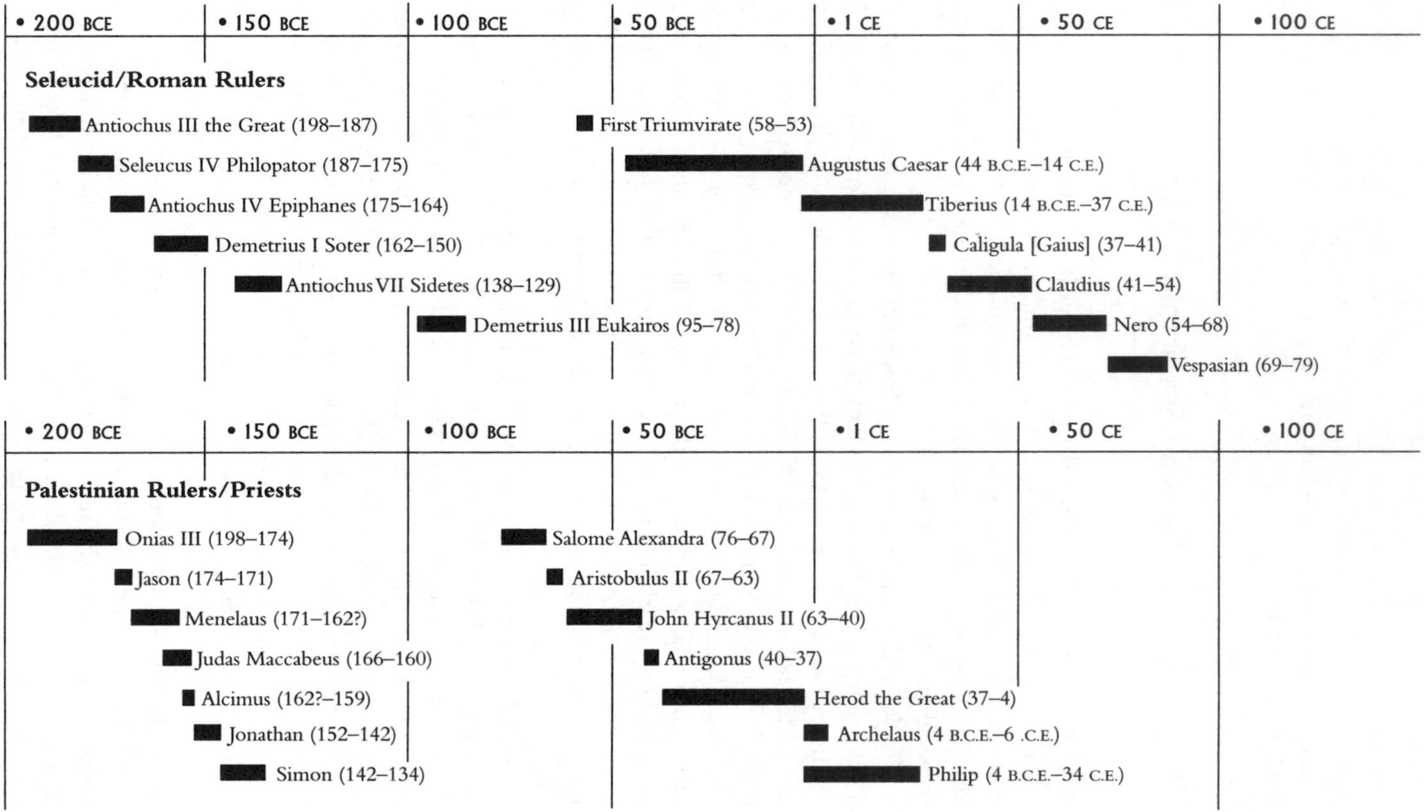

• 200 BCE
• 150 BCE
• 100 BCE
• 50 BCE
• 1 CE
• 50 CE
• 100 CE
Seleucid/Roman Rulers
Antiochus III the Great (198–187)
Seleucus IV Philopator (187–175)
Antiochus IV Epiphanes (175–164)
Demetrius I Soter (162–150)
Antiochus VII Sidetes (138–129)
Demetrius III Eukairos (95–78)
First Triumvirate (58–53)
Augustus Caesar (44 B.C.E.–14 C.E.)
Tiberius (14 B.C.E.–37 C.E.)
Caligula [Gaius] (37–41)
Claudius (41–54)
Nero (54–68)
Vespasian (69–79)
• 200 BCE
• 150 BCE
• 100 BCE
• 50 BCE
• 1 CE
• 50 CE
• 100 CE
Palestinian Rulers/Priests
Onias III (198–174)
Jason (174–171)
Menelaus (171–162?)
Judas Maccabeus (166–160)
Alcimus (162?–159)
Jonathan (152–142)
Simon (142–134)
Salome Alexandra (76–67)
Aristobulus II (67–63)
John Hyrcanus II (63–40)
Antigonus (40–37)
Herod the Great (37–4)
Archelaus (4 B.C.E.–6 .C.E.)
Philip (4 B.C.E.–34 C.E.)

• 200 BCE • 150 BCE • 100 BCE • 50 BCE • 1 CE • 50 CE • 100 CE

Palestinian Rulers/Priests

- John Hyrcanus I (134–104)
- Aristobulus I (104–103)
- Alexander Jannaeus (103–76)
- Herod Antipas (4 B.C.E.–39 C.E.)
- Pontius Pilate (26–36)
- Herod Agrippa I (37, 40–44)

• 200 BCE • 150 BCE • 100 BCE • 50 BCE • 1 CE • 50 CE • 100 CE

Events

- Teachers minist ry begins [Standard Model] (176)
- Maccabean Revolt (168)
- Antiochus IV desecrates the Temple (167)
- Jews throw off Syrian rule (165)
- Rededication of the Temple (164)
- Death of Judas Maccabeus (160)
- Samaritan temple destroyed by Hyrcanus I (113)
- Teacher's ministry [New Model] (late second or early first century B.C.E.)
- Wicked Priest active (first decades of first century B.C.E.)
- Demetrius III Eukairos [Syrian king] invades Palestine (88)
- Civil war between Aristobulus II and Hyrcanus II (67)
- Aemilius Scaurus leads Pompey's armies into Judea (63)
- Birth of Jesus of Nazareth (6 B.C.E.)
- Crucifixion of Jesus of Nazareth (31)
- Apostle Paul writes *Letter to the Galatians* (ca. 50)
- First Jewish revolt (66)
- Romans destroy Qumran [Standard Model] (68)
- Roman forces destroy Herod's Temple (70)
- Pliny the Elder writes *Natural History* (77)
- Roman forces destroy Masada (73–74)
- Josephus writes *War* (78) and *Antiquities* (ca. 95)

Reading a Dead Sea Scroll

In order to read a Dead Sea Scroll with proper appreciation and a modicum of critical acumen, it's important to know what you are reading. That may seem trite, but it's true. How does one go from a hugger-mugger of over 15,000 tiny scraps of skin and ink to about 900 full-blown manuscripts, and from there to published texts and translations? You should have some idea of the various steps involved in the process. Only then can you begin to think for yourself about what you will be reading in the following pages. Understanding the process by which the scrolls have been put together will help you to avoid the reader's cardinal sin—trusting an author too much. If we have certain ideas to present, we want you to be persuaded, not simply take our word for it. We want you to know just how much reconstructing the scrolls can be a matter of judgment (possibly mistaken) and uncertainty. We also want you to be able to make sense of the various sigla, brackets, and other paraphernalia that decorate the translations in this book.

As noted in the Introduction, the first seven Dead Sea Scrolls were discovered more or less intact. That can be said of very few of the hundreds of works that came to light subsequently. The early members of the scrolls editorial team found themselves facing an enormously complex jigsaw puzzle. After a short time, they worked out a *modus operandi*. Thousands of fragments were spread out on the tables of the Palestine Archaeological Museum, flattened under glass. The editors would walk from table to table, scrutinizing the fragments and trying to match them with this or that grouping they had already isolated. One of the editors, John Allegro, has described the guiding principle of those early efforts:

> One of the saving factors has been that of the four hundred [later, eight hundred] or so manuscripts we have had to deal with, surprisingly few were written by the same scribe, so that by recognizing the idiosyncrasies of one's own scribes one could be fairly sure that the piece belonged to his document.*

Handwriting was thus the foremost criterion that the editors used to separate fragments into piles and then into manuscripts. A second important guide was the skin on which the texts were inscribed. The treated hides of goats, ibex, and even gazelle used for the scrolls are not uniform in thickness or color.

*J. Allegro, *The Dead Sea Scrolls: A Reappraisal* (New York: Penguin, 1964), 55–56.

Each skin is, so to speak, its own animal: one might be thick, another thin; one might have a reddish cast, another could be nearly black. Study of the differences in the skins was therefore important for figuring out how to group fragments. But the skins could sometimes be misleading. Though they might have been uniform shortly after they were first placed in the caves, when they came out of the caves as manuscript fragments, they could differ markedly in appearance. The reason: the variable conditions in which they had spent the past two millennia. Some fragments were exposed to more light than others, some to more moisture or a different soil chemistry. Still, in general, handwriting and the appearance of the skins were reasonably trustworthy as dual criteria guiding the early work of separating out scrolls. For the hundred or so texts written not on skin, but on papyrus, scrutiny of the patterns of the plant fibers in the papyrus helped in the separating.

Work on proper identification of the fragments continues to this day. Although the early editors did their work of sorting admirably well, they were not infallible. Sometimes they made mistakes; in fact, we suggest a few that we think we've caught in the pages that follow (for example, see *Assorted Manuscripts,* text 121). Scholars continue to assess older conclusions. Advancing technology holds the promise of new approaches, although, since in most cases there is little doubt about the sorting, help will come mostly "at the margins." In this vein, researchers at Brigham Young University have recently begun to extract DNA from some of the fragments. Extraction does minimal damage to the materials, and DNA analysis makes it possible to identify the individual animal from which each fragment came. Where there is some question about a given fragment, or where fragments have never been assigned to any manuscript (there is a fairly sizable group of such pieces, all extremely tiny), this new approach may accomplish a modest breakthrough.

Once the early editors had grouped the fragments of a given manuscript together on one or more plates, they had photographs taken. Also, each manuscript was assigned a "Q-number," indicating which cave it had come from. For example, 4Q242 means Cave 4 of Q(umran), the 242nd manuscript from that cave. (This system did not yet exist when the first seven scrolls were discovered, so they have no number. They are designated by abbreviations of their names; e.g., 1QS means: Cave 1 of Q(umran), *Serek* [Hebrew for "order"].) As work progressed and new fragments were identified, or it became clear that questionable assignments were in fact mistaken and fragments were removed, the shape of a given manuscript changed, and new photographs were taken. Today we can study the entire sequence of photographs for each manuscript. For the most part, these photographs were taken under infrared light. Time had so blackened many of the fragments that the writing on them was nearly invisible to the naked eye. Infrared photography rendered the invisible visible. The use of infrared explains why you seldom see color photographs of the more fragmentary manuscripts; in the 1950s, color infrared photography was not yet possible (now it is).

Because these photographs were usually so much more legible than the manuscripts themselves, the early editors worked mostly with the photographs, and subsequent scholars have continued this practice. Autopsy of the original manuscript is still important, for it can resolve uncertainties (is this odd mark ink or just a spot on the skin?), but research on the scrolls centers on the photographs. Here too technology promises to improve our understanding in the future. Photographic methods developed for aerial reconnaissance have been brought down to earth and are now being applied to the scrolls. Researchers are beginning to use infrared imaging systems enhanced by electronic cameras and computer image-processing technology. Like the magical liquid we applied as children to reveal invisible ink, this method has brought out writing on fragments so dark that nothing was visible before, even in conventional infrared photographs. "We were using infrared photography like a blunt instrument," Bruce Zuckerman, one of the pioneers in applying the new techniques, has said. "Now we can sharpshoot, be precise and push technology beyond anything we've done before." So far the method has been applied to the *Tales of the Patriarchs* (text 4), with salutary results.

Working with the photographs today, a scrolls scholar will attempt to reconstruct the original manuscript as much as possible. (The early editors, overwhelmed as they were with multiple lifetimes of material, usually attempted more limited reconstruction. Thus, the fragments in the early volumes of *DJD* were often simply arranged by size from largest down to smallest.) Usually a scholar will not choose an ordinary photograph, but rather a transparency made from the photographic negative. The transparency is placed on a light table, the sort you often see in camera stores for use with slides. The scholar may work with two copies of the transparency simultaneously, sliding one on top of the other to try joining fragments, or checking an uncertain letter by sliding well preserved options for the letter underneath it, to see how the remaining bits of ink line up. Magnification is helpful to a degree. A jeweler's loupe, with a strength of 8x–12x, works best; too much magnification results in pixilation (all you see are dots). In recent years, great strides have been made with computer digital imaging of the texts. Many scholars today view high-resolution digital images of the scrolls on desktop computers, using software such as Adobe Photoshop to magnify, manipulate, and enhance the ancient letters.*

*See Bruce Zuckerman and Kenneth Zuckerman. "Photography and Computer Imaging." *Encyclopedia of the Dead Sea Scrolls* (ed. Lawrence H. Schiffman and James C. VanderKam; New York: Oxford University Press, 2000), 2.669–75.

A guiding principle for manuscript reconstruction is the recognition of congruent patterns of damage. Consider: as a scroll lay decomposing on the floor of its cave, it rotted away layer by layer, from the outside in. The scroll might also have been visited by insects or rats, which would eat away at the edges or at a fold. Worms could bore into the scroll. Assuming that the vermin ate through more than one turn of the scroll, more than a single thickness of skin, the damage pattern of the outer layer will continue some distance into the interior layers. An analogy would be the patterns of damage in your rolled-up morning newspaper left by the teeth of your overeager dog that brought it to you. The puncture marks and tears go several layers deep, right into the sports section.

Scholars study these patterns of damage, for they can help determine how surviving fragments of a scroll were positioned when it was intact. If two fragments manifest a congruent pattern, then they must once have been in some physical relation to one another. Perhaps one fragment originated near the center of the rolled scroll, and the other came from an outer layer overlying the first fragment. If the scholar can identify fragments that come from three contiguous columns, he or she is off to the races. He or she need merely measure the distance between fragments. The distance between consecutive layers of a rolled scroll will change by a mathematically predictable amount, decreasing as you move toward the center. Having identified three consecutive fragments, you can then calculate the diameter of the scroll at the point where the fragments stood, using the mathematical formula for the geometric shape of a regular spiral. (If you picture a scroll edge-on, you will see that from that perspective it actually is a tight spiral. If it's not too late, have a look at your damaged rolled newspaper, edge-on.)

At this juncture in the editing process a scholar will usually make a scale drawing of the scroll showing the proposed relation between the fragments. The photographs will not depict such relations, of course, so a drawing is needed. Now begins in earnest the difficult process of reading the words and trying to figure out what might have been lost in the portions of the scroll that have perished. The researcher copies or traces all the fragments and words from the photographs. In most cases the result is a series of legible letters or words that breaks off because of damage to the scroll, only to pick up a bit farther on. If the scholar is to have any chance of understanding a fragmentary scroll, he or she must try to imagine what was happening in the damaged, lost sections. How do the preserved portions relate? What is the flow of thought? Here the scale drawing helps, for one can lightly draw in a few tentative words, tracing letters so as to use the very handwriting that appears in the scroll. It's important to use the ancient scribe's actual letter forms, because the size of ancient handwriting varied as much as modern handwriting does. A break large enough for ten letters in one hand may support only five in another, larger, handwriting.

Of paramount importance is determining the width of the original column. Unfortunately, the full width is only occasionally preserved in some of the fragments of a manuscript, so certainty on this question is often elusive. On a good day one gets a little help. The scholar may recognize a broken biblical quotation, for example, or a broken quotation from a known extrabiblical writing, even another Dead Sea Scroll. Filling out the broken quotation may reveal the column's width. The quotation of Zechariah 2:8 works that way in frag. 2 of *An Aramaic Text on the Persian Period* (text 148), for example. Knowing the width is crucial, for with that information, one also knows how much text is missing, how much preserved. The resulting parameters will guide the reconstruction of ideas. If, say, half a line is missing, then it's unlikely that the idea or statement in the preserved half can simply be extrapolated into the next preserved section. Too much is missing. But if only one or two words are missing, the flow of ideas is generally not too badly disrupted, and confident reconstruction is possible.

Constant interaction goes on between the scholar's mind—his or her "theory of the text"—and what can be read and understood in the fragmentary manuscript. Imagination is important, but so is the opposite pole, restraint. Reconstructing a Dead Sea Scroll, for all it may resort to technology and sophisticated methods, is no science. It is an art. Like all art, it requires inspiration, intuition, and the clamp-jawed determination of a pit bull. An intractable problem may gnaw at the mind for months, and then suddenly, in a moment, the solution becomes obvious. Yet paradoxically, when done best, this art is not creative, for the result is no new creation. The goal is to re-create an ancient writer's work.

Having done as much reconstruction of the fragmentary manuscript as he or she can (someone else may later do better; scholarship is cumulative), the scholar prepares a *transcription*. This is the term for a rendering of the text into standard Hebrew or Aramaic book-style lettering. If you were to type out a handwritten note from a friend, that would be a transcription. The scholar does the same with the ancient text. He or she also labels fragments and columns using a standard system. A fragment can, of course, contain parts of more than one column. Labeling will then indicate "Frag. 1 Col. 1" and "Frag. 1 Col. 2," for example. At other times a column may be composed of several fragments joined together. The label might then read "Col. 1 (Frags. 1+2+3)." Lines in the transcription are numbered, reading from the top of the column to the bottom. Numbering does not necessarily begin with 1. Several lines may be known to be missing, and the first line might be l. 4, or l. 15. Much of this labeling carries over into the next step, the translation. We have included such labels in our translations throughout the following pages.

The transcription indicates uncertain letters in the text with standard sigla, which also signal the degree of uncertainty. And scholars use different types of brackets to communicate additional types of information. Square brackets [ ], for example, surround reconstructed words. We have ourselves used square brackets for that purpose throughout the book. Square-bracketed portions may be simple guesses, calculated probabilities, or virtually certain: broken biblical quotations filled out, for example, or wording that overlaps with another scroll. If you see square brackets, you should be cautious about the words inside. Portions in square brackets do not actually appear in the scroll.

Simultaneously with the transcription one prepares a translation. Note: not *the* translation—*a* translation. There is no single translation equivalent for many words, not to speak of phrases or entire texts. Some words have many possible rough equivalents. Other words, phrases, and idioms in one language lack exact counterparts in another language. For example, none of the European languages possesses an exact equivalent for the English phrase "bend over backward." The unfortunate inhabitants of Germany, Italy, and France, among others, must make do with a translation equivalent like "try very hard." A little thought, however, will convince you that "try very hard" does not really convey the entire meaning or any of the nuance of the other phrase. In fact, exact translation between two languages is impossible. To truly read Goethe, you must learn German. So scholars prepare *a* translation of each transcription.

Essentially, that is what you will be reading in the following pages: translations of transcriptions that we have prepared for each Dead Sea Scroll in the book. Translation is the last step in an intricate and frequently uncertain process of reconstruction. In the process we have consulted and profited from the work of many colleagues worldwide (see the Bibliography). We have done our best to present flowing, idiomatic translations, so far as that has been possible given the frequently fragmentary materials. Throughout our work we have been mindful of the Italian apothegm: "*Traduttore traditore*" ("The translator is a traitor"). Translators betray both what they translate and the readers of their translation. By their very effort they violate the original. Yet we are not unduly concerned, nor in the least repentant. Any damage is for a worthy cause and is not irreparable. Much of the beauty, the concision, the power of the Hebrew and Aramaic in which the scrolls are couched will continue to reside, untranslatable, where nature has decreed it must. And we are not really traitors to you, the reader, for we have drawn your attention to our betrayal from the very first. Forewarned, you go forward fully armed. If we have perhaps transported at least most of the meaning of the words across time, space, and linguistic distance, we shall have succeeded in a principal aim.

How to Read This Book

Italics:
Explanatory headings.

A return to the subject of oaths.

As for the passage "observe what comes out of your lips" (†Deut. 23:24), [7]it means to abide by every binding oath in which a man promises [8]to do anything from the Law: he may not break it, even at the price of death. Every[9] promise a man makes to depart from the Law he shall not keep, even at the price of death.

Brackets:

Square brackets surround lost areas in the scroll due to various types of damage.

Parentheses enclose various types of helpful information. In this case "son of man" is another possible translation of a partial word.

Words that have been erased but are of interest are placed between curly brackets.

[28][above another.] Thus for the son of [Your] maid[servant (*or* son of m[an) . . .] You have <enlarged> his inheritance [29]through the knowledge (?) of Your {righteousness} truth. According to his knowledge and [his . . .]

Angle brackets indicate errors in the original manuscript and a possible solution.

A question mark in parentheses indicates that the preceding word is less than certain due to a difficulty understanding the original language.

NUMBERS:

Q (Qumran) numbers indicate the number of the cave—in this case 4—and the manuscript—in this case the 266th from cave 4.

Frag. indicates the number of the fragment—or in this case group of fragments—for the manuscript being translated.

Superscript numbers indicate the line number (*not* verse number!) of the fragment.

4Q266 Frag. 4–6 Col. 1 [6][. . .] the mighty ones when they are smitten [. . .] [7][. . . who hold] fast to His holy name [. . .] [8][. . .] for in Judah [. . .] [9][. . .] to Israel when he appears [. . .] to teach [10][. . .]

[2] [During the day, *x* songs and] sixtee[n wor]ds of [praise].

Col. indicates the column number of the fragment or group of fragments. In the case of the more complete manuscripts such as 1QS and 1QH boldface numbers refer to columns.

SYMBOLS:

An *x* in brackets indicates an unknown number.

II
Texts

1. The Damascus Document (CD)

Geniza A + B, 4Q266–272

The Jewish scholar Solomon Schechter first discovered portions of the *Damascus Document* among manuscripts from the Cairo Geniza and published them in 1910 under the title *Zadokite Fragments.* The name is derived from the frequent mention of the "sons of Zadok" in the text. Schechter believed that the writing originated in a Jewish sect of about the first century B.C.E., although the two manuscripts he published (Geniza texts A and B) were themselves medieval copies dating from the tenth and twelfth centuries C.E., respectively. The dating of the *Zadokite Fragments* remained an issue for decades. Many scholars agreed with Schechter, but many others dismissed his theory, preferring to date the *Document* centuries later.

The discovery of the Dead Sea Scrolls settled the question in Shechter's favor. The texts from Cave 1, especially the *Charter of a Jewish Sectarian Association* (text 7), clearly stemmed from the same circles that composed the *Damascus Document* and used much of the same religious terminology. When fragments of the *Document* itself were found in Caves 4 and 5, then, the discovery simply confirmed what most scholars had already concluded: the Dead Sea sect was the source of the *Damascus Document.* Moreover, it was to all appearances one of the group's most important texts, containing clues to its history, theology, and conception of its role in history.

Reading the *Damascus Document* can be a frustrating experience. Although many broad themes are easy to notice—the greatness of God and his covenant with Israel, the perfidy of apostates, the necessity of obeying the rules of God and the group, and so on—the train of thought rambles from subject to subject, with many digressions, asides, and pauses to explain a difficult or important quotation from Scripture. Apparently the *Document* was expanded at different times, often without care for the lucidity of the discourse.

Despite its occasional obscurities, however, the book can be easily divided into two broad sections: the "Exhortation" and the "Laws." The Exhortation is a sermon or perhaps a collection of sermons describing how God has always judged the wicked and rewarded the faithful throughout the history of Israel. In view of this pattern, the author exhorts his listeners to be faithful to God, to be particularly careful of obeying his laws, and to avoid living by the principle of selfishness he calls, from a biblical phrase, "the willful heart."

Two kinds of material comprise the Exhortation: the sermon proper and biblical commentary. While the sermon itself is based on biblical themes and sometimes quotes verses from the Bible, the commentary sections go into particular passages in great depth, picking out certain phrases for symbolic or allegorical expansions that relate to the life of the sect. These distinctive passages seem to have been added after the original Exhortation was composed, as they sometimes interrupt the train of thought.

The section on the Laws, a rule book similar to the Mishnah of later centuries, is more tightly written than the Exhortation, and details the kinds of behavior—moral, legal, and cultic—that the Exhortation urges in more general terms. The rules themselves fall into two groups: the rules for "those living in cities" (A 12:19), paraphrasing or expanding biblical laws, and the rules for "those living in camps" (A 12:22–23), i.e., sectarian enclaves. The camp rules are oriented to communitarian life; they describe the internal lines of authority of the camp and specify sanctions to be carried out against violators of particular rules, quite in the manner of the *Charter* and sometimes with verbatim parallels to it.

It is likely that sectarian authors added the commentaries embedded in the Exhortation and the camp rules of the Laws some time after the original *Damascus Document* was written. As originally conceived, the *Document* was less sectarian than it was later made to appear, consisting of the Exhortation originally addressed to all Israel and the city rules, also, in intent, binding on all religiously serious Israelites. This first version might have been composed as early as the third century B.C.E., although it is impossible to tell for sure. Later, members of the *Yahad,* finding the text's warnings against apostasy and call to obedience thoroughly in line with their own thinking, revised and expanded it to reflect their views, perhaps adding additional glosses and explanatory comments to both the Exhortation and the Laws with the passage of time. Scholars have been able to detect editorial expansions between the A and B Geniza texts, and perhaps there was never a final, canonical, version of the *Document.*

Besides the two Geniza texts (A contains sixteen columns, B two), which preserve the longest consecutive sections of the text, the remains of seven copies were found in the Qumran caves. Only the sections that are not paralleled in the Geniza texts are translated here. The translation attempts to use all of the available material to restore as much of the *Document* in its original order as possible, but the sequence of many of the sections in the Laws is uncertain. The order given here generally follows the outline established by the current official editor of the Cave 4 manuscripts of the *Document,* Joseph Baumgarten.

The text, in its final form, is addressed to "those entering the new covenant in the land of Damascus" (A 6:19). Whether a literal Damascus is meant or whether the name is instead another of the symbolic pseudonyms known from other Dead Sea Scrolls is uncertain, and much debated; but such references have given the book its modern name. The letters "CD" (for "Covenant of Damascus") are the most common abbreviation used to refer to this text.

The Exhortation

Only fragments remain of the opening paragraphs of the Damascus Document. *The translation that follows is pieced together from 4Q266 and 4Q268. Enough can be recovered to tell that several of the themes of the entire work are foreshadowed in the introductory paragraphs: the necessity of obedience to God, the perfidy of the wicked, the insight of the pious into the future, the importance of observing the proper times of worship, the special revelation given to the "Children of Light." This portion probably comes from the sectarian reworking of the document.*

4Q266 Frag. 1 [1][. . . the Chil]dren of Light to avoid the wa[ys of evil . . .] [2][. . .] until the time appointed for punishment is past [. . .] [3][. . .] God [saw] all her deeds, that they brought all [. . .] [4][. . .] to the Boundary-Shifters and all of it will be done [in the era of] [5]wickedness [. . . listen] to me, for now I shall make known to you [. . .] [6]the awesome [. . .] His wonderful [miracles] I shall relate to y[ou, hidden] [7]from humanity [. . .] heavens, who lives [. . .] [8]in the deepest [. . .] [9]he has sealed [. . .] [10–13][. . .] [14]in the commandments [. . .] [15]in the offering [. . .] and they did not obey [16]the voice of Moses [. . .] they went about spread]ing [17]lies about His laws and from God's covenant [they strayed . . .] [18]both small and great [. . .] [19]Please tell us about [your ways . . .] [20]your conversation [. . .] [21]you appeared and understood [. . .] [22]they shall restore the [. . . and I am dust] [23]and ashes [. . .] [24]give he[ed . . .] **4Q268 Frag. 1 (= 4Q266 Frag. 2 Col. 1)** [1][. . .] later [generations] for surely they will come to pass [. . .] [2][. . .] what is its beginning and what its ending [. . .] [3][. . . be]fore it comes upon them [. . .] [4][. . . for it is not permitted] to celebrate th[eir] holidays too early or too late. [. . .] [5][. . . Yes,] periods of God's w[rath] are decreed [for a people who know him not] [6][and He has established times of] favor for those who seek His commandments and to [those who live blamelessly in] [7]the proper way. [He uncovered their] e[yes] to the hidden things and opened their ears that [they might hear deep things] [8]and understand future events before they happen to them.

This epigraph sets the tone for what is to follow: an exposition of how God punishes the wicked while leaving a righteous remnant to live exemplary lives. The Geniza manuscript A begins at this point.

Geniza A Col. 1 [1]So listen, all you who recognize righteousness, and consider the deeds of [2]God. When He has a dispute with any mortal, He passes judgment on those who spurn Him.

A description of Israel's sin resulting in exile, and God's mercy on the generation that returned from exile.

[3]For when Israel abandoned Him by being faithless, He turned away from Israel and from His sanctuary [4]and gave them up to the sword. But when He called to mind the covenant He made with their forefathers, He left a [5]remnant for Israel and did not allow them to be exterminated. In the era of wrath—three hundred [6]and ninety years at the time He handed them over to the power of Nebuchadnezzar king of Babylon—[7]He took care of them and caused to grow from Israel and from Aaron a root of planting to inherit [8]His land and to grow fat on the good produce of His soil. They considered their iniquity and they knew that [9]they were guilty men, and had been like the blind and like those groping for the way [10]twenty years. But God considered their deeds, that they had sought Him with a whole heart. [11]So He raised up for them a teacher of righteousness to guide them in the way of His heart. He taught [12]to later generations what God did to the generation deserving wrath, a company of traitors. [13]They are the ones who depart from the proper way. That is the time of which it was written, "Like a rebellious cow, [14]so rebelled Israel" (Hos. 4:16).

The Man of Mockery. This paragraph, which introduces the principal religious opponent of the sect, appears to have been added later.

When the Man of Mockery appeared, who sprayed on Israel [15]lying waters, he led them to wander in the trackless wasteland. He brought down the lofty heights of old, turned aside [16]from paths of righteousness, and shifted the boundary marks that the forefathers had set up to mark their inheritance, so that [17]the curses of His covenant took hold on them. Because of this they were handed over to the sword that avenges the breach of [18]His covenant.

The sins of the generation of wrath and their punishment.

For they had sought flattery, choosing travesties of true religion; they looked for [19]gaps in the law; they favored the fine neck. They called the guilty innocent, and the innocent guilty. [20]They overstepped covenant, violated law; and they conspired together to kill the innocent, for all those who lived [21]pure lives they loathed from the bottom of their heart. So they persecuted them violently, and were happy to see the people quarrel. Because of all this God became very angry **Col. 2** [1]with their company. He annihilated the lot of them, because all their deeds were uncleanness to Him.

[2]So now listen to me, all members of the covenant, so I can make plain to you the ways [3]of the wicked (**4Q267** adds: so you can leave the paths of sin). God, who loves true knowledge, has positioned Wisdom and Cleverness in front of Him; [4]Cunning and True Knowledge wait on Him. He is very patient and forgiving, [5]covering the sin of those who repent of wrongdoing.

But Strength, Might, and great Wrath in the flames of fire [6]with all the angels of destruction shall come against all who rebel against the proper way and who despise the law, until they are without remnant [7]or survivor, for God had not chosen them from ancient eternity. Before they were created, He knew [8]what they would do. So He rejected the generations of old and turned away from the land [9]until they were gone.

He knows the times of appearance and the number and exact times of [10]everything that has ever existed and ever will exist before it happens in the proper time, for all the years of eternity. [11]And in all of these times, He has arranged that there should be for Himself people called by name, so that there would always be survivors on the earth, replenishing [12]the surface of the earth with their descendants. He taught them through those anointed by the holy spirit, the seers of [13]truth. He explicitly called them by name. But whoever He had rejected He caused to stray.

A homily on the willful heart.

[14]So now, my children, listen to me that I may uncover your eyes to see and to understand the deeds of [15]God, choosing what pleases Him and hating what He rejects, living perfectly [16]in all His ways, not turning away through thoughts caused by the sinful urge and lecherous eyes.

For many [17]have gone astray by such thoughts, even strong and doughty men of old faltered through them, and still do.

When they went about in their willful [18]heart, the Guardian Angels of Heaven fell and were ensnared by it, for they did not observe the commandments of God. [19]Their sons, who were as tall as cedars, and whose bodies were as big as mountains, fell by it.

[20]Everything mortal on dry land expired and became as if they had never existed, because they did [21]their own will, and did not keep the commandments of their Maker, until finally His anger was aroused against them.

Col. 3 [1]By it the sons of Noah and their families went astray, and by it they were exterminated.

[2]Abraham did not live by it and was considered God's friend, because he observed the commandments of God and he did not choose to follow [3]the will of his own spirit; and he passed them on to Isaac and to Jacob and they too observed them. They too were recorded as friends [4]of God and eternal partners in the covenant.

But the sons of Jacob went astray by them and were punished for [5]their errors. In Egypt their descendants lived by their willful heart, too obstinate to consult [6]the commandments of God, each one doing what was right in his own eyes. They even ate blood; and the men were exterminated [7]in the wilderness. <God commanded> them at Kadesh "Go up and possess <the land"; but they chose to follow the will of> their spirit; and they did not listen [8]to their Maker's voice or the commandments of their teacher; instead they grumbled in their tents. So God became angry [9]with their company.

Their sons perished because of it. Their kings were exterminated because of it. Their heroes [10]perished because of it. Their land was devastated because of it, and because of it the members of the forefathers' covenant committed sin, and so were handed over [11]to the sword because they abandoned the covenant of God, and chose their own will, and followed their own willful [12]heart, each man doing his own will.

But when those of them who were left held firm to the commandments of God [13]He instituted His covenant with Israel forever, revealing [14]to them things hidden, in which all Israel had gone wrong: His holy Sabbaths, His glorious festivals, [15]His righteous laws, His reliable ways. The desires of His will, which Man should carry out [16]and so have life in them, He opened up to them. So they "dug a well," yielding much water. [17]Those who reject this water He will not allow to live.

And although they had wallowed in the sin of humanity and in impure ways [18]and said, "Surely this is our business," God in His mysterious ways atoned for their iniquity and forgave their transgression. [19]So He built for them a faithful house in Israel, like none that had ever appeared before; and even [20]at this day, those who hold firm to it shall receive everlasting life, and all human honor is rightly theirs, as [21]God promised them by Ezekiel the prophet, saying, "The priests and the Levites and the sons of **Col. 4** [1]Zadok who have kept the courses of My sanctuary when the children of Israel strayed [2]from Me, they shall bring Me fat and blood" (Ezek. 44:15).

This interpretive comment appears to be a later addition.

"The priests": they are the repentant of Israel, [3]who go out of the land of Judah and the Levites are those accompanying them; "and the sons of Zadok": they are the chosen of [4]Israel, the ones called by name, who are to appear in the Last Days.

This is the precise account [5]of their names by their generations, and the time they appeared, the number of their troubles and the years of [6]their sojourn and the precise account of their deeds.

The section that now begins explains that the "present age" is under the power of Belial, that is, Satan. Part of the beginning has been lost.

<. . .> holiness <. . .> whom God atoned [7]for, and they acquitted the innocent and condemned the guilty, as well as all who come after them [8]who act according to the interpretation of the Law by which the forefathers were taught, until the age is over, [9]that is, the present time. Like the covenant God made with the forefathers to atone [10]for their sin, so shall God atone for them. When the total years of this present age are complete, [11]there will be no further need to be connected to the house of Judah, but instead each will stand on [12]his own tower; "the wall is built, the boundary removed" (Mic. 7:11).

But in the present age [13]Belial is unrestrained in Israel, just as God said by Isaiah the prophet, the son of [14]Amoz, saying, "Fear and pit and snare are upon thee, dweller in the land" (Isa. 24:17).

The three traps of Belial. This section, explaining the text just quoted, discloses some important ethical principles of the Qumran group that, in its members' eyes, differentiated them from other groups: their opposition to polygamy, to the amassing of wealth, to defiling the Temple in Jerusalem, and to marriage between uncles and nieces.

The true meaning of this verse [15]concerns the three traps of Belial about which Levi son of Jacob said [16]that Belial would catch Israel in, so he directed them toward three kinds of [17]righteousness.

The first is fornication; the second is wealth; the third is [18]defiling the sanctuary. Who escapes from one is caught in the next; and whoever escapes from that is caught [19]in the other.

The Shoddy-Wall-Builders who went after "Precept"—Precept is a Raver [20]of whom it says, "they shall surely rave" (Mic. 2:6)—they are caught in two: fornication, by taking [21]two wives in their lifetimes, although the principle of creation is "male and female He created them" (Gen. 1:27) **Col. 5** [1]and those who went into the ark "went into the ark two by two" (Gen. 7:9). Concerning the Leader it is written [2]"he shall not multiply wives to himself" (Deut. 17:17); but David had not read the sealed book of the Law [3]in the Ark; for it was not opened in Israel from the day of the death of Eleazar [4]and Joshua and the elders who served the goddess Ashtoret. It lay buried [5]<and was not> revealed until the appearance of Zadok. Nevertheless the deeds of David were all excellent, except the murder of Uriah [6]and God forgave him for that.

They also defile the sanctuary, for they do not [7]separate clean from unclean according to the Law, and lie with a woman during her menstrual period. Furthermore they marry [8]each man the daughter of his brother and the daughter of his sister, although Moses said, "Unto [9]the sister of your mother you shall not draw near; she is the flesh of your mother" (Lev. 18:13). But the law of consanguinity is written for males [10]and females alike, so if the brother's daughter uncovers the nakedness of the brother of [11]her father, she is the flesh <of her father>.

Also they have corrupted their holy spirit, and with blasphemous language [12]they have reviled the statutes of God's covenant, saying, "They are not well-founded." [13]They continually speak abhorrent things against them. "All of them are kindlers and lighters of brands" (Isa. 50:11); "the webs of [14]a spider are their webs and the eggs of vipers are their eggs" (Isa. 59:5). Whoever touches them [15]shall not be clean. The more he does so, the more he is guilty, unless he is forced.

After the interpretive section, the train of thought continues: just as the present age is an age of wickedness, God's ways in the past reveal how he punishes sin and provides for the faithful of Israel.

For in times past, God punished [16]their deeds and His wrath burned against their misdeeds, for "they are a people without insight" (Isa. 27:11); [17]"they are a people wandering in counsel, for there is no insight in them" (Deut. 32:28). For in times past [18]Moses and Aaron stood in the power of the Prince of Lights and Belial raised up Yannes and [19]his brother in his cunning when seeking to do evil to Israel the first time.

[20]In the time of destruction of the land the Boundary-Shifters appeared and led Israel astray [21]and the land was devastated, for they had spoken rebellion against the commandments of God through Moses and also **Col. 6** [1]through the anointed of the spirit; and they prophesied falsehood to turn Israel from following [2]God. But God called to mind the covenant of the

forefathers; and He raised up from Aaron insightful men and from Israel [3]wise men and He taught them and they dug the well: "the well the princes dug, the nobility of the people [4]dug it with a rod" (Num. 21:18).

The symbolic interpretation of the verse last quoted.

The Well is the Law, and its "diggers" are [5]the repentant of Israel who went out of the land of Judah and dwelt in the land of Damascus; [6]because God had called them all princes, for they sought him and [7]their honor was not denied by a single mouth. And the "rod" is the interpreter of the Law of whom [8]Isaiah said, "he brings out a tool for his work" (Isa. 54:16). The "nobility of the people" are [9]those who come to "dig the well" by following rules that the Rod made [10]to live by during the whole era of wickedness, and without these rules they shall obtain nothing until the appearance of [11]one who teaches righteousness in the Last Days.

The continuation of the exhortation. These paragraphs read like a conclusion, and they may have occurred at the end of an earlier form of the text. The author summarizes the way of life expected of those who enter the sect.

None who have been brought into the covenant [12]shall enter into the sanctuary to light up His altar in vain; they shall "lock [13]the door," for God said, "Would that one of you would lock My door so that you should not light up my altar [14]in vain" (Mal. 1:10). They must be careful to act according to the specifications of the Law for the era of wickedness, separating [15]from corrupt people, avoiding filthy wicked lucre taken from what is vowed or consecrated to God [16]or found in the Temple funds. They must not rob "the poor of God's people, making widows' wealth their booty [17]and killing orphans" (Isa. 10:2). They must distinguish between defiled and pure, teaching the difference [18]between holy and profane. They must keep the Sabbath day according to specification and the holy days [19]and the fast day according to the commandments of the members of the new covenant in the land of Damascus, [20]offering the holy things according to their specifications. Each one must love his brother [21]as himself, and support the poor, needy, and alien. They must seek each the welfare of **Col. 7** [1]his fellow, never betraying a family member [2]according to the ordinance. Each must reprove his fellow according to the command, but must not bear a grudge [3]day after day. They must separate from all kinds of ritual impurity according to their ordinance, not befouling [4]each his holy spirit, just as God has told them so to do. In short, for all who conduct their lives [5]by these laws, in perfect holiness, according to all the instructions, God's covenant stands firm [6]to give them life for thousands of generations (**Geniza B** adds: as it is written, "He keeps the covenant and loyalty to those who love Him and keep His commandments for a thousand generations" [Deut. 7:9]).

An addendum on marriage. This paragraph might have been misplaced in antiquity; it belongs with the laws. Some have taken these words, apparently providing for the special needs of married members, to imply the presence also of unmarried or celibate members of the sect.

But if they live in camps according to the rule of the land (**Geniza B** adds: which existed in ancient times) and marry [7]women (**B** adds: as is the custom of the Law) and beget children, then let them live in accordance with the Law, and by the ordinance [8]of vows according to the rule of the Law, just as it says, "Between a man and his wife, and between a father and his [9]sons" (Num. 30:17).

The fulfillment of prophecy, indicating the inevitability of punishment on those who reject God's laws. Geniza B has a different version of this passage. Note the interpretive section embedded in this paragraph.

But all those who reject the commandments and the rules <shall perish>. When God judged the land, bringing the just deserts of the wicked [10]to them, that is when the oracle of the prophet Isaiah son of Amoz came true, [11]which says, "Days are coming upon you and upon your people and upon your father's house that [12]have never come before, since the departure of Ephraim from Judah" (Isa. 7:17), that is, when the two houses of Israel separated, [13]Ephraim departing from Judah. All who backslid were handed over to the sword, but all who held fast [14]escaped to the land of the north, as it says, "I will exile the tents of your king [15]and the foundation of your images beyond the tents of Damascus" (Amos 5:27). The books of Law are the tents of [16]the king, as it says, "I will re-erect the fallen tent of David" (Amos 9:11). The "king" (**4Q266:** the images) is [17]the congregation and the "foundation of your images" is the books of the prophets [18]whose words Israel despised. The star is the Interpreter of the Law [19]who comes to Damascus, as it is written, "A star has left Jacob, a staff has risen [20]from Israel" (Num. 24:17). The latter is the Leader of the whole nation; when he appears, "he will shatter [21]all the sons of Sheth" (Num. 24:17). They escaped in the first period of God's judgment, **Col. 8** [1]but those who held back were handed over to the sword.

The fulfillment of prophecy, alternate version (Geniza B).

Col. 19 [7]When the oracle of the prophet Zechariah comes true, "O sword, be lively and smite [8]my shepherd and the man loyal to Me—so says God. If you strike down the shepherd, the flock will scatter. [9]Then I will turn My power against the little ones" (Zech. 13:7). But those who give heed to God are "the poor of the flock" (Zech. 11:7): [10]they will escape in the time of punishment, but all the rest will be handed over to the sword when the Messiah of [11]Aaron and of Israel comes, just as it happened during the time of the first punishment, as [12]Ezekiel said, "Make a mark on the foreheads of those who moan and lament" (Ezek. 9:4), [13]but the rest were given to the sword that makes retaliation for covenant violations.

The lesson to be drawn from the fulfillment of prophecy: be faithful!

Col. 8 [1]And such is the verdict on all members of the covenant who [2]do not hold firm to these laws: they are condemned to destruction by Belial. That is the day [3]on which God shall judge (**4Q268** adds: as He has said), "The princes of Judah were those (**B**: like Boundary-Shifters) on whom I shall pour out wrath (**B** adds: like water)" (Hos. 5:10). [4]Truly they were too sick to be healed; every kind of galling wound adhered to them (**B** adds: Truly they had entered the covenant repenting) because they did not turn away from traitorous practices; [5]they relished the customs of fornication and wicked lucre. Each of them vengefully bore a grudge [6]against his brother, each hating his fellow; each of them were indifferent to their closest relatives [7]but drew near to indecency; they vaunted themselves in riches and in ill-gotten gains; each of them did just what he pleased; [8]each chose to follow his own willful heart. They did not separate from the people (**B** adds: and their sin), but arrogantly threw off all restraint, [9]adopting the customs of the wicked, of whom God had said, "Their wine is venom of snakes, [10]the cruel poison of vipers" (Deut. 32:33).

A pause for interpretation of the verse quoted. The "chief of the kings of Greece" may refer to Antiochus Epiphanes, the Gentile ruler of Palestine at the time of the Maccabean rebellion. The sect believed that their opponents did not understand that the persecutions of that time were caused by the nation's disobedience.

"The snakes" are the kings of the Gentiles, and "their wine" is [11]their customs and "the poison of vipers" is the chief of the kings of Greece, who comes to wreak [12]vengeance on them. But the "Shoddy-Wall-Builders" and "White-washers" understood none of these things, for [13]one who deals in mere wind, a spewer of lies, had spewed on them (**B** reads slightly differently: one who walks in wind, and who deals in storms, one who preaches lies to men), one on whose entire company God's anger had burned hot.

Despite the nation's perfidy, God will remain faithful to his covenant.

[14]But as Moses said (**B** adds: to Israel), "It is not for your righteousness or the integrity of your heart that you are going to dispossess [15]these nations, but because He loved your ancestors and because He has kept his promise" (Deut. 9:5; 7:8). [16]Such is the verdict on the repentant of Israel, those who turn away from the usages of the common people. Because God loved [17]the forefathers who bore witness (**B** adds: to the people) following Him (**B**: following God), so too He loves those who follow them, for to such truly belongs [18]the covenant of the fathers. But against His enemies, the Shoddy-Wall-Builders, His anger burns. (**B**: But He hates and despises the Shoddy-Wall-Builders and His anger burns hot against them and all who follow them.)

A summary of the "moral" of the exhortations. The reference to Jeremiah (only in the A manuscript) is obscure.

So there is one fate for [19]everyone who rejects the commandments of God and abandons them to follow their own willful heart. [20]This is the word that Jeremiah spoke to Baruch son of Neriah, and Elisha [21]to Gehazi his servant.

The B manuscript's version of the "moral" of the exhortations. The version of the Damascus Document *of which the B manuscript is a later copy was more thoroughly revised to reflect the outlook of the sect. Thus two distinct versions of the text circulated in ancient times, and taken together the Geniza copies preserve both versions.*

B Col. 19 [33]So it is with all the men who entered the new covenant [34]in the land of Damascus, but then turned back and traitorously turned away from the fountain of living water. [35]They shall not be reckoned among the council of the people, and their names shall not be written in their book from the day **20**[1]the Beloved Teacher dies until the Messiah from Aaron and from Israel appears. Such is the fate for all [2]who join the company of the men of holy perfection and then become sick of obeying virtuous rules. [3]This is the type of person who "melts in the crucible" (Ezek. 22:21).

When his actions become evident he shall be sent away from the company [4]as if his lot had never fallen among the disciples of God. In keeping with his impiety [5]the most knowledgeable men shall punish him until he returns to take his place among the men of holy perfection. [6]When his actions become evident, according to the interpretation of the Law which [7]the men of holy perfection live by, no one is allowed to share either wealth or work with such a one, [8]for all the holy ones of the Almighty have cursed him.

Such is the fate for all who reject the commandments, whether old or [9]new, who have turned their thoughts to false gods and who have lived by their willful [10]hearts: they have no part in the household of Law.

[11]They will be condemned along with the Men of Mockery, because they have uttered lies against the correct laws and rejected [12]the sure covenant that they made in the land of Damascus, that is, the New Covenant. [13]Neither they nor their families shall have any part in the household of Law.

Now from the day [14]the Beloved Teacher passed away to the destruction of all the warriors who went back to [15]the Man of the Lie will be about forty years. Now at that time [16]God's anger will burn against Israel, as He said, "Neither king nor prince" (Hos. 3:4) nor judge nor [17]one who exhorts to do what is right will be left. But those who repent of the sin of Jacob have kept God's covenant. Then each will speak [18]to his fellow, vindicating his brother, helping him walk in God's way, and God shall listen [19]to what they say, and hear it, and "a record-book has been written f[or him] of those who fear God and honor [20]his name" (Mal. 3:16) until salvation and righteousness are revealed for those who fear God. "And you shall again know the innocent [21]from the guilty, those who serve God and those who do not" (Mal. 3:18). "He keeps faith [with thousands] of those who love Him [22]and to those who keep him for a thousand generations" (Exod. 20:6).

As for those separatists who left the city of the sanctuary [23]and relied on God in the time of Israel's unfaithfulness, but defiled the Temple: they shall return again [24]to the way of the people in a few matters [. . .] Each of them shall be judged in the holy council according to his spirit.

[25]But all of the members of the covenant who breached the restrictions of the Law, when [26]the glory of God appears to Israel they shall be excluded from the midst of the camp, and with them all who did evil in [27]Judah when it was undergoing trial.

The end of the exhortations.

But all who hold fast to these rules, going out [28]and coming in according to the Law, always obeying the Teacher and confessing to God as follows:

"We have wickedly sinned, [29]we and our ancestors by living contrary to the covenant laws; just [30]and true are Your judgments against us" and do not act arrogantly against His holy laws and [31]His righteous ordinances and His reliable declarations and who discipline themselves by the ancient laws [32]by which the members of the *Yahad* were governed and listen attentively to the Teacher of Righteousness, not abandoning [33]the correct laws when they hear them: they will rejoice and be happy and exultant. They will prevail over [34]all the inhabitants of the earth. Then God will make atonement for them and they will experience His deliverance because they have trusted in His holy name.

The Laws

The rules that follow were not intended to be an exhaustive scheme for righteous living, but a summary of important points that would serve to guide the righteous Israelite in areas where controversy might arise.

The main section of the laws deals with rules applying to Israel as a whole ("those living in the cities of Israel"). A shorter section at the end contains regulations for the internal life of the sect ("those living in camps").

The opening portions of the laws are available only in the fragmentary scrolls from Cave 4. The order of the fragments from different scrolls is hypothetical.

4Q266 Frag. 5 (= 4Q267 Frag. 5) Col. 1 [8][. . .] the mighty ones in what is re[vealed . . .] [9][. . . who hold] fast to His [ho]ly name [. . .] [10][. . .] for in Judah is fo[und a conspir]acy [11][to return to the sins of their ancestors . . .] to Israel when he appears [. . .] [12][. . . in the inhabitants of Jerusal]em and all who re[main . . .] [13][. . .] each according to [his] spirit [. . .] [14][. . . the stubborn in spir]it shall be banished at the command of the Overseer [. . .] [15][. . .] all the repentant of Israel [. . .] [16][. . . the so]ns of Zadok, the priests, are the [. . .] [17]the most recent [interpretation] of the Law.

Now these are the laws for the wi[se man . . .] [18][. . . to teach] them to all Israel, for it will not [. . .] [19][. . .] to live blame[lessly] in his ways [. . .] **Col. 1 c–d** [2][. . .] for all the upright of heart in I[s]rael [. . . who kept] his laws, they considered righteous [. . .]

Certain acts are grounds for excommunication or severe discipline. Idolatry, sexual sin, withholding what is due to the priests, rebellion, and certain ritual offenses are all serious transgressions.

4Q270 Frag. 2 Col. 1 [10][. . . who sacrifices to sa]tyrs or asks guidance from a necromancer or a medium [11][. . .] or who profanes the [holy]

Name [12–16][. . . or any woman who has a bad reputation while] a virgin in the house of [17][her father . . .] another man lies with her [18][. . . or app]roaches his wife in the time of [19][her impurity . . .]

Col. 2 [6][. . . to] the Aaronites belongs the planting of [. . .] [7][. . . the firstfruits of] all that they have, the tithe of do[mestic animals, whether cattle] [8]or sheep, the redemption mone[y of the firstlings of] unclean [beas]ts, the redemption money of the first[born human, the first shearing of] [9]the flock, and the assessment money for their own redemption; [every sin for which restitution is made which] [10]cannot be returned; "a fifth must be added to it" (Lev. 27:31) or [. . .] [11]by their names, defiling His holy spirit [. . .] [12]or is afflicted with a skin disease or an unc[lean] bodily discharge [. . . or] [13]reveals the secret of his people to the Gentiles or curses o[r speaks] [14]rebellion against those anointed by the Holy Spirit or who speaks lies [against . . .] [15]God's command or slaughters a domestic or wild animal with a living fetus [in it or who lies with] [16]a pregnant woman when her monthly period [ceases . . . or lies with a man] [17]as one lies with a woman: these are the ones who violate the [Way . . .] [18]God has decreed to remove [. . .]

[19]So listen now, all you experts in righteousness, [who obey the To]rah, [I will reveal to] [20]you the ways that lead to life and the paths that lead to destruction; I will open [your eyes [. . . in their traps] [21]do not be caught; and when you understand the things that have happened in every generation [. . .]

Rules for the priests. Improper recitation of Scripture, profaning the Temple, and eating holy food in an impure state are all grounds for expulsion.

4Q266 Frag. 5 Col. 2 (= 4Q267) [1][. . . Aar]on and all w[ho speak too quickly or in a harsh voice] [2][or who does] not speak his words clearly to make [his voice] heard, [none of these shall read from the book of] [3][the Law,] lest he incur the penalty of death [. . .] [4][. . . to assist] his brothers, the priests, in the worship [. . .] [5]Any of the Aaronites who is captured by the Gentiles [. . . may not come] [6]to profane the Temple by their impurity, he may not approach the worship [. . . he may not go] [7]within the curtain or eat of the holy [food . . .] [8]any Aaronite who befouls the wor[ship of God . . .] [9]to instruct with him in the council of the people; and also [. . .] to betray the truth [. . .] any of the [10]Aaronites whose name is dropped from the truth [. . .] [11]in his willful heart to eat any of the holy [food . . .] [12]of Israel the counsel of the Aaronites [. . .] if he has eaten any of] [13]the food and become guilty by consuming blood [. . . he shall not be named] [14]in their genealogy.

This is the rule for those living in [the cities of Israel . . .] [15]holine[ss in] their [camps and] their cities in a[ll . . .]

This section is an interpretation of the law concerning "leprosy," or infectious skin diseases, in Leviticus 13–14. It displays a rudimentary knowledge of the circulation of the blood through arteries, a phenomenon not fully described until the seventeenth century by William Harvey.

4Q272 Frag. 1 (= 4Q266 Frag. 6) Col. 1 [1][. . . a sore or] scab or in[flammation . . .] [2][. . . a sore of any kind and a scab due to a wound from a piece of wood or] stone. In the case of a wound, when the spirit comes [and possesses the artery, the blood stops] [3][flowing] above and below the wound, and the artery [. . .] [4–5][The priest shall examine the] healthy [skin] and the diseased skin [. . . If] the diseased skin is [greater than] [6][the healthy skin, he shall isolate him] until [the tissue] grows back [and] [6a][until] the blood [re]turns to the artery. [Then] on [the seventh day] the priest [shall examine him] and compare. [7][If the spir]it of life rises and falls [and] the tissue has grown back, [8][he is healed . . .] the scab, the priest shall not examine the skin of the bo[dy] [9][. . . If the] sore or the sc[ab] is lower [than the skin . . .] [10][and the priest sees] that it looks like raw flesh [. . .] [11][. . . a skin disease has taken ho]ld in the healthy skin, and according to [this] regulation [. . .] [12][. . . The priest shall examine on the seve]nth [day]. If the [healthy] [13][tissue] has given way [to diseased tissue, . . . it is an in]curable [skin disease.]

The skin diseases ("scall") of the hair of head and beard (Lev. 13). The conditions described may refer to kwashiorkor, caused by protein deficiency, or to favus.

4Q266 Frag. 6 Col. 1 [5]The regulation pertaining to scall of the head and be[ard . . .] [6][. . . The priest shall examine it;] if the spirit has entered into the head or the beard to possess [7][the artery and the disease] spro[uts underneath the ha]ir and makes it resemble thin yellow growth; for it is like grass [8]with a worm under it, which then cuts its root and the blossom dries up. As for the verse [9]that says, "The priest shall order the head to be shaven without shaving the scall" (Lev. 13:33), this is so that [10]the priest can count the diseased and healthy hairs. He shall examine the skin, and if the [11]diseased tissue has encroached on the healthy tissue after seven days, the man is unclean. But if the diseased parts have not encroached [12]on the h[ealthy], and the artery is full of [bl]ood and the sp[ir]it of life rises and falls in it [he is healed] [13][from] this disease.

Such is the regulation of the l[aw] pertaining to infectious skin disease so that the Aaronites can separate [. . .]

Uncleanness caused by bodily discharges. These regulations are based on the laws of Leviticus 15.

The man with a discharge (see Lev. 15:1–18).

14The regulation pertaining to the man with a bodily discharge. Every man who [has a discharge] 15from [his] flesh [o]r w[ho] allows [hi]mse[lf] thoughts of depravity or [who . . .] 16[. . .] contact with him [is like the contact with . . .] **4Q272 Frag. 1 Col. 2** 6he shall wash his clothes [and bathe in water . . .] 7whoever touches him [shall bathe in water . . .]

The woman with a discharge (see Lev. 15:19–30).

4Q266 Frag. 6 Col. 2 1[The regulation pertaining to the woman with a bodily discharge . . . Whoever] has intercourse 2[with a menstruating woman] contracts the [defile]ment caused by menstruation; and if she sees a discharge a[gain] but not 3[during her] seven-day [menstrual period], she shall not eat of the consecrated food or e[nter] 4the sanctuary until the sun sets on the eighth day.

Purification after childbirth (see Lev 12).

5A woman who [becomes pregna]nt and bears a male child [shall be unclean] seven [days] 6[a]s [the days of her] menstrual [flow. And on the eighth day the flesh of his] foreskin [shall be circumcised.] 7[Thirty-three days she shall remain in blood purification. And if she bears a female,] 8[she shall be unclean two weeks as with] her [menstrual f]low. Sixty-six days she shall remain in blood 9purification; and she] shall not eat [any consecrated food or enter the sanctuary, 10fo]r this is a capital crime [. . . she shall give] 11[the c]hild to a nurse who is in a state of ritu[al purity . . .] 12[and] if [she] cannot afford [a lamb, let her get a turtledove or pigeon for a whole burnt offering 13and] exchange for t[he lamb . . .]

Regulations about harvest, gleaning, and tithes.

4Q266 Frag. 6 Col. 3 4[These shall be given as priestly levies: . . . and] the single bunches of the vi[neyard: up to ten grape]s [make the bun]ches 5[. . .] and all the gleanings [up to a seah for the area sown with a s]ea[h of seed]; [6][a vineyard] that has no seed in it, there is no [levy] in it or grape-gleanings [7]and (there is not) a maximum of ten [grapes] in its bunches.

4Q270 Frag. 3 Col. 2 (= 4Q267 Frag. 6) [15][As for] that which is beaten from the olive tree [and the fruit of its yield,] if the yield is in good condition, the beaten olives, [one-] [16][thirti]eth, [should be . . . from] it; but if the field has been trampled down or [burned] [17][with fire and there was separated out] a seah for each area sown with a seah of seed, it is subject to tithe; and if [18][one person] shall glean one [seah] from it in one day, it is subject to the priestly levy, a tenth of [19][an ephah . . .] the loaves for the priestly gift for all the families of Israel who eat bread [20][. . .] to set aside for an offering once a year: one-tenth of an ephah there will be for one (loaf) [. . .] [21][. . . before they] have been completed for Israel let no man [re]move **Col. 2a** [1][. . .] t[he] unleave[ned bre]ad [. . .] [2][. . .] the best grain [. . .]

Measurements and offerings (see Ezek. 45:11–15).

4Q271 Frag. 2 [1][. . .] from the threshing floor shall bring down the tenth of the h[omer, which is the] ephah [2][. . .] the ephah and the bath, the two of them are the same measurement. From [the wheat,] a sixth of [3][an ephah for each homer, and a tenth of a bath for the fruit of] the trees. One must not set apart for an offering o[ne] lamb out of every hundred [4][. . . one must not] eat [. . . from the threshing floor] and from the garden, until [the pries]ts stretch out their hand [5][to ble]ss first of all. [. . .] to a man, he may sell it and when he [. . .] and then he shall be free of obligation [6][. . .] a field mixed [7][. . .]

Various rules of purity with respect to Gentile meat, metals, corpse impurity, and the qualifications for sprinkling for impurity.

4Q271 Frag. 2 [8]One must never bring [Gentile meat in the blood of their sacrifices . . . or any such blood on] his [clo]thing into the zone of purity; nor is one to bring any portion of [9]gold or silver [or bronze] or tin or le[ad that the Gentiles used to make i]dols. No one can bring [10]it into the zone of puri[ty, unless it is ne]w, straight from the furnace [. . .] No one can br[ing] any skin or garment or part of [11]any too[l] with which [w]ork [is done] that is unclean by reason of a cor[pse, un]less it has been sprinkled according the regulation [12][. . .] impurity, in the era of wickedness, a man is pu[re from all unclean]ness, who [13][sees the sunset. But any young man who] is [no]t old enough to be included among the re[gistrants shall not sprinkle . . .]

Immediately preceding this section is a section on the woman suspected of adultery (Num. 5:11–31), but it is too fragmentary for accurate translation. Following it are various rules among which are those on full disclosure in business, including betrothal, which is considered a commercial transaction.

4Q271 Frag. 3 Col. 1 [1][. . .] with silver [. . .] [2][. . . and his means are not su]fficient for re[payment], and the year of [jubilee] shall arrive [. . .] [3][. . .] God will release hi[m from all] his obligations.

Prohibition of cross-dressing (Deut. 22:5).

[The garments of a male] should not [4][be worn by man and woman] alike, for that is an abhorrent thing.

Full disclosure in business transactions, including betrothal.

As for the verse that says "When [you sell] [5][anything or buy anything from] your neighbor, do not defraud him" (Lev. 25:14). Now this is the mean[ing . . .] [6][. . . he must be frank about] all that he is aware of that is found [in whatever he is selling;] [7][if there is a fault in it] and he is aware of it, he is cheating him, whether it is human or animal.

And if [8][a man betroths his daughter to another ma]n, he shall tell him about all her defects, lest he bring upon himself the judgment of [9][the curse, which say]s, "Cursed is he who leads the blind astray on the road" (Deut. 27:18). Moreover, he should not give her to someone who is not proper for her, for [10][this is a case of "forbidden mixtures," like plowing with an o]x and ass, or clothing made of wool and flax together.

Rules concerning women with a history of promiscuity.

Let no man bring [11][a woman into the covenant of holi]ness whom he knew to "do the deed" for a trifle or whom he knew [12][to "do the deed" while in the house of] her father; or a widow who has had intercourse after she became a widow, or any [13][woman who has a] bad [repu]tation while a virgin in the house of her father. Let no man marry such a one unless [14][she is examined by] dependable and knowledgeable [women] who are selected at the command of the Overseer who is over the [15][general membership; the]n he may marry her, but when he marries her let him do according to the re[gul]ation [and not] tell others about [her . . .]

Rules on taking oaths. The translation of Geniza A resumes here.

Geniza A Col. 15 [1][A man must not sw]ear either by Aleph and Lamedh (*Elohim*) or by Aleph and Daleth (*Adonai*), but rather by the oath of those who enter [2]into the covenant vows. He must not make mention of the Law of Moses, because the Name of God is written out fully in it, [3]and if he swears by it, and then commits a sin, he will have defiled the Name. But if he has sw[orn] by the covenant vows in front of [4]the judges, if he has violated them, he is guilty; he should then confess his sin and make restitution and then he will not bear the burden of sin [5]and die.

Whoever enters the covenant, for all Israel this is a perpetual observance: any children who reach [6]the age to be included in the registrants, they shall impose the covenant oath upon them.

This is an excursus on the procedure for becoming a member of the Yahad, *apparently suggested by the topic of oaths, since an oath was administered to new members.*

This [7]is the rule during all the era of wickedness for all who repent of their wicked ways: On the day he speaks [8]to the Overseer of the general membership, they shall register him by the oath of the covenant that [9]Moses made with Israel, the covenant to ret[urn] to the Law of Moses with a whole heart, and [with] a who[le] [10]soul to that which is found therein to do during al[l] the era of [wickedness]. No one is allowed to tell him [11]the rules until he appears before the Overseer, so that he, the Overseer, is not fooled by him when he examines him; [12]and when he imposes upon him the oath to return to the Law of Moses with a whole heart and with a whole soul, [13]they are innocent with respect to him if he proves false.

Everything that is revealed from the Law for the multitude of the [14]Camp, and in which he (the postulant) has imperfect knowledge, the Overseer should tell him and command him to study [15]for one full year; and then according to his knowledge he may draw near.

But no one who is a fool or insane may enter; and no simpleton or ignoramus [16]or one with eyes too weak to see or lame or crippled or deaf or minor child, [17]none of these shall enter the congregation, for the holy angels are in your midst.

Col. 16 [1][. . .] with you a covenant, and with all Israel. Therefore let a man take upon himself the oath to return to [2]the Law of Moses, for in it everything is laid out in detail. But the specification of the times during which all Israel is blind to [3]all these rules is laid out in detail in the "Book of Time Divisions by [4]Jubilees and Weeks." On the day a man takes on himself the oath to return [5]to the Law of Moses the Angel of Obstruction will leave him, if he keeps His words. [6]That is why Abraham was circumcised on the day he gained true knowledge.

A return to the subject of oaths.

As for the passage "observe what comes out of your lips" (Deut. 23:24), [7]it means to abide by every binding oath in which a man promises [8]to do anything from the Law: he may not break it, even at the price of death. Every [9]promise a man makes to depart from the Law he shall not keep, even at the price of death.

[10]Concerning a woman's oath: The passage that speaks of her husband annulling her oath (Num. 30:9) means he should not [11]annul an oath if he does not know whether it should be allowed to stand or be annulled. [12]If it violates the covenant he should annul it and not allow it to stand. The rule also applies to her father.

Offerings and vows to God.

[13]Concerning the rule of freewill offerings: A man shall not vow to the altar anything stolen, nor [14]shall the priests accept it from an Israelite.

A man shall [not] consecrate the food [15]of his mouth to God, for that is referred to by the passage, "Men trap each other with what is consecrated to God" (Mic. 7:2); nor should [16]a man consecrate any [. . .] And the rule also applies if he [17]consecrates part of a field he owns himself [. . .] [18]The one who so vows shall be punished [. . .] money of its value [. . .] [19]to the judges [for a fair decision and to evaluate . . . after the thing is vowed . . .] [20]If [it is gained by extortion, the extorter shall pay, if he has not spoken the truth to his fellow . . . As for the verse that says,]

Col. 9 [1]"Anything <MS.: any man> a man proscribes" (Lev. 27:28), if a human being is proscribed, he shall be put to death by the laws of the Gentiles.

Accusations against fellow Israelites.

[2]As for the passage that says, "Take no vengeance and bear no grudge against your kinfolk" (Lev. 19:18) any covenant member [3]who brings against his fellow an accusation not sworn to before witnesses [4]or who makes an accusation in the heat of anger or who tells it to his elders to bring his fellow into disrepute, the same is a vengeance-taker and a grudge-bearer.

[5]It says only, "On his enemies God takes vengeance, against his foes he bears a grudge" (Nah. 1:2).

[6]If he kept silent day by day and then in the heat of anger against his fellow spoke against him in a capital case, [7]this testifies against him that he did not fulfill the commandment of God which says to him, "You [8]shall reprove your fellow and not bear the sin yourself" (Lev. 19:17).

Another law about oaths.

About oaths. The passage [9]that says, "You may not seek a remedy by your own power" (1 Sam. 25:26), a man who makes someone take an oath out in the countryside [10]and not before judges or at their bidding: such a one has "sought a remedy by his own power."

Lost property.

Everything that is lost [11]and it is not known which of the men of the camp stole it, its owner shall pronounce a malediction [12]by the covenant oath and whoever hears it, if he knows and does not tell, is guilty.

Restitution in the absence of an owner.

[13]Every sin for which restitution is to be made in the absence of an owner to whom it is to be paid, the one making restitution shall confess to the priest [14]and it shall belong to the priest alone, aside from the ram of expiation. So also every lost item that is found with no [15]owner present shall belong to the priests, if the one who found it does not know the proper thing to do with it. [16]If no owner is found, they shall have custody of it.

The law of witnesses.

Anything in which a man shall violate the Law [17]and his fellow sees it, he alone, if it is a capital case, he shall tell him of it [18]to his face in a denunciation to the Overseer, who shall then personally make a written note of it, until he does it [19]again in the presence of a sole witness, who again makes it known to the Overseer. If he is caught doing it yet again by one [20]witness, his fate is sealed. But if there are only two witnesses, who yet disagree [21]about the offense, then the man should be banned only from the community meal, if they are reliable, and if [22]the day the man saw the offense, he tells the Overseer. Two [23]reliable witnesses may bring charges in a property case; only one is required for a ban from the community meal. **Col. 10** [1–2]A witness who is not old enough to be enrolled among those numbered as fearing God may not be admitted before the judges to put anyone to death on his evidence. [2–3]No one who has knowingly violated a single word of the commandment will be considered a reliable witness against his fellow until he is considered fit to return to full fellowship.

Qualifications for judges.

[4]This is the rule for the judges of the nation. They shall be ten men in all chosen [5]from the nation at the proper time: four from the tribe of Levi and Aaron, and from Israel [6]six men learned in the Book of Meditation and in the basic covenant principles, from the age of [7]twenty-five to sixty. No one above the age [8]of sixty shall hold the office of judge of the nation, because when Adam broke faith, [9]his life was shortened, and in the heat of anger against the earth's inhabitants, God commanded [10]their minds to regress before their life was over.

The amount of water necessary for purification.

About purification by water. A man may not [11]wash himself in water that is filthy and too shallow to make a ripple. [12]A man may not purify any vessel in such water or in any stone cistern that does not have enough water in it [13]to make a ripple and that something unclean has touched, for its water will defile the water of the vessel.

Rules on keeping the Sabbath. This subject receives the greatest amount of attention, reflecting its importance to the sect.

[14]About the Sa[bb]ath, how to keep it properly. A man may not work on the [15]sixth day from the time that the solar orb [16]is above the horizon by its diameter, because this is what is meant by the passage, "Observe the [17]Sabbath day to keep it holy" (Deut. 5:12).

On the Sabbath day, one may not speak any [18]coarse or empty word.

One is not to seek repayment of any loan from his fellow.

One may not go to court about property or wealth.

[19]One may not discuss business or work to be done the next day.

[20]A man may not go about in the field to do his desired activity on [21]the Sabbath.

One may not travel outside his city more than a thousand cubits.

[22]A man may not eat anything on the Sabbath day except food already prepared. From whatever was lost [23]in the field he may not eat, and he may not drink unless he was in the camp.

Col. 11 [1]If he was on a journey and went down to bathe, he may drink where he stands, but he may not draw water into [2]any vessel.

One may not send a Gentile to do his business on the Sabbath day.

[3]A man may not put on filthy clothes or clothes kept in fleece unless [4]he launders them in water or if they scrub them with spice.

A man may not voluntarily cross Sabbath borders [5]on the Sabbath day.

A man may walk behind an animal to graze it outside his city [6]up to two thousand cubits. One may not raise his hand to hit it with a fist. If it is [7]uncooperative, he should leave it inside.

A man may not carry anything outside his house, nor should he [8]carry anything in. If he is in a temporary shelter, he should not take anything out of it [9]or bring anything in.

No one should open a sealed vessel on the Sabbath. No one should carry [10]medicine on his person, either going out or coming in, on the Sabbath. No one should pick up stone and dust [11]in an inhabited place. No caregiver should carry a baby on the Sabbath, either going out or coming in.

[12]No one should provoke his servant, his maid, or his employee on the Sabbath.

[13]No one should help an animal give birth on the Sabbath; and if it falls into a well [14]or a pit, he may not lift it out on the Sabbath.

No one should rest in a place near [15]to Gentiles on the Sabbath.

No one should profane the Sabbath for wealth or spoil on the Sabbath.

[16]Any living human who falls into a body of water or a cistern [17]shall not be helped out with ladder, rope, or tool.

No one should offer any sacrifice on the Sabbath [18]except the Sabbath whole burnt offering, for so it is written, "besides your Sabbaths" (Lev. 23:38).

The last law suggested the topic of sacrifices.

No one should send [19]a whole burnt offering, cereal offering, incense offering, or wood offering to the altar through anyone impure by any [20]of the impurities, thus allowing him to defile the altar; for it is written, "The sacrifice [21]of the wicked is abhorrent; but the prayer of the righteous is like an offering received with favor" (Prov. 15:8). No one who enters the [22]house of worship shall enter in impurity, with garments requiring ritual laundering. When the trumpets for assembly are blown, [23]let him go earlier or later so that they need not stop the whole service, [fo]r it is a place of **Col. 12** [1]holiness.

The holiness of the sanctuary applies to the city itself. A similar point of view is taken by the Temple Scroll.

A man may not lie with a woman in the city of the Temple, defiling [2]the city of the Temple by their uncleanness.

A law counseling flexibility in the treatment of the demon-possessed. Lesser violations of the ritual law should be treated by confinement, not execution, as we would say, "for reasons of insanity."

Everyone who is controlled by the spirits of Belial [3]and who advises apostasy will receive the same verdict as the necromancer and the medium; but all such who go astray [4]to defile the Sabbath and the festivals shall not be put to death, for it is the responsibility of human beings [5]to keep him in custody. If he recovers from it, they must watch him for seven years and afterwards [6]he may enter the assembly.

Laws relating to contact with Gentiles.

Let no one attack any of the Gentiles with intent to kill [7]for the sake of wealth and spoil, nor may anyone carry away any of their wealth, so that they may not [8]blaspheme, except by the counsel of the commonwealth of Israel.

No one may sell a clean animal [9]or bird to the Gentiles, lest they sacrifice them to idols; neither from his threshing floor [10]or from his winepress shall he sell to them, in all his property; his servant and his maidservant he may not sell [11]to them, for they have entered with him into Abraham's covenant.

Laws relating to impure foods.

No one may defile himself [12]with any creature or creeping thing by eating them, from the larvae of bees to any living [13]creature that crawls in the water; and the fish may not be eaten unless they are split open [14]while living and their blood poured out. All species of locust must be put in fire or water [15]while they are alive, because that befits their nature. Every piece of wood or stone [16]or dust that is desecrated by human uncleanness, with stains of oil: according to their [17]uncleanness, whoever touches them will become unclean. Every instrument, nail, or peg in the wall of [18]a house where a corpse lies shall be unclean, with the same impurity as a work tool.

Summary and conclusion to the laws for Israel in general.

[19]The regulations above are the rule for those who live in the cities of Israel, with these regulations to separate [20]unclean from clean and to discriminate between holy and profane. These are the rules [21]for the sage to live by with all that is living, according to the regulation for every occasion. If [22]the seed of Israel lives according to this law, they shall never know condemnation.

Rules for those living in camps.

This is the rule for those who live in [23]camps, who live by these rules in the era of wickedness, until the appearance of the Messiah of Aaron **Col. 13** [1]and of Israel: up to ten men at least, for thousands, and hundreds, and fifties, [2]and tens. For every group of ten, a priest knowledgeable in the Book of Meditation should always be present; by [3]his command all shall be ruled. If he is not qualified in these rules and a Levite is qualified in [4]them, then the allotment shall proceed in all its ways at his command, all the members of the camp. But if [5]it is a case of the law of skin diseases, then the priest must come and be present in the camp, and the Overseer [6]shall instruct him in the details of the Law, and even if the priest is ignorant, it is he who must isolate the one suffering from skin disease, because that duty [7]is the priests' alone.

Qualifications for an Overseer.

This is the rule for the Overseer of a camp. He must teach the general membership about the works [8]of God, instruct them in His mighty miracles, relate to them the future events coming to the world with their interpretations; [9]he should care for them as a father does his children, taking care of all their problems as a shepherd does for his flock. [10]He should loosen all their knots, that there be no one oppressed or crushed in his congregation.

[11]He shall observe everyone who is added to his group as to his actions, his intelligence, his ability, his strength, and his wealth [12]and write him down by his place according to his share in the allotment of Light.

Relationships with outsiders.

No members of the camp are allowed [13]to bring anyone into the group except by permission of the Overseer of the camp; [14]and none of the members of God's covenant should do business with corrupt people, [15]except hand to hand. No one should do any buying or selling unless he has informed [16]the Overseer who is in the camp and taken counsel (with him), [lest they err unwittingly. Likewise] with [an]y man who m[arr]ies a wom[an] [17]let [it be with] the counsel (of the Overseer); and likewise (**4Q266** adds: let him instruct) a man who wishes to divorce. He shall edu[cate their sons and daughters] [18][and young children] in a spirit of meekness and love of mercy. He must not bear against them [a grudge in anger] [19][and wrath for] their [tr]ansgressions. And one who is not bound [. . .]

[20]This is the <rule for> those living in camps, for all [. . .] [21][If any have broken] these rules, they will not prosper when they live in the land [. . .]

A second section of the camp rules begins here. These rules seem to apply to the camps in full convention, instead of considered individually.

[22]These are the re[gulation]s for the Instructor [. . .] [23][. . . when the verse comes true that says, "There shall come upon your people days] **Col. 14** [1]that have not been seen since the day Ephraim separated from Judah" (Isa. 7:17). But as for all who live by these rules, [2]God's covenant stands firm for them, delivering them from all the traps of corruption; but "the ignorant pass them by and are punished" (Prov. 22:3, 27:12).

Rank within the camps.

[3]The rule of dwelling in all the camps. All shall be mustered by their names: the priests first, [4]the Levites second, the children of Israel third, the proselyte fourth. Then they shall be recorded by name, [5]one after the other: the priests first, the Levites second, the children of Israel [6]third, the proselyte fourth. In the same order they shall sit, and in the same order they will inquire of all.

Qualifications for the presiding priest and general Overseer. For more on the mysterious Book of Meditation, see the introductions to the Charter for Israel in the Last Days *(text 8) and the* Secret of the Way Things Are *(text 105).*

The priest who presides [7]at the head of the general membership must be between thirty to sixty years old, learned in the Book of Meditation [8]and in all the regulations of the Law, speaking them in the proper way. The Overseer of [9]all the camps must be between thirty and fifty years old, master of every [10]secret of men and of every deceptive utterance. At his command the members of the congregation shall enter, [11]each in his turn. Anything that any man might have to say, let him say it to the Overseer, including [12]any kind of dispute or legal matter.

Contributions for the needs of camp members.

This is the rule of the general membership for meeting all their needs: a wage of [13]two days every month at least shall be given to the Overseer. Then the judges [14]will give some of it for their wounded, with some of it they will support the poor and needy, and the elder [15][bent with age], the man with a skin disease, whoever is taken captive by a foreign nation, the girl [16]without a near kinsman, the boy without an advocate; and for whatever is common business, so that [17]the common house should not be cut off.

This is the exposition for those who live in the ca[mps, and these are the pillars of [18]the foundations of] the assembly.

Rules dealing with punishments for infraction of the rules. Some of these rules are the same as those found in the Charter of a Jewish Sectarian Association *(text 7).*

And this is the exposition of the regulations by which [they shall be governed [19]until the appearance of the Messi]ah of Aaron and of Israel, so that their iniquity may be atoned for. [Cereal offering and sin offering . . .]

[20][Who]ever [li]es knowingly in a matter of money shall be ex[pelled from the common me]al [21][. . . and suffer redu]ced rations six days; and whoever spea[ks . . .] [22][and whoever bears a grudge against his neighbor, which] is not lawful, [shall suffer re]duced rations [. . .] **4Q266 Frag. 10 Col. 2** [1][. . . shall be expelled two] hundred days and suffer reduced rations one hundred days. If he has born a grudge in a capital case, he shall not ever come back.

[2][Whoever . . .] his fellow without taking counsel shall be [ex]pelled one year and suffer reduced rations [3]s[ix months.]

Whoever speaks audibly a coarse word shall suffer reduced rations t[went]y [4][days, and expelled] three month[s.

Whoever] speaks while [another is speaking] and disturbs him [5][will suffer reduced rations ten] days.

[Whoever lies do]wn [and] sleeps in the [general me]etin[g . . .] [6][shall be expelled] thirty days [and] suffer reduced rations ten days.

[And likewise for whoever lea]ves [7][with]out the permission of the g[en]eral membership, [for n]o [reason,] up to three ti[mes in] one [meeting,] [8][shall suffer reduced rations] ten days. If [he continues] to leave [the meeting, he shall suffer reduced rations thirty] [9]days.

Whoever goes around [naked] in front [of his] fellow [in the house or whoever goes about naked outside before] [10]the world must be expelled for six [months . . . Whoever] [11]brings his penis out of [his] clothing, [being dressed in rags, and his nakedness is seen, shall be expelled for thir]ty [12][da]ys and shall suffer reduced rations ten.

Whoever laughs foolish[ly in an audible voice must be expelled] [13][th]irty days and suffer reduced rations fif[teen] days.

[Whoever puts out] his le[ft ha]nd [14][to gestu]re with it must suffer reduced rations [ten days.

Whoever] spreads [slander] [15][about his nei]ghbor [must be banned from the common meal for one year . . .]

4Q270 Frag. 7 Col. 1 [6][Whoever spreads slander about the general membership] [7][is to be sent away and must never] return a[gain. If he complains about his fellow unlawfully, he must suffer reduced rations six] [8][months.

The man] whose [spirit] deviates [from the fundamentals of the *Yahad,* proving unfaithful to the truth, and walking in his willful heart,] [9][mu]st be [expelled two years and su]ffer reduced rations sixty [days. When his two years are complete, the general membership will inquire] [10]about [his] ca[se; if he draws near, let them] write [him down in his rank and then he may be examined about the law . . .]

. . . [11][Who]ever rejects the ruling of the general membership shall depart and [never return.

Whoever takes his] [12]food outside contrary to the rules must return it to the one he took it from. [. . .]

Whoever approa[ches] [13]to fornicate with his wife, which is not according to the regulation, shall depart and never return.

[Whoever complains] against the fathers, [14][he must leave] the congregation and never return; [but if] against the mothers, he must suffer reduced rations ten days, for the mothers have no such status within [15][the congregation.

These are the] regulations by wh[ich they judge] all who are disciplined.

Procedure for punishment of the offender.

Whoever [16][is disciplined] must come and tell it to the priest who presides over **4Q266 Frag. 11** [1]the general membership, he must receive his verdict willingly, just as it says through [2]Moses concerning the person who sins unwittingly, that they shall bring [3]his sin offering [or] his guilt offering; and concerning Israel it is written, "I shall go [4]to the ends of heaven and I will not smell the odor of your incense" (Lev. 26:31). In another place [5a]it is written, "Rend your hearts and not your garments" (Joel 2:13), [5]and, "Return to God with weeping and fasting" (Joel 2:12). Anyone who rejects these regulations, [6]which are in keeping with the statutes found in the Law of Moses, shall not be considered [7]one of those who belong to his truth, for his soul is repulsed by righteous discipline. [8]He shall be sent away in the presence of the general membership for the crime of rebellion, and the priest who presides over the general membership shall speak, and raise his voice [9]and say:

Blessed art Thou! Thou art the All, in thy hands are all things, and Maker of All, who hast established [10]the [p]eoples by clans and tongues and nations, then led them astray in a wasteland without [11]a way, but Thou hast chosen our fathers, Thou hast given to their descendants the statutes of Thy truth, [12]and the judgments of Thy holiness, which, if humankind shall do, they shall have life; and boundaries hast Thou made [13]for us, and they that transgress them Thou hast cursed; but we are Thy redeemed people, and the sheep of Thy pasture. [14]Indeed, Thou hast cursed the transgressors; but Thou hast made us firm.

Then the excommunicated shall leave. Anyone [15]who uses any of their property or who greets him or who agrees with him, [16]this matter shall be recorded by the Overseer with an engraving tool, and his fate is sealed.

And all [17][those who live in] camps shall convene on the third month and curse those who stray from the Law to the right [18][or to the left.]

Conclusion of the rule.

This is the exposition of the regulations that they shall follow during the era [19][of wickedness, for which] they are [respon]sible [in al]l the times of wrath and the stages of their journeys, for all those [20][who live in their camps and all those who live in their cities.

Behold, al]l of this is [o]n the basis of the most [recent in]terpreta[tion] of the Law.

—E.M.C.

2. A Commentary on Habakkuk

1QpHab

Almost all of the Dead Sea Scrolls that are not themselves copies of biblical books are still connected in some way with the Scriptures of Israel. The poetic compositions, however creative, are still suffused with biblical phrases; the legal texts are based openly or implicitly on scriptural precedents; and the narratives of the past or predictions of the future are retellings or refashionings of sacred stories or prophecies.

The biblical connection comes to expression most clearly in texts that specifically attempt to explain or decipher biblical texts. Sometimes the ancients "explained" the text by rewriting or paraphrasing it, as in *Tales of the Patriarchs* (text 4) or the *Words of Moses* (text 5). Often, though, they simply commented on the Bible, verse by verse. Sometimes the texts under consideration are chosen because of their relevance to a particular theme, as in the *Last Days* (text 25), which consists of explanations of verses about Israel's future destiny; sometimes continuous passages or books are treated in order, as in the present text, the *Commentary on Habakkuk*.

It is very characteristic of the Dead Sea sect that they often considered the Bible a puzzle to be solved or an enigma to be unraveled. Its characteristic word for the activity of interpretation was *pesher,* which as a rule refers to the interpretation of dreams. The biblical Daniel serves as the ideal interpreter of this type: he interprets dreams (Dan. 2; 4) and visions (the "handwriting on the wall," Dan 5), not through native ability but because God has revealed the secrets to him. The Qumran scribes understood their task in the same way: to penetrate the secrets of Scripture not through reflection on the text itself, but through openness to the revelation of God.

The result of this activity is a series of commentaries (perhaps "interpretations" is a better word) that themselves often partake of the unreality of dreams. The writers saw their own group's history in the words of Scripture, foretold long ago, but are cautious about naming names. Instead, they use symbolic titles with biblical overtones: the Teacher of Righteousness, the Wicked Priest, the Man of the Lie. When they find these characters in the words of the Bible, the disconcerting outcome is not a decoded message, but one code translated into another code.

The *Commentary on Habakkuk* was among the first cache of scrolls from Cave 1, and has itself been the subject of several commentaries. The first step in understanding the commentary is to understand the background of the original book. Habakkuk delivered his prophecy in the sixth century B.C.E. His native Judah was then threatened by two forces: the Chaldeans, or Babylonians, under Nebuchadnezzar, who were then in the process of conquering the small kingdoms of the Near East, and internal religious strife between the pious worshipers of the Lord and the ungodly. The main thrust of the biblical book is to ask where God is in the midst of this misery and whether there is a divine plan.

The Qumran writer uses the biblical book as a pattern to understand his own times. As in the biblical book, Israel is again threatened by a foreign power: not the Chaldeans this time, but a group he calls the Kittim, or "Westerners," in the opinion of most scholars today the Romans. And again, Israel is suffering from internal strife between the wicked and the pious, exemplified by the conflict between the Teacher of Righteousness and his opponents, the Man of the Lie and the Wicked Priest. All the statements in the first two chapters of Habakkuk are made to refer to these circumstances (the third chapter, consisting of a hymn of praise, is not included in the *Commentary*).

The modern attempt to decode the Qumran "recoding" of Habakkuk has centered on the identification of the Kittim. As noted, most now agree that the Kittim are the Romans, and their arrival in Israel—so dreaded by the writer of the commentary—in fact took place in 63 B.C.E. The commentary must have been written around that time, and the latest carbon-14 tests in fact point to the first century B.C.E. as the period when the Cave 1 copy was made. (The paleographical date places the scroll late in the first century B.C.E.) That the activity of the Teacher, the Priest, and the Man of the Lie also belongs to this period is still disputed (see the Introduction, pp. 27–33).

The first portion of the commentary focuses on the religious strife in Israel. Unfortunately, the first column survives only in fragments.

Col. 1 1["The oracle that the prophet Habakkuk saw. How long have] I cried out, and 2[You do not hear? I cry out 'Injustice!' and You do not liberate us" (1:1–2).

This refers to the en]treaty of the generation 3[. . . the events to] come upon them 4[. . . they] cried out for 5[. . .].

["Why do You let me see such wickedness, why do You be]hold such [tur]moil?" (1:3a).

6[This refers to . . . those who rejected the Law of] God with tyranny and treason.

[7][“Robbery and injustice are in front of me; strife and conflict continue” (1:3b).]

[8][This refers to . . .] in[justice] and strife [. . .] [9][. . . conten]tion and [. . .] is [10][. . .]

“Therefore Law declines, [11][and true judgment never comes forth” (1:4a).

This means] that they rejected God’s Law [12][. . .]

[“For the wicked man hems in] the righteous man” (1:4b).

[13][The “wicked man” refers to the Wicked Priest, and “the righteous man”] is the Teacher of Righteousness. [14][. . .]

[“There]fore judgment comes out [15][perverted” (1:4c).

This means that . . .] not [. . .] [16][. . .]

The following passage expresses something of the writer’s view of Israel’s history. He believes that “traitors” to God’s law trouble the nation at crucial times: the present (those who disbelieve in the Teacher), the past (the unfaithful at the time of Israel’s return from exile, the “new covenant”), and the future (those who disbelieve in the “anointed priest,” the Messiah of Aaron).

[“Look, traitors, and see,] [17][and be shocked—and amazed—for the LORD is doing something in your time that you would not believe it if] **Col. 2** [1]told” (1:5).

[This passage refers to] the traitors with the Man of the [2]Lie, because they have not [obeyed the words of] the Teacher of Righteousness from the mouth of [3]God. It also refers to the trai[tors to the] New [Covenant], because they did not [4]believe in God’s covenant [and desecrated] His holy name; [5]and finally, it refers [to the trai]tors in the Last [6]Days. They are the cru[el Israel]ites who will not believe [7]when they hear everything that is to c[ome upon] the latter generation that will be spoken by [8]the Priest in whose [heart] God has put [the ability] to explain all [9]the words of his servants the prophets, through [whom] God has foretold [10]everything that is to come upon his people and [the Gentiles].

The coming of the Romans. Their cruelty and military prowess were already legendary.

“For I am now about to raise up [11]the Chaldeans, that br[utal and reckle]ss people” (1:6a).

[12]This refers to the Kittim, w[ho are] swift and mighty [13]in war, annihilating many people, [and . . .] in the authority of [14]the Kittim and the wic[ked . . .] and have no faith in [15]the laws of [God.]

["They range across the land to seize dwellings not their own" (1:6b).

[16][This refers to the Kittim . . .] [17][. . .] **Col. 3** [1]and they cross the plain, attacking and pillaging the cities of the land, [2]for that is what it means when it says, "to seize dwellings not their own" (1:6b).

"Dire [3]and dreadful are they; their law and their fame come from themselves alone" (1:7).

[4]This refers to the Kittim, the fear and dread of whom are on all [5]nations. By intention their only thought is to do evil, and in deceit and trickery [6]they conduct themselves with all the peoples.

"Swifter than panthers their horses, faster [7]than desert wolves. Their horses, galloping, spread out, from afar [8]they fly like a vulture intent on food, all of them bent on violence, [9]their faces ever forward" (1:8–9a).

[This refers to] the Kittim, who [10]trample the land with [their] horses and with their beasts. From far away [11]they come, from the seacoasts, to eat up all the peoples like an [12]insatiable vulture. In anger and [hostility and in] wrath and arrogance [13]they speak with all [the peoples, for] that is what it means when [14]it says, ["their faces ever forward."]

["They will gather] captives [like sa]nd" (1:9b).

[15][This refers to . . .] [16–17][. . .]

["At kings] **Col. 4** [1]they mock, potentates they laugh to scorn" (1:10a).

This means that [2]they sneer at many people and deride the nobility; [3]they jeer at kings and princes, and ridicule a throng of people.

"They [4]laugh at every fortress; they pile up dirt and capture it" (1:10b).

[5]This refers to the rulers of the Kittim who deride [6]the fortresses of the peoples and with a sneer laugh at them. [7]With a great army they surround them to capture them, and with fear and terror [8]the fortresses fall into their power. Then they destroy them because of the crimes of those who dwell [9]there.

The arrival of the Romans in Israel was, in the commentator's words, "by the advice of a family of sinners." Both of the warring factions in Israel in the first century B.C.E. *had an interest in Roman intervention. From the commentator's standpoint, no good, beyond the manifestation of God's judgment, can come of the Roman presence.*

"Then a wind passes and they are gone, having caused devastation; this power has become [10]their god" (1:11).

This refe[rs t]o the rulers of the Kittim, [11]who cross the land by the advice of a family of sinn[ers]: each [12]before his fellow, [their] rulers come, one after the other, [13]to devastate the la[nd. When it says] "this power has become their god," [14]this means [. . . a]ll the peoples [15–16][. . .]

The only solution for the faithful, as in Habakkuk's day, is to remain loyal to God's law.

["But You] [17][are eternal, O LORD, my holy God, we will not die.] **Col. 5** [1]You have marked them for judgment; O Rock, You have made them for rebuke. Eyes too pure [2]to see evil, You cannot even watch wrongdoing" (1:12–13a).

[3]This passage means that God will not exterminate his people through the Gentiles; [4]on the contrary, He will give the power to pass judgment on the Gentiles to his chosen, and it is at their rebuke that [5]all the wicked of His people shall be condemned. The chosen are those who have observed His commandments [6]in the time of their distress, for that is what it means when it says, "eyes too pure to see [7]evil" (1:13a). That means that they have not let their eyes lead them into fornication during the time of [8]wickedness.

The reference to the "family of Absalom" in the following passage has puzzled scholars for decades. Is Absalom another code name or a real historical figure? The biblical Absalom was a son of King David who revolted against his father's rule. But there was also an Israelite nobleman named Absalom in the first century B.C.E. who was the uncle and father-in-law of Aristobulus II (see the Introduction, pp. 30–31), and presumably a member of the Sadducean faction. It is possible that he is the one the text refers to.

"How can you look on silently, you traitors, when [9]the wicked destroys one more righteous than he?" (1:13b).

This refers to the family of Absalom [10]and the members of their party, who kept quiet when the Teacher of Righteousness was rebuked, [11]and they did not help him against the Man of the Lie, who had rejected [12]the Law in the presence of their entire [company.]

The assertion that the Kittim sacrifice to their standards (military insignia bearing likenesses of the gods or divinized kings, mounted on a staff) is one of the clearest indications that they are the Romans. It is well documented that the Roman legions burned incense to their standards.

"You made humanity as helpless as fish in the sea, [13]like something a worm could rule over. He draws them [all] out [with a hook], pulls them in with his net, [14]gathers them with [his dragnet. Therefore he sacrifices] to his net, therefore he is happy [15][and rejoices and burns incense to his dragnet; for by them] his lot in life [is enriched] [16][and his food is wholesome" (1:14–16).

This refers to . . .] **Col. 6** [1]the Kittim, and they added to their wealth by all their plunder [2]like the fish of the sea. And when it says, "therefore he sacrifices to his net [3]and burns incense to his dragnet" (1:16a), this means that they [4]sacrifice to their standards, and that their weapons are [5]what they worship. "For by them his lot in life is enriched and his food is wholesome" (1:16b), [6]means that they impose the yoke of their [7]taxes—their "food"—on all the peoples yearly, [8]thus ruining many lands.

"Therefore he keeps his sword always drawn [9]to kill nations without pity" (1:17).

[10]This refers to the Kittim who destroy many people with the sword, including [11]boys, adults, old men, women, and children. Even on "the child in the [12]womb they have no mercy" (Isa. 13:18).

According to this section, the Teacher himself, like Daniel, received divine communications explaining the words of the prophets. He himself may have pioneered the pesher approach to biblical interpretation.

"So I will stand on watch [13]and station myself on my watchtower and wait for what He will say [14]to me, and [what He will reply to] my rebuke. Then the LORD answered me [15][and said, Write down the vision plainly] on tablets, so that with ease [16][someone can read it" (2:1–2).

This refers to . . .] **Col. 7** [1]then God told Habakkuk to write down what is going to happen to [2]the generation to come; but when that period would be complete He did not make known to him. [3]When it says, "so that with ease someone can read it," [4]this refers to the Teacher of Righteousness to whom God made known [5]all the mysterious revelations of his servants the prophets.

"For still the prophecy is for [6]a specific period; it testifies of that time and does not deceive" (2:3a).

[7]This means that the Last Days will be long, much longer than [8]the prophets had said; for God's revelations are truly mysterious.

Again, as in the Commentary on Habakkuk *1:12–13, the writer exhorts the righteous to remain faithful and patient throughout the time of suffering.*

[9]"If it tarries, be patient, it will surely come true and not [10]be delayed" (2:3b).

This refers to those loyal ones, [11]obedient to the Law, whose hands will not cease from [12]loyal service even when the Last Days seems long to them, for [13]all the times fixed by God will come about at their proper time as He ordained [14]that they should by his inscrutable insight.

"See how bloated, not smooth, [15][his soul is!" (2:4a).]

This means that [their punishment] will be twice as much for them [16][and they will not] find favor when they come to judgment [. . .] [17][. . .]

The writer here contemplates the final judgment. How may one escape the wrath to come? By obedience to the Law and loyalty to the Teacher. It is not clear if the Teacher here mentioned is the founder of the sect or a Teacher who will appear later. The sect appeared to believe both in a present and future Teacher of Righteousness. Whether they were one and the same is still debated.

["As for the righteous man, by loyalty to him one may find life" (2:4b).]

Col. 8 [1]This refers to all those who obey the Law among the Jews whom [2]God will rescue from the place of judgment, because of their suffering and their loyalty [3]to the Teacher of Righteousness.

The Teacher's nemesis, the Wicked Priest, is here introduced. Because he was both a priest and also a "ruler of Israel" (ll. 9–10 below) most scholars believe that he must have been one of the Hasmonean priest-kings of the second and first centuries B.C.E. *He appears to have been originally a figure that the Teacher and his followers could trust (he had a "reputation for reliability," literally "was called by the name of truth"), but then proved to be proud, selfish, and greedy.*

"And indeed, riches betray the arrogant man and he will not [4]last; he who has made his throat as wide as Hades, and who, like Death, is never satisfied. [5]All the Gentiles will flock to him, and all the peoples will gather to him. [6]Look, all of them take up a taunt against him, and invent sayings about him, [7]saying, 'Ho, one who grows large on what is not his, how long will he burden himself down [8]with debts?' " (2:5–6).

This refers to the Wicked Priest, who [9]had a reputation for reliability at the beginning of his term of service; but when he became ruler [10]over Israel, he became proud and forsook God and betrayed the commandments for the sake of [11]riches. He amassed by force the riches of the lawless who had rebelled against God, [12]seizing the riches of the peoples, thus adding to the guilt of his crimes, [13]and he committed abhorrent deeds in every defiling impurity.

The fate of the Wicked Priest. He fell into the hands of his enemies and was tortured; yet it would be his successors, the "later priests of Jerusalem," who would lose their riches to the Romans. It is not clear if the Wicked Priest died as a result of his mistreatment.

"Look, suddenly [14]your creditors will appear, your enemies will rouse themselves and you will become booty for them. [15]Yes, you yourself have plundered many nations, now the rest of the peoples will plunder you" (2:7–8a).

[16][This refers to] the priest who rebelled [17][and violated] the commandments of [God . . . they mis]treated him [. . .] **Col. 9** [1]his afflictions with the punishments due to such wickedness, perpetrating upon him the horrors of painful [2]diseases, acts of retaliation against his mortal body. But the verse that [3]says, "Yes, you yourself have plundered many nations, now the rest of [4]the peoples will plunder you" (2:7–8a), refers to the later priests of Jerusalem, [5]who will gather ill-gotten riches from the plunder of the peoples, [6]but in the Last Days their riches and plunder alike will be handed over to [7]the army of the Kittim, for they are "the rest of the peoples."

[8]"For the murder of a man and injustice in the land, the city and all who live in it" (2:8b).

[9]This refers to the Wicked Priest. Because of the crime he committed against the Teacher of [10]Righteousness and the members of his party, God handed him over to his enemies, humiliating him [11]with a consuming affliction with despair, because he had condemned [12]his chosen.

"Ah, you who amass evil plunder for your own house, placing [13]your perch in a high place to escape the clutch of disaster—you have given shameful advice [14]to your house, destroying many peoples and the sinners of your soul. Surely even [15]the stonew[ork] from the wall will denounce you, a rafter in the ceiling will [echo it"] (2:9–11).

[16][This refers] to the p[ries]t who [. . .] [17][. . .] **Col. 10** [1]that its stones were laid by tyranny and the wooden rafters by robbery. The verse that [2]says, "destroying many peoples and the sinners of your soul" (2:10b). [3]refers to the place of judgment, when God will pronounce [4]sentence in the presence of many peoples; from there He will bring him up for judgment, [5]and in their presence He will condemn him and punish him with fire and brimstone.

The Man of the Lie, or the Spreader of Lies, was the leader of a rival party to that of the Teacher. He and his group—possibly the Pharisees—held a competing interpretation of the Law of Moses.

"Woe to [6]you who build a city by bloodshed, who found a town by vice! Indeed [7]this prophecy is from the LORD of Hosts: peoples will toil just for enough fire, [8]nations will wear themselves out for nothing" (2:12–13).

[9]This refers to the Spreader of Lies, who deceived many, [10]building a worthless city by bloodshed and forming a community by lies [11]for its own glory, making many toil at useless labor, teaching them [12]to do false deeds. In the end, their toil will be for nothing. As a result, they will undergo [13]fiery punishments because they blasphemed and reviled God's chosen ones.

[14]"The earth will be full of the knowledge of the LORD's glory as waters [15]cover the sea" (2:14).

This means [that] [16]when they repent [. . .] [17][. . . Spreader of] **Col. 11** [1]Lies, and afterwards true knowledge will be revealed to them, as water of [2]the sea for abundance.

The Priest persecutes the Teacher. This paragraph has been intensely studied for clues to the identity of both Priest and Teacher. It appears that the Teacher, after his "rebuke" (see 5:10 above), went into exile; but the Priest, wishing to finish off the Teacher and his followers, hunted him down and confronted the Teacher and his followers on the Day of Atonement. Since it is unlikely that the Priest, if he were high priest, would be hunting his enemies on that holy day, when he had important ritual duties to perform, the day referred to must have been celebrated according to the sectarian calendar.

"Woe to the one who gets his friend drunk, pouring out [3]his anger, making him drink, just to get a look at their holy days" (2:15).

[4]This refers to the Wicked Priest, who [5]pursued the Teacher of Righteousness to destroy him in [6]the heat of his anger at his place of exile. At the time set aside for the repose of [7]the Day of Atonement he appeared to them to destroy them [8]and to bring them to ruin on the fast day, the Sabbath intended for their repose.

More on the fate awaiting the Wicked Priest.

"You are satisfied with [9]disgrace, not honor? So go ahead and drink until you stagger; [10]the cup of the LORD's right hand will come around for you, and then shame [11]will cover your honor" (2:16).

[12]This refers to the priest whose disgrace became greater than his honor, [13]because he had not circumcised his heart's foreskin, and he walked in the ways of [14]drunkenness in order to put an end to thirst. But the cup of God's wrath [15]will destroy him, increas[ing only his dis]honor and pain [. . .] [16][. . .]

[17]["For the crimes perpetrated against Lebanon he will bury you, for the robbery of beasts,] **Col. 12** [1]he will smite you; because of murder and injustice in the land, he will destroy the city and all who live in it" (2:17).

[2]The passage refers to the Wicked Priest, that he will be paid back [3]for what he did to the poor, for "Lebanon" refers to [4]the party of the *Yahad,* and "beasts" refers to the simple-hearted of Judah who obey [5]the Law. God will condemn him to utter destruction, [6]just as he planned to destroy the poor. As for the verse that says, "because of murder in the [7]city and injustice in the land," "the city" refers to Jerusalem, [8]where the Wicked Priest committed his abhorrent deeds, defiling the [9]Temple of God. "Injustice in the land" refers to the cities of Judah where [10]he stole the assets of the poor.

The commentary ends with straightforward condemnation of Gentile idolatry.

"What good is an idol that someone makes? It is only [11]an image, a source of false teaching—though indeed the manufacturer trusts his own products, [12]making for himself false gods without a voice!" (2:18).

This refers to all [13]idols of the Gentiles that they made to worship and bow down to, [14]though they will not save them on the day of judgment.

"Woe [15]to those [who say] to mere wood, 'Be alert,' or 'W[ake up,'] to dumb [st]one. [16][Can it enlighten you? It may indeed be covered with gold and silver,] [17][but there is no life in it. But the LORD really is in his holy temple.] **Col. 13** [1]Keep silence before him, all the earth" (2:19–20).

This refers to all the Gentiles [2]who have worshiped stone and wood. In the day of [3]judgment God will exterminate all those who worship false gods, [4]as well as the wicked, from the earth.

—E.M.C.

3. A Commentary on Micah

1Q14

The very fragmentary *Commentary on Micah* contains tantalizing references to the Teacher of Righteousness and his enemy, the Spreader of Lies, but the restoration of the surrounding text is hypothetical.

Frags. 8–10 [1][". . .] for the sin [2][of Jacob is all of this and for the transgressions of the House of Israel. What is Jac]ob['s sin?] Behold, it is [3][Samaria. What are the high places of Judah? Behold, it is Jer]usa[lem." (1:5). "I will make Samaria] [4][a heap in the open country, a place for planting vineyards" . . . (1:6).] This refers to the Spreader of Lies, [5][who will lead astray the]

simple-hearted. "And what are Judah's high places? [6][Behold, they are Jerusalem." (1:5). This refers t]o the Teacher of Righteousness who himself [7][shall teach the law to his par]ty and to all those who are willing to be added to the chosen of [8][God, the ones who observe the law] in the party of the *Yahad* who will be saved on the Day of [9][Judgment . . .] [10][. . . As for the verse that says, "I will make Samaria as] a heap of [the] open country [11][a place for planting vineyards; and I will pour down her stones into the valley, and I will uncover her foundations (1:6).] A[ll her idols . . ." (1:7).]
—E.M.C.

4. Tales of the Patriarchs

1QapGen

This charming collection of stories is one of a fair number of Dead Sea Scrolls that scholars assign to the category "rewritten Bible." The category is a broad one, embracing many different methods of rewriting the Bible; some examples do little more than select and rearrange portions of Scripture, apparently intending by such juxtapositioning to clarify the relationship and proper interpretation of the portions involved. The present text is more adventurous. Although at points the author simply presents the text of Genesis more or less as he knew it, more often he adds details—and even whole sections—drawn from extrabiblical sources or oral traditions. The author attempts to give the proper spin to the biblical text at crucial points where, in his view, dangerous misinterpretation is possible.

A clear example of this concern is the case of Abraham's wife, Sarah, and an unnamed Egyptian pharaoh. (Throughout the surviving portions of *Tales,* however, Abraham is referred to as "Abram," and Sarah as "Sarai"; the reason is that these portions of the *Tales* correspond to chapters of Genesis that precede Genesis 17, the biblical portion wherein Abraham and Sarah receive their new, but to us more familiar, names.) According to Genesis 12, this pharaoh took Sarah from Abraham when the patriarch had gone down to the pharaoh's territory in search of food. Our author had a definite view of the chronology of Genesis, even where the Bible says nothing of such matters directly, and believed that Sarah must have been with the pharaoh for some two years. Had she then been violated repeatedly? If so, this was a sordid tale indeed, bringing shame upon the Jewish people. To obviate this implication of the biblical text, our author decided that the pharaoh must be shown to have been impotent the entire time. Then, of course, Sarah's purity would have been preserved. So he introduced a long addition to the biblical text at the proper point, explaining that God smote the pharaoh with "a baneful spirit." Because of this spirit's effect—a disgusting discharge, perhaps gonorrhea—not just the pharaoh, but all his men were rendered impotent. Only with the help of the righteous Abraham's prayer on his behalf was the Egyptian monarch cured, and then only on condition of Sarah's restoration to her husband.

The description of Abraham's prayer is noteworthy: "So I prayed for him, that blasphemer, and laid my hands upon his head. Thereupon the plague was removed from him, the evil spirit exorcised from him, and he was healed" (20:28–29). This is a description of an exorcism, one roughly contemporary with the New Testament passages that record the frequent exorcisms performed by Jesus of Nazareth. The scroll's description is particularly reminiscent of an exorcism described in Mark 9. Jesus' disciples had tried and failed to exorcise a spirit that continually threw a young boy into convulsions. Jesus had to perform the exorcism himself. Later, when asked by his disciples why they had failed, Jesus replied, "This kind can come out only through prayer" (Mark 9:29).

Another example of the author's concern with the purity of Abraham's line appears in what may first seem but an insignificant detail added to the biblical text. After the Flood, Noah's family was essentially in the same situation as Adam, Eve, and their children. With no other people around, whom could the young people marry? The Bible is silent on this problem, though it does provide genealogical information about Noah's sons and grandsons. The scroll adds details about Noah's granddaughters. The author claims the following: Shem, Noah's oldest son, had five sons and five daughters; Ham had four sons and seven daughters; and Japheth had the reverse: seven sons and four daughters. The point: for the chosen lineage of Shem, intermarriage with the lines of his brothers might introduce corruption; thus, his sons married his daughters. For the other two sons, intermarriage of their lines was not dangerous, so they had congruent numbers of sons and daughters who could then marry their cousins.

In such ways the author of this rewritten Bible text dealt with the patriarchs Enoch, Lamech, Noah and his sons, and Abraham.

The very fragmentary earliest surviving portions of the text concern the period before the great Flood. Cols. 0–1 evidently describe the depraved condition of humanity at that time, with reference in particular to the illicit marriages between human women and fallen angels, known as Watchers (Gen. 6:2–4). According to the extrabiblical 1 Enoch, the Watchers also taught humanity all manner of evil. As a punishment they were "bound on the earth for all the days of eternity" (1 Enoch 14:4), an idea to which the New Testament also alludes in the Gospels and especially in the book of Revelation.

Col. 0 [2][. . .] for withal we shall receive a stranger [. . .] [5][. . . in the da]y of your wrath you will be strong and will be established. Who is he [6][who . . .] the heat of your wrath? [7][. . .] the humble and lowly quivering and trembling [8][. . .] And now, as is clear, we are bound [10][. . .] your wrath shall slay [. . .] [11][. . .] by your wrath; [. . .] after we go to the house of [. . .] the Great [H]oly One. [12]And now, your hand has drawn near to smite [. . .] and to cause to pass away all [13][. . .] for we are bound [before] a fire that has been seen [. . .] [15][. . .] and being smitten from their rear and n[o] longer[. . .] [18][. . .] before the Lord of the Earth. **Col. 1** [1][. . .] and with women [2][. . .] and also the mystery of wickedness that [3][. . .] and the mystery that [4][. . .] and sicknesses [. . .] [10]medicines, magicians and di[viners . . .] [25][. . .] for a curse on all flesh [26][. . .] and when they rest, it will be rest for you [27][. . .] to the earth, and to descend to it [. . .] the people [28][. . .] they do [not] know how to make human beings for the earth [29][. . .] he made for them, and also for all flesh.

Lamech, Noah's father, suspects that his newborn son may in fact not be his own, but rather the product of an illicit union between his wife, Bitenosh, and one of the Watchers.

Col. 2 [1]Then I decided that the conception was at the hands of Watchers, that the seed had been planted by Holy Ones or Nephil[im]. [2]I was in a turmoil because of this infant. [3]Then I, Lamech, hurriedly went in to [my] wi[fe], Bitenosh, [and I said to her,] [4]["I adjure you by . . .] and by the Most High, by the Lord, the Great One, by the King of all Et[ernity . . . have you conceived] [5][by one of] the Sons of Heaven? Tell me every detail truthfully [. . .] [6][in truth] make it known to me, without lies. Was this [. . .] [7]by the King of Eternity. You are to speak with me in utter truth, without lies [. . .]"

Bitenosh allays Lamech's suspicions by recalling the time when Noah would have been conceived.

[8]Then Bitenosh, my wife, replied to me very passionately, we[eping . . .] [9]She said, "O, my brother, my lord, remember my voluptuousness [. . .] [10]in the heat of lovemaking, and my ardent response. I [am telling

you] the whol[e] truth [. . .]" [11]and my mind was then changed. [12]Now when my wife Bitenosh saw that my disposition had changed, [. . .] [13]Then she restrained her anger, speaking with me and saying, "O, my lord, my [brother, remember] [14]my pleasure. I swear to you by the Great Holy One, by the King of He[aven . . .] [15]that this seed comes from you, this conception was by you, the planting of [this] fruit is yours [. . . It was] [16]not by any stranger, neither by any of the Watchers, nor yet by any of the Sons of Heav[en. Why has] [17]your expression been so altered, your mood so depressed? [. . .] Surely [18]I am speaking with you truthfully."

Still confused by the baby's glorious appearance, Lamech travels to consult with Methuselah, his father, asking him to inquire of Enoch, his grandfather. Enoch was thought to understand many hidden matters.

[19]Thereupon I, Lamech, ran to Methuselah my father, and [told] him everything, [so that he would go ask Enoch,] [20]his father, and come to understand the whole matter with certainty. For he, Enoch, is beloved and a friend [of God, and with the Holy Ones] [21]has his lot been cast. They reveal everything to him. When Methusel[ah] heard [of these matters,] [22]he set out for his father Enoch, in order to learn from him the truth of the whole affair [. . .] [23]his will. Then he went the length of the land of Parvaim, and there he found Enoch [his father with the Holy Ones.] [24]He [sa]id to Enoch, his father, "O, my father, my lord, I [have come] to you [. . . Hear] [25]what I say to you. Do not be angry with me that I have come here [. . .]"

Col. 3 apparently contained the beginning of Enoch's reply to Methuselah. Enoch began by referring to the descent of the Watchers to take human wives, which occurred in Jared's day.

Col. 3 [3]For in the days of Jared, my father [. . .]

Enoch's reply continues.

Col. 5 [2]And to you, Methuselah [my] so[n . . .] this lad. [3]Behold, when I, Enoch [. . . and not] by the Sons of [4]Heaven, but by Lamech, your son [. . .] [5]and he did not resemble [. . .] [7]Lamech your son fears his appearance [. . .] [8]in very truth that [. . .] [9]And now, I say to you, my son, and reveal to you [that . . .] then in truth [. . .] [10]Go, say to Lamech your son [. . .] [11]and they put him in the earth and every deed of the [Sons of Heaven . . .] [12]he lifted his face to me, and his eyes shone like the su[n . . .] [13]this lad fire, and he [. . .] [16]then they were confused and ceased [. . .] [17]eternity, giving [. . .] [18]doing great violence; they will do it until [. . .] [19]and going up, and all the paths of [. . .] [20]And now I declare to you by the mystery [. . . Lamech] [21]your son. I declare by this great mystery [. . .] [22]in his days the deed, and behold, [. . .] [23]blessing the Lord of All [. . .]

Methuselah returns to Lamech and tells him the secret things that Enoch had revealed, especially that Noah is truly his son.

[24]Now when Methuselah heard [these things . . .] [25]And spoke secretly with Lamech his son [. . .] [26]Now when I, Lamech, heard [these things . . .] [27]see, that he brought forth from me [. . .]

The setting has shifted, and now the adult Noah speaks in his own words. In cols. 7–18 he remains the hero and is made to speak in the form of a "testament" or "last words" (compare texts 39, 40, and 136–138). Throughout these columns a marked affinity exists with the presentation of the same subjects in Jubilees *(text 42).*

[29][A copy:] The Book of the Words of Noah [. . .] **Col. 6** [1]from iniquity, and in the crucible of she who bore me I sprouted for righteousness. So when I emerged from my mother's womb, I was planted for righteousness, [2]and it was righteousness that I practiced all of my days. I continued to walk in the paths of the eternal truth, accompanied by a holy [. . .] [3]righteousness hastened on my paths, and to warn me about the [. . .] of falsehood that lead to darkness and to [. . .] [4][. . .] I girded my loins with a vision of righteousness, and wisdom as a robe [. . .] [5][. . .] all the paths of violence.

Noah marries and has sons. Compare Genesis 5:32 and Jubilees *4:33. Note the emphasis placed on marriage only to one's first cousin, said to be established by "the law of the eternal statute." At the time our text was written, this must have been a controversy, as it is in* Jubilees *(text 42), the* Damascus Document *(text 1), the* Temple Scroll *(text 155), and other Dead Sea Scrolls. The opposing view, held by the Pharisees and perhaps others, preferred marriage between uncle and niece.*

[6]Th[e]n I, Noah, became a man; I laid hold of righteousness, and I grasped the [. . .] [7][. . .] I took Emzara his daughter as my wife, and she

conceived and bore me three sons [and also] [8][daughters]. Then I took wives for my sons from my brother's daughters, and I gave my daughters to my brother's sons, in accordance with the law of the eternal statute. [9][. . .] the Most High to humanity. And when, in my days, the number that I had calculated reached full measure [10][. . .] ten jubilee periods, at that point the period for my sons taking their wives was complete.

The coming Flood is announced to Noah by a mighty Watcher. These Watchers were identified by early biblical interpreters with the Nephilim of Genesis 6. Note that Noah calculates the time of the coming Flood as he calculated above the time for his sons' marriages: our text is very concerned with matters of chronology left unclear in the Bible, another way in which it resembles Jubilees.

[11][. . .] heaven. In a vision I saw, had it made known, and came to realize the deed of the Sons of Heaven, and what [. . .] [12]heaven. I hid this mystery in my heart, revealing it to no one. [13][. . . came] to me, and a mighty Watcher to me as a messenger, and as an emissary of the [Great] Holy One [. . .] [14]And in a vision he spoke with me, and stood before me [. . .] [15]an emissary of the Great Holy One proclaimed to me in a voice, "To you they say, 'Noah! [. . .] [16][. . .].' " So I calculated concerning all the activity of those who dwell upon the earth; I knew, and made known, all [. . .][17]they shall be prosperous, and they have chosen them [. . .] [18][. . .] two weeks (of years). Then, sealing [. . .] [19][. . .] the blood that the Nephilim had shed. I was serene, and I waited until [. . .] [20][. . .] holy ones who [mated] with hum[an] women [. . .] [23][. . .] I, Noah, [fo]und great favor and truth [. . .] [24][. . .] Most High, a day [. . .]

The Flood itself is recounted in several very fragmentary columns of the scroll. Noah, singled out as the one righteous man on earth, rejoices and praises God.

[25][. . .] until the floodgates of heaven [26][opened . . . destroying] humanity and cattle and wild animals and birds [. . .] **Col. 7** [1][. . .] upon them. The earth and all that was upon it, in the seas and on the mountains [2][. . .] all the constellations, the sun, the moon, and the stars. And the Watchers [. . .] [5][. . .] "I hereby grant you your reward from me" [. . .] [7][. . . thus spoke the emissary of] the Great Holy One. I rejoiced at the words of the Lord of Heaven, and shouted for joy [8][. . .]

Col. 10 [10]to the king of all the ages, forever and ever, for all eternity.

Sacrifice of thanksgiving and debarkation from the Ark. Compare Genesis 8:20 and Jubilees *6:1–3.*

[11]Then upon the earth [. . .] and he took from [. . .] [12]finding. Behold, [. . .] the ark came to rest upon one of the mountains of Ararat. And eternal fire [. . .] [13][. . .] and I atoned for all the earth; and a choice [. . .] [14]the [kid of the goat] first, and after it came [. . .] I burned the fat upon the fire, and second [. . .] [15][. . . I] poured out their blood at the base of the altar, [and] I burned the entirety of their flesh upon the altar; then, third, the turtledove [16][. . .] on the altar as an offering [. . .] upon it I placed fine flour soaked with oil together with frankincense as a grain offering. [17][. . .] Upon all of them I was sprinkling salt. Then the savor of my burnt offering ascended to [he]aven.

[18]Then the Most High [. . .]

Col. 11 [1][. . .] I, Noah, was in the door of the ark with the lion in fr[ont . . .] [9][. . .] for the mountains and the deserts, for the [. . .] no [10][. . .] four.

[11][Then] I, Noah, debarked and walked about the length and breadth of the land [. . .] [12][. . .] upon it, pleasure in their leaves and in their fruit. For the whole land was filled with grass, herbs and grain.

Then I praised the Lord of [13][Heaven, for] it is he who works praise forever, and the glory is his. Again I blessed him because he had mercy upon the earth, and because he removed and destroyed from upon it [14]all who work violence, evil, and deceit, but rescued a righteous man for [. . .] for all creation, for his own sake.

God makes a covenant with Noah, including the prohibition of eating blood. Compare Genesis 8:21–9:17 and Jubilees *6:4–16.*

[15][And the Lord of] Heaven [appeared] to me; he spoke with me, and said to me, "Noah, do not fear! I am with you, and with those sons of yours who will be like you, forevermore. [16][. . .] the earth, and rule over them all [. . .] and over its deserts and its mountains, and over all that is in them. Behold, I hereby [17][gr]ant to you and to your sons everything as food, along with the vegetables and herbs of the earth; only you shall consume no blood. The terror and fear of you [18][. . .] forever. [. . .] [19][. . .] I to you [that] your sons shall corrupt [. . .] [20–24][. . .]

Col. 12 [1][. . .] And it served as a sign for me in the cloud, and as a [. . .] [2][. . . e]arth [3][. . .] it was revealed to me [4–7][. . .] [8][. . . one among] the mountains of Ararat.

The children of Noah's sons, Shem, Ham, and Japheth—including daughters unmentioned in the Bible or Jubilees. *Compare* Jubilees *7:18–19.*

Afterward I descended to the foot of this mountain, I, my sons and my grandsons [9][. . .] Behold, the devastation upon the earth was large-scale. [Sons and da]ughters were bo[rn] to [me] after the Flood. [10][To Shem, my] eldest [son], a son was born first—namely Arpachshad, two years after the Flood. All of the sons of Shem were [11][Elam, Ash]ur, Arpachshad, Lud, and Aram, along with five daughters. And [the sons of Ham: Cush, Egyp]t, Put, and Canaan, together with seven [12]daughters. And the son[s] of Japheth: Gomer, Magog, Madai, Javan, Tubal, Moshok, Tiras, together with four daughters.

Noah's sacrifice. Compare Genesis 9:20 and Jubilees *7:1–6.*

[13]Then I began to cultivate the earth together with all my sons. I planted a large vineyard on Mount Lubar; when four years had passed, it produced wine for me [14][. . .] all. And when the first festival [came], on the first day of that festival, which is in the [first] month, [15][. . .] that belonged to my vineyard. I opened this vessel and began to drink it on the first day of the fifth year since planting. [16][. . .] On this day, I invited my sons, grandsons and all of our wives and daughters, and we gathered together, and we went [17][to the place of the altar.] And I was blessing the Lord of Heaven, God Most High, the Great Holy One, for he rescued us from destruction. [18][. . .]

Having fallen asleep drunk, Noah sees a vision involving a cedar and an olive tree. Compare Genesis 9:21–23 and Jubilees *7:7–13.*

Col. 13 [8][. . .] and the beasts of the field [. . .] and animals that creep upon the dry ground, exchanging [. . .] [9][of gold and silver], stones and clay were cutting down and taking some of it for themselves. I continued watching the gold and silver ones [10][. . .], the iron one and the trees: all of them were cutting down and taking some of it for themselves. I watched the sun, moon, [11][and] stars cutting down and taking some of it for themselves. I continued to watch until they consumed it, then released the earth and the water. The [12]water ceased, and it ceased.

[13]I then turned to watch the olive tree, and behold, the olive tree grew tall, with many perfumed blossoms in the radiance of its dense foliage [. . .] [14]fru[it . . .] and I gazed upon them. I considered this olive tree, and espe-

cially the abundance of its leaves [. . .] [15][. . .] attaching to it. And I wondered at this olive tree, amazed at the exceeding abundance of its leaves [. . . Then I saw] [16][four] winds of heaven, blowing with destructive force upon this olive tree, stripping it of leaves and breaking it. First [17][. . .] a western [wind] battered it, shaking off some of its leaves and fruit, scattering them in every direction. After it [. . .] [18][. . .] and some of the fruit [. . .]

Col. 14 [7][. . .] knowing [. . .] [8][. . .]

The interpretation of the vision is revealed to Noah.

[9][. . .] Give hee[d], and listen! The great cedar is you [. . .] standing before you in the dream on the summit of the mountains [. . .] [10][. . .] truth. The shoot that emerged from it and grew to a great height represents three s[o]ns [. . .] [11][. . . In that] you saw the first shoot as attached to the stump of the cedar, [. . .] and wood from it [. . .] [12][. . .] all of his days he shall not separate from you, and his progeny shall call themselves by your n[am]e. [. . .] [13][. . .] shall emerge as a righteous planting for all [. . .] [14][. . .] surely existing forever. In that you saw the shoot attached to the st[um]p of [. . .] [15][. . .] And in that you saw [. . .] the oth[e]r shoot [. . .] [16][. . .] some of its branches intertwined with the branches of the first shoot: two s[o]ns [. . .] [17][. . .] from the land [. . .] to the north [. . .] And in that you saw some of their branches intertwined with those of the first shoot, [18][. . .] placing upon the earth [. . .] and not [. . .] [19]You revealed the mystery as far as [. . .] [20–21][. . .] [22][. . .] to their east he sent [. . .] [23–26][. . .] [27][. . .] the cedar [. . .]

Col. 15 [8]And I [. . .] [9][. . .] In that you saw all of them [. . .], they will apostatize; the majority of them will be evil. In that you saw [10]the man coming from the south of the land, the sickle in his hand, and fire with him: he has torn and [. . .] [11][. . . and goo]dness he is [. . .], who shall come from the south of the land [. . .] [12][. . .] and evil. He shall hurl upon the fire all who reb[el . . .] [13]and he shall come between the [. . .]. In that you saw [. . .] [14][. . .] with them a cord, four angels [. . .] [15][. . .] to them a cord from all [. . .] the earth that [. . .] [16][. . .] and large and [. . .] [17][. . .] [18][. . .] between all the peoples. And all of them will be serving and dominated by [. . .] [19][. . .] Be not amazed about it [. . .] and do not [. . .] [20][. . .] He has made all known to you in righteousness, and thus is it written about you [. . .] [21][Then] I, Noah, [awoke] from my sleep, and the sun [. . .] [22][. . .] I to [. . .] because I was blameless [. . .] [23]the righteous man [. . .]

The division of the earth among Noah's sons, Japheth, Shem, and Ham. Compare Genesis 10 and Jubilees *8:10–30.*

Col. 16 [8][. . .] [9]the bay lying between them, the headwater in a spring as far as the River Tina, and the riverhead [. . .] [10]all the land of the north until it reached [. . .] [11][and] this portion crossed the waters of the Mediterranean until it reached [. . .] [12]he apportioned by lot to Japheth and to his sons as an everlasting inheritance.

[14]The second lot for an everlasting inheritance fell to Shem and his sons. [15][. . .] the waters of the River Tina em[pt]y [. . .] [16]until the River Tina [. . .] [17][to] the Great Salt Sea. And this boundary went as a spring from this inlet [. . .] [18][. . .] that faces westward, and it crossed [. . .] [19][. . .] until it reached the [. . .] [20][. . .] to the east [. . .]

The division of the portions of Shem, Ham, and Japheth among their sons. Compare Genesis 10 and Jubilees *9:1–13.*

Col. 17 [7][And] my son Shem [di]vided his inheritance among his sons. The first lot fell to [El]a[m] in the north, along the Tigris River until it reached the R[e]d [8]Sea, and north to the river's source, then turn[ing] to the west toward Ashur's portion, to the point where the latter met the Tigris. [. . .] After him, [9]the land between the two rivers fell to Aram, until it reaches the beginning of Mo[unt Ashur . . .] until the [Land of] Ararah [. . .] [10]fell this Mountain of the Bull; and this portion crossed over and continued until it met Magog's portion, and to [. . .] north-[11]east, which extends from the center of this bay by the source of the three portions and along the sea, to Arpachshad [. . .] [12]to the [boundary] that faces the south, all the land that the Euphrates waters and all [. . .] [13][. . .] all the valleys and plains that are between them, together with the island in the midst of the bay [. . .] [14][. . .] as far as the sons of Gomer [. . .] and Amana until it reaches the Euphr[ates . . .] [15][. . .] the portion that he allotted to him, and that Noah his father had given him.

[16]Japheth [also] divided his inheritance among his sons. First, to Gomer he allotted the north extending to the River Tina. After him, he gave portions to Magog, then [17]to Madai, then to Javan. The latter he allotted all the islands along the coast of Lud's portion, and what lay between the bay alongside L[u]d's portion and the second ba[y], that of Tubal. [. . .] [18][. . .] in the land. And to Moshok, the sea [. . . And] to Tiras [. . .] the [f]our [islands] in the bay belonging to [19][the sea bordering] the [po]rtion of the sons of Ham [. . .]

The hero of the story is now Abraham. This portion apparently concerns the building of the altar at Bethel. Compare Genesis 12:1–7.

Col. 19 [6][. . . And there I built] the [altar, and called] ther[e upon the name of G]o[d . . .] And I said, "You are indeed [7][the Etern]al [G]od for m[e], [. . .]." Previously, I had not reached the holy mountain; so I journeyed [8]to [. . .] and I continued traveling to the south [. . .] until I reached Hebron—though Hebron had yet to be built—and I lived [9][th]ere [for two years].

Suffering from a famine, Abraham and his family go to Egypt.

Now, there was a famine in all that land, but I heard that in Egypt there w[as] g[ra]in. So I journeyed [10]to [enter] the land of Egypt [. . . and] I [reached] the Carmon River, one of the [11]branches of the Nile [. . .] Until this point we were still within our own land, [but] now I [cr]ossed the seven branches of this river that [. . .] [12][. . .] Now we had crossed our land and entered the land of the children of Ham, the land of Egypt.

Abraham has an ominous dream.

[13]I, Abram, had a dream the night of my entry into the land of Egypt. In my dream, I saw a cedar tree and a [14]date palm gro[wing] from [a single] roo[t]. Then people came intending to cut down and uproot the [c]edar, thereby to leave the date palm by itself. [15]The date palm, however, objected, and said, "Do not cut the [c]edar down, for the two of us grow fr[om] but a [sin]gle root." So the cedar was spared because of the date palm, [16]and was not cut down.

Abraham relates the dream to his wife, Sarah, and interprets its meaning.

Then I started from my sleep while it was still night, and said to Sarai, my wife, "I have had a [17]dream and no[w] am fearful [because of] it." She replied, "Tell me your dream so I may understand." So I began to explain it to her, [18]and I also [explained its significance.] I said, "[. . . men will come] intending to kill me while sparing you. Notwithstanding, this is the kindness [19][that you can do for me.] In every [place] where [we shall go, say] concerning me, 'He is my brother.' Thus I may live because of you and my life be spared owing to you. [20][. . . they will attempt] to sepa[ra]te us and to kill me." Then Sarai wept at my words that night. [21][. . .] and the

Pharaoh of Zo[an . . .] Sarai n[o longer wanted] to go to Zoan [22][with me, and she was] exceedingly [careful for five year]s lest any man attached to the Pharaoh of Zoan should see her.

Nevertheless, after five years had passed [23][there came] three men, councilors from the Egyptian court [and advisers] of the Pharaoh of Zoan. They came having heard of [my] words and my wife, and kept plying me [24][with many gifts.] They as[ked] me [for knowledge] of goodness, wisdom, and righteousness, so I read to them the [Book] of the Words of Enoch. [25][. . .] in the famine that [. . .] the Book of the Words of Enoch [. . .] [26][. . .] with much eating and drinking [. . .] wine [. . .]

The pharaoh's advisers return to him, including one named Hyrcanos, who describes Sarah's wondrous beauty in a poem.

Col. 20 [2][. . .] How splen[did] and beautiful is the aspect of her face, and how [. . .] [3][And] h[ow] supple is the hair of her head. How lovely are her eyes; how pleasant her nose and all the radiance of [4]her face [. . .] How shapely is her breast, how gorgeous all her fairness! Her arms, how comely! Her hands, [5]how perfect—how [lovely] is every aspect of her hands! How exquisite are her palms, how long and delicate all her fingers!

Her feet, [6]how attractive! How perfect are her thighs! Neither virgins nor brides entering the bridal chamber exceed her charms. Over all [7]women is her beauty supreme, her loveliness far above them all. Yet with all this comeliness, she possesses great wisdom, and all that she has [8]is beautiful.

The Pharaoh of Zoan takes Sarah for himself. Abraham grieves and prays for God to judge the pharaoh and protect Sarah.

When the king heard Hyrcanos' words and those of his companions—for the three of them spoke of one accord—he desired her very much. So he sent [9]immediately and had her brought to him. He saw her and was amazed at her beauty. Thereupon, he took her as his wife and sought to kill me, but Sarai said [10]to the king, "He is my brother." Thus she benefited me and I was spared—I, Abram—by her good graces, and not killed. Then I wept copiously—I, [11]Abram—both I and Lot, my nephew, that night when Sarai was taken from me by force.

[12]That night I prayed, entreating and seeking mercy. In anguish, tears running down my cheeks, I said, "Blessed are You, O God Most High, Eternal [13]Lord, for You are Lord and Master over all. Over all the kings of the earth You are Lord, to work justice among them. And now, [14]I seek redress, O Lord, against the Pharaoh of Zoan, king of Egypt, for my wife has been

taken from me by force. Render me a verdict against him, and display Your mighty hand [15]against him and all his house. May he not be empowered this night to defile my wife! Thus they may know You, O my Lord, that You are Lord over all the kings [16]of the earth." So I wept and spoke to none.

God answers Abraham's prayer, sending an afflicting spirit against the pharaoh.

That night God Most High sent a baneful spirit to smite him and every man of his household, an evil [17]spirit that continued to afflict him and every man of his household. Consequently, he was unable to have sexual relations with her; indeed, he did not have intercourse with her even though she was with him [18]two full years. At the end of two years the plagues and afflictions grew yet more severe against him and every man of his household, so he sent messengers [19]calling for all [the wise men] of Egypt, along with all the magicians and healers of Egypt, thinking that perhaps they could cure him and his household of this pestilence. [20]Yet none of the healers, magicians, and wise men were able to cure him; on the contrary, the spirit afflicted all of them too, [21]so that they fled.

Abraham agrees to exorcise the pharaoh's evil spirit in return for Sarah's being restored to him. The pharaoh rewards them and has them escorted out of Egypt.

Then Hyrcanos came to me, asking me to come pray for the [22]king, and to lay hands upon him and cure him—for [he had seen me] in a dream. But Lot replied, "My uncle, Abram, is unable to pray for [23]the king while Sarai, his wife, remains with him. Now, go tell the king to send his wife to her husband. Then he will pray for him and he will be cured." [24]When Hyrcanos heard Lot's words, he went and told the king, "All these smitings and plagues [25]by which my lord the king has been smitten and afflicted are because of Sarai, the wife of Abram! Let him return Sarai to Abram, her husband, [26]and this plague will depart from you, that is, the spirit causing the discharges of pus."

So he called me to himself and asked me, "What have you done to me because of your wife [Sar]ai? You told [27]me, 'She is my sister,' yet she was actually your wife! I took her as my own wife! Here she is; take her, go, depart from [28]all the provinces of Egypt! But first, pray for me and my house that this evil spirit may be exorcised from us." So I prayed for him, that blasphemer, [29]and laid my hands upon his [he]ad. Thereupon the plague was removed from him, the evil [spirit] exorcised [from him,] and he was healed. The king rose and gave [30]to me on that [day] many gifts, and the king swore to me with an oath that [he had not touched] her. Then he returned Sarai [31]to me. The king gave her much [silver and g]old, and great quantities of linen and purple-dyed garments. [. . . He put them] [32]before her, and before Hagar as well. He restored her to me and assigned men to escort [me out of Egypt . . .]

Abraham returns to Canaan.

[33]So I, Abram, left, with many, many flocks, together with silver and gold, and went up from [Egyp]t. [Lot,] [34]my nephew, accompanied me, and he also had acquired many flocks for himself, and had taken a wife from among the daughters [of Egypt]. I [cam]ped [with him] **Col. 21** [1][in] each of my former encampments until I reached Bethel, where I had once erected an altar. Now I rebuilt it [2]and offered up burnt offerings and a cereal offering to God Most High. There I called upon the name of the Eternal Lord and praised the name of God. I blessed [3]God and gave thanks to Him there for all the flocks and goods He had given me, and for the good that He had done me, and because He had returned me [4]to this land safely.

Lot separates from Abraham and goes to live in Sodom. Genesis 13:6–7 explains that the land could not support both of them, for their flocks were too numerous; also, their herders were fighting one another. The Tales *downplays these difficulties. God appears to Abraham in a vision.*

[5]After this day Lot separated from me because of the actions of our shepherds. He went to live in the valley of the Jordan, taking all his flocks [6]with him. I also added greatly to what he had. He pastured his flocks and kept on the move until he reached Sodom, where he bought himself a house [7]and settled down to live. I myself continued living on the mountain of Bethel, and thought it unwise that my nephew Lot had separated from me.

[8]Thereafter God appeared to me in a vision of the night and told me, "Go up to Ramath Hazor, which is on the north of [9]Bethel where you now live, and lift up your eyes. Look to the east, west, south, and north. Survey all [10]this land that I am about to give to you and your descendants forever." So I went up the next day to Ramath Hazor and surveyed the land from [11]that height, from the River of Egypt to Lebanon and Senir, and from the Mediterranean to the Hauran, and all the land of Gebal as far as Kadesh, and all the [12]Great Desert to the east of the Hauran and Senir as far as the Euphrates. And He said to me, "I will give all this land to your descendants; they will inherit it forever. [13]Moreover, I will multiply your descendants like the dust of the earth that none can count. Your descendants shall be numberless. Arise, walk about, go [14]see how long and how wide it is, for I will give it to you and to your descendants after you, forever."

Abraham surveys the promised land.

[15]Then I went—I, Abram—traveling in a circuit to survey the land. I began the circuit at the Gihon River, traveling along the Mediterranean until [16]I reached the Mount of the Ox. I circled from the coast of this great saltwater sea, skirting the Mount of the Ox, and continued eastward through the breadth of the land [17]until I came to the Euphrates River. I journeyed along the Euphrates until I reached the Red Sea in the east, whence I followed the coast of [18]the Red Sea until I came to the tongue of the Reed Sea, jutting out from the Red Sea. From there I completed the circuit, moving southward to arrive at the Gihon [19]River. Afterwards I returned home safely and found all my men well.

Shortly thereafter I went to dwell at the Oaks of Mamre that are in Hebron, [20]actually somewhat to the northeast of Hebron. There I built an altar and offered up a burnt offering and a cereal offering to God Most High. I ate and drank there, [21]I and all the men of my household, and invited Mamre, Arnem, and Eshkol, three Amorite brothers and my friends. They ate and drank together [22]with me.

Abraham battles the four kings of the east. Compare Genesis 14, whose narrative this portion of the Tales *elaborates considerably. The author of the* Tales *is also concerned to update or identify the biblical names of peoples and places.*

[23]Prior to those days Chedorlaomer, the king of Elam, Amraphel, the king of Babylon, Arioch, the king of Cappadocia, and Tidal, the king of Goiim, which [24]lies between the two rivers, had come. They had waged war on Bera, the king of Sodom, Birsha, the king of Gomorrah, Shinab, the king of Admah, [25]Shemiabad, the king of Zeboiim, and the king of Bela. All these gathered themselves together to battle in the Valley of Siddim. Now, the king of [26]Elam and the kings with him proved stronger than the king of Sodom and all his allies. Thus they imposed tribute upon them.

For twelve years they continued [27]to pay their tribute to the king of Elam, but in the thirteenth they rebelled against him. Consequently, in the fourteenth year the king of Elam sallied forth with all [28]his allies, and they ascended by way of the desert. They smote and plundered beginning from the Euphrates. They kept smiting—smiting the Rephaim who were in Asteroth [29]Kernaim, the Zumzammim who were in Amman, the Emim [who were in] Shaveh Hakerioth, and the Horites who were in the mountains of Gebal—until they reached El [30]Paran, in the desert. Then they turned back and struck [En-mishpat and the people] who were in Hazazon Tamar. [31]Thereupon the king of Sodom went out to confront them, along with the king of [Gomorrah, the k]ing of Admah, the king of Zeboiim, and the king of Bela. [They wa]ged war [32]in the Valley of [Siddim] with Chedorla[omer, the king of Elam, and the kings] who were his allies. The king of Sodom was put to flight, while the king of Gomorrah [33]fell into pits [of tar . . .] The king of Elam plundered all the flocks of Sodom and [34][Gomorrah . . .]

And Lot, Abram's nephew who had been living in Sodom, was taken captive **Col. 22** [1]along with them, he and all his flocks. One of the herdsmen of the [2]flock that Abram had given Lot escaped from the captives and came to Abram—at the time Abram [3]dwelled in Hebron. The herdsman informed him that his nephew Lot and all his flocks had been taken into captivity, but that Lot had not been killed. He also told him that [4]the kings were marching along the trail of the Great Valley toward their own territory, taking captives and plunder, smiting and killing, heading [5]for the city of Damascus.

Abram wept over his nephew Lot, but then gathered his strength and arose [6]to select from among his servants elite warriors, three hundred and eighteen of them. Arnem, [7]Eshcol, and Mamreh set out with him. He pursued the kings as far as Dan, where he found them [8]encamped in the Valley of Dan. He attacked by night from four directions, killing [9]some of them that night. Some he slaughtered, others he pursued; they fled before him [10]until they reached Helbon, located to the north of Damascus. Thus Abram recovered from them everyone they had taken captive [11]and everything they had taken as spoils, and despoiled their own property as well. He further saved his nephew Lot and all his flocks. All [12]those who had been captured he brought back.

The king of Sodom heard that Abram had recovered all the captives [13]and plunder, so he went up to meet him. He came to Salem, that is, Jerusalem, whereas Abram was encamped in the Valley [14]of Shaveh, that is, the Valley of the King, the Valley of Beth Hakerem. Now Melchizedek, the king of Salem, provided [15]food and drink for Abram and all the men with him. He himself was a priest of God Most High, and he blessed [16]Abram, saying, "Blessed be Abram by God Most High, the Lord of heaven and earth. Blessed be God Most High [17]who has closed your grasp about your enemies." Then Abram gave him a tithe of all the flocks that had belonged to the king of Elam and his allies.

[18]At that point the king of Sodom drew near and said to Abram, "My lord Abram, [19]give me my men, the captives with you, whom you have rescued from the king of Elam; as for the plunder, [20]let it all pass to you." Abram replied to the king of Sodom, "I lift my [21]hand and swear this day by God Most High, the Lord of heaven and earth: I shall not take even a thread or sandal strap [22]from all that is yours, lest you go on to say 'All Abram's

wealth derives from plunder of what [23]once was mine.' I exempt from this oath what my men have already eaten, and the portion belonging to the three men who [24]marched with me. They are sovereign over their own portion, and can restore it to you or not." So Abram returned all the plunder and [25]captives, giving them to the king of Sodom. As for all the captives accompanying him who were natives of this land, these he freed [26]and sent on their way.

God appears to Abraham in a vision and promises that Eliezer shall not be his heir. Compare Genesis 15:1–4; the Tales *manifests a clear concern with chronology here, for Genesis says nothing about how long Abraham had been in various places. The dialogue between God and Abraham is also markedly different, here emphasizing Abraham's wealth much more than the biblical narrative does.*

[27]After these events God appeared to Abram in a vision and said to him, "Consider, ten full years [28]have passed since the day that you left Haran. Two you spent here, seven in Egypt, and one [29]has passed since you returned from Egypt. Now, take an accounting of all that you possess; note how your possessions have doubled and more, compared to [30]what you took with you the day you left Haran. So fear not, I am with you. I shall be your [31]support, your strength. I myself shall be your shield and buckler against any foe mightier than you. Your wealth and flocks [32]shall multiply exceedingly."

Abram replied, "My Lord God, my wealth and flocks are already vast. But what good are [33]all [th]ese things to me, inasmuch as when I die, I go childless, having no sons? In fact, one of my household staff will inherit what I have. [34]Eliezer, a member of [my household staff], that [. . .] young man is set to be my heir." God said to him, "No, this man shall not be your heir, but rather one who shall be [your own] issue."

—M.O.W.

5. The Words of Moses

1Q22

The authors of the Dead Sea Scrolls found the Bible a limitless source of wisdom and instruction, but on occasion they found it necessary to rewrite portions of it to enhance the message they found in it—or wanted to find in it. Sometimes biblical stories were rewritten—such as *Tales of the Patriarchs* (text 4)—probably to increase their entertainment value. Other portions, such as the *Temple Scroll* (text 155), represent rewritten and expanded legal material with controversial or new laws added, highlighted, or explained.

The text here translated, the *Words of Moses,* follows a similar plan. Although fragmentary (and reconstructed with remarkable acumen by J. T. Milik), the scroll apparently was a rewriting of parts of Moses' last farewell as given in the book of Deuteronomy. Since most of the composition has perished, we can only guess what purpose lay behind its writing. The parts that remain emphasize the dangers of apostasy and the judgment that inevitably follows—a theme quite in keeping with the original book.

The introductory passage recalls Deuteronomy 1:3.

Col. 1 [1][God called] to Moses [on the fortieth] year after the [children of I]sra[el] lef[t the land of E]gypt, in the [el]eventh mo[nth], [2]on the first day of the [mo]nth, saying, [Convene] the entire na[ti]on and go up to [Mount Nebo] and stand [ther]e, you [3]and Elea[zar so]n of Aaron. Ex[plain to the family] heads, to the Lev[i]tes, and all the [priests] and command the children of [4]Israe[l] the words of the Law that [I] have commanded [you] on Mount S[i]nai to command t[hem] in the[ir] hearing.

This passage recalls Deuteronomy 4:25–28, except that the author adds to the prediction of idolatry a further one concerning breaking the laws of the festival calendar—a topic much on the minds of the Yahad *and earlier groups such as the circles that produced* Jubilees.

[5]Explain thorou[ghly everything] that I [deman]d of them and [call as witnesses against] them Heaven and [Earth, for] [6]wha[t] I command [them will] not be to their [li]king, or to [their] descendants' liking, [all] the days that they [live on the la]nd. Indeed [7]I declare [to you] that they will abandon [Me and ch]oo[se to follow the idols of the] Gen[tiles and] their [ab]ominations and their [fil]thy deeds, [and they will worship] the [8]fals[e god]s, which will become a tr[ap and] snare, and they will vi[olate every sacred assem]bly and covenant Sabbath [and the festivals], the very ones [9]I am commanding them today [to ob]serve.

A paraphrase of Deuteronomy 28:15.

[They will suffer a] great [defeat] within the very land [that they] are about to cross [10][the] Jordan [to poss]ess. And so it will be, [th]at all the curs[es] will come upon them and catch them un[til] they perish and until [11]they are de[stroyed] and they will know [that] a just judgment has been [passed] on them.

Deuteronomy 31:7 states only that Moses summoned Joshua. The addition here of Eleazar the priest as a co-ruler of Israel is characteristic of the Dead Sea sect.

So Moses called Eleazar son of [12][Aaron] and Joshu[a son of Nun and said to] them, Repeat [all the words of the Law up to] the very end [. . .]

Here the author combines the gist of Deuteronomy 27:9–19 with Deuteronomy 6:10–11.

Col. 2 [1][I]srael and hear! This very [da]y [you become a peo]ple belonging to the Lord [your God], so [you] should o[bserve my regulations] and my testimonies [and] my [commandments th]at [2][I am] commanding you [to]day, [doing them just] as [you] are about to cross the [Jordan], and [I shall give] you [3]large and [beautiful] cities and houses full of eve[ry good thing, vineyards and olive trees] that [you did] n[ot plant and cis]terns [that you] did not [4][d]ig; and you will eat and be satisfied. [Be careful] lest your [hea]rt grow proud and you [forget what] I [command you] today; [5][for] it is [your] life and length of [your] days.

Here the author combines themes and expressions from Deuteronomy 1:9–18 and 11:17.

[So] Moses [called] and [said to the children of I]srael, It is now forty [6][years] since we c[ame out of] the land of [Egypt.] This very [day the Lor]d our [God has expressed the]se [wor]ds from [his] mouth: [7][all] his [sta]tutes [and] all [his] <regulations> (sta[tutes]). [H]ow [shall I bear alone] your trouble [and your burdens and your quarreling?] So it shall be, [8][when] I [finish giving] the covenant and commanding [the] w[ay tha]t you should walk in, [appoint for yourself wise men who] should explain [9][to you and to] your [children] all [these] words of the L[aw]. Be [very careful] of yourselves [to do them lest] his anger burn and his wrath ignite [10]against you, [and] He closes the heavens above from raining [upon you], and the [waters below the earth] from giving you [11][produce].

This section concerns the sabbatical year, combining material from Deuteronomy 15 and Leviticus 25. The reconstruction is especially uncertain.

Moses [spoke again] to the children of Israel, These are [the commandments that God commanded] to obey [. . .] **Col. 3** [1][Every seventh y]ear, [the] sabbath of [the land you shall keep. And the sabbath of the] la[nd shall be for you] food for [you and for the domestic animals and for the beasts of] the fi[eld] [2][. . . and whatever is le]ft over is for [the poor of] your [brothers] who are in [the land. No one] shall s[ow his field or] prune [his vineyard. No] ma[n] 3[shall harvest the aftergrowth of his harvest, nor shall he] gather for [himself anything. You shall keep] al[l th]es[e words of the] covenant, 4[to do them. And] it shall be, when [you hearken] to do [this commandment], and remit [the debt in] thi[s y]ear, [. . .]

—E.M.C.

6. The Book of Secrets

1Q27, 4Q299–301

"Where shall wisdom be found, and where is the place of understanding?" Such was the cry of the author of Job (28:12), and an entire literature, even a literary movement, stood behind that cry. "Wisdom books" are the biblical writings that embody this search for understanding: Proverbs, Ecclesiastes (or Koheleth), and Job. Indeed, almost every culture of the ancient Near East had its own representative books of wisdom, and the oldest collections of proverbs are not Israelite, but Egyptian, and go back to the late third millennium B.C.E.

Often the collections of proverbs are framed by what scholars call an "instruction," that is, the literary device of a wise sage instructing his pupils or his children in the ways of wisdom. Sometimes the instruction is patently fictional, and the sage who "speaks" through the proverbs is anonymous; sometimes the teacher is a real historical figure, such as Jesus ben Sira, who wrote the book of Sirach, or Ecclesiasticus, in the second century B.C.E. Several compositions among the Dead Sea Scrolls are wisdom instructions, including the *Book of Secrets* and the longer work called the *Secret of the Way Things Are* (text 105). In the *Book of Secrets,* although the name of the sage is not preserved, one can hear the distinctive voice of a real, and redoubtable, teacher.

The wisdom movement in Israel had fairly humble beginnings in homely proverbs, but grew to produce intense speculation about God's ways of governing the world. The idea that a basic order lay hidden behind the apparent randomness and injustice of daily life was fundamental to the religion of the ancients, and this divine order was in Israel known as *hokhmah,* "wisdom." But the difficulty of grasping the essence of wisdom through practical maxims later led to deeper ruminations on God's way with the world. Ben Sira came to identify God's pattern with the Law revealed to Israel, in this way reconciling ancient "philosophy" with Israel's covenant faith.

The scroll writers generally took a different tack in their wisdom instructions. Although honoring the Law as much as Ben Sira, the hiddenness of the divine pattern impressed them as much as its splendor. It was clear to them that, unaided, the human mind could not grasp wisdom; it would have to be given to individuals as a gift. Certain men, then, were singled out to be the lucky recipients of revelation, and they would then know the "secrets" of God, especially the "secret of the way things are," a sectarian title for divine *hokhmah*. The scroll writers did not believe that the unaided human mind, however pious, could understand the ways of God. The path to true understanding was through revelation, not reason.

The order of the fragments below is topical and does not necessarily reflect the original order of the *Book of Secrets*.

The "instructor" announces his intention to reveal his learning to all who are interested, even the benighted Gentiles.

4Q301 Frag. 1 [1][. . .] I shall speak out freely, and I shall express my various sayings unto you [. . .] [2][. . . those who would understand pa]rables and riddles, and those who would penetrate the origins of knowledge, along with those who hold fast to [the wonderful mysteries . . .] [3][. . .] those who walk in simplicity as well as those who are devious in every activity of the deeds of [humanity . . .] [4][those with a stiff] neck, [a hard] pate, [all] the mass of the Gentiles, with [. . .]

The instructor asks the motivation for learning. It must not be for worldly power and privilege.

Frag. 2b [1][. . .] Now what good is the riddle to you, you who search for the origins of knowledge? [2][. . .] a parable? Why is it splendid to you, for it is [. . .] What is a prince [. . .] [3][. . .] without strength, and he dominates him with a whip that cost nothing. Who would say [4][. . .] who among you seeks the presence of Light and Illu[mination] [5][. . .] the plan of memory without [. . .] [6][. . .] by the angels of [. . .] [7][. . .] those who praise [. . .]

In times past people ignored this teaching and disaster came upon them.

4Q300 Frag. 3 [2]so that they would know the difference between g[ood and evil and between lies and truth and they understood secrets of sin . . .]

[3]all their wisdom. **1Q27 Frag. 1 Col. 1** [3][. . . all their wisdom.] But they did not know the secret of the way things are nor did they understand the things of old and they did not [4]know what would come upon them, so they did not rescue themselves by means of the secret of the way things are.

The time for ignoring the true wisdom is past. Those who have not reformed their lives by means of it will soon be eliminated.

[5]This shall be the sign that this shall come to pass: when the times of evil are shut up and wickedness is banished in the presence of righteousness, as darkness in the presence of [6]light, or as smoke vanishes and is no more, in the same way wickedness will vanish forever and righteousness will be manifest like the sun. [7]The world will be made firm and all the adherents of the secrets of <sin> (MS.: wonder) shall be no more. True knowledge shall fill the world and there will never be any more folly. [8]This is all ready to happen, it is a true oracle, and by this it shall be known to you that it cannot be averted.

It is not enough simply to honor goodness or desire truth. The attainment of wisdom lies beyond human effort, and it is beyond the reach of the rich.

It is true that all [9]the peoples reject evil, yet it advances in all of them. It is true that truth is esteemed in the utterances of all the nations—[10]yet is there any tongue or language that grasps it? What nation wants to be oppressed by another that is stronger? Or who [11]wants his money to be stolen by a wicked man? Yet what nation is there that has not oppressed its neighbor? Where is the people that has not [12]robbed the wealth [of another? . . .]

Even the so-called righteous have fallen short of the ideals of true wisdom.

4Q299 Frags. 3a–b Col. 2 [2]what should we call [a man who . . . his] deeds [. . .] [3]but every deed of the righteous has been judged im[pure. And what] should we call a ma[n who . . . Call no one on earth] [4]wise or righteous, for it is not a human possession [. . .] and no[t . . . wisdom is hidden,] [5]except for the wisdom of cunning evil, and the s[chemes of Belial . . .] [6]a thing that ought never to be done again, except [. . .] [7]the command of his Maker; and what shall a m[an] do [and live? . . . he who] [8]has violated the command of his Maker shall have his name erased from the mouth of all [. . .]

God knows all hidden things; indeed, he has determined how everything should come about.

[9][. . .] So listen, you who hold fast [to the wonderful secrets . . .] [10]of eternity, and the plots behind every deed, and the pur[pose of . . . He knows] [11]every secret and stands behind every thought, He does every [. . . the Lord of all] [12]is H[e, fr]om long ago He established it, and forever [. . .] [13][. . .] the purpose of the times of birth He opened up to [. . .] [14][. . .] for He tests our heart, and gives to us as an inheritance [. . .] [15][. . .] every secret, and the limits of every deed; and what [. . .] [16][. . .] the Gentiles, for He created them and [their] deeds [. . .]

Magicians and soothsayers have not been able to penetrate God's secrets.

4Q300 Frag. 1a Col. 1 [4][. . . de]ed of anger and work of [. . .] **Frags. 1a–b Col. 2** [1][Consider the sooth]sayers, those teachers of sin. Say the parable, declare the riddle before we speak; then you will know if you have truly understood. [2][. . .] your foolishness, for the seal of the vision is sealed up from you, and you have not properly understood the eternal mysteries and you have not become wise in understanding. [3][. . .] for you have not properly understood the origin of wisdom; but if you should unseal the vision [4][. . .] all your wisdom, for to you is the par[able . . .] Hear now what is [5][the] hidden [wisdom . . .] shall not be [. . .] [6][v]ision [. . .]

The secret of true wisdom is as hidden as God's design of the natural world. He created the heavenly bodies to regulate human life.

4Q299 Frag. 5 [1][. . . light]s of the stars for a m[emo]rial of [His] name [. . .] [2][. . . hidden] things of the mysteries of Light and the ways of Darkne[ss . . .] [3][. . .] the times of heat with the period[s of cold . . .] [4][. . . the breaking of day] and the coming of night [. . .] [5][. . .] the times of birth [. . .]

He created the earth with its rivers and streams perpetually filled by the gift of rain.

Frag. 6 Col. 1 [1][. . .] waters [2][. . .] their [. . .] [3][. . .] their work, they shall be strong [4][. . . lightni]ng he made in perpetuity, showers [5][. . . wat]er and they give to drink by measure [6][. . .] he speaks to them and they give [7][. . .] by His might He created [8][. . .] its mountains all

[9][. . .] all that springs forth from it [10][. . .] from its center stretches out [11][. . .] their [. . .] time after time [12][. . .] to teach to all [13][. . .] from the dust of their frame [14][. . .] all their pools and the chamber of [15][. . .] he gave dominion to strengthen [16][. . .] all strength [17][. . .] and strengthens all [18][. . .] the work of man [19][. . .] his [wo]rk.

Wisdom is available by humble submission to the unchangeable plan of God.

Frag. 8 [5][. . .] and what shall a man understand without knowledge and without hearing [. . .] [6][. . .] insight, the impulse of [our] heart with great intelligence, he uncovered our ears that we [might hear . . .] [7][. . .] He created insight for all those who pursue true knowledge and [. . .] [8][. . .] all wisdom is from eternity, it may not be changed [. . .] [9][. . .] He locked up behind the waters, so that [not . . .] [10][. . .] the heaven above heaven [. . .]

True wisdom is also found among his people Israel.

4Q301 Frags. 3a–b [4][. . .] and He is well known for His patience, and [mighty] in His great anger, and [splendid] [5][. . .] He in His numerous acts of mercy, and terrible in His wrathful purposes, and honored [. . .] [6][. . .] and over the land He made him ruler, and God is honored among His holy people, and splendid [7][among] His chosen, yes, splendid [. . .] his [hol]iness, great in the blessings of [. . .] [8][. . .] their splendor and [. . .] when the era of wickedness is at an end, and [evil]doing [. . .]

—E.M.C.

7. Charter of a Jewish Sectarian Association

1QS, 4Q255–264a, 5Q11

Discovery can be a deceitful process. What is discovered, and when, frequently depends on nothing so much as sheer chance. Unavoidably and often, the order of discovery is a decisive factor in historical reconstructions—to the detriment, occasionally, of accurate understanding. The fortuitous is not always fortunate. But that is not the case with the present text.

It was among the first seven scrolls found and has been central to discussions about the Dead Sea Scrolls ever since. But this work's centrality has depended less on the accident that it was among the first scrolls discovered (though that has been a factor) than on its character, and on the fact that the Cave 1 copy was virtually intact. Also, the sheer number of copies of this work discovered in the caves—thirteen, almost as many as copies of Genesis and Exodus, and more than almost any of the other books of the Bible—dictates this work's centrality in any attempt to understand the phenomenon of the scrolls. Clearly sectarian, this writing uses striking language and imagery to express the mindset of outsiders.

Scholars commonly refer to this work as the "Community Rule." According to the Standard Model described in the Introduction, this work is supposed to have governed a community living at Qumran. But that idea is at least partly wrong; the work itself refers to various groups or chapters scattered throughout Palestine. Therefore it did not attach specifically to the site of Qumran (whatever the connection of the Dead Sea Scrolls to the site, and whatever the nature of that site). This text does not merely reflect a small community living there. Since "community" usually implies a definite and restricted geographical location and thereby calls this mistaken notion to mind, it seems better to find a different word for the text's users. As we have explained in the Introduction, to avoid the misleading connotations of various possible English semiequivalents we have decided to use one of the association's most common self-designations, *Yahad,* "unity."

The present text is essentially a constitution or charter for the *Yahad.* That it is a charter becomes clear by comparison with charters from elsewhere in the contemporary Greco-Roman world. Research by Moshe Weinfeld and Matthias Klinghardt, among others, has shown that virtually every structural element of this ancient Jewish writing has analogs in the charters of guilds and religious associations from Egypt, Greece, and Asia Minor. Yet it seems that something more is going on in this writing than simply chartering a club.

The first-century Jewish historian Josephus described the major Jewish groups as philosophical schools, not clubs. His portrayal is usually dismissed by scholars as a misleading adaptation of the true Jewish situation, done for the sake of his Greek-reading audience. If, however, we give the historian's characterization a bit more credence, we note that in some ways the group described by our text indeed was more like a philosophic academy than a club. Such academies were more all-embracing than clubs generally tended to be, more definitive of the members' total worldview; clubs were more nearly analogous to our guilds or unions. In his classic 1933 study *Conversion,* A. D. Nock delineated the hallmarks of the philosophies: they offered intelligible explanations of phenomena, offered a life with discipline, fostered ideal types (saints), had the influence of a living teacher, made a literary appeal, and demanded a change in lifestyle akin to the Judeo-Christian concept of conversion. All of these elements are present here. Thus, though the group described by our charter was *formed* like a club, it *functioned* more like a philosophic academy.

As the work describes it, the association is made up of priests, Levites (a secondary priestly order), "Israel," and Gentile proselytes. In this context "Israel" means not the generality of Jews, but only those who accept the teachings of the group. Other Jews, along with the surrounding Gentile nations, are considered "Men of Perversity" who "walk in the wicked way." Entry into the group is through conversion. Following repentance from sin, the initiate begins a two-year process leading to full membership. During this period he (women are not specifically mentioned) receives instruction in the group's secret knowledge and passes through progressively higher stages of purity. Some of the convert's wealth (according to 7:6–8 he retained an unspecified portion of his funds) is merged with that of the group, a marked similarity to the practice of early Christians described in the New Testament book of Acts. Eventually the association assigns him a rank based upon his obedience to the Law of Moses as they understand it. Rank and advancement in group life depend in large measure upon doing "works of the Law" (Hebrew, *maase ha-torah*), a phrase significant also in writings of the apostle Paul.

Each chapter of the association has a leader known as the Instructor, probably the foremost priest, who guides deliberations about rules for the group's government, association funds, and biblical interpretation. Indeed, the heading of the text from Cave 1 states that this copy belonged to an Instructor, who may well have referred to the work when instructing new converts.

Decisions are by majority rule. The local chapters comprise at least ten men who meet for meals and Bible study. Each year they conduct a full review of the membership. At that time a man's rank can change, for better or worse, according to his behavior and biblical understanding.

The use of military terminology is notable. Members are described as "volunteers" and are organized into groups of thousands, hundreds, fifties, and tens. The method of organization is that of the holy war conducted under Moses and Joshua when Israel first attacked the Canaanites and took possession of the land of Israel. This choice of terminology was, of course, deliberate. The group thought of itself as warriors awaiting God's signal to begin the final war against the nations and the wicked among the Jews. Meanwhile they sought to live in a heightened state of purity, as the Bible required for holy warriors.

Among the Jews, similar purity groups are known from rabbinic literature. Designated by the Hebrew term *haburot,* these other Jewish purity groups (perhaps made up of Pharisees) required an oath of admittance and ate their meals together. Further similarities between our group and the *haburot* include a period of probation for prospective members and separation from the generality of Jews. Some early Christian groups also organized themselves in similar fashion, so far as the details are described in the book of Acts.

Many of this work's theological ideas are familiar to us from other Jewish writings and early Christianity (which was, of course, itself a Jewish movement when it began). As with Christianity, members of the association envision themselves as entering a new covenant with God, truly fulfilling the old Mosaic covenant. The charter calls this new covenant variously the Covenant of Mercy, the Covenant of the Eternal *Yahad,* the Eternal Covenant, and the Covenant of Justice. Believers are presently living in an era when Satan (here called Belial) rules the world. The New Testament terms Satan "the Prince of this world." Ultimately, that fact explains why believers, who know and live by the truth, have such difficulties in this world. Believers are Children of Light, nonbelievers Children of Darkness—terminology also used in the New Testament. Among other names, the association calls itself "The Way" (e.g., 9:18), a self-designation that some of the first Christians also used (Acts 9:2).

In the future the charter anticipates a "gracious visitation" of God. Then adherents will enter into the Day of Vengeance, and this world's power structures will be overturned: the last shall be first and the first, last. Those who enter the *Yahad* of God can anticipate long life, bountiful peace, multiple progeny, and eventually life everlasting. One passage of the text may speak of the hope of resurrection (11:16–17). Believers will one day receive a "crown of glory" and a "robe of honor." On the other hand, everyone not belonging to the group is fated to everlasting damnation, an eternity of torture by the evil "angels of perdition," all the while burning in utter darkness. The charter's long descriptive passages on hell and the fate of unbelievers are chilling, their detail doubtless a reflection of the almost palpable hatred of outsiders.

Particularly striking is the notion of hidden teaching, called the "mystery." Early Christianity and rabbinic Judaism also embraced similar but distinct notions of "continuing revelation" not known to outsiders. This is the idea that God continued to reveal new truth in their own day and that the Bible was neither the only, nor the final, repository of his communication with humankind. Paul speaks often of "the mystery that has been hidden throughout the ages and generations but has now been revealed to his saints" (Col. 1:26). The rabbis thought of themselves as tradents, "handers-down" of additional revelation given to Moses at Sinai, the "oral law"—passed on from generation to generation only by word of mouth. This revelation could not be found in the Bible. Likewise, the mystery cults of the Greco-Roman world promised their initiates insight into some otherwise unattainable secret to life. In no small part this common emphasis on mysterious new revelation expressed a dissatisfaction with centuries-old cults and religious teachings. Among Jews, for example, many thinking people in the period of the New Testament had difficulties with the notion of animal sacrifice. As the New Testament book of Hebrews formulates the issue, "It is impossible for the blood of bulls and goats to take away sins" (10:4). Thus, for the author of Hebrews, sacrifices are ineffectual and pointless in the light of what Jesus has accomplished.

The members of this charter's association likewise believed that sacrifice was in itself ineffectual. They were not so radical as the early Christians, however, and could not simply discontinue sacrifice altogether, since it was, after all, commanded by God and regulated in great detail by the writings of Moses. They conceived of themselves as atoning for sin through sacrifice offered in the context of prayer, righteousness, and blameless behavior (9:4–5). Without the proper inner attitude, sacrifice meant nothing (3:11).

Perhaps the most striking conceptual—even verbal—similarity between early Christian thought and that of this charter is the notion of community as temple. Paul speaks of the believers being "built upon the foundation of the apostles and prophets, with Christ Jesus himself as the cornerstone. In him the whole structure is joined together and grows into a holy temple in the Lord; in whom you also are built together spiritually into a dwelling place for God" (Eph. 2:20–22). Our text describes the believers as a "temple for Israel and . . . Holy of Holies . . . the tested wall, the precious cornerstone whose foundations shall neither be shaken nor swayed . . . a blameless and true house in Israel" (8:5–9). Thus both early Christians and members of this association conceived of themselves abstractly as the true temple. They had replaced the physical structure in Jerusalem. This was an idea with a transcendent implication, since the Bible could be read as saying that God lived in the Jerusalem temple. For both of these groups, God did not dwell in that mere hollow edifice built by human hands. He lived in them.

The charter underwent literary development in the course of use and circulation among local chapters of the association. Sometimes the changes were profound. Still, it remains unclear just how much the changes in the text reflect changes in the actual life of the membership. We are all familiar with the phenomenon in our own culture whereby laws remain on the books that are no longer enforced, while new ones that get passed may or may not supersede the older legislation even when, theoretically, they should.

We have provided a translation of the text known as 1QS, with damaged portions filled in from time to time on the basis of other, more fragmentary, copies from Cave 4. Though 1QS is the best preserved copy of the *Charter,* it represents only one of three basic forms of the work and is arguably the latest form of the *Charter.* To represent to the reader something of the nature of the differences among the different forms of the *Charter,* a second, apparently earlier, version of col. 5 is appended to the end of the translation that follows.

The work begins by characterizing the covenant to which members are to commit themselves. The author further describes the ideal community in general terms, and explains the role to be taken by an Instructor as a teacher for the community.

Col. 1 [1]A text belonging to [the Instructor, who is to teach the Ho]ly Ones how to live according to the book of the *Yahad*'s Rule. He is to teach them to seek [2]God with all their heart and with all their soul, to do that which is good and upright before Him, just as [3]He commanded through Moses and all His servants the prophets. He is to teach them to love everything [4]He chose and to hate everything He rejected, to distance themselves from all evil [5]and to hold fast to all good deeds; to practice truth, justice, and righteousness [6]in the land, and to walk no longer in a guilty, willful heart and lustful desires, [7]wherein they did every evil thing. He is to induct all who volunteer to live by the laws of God [8]into the Covenant of Mercy, so as to be joined to God's society and walk faultless before Him, according to all [9]that has been revealed for the times appointed them. He is to teach them both to love all the Children of Light—each [10]commensurate with his rightful place in the council of God—and to hate all the Children of Darkness, each commensurate with his guilt [11]and the vengeance due him from God.

All who volunteer for His truth are to bring the full measure of their knowledge, strength, and [12]wealth into the *Yahad* of God. Thus will they purify their knowledge in the verity of God's laws, properly exercise their strength [13]according to the perfection of His ways, and likewise their wealth by the canon of His righteous counsel. They are not to deviate in the smallest detail [14]from any of God's words as these apply to their own time. They are neither to advance their holy times nor to postpone [15]any of their prescribed festivals. They shall turn aside from His unerring laws neither to the right nor the left.

Next is described a ceremony for initiating new members into the community.

[16]All who enter the *Yahad*'s Rule shall be initiated into the Covenant before God, agreeing to act [17]according to all that He has commanded and not to backslide because of any fear, terror or persecution [18]that may occur during the time of Belial's dominion. While the initiates are being inducted into the Covenant, the priests [19]and the Levites shall continuously bless the God of deliverance and all His veritable deeds. All [20]the initiates into the Covenant shall continuously respond "Amen, amen."

[21]The priests are to rehearse God's gracious acts made manifest by mighty deeds, [22]heralding His loving mercies on Israel's behalf. The Levites

in turn shall rehearse [23]the wicked acts of the children of Israel, all their guilty transgressions and sins committed during the dominion [24]of Belial. All the initiates into the Covenant are to respond by confessing, "We have been wicked, [25]transgressed, and [sin]ned. We have been wicked—we and our fathers before us—walking [26][in rebellion to the laws] of truth and righteousness, [wherefore God] has judged us, both we and our fathers. **Col. 2** [1]Yet He has also requited us with the loving deeds of His mercy, long ago and forevermore."

Then the priests are to bless all [2]those foreordained to God, who walk faultless in all of His ways, saying "May He bless you with every [3]good thing and preserve you from every evil. May He enlighten your mind with wisdom for living, be gracious to you with the knowledge of eternal things, [4]and lift up His gracious countenance upon you for everlasting peace." The Levites in turn shall curse all those foreordained to [5]Belial. They shall respond, "May you be damned in return for all your wicked, guilty deeds. May the [6]God of terror give you over to implacable avengers; may He visit your offspring with destruction at the hands of those who recompense [7]evil with evil. May you be damned without mercy in return for your dark deeds, an object of wrath [8]licked by eternal flame, surrounded by utter darkness. May God have no mercy upon you when you cry out, nor forgive so as to atone for your sins. [9]May He lift up His furious countenance upon you for vengeance. May you never find peace through the appeal of any intercessor." [10]All the initiates into the Covenant shall respond to the blessers and cursers, "Amen, amen."

Many movements founded on repentance face the problem of the initiate who is not truly converted. The following section addresses this problem.

[11]Then the priests and Levites shall go on to declare, "Damned be anyone initiated with unrepentant heart, [12]who enters this Covenant, then sets up the stumbling block of his sin, so turning apostate. It shall come to pass, [13]when he hears the words of this Covenant, that he shall bless himself in his heart, saying 'Peace be with me, [14]though I walk in the stubbornness of my heart' (Deut. 29:18–19). Surrounded by abundant water, his spirit shall nevertheless expire thirsty, without [15]forgiveness. God's anger and zeal for His commandments shall burn against him for eternal destruction. All the [16]curses of this Covenant shall cleave to him, and God shall separate him out for a fate befitting his wickedness. He shall be cut off from all the Sons of Light because of his apostasy [17]from God, brought about by unrepentance and the stumbling block of sin. He shall cast his lot with those damned for all time." [18]The initiates are all to respond in turn, "Amen, amen."

Annual review of the membership.

[19]They shall do as follows annually, all the days of Belial's dominion: the priests shall pass in review [20]first, ranked according to their spiritual excellence, one after another. Then the Levites shall follow, [21]and third all the people by rank, one after another, in their thousands and hundreds [22]and fifties and tens. Thus shall each Israelite know his proper standing in the *Yahad* of God, [23]an eternal society. None shall be demoted from his appointed place, none promoted beyond his foreordained rank. [24]So shall all together comprise a *Yahad* whose essence is truth, genuine humility, love of charity and righteous intent, [25]caring for one another after this fashion within a holy society, comrades in an eternal fellowship.

Who is to be excluded from God's society and why.

Anyone who refuses to enter [26][the society of G]od, preferring to continue in his willful heart, shall not [be initiated into the *Ya*]*had* of His truth, inasmuch as his soul **Col. 3** [1]has rejected the disciplines foundational to knowledge: the laws of righteousness. He lacks the strength to repent. He is not to be reckoned among the upright. [2]His knowledge, strength and wealth are not to enter the society of the *Yahad*. Surely, he plows in the muck of wickedness, so defiling stains [3]would mar his repentance. Yet he cannot be justified by what his willful heart declares lawful, preferring to gaze on darkness rather than the ways of light. With such an eye [4]he cannot be reckoned faultless. Ceremonies of atonement cannot restore his innocence, neither cultic waters his purity. He cannot be sanctified by baptism in oceans [5]and rivers, nor purified by mere ritual bathing. Unclean, unclean shall he be all the days that he rejects the laws [6]of God, refusing to be disciplined in the *Yahad* of His society.

For only through the spirit pervading God's true society can there be atonement for a man's ways, all [7]of his iniquities; thus only can he gaze upon the light of life and so be joined to His truth by His holy spirit, purified from all [8]iniquity. Through an upright and humble attitude his sin may be covered, and by humbling himself before all God's laws his flesh [9]can be made clean. Only thus can he really receive the purifying waters and be purged by the cleansing flow. Let him order his steps to walk faultless [10]in all the ways of God, just as He commanded for the times appointed to him. Let him turn aside neither to the right nor the left, nor yet [11]deviate in the smallest detail from all of His words. Then indeed will he be accepted by God, offering the sweet savor of atoning sacrifice, and then only shall he be a party to the Covenant of [12]the Eternal *Yahad*.

A theoretical discussion of the two spirits that control humankind and determine who is good and who is evil, why upright people sin and why the good suffer, and what the manifestations are of both spirits.

[13]A text belonging to the Instructor, who is to enlighten and teach all the Sons of Light about the character and fate of humankind: [14]all their spiritual varieties with accompanying signs, all their deeds generation by generation, and their visitation for afflictions together with [15]eras of peace.

All that is now and ever shall be originates with the God of knowledge. Before things come to be, He has ordered all their designs, [16]so that when they do come to exist—at their appointed times as ordained by His glorious plan—they fulfill their destiny, a destiny impossible to change. He controls [17]the laws governing all things, and He provides for all their pursuits.

He created humankind to rule over [18]the world, appointing for them two spirits in which to walk until the time ordained for His visitation. These are the spirits [19]of truth and falsehood. Upright character and fate originate with the Habitation of Light; perverse, with the Fountain of Darkness. [20]The authority of the Prince of Light extends to the governance of all righteous people; therefore, they walk in the paths of light. Correspondingly, the authority of the Angel [21]of Darkness embraces the governance of all wicked people, so they walk in the paths of darkness.

The authority of the Angel of Darkness further extends to the corruption [22]of all the righteous. All their sins, iniquities, shameful and rebellious deeds are at his prompting, [23]a situation God in His mysteries allows to continue until His era dawns. Moreover, all the afflictions of the righteous, and every trial in its season, occur because of this Angel's diabolic rule. [24]All the spirits allied with him share but a single resolve: to cause the Sons of Light to stumble.

Yet the God of Israel (and the Angel of His Truth) assist all [25]the Sons of Light. It is actually He who created the spirits of light and darkness, making them the cornerstone of every deed, [26]their impulses the premise of every action. God's love for one spirit **Col. 4** [1]lasts forever. He will be pleased with its actions for always. The counsel of the other, however, He abhors, hating its every impulse for all time.

[2]Upon earth their operations are these: one enlightens a man's mind, making straight before him the paths of true righteousness and causing his heart to fear the laws [3]of God. This spirit engenders humility, patience, abundant compassion, perpetual goodness, insight, understanding, and powerful wisdom resonating to each [4]of God's deeds, sustained by His constant faithfulness. It engenders a spirit knowledgeable in every plan of action, zealous for the laws of righteousness, holy [5]in its thoughts, and steadfast in purpose. This

spirit encourages plenteous compassion upon all who hold fast to truth, and glorious purity combined with visceral hatred of impurity in its every guise. It results in humble deportment [6]allied with a general discernment, concealing the truth, that is, the mysteries of knowledge. To these ends is the earthly counsel of the spirit to those whose nature yearns for truth.

Through a gracious visitation all who walk in this spirit will know healing, [7]bountiful peace, long life, and multiple progeny, followed by eternal blessings and perpetual joy through life everlasting. They will receive a crown of glory [8]with a robe of honor, resplendent forever and ever.

[9]The operations of the spirit of falsehood result in greed, neglect of righteous deeds, wickedness, lying, pride and haughtiness, cruel deceit and fraud, [10]massive hypocrisy, a want of self-control and abundant foolishness, a zeal for arrogance, abominable deeds fashioned by whorish desire, lechery in its filthy manifestation, [11]a reviling tongue, blind eyes, deaf ears, stiff neck, and hard heart—to the end of walking in all the ways of darkness and evil cunning.

The judgment [12]of all who walk in such ways will be multiple afflictions at the hand of all the angels of perdition, everlasting damnation in the wrath of God's furious vengeance, never-ending terror and reproach [13]for all eternity, with a shameful extinction in the fire of Hell's outer darkness. For all their eras, generation by generation, they will know doleful sorrow, bitter evil, and dark happenstance, until [14]their utter destruction with neither remnant nor rescue.

The struggle of good and evil, and good's ultimate triumph.

[15]The character and fate of all humankind reside with these spirits. All the hosts of humanity, generation by generation, are heirs to these spiritual divisions, walking according to their ways; the outworking of every [16]deed inheres in these divisions according to each person's spiritual heritage, whether great or small, for every age of eternity. God has appointed these spirits as equals until the [17]last age, and set an everlasting enmity between their divisions. False deeds are thus an abomination to the truth, whereas all the ways of truth are for perversity equally a disgrace. Fierce [18]dispute attends every point of decision, for they can never agree. In his mysterious insight and glorious wisdom God has countenanced an era in which perversity triumphs, but at the time appointed [19]for visitation He shall destroy such forever. Then shall truth come forth in victory upon the earth. Sullied by wicked ways while perversity rules, at [20]the time of the appointed judgment truth shall be decreed. By His truth God shall then purify all human deeds, and refine some of humanity so as to extinguish every

perverse spirit from the inward parts [21]of the flesh, cleansing from every wicked deed by a holy spirit. Like purifying waters, He shall sprinkle each with a spirit of truth, effectual against all the abominations of lying and sullying by an [22]unclean spirit. Thereby He shall give the upright insight into the knowledge of the Most High and the wisdom of the angels, making wise those following the perfect way. Indeed, God has chosen them for an eternal covenant; [23]all the glory of Adam shall be theirs alone. Perversity shall be extinct, every fraudulent deed put to shame.

Until now the spirits of truth and perversity have contended within the human heart. [24]All people walk in both wisdom and foolishness. As is a person's endowment of truth and righteousness, so shall he hate perversity; conversely, in proportion to bequest in the lot of evil, one will act wickedly and [25]abominate truth. God has appointed these spirits as equals until the time of decree and renewal. He foreknows the outworking of their deeds for all the ages [26][of eternity.] He has granted them dominion over humanity, so imparting knowledge of good [and evil, de]ciding the fate of every living being by the measure of which spirit predominates in hi[m, until the day of the appointed] visitation.

Rules for the conduct of the community. In the first section the rules are general and abstract.

Col. 5 [1]This is the rule for the men of the *Yahad* who volunteer to repent from all evil and to hold fast to all that He, by His good will, has commanded. They are to separate from the congregation of [2]perverse men. They are to come together as one with respect to Law and wealth. Their discussions shall be under the oversight of the Sons of Zadok—priests and preservers of the Covenant—and according to the majority rule of the men of [3]the *Yahad,* who hold fast to the Covenant. These men shall guide all decisions on matters of Law, money, and judgment.

They are to practice truth together with humility, [4]charity, justice, lovingkindness, and modesty in all their ways. Accordingly, none will continue in a willful heart and thus be seduced, not by his heart, [5]neither by his eyes, nor yet by his lower nature. Together they shall circumcise the foreskin of this nature, this stiff neck, and so establish a foundation of truth for Israel—that is to say, for the *Yahad* of the Eternal [6]Covenant. They are to atone for all those in Aaron who volunteer for holiness, and for those in Israel who belong to truth, and for Gentile proselytes who join them in community. Both by trial and by verdict [7]they are to condemn any who transgress a regulation.

General foundational precepts regarding entry into the group's new covenant.

These are the regulations that govern when they are gathered together as a community. Every initiate into the party of the *Yahad* [8]is to enter the covenant in full view of all the volunteers. He shall take upon himself a binding oath to return to the Law of Moses (according to all that He commanded) with all [9]his heart and with all his mind, to all that has been revealed from it to the Sons of Zadok—priests and preservers of the Covenant, seekers of His will—and the majority of the men of their Covenant [10](that is, those who have jointly volunteered for His truth and to live by what pleases Him). Each one who thus enters the Covenant by oath is to separate himself from all of the perverse men, they who walk [11]in the wicked way, for such are not reckoned a part of His Covenant. They "have not sought Him nor inquired of His statutes" (Zeph. 1:6) so as to discover the hidden laws in which they err [12]to their shame. Even the revealed laws they knowingly transgress, thus stirring God's judgmental wrath and full vengeance: the curses of the Mosaic covenant. He will bring against them [13]weighty judgments, eternal destruction with none spared.

The mention of outsiders inspires a digression criticizing them. Clearly involvement with such people was a dangerous attraction for some members of the community.

None of the perverse men is to enter purifying waters used by the Men of Holiness and so contact their purity. (Indeed, it is impossible to be purified [14]without first repenting of evil, inasmuch as impurity adheres to all who transgress His word.) None is to be yoked with such a man in his work or wealth, lest "he cause him to bear [15]guilt" (Lev. 22:16). On the contrary, one must keep far from him in every respect, for thus it is written:"Keep far from every false thing" (Exod. 23:7). None belonging to the *Yahad* is to discuss [16]with such men matters of Law or legal judgment, nor to eat or drink what is theirs, nor yet to take anything from them [17]unless purchased, as it is written "Turn away from mere mortals, in whose nostrils is only breath; for of what account are they?" (Isa. 2:22). Accordingly, [18]all who are not reckoned as belonging to His covenant must be separated out, along with everything they possess; the Man of Holiness must not rely upon futile [19]actions, whereas all who do not know His Covenant are futility itself. All those who despise His word, He shall destroy from upon the face of the earth. Their every deed is an abomination [20]before Him, all that is theirs being infested with impurity.

Stipulations governing the examination of initiates.

When anyone enters the Covenant—to live according to all these ordinances, to make common cause with the Congregation of Holiness—they [21]shall investigate his spiritual qualities as a community, each member taking part. They shall investigate his understanding and works vis à vis the Law, guided both by the Sons of Aaron, who have jointly volunteered to uphold [22]His Covenant and to observe all of the ordinances that He commanded them to execute, and by the majority of Israel, who have volunteered to return, as a community, to His Covenant. [23]They are to be enrolled by rank, one man higher than his fellow—as the case may be—by virtue of his understanding and works. Thus each will obey his fellow, the inferior his superior. They shall [24]examine spiritual qualities and works annually, promoting a man because of his understanding and perfection of walk, or demoting him because of failure.

How shall those higher in rank reprove their inferiors? Several rules govern this potentially divisive issue.

Each man is to reprove [25]his fellow in truth, humility and loving-kindness. He should not speak to him in anger, with grumbling, [26]with a [stiff] neck or with a wickedly [zealous] spirit. He must not hate him because of his own [uncircumcised] heart. Most assuredly he is to rebuke him on the day of the infraction so that he does not **Col. 6** [1]continue in sin. Also, no man is to bring a charge against his fellow before the general membership unless he has previously rebuked that man before witnesses.

General principles of organization intended to govern the various local chapters of the community in their joint meals and study of the Bible.

By these rules [2]they are to govern themselves wherever they dwell, in accordance with each legal finding that bears upon communal life. Inferiors must obey their ranking superiors as regards work and wealth. They shall eat, [3]pray and deliberate communally. Wherever ten men belonging to the party of the *Yahad* are gathered, a priest must always [4]be present. The men shall sit before the priest by rank, and in that manner their opinions will be sought on any matter. When the table has been set for eating or the new wine readied [5]for drinking, it is the priest who shall stretch out his hand first, blessing the first portion of the bread or the new wine. [6]In any place where is gathered the ten-man quorum, someone must always be engaged in study of the Law, day and night, [7]continually, each one taking his turn. The general membership will be diligent together for the first third of every night of the year, reading aloud from the Book, interpreting Scripture, and [8]praying together.

Procedural rules for the public meetings of the chapters.

This is the rule for the session of the general membership, each man being in his proper place. The priests shall sit in the first row, the elders in the second, then the rest [9]of the people, each in his proper place. In that order they shall be questioned about any judgment, deliberation, or matter that may come before the general membership, so that each man may state his opinion [10]to the party of the *Yahad.* None should interrupt the words of his comrade, speaking before his brother finishes what he has to say. Neither should anyone speak before another of [11]higher rank. Only the man being questioned shall speak in his turn. During the session of the general membership no man should say anything except by the permission of the general membership, or more particularly, of the man [12]who is the Overseer of the general membership. If any man has something to say to the general membership, yet is of a lower rank than whomever is guiding the deliberations of the party of the [13]*Yahad,* let him stand up. He should then say, "I have something to say to the general membership." If they permit, he may speak.

The work returns yet again to the topic of initiates into the community. Here are elaborated specific procedures for a two-year process of admission by steps into full membership.

If anyone of Israel volunteers [14]for enrollment in the party of the *Yahad,* the man appointed as leader of the general membership shall examine him regarding his understanding and works. If he has the potential for instruction, he is to begin initiation [15]into the Covenant, returning to the truth and repenting of all perversity. He shall be made to understand all the basic precepts of the *Yahad.* Subsequently in the process, he must stand before the general membership and the whole chapter shall interrogate him [16]about his particulars. According to the decision of the society of the general membership, he shall either proceed or depart.

If he does proceed in joining the party of the *Yahad,* he must not touch the pure food [17]of the general membership before they have examined him as to his spiritual fitness and works, and not before a full year has passed. Further, he must not yet admix his property with that of the general membership. [18]When he has passed a full year in the *Yahad,* the general membership shall inquire into the details of his understanding and works of the Law.

If it be ordained, [19]in the opinion of the priests and the majority of the men of their Covenant, then he shall be initiated further into the secret teaching of the *Yahad.* They shall also take steps to incorporate his property, putting it under the authority of the [20]Overseer together with that of the general membership, and keeping an account of it—but it shall not yet be disbursed along with that of the general membership.

The initiate is not to touch the drink of the general membership prior to [21]passing a second year among the men of the *Yahad.* When that second year has passed, the general membership shall review his case. If it be ordained [22]for him to proceed to full membership in the *Yahad,* they shall enroll him at the appropriate rank among his brothers for discussion of the Law, jurisprudence, participation in pure meals, and admixture of property. Thenceforth the *Yahad* may draw upon his counsel and [23]judgment.

A penal code, setting forth case-by-case violations and penalties. Many of these have to do with breaches of discipline and order, while others concern ethical shortcomings. The code begins with laws governing speech.

[24]These are the rules by which cases are to be decided at a community inquiry.

If there be found among them a man who has lied [25]about money and done so knowingly, they shall bar him from the pure meals of the general membership for one year; further, his ration of bread is to be reduced by one-fourth.

Anyone who answers [26]his comrade defiantly or impatiently, thereby rejecting the instruction of his fellow and rebelling against the orders of his higher-ranked comrade, [27]has usurped authority; he is to be punished by reduced rations and [exclusion from the pure meals] for one year.

Anyone who speaks aloud the M[ost] Holy Name of God, [whether in . . .] or **Col. 7** [1]in cursing or as a blurt in time of trial or for any other reason, or while he is reading a book or praying, is to be expelled, [2]never again to return to the party of the *Yahad.*

If anyone speaks angrily against one of the priests who are inscribed in the book, he is to be punished by reduced rations for [3]one year and separated from the pure meals of the general membership, eating by himself. If, however, he spoke without premeditation, he shall suffer reduced rations for only six months.

Anyone who knowingly lies [4]is to be punished by reduced rations for six months.

The man who accuses his comrade of sin, fully aware that he cannot prove the charge, is to suffer reduced rations for one year [5]and be separated from the pure meals.

Laws governing fraud and grudges.

Whoever speaks with his companion deceitfully or knowingly practices fraud is to be punished by reduced rations for six months.

If a man is [6]drawn unawares into a fraudulent scheme by his comrade, then he is to be punished by reduced rations for only three months.

If money belonging to the *Yahad* is involved in a fraudulent scheme and lost, the man responsible must repay the sum [7]from his own funds. [8]If he lacks sufficient resources to repay it, then he is to suffer reduced rations for sixty days.

Whoever nurses a grudge against his companion—in blatant disregard of the *Yahad* statute about reproof on the selfsame day—is to be punished by reduced rations for six months <one year.> [9]The same applies to the man who on any matter takes vengeance into his own hands.

Laws governing public meetings and communal meals of the chapters. Coarse behavior, public indecency, spitting, and gesturing with the left hand are all forbidden; spitting and using the left hand carried overtones of sorcery in the ancient world.

Whoever speaks foolishness: three months.

Anyone interrupting his companion while in session: [10]ten days.

Anyone who lies down and sleeps in a session of the general membership: thirty days.

The same applies to the man who leaves a session of the general membership [11]without permission and without a good excuse three times in a single session. Up to the third time he shall be punished by reduced rations only ten days. But if they have risen for prayer [12]when he leaves, then he is to suffer thirty days' reduced rations.

Anyone who walks about naked in the presence of a comrade, unless he be sick, is to be punished by reduced rations for six months.

[13]A man who spits into the midst of a session of the general membership is to be punished by reduced rations for thirty days.

Anyone who brings out his penis from beneath his clothing—that is, his clothing is [14]so full of holes that his nakedness is exposed—is to be punished by thirty days' reduced rations.

Anyone who bursts into foolish horselaughter is to be punished by reduced rations for thirty [15]days.

A man who draws out his left hand to gesture during conversation is to suffer ten days reduced rations.

Laws concerning various degrees of rebellion against the community and its teaching.

The man who gossips about his companion [16]is to be barred for one year from the pure meals of the general membership and punished by reduced rations. But if a man gossips about the general membership, he is to be banished from them [17]and may never return.

The man who murmurs against the secret teaching of the *Yahad* is to be banished, never to return. But if he murmurs against a comrade [18]and cannot prove the charges, he is to be punished by reduced rations for six months.

The man whose spirit deviates from the secret teaching of the *Yahad,* such that he forsakes the truth and [19]walks in the stubbornness of his heart—if he repents, he is to be punished by two years of reduced rations. During the first, he is not to touch the pure food of the general membership; [20]during the second, he is not to touch their drink. He shall rank lower than all the men of the *Yahad*. When [21]two full years have passed, the general membership shall inquire into his particulars. If they allow him to proceed, he shall be enrolled at the appropriate rank and thereafter take part in discussions of community precepts.

[22]Any man who, having been in the party of the *Yahad* for ten full years, [23]backslides spiritually so that he forsakes the *Yahad* and leaves [24]the general membership, walking in his willful heart, may never again return to the party of the *Yahad*.

Also, any man belonging to the *Ya*[*had* who sh]ares [25]with him his own pure food, his own wealth [or that of] the *Yahad,* is to suffer the same verdict: he is to be exp[elled.]

This section of the text bears an uncertain relationship to the previous portions. Some scholars believe that an "inner council" of elite members is here described; others, that this and several following sections of the text represent an early, original manifesto that was later expanded. On this second understanding, the whole community, not just an elite, is being described. Several of the Cave 4 copies of the Charter *suggest that this second understanding, or some more nuanced version of it, is indeed correct.*

Col. 8 [1]In the party of the *Yahad* there shall be twelve laymen and three priests who are blameless in the light of all that has been revealed from the whole [2]Law, so as to work truth, righteousness, justice, loving-kindness, and humility, one with another. [3]They are to preserve faith in the land with self-control and a broken spirit, atoning for sin by working justice and [4]suffering affliction. They are to walk with all by the standard of truth and the dictates proper to the age.

When such men as these come to be in Israel, [5]then shall the party of the *Yahad* truly be established, an "eternal planting" (*Jubilees* 16:26), a temple for Israel, and—mystery!—a Holy [6]of Holies for Aaron; true witnesses to justice, chosen by God's will to atone for the land and to recompense [7]the wicked their due. They will be "the tested wall, the precious cornerstone" (Isa. 28:16) whose [8]foundations shall neither be shaken nor swayed, a fortress, a Holy of Holies [9]for Aaron, all of them knowing the Covenant of Justice and thereby offering a sweet savor. They shall be a blameless and true house in Israel, [10]upholding the covenant of eternal statutes. They shall be an acceptable sacrifice, atoning for the land and ringing in the verdict against evil, so that perversity ceases to exist.

When these men have been grounded in the instruction of the *Yahad* for two years—provided they be blameless in their conduct—[11]they shall be set apart as holy in the midst of the men of the *Yahad*. No biblical doctrine concealed from Israel but discovered by the [12]Interpreter is to be hidden from these men out of fear that they might backslide.

When such men as these come to be in Israel, [13]conforming to these doctrines, they shall separate from the session of perverse men to go to the wilderness, there to prepare the way of truth, [14]as it is written, "In the wilderness prepare the way of the LORD, make straight in the desert a highway for our God" (Isa. 40:3). [15]This means the expounding of the Law, decreed by God through Moses for obedience, that being defined by what has been revealed for each age, [16]and by what the prophets have revealed by His holy spirit.

Rules for community discipline, more general than those previously stipulated in the penal code. Notably harsher at points, they may constitute an earlier version of that code.

No man belonging to the Covenant of the [17]*Yahad* who flagrantly deviates from any commandment is to touch the pure food belonging to the holy men. [18]Further, he is not to participate in any of their deliberations until all his works have been cleansed from evil, so that he is again able to walk blamelessly. They shall admit him [19]into deliberations by the decision of the general membership; afterwards, he shall be enrolled at an appropriate rank. This is also the procedure for every initiate added to the *Yahad*.

[20]These are the rules by which the men of blameless holiness shall conduct themselves, one with another. [21]Any covenant member of the *Yahad* of Holiness (they who walk blamelessly as He commanded) [22]who transgresses even one commandment from the Law of Moses intentionally or deviously is to be expelled from the party of the *Yahad,* [23]never to return. Further, none of the holy men is to do business with that man or advise him on any [24]matter whatsoever.

But if the sinner transgressed unintentionally, then he is to be separated from the pure food, community deliberations, [25]and jurisprudence for two years. He may return to study sessions and deliberations if he does not again sin by inadvertence for two full years. **Col. 9** [1]A single unintentional sin may be punished by this two-year process, but the intentional sinner shall never again return. Only the accidental sinner [2]shall be tested by the general membership over a two-year period for blameless conduct and right understanding. Afterwards, he may be enrolled at the appropriate rank within the *Yahad* of Holiness.

The purpose of the community, its manifesto, is reiterated. This statement ends by looking forward to the arrival of a prophet—perhaps the "prophet like Moses" predicted by the book of Deuteronomy, or perhaps a herald such as John the Baptist became for early Christians—and two messiahs, one priestly and one presumably in the royal line of David.

[3]When, united by all these precepts, such men as these come to be a community in Israel, they shall establish eternal truth [4]guided by the instruction of His holy spirit. They shall atone for the guilt of transgression and the rebellion of sin, becoming an acceptable sacrifice for the land through the flesh of burnt offerings, the fat of sacrificial portions, and [5]prayer, becoming—as it were—justice itself, a sweet savor of righteousness and blameless behavior, a pleasing freewill offering.

At that time the men [6]of the *Yahad* shall withdraw, the holy house of Aaron uniting as a Holy of Holies, and the synagogue of Israel as those who walk blamelessly. [7]The sons of Aaron alone shall have authority in judicial and financial matters. They shall decide on governing precepts for the men of the *Yahad* [8]and on money matters for the holy men who walk blamelessly. Their wealth is not to be admixed with that of rebellious men, who [9]have failed to cleanse their path by separating from perversity and walking blamelessly. They shall deviate from none of the teachings of the Law, whereby they would walk [10]in their willful heart completely. They shall govern themselves using the original precepts by which the men of the *Yahad* began to be instructed, [11]doing so until there come the Prophet and the Messiahs of Aaron and Israel.

Rules for the Instructor who is to teach the Yahad.

[12]These are the statutes for the Instructor. He is to conduct himself by them with every living person, guided by the precepts appropriate to each era and the value of each person. [13]He is to work the will of God according to what has been revealed for each period of history, studying all the wise legal findings of earlier times, as well as every [14]statute applying to his own time. He is to discern who are the true Sons of Righteousness and to weigh each man's spiritual qualities, sustaining the chosen ones of his own time in keeping with [15]His will and what He has commanded. In each case he shall decide what a man's spiritual qualities mandate, letting him enter the *Yahad* if his virtue and understanding of the Law [16]measure up. By the same standards he shall determine each man's rank.

The Instructor must not reprove the Men of the Pit, nor argue with them about proper biblical understanding. [17]Quite the contrary: he should conceal his own insight into the Law when among perverse men. He shall save reproof—itself founded on true knowledge and righteous judgment—for those who have chosen [18]the Way, treating each as his spiritual qualities and the precepts of the era require. He shall ground them in knowledge, thereby instructing them in truly wondrous mysteries; if then the secret Way is perfected among [19]the men of the *Yahad*, each will walk blamelessly with his fellow, guided by what has been revealed to them. That will be the time of "preparing the way [20]in the desert" (Isa. 40:3). He shall instruct them in every legal finding that is to regulate their works in that time, and teach them to separate from every man who fails to keep himself [21]from perversity.

These are the precepts of the Way for the Instructor in these times, as to his loving and hating: eternal hatred [22]and a concealing spirit for the Men of the Pit! He shall leave them their wealth and profit like a slave does his master—presently humble before [23]his oppressor, but a zealot for God's law whose time will come: even the Day of Vengeance. He shall work God's will when he attacks the wicked and [24]exercise authority as He has commanded, so that He is pleased with all that is done, as with a freewill offering. Other than God's will he shall delight in nothing, [25]finding pleasure only in [ev]ery word of His mouth. He shall desire nothing that He has not command[ed,] ceaselessly seeking the [la]ws of God. [26]He shall bless his Creator [for all of His good]ness, and re[count His loving-kindness] in all that is to be.

The times when the Instructor is to lead in prayer.

[With pray]er shall he bless Him **Col. 10** [1]at the times ordained of God: when light begins its dominion—each time it returns—and when, as ordained, it is regathered into its dwelling place; when night begins [2]its watches—as He opens His storehouse and spreads darkness over the earth—and when it cycles back, withdrawing before the light; [3]when the luminaries show forth from their holy habitation, and when they are regathered into their glorious abode; when the times appointed for new moons arrive, and when, as their periods require, [4]each gives way to the next. Such renewal is a special day for the Holy of Holies; indeed, it is a sign that He is unlocking eternal loving-kindness each time [5]these cycles begin as ordained, and so it shall be for every era yet to come.

A lengthy sample prayer of the sort that the Instructor was to deliver in celebration of holy times. This prayer is clearly connected in language and style to the Thanksgiving Hymns *(text 12). The times specified are particularly related to the solar calendar found in so many of the Dead Sea Scrolls. One earlier form of the* Charter *contains instead of this prayer a calendrical discourse (see* Calendar of the Heavenly Signs, *text 71).*

On the first of each month in its season, and on holy days laid down for a memorial, in their seasons [6]by a prayer shall I bless Him—a statute forever engraved. When each new year begins and when its seasons turn, fulfilling the law [7]of their decree, each day as set forth, day after day: harvest giving way to summer, planting to the shoots of spring, seasons, years, and weeks of years.

[8]When weeks of years begin, jubilee by jubilee, while I live, on my tongue shall the statute be engraved—with praise its fruit, even the gift of my lips.

[9]With knowledge shall I sing out my music, only for the glory of God, my harp, my lyre for His holiness established; the flute of my lips will I lift, His law its tuning fork. [10]At break of day and darkling sky shall I enter the covenant of God, and when they depart I shall recite His laws; then shall I prescribe [11]my bounds, never to turn back.

By His law shall I convict myself, my wickedness the measure, my sin before my eyes, as a statute engraved. To God shall I say "O, my Righteousness," [12]to the Most High "O, Seat of my good, source of knowledge and

Fount of holiness; height of glory, Almighty, eternal Splendor." What He teaches me, [13]that shall I choose; as He judges me, so shall I delight.

When first I begin campaign or journey, His name shall I bless; when first I set out or turn to come back; [14]when I sit down or rise up, when I spread my bed, then shall I rejoice in Him.

I will bless Him with the offering, the issue of my lips when in ranked array; [15]before I lift hand to mouth to savor the delightful bounty of the earth; when fear or terror break out, in habitation of dire straights or desolation, [16]Him shall I praise.

Upon His miracles and deeds of power shall I meditate; upon His loving-kindness I shall rely all the day. Then shall I know that in His hand resides the judgment [17]of all the living, and all His works are truth. When distress breaks out I shall praise Him, and in His salvation shall I rejoice.

The prayer turns from holy times to ethical behavior, with a focus on the coming "Day of Vengeance." This term refers to the time of war when the people of God will rise up and take their rightful place at the head of the nations.

To no man shall I return [18]evil for evil, I shall pursue a man only for good; for with God resides the judgment of all the living, and He shall pay each man his recompense. My zeal shall not be tarnished by a spirit [19]of wickedness, neither shall I lust for riches gained through violence.

The multitude of evil men I shall not capture until the Day of Vengeance; yet my fury shall not [20]abate from Men of the Pit, and I shall never be appeased until righteousness be established.

I shall hold no angry grudge against those repenting of sin yet neither shall I love [21]any who rebel against the Way; the smitten I shall not comfort until their walk be perfected. I shall give no refuge in my heart to Belial.

Next the focus turns to the use of the tongue. This portion is reminiscent of the New Testament book of James (3:1–12) and its warnings on the danger of an uncontrolled tongue.

In my mouth shall be heard [22]neither foolishness nor sinful deceit; neither fraud nor lies shall be discovered between my lips. Rather, the fruits of holiness will be upon my tongue—abominations [23]will not be found thereon.

For thanksgiving shall I open my mouth, the righteousness of God shall my tongue recount always. Human rebellion, made full [24]by sin, as vain I shall purge from my lips; impure and crafty design I shall expunge from my mind.

Counseled by wisdom, I shall recount knowledge; [25]both prudent and wise, I shall compass it close about, so to preserve faith and strict judgment—conforming to the righteousness of God.

I shall mete out [26]the statute by the measure proper to each time and [. . . dispense] righteousness and loving-kindness to those cast down, even strong encouragement to those who are fearful.

Col. 11 [1][I shall teach] the errant of spirit understanding, instructing those who murmur with wisdom—so humbly to answer the haughty with broken spirit them who [2]oppress, scorn, speak vainly, and are zealous only for wealth.

God is the source of whatever goodness the worshiper may claim, and the truths that he possesses—hidden from other people—are given by God.

As for me, my justification lies with God. In His hand are the perfection of my walk and the virtue of my heart. [3]By His righteousness is my transgression blotted out. For from the fount of His knowledge has my light shot forth; upon his wonders has my eye gazed—the light of my heart upon the mystery [4]of what shall be.

He who is eternal is the staff of my right hand, upon the Mighty Rock do my steps tread; before nothing shall they retreat. For the truth of God—[5]that is the rock of my tread, and His mighty power, my right hand's support. From His righteous fount comes my justification, the light of my heart from His wondrous mysteries.

Upon the eternal [6]has my eye gazed—even that wisdom hidden from men, the knowledge, wise prudence from humanity concealed. The source of righteousness, gathering [7]of power, and abode of glory are from fleshly counsel hidden.

To them He has chosen all these has He given—an eternal possession. He has made them heirs in the legacy [8]of the Holy Ones; with the Angels has He united their assembly, a *Yahad* party. They are an assembly built up for holiness, an eternal Planting for all [9]ages to come.

As for me, to evil humanity and the counsel of perverse flesh do I belong. My transgressions, evils, sins, and corrupt heart [10]belong to the counsel of wormy rot and those who walk in darkness.

Surely a man's way is not his own; neither can any person firm his own step. Surely justification is of God; by His power [11]is the way made perfect. All that shall be, He foreknows, all that is, His plans establish; apart from Him is nothing done.

As for me, if [12]I stumble, God's loving-kindness forever shall save me. If through sin of the flesh I fall, my justification will be by the righteousness of God which endures for all time.

[13]Though my affliction break out, He shall draw my soul back from the

Pit, and firm my steps on the way. Through His love He has brought me near; by His loving-kindness shall He provide [14]my justification.

By His righteous truth has He justified me; and through His exceeding goodness shall He atone for all my sins. By His righteousness shall He cleanse me of human [15]defilement and the sin of humankind—to the end that I praise God for His righteousness, the Most High for His glory.

The prayer closes by reflecting on the greatness of God and human unworthiness.

Blessed are You, O my God, who has opened to knowledge [16]the mind of Your servant. Establish all of his works in righteousness; raise up the son of Your handmaiden—if it please You—to be among those chosen of humankind, to stand [17]before You forever.

Surely apart from You the way cannot be perfected, nor can anything be done unless it please You. You teach [18]all knowledge and all that shall be, by Your will shall it come to pass. Apart from You there is no other able to contest Your counsel, fathom [19]the design of Your holiness, penetrate the depth of Your mysteries, or apprehend Your wonders and surpassing [20]power.

Who can Your glory measure? Who, indeed, is man among Your glorious works? [21]As what can he, born of a woman, be reckoned before You? Kneaded from dust, his body is but the bread of worms; he is so much spit, [22]mere nipped-off clay—and for clay his longing. Shall clay contest, the vessel plumb counsel?

The version of 5:1–20 found in 4Q256 col. 9 and 4Q258 col. 1. In general, the version of the Charter *found in these Cave 4 copies is shorter (4Q258 is lacking cols. 1–4 entirely), lacks biblical quotations found in 1QS, and is stylistically less given to rhetoric. Notable too is the absence of any reference to the "Sons of Zadok," who lead the group's deliberations according to 1QS col. 5.*

Col. 5 [1]A legal finding for the Instructor concerning the men of the Law who volunteer. They are to repent from all evil and to hold fast to all that He has commanded. [2]They are to separate from the congregation of perverse men. They are to come together as one with respect to Law and wealth. Their discussions shall be according to majority rule regarding all matters [3]of Law and money.

They are to practice humility, charity, justice, loving-[kindness, and mod]esty in all their ways. [4][Accordingly,] none will continue in a willful heart and thus be seduced; rather, they are to establish a [foundation] of truth for Israel—a *Yahad* for all [5]those in Aaron who volunteer for holiness, a house of truth for Israel and for Gentile proselyte[s] who join th[em] in community. Every initiate into the party of the [6][*Yah*]*ad* is to ta[ke] upon himself a binding oath to [return t]o the [L]aw of Mos[es] with all his heart and with all his mind, to all that has been revealed from [7]the L[aw ac]cording to the party of the me[n] of the *Yaha*[*d*. Each is to separate himself from all of the] perverse [men;] none of the perverse men is to enter purifying waters used by the Men of [8][Holine]ss, and one shall not eat with such a man. None of the [m]en of the *Yahad* is [to discuss] with such men matters of [9][Law] or legal judgment; [none is to be yoked] with such a man in his wealth or work. Nor shall any man of the Men of Holiness eat [10][from their wealth, nor] yet [take any]thing [from them.] They shall not depend on [any of the wo]rks of vanity, for vanity defines all who [do not know [11]His Covenant. All those who despi]se His word, He shall destroy from upon the face of the earth. Their deeds are an abomina[tion] bef[ore Him, a]ll [that is theirs being infested with impurity.]

—M.O.W.

8. Charter for Israel in the Last Days

1QSa (1Q28a), 4Q249a–i

This short work—only two columns of Hebrew text—was inscribed as an appendix to the Cave 1 copy of the foregoing *Charter of a Jewish Sectarian Association* (text 7). Only this one copy exists with certainty (nine additional copies inscribed in Cryptic Script A may also have been found, but they are so fragmentary that identification is problematic). The work reflects many of the same ideas as the longer charter, but unlike that writing, this composition is specifically intended for an ideal future, which it calls the "Last Days." The author imagines that when this millennium fully breaks forth, the *Yahad* will lead a final war against the Gentiles. All Israel—including here women and children—will mobilize and, now realizing their error in not earlier accepting the group's views, come to the *Yahad* and join it for Armageddon. This composition is a blueprint for central aspects of military organization in the coming war, and in both language and concept is closely related to the *War Scroll* writings (see text 11).

Two aspects of this text are particularly remarkable. First, it describes a banquet or feast in which all Israel will take part in the Last Days. The feast is associated with the arrival of the "Messiah of Israel" and is comparable with the early Christian *agape,* or "love," feasts described by such ancient writers as Hippolytus. These Christian meals were attached to the sacrament of communion. We read in the New Testament and other early Christian literature of disorderly behavior associated with these meals. Thus the strict regulation of the banquet described here finds a context. Doubtless this future banquet was an idealization of the *Yahad*'s ordinary practice. According to text 7, it regularly held less exalted communal meals. The connection of the meal here to the arrival of the messiah further recalls Christian imagery of the "marriage supper of the Lamb," the great banquet at which believers are said to join Jesus after all evil has been vanquished (Rev. 19:6–9).

The second remarkable aspect of this writing is its possible reference in 2:11 to God's "fathering" of the Messiah of Israel, that is, of the war leader who was to arise from the line of David. The Hebrew verb used here is *holid,* the same verb used in the biblical "begetting" passages. Because it has been damaged, however, this passage of our text has long been controversial. The reading of the Hebrew letters is difficult, but the scholars who saw the manuscript when it was first discovered (when it was more legible than it is today; the texts have deteriorated) agreed on this reading. Yet the most recent examinations of the difficult passage continue to breed controversy. Geza Vermes, of Oxford, wrote in 1994: "This reading, which has been queried by many, including myself in [the past], seems to be confirmed by computer image enhancement." But in the same year Émile Puech, also relying upon improved photographic technology, came to a different conclusion: the difficult letters should be read as another verb meaning "be revealed." The matter requires further study, but for now the reading of the earliest scholars should probably be preferred, simply because they were able to study the text in its less deteriorated state.

If the traditional reading is correct, then this Qumran text is describing a messianic figure who is in a special way a "son of God." The notion that a messiah would be such is, of course, an idea held in common with early Christianity.

General instructions for the final incorporation of all Israel into the Yahad.

Col. 1 [1]This is the rule for all the congregation of Israel in the Last Days, when they are mobilized [to join the *Yahad*. They must l]ive [2]by the law of the Sons of Zadok, the priests, and the men of their Covenant, they who ce[ased to walk in the w]ay [3]of the people. These same are the men of His party who kept His Covenant during evil times, and so aton[ed for the lan]d.

[4]As they arrive, all the newcomers shall be assembled—women and children included—and read [5][a]ll the statutes of the Covenant. They shall be indoctrinated in all of their laws, for fear that otherwise they may sin accidentally.

Rules for the childhood education of the troops. The mysterious "Book of Meditation" is also mentioned in the Damascus Document *(text 1) and the* Secret of the Way Things Are *(text 105).*

[6]The following is the policy for all the troops of the congregation, and it applies to every native-born Israelite. From [early ch]ildhood each boy [7]is to be instructed in the Book of Meditation. As he grows older, they shall teach him the statutes of the Covenant, and [he will receive] [8][in]struction in their laws. For ten years he is to be considered a youth.

Male rite of passage into adulthood and the army at age twenty. Female incorporation at marriage.

Then, at a[ge] twenty, [he shall be enrolled] [9][in] the ranks and take his place among the men of his clan, thereby joining the holy congrega[tion.] He must not app[roach] [10]a woman for sexual intercourse before he is fully twenty years old, when he knows [right] [11]from wrong. With the marriage act she, for her part, is received into adult membership. From this time on he may bear witness to the statutes of the Law, and take his place among the ranks for the ceremonial proclamation of the ordinances.

Rules governing eligibility for service to the congregation and the army, at ages twenty-five, thirty, and older.

[12]At age twenty-five, he is eligible to take his place among the pillars of the holy [13]congregation and to begin serving the congregation.

When he is thirty years old, he may begin to take part in legal disputes. [14]Further, he is now eligible for command, whether of the thousands of Israel, or as a captain of hundreds, fifties, or [15]tens, or as a judge or official for their tribes and clans. Command appointments shall [be decided by] the Sons of [16][Aar]on, the priests, advised by all the heads of the congregation's clans. Anyone so destined must take his pla[ce] in service publicly, [17][and likewise go for]th to battle and return while the congregation looks on.

In proportion to his intelligence and the perfection of his walk, let each man strengthen his loins for his assignm[ent among the tr]oops, [18]for the performance of his works among his brothers. [What]ever his rank, high or low, let [ea]ch man seek honor for himself, striving to outdo his fellow.

[19]When a man is advanced in age, let him be assigned a task in the se[rvi]ce of the congregation that is commensurate with his remaining strength.

The place of the dull-witted.

No dull-witted man [20]is to be ordained to office as a leader of the congregation of Israel; neither may he be a le[ga]l disputant, nor perform a task for the congregation. [21]He may not receive command in the war that will bring the Gentiles to their knees. Still, he may be enlisted in the ranks of his clan [22]and serve as a laborer or such, as his capacities permit.

The role of the Levites.

Now the Sons of Levi shall each receive a specific assignment [23]from the Sons of Aaron. In general, they shall lead the whole congregation out to battle and back, each man in ranked array, commanded by the heads of [24]the congregation's clans: officers and judges and officials, in the number required by their armies. The Levites shall be overseen by the Sons of Aaron, the priests, [25]and all the heads of the congregation's clans.

Whenever the entire congregation is required to assemble, whether to deliver a legal verdict, [26]as a party of the *Yahad,* or as a war council, then the Levites shall consecrate them for three days, ensuring that everyone who comes [27]is properly prep[ared for the counc]il.

Membership in the party of the Yahad.

These are the men appointed to the party of the *Yahad:* from the age of tw[enty], all the [28][wis]e of the congregation, the understanding and knowledgeable—who are blameless in their behavior and men of ability—together with the [29]tri[bal officials,] all judges, magistrates, captains of thousands, [hundreds,] **Col. 2** [1]fifties, and tens, and the Levites, each a full mem[ber of his div]ision of service. These are [2]the men of reputation, who hold commissions in the party of the *Yahad* in Israel [3]that sits before the Sons of Zadok, the priests.

Those excluded from assemblies. Some are disallowed because of cultic impurity, others because of physical infirmity, which was regarded as a mark of sin.

No man who suffers from a single type of the uncleanness [4]that affects humanity shall enter their assembly; neither is any man so afflicted [5]to receive an assignment from the congregation. No man with a physical handicap—crippled in both legs or [6]hands, lame, blind, deaf, dumb, or possessed of a visible blemish in his flesh—[7]or a doddering old man unable to do his share in the congregation—[8]may en[ter] to take a place in the congregation of the m[e]n of reputation. For the holy [9]angels are [a part of] their congregation.

If [one] of these people has some[thing] to say to the holy congregation, [10]let an oral [de]position be taken, but the man must n[ot] enter [the congregation,] for he has been smitten.

The messianic banquet. The Yahad *believed that in the Last Days two messiahs would emerge from its own ranks, one a priest, the other a royal commander for the armies.*

[11]The procedure for the [mee]ting of the men of reputation [when they are called] to the banquet held by the party of the *Yahad,* when [God] has fa[th]ered [12]the Messiah (*or* when the Messiah has been revealed) among them: [the Priest,] as head of the entire congregation of Israel, shall enter first, trailed by all [13][his] brot[hers, the Sons of] Aaron, those priests [appointed] to the banquet of the men of reputation. They are to sit [14]be[fore him] by rank. Then the [Mess]iah of Israel may en[ter,] and the heads [15]of the th[ousands of Israel] are to sit before him by rank, as determined by [each man's comm]ission in their camps and campaigns. Last, all [16]the heads of [the con]gregation's cl[ans,] together with [their] wis[e and knowledgeable men,] shall sit before them by [17]rank.

[When] they gather [at the] communal [tab]le, [having set out bread and w]ine so the communal table is set [18][for eating] and [the] wine (poured) for drinking, none [may re]ach for the first portion [19]of the bread or [the wine] before the Priest. For [he] shall [bl]ess the first portion of the bread [20]and the wine, [reac]hing for the bread first. Afterw[ard] the Messiah of Israel [shall re]ach [21]for the bread. [Finally,] ea[ch] member of the whole congregation of the *Yahad* [shall give a bl]essing, [in descending order of] rank.

This procedure shall govern [22]every me[al], provided at least ten me[n are ga]thered together.

—M.O.W.

9. Priestly Blessings for the Last Days

1QSb (1Q28b)

This collection of blessings expresses important aspects of the *Yahad*'s ideology regarding the Last Days. The leader of the *Yahad,* called "the Instructor," was to recite these blessings, perhaps upon the occasion (described in text 8) when all Israel was being mustered as new members. He would bless first the general membership, then two unidentifiable groups (the text here being so fragmentary that the identities are obscure), the Zadokite priests, the messianic high priest, and finally the Prince of the Congregation, or military messiah.

In this text we find mention of the group's belief that they would someday be joined to the angels. The priests, in particular, are envisioned as serving in a future temple with the "Angels of the Presence." With these exalted beings the priests would "order destiny," that is, determine the course of events on earth. Thus the group held no mean view of their own importance. We also read of the group's intense hatred for their enemies and of their confident belief in ultimate victory, not only over other Jews, but over the entire earth. As in text 8, the notion of a final war against the Gentiles is prominent, and selected portions of the Bible are understood as applying to the son of David (Prince of the Congregation) who will lead that campaign.

Only this one copy of the work has survived, as an appendix to text 7.

A blessing on the faithful of the Yahad.

Col. 1 [1]Words of blessing belonging to the Instructor, by which to bless those who fear [God, those who do] His will and keep His commandments, [2]who hold fast to His holy co[ven]ant and walk blameless [in all the paths of] His [truth,] whom He chose for an [3]eternal covenant th[at should en]dure forever.

"May the L[ord] bless you [from His holy habitation;] may He throw open for you an everla[st]ing fount from hea[ven], [4]ne[ver fail]ing. [. . .] [5]May He [gra]ce you with every blessing [of the heavenlies]; [may He teach] you the knowledge of the angels! [6][. . . May He open for you] an eternal [fou]nt; may He never wi[thhold living water from] the thirsty. You sha[ll be] [7][. . . May He] deliver you from all [your enemies; may He smite] whom you hate so that none sur[vive.]"

Remnants of a blessing on the second of two unidentifiable groups or individuals. (The blessing on the first is too fragmentary to translate.)

Col. 2 [22][. . .] "May the Lord grace you with the [holy] sp[irit . . . with all] [23]His [rewa]rds may He delight you; May He grace you [with . . .] [24]May He grace you with the holy spirit and loving-[kindness . . .] [25]and with an eternal covenant may He grace you, causing [you] greatly to rejoice [. . .] [26]May He grace you with righteous judgment, [. . . that you not] stumb[le . . .] [27]May He look graciously upon all your works [. . . May He grace you] [28][with] eternal truth [. . . May He look graciously] upon all your descen[dants . . .]"

Col. 3 [1]" 'May the LORD lift up His countenance upon you' (Num. 6:26); [may He delight in] the savor [of your sacrifices.] May He choose all who abide in [your] pries[thood.] [2]May He be specially present at all your holy times and fest[ivals . . .] all your seed. May He lift up [3]His countenance toward your entire congregation! May He place [a crown] upon your head [. . .] [4]with [perpetual] glo[ry. May He] sanctify your descendants with glory without end! May He lif[t up His countenance toward . . .] [5][. . .] May He grant you eter[na]l [pea]ce and a kingdom of [. . .] [6][. . .] from the flesh, and with the h[oly] angels [. . .] [7]May He wage war [at the head] of your thousands [to exterminate] a perver[se] generation . . .

[18][. . . to bring to their kn]ees ma[n]y pe[opl]es on your behalf, and not [19][. . .] all the wealth of the earth to turn you away from the [eternal] fount [20][. . . S]eek him, for God has laid all the foundations of [21][. . .] He has established peace for you forever and ever."

A blessing for the Zadokite priests.

[22]Words of blessing belonging to the Inst[ructor, by which to bless] the Sons of Zadok, the priests, chosen [23]by God to uphold His covenant for[ever, to pr]ove His precepts among His people, and to teach them [24]as He commanded. They have truly held fast [to His covenant], righteously observing all His statutes and walking as [25]He chose.

"May the Lord bless you from His [ho]ly [habitation]! May He set you, perfected in honor, in the midst of [26]the Holy Ones; [may He re]new for you the [eternal] covenant of the priesthood. May He make a place for you in the holy [habitation]. [27]May He ju[dge a]ll princes by the measure of your works, all [leaders] of the nations by [28]what you say. May He make the firstfruits of [every pleas]ing thing your inheritance; may He bless all mortal counsel by your hand!"

A blessing on the messianic high priest.

Col. 4 [22][. . . "For] He has chosen you [. . .] [23]and to place you at the head of the Holy Ones and with you to bl[ess . . .] by your hand [24]the men of God's society, rather than by the hand of a prince [. . .] May you [25][abide forever] as an Angel of the Presence in the holy habitation, to the glory of the God of host[s. May you] serve in the temple of [26]the kingdom of God, ordering destiny with the Angels of the Presence, a party of the *Yahad* [with the Holy Ones] forever, for all the ages of eternity!

Surely [27][all] His [pr]ecepts are truth! May He establish you as holy among His people, as the 'greater [light' (Gen. 1:16) to illumine] the world with knowledge, and to shine upon the face of many [28][with wisdom leading to life. May He establish you] as consecrated to the Holy of Holies! [You shall] indeed [be sanc]tified to Him, glorifying His name and His Holy Ones!

Col. 5 [17][. . . F]or He has ord[ained you to the priesthood . . .] [18][wi]th never-[ending] time [and] with all the ages of eternity. May He never gi[ve] your glory [to another . . . May] [19]God [put] the fear of you [upon] all who hear a report of you, and of your majesty [upon all who . . .]"

A blessing for the Prince of the Congregation, a Davidic war leader who was to arise in the Last Days. Much of the language of this blessing is drawn from Isaiah 11, which has often been interpreted by both Jews and Christians as speaking of the Messiah.

[20](Words of blessing) belonging to the Instructor, by which to bless the Prince of the Congregation who [. . .] [21]And He shall renew for him the Covenant of the [*Ya*]*had,* so as to establish the kingdom of His people forev[er, that "with righteousness He may judge the poor,] [22][and] decide with equity for [the me]ek of the earth" (Isa. 11:4), walk before Him blameless in all the ways of [His heart,] [23]and establish His covenant as holy [against] the enemy of those who seek H[im.]

"[May] the Lord li[ft] you up to an eternal height, a mighty tower in a wall [24]securely set on high! Thus may you 'be r[ighteous] by the might of your [mouth,] lay waste the earth with your rod! With the breath of your lips [25]may you kill the wicked!' (Isa. 11:4, modified). May He give [you 'the spirit of coun]sel and may eternal might [rest upon you], the spirit of knowledge and the fear of God' (Isa. 11:2). May 'righteousness [26]be the belt [around your waist, and faithful]ness the belt around your loins' (Isa. 11:5). May He 'make your horns iron and your hoofs bronze!' (Mic. 4:13). [27]May you gore like a bu[ll . . . May you trample the nati]ons like mud in the streets! For God has established you as 'the scepter' (Num. 24:17) [28]over the rulers; bef[ore you peoples shall bow down, and all nat]ions shall serve you. He shall make you mighty by His holy name, [29]so that you shall be as a li[on among the beasts of the forest;] your [sword will devour] prey, with none to resc[ue.] Your [sw]ift steeds shall spread out upon [the earth . . .]"

—M.O.W.

10. Tongues of Fire and Prayer of Praise

1Q29, 4Q376, 4Q408

Exodus 28 describes Israel's high priest's garments and equipment, and though the entire description is shot through with awe and mystery, nothing in the description has more captured the imagination of readers than the sparse account of the two oracle stones called the Urim and the Thummim. The Bible suggests that the high priest would rely upon the Urim and Thummim to discover God's will (Num. 27:21; 1 Sam. 28:6); presumably this form of divination responded only to "yes" and "no" questions, and according to how the question was phrased, the priest's blind selection of one stone or the other from their pouch would reveal the answer. That, at least, is how modern scholars generally understand the mechanism. *Tongues of Fire,* however, and the traditions of Josephus (*Ant.* 3.214–215) share a much more miraculous expectation. They agree in indicating that God would make the answer known by causing the appropriate stone to shine forth with a brilliant light.

This is not the only respect in which modern scholarship differs from ancient Jewish understanding of the Urim and Thummim. Most English translations of Exodus 38:30 indicate that the stones were carried in a pouch or pocket on the priest's breastplate. Jewish tradition, on the contrary, has understood that these stones were part of the breastplate itself. *Tongues of Fire* agrees with this latter understanding, and so does Josephus.

The author of *Tongues of Fire* expected that the Urim and Thummim would be called upon for especially momentous decisions. The remaining fragments of the work describe their use to decide whether a prophet was true or false and to decide military strategy.

For other occurrences of the Urim and Thummim among the Dead Sea Scrolls, see the *Commentaries on Isaiah* (text 21), the *Last Days* (text 25), *A Collection of Messianic Proof Texts* (text 26), and the *Temple Scroll* (text 155).

The only other occurrence of the term "anointed priest" in the scrolls is in the Test of a True Prophet *(text 90).*

4Q376 Frag. 1 Col. 1 [1][. . .] the anointed priest [2][upon whose head has been poured the anointing oil . . . and he shall offer a bul]l from the herd and a ram [3][. . .] for the Urim [. . .]

This fragment shows that the Urim was used to test whether a prophet was true or false. Lines 3 and 5 indicate a negative response in this case. Compare the Test of a True Prophet *(text 90).*

1Q29 Frag. 1 (with **4Q376 Frag. 1 Col. 2** and **4Q408 Frag. 11)** [1][. . .] [2][. . .] the stone, just as [the LORD commanded . . .] [3][. . . and they shall give you light (?) and it (the cloud?) shall come forth] with it (?), with tongues of fire. [The left-hand stone that is on its left side shall be uncovered] [4][before the whole congregation until] the priest finishes speaking. [And after the cloud has been lifted . . . And you shall observe] [5][and do all that] the prop[het shall s]ay to you [. . .] [6][. . . and the prophet] who counsels rebellion [. . .] [7][. . . to] the LORD [your] God [. . .]

A positive response.

Frag. 2 [1][. . .] [2][. . . the] right-hand [s]tone when the pri[est] comes out [from . . .] [3][. . .] three tongues of fire from [the right-hand stone . . .] [4][. . .] and after he goes up then [. . .] shall be clos[ed . . .]

Frags. 3–4 (with **4Q408 Frag. 2)** [1][. . .] [2][. . . the L]ORD your God [. . .] [3][. . . al]l Israel [shall answer . . .] [4][. . . O LOR]D, in all Your judgments [. . .] [5][. . . an] abundance of strength, honored [and awesome . . .]

4Q376 Frags. 5–7 [1][. . .] these words, according to all [. . .] [2][. . . and the]n the priest shall interpret all His will, a[ll . . .] [3][. . .] the congregation. [. . .]

[4][. . . O Children of I]s[rae]l, keep all of these words [. . .] [5][. . . to d]o al[l . . .] [6][. . .] the number of com[mandments (?) . . .] [7][. . .] their [. . .]

The use of the oracle stones for help with military strategy. Joshua used them in this way according to Numbers 27:21.

Frag. 1 Col. 3 [1][. . .] according to this entire commandment. And if the Leader of the whole congregation is in the camp and [. . .] [2]his enemy and Israel is with him, or if they march on a city to throw up a siege against it, or in respect to any matter that [. . .] [3]to the Leader [. . .] the field is far (?) [. . .]

This perhaps final prayer praises God for creating day and night and the lights to rule them. In this regard the text is similar to other poetic accounts of the heavenly cycles among the scrolls; note for example the Charter of a Jewish Sectarian Association *10:1–5 (text 7) and the* Thanksgiving Hymns *20:7–14 (text 12).*

4Q408 Frags. 3–3a [1][. . .] under[standing . . .] [2][. . .] to You there to do [. . .] [3][. . .] the God of Israel [who] creates together (*or* for the *Yahad*) [. . .] [4][. . . Mos]es [called] to all Israel when they saw [. . .] [5][. . . when] His glorious ornaments shine forth from [His] hol[y] habitation [. . .] all [Israel shall] answer [6][. . . Ble]ssed {is the LORD} are You, O Lord, [who] are righteous in all Your ways, who are [mi]ghty in power, who are f[aithful in] Your [jud]gments, who are trustworthy [7] in a[ll Your precepts], who are understanding with a[ll in]sight, who shake off (?) [with] all might, who lead to bring out [. . .] [8]because You created the morning, a sign to reveal the dominion of light as a boundary for the day at the be[ginning . . .] [9]for their service, to bless Your holy name. When they saw that the light is good and [when they recognized] that in all [. . .] [10][. . .] men, because [You] crea[ted] the evening, a sign to reveal the dominion of [darkness as a boundary for the night . . .] [11][. . .] from toil, to bless [Your holy name when] they saw [that all the stars were good . . .]
—M.G.A.

11. The War Scroll

1QM, 4Q491–496

Armageddon: the war to end all wars. These words stir up images of inevitable conflict, the final focus on the dark side of human nature, the ultimate catharsis that ushers in an age of peace. All of these issues come to a head in the *War Scroll,* a text that describes the eschatological last battle in gory detail, as righteousness is fully victorious and evil is forever destroyed. This vivid account gives us insight into how, at about the time of Jesus, some Jews conceived of Armageddon.

The first lines of the scroll (1QM 1:1–7) lay the framework for a three-stage conflict between the Sons of Light—that is, members of the *Yahad* (see 1QS 3:13, text 7)—and the Sons of Darkness. The first battle finds the adversaries led by the Kittim of Assyria. (Although the name Kittim is most often used in the scrolls as a reference to the Romans, its basic sense seems to have been "archetypical bad guys.") The Kittim of Assyria come in alliance with the biblical enemies Edom, Moab, Ammon, and Philistia. Cooperating with this unholy alliance are the "violators of the covenant": Jews who had spurned the message of the *Yahad,* and in so doing aligned themselves with the Sons of Darkness.

The second stage expands the war's influence to the Kittim who dwelt in Egypt, and then finally to the Kings of the North.

Although this war is said to extend over forty years, the writer of the scroll was particularly concerned with the details of the very final day of battle. After six bloody engagements during this last battle, the Sons of Light and Sons of Darkness are deadlocked in a 3–3 tie. In the seventh and final confrontation "the great hand of God shall overcome [Belial and al]l the angels of his dominion, and all the men of [his forces shall be destroyed forever]" (1QM 1:14–15).

Along the way, in true apocalyptic fashion, the scroll goes into elaborate detail concerning the battle trumpets (2:15–3:11), banners (3:12–5:2), and operational matters (5:3–9:16). Then turning to the liturgical, priestly prayers for the various phases of the conflict are recorded (9:17–15:3). Finally, the seven savage engagements of the final day of battle are detailed (15:4–18:8), culminating in a ceremony of thanksgiving on the day following the victory (18:10–19:14).

As with biblical representatives of apocalyptic literature, Ezekiel 38–39 and the Revelation to John as pertinent examples, one can easily lose sight of the primary purpose of the work. It is not to be found in the intricate and often mysterious details of the text. Rather, the author was concerned with the tribulation and hopelessness that his readers were currently experiencing. He built his encouragement on a biblical theology of rescue: the defeat of Goliath at the hand of David (1QM 11:1–2), and Pharaoh and the officers of his chariots at the Red Sea (11:9–10). Coupled with this aspect was his understanding that great suffering was part of God's will for the redeemed. Indeed, God's crucible (17:9) was seen as a necessary component of human existence so long as evil continued to exist in the world. Ultimately, God's purpose was to exalt the Sons of Light and to judge the Sons of Darkness. The message is one of hope. In the face of such perverse evil, the Sons of Light are encouraged to persevere to the end. God was preparing to intervene and bring a permanent solution for the problem of evil.

The scroll itself is one of the first seven texts found by the Bedouin in 1947. Nineteen columns of text are preserved, lacking only a few lines at the bottom edge and the final page or pages of the composition (see text 63). Although six additional manuscripts were found seven years later in Cave 4 (4Q491–496), they are only moderately helpful in reconstructing the missing portions of 1QM.

The description of the eschatological war.

Col. 1 [1]For the In[structor, the Rule of] the War. The first attack of the Sons of Light shall be undertaken against the forces of the Sons of Darkness, the army of Belial: the troops of Edom, Moab, the sons of Ammon,

[2]the [Amalekites,] Philistia and the troops of the Kittim of Assyria. Supporting them are those who have violated the covenant. The sons of Levi, the sons of Judah, and the sons of Benjamin, those exiled to the wilderness, shall fight against them [3]with [. . .] against all their troops, when the exiles of the Sons of Light return from the Wilderness of the Peoples to camp in the Wilderness of Jerusalem. Then after the battle they shall go up from that place [4]a[nd the king of] the Kittim [shall enter] into Egypt. In his time he shall go forth with great wrath to do battle against the kings of the north, and in his anger he shall set out to destroy and eliminate the strength of [5]I[srael. Then the]re shall be a time of salvation for the People of God, and time of dominion for all the men of His forces, and eternal annihilation for all the forces of Belial. There shall be g[reat] panic [6][among] the sons of Japheth, Assyria shall fall with no one to come to his aid, and the supremacy of the Kittim shall cease, that wickedness be overcome without a remnant. There shall be no survivors [7]of [all Sons of] Darkness.

[8]Then [the Sons of Rig]hteousness shall shine to all ends of the world, continuing to shine forth until the end of the appointed seasons of darkness. Then at the time appointed by God, His great excellence shall shine for all the times of [9]e[ternity;] for peace and blessing, glory and joy, and long life for all Sons of Light. On the day when the Kittim fall there shall be a battle and horrible carnage before the God of [10]Israel, for it is a day appointed by Him from ancient times as a battle of annihilation for the Sons of Darkness. On that day the congregation of the gods and the congregation of men shall engage one another, resulting in great carnage. [11]The Sons of Light and the forces of Darkness shall fight together to show the strength of God with the roar of a great multitude and the shout of gods and men; a day of disaster. It is a time of [12]distress fo[r al]l the people who are redeemed by God. In all their afflictions none exists that is like it, hastening to its completion as an eternal redemption. On the day of their battle against the Kittim, [13]they shall g[o forth for] carnage in battle. In three lots the Sons of Light shall stand firm so as to strike a blow at wickedness, and in three the army of Belial shall strengthen themselves so as to force the retreat of the forces [14][of Light. And when the] banners of the infantry cause their hearts to melt, then the might of God will strengthen the he[arts of the Sons of Light.] In the seventh lot the great hand of God shall overcome [15][Belial and al]l the angels of his dominion, and all the men of [his forces shall be destroyed forever.]

The annihilation of the Sons of Darkness and service to God during the war years.

[16][. . .] the holy ones shall shine forth in support of [. . .] the truth

for the annihilation of the Sons of Darkness. Then[. . .] [17][. . .] a great [r]oar [. . .] they took hold of the implement[s of war . . .] [18][. . .] [19][. . . chiefs of the tribes . . . and the priests,] [20][the Levites, the chiefs of the tribes, the fathers of the congregation . . . the priests and thus for the Levites and the courses of the heads of] **Col. 2** [1]the congregation's clans, fifty-two. They shall rank the chiefs of the priests after the Chief Priest and his deputy; twelve chief priests to serve [2]in the regular offering before God. The chiefs of the courses, twenty-six, shall serve in their courses. After them the chiefs of the Levites serve continually, twelve in all, one to a [3]tribe. The chiefs of their courses shall serve each man in his office. The chiefs of the tribes and fathers of the congregation shall support them, taking their stand continually at the gates of the sanctuary. [4]The chiefs of their courses, from the age of fifty upwards, shall take their stand with their commissioners on their festivals, new moons, and Sabbaths, and on all days of the year. [5]These shall take their stand at the burnt offerings and sacrifices, to arrange the sweet-smelling incense according to the will of God, to atone for all His congregation, and to satisfy themselves before Him continually [6]at the table of glory. All of these they shall arrange at the time of the year of remission. During the remaining thirty-three years of the war the men of renown, [7]those called of the congregation, and all the heads of the congregation's clans shall choose for themselves men of war for all the lands of the nations. From all the tribes of Israel they shall prepare [8]capable men for themselves to go out for battle according to the summons of the war, year by year. But during the years of remission they shall not ready men to go out for battle, for it is a Sabbath [9]of rest for Israel. During the thirty-five years of service the war shall be waged. For six years the whole congregation shall wage it together, [10]and a war of divisions shall be waged during the twenty-nine remaining years. In the first year they shall fight against Aram-naharaim (Mesopotamia), in the second against the sons of Lud, in the third [11]they shall fight against the rest of the sons of Aram: Uz, Hul, Togar, and Mesha, who are beyond the Euphrates. In the fourth and fifth they shall fight against the sons of Arpachshad, [12]in the sixth and seventh they shall fight against all the sons of Assyria and Persia and the easterners up to the Great Desert. In the eighth year they shall fight against the sons of [13]Elam, in the ninth year they shall fight against the sons of Ishmael and Keturah, and during the following ten years the war shall be divided against all the sons of Ham [14]according to [their] c[lans and] their [terri]tories. During the remaining ten years the war shall be divided against all [the sons of Japhe]th according to their territories. [15][. . .]

The description of the trumpets.

[16][The Rule of the Trumpets: the trumpets] of alarm for all their service for the [. . .] for their commissioned men, [17][by tens of thousands and thousands and hundreds and fifties] and tens. Upon the t[rumpets . . .]

[18][. . .] [19][. . . which . . .] [20][. . . they shall write . . . the trumpets of] **Col. 3** [1]the battle formations, and the trumpets for assembling them when the gates of the war are opened so that the infantry might advance, the trumpets for the signal of the slain, the trumpets of [2]the ambush, the trumpets of pursuit when the enemy is defeated, and the trumpets of reassembly when the battle returns. On the trumpets for the assembly of the congregation they shall write, "The Called of God." [3]On the trumpets for the assembly of the chiefs they shall write, "The Princes of God." On the trumpets of the formations they shall write, "The Rule of God." On the trumpets of the men of [4]renown {they shall write}, the heads of the congregation's clans when they are assembled at the house of meeting, they shall write, "The Testimonies of God for a holy congregation." On the trumpets of the camps [5]they shall write, "The Peace of God in the camps of His holy ones." On the trumpets for their campaigns they shall write, "The Mighty deeds of God to scatter the enemy and to put all those who hate [6]justice to flight and a withdrawal of mercy from all who hate God." On the trumpets of the battle formations they shall write, 'Formations of the divisions of God to avenge His anger on all Sons of Darkness." [7]On the trumpets for assembling the infantry when the gates of war open that they might go out against the battle line of the enemy, they shall write, "A Remembrance of requital at the appointed time [8]of God." On the trumpets of the slain they shall write, "The Hand of the might of God in battle so as to bring down all the slain because of unfaithfulness." On the trumpets of ambush they shall write, [9]"Mysteries of God to wipe out wickedness." On the trumpets of pursuit they shall write, "God has struck all Sons of Darkness, He shall not abate His anger until they are annihilated." [10]When they return from battle to enter the formation, they shall write on the trumpets of retreat, "God has gathered." On the trumpets for the way of return [11]from battle with the enemy to enter the congregation in Jerusalem, they shall write, "Rejoicings of God in a peaceful return."

The description of the banners.

[13]The Rule of the Banners of the whole congregation according to their formations. On the grand banner which is at the head of all the people they shall write, "People of God," the names "Israel" and [14]"Aaron," and the

names of the twelve tribes of Israel according to their order of birth. On the banners of the heads of the camps of the three tribes [15]they shall write, "The Spirit [of God," and the names of the three tribes. O]n the standard of the tribe they shall write, "The Standard of God," and the name of the prince of the t[ribe . . .] [16]of its clans. [. . . and] the name of the prince of the ten thousand and the names of the chief[s of . . .] [17][. . .] his hundreds. On the banner [. . .] [18–20][. . .] **Col. 4** [1]On the banner of Merari they shall write, "The Offering of God," and the name of the prince of Merari and the names of the chiefs of his thousands. On the banner of the tho[us]and they shall write, "The Anger of God is loosed against [2]Belial and all the men of his forces without remnant," and the name of the chief of the thousand and the names of the chiefs of his hundreds. And on the banner of the hundred they shall write, "Hundred [3]of God, the power of war against all sinful flesh," and the name of the chief of the hundred and the names of the chiefs of his tens. And on the banner of the fifty they shall write, "Ended [4]is the stand of the wicked [by] the might of God," and the name of the chief of the fifty and the names of the chiefs of his tens. And on the banner of the ten they shall write, "Songs of joy [5]for God on the ten-stringed harp," and the name of the chief of the ten and the names of the nine men in his command.

[6]When they go to battle they shall write on their banners, "The Truth of God," "The Righteousness of God," "The Glory of God," "The Justice of God." And after these the list of their names in full. [7]When they draw near for battle they shall write on their banners, "The Right hand of God," "The Appointed time of God," "The Tumult of God," "The Slain of God." After these their names in full. [8]When they return from battle they shall write on their banners, "The Exaltation of God," "The Greatness of God," "The Praise of God," "The Glory of God," with their names in full.

[9]The Rule of the Banners of the Congregation: When they set out to battle they shall write on the first banner, "The Congregation of God," on the second banner, "The Camps of God," on the third, [10]"The Tribes of God," on the fourth, "The Clans of God," on the fifth, "The Divisions of God," on the sixth, "The Assembly of God," on the seventh, "Those called [11]by God," and on the eighth, "The Army of God." They shall write their names in full with all their order. When they draw near for battle they shall write on their banners, [12]"The Battle of God," "The Recompense of God," 'The Cause of God," "The Reprisal of God," "The Power of God," "The Retribution of God," "The Might of God," "The Annihilation by God of all the vainglorious nations." And [13]their names in full they shall write upon them. When they return from battle they shall write on their banners, "The

Deliverance of God," "The Victory of God," "The Help of God," "The Support of God," [14]"The Joy of God," "The Thanksgivings of God," "The Praise of God," and "The Peace of God."

[15][The Length of the Bann]ers. The banner of the whole congregation shall be fourteen cubits long; the banner of th[ree tribes, thir]teen cubits [long;] [16][the banner of a tribe,] twelve cubits; the banner of ten thousand, eleve[n cubits; the banner of a thousand, ten cubits; the banner of a hu]ndred, [n]ine cubits; [17][the banner of a fifty, ei]ght cubits; the banner of a ten, sev[en cubits . . .] [18][. . .]

The description of the shields.

[19][The Rule of the Shields . . .] [20][. . .] **Col. 5** [1]and on the sh[ie]ld of the Prince of the Whole Congregation they shall write his name, the names "Israel," "Levi," and "Aaron," and the names of the twelve tribes of Israel according to their order of birth, [2]and the names of the twelve chiefs of their tribes.

The description of the arming and deployment of the divisions.

[3]The Rule for Arranging the Divisions for War: when their army is complete to make a forward battle line. The battle line shall be formed of one thousand men. There shall be seven forward rows [4]to each battle line, arranged in order; the station of each man behind his fellow. All of them shall bear shields of bronze, polished like [5]a face mirror. The shield shall be bound with a border of plaited work and a design of loops, the work of a skillful workman; gold, silver, and bronze bound together [6]and jewels; a multicolored brocade. It is the work of a skillful workman, artistically done. The length of the shield shall be two and a half cubits, and its breadth a cubit and a half. In their hands they shall hold a lance [7]and a sword. The length of the lance shall be seven cubits, of which the socket and the blade comprise half a cubit. On the socket there shall be three bands engraved as a border of plaited [8]work; of gold, silver, and copper bound together like an artistically designed work. And in the loops of the design, on both sides of the band [9]all around, shall be precious stones, a multicolored brocade, the work of a skillful workman, artistically done, and an ear of grain. The socket shall be grooved between the bands like [10]a column, artistically done. The blade shall be of shining white iron, the work of a skillful workman, artistically done, and an ear of grain of pure gold inlaid in the blade; tapered toward [11]the point. The swords shall be of refined iron, purified in the furnace and polished like a face mirror, the work of a skillful workman, artistically done,

with figures of ears of grain [12]of pure gold embossed on both sides. The borders shall go straight to the point, two on each side. The length of the sword shall be a cubit [13]and a half and its width four fingers. The scabbard shall be four thumbs wide, and four handbreadths up to the scabbard. The scabbard shall be tied on either [14]side with thongs of five handbreadths. The handle of the sword shall be of choice horn, the work of a skillful workman, a varicolored design with gold and silver and precious stones.

[16]And when the [. . .] stand, they shall arrange seven battle lines, one behind the other, [17]and there shall be a space [between . . . t]hirty cubits, where the infan[try] shall stand [18][. . .] forward [. . .] [. . .] [19–20][. . .] **Col. 6** [1]seven times, and return to their position. After them, three divisions of infantry shall advance and stand between the battle lines. The first division shall heave into [2]the enemy battle line seven battle darts. On the blade of the first dart they shall write, "Flash of a spear for the strength of God." On the second weapon they shall write, [3]"Missiles of blood to fell the slain by the wrath of God." On the third dart they shall write, "The Blade of a sword devours the slain of wickedness by the judgment of God." [4]Each of these they shall throw seven times and then return to their position. After these, two divisions of infantry shall march forth and stand between the two battle lines, [5]the first division equipped with a spear and a shield and the second division with a shield and a sword; to bring down the slain by the judgment of God, to subdue the battle line [6]of the enemy by the power of God, and to render recompense to all the vainglorious nations for their evil. So the kingship shall belong to the God of Israel, and by the holy ones of His people He shall act powerfully.

The description of the deployment of the cavalry.

[8]Seven rows of horsemen shall also take position at the right and at the left of the battle line. Their rows shall be positioned on both sides, seven hundred [9]horsemen on one side and seven hundred on the other. Two hundred horsemen shall go out with one thousand men of the battle line of the infantry, and thus [10]they shall take position on all sides of the camp. The total being four thousand six hundred men, and one thousand four hundred cavalry for the entire army arranged for the battle line; [11]fifty for each battle line. The horsemen, with the cavalry of the men of the entire army, will be six thousand; five hundred to a tribe. All the cavalry that go out [12]to battle with the infantry shall ride stallions; swift, responsive, unrelenting, full-grown, trained for battle, [13]and accustomed to hearing noises and seeing all kinds of scenes. Those who ride them shall be men capable in battle, trained in horsemanship, the range [14]of their age from thirty to forty-five years. The

horsemen of the army shall be from forty to fifty years old, and they [15][. . .], helmets and greaves, carrying in their hands round shields and a lance eig[ht cubits long, . . .] [16][. . .] and a bow and arrows and battle darts, all of them prepared in [. . .] [17][. . .] and to shed the blood of their guilty slain. These are the [. . .]

The recruitment and age of the soldiers.

[18–20][. . .] **Col. 7** [1]and the men of the army shall be from forty to fifty years old. The commissioners of the camps shall be from fifty to sixty years old. The officers [2]shall also be from forty to fifty years old. All those who strip the slain, plunder the spoil, cleanse the land, guard the arms, [3]and he who prepares the provisions, all these shall be from twenty-five to thirty years old. No youth nor woman shall enter their encampments from the time they leave [4]from Jerusalem to go to battle until their return. No one crippled, blind, or lame, nor a man who has a permanent blemish on his skin, or a man affected with ritual uncleanness of [5]his flesh; none of these shall go with them to battle. All of them shall be volunteers for battle, pure of spirit and flesh, and prepared for the Day of Vengeance. Any [6]man who is not ritually clean in respect to his genitals on the day of battle shall not go down with them into battle, for holy angels are present with their army. There shall be a space [7]between all their camps and the latrine of about two thousand cubits, and no shameful nakedness shall be seen in the environs of all their camps.

The ministry of the priests and Levites.

[9]When the battle lines are arranged against the enemy, battle line against battle line, there shall go forth from the middle opening into the space between the battle lines seven [10]priests of the sons of Aaron, dressed in fine white linen garments: a linen tunic and linen breeches, and girded with a linen sash of twined fine linen, violet, [11]purple, and crimson, and a varicolored design, the work of a skillful workman, and decorated caps on their heads; the garments for battle, and they shall not take them into the sanctuary. [12]The one priest shall walk before all the men of the battle line to strengthen their hands for battle. In the hands of the remaining six shall be [13]the trumpets of assembly, the trumpets of memorial, the trumpets of the alarm, the trumpets of pursuit, and the trumpets of reassembly. When the priests go out [14]into the space between the battle lines, seven Levites shall go out with them. In their hands shall be seven trumpets of rams' horns. Three officers from among the Levites shall walk before [15]the priests and the

Levites. The priests shall blow the two trumpets of assem[bly . . . of ba]ttle upon fifty shields, [16]and fifty infantrymen shall go out from the one gate and[. . .] Levites, officers. With [17]each battle line they shall go out according to all [this] o[rder. . . . men of the] infantry from the gates [18][and they shall take positi]on between the two battle lines, and [. . .] the bat[tle . . .] [19–20][. . .]

Col. 8 [1]The trumpets shall blow continually to direct the slingmen until they have completed hurling seven [2]times. Afterwards the priests shall blow on the trumpets of return, and they shall go along the side of the first battle line [3]to take their position. The priests shall blow on the trumpets of assembly, and [4]the three divisions of infantry shall go out from the gates and stand between the battle lines, and beside them the cavalrymen, [5]at the right and at the left. The priests shall blow on their trumpets a level note, signals for the order of battle. [6]And the columns shall be deployed into their formations, each to his position. When they have positioned themselves in three formations, [7]the priests shall blow for them a second signal, a low legato note, signals for advance, until they draw near to [8]the battle line of the enemy and take hold of their weapons. Then the priests shall blow on the six trumpets [9]of the slain a sharp staccato note to direct the battle, and the Levites and all the people with rams' horns shall blow [10]a great battle alarm together in order to melt the heart of the enemy. With the sound of the alarm, [11]the battle darts shall fly out to bring down the slain. Then the sound of the rams' horns shall quiet, but on the tru[m]pets [12]the priests shall continue to blow a sharp staccato note to direct the signals of battle until they have hurled into the battle line [13]of the enemy seven times. Afterwards, the priests shall blow for them the trumpets of retreat, [14]a low note, level and legato.

According to this rule the [pr]iests shall blow for the three divisions. When [15]the first division throws, the [priests and the Levites and all the people with rams'] horns shall blow a great alarm [16]to direct the bat[tle until they have hurled seven times. Afterwards,] the priests [shall blow] for them [17]on the trumpe[ts of retreat . . . and they shall take their stan]d in their positions in the battle line, [18][. . .] and shall take up position [19][. . . the sl]ain, [20][and all the people with rams' horns shall blow a very loud battle alarm, and as the sound goes out] **Col. 9** [1]their hands shall begin to bring down the slain, and all the people shall quiet the sound of alarm, but the priests shall continue sounding on the trumpets [2]of the slain to direct the fighting, until the enemy are defeated and turn in retreat. The priests shall blow the alarm to direct the battle, [3]and when they have been defeated before them, the priests shall blow the trumpets of assembly, and all the infantry shall go out to them from the midst of [4]the front battle lines and stand, six divisions in addition to the division which is engaged in battle. Altogether, seven battle lines, twenty-eight thousand [5]soldiers, and six thousand horsemen. All these shall pursue in order to destroy the enemy in God's battle; a total annihilation. [6]The priests shall blow for them the trumpets of pursuit, and they shall divide themselves for a pursuit of annihilation against all the enemy. The cavalry [7]shall push the enemy back at the flanks of the battle until they are destroyed. When the slain have fallen, the priests shall continue blowing from afar and shall not enter [8]into the midst of the slain so as to be defiled by their unclean blood, for they are holy. They shall not allow the oil of their priestly anointment to be profaned with the blood [9]of vainglorious nations.

The description of the maneuvers of the battle divisions.

[10]Rule for changing the order of the battle divisions, in order to arrange their position against [. . .] a pincer movement and towers, [11]an arc and towers, and as it draws slowly forward, then the columns and the flanks go out from the [t]wo sides of the battle line [that] [12]the enemy might become discouraged. The shields of the soldiers of the towers shall be three cubits long, and their lances eight cubits l[on]g. The towers [13]shall go out from the battle line with one hundred shields on a side. F[or] they shall surround the tower on the three frontal sides, [14]three hundred shields in all. There shall be two gates to a tower, one on [the right and] one on the left. Upon all the shields of the tower soldiers [15]they shall write: on the first, "Mi[chae]l," [on the second, "Gabriel," on the third,] "Sariel," and on the fourth "Raphael." [16]"Michael" and "Gabriel" on [the right, and "Sariel" and "Raphael" on the left.]

[17]And[. . .] for to the four [. . . They] shall establish an ambush for the [battle line] of[. . .] [18]and[. . . they shall fal]l on the s[lain . . .]

The address of the chief priest.

[19–20][. . .] **Col. 10** [1]of our camps, and to keep ourselves from any shameful nakedness, and he (Moses) told us that You are in our midst, a great and awesome God, plundering all of [2]our enemies befo[re u]s. He taught us from of old through all our generations, saying, "When you approach the battle, the priest shall stand and speak unto the people, [3]saying, 'Hear O Israel, you are approaching the battle against your enemies today. Do not be afraid nor fainthearted. [4]Do not trem[ble, no]r be terrified because of them, for your God goes with you, to fight for you against your enemies, and to save [5]you' " (Deut. 20:3–4). Our [of]ficers shall speak to all those prepared for battle, those willing of heart, to strengthen them by the might of God, to turn back all [6]who have lost heart, and to strengthen all the valiant warriors together. They shall recount that which You s[poke] by the hand of Moses, saying: "And when there is a war [7]in your land against the adversary who attacks you, then yo[u] shall sound an alarm with the trumpets and you will be remembered before your God [8]and be saved from your enemies" (Num. 10:9). Who is like You, O God of Israel, in he[av]en and on earth, that he can do according to Your great works [9]and Your great strength?

The prayer of the chief priest.

Who is like Your people Israel, whom You have chosen for Yourself from all the peoples of the lands? [10]The people of the holy ones of the covenant, learned in the statutes, enlightened in understan[ding . . .] those who hear the glorious voice and see [11]the holy angels, whose ears are open; hearing deep things. [O God, You have created] the expanse of the skies, the host of luminaries, [12]the task of spirits and the dominion of holy ones, the treasures of [Your] gl[ory . . .] clouds. He who created the earth and the limits of her divisions [13]into wilderness and plain, and all her offspring, with the fru[its . . .] , the circle of the seas, the sources of the rivers, and the rift of the deeps, [14]wild beasts and winged creatures, the form of man and the gener[ations of] his [see]d, the confusion of language and the separation of peoples, the abode of clans [15]and the inheritance of the lands, [. . . and] holy festivals, courses of years, and times of [16]eternity. [. . .] these we know from Your understanding which [. . .] [17][. . .] Your [ears] to our cry, for [. . .] [18][. . .] his house [. . .] [19–20][. . .] **Col. 11** [1]Truly the battle is Yours, and by the strength of Your hand their corpses have been dashed to pieces so that no one can bury them. Indeed, Goliath the Gittite, a mighty warrior, [2]You delivered into the hand of David, Your servant, because he trusted in Your great name and not in sword and spear, for the battle is Yours. [3]He subdued the Philistines many times by Your holy name. Also by the hand of our kings You rescued us many times [4]because of Your mercy; not according to our works, for we have acted wickedly, nor for the acts of our rebelliousness. The battle is Yours, the strength is from You, [5]it is not our own. Neither our power nor the strength of our hand have done valiantly, but by Your power and the strength of Your great valor. Jus[t a]s You told [6]us in time past, saying: "There shall come forth a star from Jacob, a scepter shall rise out of Israel, and shall crush the forehead of Moab and tear down all sons of Sheth, [7]and he shall descend from Jacob and shall destroy the remnant from the city, and the enemy shall be a possession, and Israel shall do valiantly" (Num. 24:17, 19, 18a, c). By the hand of Your anointed ones, [8]seers of things appointed, You have told us about the ti[mes] of the wars of Your hands in order that You may {fight} glorify Yourself among our enemies, to bring down the hordes of Belial, the seven [9]vainglorious nations, at the hand of the oppressed whom You have redeemed [with powe]r and by retribution (*or* with peace); a wondrous strength. A heart that melts shall be as a door of hope. You will do to them as You did to Pharaoh [10]and the officers of his chariots in the Red Sea. You will ignite the humble of spirit like a fiery torch put to the sheaf, consuming the wicked. You shall not turn back until [11]the annihilation of the guilty. In time past You foretold [the app]ointed time for Your hand's powerful work against the Kittim, saying: "And Assyria shall fall by a sword not of man, and a sword [12]not of men shall consume him" (Isa. 31:8).

[13]For into the hand of the oppressed You will deliver the [ene]mies of all the lands; into the hands of those who are prostrate in the dust, in order to bring down all mighty men of the peoples, to return the recompense [14]of the wicked on the head of [. . . ,] to pronounce the just judgment of Your truth on all humankind and to make for Yourself an everlasting name among the people. [15][. . .] the wars, and to show Yourself great and holy before the remnant of the nations, so that [they] may know [that] [16][. . . when You] carry out judgments on Gog (Ezek. 39:11) and on all his company that are as[semb]led [abou]t [us . . .] [17][. . .] for You will do battle against them from the heave[ns . . .] [18][. . .] upon them for confusion [. . .] [19–20][. . .] **Col. 12** [1]For You have a multitude of holy ones in the heavens and hosts of angels in Your holy abode to pr[aise] Your [truth.] The chosen ones of the holy people [2]You have established for Yourself in a [community. The nu]mber (*or* The b]ook) of the names of all their host is with You in Your holy dwelling, and the n[umber of the holy one]s is in the abode of Your glory. [3]The mercies of [Your] blessing and Your covenant of peace You engraved for them with a stylus of life in order to reign o[ver them] for all time, [4]commissioning the hos[ts of] Your [e]lect by their thousands and tens of thousands together with Your holy ones [and] Your angels, and directing them [5]in battle [so as to condemn] the earthly adversaries by trial of Your judgments. With the elect of heaven [they] shall prev[ail.]

[7]And You, O God, are awe[some] in the glory of Your dominion, and the company of Your holy ones is in our midst for etern[al] support. We [shall direc]t our contempt at kings, derision [8]and disdain at mighty men. For the Lord is holy, and the King of Glory is with us together with the holy ones. Migh[ty men and] a host of angels are with our commissioned forces. [9]The Hero of Wa[r] is with our company, and the host of His spir-

its is with our steps. Our horsemen are [as] the clouds and as the mist covering the earth, [10]and as a steady downpour shedding judgment on all her offspring.

Rise up, O Hero. Take Your captives, O Glorious One. Take [11]Your plunder, O You who do valiantly. Lay Your hand upon the neck of Your enemies, and Your foot upon the backs of the slain. Crush the nations, Your adversaries, and may Your sword [12]devour guilty flesh. Fill Your land with glory, and Your inheritance with blessing, an abundance of cattle in Your fields; silver, gold, and precious [13]stones in Your palaces. O Zion, rejoice greatly, and shine with joyful songs, O Jerusalem. Rejoice, all you cities of Judah, open [14]your gate[s] forever. That the wealth of the nations might be brought to you, and their kings might serve you. All those who oppressed you shall bow down to you, and the dust [15][of your feet they shall lick. O daughter]s of my people, shout out with a voice of joy, adorn yourselves with ornaments of glory. Rule over the ki[ngdom of the . . . ,] [16][. . . and I]srael to reign eternally [. . .]

[. . .][17][. . .] them the mighty men of war, O Jerusalem [. . .] [18][Be exalt]ed above the heavens, O Lord, [and let Your glory be above all the earth . . .] [19][. . .]

The blessings of the war recited by all the leaders after the victory.

[20][. . . And the Chief Priest shall stand] **Col. 13** [1]and his brothers the [pr]iests, the Levites, and all the elders of the army with him. They shall bless, from their station, the God of Israel and all His works of truth, and they shall curse [2]Be[li]al there and all the spirits of his forces. And they shall say in response: "Blessed is the God of Israel for all His holy purpose and His works of truth. And blessed are [3]all those who serve Him righteously, who know Him faithfully.

[4]And cursed is Belial for his contentious purpose, and accursed for his guilty dominion. And cursed are all spirits of his lot for their wicked purpose.

[5]Accursed are they for all their impure unclean service. For they are the lot of darkness, but the lot of God is light [6][eterna]l.

[7]Y[o]u are the God of our fathers. We will bless Your name forever, for we are an [eter]na[l] people. You made a covenant with our fathers, and established it for their seed [8]throughout the ages of eternity. In all the appointed times of Your glory there has been a remembrance of Your [kindnesses] in our midst as a help for the remnant and provision for Your covenant [9]and to re[count] Your works of truth and the judgments of Your wondrous strength. And You, [O God,] created us for Yourself as an eternal people, and into the lot of light You cast us [10]for Your truth. You appointed the Prince of

Light from of old to assist us, for in [His] l[ot are all sons of righteous]ness and all spirits of truth are in his dominion. You yourself [11]made Belial for the pit, an angel of malevolence, his [dominio]n is in darkne[ss] and his counsel is to condemn and convict. All the spirits [12]of his lot, the angels of destruction, walk in accord with the rule of darkness, for it is their only [des]ire. But we, in the lot of Your truth, rejoice in [13]Your mighty hand. We rejoice in Your salvation, and revel in [Your] hel[p and] Your [p]eace. Who is like You in strength, O God of Israel, and yet [14]Your mighty hand is with the oppressed. What angel or prince is like You for [Your] effe[ctual] support, [fo]r from of old You appointed for Yourself a day of gre[at] battle [. . .] [15][. . .] to [sup]port truth and to destroy iniquity, to bring darkness low and to lend might to light, and to [. . .] [16][. . .] for an eternal stand, and to annihilate all the Sons of Darkness and joy for [al]l [the Sons of Light. . . .] [17][. . .]

[. . .][18][. . . f]or You Yourself appointed us for an app[ointed time . . .] [19–20][. . .] **Col. 14** [1]like the fire of His fury against the idols of Egypt."

The blessings of the war recited by all the leaders in the morning before the battle.

[2]After they have withdrawn from the slain to return to the camp, all of them shall sing the hymn of return. In the morning they shall wash their clothes, cleanse themselves [3]of the blood of the sinful bodies, and return to the place where they had stood, where they had formed the battle line before the slain of the enemy fell. There they shall all bless [4]the God of Israel and joyously exalt His name together. They shall say in response: "Blessed is the God of Israel, who guards loving-kindness for His covenant and the appointed times [5]of salvation for the people He redeems. He has called those who stumble unto wondrous [accomplishment]s, and He has gathered a congregation of nations for annihilation without remnant in order to raise up in judgment [6]he whose heart has melted, to open a mouth for the dumb to sing [God's] mighty deeds, and to teach feeble [hands] warfare. He gives those whose knees shake strength to stand, [7]and strengthens those who have been smitten from the hips to the shoulder. Among the poor in spirit [. . .] a hard heart, and by those whose way is perfect shall all wicked nations come to an end; [8]there will be no place for all their mighty men.

But we are the remn[ant of Your people. Blessed is] Your name, O God of loving-kindness, the One who kept the covenant for our forefathers. Throughout [9]all our generations You have made Your mercies wondrous for the rem[nant of the people] during the dominion of Belial. With all the mysteries of his hatred they have not lead us astray [10]from Your covenant. His spirits of destruction You have driven [away from us, and when the me]n of his dominion [condemned themselves], You have preserved the lives of Your redeemed. And You raised up [11]the fallen by Your strength, but those who are great in height You will cut dow[n to humble them. And] there is no rescuer for all their mighty men, and no place of refuge for their swift ones. To their honored men [12]You will return shame, and all [their] vain existence [shall be as not]hing. But we, Your holy people, shall praise Your name for Your works of truth. [13]Because of Your mighty deeds we shall exalt [Your] sp[lendor in all] epochs and appointed times of eternity, at the beginning of day, and at night [14]and the exit of evening and morning. For Your [glorio]us p[urpose] is great and Your wondrous mysteries are in [Your] high heavens, to [raise u]p those for Yourself from the dust [15]and to humble those from the gods.

[16]Rise up, rise up, O God of gods, and raise Yourself in power, [O King of Kings . . .] [17]let all the Sons of Darkness [scatter from before You.] Let the light of Your majesty shi[ne forever upon gods and men, as a fire burning in the dark places of the damned.] [18]Let it burn [the damned of Sh]eol, as an [eternal] burning [among the transgressors . . . in all the appointed times of eternity."]

[19][They shall repeat all the thanksgiving hymns of battle there and then return to their camps . . .] [20][. . .] **Col. 15** [1]For it is a time of distress for Isra[el, an appoin]tment for battle against all the nations. The purpose of God is eternal redemption, [2]but annihilation for all nations of wickedness. All those pr[epared] for battle shall set out and camp opposite the king of the Kittim and all the forces [3]of Belial that are assembled with him for a day [of vengeance] by the sword of God.

The final battle—the first engagement.

[4]Then the Chief Priest shall stand, and with him his brothers the p[riests], the Levites, and all the men of the army. He shall read aloud [5]the prayer for the appointed time of batt[le, as is written in the boo]k *Serekh 'Itto* (the *Rule of His Time*), including all their words of thanksgiving. Then he shall form there [6]all the battle lines, as writ[ten in the Book of the Wa]r. Then the priest appointed for the time of vengeance by [7]all his brothers shall walk about and encourage [them for the battl]e. He shall say in response: " 'Be strong and courageous, as warriors. [8]Fear not, nor be discoura[ged and let not y]our [heart be faint.] Do not panic, neither be alarmed because of them' (Deut. 20:3). Do not [9]turn back nor [flee from the]m. For they are a wicked congregation, all their deeds are in darkness; [10]it is [their] desire. [They have established al]l their refuge

[in a lie], their strength is as smoke that vanishes, and all [11]their vast assembly [is as chaff which blows away . . . de]solation (*or* their name), shall not be found. Every creature of destruction shall wither quickly away [12][like a flow]er at ha[rvest time. . . . Come,] strengthen yourselves for the battle of God, for this day is an appointed time of battle [13][for G]od against all the n[ations, . . . judgm]ent upon all flesh. The God of Israel is about to raise His hand in His wondrous [streng]th [14][against] all the spirits of wick[edness . . . m]ighty ones of the gods are girding themselves for battl[e, and] the formation[s of the] h[o]ly ones [15][are rea]dying themselves for a day of [vengeance . . .] [16]the God of I[srae]l [. . .] [17]to remove Bel[ial . . .] [18]in his place of destruction (Abaddon) [. . .] [19–20][. . .] **Col. 16** [1]until every source [of . . . is come to an end. For] the God of Israel has called out a sword against all the nations, and by the holy ones of His people He will do mightily."

[3]They shall carry out all this Rule [on] that [day] at the place where they stand opposite the camps of the Kittim. Then the priests shall blow for them the trumpets [4]of remembrance. The gates of w[ar] shall open, [and] the infantry shall go out and stand in columns between the battle lines. The priests shall blow for them [5]a signal for the formation and the columns [shall deplo]y at the sound of the trumpets until each man has taken his station. Then the priests shall blow for them [6]a second signal, [signs for confron]tation. When they stand near the battle line of the Kittim, within throwing range, each man shall raise his hand with his weapon of [7]war. Then the six [priests shall blow on the tr]umpets of the slain a sharp staccato note to direct the fighting. The Levites and all the people with [8]rams' horns shall blow [a battle signa]l, a loud noise. As the sound goes forth, the infantry shall begin to bring down the slain of the Kittim, and all [9]the people shall cease the signal, [but the priest]s shall continue blowing on the trumpets of the slain and the battle shall prevail against the Kittim.

The final battle—the second engagement.

[11]When [Belial] prepares himself to assist the Sons of Darkness, and the slain among the infantry begin to fall by God's mysteries and to test by the mysteries all those appointed for battle, [12]the priests shall blow the trumpets of assembly so that another battle line might go forth as a battle reserve, and they shall take up position between the battle lines. [13]For those employed in battle they shall blow a signal to return. Then the Chief Priest shall approach and stand before the battle line, and shall encourage [14]their heart by [the wondrous might of God and] their hands for His battle.

[15]And he shall say in response: ["Blessed is God, for] he tests the he[ar]t of

His people in the crucible. And not [. . .] have your slain [. . .] For you have obeyed from of old [16]the mysteries of God. [Now as for you, take courage and stand in the gap, do not fear when God strengthens . . .] [17–20][. . .] **Col. 17** [1]and He shall appoint their retribution with burning [. . .] those tested by the crucible. He shall sharpen the implements of war, and they shall not become blunt until [all the nations of] wickedness [come to an end.] [2]But, as for you, remember the judgment [of Nadab and Abi]hu, the sons of Aaron, by whose judgment God showed Himself holy before [all the people. But Eleazar] [3]and Ithamar He preserved for Himself for an eternal covenant [of priesthood.]

[4]But, as for you, take courage and do not fear them [. . . for] their end is emptiness and their desire is for the void. Their support is without st[rength] and they do not [know that from the God] [5]of Israel is all that is and that will be. He [. . .] in all which exists in eternity. Today is His appointed time to subdue and to humiliate the prince of the realm [6]of wickedness. He will send eternal support to the company of His redeemed by the power of the majestic angel of the authority of Michael. By eternal light [7]He shall joyfully light up the covenant of Israel; peace and blessing for the lot of God, to exalt the authority of Michael among the gods and the dominion [8]of Israel among all flesh. Righteousness shall rejoice on high, and all the children of His truth shall rejoice in eternal knowledge. But as for you, O children of His covenant, [9]take courage in God's crucible, until He shall wave His hand and complete His fiery trials; His mysteries concerning your existence."

The final battle—the third engagement.

[10]And after these words the priests shall blow for them a signal to form the divisions of the battle line. The columns shall be deployed at the sound of the trumpets, [11]until each man has taken his station. Then the priests shall blow another signal on the trumpets, signs for confrontation. When [12]the infa[ntry] has approached [the battle] line of the Kitt[im,] within throwing range, each man shall raise his hand with his weapon. Then the priests shall blow on the trumpets [13]of the slain [and the Levites and the al]l the people with rams' horns shall sound a signal for battle. The infantry shall attack the army [14]of the Kittim, [and as the soun]d [of the si]gnal [goes forth], they shall begin to bring down their slain. Then all the people shall still the sound of the signal, while the priests [15]continuously blow on [the trumpets of the slain,] and the bat[tl]e p[revail]s against the K[ittim, and the troops of Belia]l are defeated before them. [16]Thus in the th[ird] lot [. . .] to fall slain [. . .] [17–20][. . .]

The final battle—the fourth, fifth and sixth engagements. Nothing of these engagements is preserved.

The final battle—the seventh engagement.

Col. 18 [1][. . . and in the seven]th [lot], when the great hand of God shall be lifted up against Belial and against all the fo[rc]es of his dominion for an eternal slaughter [2][. . .] and the shout of the holy ones when they pursue Assyria. Then the sons of Japheth shall fall, never to rise again, and the Kittim shall be crushed without [3][remnant and survivor. So] the God of Israel shall raise His hand against the whole multitude of Belial. At that time the priests shall sound a signal [4][on the six trumpet]s of remembrance, and all the battle formations shall be gathered to them and divide against all the ca[mps of the Ki]ttim [5]to completely destroy them. [And] when the sun hastens to set on that day, the Chief Priest and the priests and the [Levites] who are [6]with him, and the chiefs [of the battle lines and the men] of the army shall bless the God of Israel there. They shall say in response: "Blessed is Your name, O God [of god]s, for [7]You have done wondrous things for Your people, and have kept Your covenant for us from of old. Many times you have opened the gates of salvation for us [8]for the sak[e of] Your [co]venant. [And you provided f]or our affliction in accord with Your goodness toward us. You, O God of righteousness, have acted for the sake of Your name."

Thanksgiving for final victory.

[10][. . .] You have [done w]onders upon wonders with us, but from of old there has been nothing like it, for You have known our appointed time. Today [Your] power has shined forth [11]for us, [and] You [have shown] us the hand of Your mercies with us in eternal redemption, in order to remove the dominion of the enemy, that it might be no more; the hand of Your strength. [12]In bat[tle You shall show Yourself strong aga]inst our enemies for an absolute slaughter. Now the day is pressing upon us [to] pursue their multitude, for You [13][. . .] and the heart of warriors You have broken so that no one is able to stand. Yours is the might, and the battle is in Your hand, and there is no [14][God like you . . .] Your [. . .] and appointed times of Your will, and reprisal [. . .] Your [enemie]s, and You will cut off from [. . .] [15]the God of I[srae]l [. . .] [16]to remove Bel[ial . . .] [17]in his place of destruction (Abaddon) [. . .] [18–20][. . . And we shall direct our contempt at kings,] **Col. 19** [1][derision and disdain at mi]ghty men. For our Majestic One is holy. The King of Glory is with us and the h[ost of His spirits is with our steps. Our horsemen are] [2][as the clouds and as the mis]t covering the earth; as a steady downpour shedding judgment on a[ll her offspring.

Rise up, O Hero,] [3][Take Your captives, O Glorious One, and ta]ke Your plunder, O You Who do valiantly. Lay Your hand upon the neck of Your enemies, and Your fo[o]t [upon the backs of] [4][the slain. Crush the nations, Yo]ur [adversaries,] and let Your sword devour flesh. Fill Your land with glory, and Your inheritance with blessing, an ab[undance of cattle] [5][in Your fields, silver and gold] in Your palaces. O Zion, rejoice greatly, and rejoice, all you cities of Ju[dah. Open] [6][your gates forever, so that] the wealth of the nations [might be brought to you, and their kings shall serve you. All they that oppressed] you shall bow down to you, [7][and they shall lick the dust of your feet. O dau]ghters of my [peo]ple, burst out with a voice of joy. Adorn yourselves with ornaments of glory, and r[ule] over the ki[ngdom of the . . .] [8][. . .] Your [. . .] and Israel for an [et]ernal dominion.

Ceremony after the final battle.

[9][Then they shall gather] in the camp that n[ig]ht for rest until the morning. In the morning they shall come to the p[la]ce of the battle line [10][where the mi]ghty men of the Kittim [fell], as well as the multitude of Assyria, and the forces of all the nations that were assembled unto them, to see whether [the mu]ltitude of slain [are dead] [11][with no one to bury them; those who] fell there by the sword of God. And the Chi[ef] Priest shall approach there [with] his [depu]ty, his brothers [the priests,] [12][and the Levites with the Leader] of the battle, and all the chiefs of the battle lines and [their officers . . .] [13][. . . together. When they stand before the s]lain of the Kitt[im, they shall pr]aise there the God [of Israel. And they shall say in response: . . .] [14][. . . to God Most High and . . .]

Col. 20 [8][. . .]

4Q491 (4QMilhamah[a])

In the publication by the original editors, the fragments of 4Q491 were considered to be the remains of a single work. This work was thought to be a form of the *War Scroll,* one with extensive portions that found no exact match in the Cave 1 copy. A thorough study of the evidence, however, suggests that 4Q491 is instead three distinct manuscripts. The original editors had been deceived by the similar appearance of these manuscripts and had mistakenly grouped three texts together.

Thus reorganized, the manuscripts can now be characterized as follows. Manuscript A represents a text similar to the Cave 1 copy, but with a fuller representation of the seven engagements of the troops in the final battle. Manuscript B appears to be a shorter, *Reader's Digest* form of the Cave 1 composition.

Manuscript C comprises a hymn that is not even related to the *War Scroll.* Rather, it is related to the *Thanksgiving Hymns* (text 12).

A variant of the blessings of the war recited by all the leaders in the morning before the battle. Compare 1QM 14:4–19.

4Q491 Manuscript A Frag. 10 Col. 2 [7][. . .] [8]in the Kitti[m . . .] [9]the infantrymen shall begin [to bring down the casualties of the Kittim. . . . And the] [10]battle [shall prevail] against the Kittim [. . .] [11]the corpses of the place of refining [shall begin] to fall by [the mysteries] of God. And the p[riests shall sound the trumpets of assembly . . .] [12]battle among the Kittim. And to the first battle formation . . .] [13]And the priest designated for the battle shall draw near and stand [be]fore [the battle formation . . .] [14]and he shall strengthen their hands by recounting His wondrous deeds. Then he shall sa[y] in response [. . . fire of] [15]vengeance, to consume among gods and men. For [He shall] not [. . .] [16]flesh, except dust (?). For now [. . .] [17]and [the fire] shall consume as far as Sheol. And the council of wickedness [. . .]

Frags. 11–15 represent a variant of 1QM cols. 16–17.

Frag. 11 Col. 2 [14][. . . He is] faithful, and the relief which His redemption [. . .] [15][. . . son]s of truth and to remove the faint of heart and to strengthen the he[art . . .] [16][. . . the batt]le today, the God of Isr[ael] shall subdue him (Belial?) [. . .] [17][. . .] with no place to stand. And [the kingdo]m shall be for God and the salvatio[n] for His people [. . .] [18][. . .] like as to Belial. But God's covenant is peace [for] Israel in all the times [of eternity . . .] [19]And after these words the priests shall blow to order the second battle with the Kit[tim. And when each man has taken] [20]his station, then the priests shall blow a second signal for advance. When they have approached the ba[ttle line of the Kittim, within throwing range,] [21]each man [shall ra]ise his hand with his battle weapon. Then the priests shall b[lo]w on the tr[umpet]s of the [slain a staccato note] [22][to direct the battle and the Levites] and all the people with rams' horns shall so[u]nd [a loud] n[ote . . . And when] [23][the sound of the blast is heard, they shall begin to bring do]wn the casualties of the guilty. The sound of the [. . .] [24][. . .]

Frag. 13 [1][. . . wi]th the gods [. . .] [2][. . .] the smallest of you shall pursue a tho[usand . . .] [3][. . . And after] these [w]ords, [the priests] shall blow [to order the third battle with the Kittim and the columns] [4][shall deploy at the sound of the trum]pets. When each m[an] has taken [his position] by division, [the priest shall blow a second blast on the trumpets for] [5][advance. When] they [have approached] the battle line of the Kittim, within throwing range, [each man] shall raise his hand [with his battle weapon. The priests shall blow, to direct] [6][the battle, on the t]rumpets of the slain, a staccato note. Then the Levites and all [the people with rams' horns shall sound a battle blast, and the formations] [7][shall be figh]ting one behind the other with no space between them. For [. . .] [8][. . . and] all the people shall answer, raising [on]e voice, and say [. . .]

Frag. 15 [1][. . .] and there is no [. . .] [2][. . .] and a processio[n . . .] [3]And behold we are taking position to advance [. . .] [4][. . .]

[5][. . . And] he shall say to them in response, "Be strong and courageous [. . .] [6][. . . For the] outstretched [hand] of God is upon all the Gentiles, [He shall] not [. . .] [7][. . .] kingship is [for God] Almighty and salvation is for His people. And y[ou . . .] [8][. . .] his [im]purity, the gods shall advance upon you with [. . .] [9][. . .] and to cast all [their] corpse[s . . .] [10][. . .] and all the spirits of [his] lot [. . .] [11][. . .] eternal, together wi[th . . .] [12][. . .] war [. . .]

Manuscript B appears to preserve a much shorter version of the War Scroll *than the one discovered in Cave 1.*

4Q491 Manuscript B Frags. 1–3 [1]Korah and his congregation [. . .] judgment [. . .] [2]before the whole congregation of [. . . jud]gment as sign[s . . .] [3]and the chief of his angels with their [forces,] to direct their hand [in] battle. [. . .] for the chariotry and the hor[semen . . .] [4]The hand of God shall strike [. . .] for eternal annihilation [. . .] they shall atone for you [. . .] all the princes [. . .] [5]His holiness in eternal [jo]y [. . .] And after [. . .] the congregation and a[ll] the prince[s . . .] shall not go to the enemy battle lines [. . .]

[6]This is the rule when they camp and [. . . and in] their divisions [. . .] around, outside [. . .] and women, young boys, and any man who is aff[licted with impurity in his flesh shall not come near] [7][the battle] line. The craftsmen [and blacksm]iths and those enlisted as [. . .] for their watches [. . .] the battle line until they return.

And there shall be two thousand cubits between the [camps and the latrine, so] [8]no nakedness might be seen in their surroundings. And when they set out to prepare for battle [so as to sub]due [the enemy,] some of them [shall be] dismissed by lot from each tribe according to those enlisted for [each] day's duty. [9]That day, men from each tribe [shall] go out from the camps to the house of me[eting . . . and] the [priest]s, the Levites, and all the chiefs of the camps [shall] go out to them. Then they shall pass before [them] there [. . .] [10]by thousands, hundreds, fifties, and tens. Each man who is not [clean in regard to his genitals] that [nig]ht [shall] no[t g]o out with them to battle. For the holy angels are with their battle lines [. . .]

[11][When] the formation standing ready to pass to all [. . .] of battle for that day [g]oes up [. . .], three formations shall stand one behind the other, and they shall establish a space between [each] battle formation. [12][Then they shall go out] to the battle in turn. These are the [infan]trymen and alongside them are [cavalry]men, [and they shall take their position between the battle] formations. But if they establish an ambush for a battle formation, the three ambushing formations shall [stay at a dist]ance and not ris[e up . . .] [13][. . .] the battle. When they [h]ear the trumpets of alarm, the [infantry]men [shall begin to bring do]wn the guilty casualties. Then the ambush shall rise up from its place and also order its [battle form]ations [. . .]

[14]The reassembly: from the right and left, from be[hind and before, the f]our direction[s . . .] in the battles of annihilation. All the battle formation[s] which engaged the en[emy] for battle [shall be gathered] [15]together. The [fi]rst battle formation shall [set out to battle] and the second shall remain stand[ing] at their post. When their period is completed, the first shall return and s[tand . . .] [16]The sec[ond foray . . .] when the battle is arrayed. When the second battle formation shall have completed their period, they shall return and t[ake their position.] [17]And the t[hird foray . . . Then the Chief Priest shall take his stand with his brothers the priests,] the Levites, and men [of the arm]y. And all the while the priests shall be sounding on the trumpets [. . .]

[. . .][18]A lin[en] sash [of twined fine linen, violet, purple and crimson, and a varicolored design, the work of a skillful workman, and decorated c]aps [on their heads. And they shall not take them into the sanctuary, f[or] they are garments for bat[tle.]

[19]According to all [this] rule [. . .] chiefs of the camp [. . .] [20]for [. . .] all [. . .] they will completely annihilate [. . .]

This manuscript, mistakenly identified as a copy of the War Scroll *and attributed to the archangel Michael, is instead a version of a hymn that is also found in the* Thanksgiving Hymns *col. 26 (text 12). The author's description of his office—seated "on a mighty throne in the congregation of the angels"—and his personal standing—"no one shall be exalted besides me"—has earned the piece the title "Self-Glorification Hymn." Is the speaker styling himself as the messiah? As a reflection of the clear note of suffering—"Who has been considered contemptible like me?"—some scholars have provocatively suggested that this hymn is evidence that some ancient Jews were expecting a suffering messiah before the time of Jesus. Or, as could be argued based on the placement of the psalm in the* Thanksgiving Hymns, *is this rather a communal experience that might find an echo in 4Q181 (text 30), in which the community is also described as being reckoned with the "gods as a holy congregation"? The debate has only just begun.*

4Q491 Manuscript C Frag. 11 Col. 1 [8][. . .] marvelous, wondrous deeds[. . .] [9][. . . in the pow]er of His might let the a[ng]e[l]s rejoice and the holy ones shout in exaltation [. . .] justly [10][. . . I]srael. He established His truth from of old, and the mysteries of His cunning in eve[ry . . .] might [11][. . .] and the company of the oppressed shall become an eternal congregation[. . .] blameless of [12][. . .] eternal, a mighty throne in the congregation of the angels. None of the ancient kings shall sit on it, and their nobles [shall] not [. . . There are no]ne comparable [13][to me in] my glory, no one shall be exalted besides me; none shall come against me. For I have dwelt on [high, . . .] in the heavens, and there is no one [14][. . .] I am reckoned with the angels and my abode is in the holy congregation. [My] desi[re] is not according to the flesh, [. . .] everything precious to me is in the glory [15][of] the holy [habit]ation. [Wh]o has been considered contemptible like me? Who is comparable to me in my glory? Who of those who sail the seas (?) shall return telling (?) [16][of] my [equa]l? Who has born[e] troubles like me? And who like me [has refrain]ed from evil? I have never been taught, but no teaching compares [17][with my teaching.] Who then shall assault me when [I] ope[n my mouth?] Who can endure the utterance of my lips? Who shall challenge me and compare with my judgment? [18][. . . Fo]r I am reck[oned] with the angels, [and] my glory with that of the sons of the King. Neither [pure go]ld, nor the renowned gold of Ophir [19][. . .]

To [20][. . . rejoice, you] righteous among the angels of [. . .] in the holy habitation. Praise Him in song [. . .] [21][. . . P]roclaim with heartfelt joy [. . .] joyously forever without c[easing . . .] [22][. . .] to raise up the horn on h[igh . . .] [23][. . .] to make known His power in might [. . .]

4Q493 (4QMilhamah^c)

This fragment is reminiscent of 1QM 7:9–9:9, but diverges markedly from the Cave 1 copy. Perhaps it represents another "deviant" version such as 4Q491 (Manuscripts A and B). But it is equally possible that this fragment may have been unrelated to the *War Scroll* literature, instead coming from a handbook on priestly duties.

[1]For the war: The priests, the sons of Aaron, shall take their stand before [the] battle formations [2]and sound a blast on the trumpets of remembrance. Afterwards they shall open the gates for the [3]infantrymen. Then the priests shall sound a blast on the trumpets of battle [to adva]nce on the battle line [4]of the Gentiles. The priests shall go out from among the slain and stand on [either] side of the [. . .] [5]beside the catapult (?) and the ballista (?). Thus they shall not profane the anointing of their priestly office [with the blood of the s]lai[n.] [6][And] they shall not approach any battle formation of the infantry. They shall sound an alarm—with a sharp note in order that the me[n of] battle [7]might set out to advance between the battle lines—on the trumpets [of the slain.] Then [they] shall [beg]in [8]to draw near to the battle. When their periods of engagement are completed, they shall sound a blast for them on the tru[mp]ets of withdrawal [9]to enter the gates. Then the second formation shall set out. According to this entire rule the Le[vites] [10]shall be signaling them at the proper time. When they set out, they shall blow a signal for them on the t[rumpets of assembly,] [11]and when [they] have comple[ted their foray,] on the trumpets of alarm, [and when] they return, they shall sound a sig[nal for them on the trumpets] [12]of as[sembly.] According to [this] ordin[ance] they sound the signal for ev[ery ba]ttle formation.

[13][. . .] upon the trumpets of the Sabbaths [it is written . . .] [14][. . . for] the regular [grain offering] and the burnt offerings it is written, [. . .]

—M.G.A.

12. Thanksgiving Hymns (The Thanksgiving Scroll)

1QH^a, 1Q35, 4Q427–432

The intensely personal tone of the songs known commonly as *Thanksgiving Hymns* stands in sharp contrast with the rest of the scrolls. The author speaks of himself in the first person and recounts an agonizing history of persecution at the hands of those opposed to his ministry. In addition, the writer describes having received an empowering spirit granting him special insight into God's will (1QH^a 4:38), opening his ears to wonderful divine mysteries (9:23), using him as a channel of God's works (12:9), and fashioning him as a mouthpiece for God's words (16:17). Indeed, in col. 26, he claims that no one compares with him, because his office is among the heavenly beings. These are bold affirmations for any leader, reminiscent of various messianic claimants of both ancient and more recent history.

The unique personal presentation of the work and the self-conscious divine mission of the author have led many researchers to conclude that the psalms were written by the Teacher of Righteousness himself. Some students have attempted a more refined analysis in order to isolate "true" Teacher psalms at the center of the collection (cols. 10–16 according to one, 13–16 in the eyes of another; see Hymns 10–13, 15–20, 23), noting that the themes of personal distress and affliction as well as the claim of being the recipient or mediator of revelation are especially strong here. Only one thing is sure: the debate will continue.

The name for this collection of psalms reflects the repeated introductory phrase, "I give thanks to You, O Lord." A secondary formula, "Blessed are You, O Lord," appears as a variant. Given the fragmentary nature of the manuscript, only twenty of these introductions are evident, but at least ten additional songs can be identified on the basis of context. The original work may have contained as many as fifty psalms. The large percentage of overlap between the eight surviving manuscripts, indicating that somewhat more than half of the total text has survived, supports this possibility.

Old Testament vocabulary and phraseology so abound in the *Thanksgiving Hymns* that readers feel they have entered a virtual mosaic of biblical quotations. The Psalms, Isaiah (especially chaps. 40–55), Jeremiah, Ezekiel, Job, and Proverbs are the prominent sources. Yet, surprisingly, only one passage can be considered an actual quotation (1QH^{a} 10:31–32 quotes Ps. 26:12). It thus follows that, in stark contrast to the New Testament and rabbinic literature, there are no quotation formulas: "thus says the Lord"; "as it is written in the book of . . ." The only possible such formula appears in 1QH^{a} 4:24, where reference is made to the fact that God spoke through Moses. Nevertheless, despite the absence of actual quotations, biblical imagery and language do prevail.

The large number of copies of the *Thanksgiving Hymns*—and the few significant differences between them—underscore the importance of the composition. *Thanksgiving Hymns* may have enjoyed a "canonical" status among some ancient readers.

The order of the columns presented here differs from the early publications. We have followed the lead of Emile Puech* and clues to the structure in the recent official publication of the Cave 4 manuscripts by Eileen Schuller.

The hymns are numbered consecutively, totaling thirty-four in all. There were probably at least two before col. 3 and several others whose introductory formula, "I give

*Emile Puech, "Quelques aspects de la restauration du Rouleau des Hymnes (1QH)," *Journal of Jewish Studies* 39 (1988): 38–55.

thanks to You, O Lord," has been lost. In keeping with the opinion of those who have studied the Thanksgiving Hymns *in detail, each hymn is identified as originating with the community or the Teacher (see the introduction to this text).*

Hymn 1. A community hymn of thanksgiving for God's holiness and strength while acknowledging the sin and weakness of humankind.

Col. 3 [13][. . . yo]u rebelled [. . .] [14][. . . op]pressed ones [. . .] [15][. . .] His mercies upon the poor [ones . . .] [16][. . .] And who establishes [. . .] [17][. . .] and who establishes the warrior[s . . .] [18][. . .] eternity. And who conside[rs . . .] [19][. . .] previously.

[. . .] [20][. . .] Your [stre]ngth [. . .] [23][. . .] [24][. . .] by measure through all the years of eternity [. . .] [25][. . .] every seal [. . .] [26][. . .] humankind, according to his insight and [. . .] [27][. . .] His kingdom. Who has done all of these things? [. . .] [28][. . .] and delight is Yours, and in righteousness You set [. . .] [29][. . .] before You [. . .] and the vessel of c[lay . . .] [30][. . .] he shall answer, You are honored above all g[ods . . .] [31][. . .] holiness, and just as it is Your desire to [. . .] [32][. . .] for Your name You shall [. . .] in the h[oly] assembly [. . .] **Col. 4** [13][. . .] from a low measure [. . .] [14][. . .] revealed without justic[e . . .] in the spirit [15][. . .] fire devours [. . .] desire without [16][. . .] on dry ground and a hind[rance . . . w]ithout justice [17][. . .] encountering very suddenl[y . . .] as wa[x melts . . .] [18][. . .] judgment by the spirit seeks [You . . .] [19][. . .] deceitfully with [. . .] commandment. By the spirit as [. . .] [20][. . .] with the floggings of m[en . . .]

Hymn 2. A community hymn of thanksgiving to God for delivering the psalmist from sin and judgment. The first running text begins here.

[21][I give thanks to You, O Lord, for] from hidden things whic[h . . . wh]ich they do not overtake them in [. . .] [22][. . .] and from the judgment of the tim[es of wickedness . . . th]oughts of wickedness [. . .] [23][. . .] and by the judgment of [. . . You have delivered] Your servant from all his sins [. . . and by the abundance of] Your compassion, [24][just as You spoke] by Moses [that You would forgive transgression,] iniquity, and sin and make atonement for [iniquity] and faithlessness. [25][For] the foundations of the mountains [shall quake], fire [shall burn] in Sheol below, and [You shall . . .] the [. . .] by Your judgments. [26][. . .] for those who serve You in faithfulness [th]at their offspring might be in Your presence forever. And You have determined [. . .] there, [27][forgiving every] transgression and casting away all their [iniquities], giving them all the glory of man (*or* Adam) as an inheritance [along with] long life.

Hymn 3. A community hymn of thanksgiving to God for his righteousness.

[29][I give thanks to You, O Lord, . . .] by the spirits which You have given me. I will [fin]d the proper reply to declare Your righteous deeds, patience, [30][abundant loving-kindne]ss, the deeds of Your strong right hand, forgiveness of the sins of my ancestors; p[raying] and making supplication for [31][. . .] my deeds and the perverseness of my heart. For in filth I have wallowed and from the council of [. . .] I [. . .] and I did not join myself [32][to Your congregation. (?) . . .] righteousness is Yours, and praise belongs to Your name forev[er. . . .] Your righteousness. Let [Your servant (?)] be ransomed [33][and] the wicked perish. I have understood that [You determine] the way of the one You have chosen, and in the insight [34][of Your truth You] keep him from sinning against You; restoring to him his humility by Your chastisements, and by [Your] tria[ls . . .] his heart. [35][Keep] Your servant from sinning against You and from stumbling over all the words of Your will. Strengthen [. . .] against the spirits of [36][wickedness to] walk in all that You love, and despise all that You hate, [and to do] that which is good in Your eyes. [37][Destroy] their [domi]nion in my bowels, for Your servant has a fleshly spirit.

Hymn 4. A community hymn of thanksgiving to God for making his glory known.

[38][I give thanks to You, O Lord, for] You have spread [Your] holy spirit over Your servant [. . .] his heart [39][. . .] and I examine every human covenant [. . .] they shall find it [40][. . .] and those who love it [. . .] forever and ever. **Col. 5** [12][. . .] [13][. . .] that fools might understand [. . .] of eternity [14][. . .] and that humankind might understand [. . .] flesh and the council of the spirit[s . . .] they walked [. . .]

Hymn 5. A community hymn of thanksgiving that God revealed the mysteries of his plan to the righteous. This hymn and hymns 8, 9, 18, 26, 29, 30, 31, and 33 begin with "Blessed are You" rather than the more common "I give thanks." These hymn divisions are not recognized by all experts..

[15][. . . Blessed are] You, O Lord, w[ho . . .] breadth of [. . .] in the power of Your strength [16][. . .] with an abundance of good [. . .] and the zeal of [Your] judgment [. . . un]searchable. All [17][. . .] all understanding and [. . .] and the mysteries of the plan and the mysterie[s of . . .] You have determined [18][. . .] holiness is from [eternity] past to the end of time. You are [the Lord . . . of the] holy ones [19][. . . the council of Your truth] and in the mysteries of Your wonder [You have made known to me be]cause of Your glory, and the depth of [Your insight You have made

me understand, and the source of] Your insight [You] have not [20][hidden.] You have revealed the paths of truth and the works of evil, wisdom, and foll[y . . .] righteousness [21][. . .] their works. Truth and [. . .] and folly [. . .] [22][. . .] and eternal mercies to all [who walk] in peace, but ruin [. . .] [23]their [. . .] eternal glory [. . . and] eternal joy for the work of [. . .] [24][. . .]

And it is these which [You] de[termined . . .] to judge them. [You determined] [25]all Your works before You created them, together with the host of Your spirits and the assembly of [Your holy ones,] Your holy expanse [and all] [26]its hosts, together with the earth and all that springs from it, in the seas and the deeps [according to] all Your designs for the end of time [27]and the eternal visitation. For You have determined them from of old, and also the work of [unrighteousness . . .] in them so that [28]they may tell of Your glory throughout all Your dominion, for You have shown them that which shall not [. . .] of old and creating [29]new things, breaking down those things established from of old and [setting up] that which shall be forever. For You [. . .] and You continue [30]forever and ever. By the mysteries of Your insight [You] assigned all these things to make Your glory known. [But what is] the spirit of flesh that it might understand [31]all these things and obtain insight into the council of [Your] great [wonders?] And what is one born of woman among all [Your] awesome [works]? He is but [32]an edifice of dust, kneaded with water, [. . .] his foundation is obscene shame [. . .] and a perverted spirit ruled [33]him.

If he acts wickedly, he will become [a sign for] eternity and a sign to the generations, [. . . to all] flesh. Only by Your goodness [34]shall a man be justified, and by the abundance of [Your] compass[ion . . .] with Your splendor You glorify him, and You [satisfy him with an abu]ndance of delights; with eternal peace [35]and long life. For [You have spoken and] Your word will not depart.

And I, Your servant, know, [36]by the spirit which You placed in me [that Your words are true] and all Your works are just and Your word will not depart. And [. . .] [37]Your times are appointed [. . . c]hosen for their delight. And I shall know [. . .] [38]and wicked [. . .] to consider [. . .] [39][. . .] Your [s]pirits and [. . .] [40][. . .] **Col. 6** [12][. . .] in Your people and [. . .] [13][. . .] our ears [. . .] men of truth and [. . .] [14][. . .] insight and seekers of understanding [. . . lov]ers of compassion and the humble of spirit, purified of [15][. . . by] affliction and purified by the crucible of [. . .] who strengthen themselves until [. . .] Your judgments [16][. . .] and those watching out for Your salvation [. . .] and You have established Your statutes [among them] to do [17][. . . to jud]ge the world and to distribute the inheritance among all [. . .] of holiness for fu[ture] generations and all [18][. . .] their works with [. . .] the men of Your vision.

Hymn 6. A community hymn of thanksgiving to God, who gives understanding.

[19][I give thanks to You,] O Lord, who places understanding in the heart of [Your] serv[ant,] [20][so that he might . . . al]l of these things and [. . .] and refrain from wanton works of wickedness, and bless [21][Your holy name and the words o]f Your will. [That he might walk in all whi]ch You love, and abhor all which [22][You hate . . .] Your servant [. . .] humankind. For by their spirits You distinguish between [23]the good and the wicked, [. . .] their work. And I know by Your understanding, [24]that by Your favor for m[an . . .] Your holy [sp]irit, and thus You bring me to Your understanding. As [25]I draw near, I become zealous against all those who practice wickedness and men of deceit. For none who are near You speak against Your command, [26]and none who know You pervert Your words. For You are righteous, and all Your chosen ones are truth. All injustice [27][and wi]ckedness You destroy forever. Thus Your righteousness is revealed before all Your creatures.

[28]And I know by the abundance of Your goodness, and by the oath I took upon myself that I should not sin against You [29][and] that I should not do anything which is evil in Your eyes. And thus I was brought into association (*or* in the *Yahad*) with all the men of my council. In accordance with [30]a man's insight I will advance him, and in accordance with the abundance of his inheritance I will love him. I will not consider an evil man, nor shall I acknowledge a b[rib]e from the w[icked.] [31]I will [not] exchange Your truth for wealth, nor any of Your judgments for a bribe. For wh[en You draw a ma]n [near], [32][I lov]e him, and when You remove him, I will abhor him. Indeed, I will not bring into the council of [Your] t[ruth those who] have turned [33][from] Your covena[nt.]

Hymn 7. A community hymn of thanksgiving to God, who forgives those who repent and judges the wicked.

[34][I give thanks to You,] O Lord, in accordance with Your great strength and Your abundant wonders, forever and ev[er . . .] and [Your] great [35][mercy . . .] Who forgives those who turn from sin, but judges the iniquity of the wicked. [You love righteousness] with a generous [36][heart (?) . . .] but You hate injustice forever. And as for me, Your servant, You have favored me with the spirit of knowledge [. . . t]ruth [37][. . .] and to abhor every unjust way. So I love You freely and with all [my] heart [I bless]

You, [38][I give thanks for] Your insight. For this gift has come from Your hand and without [. . .] [39][. . .] thus flesh shall rule [. . .] [40][. . .] him and You built the [. . .] with help [. . .] [41][. . .] the expanse upon the wings of the wind and [. . .] **Col. 7** [12][. . . In] Your w[ill] I have obtained insight [. . .] [13][. . .] Your wo[nder] how can we repay? For You have rewarded us and [. . .] done wonders [. . .] [14][. . .] they are not able to understand the glory of [. . . and to decla]re [Your] wonder[s . . .] [15][. . . for they have pr]aised You according to their insight. And according to Your knowledge [in] Your [g]lory [. . .] [16]You opened [. . .] unceasingly; from age to age they proclaim and seas[on to season they bless aloud . . .] [17][. . .] and as for us, we have been called together, and with those who know [we are instruc]ted by You and sing out f[or joy because of the abundance of] [18][Your] mercies [. . . lou]dly with Your mighty ones, and we will wondrously declare together in the knowledge of [God and with . . .] [19]in [the] congrega[tion of . . .] and our offspring [You] have taught [wit]h humankind in the mid[st of the peo]ple [. . .] [20]because [. . .] great wonder [. . .]

Hymn 8. A community hymn to God, who created both the righteous and the wicked; all things are his works.

[21]B[lessed are You, O Lord, . . .] who understands the comma[ndment(s) . . . a loud] cry [for those who magnify the majesty of . . .] [22][. . .] And they [shall l]ove You forever and [. . .] [23][. . .] And I love You freely and with all my heart, and with all my being I have cleansed [. . .] [24][that I might not] depart from all that You have commanded. I will take hold of many (*or* the general membership) from [. . . so that I might not] [25]depart from all Your statutes.

I know by Your understanding that it is not by human strength [. . .] a man's [26]way is [not] in himself, nor is a person able to determine his step. But I know that in Your hand is the inclination of every spirit [. . . and all] his [works] [27]You have determined before ever You created him. How should any be able to change Your words? You alone have [creat]ed [28]the righteous one, and from the womb You established him to give heed to Your covenant at the appointed time of grace and to walk in all things, nourishing himself [29]in the abundance of Your compassion, and relieving all the distress of his soul for an eternal salvation and everlasting peace without want. Thus You raise [30]his glory above the mortal.

But the wicked You created for [the time of] Your [w]rath, and from the womb You set them apart for the day of slaughter. [31]For they walk in a way which is not profitable, and they reject Your covenant [and] their soul abhors Your [truth.] They have no delight in all that [32]You have commanded, but they have chosen that which You hate. All [. . .] You have prepared them in order to execute great judgments among them [33]before all Your creatures that they might be a sign [. . .] eternal, so that all might know Your glory and great power. [34]And what indeed is a mere human that it might have insight into [. . .] how is dust able to determine its step?

[35]You Yourself have formed the spirit, and its activity You have determined, [. . .] and from You is the way of all life. I know that [36]no wealth compares with Your truth, and [. . .] Your holiness. I know that You have chosen them above all [37]and forever they shall serve You. You will not receive [a bribe . . .] nor a cover-up for the deeds of wickedness, for [38]You are a God of truth, and You [abhor] all injustice [. . .] shall not be before You. [For] I know [39]that [. . .] is Yours [. . .] do and I shall [. . .] Your holiness [. . .] [40][. . .] for in [. . .] **Col. 8** [10][. . .] all [. . .] [11][. . .] He brought into the number of [12][. . .] in heaven and on earth [13][. . .] to sanctify without [. . .] and in Your hand is the judgment of them all [14][. . .] forever. [. . .] source of wickedness [. . .] and what are they regarded [. . .] [15][. . .] to sanctify in accordance with all [Your] works [. . .] and nothing is done [16][. . .] and stiff-necked spirit [. . .] to silence [. . .] and according to Your counsel he (?) visited [. . .] [17][. . .] to give ear to a glorious voice [. . .] with [. . .] [18][. . .] a perverse [sp]irit of injustice [. . .] to [. . .] [19][. . .] [20]by [Your] ho[ly] spirit [. . .] and he (?) shall not [. . .] [21][Your] hol[y] spirit [. . .] the fullness of [heav]en [and] earth [. . .] Your [g]lory, the fullness of [. . .] [22]And I know that in [Your] will for man You have multiplied [. . .] Your truth in all [. . .] [23]and the place of righteousness [. . .] which You appointed him [. . .] to stumble in all [. . .] [24]And as I come to know all these things [I] will find the proper reply, prostrating myself and [. . .] for my rebellion, seeking a spirit of [. . .] [25]encouraging myself by [Your] h[oly] spirit, clinging to the truth of Your covenant, [serv]ing You in truth and a perfect heart, and loving [Your holy name.]

Hymn 9. A community hymn of blessing for the wonders of God's creation.

[26]Blessed are You, O Lord, Creator of [a]ll things and gr[eat] in deed because all things are Your works. Behold, You have determined to b[e] merciful [with me] [27]and be gracious to me by the spirit of Your compassion and [the . . . of] Your glory. You alone possess righteousness, for You have done al[l these things.] [28]And because I know that You have recorded the spirit of

the righteous, I myself have chosen to purify my hands in accordance with Your wil[l.] The soul of Your servant a[bho]rs every [29]work of injustice. I know that no one can be righteous apart from You. And I entreat Your favor by that spirit which You have given [me], to fulfill [30]Your [mer]cy with [Your] servant for[ever], to cleanse me by Your holy spirit, and to bring me near by Your grace according to Your great mercy [. . .] in [. . .] [31]standing [. . .] the place of [Your] wi[ll] which You have chos[en] for those who love You and keep [Your] comma[nd]ments [32]before You [fore]ver [. . . has not] been mingled with the spirit of Your servant, and with all the deed[s of inju]st[ice.] [33][. . .] And do not allow [. . .] before him any affliction which causes a falling away from the statutes of Your covenant. For [. . .] [34]g[lo]ry, and Yo[u are . . .] and compassionate, patient [and . . .] mercy and truth and forgiving transgression [. . .] [35]and moved to pity upon [. . .] and those who keep [Your] precep[ts], turning to You with faith and with a perfect heart [. . .] [36]to serve You [and to do that which is] good in Your eyes. Do not turn the face of Your servant away [. . .] the son of [Your] maidservant [. . .] [37][. . .] And I, because of Your words [. . .] **Col. 9** [5]eternal [. . .] [6]in them and jud[gment . . .] For [. . .] and [. . .] [7]and source of stren[gth . . .] great in counsel [. . .] without number, and Your zeal [8]before [. . .] patient in judgment [and Yo]u are justified by all Your works. [9]By Your wisdom [You have establish]ed the successive [generations] and before You created them You knew {all} their works [10]forever and ever. [For apart from You no]thing is done, and without Your will nothing is known. You have formed [11]every spirit and [You determined their] de[eds] and judgment for all their works.

You have stretched out the heavens [12]for Your glory, You [formed] all [their hosts] according to Your will, and the powerful spirits according to their laws, before [13]they became [Your holy] angels [. . .], as eternal spirits in their dominions, luminaries for their mysteries, [14]stars according to [their] paths, [and all the storm winds] according to their task, meteors and lightning bolts according to their service, and the storehouses [15]designed for their needs [. . .] for their secrets.

You have created the earth with Your strength, [16]seas and deeps [. . . and] their [. . .] You have determined in Your wisdom, and all that is in them [17]You have determined according to Your will. [You appointed them] for the spirit of man whom You have formed upon the earth, for all the days of eternity [18]and the everlasting generations in accordance with [their] w[orks . . .] in their ordained seasons. You apportioned their service in all their generations and judgm[en]t [19]for its appointed times for the domini[on . . .] their [. . .] for successive generations and the punishment for their retribution as well as [20]all their afflictions. [. . .] You have apportioned it to all their offspring according to the number of everlasting generations [21]and for all the years of eternity [. . .] and in the wisdom of Your knowledge You determined their destiny before [22]they came into existence and according [to Your will] everything come[s to pass], and nothing happens apart from You.

[23]These things I know through Your understanding, for You have opened my ears to wonderful mysteries even though I am a vessel of clay and kneaded with water, [24]a foundation of shame and a spring of filth, a melting pot of iniquity and a structure of sin, a spirit of error, perverted without [25]understanding and terrified by righteous judgments. What can I say that is not known and declare that is not told? Everything [26]is engraved before You with the ink of remembrance for all the times of eternity, for the numbered seasons of eternal years in all their appointed times. [27]Nothing is hidden, nor does anything exist apart from Your presence. How shall a man explain his sin, and how shall he defend his iniquities, [28]and how can he return injustice for righteous judgment? You are God of knowledge, all righteous works and true counsel belong to You; [29]sinful service and the deceitful works belong to the sons of men.

You created [30]breath for the tongue, and You know its words. You determined the fruit of the lips before they came about. You appoint words by a measuring line [31]and the utterance of the breath of the lips by calculation. You bring forth the measuring lines in respect to their mysteries, and the utterances of breath in respect to their reckoning in order to make known [32]Your glory and recount Your wonders in all Your works of truth and Your righteous jud[gments] and to praise Your name [33]openly, so that all who know You might bless You according to their insight forever [and ever.]

And You, in Your compassion [34]and Your great mercies, have steeled the spirit of man against the agony of [. . .] You have cleansed it from the abundance of iniquity, [35]that it might recount Your wonders before all Your creatures. [. . .] the judgments of my afflictions, [36]and to humankind all the wonders which You have confirmed in [me before hu]mankind.

Hearken, [37]O wise men, you who meditate upon knowledge but are reckless. Be of steadfast mind [. . .] increase prudence. [38]O you righteous, put an end to injustice. All you whose way is perfect take hold of [. . .] of the destitute. [39]Be patient and do not reject any [of the commandments of God. But the fo]olish at heart do not understand [40]these things, but by the counsel of [Your] tru[th . . .] [41][. . . and the bru]tal will gna[sh their teeth . . .] **Col. 10** [3–4][. . .]

Hymn 10. A true Teacher hymn of thanksgiving to God for his salvation.

[5][I give thanks to You, O Lord, for You set straight] all the works of injustice [in my heart . . .] [6][. . . You] set [the guardians of truth against my iniquity and the reprov]ers of righteousness against [my] every wr[ongdoing . . .] [7][. . .] the wound afflic[ted upon] me, [comforters of strength . . .] and proclaimers of joy for [my] deep so[rrow,] [8][proclaiming p]eace for all [my] destruction [. . .] the strong to make me lose heart, and those who encourage [me] [9]in the face of [afflict]ion. Then You give the appropriate reply to my unci[rcumcised] lips, and You support my soul by strengthening my loins [10]and restoring my strength. You determine my steps within the domain of wickedness. So I become a trap for the rebellious, and a cure for all [11]who turn from rebellion; prudence for the fool, and a steadfast mind for all the reckless. You have appointed me as an object of shame [12]and derision to the faithless, but a foundation of truth and understanding for the upright. And because of the iniquity of the wicked, I have become [13]slander on the lips of the brutal, and scoffers gnash their teeth. I have become a taunt-song for the rebellious, [14]and the assembly of the wicked have stormed against me. They roar like a gale on the seas; when their waves churn, [15]they cast up slime and mud. But You have appointed me as a ensign for the chosen of righteousness, and an informed mediator of wonderful mysteries, so as to test [16][the men] of truth and to try the lovers of correction. I have become a man of contention for the mediators of error, [17]but a purveyor of peace unto all the seers of righteousness. I have become impassioned against those who seek flat[tery], [18][so that all] the men of deceit roar against me, as the sound of the thunder of mighty waters. [All] their thoughts are as the plots of Belial [19]and they have transformed a man's life, whom You established by my word and whom You taught understanding, into a pitfall. [20]You placed it in his heart to open up the source of knowledge to all who understand. But they have changed them, through uncircumcised lips [21]and a strange message, into a people with no understanding, that they might be ruined in their delusion.

Hymn 11. A true Teacher hymn, according to some researchers, of thanksgiving to God for protection.

[22]I give thanks to You, O Lord, for You have placed me in the bundle of the living, [23]and You protect me from all the snares of the pit. Ruthless men seek my life, while I hold fast [24]to Your covenant. They are the fraudulent council for the congregation of Belial; they do not know that my appointment is from You. [25]By Your mercies You save my life, for my very steps are

from You. Their attack on my life is from You [26]that You might be honored by the judgment of the wicked, and that You might display Your might through me against the children [27]of men, for I stand in Your mercy. And I said, mighty men have camped against me, they have surrounded me with all [28]their weapons of war. Arrows burst forth unceasingly, and the blade of the spear devours trees with fire. [29]Like the roar of mighty waters is the clamor of their voice, a cloudburst and a downpour to destroy many. Wickedness and fraud burst forth to the stars [30]when their waves pile high. As for me, though my heart melts like water, my soul shall hold fast to Your covenant. [31]But as for them, the net that they spread for me will catch their own foot. And snares, which they hid to take my life, they themselves fell into. Meanwhile, "My foot stands on level ground; [32]far from their congregation I will bless Your name" (Ps. 26:12).

Hymn 12. A true Teacher hymn of thanksgiving to God for deliverance from persecution.

[33]I give thanks to You, O Lord, for Your eye sta[nds] over my soul, and You have delivered me from the jealousy of the mediators of lies [34]and from the congregation of those who seek flattery. You have redeemed the soul of the poor one, whom they planned to put to an end, [35]pouring out his blood because he served You. Because they [did not kn]ow that my steps are directed by You, they appointed me for shame [36]and scorn in the mouth of all those who seek deceit. But You, my God, have helped the soul of the destitute and the poor [37]against one stronger than he. You have redeemed my soul from the hand of the mighty. In the midst of their reviling You have not terrified me, [38]that I might abandon Your service for fear of ruin at the hands of the wicked, or exchange a steadfast mind which [. . .] for a delusion. [39][. . .] statutes, and by testimonies You established me to strengthen [40][the flesh . . . des]truction for all [their] offspring [41][. . . a tongue] according Your teachings and [. . .] **Col. 11** [2][. . .] and in me [. . .] [3][. . .] [4][. . .] You have made my face to shine [. . .] [5][. . .] for Yourself, with eternal glory together with all [. . .]

Hymn 13. A true Teacher hymn of thanksgiving to God for deliverance from the torments of enemies.

[6][. . .] Your mouth, and You have delivered me from [. . .] and from [. . .] [7][. . .] now [my] soul [. . . for] they did [not] esteem me. They set [my] soul as a boat in the depths of the sea, [8]and as a fortified city befo[re

her enemy.] I am in distress, as a woman about to give birth to her first born. For her pangs come over her, [9]and she has excruciating pain at the mouth of her womb, writhing in the womb of the pregnant one. For children come into life through the crashing waves of death, [10]and she who is pregnant with a male child is afflicted by her birth pains. For through the crashing waves of death she delivers a male child, through the pains of Sheol there bursts forth [11]from the womb of the pregnant one, a wonderful counselor with his strength. A male child is safely delivered from the crashing waves. Into the one who is pregnant with him rush all [12]the crashing waves, and excruciating pains when they are born, and terror to their mothers. And when he is born, all pangs come suddenly [13]to the womb of the pregnant one. But she that is pregnant with wickedness experiences excruciating pain, and the crashing waves of the pit for all works of terror. [14]And the foundations of the wall break as a ship upon the water, and the clouds thunder with a roar. Those who sit in the dust, [15]as well as those who go down to the seas, are terrified by the roar of the water, and their wise men are for them as sailors on the deeps. For [16]all their wisdom is swallowed up by the roar of the seas, when the ocean depths boil over the springs of water, and they are tossed up to the towering waves [17]and crashing waves by their roar. And when they are tossed up, Sh[eo]l [and Abaddon] shall open. [And al]l the arrows of the pit, [18]when they descend into the deep, shout out, and the gates [of Sheol] open [for all] the works of wickedness. [19]Then the doors of the pit shut up the one who is pregnant with injustice, and the eternal bars shut up the spirits of wickedness.

Hymn 14. A community hymn of thanksgiving to God, who delivers earthly humankind.

[20]I give thanks to You, O Lord, for You have redeemed my soul from the pit. From Sheol and Abaddon [21]You have raised me up to an eternal height, so that I might walk about on a limitless plain, and know that there is hope for him whom [22]You created from the dust for the eternal council. The perverse spirit You have cleansed from great transgression, that he might take his stand with [23]the host of the holy ones, and enter together (*or* in the *Yahad*) with the congregation of the sons of heaven. And for man, You have allotted an eternal destiny with the spirits [24]of knowledge, to praise Your name together with shouts of joy, and to recount Your wonders before all Your creatures. But I, a creature of [25]clay, what am I? Kneaded with water, for whom am I to be reckoned, and what is my strength? For I have taken my stand within the domain of wickedness, [26]and I am with the wretched by lot. The soul of the poor dwells with great tumults, thus great disasters accompany

my steps. [27]When all the traps of the pit open, and all the wicked snares and the net of the wretched ones are spread out on the water, [28]when all the arrows of the pit fly off without returning and burst forth without hope, when the measuring line falls upon judgment and the lot of wrath [29]upon those who are abandoned, when the outpouring of wrath upon the pretenders and the time of anger for all which belongs to Belial, when the snares of death have surrounded with no escape, [30]then the torrents of Belial shall go over all the high banks, like a fire that devoured all their channels (?), so as to destroy every green tree [31]and dry tree alongside their tributaries. It spreads with sparks from the flames, until all that drink from them are gone. It devours the cliffs of clay [32]and the plains; the foundations of the mountains are set to burning and the roots of flint become torrents of pitch. It devours right down to the great deep. [33]The torrents of Belial burst through into Abaddon, and the plotters from the deep make an uproar with the noise of those who belch forth slime. The earth [34]shouts out, because of the disaster which comes about in the world, and all its plotters scream. All who are upon it behave as if mad, [35]and they melt away in the great disaster. For God thunders with the roar of His strength and His holy dwelling roars forth in His glorious truth. [36]Then the heavenly hosts shall raise their voice and the everlasting foundations shall melt and quake. The war of the heroes [37]of heaven shall spread over the world and shall not return until an annihilation that has been determined from eternity is completed. Nothing like this has ever occurred.

Hymn 15. A true Teacher hymn of thanksgiving to God for protection against the powers of destruction.

[38]I give thanks to You, O Lord, for You have become a wall of strength for me [39][and You have rescued me from al]l destroyers and all [. . .] You hide me from the terrifying disasters [. . .] [40][. . .] a troop shall not come, a div[ision of warriors when joined . . .] [41][. . .] in the mysteries of [. . .] [42][. . .] in its environs, lest a warr[ior] shoot [. . .] **Col. 12** [2][. . .] But I, when I lay hold of [. . .] [3][. . .] [4][. . . You set] my feet upon a rock [. . .] [5][. . . You lead me in] the everlasting way and on the paths which You have chosen [. . .]

Hymn 16. A true Teacher hymn of thanksgiving to God for salvation through the covenant.

[6]I give thanks to You, O Lord, for You have made my face to shine by Your covenant, and [. . .] [7][. . .] I seek You, and as an enduring dawning, as

[perfe]ct ligh[t,] You have revealed Yourself to me. But these Your people [go astray.] [8]Fo[r] they flatter themselves with words, and mediators of deceit lead them astray, so that they are ruined without knowledge. For [. . .] [9]their works are deceitful, for good works were rejected by them. Neither did they esteem me; even when You displayed Your might through me. Instead, they drove me out from my land [10]as a bird from its nest. And all my friends and acquaintances have been driven away from me; they esteem me as a ruined vessel. But they are mediators of [11]a lie and seers of deceit. They have plotted wickedness against me, so as to exchange Your law, which You spoke distinctly in my heart, for flattering words [12]directed to Your people. They hold back the drink of knowledge from those who thirst, and for their thirst they give them vinegar to drink, that they might observe [13]their error, behaving madly at their festivals and getting caught in their nets.

But You, O God, reject every plan [14]of Belial, and Your counsel alone shall stand, and the plan of Your heart shall remain forever. They are pretenders; they hatch the plots of Belial; [15]they seek You with a double heart, and are not founded in Your truth. A root producing poison and wormwood is in their scheming. [16]With a willful heart they look about and seek You in idols. They have set the stumbling block of their iniquity before themselves, and they come [17]to seek You through the words of lying prophets corrupted by error. With mocking lips and a strange tongue they speak to Your people [18]so as make a mockery of all their works by deceit. For they did not choose the wa[y of] Your [heart] nor attend to Your word, but they said [19]concerning the vision of knowledge, "It is not sure," and concerning the way of Your heart, "It is not the way."

But You, O God, shall answer them by judging them [20]in Your strength [according to] their idols and the multitude of their transgressions, in order that they, who have turned away from Your covenant, might be caught in their own schemes. [21]You shall cut off in ju[dgm]ent all deceitful men; seers of error shall no longer be found. For there is no deception in any of Your works, [22]and no deceit in the deliberation of Your heart. Those who are in harmony with You shall stand before You forever, and those who walk in the way of Your heart [23]shall be secure forevermore. I myself, when I hold fast to You, stand up straight and arise against those who disdain me; my hands are against all who despise me. For [24]they esteem [me] not [thou]gh You display Your might through me, and reveal Yourself to me in Your strength as perfect light. You do not cover with shame the faces [25]of all those who are sought by me, who are meeting together (*or* in the *Yahad*) in accordance with Your covenant. Those who walk in the way of Your heart have listened to me; they are drawing themselves up before You [26]in the council of the holy ones. You cause their judgment to endure forever and truth to go forth without obstruction. You do not allow them to be led astray at the hand of the scoundrels [27]when they plot against them. You put the fear of them in Your people and You make them a war club to all the peoples of the lands so as to cut off in judgment all [28]those who transgress Your word.

But by me You have illumined the face of many (*or* the general membership) and have strengthened them uncountable times. For You have given me understanding of the mysteries of [29]Your wonder, and in Your wondrous council You have confirmed me; doing wonders before many (*or* the general membership) for the sake of Your glory, and making known [30]Your mighty deeds to all living. What is mortal man in comparison with this? And where is the vessel of clay that is able to carry out wondrous deeds? For he is sinful [31]from the womb and in the guilt of unfaithfulness until old age. I know that man has no righteousness, nor does the son of man walk in the perfect [32]way. All the works of righteousness belong to God Most High. The way of man does not last except by the spirit which God created for him, [33]to perfect a way for humankind so that they may know all His works by His mighty power and the abundance of His mercies upon all those [34]who do His will.

But as for me, fear and trembling have taken hold of me and all my bones break apart. My heart melts as wax over the fire, and my knees become [35]as water which is poured down over a slope. For I remember my guilt together with the unfaithfulness of my fathers, when the wicked rise against Your covenant [36]and the scoundrels against Your word. I said in my transgression, I am abandoned by Your covenant. But when I remembered the power of Your hand together with [37]the abundance of Your mercies, I stood upright and firm and my spirit grew strong to stand against affliction. For [I] rested [38]in Your mercies and the abundance of Your compassion. For You atone for iniquity and purif[y] man from guilt by Your righteousness. [39]But not for man, [but for] Your [glory] You have worked, for You created both the righteous and the wicked [. . .] [40][. . .] I will hold fast to Your covenant until [. . .] [41][. . . befor]e You. For You are truth, and all [Your] w[orks] are righteousness [. . .] **Col. 13** [3]to the day with [. . .] [4]Your forgiveness and the abundance [of Your mercies . . .] [5]And when I realized this, [You] comforted [me . . .] [6]in accordance with Your will, and by Your hand is the judgment of them all [. . .]

Hymn 17. A true Teacher hymn of thanksgiving to God, who has not forsaken his own.

[7]I give thanks to You, O Lord, for You have not forsaken me while I sojourned among a people [. . . and not] according to my guilt have [8]You

judged me. Nor have You abandoned me to the plots of my evil inclination, but You have rescued my life from the pit. You have given [. . .] among [9]lions, who are appointed for the children of guilt; lions, who break the bones of the mighty and drink the blo[od] of warriors. You assigned [10]my dwelling with many fishermen, they who spread their net on the surface of the water, and hunt for the children of injustice. [11]You have established me there for judgment. You have strengthened the counsel of truth in my heart, and waters (?) of the covenant for those who seek it. But You shut the mouth of the young lions whose [12]teeth are like a sword, and whose fangs are as a sharp spear. All their evil plans for abduction are like the poison of serpents; they lie in wait, but have not [13]opened their mouths wide against me. For You, O my God, have concealed me from humankind, and Your law You have hidden in [me] until the time [14]You reveal Your salvation to me. For in my soul's distress You did not abandon me, but You heard my cry in the bitterness of my soul. [15]You recognized my grievous cry by my sigh and You delivered the life of the destitute one from the den of lions who sharpen their tongue as a sword. [16]And You, O my God, have shut their teeth, lest they tear the soul of the destitute and poor to pieces. And their tongue is drawn in [17]as a sword into its sheath, so that it might not strike the soul of Your servant. And so that You might display Your might through me against humankind, You have done wondrous deeds [18]with the poor. You have brought him into the crucib[le like g]old to be worked by the fire, and as silver, which is refined in the smelter of the smiths to be refined seven times. [19]But the wicked of the people rush against me with their afflictions, and all the day long they crush my soul.

[20]But You, O my God, turn the tempest to a whisper, and the life of the distressed You have brought to safety as a bir[d from the snare and] as prey from the power of [21]lions.

Hymn 18. A true Teacher hymn of thanksgiving or blessing to God, who does not forsake those who turn to him despite the torments of the wicked.

[22]{I give thanks to You} Blessed are You, O Lord, for You have not abandoned the orphan, and You have not despised the poor. For Your strength [is unboun]ded and Your glory [23]without measure. Your ministers are wondrous warriors. A humbled people are in the sweepings at [Your] feet [and You have done a miracle as well] with those heedless of [24]righteousness to bring them up from out of the desolation together with all of those {heedless} lacking mercy. But I myself have become [. . .] strife [25]and contentions for my fellows, jealousy and anger to those who have entered into my covenant, a grumbling and a complaining to all who are my comrades.

Ev[en those who sha]re my bread [26]have lifted up their heel against me, and all those who have committed themselves to my counsel speak perversely against me with unjust lips. The men of my [coun]cil rebel [27]and grumble round about. And concerning the mystery which You hid in me, they go about as slanderers to the children of destruction. Because [You] have exal[ted Yourself] in me, [28]and for sake of their guilt, You have hidden in me the spring of understanding and the counsel of truth. But they devise the ruination of their heart; [and with the words of] Belial they have exhibited [29]a lying tongue; as the poison of serpents it bursts forth continuously. As those who crawl in the dust, they lie in wait so as to lay hold [of the poison] of serpents [30]for which there is no charm. And it has become an incurable pain and a tormenting agony in the bowels of Your servant, causing [my spirit] to stumble and putting an end to [31]my strength so that I might not stand firm. They overtake me in narrow places, where there is no place of refuge, nor when they [. . .] They intone [32]their dispute against me on the lyre, and compose their complaint to music; together with ruin and desolation. Searing pains have se[ized me] and pangs as the convulsions of [33]one giving birth. My heart is tormented within me. I have put on the garment of mourning, and my tongue clings to the roof of my mouth. For they have surrounded me [with . . .] of their heart, and their desire [34]has appeared to me as bitterness. The light of my countenance becomes dark, and my splendor is transformed to gloom.

But You, O my God, [35]have opened a wide space in my heart, but they continue to press in, and they shut me up in deep darkness, so that I eat the bread of groaning, [36]and my drink is tears without end. For my eyes have become weak from anger and my soul by daily bitterness. Grief and misery [37]surround me, and shame is upon my face. My bread has become strife, and my drink contention. They enter my bones, [38]causing my spirit to stumble and putting an end to my strength. In accordance with the mysteries of transgression, they are perverting the works of God by their guilt. For I have been bound with ropes [39]which cannot be pulled loose, and with fetters which cannot be broken. A strong wall [surrounds me;] iron bars and [bronze] gates [which can no]t be opened. [40]My prison is reckoned with the deep without [escape . . . the torrents of], [41][Be]l[i]al encompass my soul [. . .]

Hymn 19. A true Teacher hymn of thanksgiving to God for rescuing the righteous one from the wicked congregation.

Col. 14 [4][. . .] [5]my heart in contempt [. . .] [6]and disaster without bounds, destruction without [. . . But You, O my God,] [7]have opened my ears [to the admon]ition of those who rebuke righteously, with [. . . You rescued me] [8]from the congregation [of fra]ud and the council of violence, and brought me into the council of [Your holiness . . .] guilt. [9]I know there is hope for those who turn from rebellion, and for those who abandon sin in [. . .] to walk [10]in the way of Your heart without injustice. I am comforted despite the roar of the people and the clamor of kingdoms when they gather themselves together. [For] I [kn]ow that [11]You will soon raise up survivors among Your people and a remnant among Your inheritance. You will refine them so that they may be cleansed from guilt.

For all [12]their works are in Your truth, and in Your mercies You will judge them with abundant compassion and bountiful forgiveness, teaching them according to Your word. [13]According to Your upright truth You determined them in Your counsel for Your glory. For Your sake You have worked to make the law and truth great for [. . .] [14]the men of Your council among humankind, to recount Your wonders to successive generations and [med]itate unceasingly on Your mighty works.

[15]All the peoples shall know Your truth and all nations Your glory. For You have brought [Your] t[ruth and g]lory [16]to all the men of Your council, in the lot together with the angels of presence. And there is no mediator for [Your] ho[ly ones . . .] [17]its fruit, for [. . .] They will return at Your glorious word and they shall be Your princes in the [eternal] lo[t. . . .] [18]a blossom, as a flo[wer that blooms for] eternal [splend]or, to raise up a shoot to be the branches of an eternal planting. It will cast shade over all the wor[ld and its branches will reach] [19]as far as the heaven[s] and its roots to the depths. All the rivers of Eden [shall water] its [b]r[anch]es.

There shall be [seas without] [20]limits and they shall encircle the world without end, and as far as Sheol [. . .] the spring of light shall become an everlasting fountain [21]without turning aside. In its brilliant flames all the child[ren of injustice] shall burn, [and it shall] become a fire which burns up all the men of [22]guilt completely. They who committed themselves to my testimony have let themselves be seduced by [false] inter[preters, so as to bring the stranger] into the service of righteousness.

[23]But You, O God, have commanded them to gain profit from their ways by [walking] in the way of [Your] holin[ess.] The uncircumcised, the defiled, and the violent [24]do not traverse it. They stagger away from the way of Your heart and in the destruction [of their sin] they [stumb]le. Like a counselor, Belial is [25]with their heart. [They establish] a scheme of wickedness; they wallow in their guilt. [. . .] I have [become] as a sailor on a ship in the raging [26]seas; their waves and all their breakers come over me. A staggering wind roars [without] calm to revive the soul nor any [27]paths to make a straight way over the waters. The depths roar to my groaning and [my] lif[e approaches] the gates of death. I am

[28]as one who enters a fortified city and seeks shelter behind a high wall until his deliverance. I rejo[ice] in Your truth, my God, for You [29]set a foundation upon the rock, beams upon a just measuring line and tru[e] plumb line, to [ma]ke the tested stones into a [30]strong building which shall not be shaken. All who enter it shall not totter. For the stranger may not enter her [gat]es; armored doors do not allow [31]entry, and strong bolts which do not shatter. A troop with its weapons of war may not enter in, though all the s[words] of [32]wicked wars be destroyed.

Then the sword of God shall hasten to the time of judgment and all the children of His truth shall awaken to put an end to [the children of] [33]wickedness, and all the children of guilt shall be no more. The hero shall draw his bow, and the fortification shall open [. . .] [34]as an open country without end. The eternal gates shall open to bring out the weapons of war, and they shall be migh[t]y from one end of the world to the other [35][. . .] But there is no escape for the creatures of guilt, they shall be trampled down to destruction with no rem[nant. And there is no] hope in the abundance of [. . .] [36]and for all the heroes of war there is no refuge.

For [victory belongs] to God Most High [. . .] [37]Raise the ensign, O you who lie in the dust, and let the worms of the dead lift a banner for [. . .] they cut [. . .] [38]in the battles of the arrogant. And He shall cause a raging flood to pass through, which shall not enter the fortified city [. . .] [39][. . .] for plaster and as a beam for [. . .] [40]truth [. . .] **Col. 15** [4][. . .] I am speechless [. . .] these [. . .] [5][. . .] my [ar]m is shattered at the shoulder, and my foot has sunk in the mire. My eyes are sealed shut from seeing [6]evil, my ears from hearing of bloodshed, and my heart is stupefied because of evil plotting. For Belial is manifest when the true nature of their being is revealed. [7]All the foundations of my frame crumble. My bones are separated, and my bowels are like a ship in a raging [8]storm. My heart roars as to destruction, and a spirit of staggering overwhelms me. All because of the ruin caused by their sin.

Hymn 20. A true Teacher hymn of thanksgiving to God, who sustains his own.

[9]I give thanks to You, O Lord, for You have sustained me with Your strength, and Your holy spirit [10]You have spread out over me so that I will not falter. You have strengthened me before the wars of wickedness, and in all their devastation [11]You have not shattered me for the sake of Your covenant. You set me up as a strong tower, as a high wall. Upon the rock You have established [12]my frame, and eternal foundations for my footing. All my walls are tested walls, which will not be shaken.

[13][And] You, my God, have appointed me as a holy counsel to the weary. You [have taught me] Your covenant and my tongue is as one of Your disciples. [14]But there is no word for the spirit of disasters, nor a proper reply for any of the children of guilt. For lying lips shall be speechless. [15]For all who attack me You will condemn to judgment, so that in me You might divide between the righteous and the ungodly. [16]For You know the intention of every work, and every reply You discern. You have established my heart [17][in accordance with] Your [te]aching and Your truth, setting my steps straight in the paths of righteousness, so that I may walk in Your presence in the domain of [18][the righteous o]nes in paths of glory {and life} and peace without t[urning and ne]ver ceasing.

[19]But You know the inclination of Your servant, that [I have] not [relied on my own power] to exalt [myself,] [20]finding security in my strength. Nor have I any fleshly refuges [. . .] no works of righteousness to rescue myself from [. . .] [21][with]out forgiveness. I lean on the mult[itude of Your compassion and in the abundance of] Your mercy I await, causing [22]the plant to blossom and a shoot to grow up; taking refuge in Your strength and [. . . For in] Your righteousness You have stood me [23]in Your covenant, and I have taken hold of Your truth.

And Yo[u . . .] and You have appointed me as a father to the children of mercy [24]and as a guardian to men of portent. They open the mouth wide like a nursing ch[ild . . .] and as a child delights in the embrace of [25]its guardian. And You have given me victory over all who condemn me, and the [rem]nant of those who warred against me are sh[attered.] Those who [26]prosecuted me are as chaff before the wind, and my dominion is over [. . . And You,] my [Go]d, have helped my soul, and You have exalted my horn [27]on high. I shine forth in sevenfold light, in l[ight which] You have [esta]blished for Your glory. [28]For You are as an [eter]nal light for me, and You establish my foot upon the level gr[ound . . .]

Hymn 21. A community hymn of thanksgiving to God, the only wise and righteous one.

[29]I give thanks [to You, O Lord], for You have given me discernment into Your truth, [30]and Your wondrous mysteries You have made known to me, and Your mercies for a [rebellious] man and Your abundant compassion for those who are perverted of heart. [31]For who is like You among the gods, O Lord? And who is as Your truth? And who can be justified before You, when he enters into judgment? [32]None of the spiritual hosts is able to answer to Your punishment, and none can stand firm before Your anger. But all the children [33]of Your truth You bring before You in forgiveness, cleansing them from

their rebellious acts in the multiplicity of Your goodness, and by the abundance of Your compassion [34]maintaining them before You forever and ever.

For You are an eternal God, and all Your ways endure for eternity [35]without end; there is none beside You. And what then is the man of vacuity and the master of vanity, that he should clearly understand Your wondrous [36]mighty works?

Hymn 22. A community hymn of thanksgiving to God, who treats the psalmist with mercy and forgiveness.

[37][I give thanks to Y]ou, O Lord, for You have not cast my lot in the fraudulent assembly, nor have You set my portion in the council of the pretenders. [38]But You call me to Your mercies, to [Your] forgiveness [You have brought me,] and in the abundance of Your compassion for all the [righteous] judgments. [39][But as for me, I am an unclean man; from the womb of her who conceived me I was in the guilt of unfaithfulness, from the breasts of my mother I was in] injustice, and at the bosom [40][of my nursemaid an abundance of impurity. From my youth I was characterized by bloodshed, and until my old age by iniquity of flesh. But You, my God, have established] [41][my foot in the way of Your heart; at the report of Your wonder You have opened my ears and my heart to understand Your truth . . .] **Col. 16** [1][. . . I shut my ear to Your teaching until You gave me insight; a perverted spirit without] [2][knowledge You expelled from my bowels and You glorified me . . . I am no longer a stumbling block] [3][of iniquity. For You reveal Your salvation and] Your righteousness You establish forever. For no [one knows his way; all these things] [4]You [have don]e [for Your glory.]

Hymn 23. A true Teacher hymn of thanksgiving to God, who made the psalmist a fountain of blessing.

[5]I g[ive thanks to You, O Lord, for] You set me by a fountain which flows in a dry land, a spring of water in a desolate land, a well watered [6]garden [and a pool . . .] You [plan]ted a stand of juniper and pine together with cypress for Your glory; trees of [7]life at the secret spring, hidden among all the trees by the water so that a shoot might grow up into an eternal planting. [8]Taking root before they shoot up, they stretch out their roots to the watercourse, that its trunk might be open to the living water [9]and become an eternal fountain. On its leafy branches every the wild animal of the forest shall graze, and its trunk shall become a gathering place to all who pass [10]and its branches roosts for all the birds. All the tre[es] by the water rise over it, for in their stand they grow tall, [11]but they do not stretch out their root

toward the watercourse. The shoot of h[o]liness grows up into a planting of truth, hidden [12]and not esteemed. And because it is not known its secret is sealed up.

But You, O [G]od, You protect its fruit with the mystery of powerful warriors, [13]holy spirits, and the whirling flame of fire so that none may [come to the] fountain of life, nor with eternal trees [14]drink the waters of holiness, nor make his fruit flourish with [the plan]t of the heavens. Namely, the one though he sees has not recognized, [15]and considering has not believed in the spring of life and so gives [. . .] eternal. I have become the mockery of flooding rivers, [16]for they toss up their slime over me.

[17]But You, O my God, have placed Your words in my mouth, as showers of early rain, for all [who thirst] and as a spring of living waters. The heavens shall not fail to open, [18]nor shall they run dry, but shall become a stream pouring out up[on . . .] water and then to seas without en[d.] [19]Those hidden away flow suddenly [. . .] and they shall become a de[luge for every] [20]green and dry tree; a lake for every wild animal and bi[rd . . . . as] lead in mighty water[s,] [21][. . .] fire and they dry up. But the planting of fruit [. . .] eternally, to a glorious Eden and frui[t . . .] [22]And by my hand You have opened their spring with [its] channels [. . .] turning in accordance with the proper measurement, and the stand [23]of their trees according to the plumb line of the sun for [. . .] glorious branches. When I extend my hand to weed [24]its ditches, its roots stretch out into the flinty stone and [. . .] their trunk in the earth. In the time of heat it retains [25]its strength. But if I withdraw my hand, it shall become like a junip[er in the wilderness;] its trunk as nettles in a barren land, and its ditches [26]shall produce thorns and thistles, briars and weeds [. . . on] its banks turn into worthless trees. In [27]the heat its leaves wither and are not restored by the spri[ng of water . . . my] dwelling is with the sick, and [my] heart k[no]ws [28]agonies.

I have become like a man who is forsaken by [. . .] there is no refuge for me. For my agony breaks out [29]to bitterness, and an incurable pain without stopping, [. . . ro]ars over me, like those who descend into Sheol. Among [30]the dead my spirit searches, for [my] li[fe] goes down to the pit [. . .] my soul is faint day and night [31]without rest. And my agony breaks out as a burning fire shut up within [my] b[ones] whose flame consumes for days on end, [32]putting an end to my strength without ceasing and destroying my flesh without end. The billows break over me [33]and my soul is completely worn down. For my strength is departed from my body, my heart is poured out as water, [34]and my flesh is melted as wax. The strength of my loins has become a calamity, my arm is broken from the shoulder, [and I am no]t [able] to swing my hand. [35]My [foo]t is caught in fetters, my knees become as water, and I am not able to take a step; there is no sound to the tread of my feet. [36][. . .] are pulled loose by stumbling chains, and my tongue You had exalted in my mouth, but no longer. No more can [37]my [tong]ue give forth its voice for instru[ction] to revive the spirits of those who stumble, and to support the weary with a word. The voice of my lips is silent [38][. . .] with chains of judgment [. . .] or in the bitterness [. . .] heart [. . .] dominion [39][. . .] the earth [. . .] [40][. . .] they have been silenced as not [41][. . .] humankind, not [. . .]

Hymn 24. A community hymn of thanksgiving for God's compassion and glory.

Col. 17 [1][. . .] [2][. . .] by night and [. . .] [3][. . .] without compassion. In wrath He awakes mistrust and completely [. . .] [4]the breakers of death and Sheol are over my couch. My bed lifts up a lamentation, [and my pallet] a sound of groanings. [5]My eyes are as a moth in a furnace, and my weeping is as brooks of water. My eyes fail for rest, [and . . .] stands [6]at a great distance from me, and my life has been set aside. But as for me, from ruin to desolation, from pain to agony, and from travails [7]to torments, my soul meditates on Your wonders. In Your mercy You have not rejected me. Time [8]and time again my soul delights in the abundance of Your compassion. I give an answer to those who would wipe me out, [9]and reproof to those who would cast me down. I will condemn his verdict, but Your judgment I honor, for I know [10]Your truth. I shall choose my judgment, and with my agony I am satisfied, for I have waited upon Your mercy. You have put [11]a supplication in the mouth of Your servant, and You have not rebuked my life, nor have You removed my well-being. You have not forsaken [12]my hope, but in the face of affliction You have restored my spirit. For You have established my spirit and know my deliberations. [13]In my distress You have soothed me, and I delight in forgiveness. I shall be comforted for former sin. [14]I know that there is hope in Your mercy, and an expectation in the abundance of Your power. For no one is justified [15]in Your jud[g]ment, and no one is bl[ameless in] Your litigation. One man may be more righteous than another, or one person may be wiser [than his fell]ow, [16]humanity is more honored than a vessel of c[lay], and one spirit may surpass another spirit; but as for Your mighty str[ength], no [17]power can compare. To Your glory there are no [bounds, and] to Your wisdom there is no measure, nor is there [. . .] [18]and for everyone who has forsaken it [. . .]

But in You, I [. . .] [19]with me, and not [. . .] [20]And when they plot [. . .] against me, [. . .] and if the face shows shame [. . .] [21]for me. And You [. . .] You strengthened my enemies against me as a stumbling block to [. . .] [22]men of war [. . . sh]ame of face and reproach for those grumble against me.

[23]But You, O my God, for [. . .] You plead my case. For in the mystery of Your wisdom You have reproved me. [24]You hide the truth in [its time . . . until] its appointed time. Your chastisement has become joy and gladness to me, [25]and my agonies have become an et[ernal] healing and unending [. . .] The contempt of my enemies has become a glorious crown for me, and my stumbling, eternal strength. [26]For by [Your . . .] and Your glory, my light has shined forth, for You have caused light from darkness [27]to shine for me [. . . You bring healing for] my wounds; for my stumbling, wonderful strength; an infinite space [28]for the distress of [my] soul. [You are] my place of refuge, my stronghold, the rock of my strength and my fortress. In You [29]I take refuge from all [. . .] for an eternal escape.

For You from my father [30]have known me, from the womb [You have set me apart and from the belly of] my mother You have rendered good to me. From the breasts of she who conceived me, Your compassion [31]has been mine. And in the embrace of my nurse [. . .] and from my youth You have shined the insight of Your judgment on me. [32]With a sure truth You have supported me, and by Your holy spirit You have delighted me; even until this day [. . .] [33]Your righteous chastisement is with my [. . .] and the protection of Your peace delivers my soul. With my steps is [34]abundant forgiveness and bountiful compassion when You enter into judgment with me. Until old age You shall provide for me, for [35]my father did not know me, and my mother abandoned me to You. For You are a father to all the children of Your truth, and You rejoice [36]over them as a loving mother over her nursing child. As a guardian with his embrace, You provide for all Your creatures.

Hymn 25. A community hymn of thanksgiving to God for his strength and wisdom.

[38][I give thanks to You, O Lord, for] You have increased without num[ber] [39][. . .] Your name by doing wonders [. . .] [40][. . . with]out ceasing [. . .] [41][. . .] his insight and [they] praised [. . .] **Col. 18** [3][. . .] the plan of Your heart [. . .] [4][. . .] and without Your will it shall not be. No one understands all [Your] wisd[om] [5][and the counsel of] Your [mysteries] no one observes. What then is man? He is but dirt [. . .] [6][. . . from dust] he was formed and to dust he returns. But You give him insight into wonders such as these, and make him know the counsel [of Your] tr[uth.] [7]I am but dust and ashes, what can I plan unless You delight in it? And what can I consider for myself [8]apart from Your will? How can I show myself strong, unless You maintain me? How can I understand, unless You have formed it [9]for me? What can I speak, unless You have opened my mouth? And how can I reply, unless You have given me insight?

[10]Behold, You are Chief of the gods and King of the glorious, Lord of every spirit and Ruler over every creature. [11]Apart from You nothing is done, nor is there any knowing without Your will. There is no one beside You [12]and no one approaches You in strength. No one can compare to Your glory and as to Your strength, there is no price. [13]Who among all the celebrated creatures of Your wonder can maintain the strength to take a stand before Your glory? [14]So what then is he, who returns to his dust, that he should maintain str[en]gth? Only for Your glory have You done all of these things.

Hymn 26. A community hymn of thanksgiving to God, who has revealed himself.

[16]Blessed are You, O Lord, God of compassion [and rich] in mercy, for You have made [th]e[se things] known that I might declare [17]Your wondrous works, and not keep silent day and n[ight.] All power is Yours [. . .] [18]by Your mercy, in Your great goodness and abun[dance of compassion. I] shall delight in [Your] fo[rgiveness,] [19]for I rest in Your truth [. . .] [20]from Your will and without [. . . and without] Your rebuke there is no stumbling [. . . nor any] [21]agony except You know [. . .] Your [. . .]

[22]And I, according to my knowledge of [Your] truth [. . .] and when I gaze upon Your glory, I tell of [23]Your wonders. When I understand the [. . . and the ab]undance of Your compassion, and in Your forgiveness [24]I hope. For You formed the spi[rit of Your servant and in] Your [wil]l You established me. You have not established [25]my sustenance upon unjust gain or wealth [. . .] and that which is made of flesh You have not established as my defense. [26]The strength of the mighty [is established] on the abundance of luxur[ies . . . and in] the abundance of corn, wine, and oil. [27]They exalt themselves with property and possession. [But the righteous are as] green [trees] by the watercourses, bearing leaves [28]and producing many branches. For You chose [them from the sons of] men that all may fatten themselves from the land. [29]To the children of Your truth You have given insight [. . .] forever. And according to their knowledge one is honored [30]above another. Thus for the son of [Your] maid[servant (*or* son of m[an) . . .] You have enlarged his inheritance [31]through the knowledge of Your truth. According to his knowledge and [his . . .]

The soul of Your servant abhors wealth [32]and unjust gain, and in the height of luxury [has he not desired . . .] my heart rejoiced in Your covenant, and Your truth [33]delighted my soul. I bloom as a lily, and my heart is opened to the eternal spring. [34]My support is in the strength from on high, and [. . .] labor, and as a flower withers in [the heat.] [35]My heart behaves as if mad in anguish and my loins tremble. My groaning enters the depths [36]and completely searches out the chambers of Sheol. I am terrified when I hear of Your judgments with powerful warriors, [37]and Your dispute with the hosts of Your holy ones in [. . .] [38]and judgment against all Your creatures, and righteousness [. . .] [39–41][. . .] **Col. 19** [4]in terror [. . .] distress from my eyes and grief [. . .] [5]in the meditation of my heart.

Hymn 27. A community hymn of thanksgiving to God, who has given humankind insight into his deeds.

[6]I give thanks to You, O my God, for You have dealt wonderfully with dust, and You have worked so very powerfully with vessels of clay. As for me, what am I? For [7]You have [enlighten]ed me in the counsel of Your truth, and You have given me insight into Your wonderful works. You put praises in my mouth, and upon my tongue [8][a psal]m; the utterance of my lips forms the foundation of joyous song. I shall praise Your mercy and consider Your strength all the [9]day. I will bless Your name continually, and I will recount Your glory among humankind; in the abundance of Your goodness [10]my soul delights. I know that Your command is truth and that in Your hand is righteousness. In Your thoughts [11]are all knowledge and in Your strength is all power; all glory is with You. In Your anger are all the agonizing judgments, [12]but in Your goodness is an abundance of forgiveness. Your compassion is for all the children of Your will, for You have made them know the counsel of Your truth, [13]and in the mysteries of Your wonder You have given them insight. For Your glory's sake You have cleansed man from transgression, so that he can purify himself [14]for You from all filthy abominations and the guilt of unfaithfulness, so as to be joined wi[th] the children of Your truth, in the lot with [15]Your holy ones, that bodies, covered with worms of the dead, might rise up from the dust to an et[ernal] council; from a perverse spirit to Your understanding. [16]That he might take his position before You with the eternal hosts and spirits [of truth], to be renewed with all [17]that shall be and to rejoice together with those who know. [. . .]

Hymn 28. A community hymn of thanksgiving to God, who has given the psalmist understanding of God's righteousness.

[18]I give thanks to You, O my God, I exalt You, my rock, and when You perform wonders [. . .] [19][. . .] For You have made known to me the counsel of truth [. . .] [20][Yo]ur [hidden thin]gs You have revealed to me, so that I might gaze upon [. . .] mercy. I know [21][that] righteousness belongs to You, and in Your mercies [. . .] and annihilation without Your compassion.

[22]But as for me, a fountain for bitter sorrow has been opened [and] distress is not hidden from my eyes [23]when I came to know the inclinations of man, [considered] the response of humankind, [and recognized the sorr]ow of sin and the grief of [24]guilt. They enter into my heart and penetrate my bones. [. . .] and moaning a lament of grief [25a]and a groan on the lyre of lamentation for all griev[ous] mourning, [25]bitter wailing until injustice has ceased, and th[ere is no longer pain] nor agony to make one weak.

Then [26]I will sing praises on the lyre of salvation and to the harp of jo[y and the timbrel of rejo]icing and the flute of praise without [27]ceasing. Who among all Your creatures is able to recount [all] Your [wonders]? Your name shall be praised by every mouth [28]forever and ever. They shall bless You according to [their] insight, [and at all times] they shall proclaim together [29]with the voice of rejoicing. There is no grief nor groaning, and injustice [shall be found no longer]. You shall make Your truth to shine forth [30]for eternal glory and everlasting peace.

Hymn 29. A community hymn.

Blessed are You, [O God, f]or You have given Your servant [31]the insight of knowledge to understand Your wonders [and the proper reply to] recount the abundance of Your mercy.

Hymn 30. A community hymn.

[32]Blessed are You, O God of compassion and grace in accordance with Your grea[t pow]er and the abundance of Your truth, and the profusion [33]of Your mercy for all Your creatures. Gladden the soul of Your servant with Your truth and cleanse me [34]in Your righteousness. For just as I waited for Your goodness, so I hope in Your mercy and Your forgiveness. [35]You have relieved my adversities and in my grief You have comforted me, for I depended upon Your compassion.

Hymn 31. A community hymn.

Blessed are You [36]O Lord, for You have done these things, and You place hymns of thanksgiving in the mouth of Your servant [. . .] [37]and a supplication for favor as well as a suitable reply. And You have established for me [. . .] [38]And I shall restr[ain . . .] [39]And You [. . .] [40]tru[th . . .] [41]and I [. . .] **Col. 20** [4][. . .] my soul is broad [. . .] [5][. . . I will dwel]l safely in a ho[ly] dwelling, [in] quietness and in ease [6][with the eternal spirits] in the tents of glory and salvation. I will praise Your name among those who fear You.

Hymn 32. This community hymn and the hymn starting at 25:34 begin with formula that is more common in the Rule *texts (see CD 12:21, text 1; 1QS 3:13, text 7; 1QSb 1:1, text 9) and the* Songs of the Sabbath Sacrifice *(see 4Q401 frags. 1–2 l. 1, Cor. 1:30, text 101).*

[7][For the Instructor: hymns of than]ksgiving and prayer, to prostrate oneself and appeal for grace unceasingly, at all times. With the coming of the light [8]from [its] domi[nion], through the course of the day in respect to its plan in accordance with the laws of the great light; as the day turns to evening with the departure of [9]the light at the beginning of the rule of darkness; the time appointed for the night. And then according to its course, when night turns to morning, at the time [10]it is gathered to its dwelling before the light, at the departure of the night and the coming of the day. This occurs continually, at all [11]the birthings of the seasons from the foundation of time. And the change of seasons in their order is determined by their signs, for all [12]their dominion by the faithful plan of the mouth of God and the destiny of that which exists shall continue. [13]There is nothing other, and beside it there has not been, nor shall it be otherwise, for the God of knowledge [14]has determined it and there is no other beside Him.

And I, the Instructor, have known You, O my God, by the spirit [15]which You gave me, and I have listened faithfully to Your wondrous counsel by Your holy spirit. [16]You have opened within me knowledge in the mystery of Your insight, and a spring of [Your] strength [. . . in the] midst. [17]There shall be an abundance of mercy, but a ruinous zeal and [You] brought to an end [. . .] [18][. . .] the majesty of Your glory as an etern[al] light [. . .] [19][. . . from] fear of wickedness, and there is no deceit [. . .] [20][. . .] appointed times of desolation. For there is no [. . .] [21][. . .] there is [n]o more insolence. For before Yo[ur] anger [. . .] [22][. . .] my trembling.

There is none righteous beside You [. . .] [23][to] give insight in all Your mysteries, and to give an answer [. . .] [24][. . .] for Your condemnation, and for Your goodness they watch. For in [Your] mercy [. . .] [25]and they know You. In the time of Your glory they rejoice, and according to [. . .] According to their insight [26]You bring them near, and according to their authority they serve You in [their] divisions. [. . .] from You [27]not to transgress Your word.

But I was taken from dust [and from clay] I was [fo]rmed [28]as a fountain of filth and obscene shame, a pile of dust and kneaded [with water

. . .] and the abode [29]of darkness. And a return to dust for a vessel of clay at the end of [. . .] in the dust [30]to the place from where it was taken. And what shall the dust answer and [. . . and what] shall it understand [31][of] its [works]? And how shall it stand its ground before the one who rebukes it [. . . ho]liness [32][. . .] eternal, stores of glory, and a fountain of knowledge and marvelous strength; and they are not [33][able] to recount all Your glory, nor to take a stand before Your anger, nor is it possible to give an answer to [34]Your chastisement. For You are righteous and there is none to compare with You. So what then is the one who returns to its dust?

[35]As for me, I am speechless. What shall I say concerning this? According to my knowledge I speak. But I am mere spit (?), a vessel of clay. What [36]shall I speak unless You open my mouth? How shall I understand unless You give me insight? What shall I s[ay] [37]unless You reveal it to my heart? How shall I make the way straight except [You] determine [my steps? How shall my foot] [38]stand fast be[fore You except I be] strengthened with power? How shall I rise up [. . .] [39]And all [. . .] [40]the [. . .] [41]as [. . .] [42]and [. . .] **Col. 21** [2][. . . tra]nsgression of one born of a wo[man] [3][. . .] Your righteousness [4][. . .] I have seen this [5][. . . How] shall I see unless You have uncovered my eyes or hear [6][unless You have unstopped my ears? . . .] my [h]eart was made desolate. For to the uncircumcised of ear, a word is revealed and the heart [7][. . .]

I know that for Yourself You have done these things, O my God. What is mere humankind [8][. . . to] do wonderfully. In Your plan to confirm and determine everything for Your glory [9][. . .] the host of knowledge, to recount powerful deeds to a mere human, and sure laws for one who is born of [10][a woman . . . You have broug]ht [. . .] into a covenant with Yourself and You have uncovered the heart of dust to guard itself [11][. . .] from the traps of judgment corresponding to Your compassion. I am a creature [12][of clay . . . of du]st and a heart of stone. With whom am I to be reckoned until this occurs? For [13][. . .] You have [gi]ven [. . .] to ears of dust, and You have engraved eternity on the heart [14][of stone . . .] You have ceased [. . .] so as to bring him into a covenant with Yourself and to stand [15][in the judgments of the witnesses] in the eternal abode, as a light of the perfect light forever; and darkness will flee [16][. . . without] end, and times of peace without bo[unds . . .] [17][. . .] I am a vessel of dust [. . .] [18][. . .] Your name.

I will open [my] mo[uth . . .] [19][. . .] inclination [. . .] [20][. . . and a hidden trap. . .] [21][. . .] a net of [the pit] is [spr]ead [. . . and on its paths are the snares of Abaddon . . .] [22][. . .] a way was opened to [walk . . .] [23][. . . in the] paths of peace, and with mere human flesh to do wonders [like these . . .] [24][. . .] and my steps [will tread] upon the hiding places for traps and spreading place[s for the net and . . .] [25][. . . How can] I, a vessel of dust, keep from being shattered and melting as wax as [it melts before the fire . . .] [26][. . .] ash heaps. How can I stand before the rag[ing] wind [. . . As for me, He establishes me in . . .] [27][. . .] and He keeps him for the mysteries of His delight. For He knows [. . .] [28][. . . unt]il annihilation, and they hide trap after trap, the snares of wickedness [. . .] [29][. . .] with injustice, and every deceitful vessel is destroyed. For not [. . .] [30][. . .] there is not, and the unjust intention is no more and the works of deceit [. . .] [31][. . .]

I am a vessel of [clay . . .] [32][. . .] How shall he strengthen himself before You? You are the God of [. . .] [33][. . .] You have made them, and apart from You nothing is made [. . .] [34][. . . I am a vess]el of dust. I know, by the spirit which You have given me [. . .] [35][. . .] injustice and deceit are poured out, and arrogance ceased [. . .] [36][. . .] the works of filth lead to sicknesses, agonizing judgments, and destruction [. . .] [37][. . .] anger and [. . .] zeal are Yours [. . .] [38][. . . and I am a] vessel of cl[ay . . .]

Col. 22 [5][. . . in the ho]ly [habitation] which is in heaven [6][. . . gr]eat and it is a wonder. But they are not able [7][. . .] Your [wonder]s and they are not able to know all [8][. . . retu]rns to its dust. I am a rebellious man and defiled [9][. . .] the guilt of wickedness. And I, in the times of wrath [10][. . .] raised up in the face of my agonies, and guarding myself [11][. . . You] made me [kno]w these things. For there is hope for man [12][. . . You] abhor. I, a vessel of clay, depend [13][. . .] my God. I know that [14]Your command is true [. . . You do not go] back [on Your word.] I, in my appointed time, take hold of [15][Your] covenan[t . . .] in my office You have appointed me. For [16][. . .] man, and You restore him; and for what [. . .] [17][. . .] vessel [. . .] You are mighty and [. . .] [18][. . .] in [. . .] without hop[e . . .] [19][. . .] I am a vessel of [clay . . .] [20–21][. . .] which [. . .] [22][. . . ev]ening and morning with [. . .] [23][. . .] man and from [. . .]

[24][. . .] we shall rejoice [. . .] they watch, and upon their courses [. . .] [25]noblemen [. . .] not [. . .] You rebuke every adversary who ruins and [. . .] [26]mine, from that time I established [. . .] and You have uncovered my ear. For [. . .] [27]he shall not enter, for [. . .] the men of the covenant were deceived by them. And [they] shall go [. . .] [28]like my frame and [. . .] before You. I have feared Your judgment [. . .] [29][. . .] Your [. . .] Who shall stand blameless in Your judgment? And what [then is man . . .] [30][. . .] I in the judgment. The one who returns to his dust, what [. . .] [31][. . .] You have opened my heart to Your understanding,

and You open [my] e[ars . . .] [32]leaning upon Your goodness. But my heart groans [. . .] [33][. . .] and my heart melts as wax because of transgression and sin.

Hymn 33. A community hymn of blessing for God who sustains everything.

[34][. . .] Blessed are You, O God of knowledge, because You have determined [. . .] [35][. . .] and this happened to Your servant for Your sake. For I know [36][. . .] Your [. . .] I hope with all my being, and Your name I bless continuously. [37][. . .] Your [. . .] do not forsake me in times of [38][. . .] and Your glory and [Your] go[od . . .] [39][. . .] upon [. . .] **Col. 23** [2]Your light, and You set the lumi[naries . . .] [3]Your light without cea[sing . . .] [4]For with You is light for [. . .] [5]and You open the ear of dust [. . .] [6]evil plan which [. . .] and You establish it in the ea[rs of] [7]Your servant forever [. . .] the [re]ports of Your wonder to shine out [8]before the eyes of all that hear [You . . .] by Your strong right hand, to lead [. . .] [9]by Your mighty power [. . .] for Your name, and he magnified himself by [Your] glor[y]. [10]Do not withdraw Your hand [. . . in order] that he may become one who holds fast to Your covenant, [11]and stands before You [. . .]

You have opened [a foun]tain in the mouth of Your servant, and on his tongue [12]You engraved with a measuring line [. . . to] declare to the human vessel his lack of understanding, and as a interpreter in these things [13]to dust like myself. And You open a foun[tain] to reprove the vessel of clay of his way, and the guilt of one born [14]of a woman according to his works; that he might open a fo[untain] of Your truth for the vessel whom You have sustained with Your strength, [15]to [raise up] according to Your truth the herald of good news, [to recount] Your goodness, bringing good news to the humble in accordance with the abundance of Your compassion, [16][to satis]fy from the fountain of kn[owledge all the trou]bled of spirit and those who mourn for eternal rejoicing. [17][And You opened the mouth of Your servant . . .] [18–20][. . .] [21][. . .] Your spoil [. . .] [22][. . .] Your land and among the sons of gods and the sons of [. . .] [23][. . .] Your [. . .] and to declare all Your glory.

As for me, what am I? For from dust I was taken and [to dust I return . . .] [24][. . . for] Your [gl]ory You have done all these things. According to the abundance of Your mercy appoint a guard over Your righteousness [25][. . .] continually until the deliverance, and mediators of knowledge for my every step, and reprovers of truth [26][. . .] For what is dust in [. . .] are they not [. . .] ashes in their hand? But You [27][. . . vessel of] clay, and [. . .] Your will; and by the sons (?) You test me [28][. . .] and for You

[. . .] for my words. Over the dust You have spread out [Your holy] spirit [29][. . .] in the slime [. . . the so]ns of gods, to unite with the sons of heaven [30][. . . fo]rever and the darkness has no response. For [31][. . .] and light You have revealed, but not to return [32][. . .] Your [ho]ly [spirit] You have spread out, atoning for guilt [33][. . .] with Your hosts, and those who walk [34][. . .] before You, for they are determined in Your truth. [35][. . .] You have wonderfully done these things for Your glory, and from righteousness [36][. . .] injustice of an abhorred vessel [37][. . .] abhorred vessel [. . .] **Col. 24** [5][. . .] [6][. . .] a vessel of flesh [7][. . .] Who shall challenge [8]My judgment [. . .] to the angels of [9][. . .] and the mysteries of transgression, changing [10]flesh to [. . . the ear]th, and there shall soar about in it all [11]the angels of the hea[vens . . .] with cords of the spirit. You have humbled [12]the heavenly beings from the place of [Your holiness; they will not serve] You in the dwelling of Your glory.

And You, [13]O man, upon the [. . . like a bir]d bound until the time of Your favor, [14]not sending [. . .] heights of power and the abundance of flesh to condemn [15]at the time of [Your wrath . . . wondro]usly, to determine in the council of Your people [16][. . .] bastards, all [. . .] [17][. . .] justice and [. . .] [18][the one abh]orred to the pit at the time of his punishment [. . .] [19][. . .] every adversary and destroyer [. . .] [20][. . .] in their wickedness, sending them away, a nation [. . .] [21][. . .] the arrogant man with those who increase unfaithfulness and o[ppression . . .] [22][. . .] many in the flesh (?) for all the spirits of [. . .] [23][. . .] they will be condemned during their lives [. . .] ungodly [24][. . .] and with judgments [25][. . .] bastards to condemn the flesh [26][. . .] their spirit to save [27][. . .] the wonder of Your mysteries You have revealed [28][. . .] to the flesh. I know [29]for [. . .] iniquity at the time of [30]all [. . .] and for every one that gazes [31][. . .] and it is not hidden [32][. . .] You have served more than the children of [33]God [. . . the] unjust acts of the peoples, [34]to strengthen them [. . . to make] guilt great [35]in their inheritance [. . .] You have [. . .] forsaken them into the hand of [36]all who se[ek their life . . .] [37][. . .] [38]over [. . .]

Col. 25 [3][. . .] just [judgme]nt [. . .] [4][. . .] he dispersed them from the position of [. . .] [5][. . .] with the assembly of Your holy ones when [You] wondrously [. . .] [6][f]orever. And the spirits of wickedness shall dwell [. . .] [7][. . .] shall no longer be, and You will destroy the place of wi[ckedness, to cast lots for] all [8]spirits of injustice who are devastated for mourning [. . .] [9]and shut up for eternal generations. When wickedness has arisen to [. . .] [10]great, I will increase them for destruction, and against all Your works [. . .] [11]Your mercy, and to know all things by Your glory and to [. . .] [12]the judgment of Your truth. You have opened the ear of the flesh and [. . . for hu]mankind in [the] deliberation of [13]Your heart, and You have made the time of testimony known to fl[esh . . .] You will judge in the heights [14]and the inhabitants of the land upon the land, and also [in Sheol below You will judge, and] among the inhabitants of [15]darkness You will contend so as to just[ify] the just and con[demn the wicked,] for there is none ap[art from You,] [16]and not to separate [. . .] blessing [. . .] [17]to [. . .]

[25]not [. . . their wickedness in the wisdom of Your glory,] and [they will] no[t recognize . . . all] [26]the deeds of [Your righteousness for iniquity . . . he]aven and in the council of the hol[y ones] [27]they will be exal[ted . . .] [28]council and [. . .] [29]those who serve [. . .] [30]and they recognize them [. . . they will sing out] [31]and praise [. . . without ceasing. I am a vessel of clay,] according to my knowledge [32]I recounted in the ass[embly of Your holy ones, ascribing greatness and wonder to the God of . . . For You are the] God of [33]knowledge, with a [loud] voice [from dawn to . . .]

Hymn 34. According to the structure that many scholars have accepted for the Thanksgiving Hymns*—true Teacher hymns in the center to which the community added on either side additional hymns written in the same style—this would be a community hymn. However, the opening lines have caused some to question this judgment. These lines—aptly called the "Self-Glorification Hymn"—appear to reflect a personal experience, one that has brought the suggestion that the speaker styled himself as the Messiah. Another version of this hymn, originally published as a version of the* War Scroll *(text 11, 4Q491 Manuscript C), adds a clear note of suffering. As a result, some scholars have suggested that this hymn is evidence that some ancient Jews were expecting a suffering messiah before the time of Jesus. If, on the other hand, this is a community experience, it might find an echo in 4Q181 (text 30), in which the community is also described as being reckoned with the "gods as a holy congregation."*

[34]For the Instructor, a ps[alm, a song . . .] [35]For [. . . none of the] ancient kings [shall sit on it,] [36][. . .] [37][. . . no one besides me shall] be exalted. **Col. 26** (ll. 1–5 are supplied from **4Q431 Frag.1** and **4Q427 Frag. 7 Col. 1**) [1][. . . my abode is in the] holy [congregation.] W[ho is] despised like m[e? Who] [2]like me has refrained from evil and compares with [me? I have never been taught, but no teaching] [3]compares with my teaching. [For] I have dwelt [on high . . . in the heavens.] [4]Who is like me among the angels? [Who shall assault me when I open my mouth? Who]

[5]can endure [the utterance of] my lips? Who [with the tongue [6]will challenge me [and compare with my judgment? For I am beloved of the king, a companion to the holy ones, and no one shall] [7]come [against me . . . and to my glory no one compares. As for me, my office is among the angels,] [8]and my glory [with that of the sons of the king. Neither with pure gold shall I . . . for myself nor the renowned gold of Ophir . . .] [9]with me and [. . . shall not be reckoned for me.

Sing praise, O beloved ones, sing to the King of glory,] [10][re]joic[e in the congregation of God. Sing for joy in the tents of salvation, praise in the holy habitation.] [11]Exalt [together with the eternal hosts, ascribe greatness to our God and glory to our King. Sanctify] [12][His] n[ame with mighty speech, and with eminent oration lift up your voices together. At all times] [13]proc[laim with a heartfelt cry, exult with eternal joy. There shall be no ceasing to bow down] [14]together [in assembly. Bless the One who performs majestic wonders, and makes known the strength of His hand by sealing up] [15]mysteries and revealing hidden things, by r[aising up those who stumble and fall, by restoring the way of those who wait for knowledge,] [16][by brin]ging down the exalted appointments of the prou[d, forever, by confirming the mysteries of majesty, and by establishing the wonders of] [17][glory.]

[He who judges with the deadly wrath . . .] (**4Q427 Frag. 7 Cols. 1–2** provides ll. 18–25) [18][. . .] with mercy, justice and the abundance of compassion, supplication [19][. . .] compassion to those who frustrate His great goodness, and a source of [20][. . . wickedness ceases . . .] [21][. . . in]solence [has ceased, the combatant ceases with his indignation . . .] [22]deceit [has ended] and there is no ignorant perverseness. Light shines out and j[oy pours forth.] [23]Mourning [has ended] and grief flees. Peace is manifest, fear ceases, a fountain for [eternal] b[lessing] opens, [24]and healing for all the eternal ages. Iniquity is ended, agony ceases as there is no sickne[ss, injustice is taken away] [25][and guilt shall be no] [26]more.

[Proclaim] and s[ay, "God, who does wonders, is great." For He brings low the haughty of] [27]spirit so that none remains. He rai[ses the oppressed from the dust to the eternal height and to the clouds of the heavens] [28]and high in stature. With [the divine beings in the congregation of the *Yahad* . . . indeed for an] [29]eternal [destruction.] Those who fall to the ground He shall rai[se up without price, and everlasting strength accompanies their step;] [30]eternal joy is in t[heir] dwellings, [perpetual glory without ceasing forever and ever.

They shall say, "Blessed is God, who does mighty wonders] [31]{to make strength known} and who gre[atly manifests His wondrous strength, who does righteously in knowledge for all His creatures and goodness before them,] [32]that they might know the covenant of [His] mercy [and the abundance of His compassion for all the children of His truth. We have known You,] [33]O God of righteousness, and You have given [us] insight [into Your truth, O King of glory. For we have seen Your zeal] [34]in Your strong power, and [we] have recognized [Your judgments in abundant compassion and wonderful forgiveness.] [35]What is mere humankind in respect to these things? H[ow shall dust and ashes be reckoned to recount these things from age to age,] [36]to take a stand in place [before You, and to enter into the *Yahad* with the sons of heaven. There is no mediator] [37]to give an answer to [Your word . . . to You. For You have established us] [38]according to [Yo]ur wi[ll] and in [. . ."] (ll. 39–42 supplied from **4Q427 Frag. 7 Col. 2**) [39]strength {to answer You} <to hear Your wonders> [. . .] [40]we speak to You and not to a cham[pion (*or* intermedi[ary) . . . You have inclined] [41]an ear to the utterance of our lips.

Procl[aim, saying, "Blessed is the God of knowledge, who stretched out] [42]the heavens with His strength, and all their designs He [determines by] His might, the earth by [His] strength [. . ."]

—M.G.A.

13. Festival Prayers

1Q34, 1Q34bis, 4Q507–509

Although not all the Jewish holidays are mentioned in the portions that have survived, the present work is probably what remains of a collection of festival prayers that once covered the entire year. Only the Day of Atonement and the Day of the Firstfruits (also called Weeks; Num. 28:26) receive explicit mention. All the prayers end with a double "Amen," a regular feature of *Yahad* liturgical texts. The *Liturgy of Blessing and Cursing* (text 64) and the *Words of the Heavenly Lights* (text 127) are particularly comparable.

A notable feature of one of the Cave 4 copies, 4Q509, is that it is an *opisthograph*. This term denotes scrolls that are inscribed on both sides, an exceptional practice in ancient times, but one that is nevertheless the case for nearly a hundred of the Qumran writings. Opisthographs did not circulate in the normal market for books, to judge from practice in contemporary Egypt; rather, they were private copies prepared not by scribes, but by scholars for their own private study. The reverse of 4Q509 contains a copy of the *War Scroll* (text 11) and has been given its own reference number, 4Q496.

Lines 1–5 likely preserve the end of a prayer for the Day of Remembrance, the first day of the seventh month. Line 6 explicitly mentions the Day of Atonement.

1Q34, 1Q34bis Frags. 2 + 1 (with **4Q509 Frag. 3)** [0][. . . and its sorrow . . .] [1][. . .] the appointed time of [our] peace [. . . For You gave us gladness for our sorrow and assembled the outcasts] [2]for the time [of . . . and] our [scat]tered for the seaso[n of . . . Your loving-kindness for our assembly are as raindrops upon] [3]the earth at the ti[me of sowing . . . and] as the showers upon [the crops in the springtime . . . and we will recount Your wonders] [4]from generation to generation. Blessed is the Lord who gladdens u[s . . .] [5][. . .]

[6]Prayer for the Day of Atonement: Remem[ber, L]ord, [the] f[estival of Your mercies and the time of return . . .] [7][. . .]

This may be a prayer for the Day of Atonement.

Frag. 3 (with **4Q508 Frag. 1) Col. 1** [1][. . .] and [he] commanded [. . .] [2][. . .] in the lot of the righ[teo]us, and for the wicked, reprisal [3][. . .] in their bones shame for all flesh. But the righteous [4][. . . to] fatten oneself by the clouds of the heavens and fruit of the earth in order to distinguish [5][between the righ]teous and the wicked. And You have appointed the wicked as our [r]ansom and by the upright [6][You shall execute] destruction upon all of our oppressors. And as for us, we will praise Your name forever [7][and ever,] because for this purpose You created us. And this is ho[w we shall answer] You: Blessed [. . .] [8][. . .]

This may also be a prayer for the Day of Atonement.

Frag. 3 (with **4Q509 Frags. 97–98 Col. 1) Col. 2** [1][. . .] a grea[t] light for the [day]time [and a lesser light for the nighttime . . .] [2][. . .] and shall not transgress their statutes. And all of them [. . .] [3][. . .] and their dominion is over all the world. But the seed of ma[n] has not understood all that You have given him as an inheritance, neither have they known You, [4][do]ing Your word, so they have acted more wickedly than all the rest. They did not attend to Your great power and so You rejected them because You do not take pleasure [5]in injustice and the wicked one shall not be established before You. But in the time of Your goodwill You chose a people for Yourself, because You remembered Your covenant. [6]So You [established] them, setting them apart from all the peoples as holy to Yourself. And You renewed Your covenant for them in a vision of Your glory and words of [7]Your holy [spirit], by the works of Your hands and the writing of Your right hand, in order to declare to them the foundations of glory, and the eternal works. [8][. . .] for [th]em a faithful shepherd [. . .] wretched and p[oor . . .]

Frag. 1 of 4Q508 is translated at 1Q34bis Frag. 3 above.

Prayers for the Day of Remembrance, the first day of the seventh month (l. 1), and for the Day of Atonement (ll. 2–6).

4Q508 Frag. 2 [1][. . .] and You dwelt in our midst [. . .] [2][Prayer for the Day of Atonemen]t: Remember, Lord, the festival of Your mercies and the time of return [. . .] [3][. . .] for You established it for us as a festival of fasting, and ever[lasting] statute [. . .] [4][. . .] and You know the things hidden and revea[led . . .] [5][. . .] You [kn]ow our inclination [. . .] [6][. . . ou]r [rising] and our lying down [. . .]

This may be another prayer for the Day of Atonement.

Frag. 3 [1][. . .] we have done wickedly [. . .] [2][. . .] and because they were more in number. [Then] You established [Your covenant] for Noah [. . .] [3][. . . You]r faithfulness with [Is]aac and Jacob [. . .] [4][. . .] You remembered the ends of [. . .]

Prayer for the Day of the Firstfruits (Feast of Weeks).

Frag. 13 [1][. . . the L]ord, for in Your love [2][. . .] Your [. . .] in festivals of glory and to sanc[tify] [3][. . .] g[rain, and] fresh wine and fresh oil [4][. . .]

Given the reference in l. 3 to the offering of produce, this may be a prayer for the Raising of the Omer, an occasion on which agricultural produce was offered to God.

Frags. 22–23 [1][. . . t]hat our mercy is in [. . .] [2][. . . the abu]ndance of Your mercies [. . .] [3][. . . the pro]duce of our land as an offer[ing . . .]

In the scrolls the bifold "Amen, Amen" (1.7) is indicative of communal prayers.

4Q509 Col. 1 (Frags. 1–4) [1][. . .] our [. . .] [2][. . .] [3][. . . mi]re of the streets [. . .] [4][. . . before Yo]u we pour out [our] co[mplaint [. . .] for all [. . .] [5][. . .] our [. . .] in the time of the [visitation (?)

. . .] forever. And He has made us glad [. . .] [6][. . . Blessed is] the Lord, who has granted us understanding in [. . .] [7][. . . forever and] ever. Amen. Amen. [. . .]

[8][. . .] Moses. And You spoke to [him . . .] [9][. . .] which are upon [. . .] [10][. . . ju]st as You commanded him [. . .] [11][. . .] with You (*or* Your people?) [. . .] [12][. . .]

Frag. 3 is translated at 1Q34bis frags. 2 + 1 above.

This may be a prayer for the Day of Atonement.

Col. 2 (Frags. 5–7) [1][. . .] [2][. . .] our blood (?) in the time of [. . .] [3][. . .] our [. . .] to meet us as [. . .] [4]in [. . .] You know all [. . .] [5]You divided and announced [. . . a]ll the curses [. . .] [6][with] us just as You spoke [. . .] [7]Behold you lie down with [your] fa[thers (?) . . .] [8–15][. . .] [16][. . . and] in the deeps and in all [. . .] [17]For from eternity You have hated [. . .] [18][. . .] the only one before You [. . .] [19]in the Last Days [. . .] [20][. . .] [21][. . .] to be careful [. . .] [22][. . .]

This, also, may be a prayer for the Day of Atonement.

Col. 3 (Frags. 8–10i, 12i–13) [1][. . .] the work [. . .] [2–3][. . .][. . .] [4][. . . the produce of] our [lan]d as an offer[ing . . .] [5][. . .] at the beginning of [. . .] [6][. . . mu]ch [. . .] [7][. . .] and our poor [. . .] [8][. . . the d]ominion of [. . .] [9–20][. . .] [21][. . . so] that [. . .] [22][. . .] and You blessed [23][. . .] which [. . .] [24–29][. . .] [30][. . .] our compassion [. . .] [31–35][. . .] [36]the banished, wandering with no [one to return them . . .] [37]without strengthen, the fallen with no [one to raise them up . . .] [38]with no one to understand, the broken with no [one to mend them . . .] [39]in [their] iniquity, [and] there is no doctor [. . .] [40]comforting those who stumble in their transgressions [. . . You rem]ember [41]the torment and weeping and you are a companion to prisoner[s . . .]

Lines 24–28 contain the end of yet another prayer, as it seems, for the Day of Atonement. Lines 29–41 might form the beginning of a prayer for the Feast of Tabernacles.

Col. 4 (Frags. 10ii, 11, 12ii, 16) [24]You have shepherded (?) and [. . .] [25]with Your [. . .] [26]and Your angels [. . .] [27]and Your inheritance [. . . Blessed is] [28]the Lord [. . .]

[29][Pra]yer for the festival of [. . .] [30]Your [. . .] whi[ch . . .] [31][. . .] [32][. . .] all [. . .] [33][. . .] to [. . .] [34][. . .] [35][. . .] for all [their] pain [. . .] [36][. . .] comfort them because of their affliction [. . .] [37][. . .] the torment of our elders and [our] honorable [men . . .] [38][. . .] youths mock them [39][. . .] they have [n]ot considered that Y[ou] [40][. . .] our wisdom [. . .] [41][. . .] and we [. . .]

Frags. 97–98 col. 1 are incorporated in 1Q34bis frag. 3 col. 2 above.

Lines 2–3 likely preserve the end of the prayer for the Second Passover. Line 5 explicitly mentions the Day of the Firstfruits (i.e., the Feast of Weeks).

Frags. 131–132ii [2][. . .] Your [g]lory [. . .] [3][. . .] Amen. A[men. . . .] [4][. . .]

[5][Prayer for the day of the] firstfruits: Remember, O L[or]d, the festival of [6][. . .] and the freewill offerings of Your will which You commanded [7][. . . we shall] present before You the firstfruits of [our] labors [. . .] [8][. . .] upon the earth to be [. . .] [9][. . .]Your [. . .] for in the day of the [. . .] [10][. . .] You consecrated [. . .] [11]the offspring of [. . .] [12–14][. . .] [15]with [. . .] [16]hol[y . . .] [17]in all [. . .]

—M.G.A.

14. A Story About the Exodus

2Q21

A striking aspect of the more recently released Dead Sea Scrolls in particular (as compared to those that have been available for many years) is the prominence of writings about Moses—or even, as they claim, by Moses. Moses as the author of many works outside the Bible may seem surprising. In fact, very few, if any, of these new writings is likely to be older than the third century B.C.E., so they are centuries too young for their claims to be given serious consideration—by us, that is. Most ancient readers undoubtedly believed that these works were just what they claimed to be. This is the phenomenon that scholars know as *pseudepigraphy,* literally "false writing." Writing under the pseudonym of Moses or another biblical luminary was common among Second Temple Jews.

We do not understand this phenomenon completely. Perhaps most puzzling to modern sensibilities is the fact that the more savvy ancients knew it occurred and yet clearly distinguished pseudepigraphy from fraud. As distinct from a fraud, the author of a pseudepigraphic writing thought of himself as a disciple of the figure in whose name he wrote; thus he was utterly sincere in attaching his ideas to the master, unlike a fraud, who was motivated by greed, the desire for power, or other less lofty sentiments. The most obvious reason to write a work under the name of Moses, of course, would be the opportunity thereby to claim his authority for one's own ideas—which one would nevertheless be persuaded were truly those of Moses.

The present work takes as its setting the time of the Exodus and the wilderness wanderings. Because it is so fragmentary, we cannot really tell what points the author hoped to make. Whether this writing was a polemic grounding its views in Mosaic authority or simply a collection of interesting campfire stories about the most famous figure in Israel's history, we cannot say. Both types are well represented among the scrolls. This work seems particularly comparable to the *Words of Moses* or *A Moses Apocryphon* (texts 5 and 91).

Preserved portions begin with a list of Aaron's sons, the priests. These priests are apparently described in glowing terms. Then, as often in texts about the wilderness wanderings, Moses is depicted going outside the camp to pray.

Col. 1 [1][. . . Nadab and] Ab[i]hu, Elea[zar and Ithamar . . .] [2][to work] justice for you in truth, and to reprove with integri[t]y [. . .]

[4][Then Moses went out]side the camp and began to pray to the LORD. Falling [on his face before the LORD, . . .] [5][he said, "O LORD, my Go]d, how can I look upon You? How shall I li[ft] my face [to You? . . .] [6]so as to fa[shi]on one people through Your [mighty d]eeds [. . .]

—M.O.W.

15. The Last Words of Judah

3Q7

The first editor of this text, M. Baillet, published it under the title "An Apocryphon Mentioning the Angel of the Presence." He was otherwise able to make very little sense of the small fragments. It remained for J. T. Milik, working on the materials over a decade later, to realize with brilliant insight that several of the fragments could be read in line with a well-known Greek work, the *Testament of Judah*. The Greek *Testament of Judah* is just one portion of a much larger work, the *Testaments of the Twelve Patriarchs,* which was very popular in early Christian circles. Scholars have long suspected that at least some of those testaments were reworkings and translations of earlier Hebrew or Aramaic writings that had originated in Jewish circles. Milik's suggestion was one step toward confirming this scholarly suspicion. Numerous other writings found among the Qumran caches tend in this same direction, and the notion now seems irrefutable: most of the Christian testaments had Jewish forebears. The recognition of this does not preclude the fact that Christians very substantially rearranged and rewrote these earlier works. Probably the early Christians also inserted entire newly written sections into what they had inherited.

The discovery of these testamentary materials in the Qumran caves has thus opened new vistas of research into these early Christian texts. For a fuller discussion of the genre testament, see the introduction to the *Words of Levi* (text 39). Additional examples of testaments found in the caves include the *Last Words of Naphtali,* the *Last Words of Kohath,* and the *Vision of Amram* (texts 40, 137, and 138, respectively).

The *Apocryphon of Judah* (text 135) may also be an early source for the Christian *Testament of Judah.* If so, then both the Hebrew text before us and that Aramaic work are ancestral to the later Greek writing. Here, then, is a clear example of the complexity of the historical process of textual transmission.

Judah was the fourth of Jacob's twelve sons. This portion of the Testament of Judah *(25:1–2) concerns the blessings to come upon the sons of Jacob and their seed in the glorious Last Days. The Hebrew text here is not very different from the previously known Greek version.*

Frags. 6 + 5 + 3 (I and my brothers will be chiefs) [1][in Israe]l. Levi [shall be at the he]ad, [I shall be second, Joseph third, Benjamin] [2][fourth, Simeon fif]th, Is[sachar sixth, Reuben seventh, then all] the tribe[s.] [3][The LORD will bless Levi,] the angel of the presence [will bless me, the Glory will bless Simon, heaven Reuben, the ea]rth [Issachar, the sea] Zebul[un,] [4][the mountains Jose]ph, the sanctua[ry Benjamin . . .]

—M.O.W.

16. A List of Buried Treasure (The Copper Scroll)

3Q15

Many aspects of the Copper Scroll set it apart from the other Dead Sea Scrolls: its language is unlike the Hebrew of most of the other scrolls;

the medium upon which it is inscribed is neither animal skin nor papyrus, but copper; and, most important, it is the only scroll that contains a list of a treasure trove. The locations where the scroll's treasures are said to be hidden are scattered widely throughout Judea, so far as it is possible to identify them; but hiding places concentrate near the Temple Mount in Jerusalem, near Jericho, and in the wilderness near the site of Qumran.

The scroll's official editor, J. T. Milik, at first believed the Copper Scroll was an Essene product, but not in any sense an official work of the sect. Rather, it was a private effort, "highly individual in character and execution, perhaps the work of a crank." As such, it was not, of course, a historical record of actual treasures buried in antiquity. The "fabulous quantity" of precious metal, in particular, placed the scroll "firmly in the genre of folklore." Later, Milik's views took a decided shift. Since he had not "found a single valid indication" for attributing the work's composition to an Essene, Milik removed the Copper Scroll from the other Cave 3 discoveries and all the other Dead Sea Scrolls. He treated it as a completely extraneous document only coincidentally found among these materials. He also revised his dating of the text and now suggested that it was written about the year 100 C.E.—a generation after the destruction of Jerusalem. To justify these new claims, Milik underscored the fact that the two copper rolls found in Cave 3 were somewhat removed from the other manuscript finds made there. "This fact," Milik wrote, "points to two independent deposits, separated by a lapse in time."

But in the last few years a number of scholars—principally P. Kyle McCarter, Al Wolters, David Wilmot, and Judah Lefkovits—have turned their attention to this mysterious text. The result has been a startlingly different understanding of the Copper Scroll.

These scholars agree that Milik's attempt to remove the Copper Scroll from the context of the other Cave 3 finds was arbitrary and special pleading. Subsequent reexamination of the archaeological evidence has counted quite decisively against Milik's dating of the scroll; it rightly belongs to the period before 70 C.E. Further, these scholars agree that Milik's identification of the Copper Scroll as a literary work of folklore cannot be right. The Copper Scroll is clearly something else—but what? Wilmot has argued that the format of the Copper Scroll points to its classification as a "list." This is a well-recognized category of texts in antiquity.

Remarkably, the pattern of clauses in the Copper Scroll formulary finds precise parallels in Greek temple inventories from the Isle of Delos. These texts, most of which date between 180 and 90 B.C.E., were records kept by the priests of the island's temple of Apollo. They detail large numbers of votive objects brought to the temple, including crowns, jugs, earrings, and coins. The parallels of form and content between these archives and the Copper Scroll point not only to the scroll's identification as a business document, but more particularly to the recognition that the text is a genuine temple inventory, listing what are presumably, therefore, genuine treasures. Supporting this conclusion is the choice of medium upon which to record these treasures. Copper was used for the safekeeping of nonliterary records, Roman public laws, and even the private discharge papers of Roman military veterans. More to the point, copper and bronze were common media of choice for the archival records of temples in the Roman period. Thus the formal characteristics and choice of writing material for the Copper Scroll constitute converging lines of evidence: this scroll is a genuine administrative document of Herod's Temple in Jerusalem.

Unlike Milik and the other members of the official editorial team, John Allegro, the maverick among the editors, early on came to the conviction that the treasure inventoried in the Copper Scroll was real. He therefore mounted two treasure-hunting expeditions: one in December 1959–January 1960 and another in March–April 1960. He employed the very latest technology then available, including mine-detecting equipment on loan from the Signals Research and Development Establishment, Christchurch. But despite this technology, he came up empty-handed and was finally halted by government authorities as his team was about to begin digging on the esplanade of the sacred Dome of the Rock—an action that might have had very serious consequences, indeed.

What Allegro perhaps neglected to consider before launching these essentially fruitless treasure hunts was the motivating power of human greed. If you know that wealth is hidden somewhere and it is within your physical and political capacity to retrieve it, you do. At the time the Copper Scroll was written, the Romans certainly possessed that power, if they could somehow obtain the knowledge. On this point the tale of the recovery of the hidden treasure of Dacia's last king is instructive.

After the defeat and suicide of the Dacian king Decebalus (106 C.E.), the Romans seized his territories and began to search for his legendary treasure. A certain Bicilis, a friend of the king, knew its secret. Taken captive and subjected to torture by the Romans, he disclosed it, directing the Romans' attention to the river Saretia, which ran in front of the king's palace. Using captives who were subsequently slaughtered to preserve secrecy, Decebalus had diverted the river from its channel and buried his gold, silver and other valuables in its bed, then returned the river to its course. Knowing where to go, the Romans went and dug up the treasures.

Thus, by pressuring an informant, the Romans were able to retrieve the stores of hidden treasure. Indeed, the emperor Trajan's column even depicts the treasure being hauled away on donkeys. The question, then, is this: did the Romans also come to know the locations of the hidden treasure of Herod's Temple, portions of which are listed so laconically in the Copper Scroll?

According to Josephus, who was himself an eyewitness and participant in the war in Rome, the answer is yes. The Romans pursued a definite policy to retrieve treasure hoards that the citizens of Jerusalem had secreted during the siege. As always, the key to their recovery lay with the interrogation of prisoners. One such, Phineas, was an official treasurer of the Temple. The historian tells us that this man delivered up to the Romans "the tunics and girdles worn by the priests . . . along with a mass of cinnamon and cassia and a multitude of other spices. . . . Many other treasures also were delivered up by him, with numerous sacred ornaments" (*Jewish War* 6.390–391). Phineas led the Romans to hidden treasures from the Temple—perhaps including some that were listed in the Copper Scroll. A second passage of Josephus's *War* notes that as a result of the recovery and subsequent release of loot by the Romans, the standard of gold throughout Syria fell to half its previous value. The spoils of war were that enormous, the rape of Judea that complete.

The probability that significant portions of treasure could escape the Romans' search techniques is minimal. Just as they retrieved the treasure of Dacia, in all likelihood the Romans also retrieved the treasure of Jerusalem and its Temple—including the treasure of the Copper Scroll—in 70 C.E.

The first cache. The Valley of Achor is on the west or southwest of Jericho. The significance of the Greek letters (e.g., KEN) that follow this and several of the subsequent descriptions remains mysterious. It is impossible to specify the precise modern equivalents of talents, minas, and the other monetary units listed here, but the treasure would have totaled many millions of dollars.

Col. 1 [1]In the ruin that is in the Valley of Achor, under [2]the steps, with the entrance at the east a distance of forty [3]cubits: a strongbox of silver and its vessels—[4]seventeen talents by weight. KEN

The second cache.

[5]In the sepulcher, in the third course of stones: [6]one hundred ingots of gold.

The third cache.

In the big cistern that is in the courtyard [7]of the peristyle, at its bottom concealed by a sealing ring, [8]across from the upper opening: nine hundred talents of silver coins.

The fourth cache. Kohlit appears in the descriptions of several caches in the Copper Scroll (cf. caches twenty-two and sixty-five), but its identification remains uncertain, as does the name's precise pronunciation.

[9]In the mound of Kohlit: votive vessels—all of them flasks—and high-priestly garmenture. [10]All the votive offerings, and what comes from the seventh treasury, are [11]impure second tithe. The cache's opening is at the edge of the aqueduct, six [12]cubits to the north of the immersion pool. CHAG

The fifth cache. The reservoir's location is unknown.

[13]In the plastered Reservoir of Manos, at the descent to the left, [14]three cubits up from the bottom: silver coins [15]totaling forty talents.

The sixth cache.

Col. 2 [1]In the salt pit that is under the steps: [2]forty-one talents of silver coins. HN

The seventh cache.

[3]In the cave of the old Washer's Chamber, on the [4]third terrace: sixty-five ingots of gold. THE

The eighth cache. The location of the Courtyard of Matthias is unknown.

[5]In the burial chamber that is in the Courtyard of Matthias: wooden vessels, along with their inventory list.

The ninth cache.

[6]In a recess in the burial chamber: vessels and seventy talents of silver coins.

The tenth cache.

[7]In the cistern opposite the eastern gate (i.e., of the courtyard), [8]at a distance of nineteen cubits: in it are vessels.

The eleventh cache.

[9]And in the conduit of the cistern: ten talents of silver coins. DI

The twelfth cache. The cistern described here may be the large ancient cistern lying just beneath the First Wall of Jerusalem.

[10]In the cistern that is under the wall on the east, [11]at the crag of the bedrock: six jars of silver coins. [12]The cistern's entrance is under the big threshold.

The thirteenth cache.

[13]In the pool that is on the east of Kohlit, in the [14]northern corner, dig down four cubits: [15]twenty-two talents of silver coins.

The fourteenth cache.

Col. 3 [1]In the courtyard of [. . .], under the southern [2]corner, (dig down) nine cubits: votive vessels of silver and gold, [3]sprinkling basins, cups, bowls, [4]and pitchers, numbering six hundred and nine.

The fifteenth cache.

[5]Under the other corner—the eastern one—[6]dig down sixteen cubits: forty [7]talents of silver coins. TR

The sixteenth cache. It remains unknown whether Milham refers to a place or a structure.

[8]In the dry well that is in Milham, on its north: [9]votive vessels, priestly clothes. Its entrance [10]is under the western corner.

The seventeenth cache.

[11]In the grave that is in Milham on the [12]northeast, under the corpse, (dig down) three cubits: [13]thirteen talents of silver coins.

The eighteenth cache.

Col. 4 [1]In the b[ig] cistern [that is north of Ko]hlit, at the pillar [2]on its north: fourteen talents of silver coins. SK

The nineteenth cache.

[3]In the aqueduct that ru[ns from the po]ol, [4]fou[rt]een cubits from the entry, silver coins [5]totaling f[if]ty-five talents.

The twentieth cache. For the Valley of Achor, compare the first cache.

[6]Between the two boulders in the Valley of Achor, [7]right at the midpoint between them, dig down three [8]cubits: there, two cauldrons full of silver coins.

The twenty-first cache. The Wadi Atsla opens to the northwest of the Dead Sea, about two kilometers from the site of Qumran.

[9]In the red dry well on the edge of the Wadi Atsla: [10]silver coins totaling two hundred talents.

The twenty-second cache.

[11]In the eastern dry well on the north of Kohlit: [12]silver coins totaling seventy talents.

The twenty-third cache. Secacah appears in the Bible at Joshua 15:61, in a list of cities located in the wilderness of Judea. The modern identification is disputed, but many scholars think that Secacah was an ancient name for the site of Qumran.

[13]In the dam of the Secacah Valley, dig down [14]three (?) cubits: twelve talents of silver coins.

The twenty-fourth cache.

Col. 5 [1]At the head of the aqueduct [of the] [2]Secacah [Valley], on the north, under the [3]big [stone], dig down [4][thr]ee cub[its]: seven talents of silver coins.

The twenty-fifth cache. The Pool of Solomon is unidentified.

[5]In the fissure that is in Secacah, to the east of [6]the Pool of Solomon: vessels of [7]votive offerings, along with their inventory list.

The twenty-sixth cache.

[8]Above Solomon's Canal, [9]sixty cubits toward the large cairn, [10]dig down [11]three cubits: twenty-three talents of silver coins.

The twenty-seventh cache. "As you go from Jericho to Secacah" is the clearest geographical description in the Copper Scroll. *The reference is presumably to a well-known path.*

[12]In the grave that is in the Wadi Ha-Kepah [13]at the point of entry as you go from Jericho to Secacah, [14]dig down seven cubits: thirty-two talents of silver coins.

The twenty-eighth cache.

Col. 6 [1]In the cave of the pillar that has two [2]openings and faces east, [3]at the northern opening, dig down [4]three [cu]bits: there, an urn [5]in which is one scroll; under it, [6]forty-two talents of silver coins.

The twenty-ninth cache.

[7]In the cave at the corner [8]of the large cairn, the one that faces [9]east, dig down at the opening [10]nine cubits: twenty-one talents of silver coins.

The thirtieth cache. The Queen's Mausoleum is unidentified, but it may have been located near Jericho, where the Hasmonean kings and queens had done considerable building and lived part of the year.

[11]In the Queen's Mausoleum, on the [12]western side, dig down twelve [13]cubits: twenty-seven talents of silver coins.

The thirty-first cache. The "ford," or crossing, "of the high priest" may have been near Jericho.

[14]At the dam by the ford of the **Col. 7** [1]High Priest, dig down [2]on the west nine [cubi]ts: twenty-[two (?)] talents of silver coins.

The thirty-second cache.

[3]In the aqueduct of [. . .] [4]the [lar]ge northe[rn] reservoir, [5]on (all) four side[s from the top], [6]measure out twenty-[fo]ur cubits: [7]four hundred talents of silver coins.

The thirty-third cache. The priestly family of Hakkoz lived near Jericho. According to Ezra 8:33 and Nehemiah 10:6, they may have been in charge of the Temple treasury in the Second Temple period.

[8]In the cave that is next to the cold-chamb[er] belonging to [9]the family of Hakkoz, dig down six cubits: [10]six jars of silver coins.

The thirty-fourth cache. Dok is about two kilometers north of Jericho.

[11]At Dok, under the eastern corner of [12]the guardhouse, dig down seven cubits: [13]twenty-two talents of silver coins.

The thirty-fifth cache. Kozibah apparently designated that portion of the Wadi Qelt stretching between Ein Qelt and Jericho.

[14]At the mouth of the wellspring of Kozibah, [15]dig down three cubits to the row of stones: [16]eighty talents of silver coins; two talents of gold coins.

The thirty-sixth cache.

Col. 8 [1][In the aq]ueduct that is on the road east of the [2]storehou[se]: [3]votive vessels and ten books.

The thirty-seventh cache.

[4]In the outer gorge, at the stone in the [5]middle of the sheepfold: dig down seventeen [6]cubits beneath it: [7]seventeen talents of silver and gold coins.

The thirty-eighth cache. Qidron is the name of the wadi immediately to the east of Jerusalem.

[8]In the dam at the mouth of the gorge of the Wadi Qidron, [9]dig down three cubits: seven talents of silver coins.

The thirty-ninth cache. According to the Tales of the Patriarchs *22:14 (see text 4), the Valley of Shaveh was another name for Beth Hakerem, located to the southwest of Jerusalem. For Beth Hakerem, compare cache forty-nine below.*

[10]In the fallow field of the Valley of Shaveh that faces [11]southwest, in the burial chamber [12]facing north, dig down [13]twenty-four cubits: sixty-six talents of silver coins.

The fortieth cache.

[14]In the courtyard in the Valley of Shaveh, at the burial chamber that is in it, dig down [15]eleven cubits: [16]seventy talents of silver coins.

The forty-first cache. The Wadi Nataf lies between Herodian and Tekoa. A dovecote resembled a large birdhouse with numerous entrances, and many birds lived there simultaneously.

Col. 9 [1]At the dovecote that is at the edge of the Wadi Nataf, measure from the edge [2]thirteen cubits and dig down seven cubits: seven [3]talents of silver coins and four stater coins.

The forty-second cache.

[4]In the second estate, at the burial chamber that faces [5]east, dig down eight [6]and one-half cubits: twenty-three and one-half talents of silver coins.

The forty-third cache. Upper and Lower Beth Horon are some sixteen kilometers to the northwest of Jerusalem, separated from each other by a wadi.

[7]At the Vaults of Beth Horon, at the burial chamber facing [8]west, in the recess, dig down sixteen cubits: [9]twenty-two talents of silver coins.

The forty-fourth cache.

[10]At the Pass: silver coins totaling one mina, and consecrated Temple offering.

The forty-fifth cache.

[11]At the wellspring near the edge of the aqueduct, [12]on the east over against the wellspring, dig down seven [13]cubits: nine talents of silver coins.

The forty-sixth cache. Beth Tamar is apparently the equivalent of Baal Tamar, near Gibeah. Note that for this deposit the command to dig and the depth as well as the amount of treasure are missing, presumably because of scribal error.

[14]At the dry well north of the mouth of Beth [15]Tamar's gorge, at the outlet of the Pele Ravine: [16]all that is in it is consecrated Temple offering.

The forty-seventh cache. Nobah is mentioned in Numbers 32:42 and Judges 8:11 as a town near Kenath on the east side of the Jordan.

[17]At the dovecote that is in the Fortress of Nobah, at the bor[der] **Col. 10** [1]on the south, in the second roof-chamber—whose entrance descends [2]from above—: nine talents of silver coins.

The forty-eighth cache. The Great Wadi is an appellation that might reasonably be applied to any of several wadis, so no certain identification is possible.

[3]In the lime-plastered cistern that has conduits drawing water from the Great [4]Wadi, at the cistern's bottom: eleven talents of silver coins.

The forty-ninth cache. Beth Hakerem is on the south of Jerusalem, at the modern Kibbutz Ramat Rachel. No treasure has been found there by modern inhabitants.

[5]At the reservoir of Beth Hakerem, on the left [6]as you enter, (dig down) ten cubits: silver coins totaling [7]sixty-two talents.

The fiftieth cache. The Wadi Zered is mentioned several times in the Bible, but its location is disputed.

[8]At the tank of the Zered Gorge, at the western burial chamber—[9]a black stone is the opening—dig down two cubits: [10]three hundred talents of silver coins, [11]gold coins, and twenty vessels containing Temple penalty fees.

The fifty-first cache. Absalom's Monument stood in the ancient Royal Valley (today's Emeq Rephaim), some thirteen hundred feet to the south of Jerusalem.

[12]Under Absalom's Monument, on the western [13]side, dig down twelve cubits: [14]eighty talents of silver coins.

The fifty-second cache.

[15]At the outlet of the water of Siloam, and under [16]the trough: seventeen talents of silver coins.

The fifty-third cache.

[17]In the [Upp]er [Pool], **Col. 11** [1]in its four corners: votive vessels, and their inventory list is next to them.

The fifty-fourth cache. The location is apparently at the southeast corner of the Temple.

[2]Under the southern corner of the Stoa, [3]at Zadok's grave, under the column of the small portico: [4]ten votive vessels, and their inventory list is next to them.

The fifty-fifth cache. This cache and those that follow through cache sixty-one are—so far as they can be identified—in the upper part of the Qidron, in the vicinity of Gethsemane.

[5]At the Throne—the peak of the cliff facing west—[6]over against Zadok's Garden, under the great [7]closing-stone that is at the garden's edge: gold coins and consecrated offerings.

The fifty-sixth cache.

[8]At the grave that is under the Knife: forty-one talents of silver coins.

The fifty-seventh cache. The Qidron Valley was the traditional location for the burial of common people, as opposed to priests and Levites. See 2 Kings 23:6 and Jeremiah 26:23.

[9]At the grave of the common people—it is ritually pure—[10]in it: fourteen votive vessels, [11]and their inventory list is next to them.

The fifty-eighth cache.

[12]In the reservoir precinct, in the reservoir [13]on the left as you enter: [14]eleven votive vessels, [15]and their inventory list is next to them.

The fifty-ninth cache.

[16]At the entry to the court[yard] of the western mausoleum, [17](at) a stove-platform near the en[try]: nine hundred [talents] of silv[er coins]; **Col. 12** [1]five talents of gold coins; sixty talents of silver coins. Its entrance is on the west.

The sixtieth cache.

[2]Under the black stone: oil vessels.

The sixty-first cache.

Under the threshold [3]of the burial bench: forty-two talents of silver coins.

The sixty-second cache. Mount Gerizim, in Samaria, was the former site of the Samaritans' own temple to the God of Israel. Even after that temple had been destroyed about 100 B.C.E., the precinct remained holy.

[4]On Mount Gerizim, under the top step of the ditch: [5]one chest and all its vessels, and silver coins totaling sixty-one talents.

The sixty-third cache. The place name is unknown; indeed, it may be an error for Beth Shemesh, the city in the southwest famously associated with Samson.

[6]At the mouth of the fountain of Beth Shem: silver and gold [7]votive vessels, and silver coins. The sum total: six hundred talents.

The sixty-fourth cache.

[8]In the big pipe of the cistern, at the point where it joins the cistern: [9]a sum total, by weight, of seventy-one talents and twenty minas.

The sixty-fifth cache. The more detailed version of the Copper Scroll *described here has never been found.*

[10]In the dry well that is north of Kohlit, with an opening on the north [11]and graves by its mouth: a copy of this inventory list, [12]with explanations and measurements and full detail for each [13]and every hidden item.
—M.O.W.

17. Apocryphal Psalms

4Q88

4Q88 is a copy of the Book of Psalms, but in addition to psalms known from the Bible, it includes works new to us. Just prior to the apocryphal psalms translated below, this scroll contained an *Address to Zion,* which has been preserved virtually intact in another Dead Sea Scroll, *Apocryphal Psalms of David* (see text 151). Preceding the *Address* was Psalm 109. Thus, the order in 4Q88 was: Psalm 109, *Address to Zion, Psalm on the Last Days,* and *Address to Judah* (the latter two given below). This scroll, and several others like it such as the *Apocryphal Psalms of David,* suggest that the precise order and content of the book of Psalms were not yet fixed when the scrolls were written.

A psalm on the Last Days, celebrating the wondrous fruitfulness expected in that time.

Col. 9 [4][. . .] Then shall they extol [5]the name of the LORD, [fo]r He comes to judge [6]every wo[r]k, to make an end of the wicked [7]from upon the earth: Evil [men] shall no more [8]be found. The heavens [shall give] their dew, [9]no ev[il within] their [boun]ds; the earth [offer up] [10]fruits in season, its [pro]duce [11]never short; fruit trees, [12]their cr[op] in their vineyards, [13]their [spring]s never failing. The poor [14]shall eat, they who [fe]ar the LORD, be satisfied.

An address to Judah. The Address to Zion, *in text 151, is similarly addressed to a place.*

Col. 10 [5][. . .] So, let heaven and earth praise [6]as one, let all the twilight stars give praise! [7]Rejoice, O Judah, rejoice, [8]rejoice and be very glad! [9]Make your pilgrimages, fulfill your vows for Belial is [10]nowhere to be found. Lift your hand on high, [11]fortify your right hand: behold, enemies [12]have perished, all who work evil been scattered. [13]For You, O LORD, are etern[al,] [14]Your glory enduring foreve[r and ev]er.
—M.O.W.

18. A Reworking of Genesis and Exodus

4Q158

4Q158 is a variety of rewritten Bible, selecting portions from Genesis and Exodus and combining them with other biblical texts. The passages that are added often come from parallel passages in the book of Deuteronomy. Sometimes, in addition to combining biblical portions, the text adds words or whole paragraphs unknown from any version of the Bible that has survived antiquity. Just what are we to make of this exercise?

At various junctures the point seems to be biblical interpretation. For example, by juxtaposing Exodus 20 with Deuteronomy 5 in frags. 7–8, the author may have sought to clarify the confusing chronology surrounding the revelation at Sinai. Most casual readers of the Bible never notice the problems that emerge when attempting to piece together a *précis* of those events. Ancient scholars did notice, however; they observed that according to the biblical narratives, Moses went up the mountain to meet God at least seven times. He is only explicitly said to descend twice. How can these facts be rationalized, and why this marathon mountain climbing? Resolving details of this sort taxed the energies and ingenuity of ancient biblical interpreters. The problems of the Sinai episode finally drove early rabbis to assert, "There is neither early nor late in the Torah!" They meant that the narratives were just not in any particular order, and when chronology was the issue, one had to rearrange the material as logic dictated. Certain aspects of 4Q158 seem to represent this sort of problem solving.

On the other hand, the reasoning behind other textual combinations represented here is obscure. Accordingly, perhaps in some measure we are dealing with a "wild" text of the Bible. We know that such wild texts—that is, forms vastly divergent from the "standard" versions—existed for many authors in Greco-Roman antiquity; we have not previously known of such for the Bible. Few wild texts of classical authors survived, mainly because of the concerted textual criticism prosecuted by ancient scholars. A case in point: at the fabled library in Alexandria, Egypt, literary critics famed in their own day worked to uncover the true text of Homer, the closest thing the Greeks had to a Bible. They pored over all the variants and allowed inferior and wild copies to perish by neglect. They simply did not copy them. Yet even wild texts might preserve a true reading here and there. In that vein, it is instructive to observe that 4Q158 adds to the familiar text of Genesis 32:25 the phrase "He held him tight." This addition also appears in an early translation of the Bible into Aramaic known as *Targum Neofiti*. *Targum Neofiti* has survived only in an early medieval copy, but many of its traditions date centuries earlier. The fact that *Neofiti* agrees with our text in adding to Genesis suggests that this reading is not merely an explication unique to our author. It may originally have been part of the biblical text.

The reader should note that Emanuel Tov and other scholars have suggested that 4Q365 (text 84) is another copy of the present writing. If so, then the two would, of course, not be separate examples of the rewritten Bible phenomenon. They would simply be two copies of the same book. This theory is difficult to verify because the two copies do not overlap.

A combination of Genesis 32:24–32 and Exodus 4:27–28, with extrabiblical additions. The writer adds to Genesis 32:30, reporting the exact wording of the blessing Jacob received from his divine visitant. The writer also transforms what Genesis 32:32 reports as a tradition—one does not eat a certain portion of the thigh muscle— into a direct command from God. Lines 16–18 constitute an addition to Exodus 4:28, but the point is unclear.

Frags. 1–2 3[J]ac[ob] was left there [a]lone; and [a man] wrestled [with him until daybreak. When the man saw that he could not prevail against Jacob, he struck him on the hip socket; 4and Jacob's hip was put out of joint] as he wrestled with him. [Still,] he held him tight; then the man said, ["Let me go, for the day is breaking." But Jacob said, "I will not let you go,] 5[unless you bless] me." So he said to him, "What is your name?" And he replied, ["Jacob." Then the man said, "You shall no longer be called Jacob, but Israel, for you have striven] 6[with God and] humans, and have prevailed." J[a]cob then asked him, "Please [te]ll me [your name."] 7[But the man said, "Why is it that you ask my name?" And he bless]ed him [there], saying, "May the LO[RD] make you fruitful, [and multiply] you [. . . May He grant you] 8[know]ledge and insight. May he preserve you from all wrongdoing, and [. . .] 9until this day and forever more [. . ."] 10Then the man went on his way, having blessed Jacob there.

Subsequently [Jacob] ca[lled the place Penuel, saying, "I have seen God face to face, and yet my life is preserved."] 11The sun rose upon him as he passed Penue[l, limping because of his hip. And the LORD appeared to Jacob] 12on that day, and said, "You shall not eat [the thigh muscle that is on the hip socket." Therefore the Israelites do not eat the thigh muscle] 13that is on the hip socket to t[his day, because he struck Jacob on the hip socket at the thigh muscle.]

[The LORD said] 14to Aaron, "Go [into the wilderness] to meet [Moses." So he went, meeting him at the mountain of God, and kissed him. Moses told Aaron all] 15the LORD's words with which He had sent him, and all [the signs with which He had charged him . . . Moses told Aaron,] 16"The LORD [has spoken] to me, saying, 'When you have brought the [people] out [of Egypt . . .'] 17to go as slaves, and consider, they number thir[ty . . .] 18the LORD, God [. . .]

This portion is a variation of Exodus 24:4–6. The second half of Exodus 3:12 apparently occupies ll. 1–2. The focus of the extrabiblical addition in ll. 6–8 is God's covenant with the patriarchs.

Frag. 4 1[. . ."When you have brought] 2the people out of Egypt, you are to worsh[ip Me on this mountain." . . . So Moses built an altar at the foot of the mountain, and set up twelve pillars, corresponding] [3]to the number of the twelve tribes [of Israel . . .] [4]Then he offered a burnt offering upon the alta[r . . . Moses took half of the blood and put it] [5]in basins, and hal[f of the] blood he dashed against the [altar . . . And God said to Moses, " . . .] [6]that I revealed to Abraham and to Isaac* [and to Jacob . . . the covenant that I made] [7]with them to b[e] their God, both theirs and the [pe]ople's [. . .] [8][for]ever [. . .]

This portion contains Exodus 20:19–21, but not in the form familiar to most readers of the Bible. Instead, the text presents a much expanded version of these verses, previously known to scholars from the Samaritan Pentateuch. Most of the expansions come from Deuteronomy.

Frag. 6 [1][like us, and live? Approach and hear everything that the LORD our God says. Then you can tell us everything the LORD our God says] [2][to you, and we will listen and obey. But do n]ot let [God] speak to u[s, or we will die." Moses said to the people, "Do not fear; for God has come only to test you] [3][and t]o put the fear of [Him upon you so that you do not sin." Then the people stood at a distance, while Moses drew near to the thick darkness where] [4]God was.

And the LORD [spoke] to Moses, s[aying, "I have heard this people's words, which they have spoken to you; they are right in all that they have spoken. If only] [5]they had such a mind as this, to fear [Me and to keep all My commandments always, so that it might go well with them and with their children forever! Now, as you have heard] [6]My words, sa[y] to them, ['I will raise up for them a prophet like you from among their own people; I will put my words in the mouth of the prophet, who shall speak to them everything that I command. Anyone] [7]who does not heed the words [that the prophet shall speak in My name, I Myself will hold accountable.

But any prophet who presumes to speak in My name a word that I have not commanded] [8]him [to] speak, or who shall sp[eak in the name of other gods—that prophet shall die. Perhaps you will say to yourself, "How can we recognize a word that the LORD has not spoken?"] [9]If a [prophet] speaks [in the name of the LORD, but the thing does not take place or prove true, it is a not a word that the LORD has spoken. The prophet has spoken presumptuously; do not be frightened by it.' "]

*The scribe first wrote "Jacob," then erased it. Presumably he erased because he meant to write "Isaac." He forgot to complete his correction and did not write over his erasure. I have filled out the portion accordingly.

This portion combines Exodus 20:12–17, Deuteronomy 5:30–31, Exodus 20:22–26, and Exodus 21:1–10, with small extrabiblical additions. The first half of l. 5 is such an addition.

Frags. 7–8 [1](Honor) your [father] and your mother, [so that your days may be long in the land that the LORD your God is about to give you. You shall not murder. You shall not commit adultery. You shall not steal. You shall not bear] [2]false witness [against] your [neighbor.] You shall not covet [your] nei[ghbor's] wife, [male or female slave, ox, donkey, or anything that belongs to your neighbor.] [3]And the LORD said to Moses, "Go say to them, 'Return to [your tents.' But you, stand here by Me, and I will tell you all the commandments, the statutes] [4]and the ordinances that you shall teach them, so that they may do them in the land that [I am about to give them as a possession." . . .]

[5]So the people returned to their individual tents, but Moses remained before [the LORD, who said to him, "Thus shall you say to the Israelites,] [6]'You have seen for yourselves that I spoke with you from heaven. You are not to mak[e gods of silver alongside Me, nor make for yourselves gods of gold. You need make for Me only an altar of earth, and sacrifice] [7]on it your burnt offerings and offerings of well-being, your sheep [and oxen; in every place where I cause My name to be remembered I will come to you and bless you. But if] [8]you make for Me [an altar of stone,] do not build it of hewn stones; for by [using] a chisel [upon it you profane it. You are not to go up by steps to My altar, lest your nakedness be exposed] [9]on it.' "

This portion contains Exodus 21:32–22:13, with a few very minor deviations from the familiar biblical text.

* **Frags. 10–12** [1]thir[ty shekels] of sil[ver, and the ox must be stoned. If someone leaves a pit open, or digs a pit and fails to cover it, and an ox or a donkey falls into it, the owner] [2]of the pit must make resti[tution by payment to its owner, while keeping the dead animal. If someone's ox hurts the ox of another, so that it dies, then they shall sell the live ox and divide] [3][t]he price; [the dead animal they shall] also [divide.] But if it was kno[wn] th[at the ox was accustomed] to gore [previously, yet its owner has failed to restrain it, the owner must restore] [4][ox for ox, but keep the dead animal.]

When someone steals an ox or a sheep, and slaughters it or s[ells it, the thief shall pay five oxen for an ox, and four sheep for a sheep.] [5][If the thief is

*The numbering of the lines for this portion in *DJD* 5 does not accord with the lines of the actual manuscript. The numbers are corrected here.

found breaking in,] and is beaten to death, no bloodguilt is incurred; but if it happens after sunrise, bloodguilt is incurred. [The thief must make restoration; if he cannot, he shall be sold for the theft. Should] 6[the animal, whether ox] or donkey or sheep, be found alive in the thief's possession, the thief shall pay double. When someone allows [a field or vineyard] to be grazed over, [or lets livestock loose in someone else's field,] 7[he must make restitution from his own field, depending] on its produce. If he allowed the whole field to be grazed over, he must [repay] from the choicest of his own field or vineyard.

[If a fire breaks out and catches in thorns,] 8[so that the stacked grain or the standing grain or the field is burned up,] the one who started the fire shall make full restitution. When someone delivers to [a neighbor money or goods for safekeeping, and they are stolen from the neighbor's house, then the thief must pay double when caught.] 9[If the thief is never caught, then] they shall bring [the ow]ner of the house before God, to determine whether or not the owner had laid hands on [the neighbor's] good[s. In any case of disputed ownership involving ox, donkey, sheep,] 10[clothing, or any other loss,] wherein one party says, "This is mine," the case shall come before the LORD. [Whoever God condemns shall pay double to the other.] 11[When someone delivers to another a donkey,] ox, sheep, or any other animal for safekeeping, [and it dies or is injured or is carried off, but no one sees it, an oath before the LORD shall decide] 12[between the two of them whether one has stolen] the property of the [oth]er. The owner must accept the oath, and no rest[itution] shall [be made. But if] it was stolen, [restitution is to be made to its owner. If it was torn by animals,] 13[let it be brought as evidence; restitution shall not be made for the remains.] If some[one] borrows an animal [from] another [and it is injured or dies,] the owner [not being present, full restitution shall be made . . .]

This is an extrabiblical addition. The precise import is no longer detectable, but God is speaking in the first person, presumably to Abraham (cf. Gen. 15) or Jacob. The setting seems to be prior to the descent of Israel into Egypt.

Frag. 14 2[all the fl]esh and all the spirits 3[. . .] as a blessing for the land 4[. . .] the peoples [. . .] this; in the land of Egypt 5shall be desolation [. . .] I shall create in [. . . I shall rescue them from] the yoke of Egypt's power, and redeem them 6from their control. I shall make them My people forever [and ever . . . I shall bring them forth] from Egypt. The seed of 7your children I [shall settle in the] land safely for[ever . . . but Egypt shall I hurl into] the heart of the sea, into the fasts 8of the deep [. . .] where they shall dwell 9. [. . bo]rders [. . .]
—M.O.W.

19. Ordinances

4Q159, 4Q513–514

Ancient Jews were generally most anxious to obey God. Yet obedience entailed putting into practice all of the biblical laws and precepts, and that is where matters got sticky. The fact was, the Bible often left out important details that one needed to know in order to obey. For example, Exodus 30:13–14 stipulates that every man twenty years and older had to pay a half-shekel (equivalent to about two weeks' wages for a day laborer) to support the activities held at the tabernacle. But the biblical text is unclear: is this payment to be made every year (the actual practice at the time of Jesus, according to Matt. 17:24–27), or one time only? Differences of opinion on matters such as this could be seriously divisive. The present work in fact argues for the second method of payment, and thus apparently against prevailing practice. This work is a collection of legal ordinances whose author, by supplying the necessary details as a supplement to the biblical text, intended to help readers obey God. In that sense it is similar to a modern "statement of faith."

In addition to the ordinance on the half-shekel payment, remains of at least eight additional rulings are preserved. One concerns the man who has a discharge from his penis (perhaps gonorrhea) and the biblical commands about such a man found in Leviticus 15:13. The Bible says the man "shall count seven days for his cleansing; he shall wash his clothes and bathe his body in running water, and then be clean." Once again, important practical details are absent from the biblical statement. When is the man to wash? On the seventh day alone? On each day of the waiting period? What is the man's purity status while waiting, and is it the same throughout the seven days? This last point would affect whether the man could touch the pure food of the community. The present work tries to answer these questions by stipulating that the affected party must bathe on the first day and then he can eat. If a man does not wash on the first day, he is not allowed to eat. The fact that this ordinance is repeated more than once suggests a polemic against a competing interpretation in which the only washing required was on the seventh day.

We do not know which parties among the Jews held to which interpretation. Frankly, many readers may not consider it important to determine who held which views—such issues may appear nothing more than legal minutiae. But we should not be so quick to dismiss them. That these arguments strike many of us this way only brings home the vast chasm separating us from those who adhered to such principles. For them, these arguments were not about minutiae, but about how to obey God. Presumably God cared about what they did, and presumably there was a right way and a wrong way to do things. For the ancient adherents, discovering that right way was imperative, for otherwise they could not obey God. Thus, to care about the Bible was to care about the details, and this sort of text was not dry and dull, but the essence of passion and life.

Ordinance concerning atonement (Lev. 16:16, 21?).

4Q159 Frag. 1 Col. 2 [1][. . .] not .[. . .] for [. . .] [2][. . . Isra]el His co[mmandment]s and to atone for all the[ir] transgressions [. . .]

Ordinance concerning produce for the poor (Deut. 23:25–26).

[3][. . . and if] one makes from it a threshing floor or a winepress, whoever comes to the threshing flo[or or winepress . . .] [4]the Israelite who has nothing may eat of it and gather for himself but for [his] househ[old he shall not (?) gather . . . Whoever enters the grain of] [5]the field may himself eat but he may not take anything to his house so as to store it. [. . .]

Ordinance concerning the half-shekel for the sanctuary (Exod. 30:11–16).

[6][. . . concer]ning [the Ransom:] the money of the valuation which a man gives as ransom for his life shall be half [a shekel in accordance with the shekel of the sanctuary.] [7]He shall give it only o[nce] in his life. A shekel is twenty gerahs in accordance with [the shekel of the sanctuary.] [8]For the six hundr[e]d thousand, one hundred talents; for the third (i.e., three thousand), half a talent, [which is thirty minas; for the five hundred, five minas;] [9]and for the fifty, one half a mi[n]a, [which is twenty-]five shekels. The total [is six thousand thirty-five and one half of a] [10]mina. [. . . me]n for ten minas; [. . .] [11][. . . fi]ve shekels of silver are a tenth of a [mina . . .] [12][. . . the shekel is equivalent to twenty gerahs in accordance with the sheke]l of the sanctuary. A hal[f of a shekel is twelve meahs and two zuzim . . .]

Ordinance concerning the ephah and bath, two dry measures of uncertain modern equivalence (Ezek. 45:11).

[13][. . .] the ephah and the bath are the same measure, [ten tenths. As the ephah of grain is the bath of wine . . .] [14][And the seah is t]hree and [one-third] tenths [and the tithe of the ephah is a tenth.]

Ordinance concerning Israelite slaves (Lev. 25:47–55).

Frags. 2–4 [1]And if [. . . to] a stranger or to the offspring of the famil[y of a stranger . . .] [2]before Isra[el,] they shall [not] serve the Gentiles; with an [outstretched] a[rm and great judgments He brought them out from the land] [3]of Egypt and commanded them that an Israelite should not be sold as a slave.

Ordinance concerning the Council of Twelve (Deut. 17:8–13). The Council was to act as a judiciary.

And [. . . te]n laymen [4]and two priests. And they shall be judged before these twelve [. . . and for every] [5]matter in Israel concerning a capital offense, they shall be consulted and whoever rebels [. . .] [6]he who has acted with a high hand shall be put to death.

Ordinance concerning wearing clothing of the opposite sex (Deut. 22:5). Although not stated, the penalty for this crime, as an "abomination," would presumably have been death.

Let not men's garments be found on a woman. Every [. . . Let not a man] [7]be covered with the mantle of a woman, nor wear a woman's tunic, because this is an [ab]omination.

Ordinance concerning nonvirgin brides (Deut. 22:13–21). Note the meager punishment for a man's false accusation in comparison with the severe consequences for misbehavior by a woman.

[8]If a man brings an accusation against a virgin of Israel, if [it is at the time] he marries her, let him speak and they shall investigate her [9]trustworthiness. If he has not lied about her, she shall be put to death, but if he has testified f[alse]ly against her, he shall be fined two minas [10][and] he may [not] divorce her all of his life. Every [girl] who [. . .]

Ordinance concerning the half-shekel for the sanctuary (Exod. 30:11–16).

4Q513 Frags. 1–2 Col. 1 [2][the shekel is equivalent to twe]nty [gerahs] in accordance with the sheke[l of the sanctuary.]

A half of [3][a shekel is tw]elve [meahs] and [two] zuzi[m . . .] and also from them is uncleanness.

Ordinance concerning the dry measures of the ephah and bath (Ezek. 45:11).

[4][The ephah and the ba]th, from which is uncleanness, are the same measure, [ten tenths. As the ephah of] grain is the bath of wine. And the seah is [5][three] and one-third [te]nths, [from which is the unclea]nness. And the tithe of the ephah [6][is a tenth.]

Ordinance concerning the daughters of priests who marry foreigners (Lev. 19:8). They were prohibited from eating any of the sacrificial portions that their fathers received from Temple offerings and ordinarily shared with them and the entire family.

Frag. 2 Col. 2 [1]to add them to the [hol]y food, for [they are] unclean [. . .] [2]mistresses of foreigners and as for all the fornication which [. . . which] [3]he prov[ided] for himself, to feed them from all the offerings of the s[acred donations . . .] [4]and for [a]ngelic food and to make acceptable atonement with them for I[srael . . .] [5]their food is [. . . of] fornication, he has borne the sin for he has profaned al[l . . .] [6]they [. . .] guilt when they profaned [. . .]

Ordinance concerning a discharge from the penis, possibly gonorrhea (Lev. 15:13). Ordinary seminal discharges, such as would take place during intercourse, would entail only three days of uncleanness.

4Q514 Frag. 1 Col. 1 [1][. . .] woman [. . .] [2]no one may eat [. . .] for all the un[cl]ean [. . .] [3]to count for [himself seven days of wa]shing. And he shall bathe and wash on the d[a]y of [his] uncleanness [. . . And no man] [4]may eat who has not begun to be clean from his seminal (?) f[low. Nor may he eat] [5]in his primary uncleanness. And on the day of their [cl]eansing, all those who are unclean of days (i.e., unclean during the seven days) shall bathe [6]and wash in water and shall become clean.

Afterwards they may eat their bread according to the law of [p]urity. [7]No one may eat who is yet in his primary uncleanness, who has not begun to be clean from his seminal flow. [8]Indeed, no one who is yet in his primary uncleanness may eat. All of those who are [un]clean of days, on the day of [9]their pu[rification] they shall bathe and wash in water and they shall be clean. Afterwards they may eat their bread [10]according to the or[dinance. No] man [shall e]at or [dr]ink with any ma[n] who prepares [11][. . .] in [. . .]

—M.G.A.

20. An Account of the Story of Samuel

4Q160

Samuel, the son of Elkanah of the tribe of Ephraim, was one of the most prominent figures in the early history of Israel. He lived at the time when the age of the judges was giving way before the nascent kingdom of Israel. The Bible portrays Samuel's mother, Hannah, as a prophetess who determined while the boy was yet unborn that he should be a Nazirite. (A Nazirite was one who vowed not to touch wine or any product of the grape, could not cut his hair, and was forbidden to approach any dead body, even that of his own parent. By reason of these vows, he was especially holy.) When Samuel was very young, his mother attached him in service to the tabernacle at Shiloh. There he served under the judge Eli. When that tabernacle was overthrown by the Philistines, we read the last of the boy Samuel, and only encounter him again later in the Bible as an adult.

Like Eli, Samuel was designated a judge, and the book of 1 Samuel describes him moving in a circuit to preside at the early sanctuaries of Bethel, Gilgal, and Mizpeh. Samuel anointed Saul the first king of Israel, and later, when Saul proved disappointing (but while he still lived) Samuel anointed David as his successor—or, perhaps better, replacement. The last episode involving Samuel occurs some time after he has died. Saul, desperate before a battle with the Philistines and conscious of his abandonment by God, sought to know the outcome of the dawning conflict. He approached the witch at Endor, and she is said to have summoned Samuel's spirit from Sheol, only to have him pronounce Saul's doom.

The present scroll is an apocryphal narrative about Samuel. The first fragment is little more than a paraphrase of a section of 1 Samuel, but the other surviving portions have a different character. They portray Samuel speaking in the first person, narrating his own life story, and praying. As with many of the other scrolls from the caves, this work manifests no sectarian connections and may well have circulated widely among Second Temple Jews.

This fragment paraphrases 1 Samuel 3:14–17, which describes God's judgment upon the house of Eli because of unfaithfulness and his announcement of this judgment to the boy Samuel.

Frag. 1 [1][F]or I sw[ear to] the house of [Eli that the iniquity of Eli's house shall not be expiated by sacrifice] [2][or offe]ring [forever." And] Samuel heard the wo[rds of the LORD . . .] [3]And Samuel slept in Eli's presence, then arose and opened the do[ors of the house of the LORD . . . Yet Samuel] [4][was afraid] to relate the oracle to Eli. But Eli spoke to him, [calling, "Samuel, my son." Samuel answered, "Here I am." Eli said,] [5]["Please, te]ll me about God's vision; do not [hide it from me. May the LORD curse you] [6][and more also,] if you hide from me any[thing of all that He told you."] [7][So] Samuel [told him everything, hiding nothing from him . . .]

A prayer of Samuel on behalf of Israel. In ll. 2–3, the prayer alludes to Psalm 40:3.

Frags. 3–5 [1][. . . O LORD, please hear] Your servant. I have never yet held back until this time, for [2][. . .] O my God, [let] them be gathered to Your people! Be a help to them, and raise them up [3][from the pit of tumult! . . . Deliver their f]ee[t] from the miry bog, [and] establish for them a rock from of old! Surely they are Your praise [4][above all other na]tions. Let Your people find refuge [in Your house,] let [Your anoint]ed sanctify themselves [to You]. In the very fury of those who hate Your people shall Your glory gain strength; [5]in lands and seas [shall Your honor increase;] fear of You shall intensify beyond that of any [god, people,] or kingdom. Then shall all the peoples of Your lands know [surely] [6]it is You Who has created [them . . .] The multitudes shall understand surely this is Your people [. . . They are] [7]Your hol[y ones,] whom You have sanctified [. . .]

Samuel rehearses the story of his life, here describing the years he spent with Eli.

Frag. 7 [2]I lived with him from festival to festival, and joined myself to him from [my youth . . .] [3]I [never] sought to cultivate favor by means of wealth, money or bribery [. . .] [4][I preferred to serve] my Lord, and chose to sleep at the foot of [Eli's] bed [. . .]

—M.O.W.

21. Commentaries on Isaiah

4Q161–165

Fragments of five commentaries on the book of Isaiah were found among the Cave 4 remains. The ten fragments of the first text have been reconstructed to yield three columns of text and commentary.

4Q161 Col. 1 (Frag. 1) [1][. . .] God [. . .] [2][. . .] Israel is [. . .] [3][. . .] the men of his army and [. . .] [4][. . .] the priests, for he [. . .]

Col. 2 (Frags. 2–6) [1]["Even if your people, Israel, were as many as the grains of the sand by the sea, only a remnant would return; for destruction is assured, [2]righteous judgment is about to overflow, it is completely predetermined. The Lord GOD of Hosts is about to act within the whole land"] (10:22–23).

[3][This refers to . . .] for [. . .] the sons of [. . .] [4][. . .] his people. [As for the verse th]at says, "Even if [your people, Israel, were as many as the grains of the sand by the sea, [5]only a remnant would return; for] des[truction is as]sured, righ[teous judgment] is about to overflow," [this refers to] [6][. . . to de]struction in the da[y of slaugh]ter, and many shall per[ish . . .] [7][. . .] shall escape to [. . .] land in truth [. . .].

The verses that follow are taken as a prophecy of the "Leader of the Nation," a common expression in the scrolls for the Davidic messiah. The interpretation apparently predicts that God will soon overthrow Israel's enemies, as he once did Egypt.

[8]"Therefore, t[hus say]s the L[ord GOD of Hosts, Don't be afraid, my people] [9][liv]ing in Zio[n, of Assyria, of the r]od [he beats you with, of the staff he raises against you as Egypt did;] [10][for] very soon [now my anger will be spent, my wrath against] their [corruption]. Then [the] [11][LORD of Hosts] will st[ir up a Lash, as when Midian was defeated at the Cliff of Or]eb; [his] own S[taff He will raise over the sea] [12][as He did against Egypt. On that day his] burd[en] will drop [from your shoulder, his yoke] [13][from your neck!"] (10:24–27).

[This refers to . . .] [14][. . .] when they return from the "wilderness of the Ge[nti]les" (cf. Ezek 20:35) [. . .] [15][. . . the Staff is the] Leader of the Nation, and afterward he will re[mo]ve [the yoke] from [them] [16][. . .]

The verses that originally referred to the advance of the Assyrians on Jerusalem are here taken as a prophecy of the Messiah's progress to the holy city.

[17]"To Ayath he comes, passes on [to Migron], at Michma[sh] [18][leaves his gear, they make the] ford, stay the night at Geba. [Ramah] si[ckens, Gibeath–] [19][Shaul flees. Shout] aloud, little Gallim! Listen close[ly, Laish! Call out, Anathoth!] [20]Madmenah [bolts,] the [in]habitants of Gebim [ha]ve become refugees. One more [day and he will stand in Nob,] [21][waving] his hand at little Zion's mount, Jerusalem's hill" (10:28–32).

[22]This saying [refers to] the Last Days, coming [. . .] [23][the Leader of the Na]tion, when he marches inland from the Plain of Akko to fight against Phil[istia . . . the Leader of] [24][the Na]tion, for there is none like him in all the cities of [. . .] [25]up to the border of Jerusalem [. . .]

The interpreter describes the war against the Kittim, who in this context may be Greeks or Romans or simply a vague eschatological foe. Interestingly, the messianic Leader of the Nation seems not to play a role in the combat, at least in the portions that are preserved.

Col. 3 (Frags. 8–10) [1]["Right now, the Lord GOD of Hosts is pruning the treetops with a hook. The tal]lest of all [are h]e[wn down,] [2][the mightiest are laid low. The forest] thickets [will be cut down] with iron tools, the trees of Lebanon, for all their majesty, [3][will fall"] (10:33–34).

[This refers to the] Kittim, wh[o] will [fall] at the hand of Israel and the humble [4][of Judah, who will . . .] all the Gentiles, and the mighty will be shattered, and [their] co[urage] will dissolve. [5][. . . The "tallest] of all will be cut down" refers to the warriors of the Kit[tim,] [6][who . . . as for the verse that say]s, "[The] forest thickets will be cut down with iron tools," t[hey are] [7][. . .] for war against the Kittim. "The trees of Lebanon, for [all their majesty,] [8][will fall": they are the] Kittim, who will be p[ut] into the power of the nobles of [Israel . . .] [9][. . .] when he flees befo[re Is]rael [. . .] [10][. . .]

When the enemies are destroyed, the new David will hold sway over all the earth, although the interpreter is careful to say that the Messiah will decide nothing without conferring with the legitimate priesthood. The messianic passage from Isaiah also plays a role in 4Q285 (text 63).

[11]["A rod will grow from] Jesse's [stock], a sprout [will bloom] from his ro[ots]; upon him wi[ll rest] the sp[irit of] [12][the LORD: a spirit of wisd]om and insight, a spirit of good coun[sel and strength], a spirit of true

know[ledge] [13][and reverence for the LORD, he will delight in reverence for] the LORD. [He will not judge only] by what [his eyes] see, [14][he will not decide only by what his ears hear;] but he will rule [the weak by justice, and give decisions] [15][in integrity to the humble of the land. He will punish the land with the mace of his words, by his lips' breath alone] [16][he will slay the wicked. 'Justice' will be the sash around] his waist, 'Tr[uth' the sash around his hips"] (11:1–5).

[17][This saying refers to the Branch of] David, who will appear in the Las[t Days, . . .] [18][. . .] his [ene]mies; and God will support him with [a spirit of] strength [. . .] [19][. . . and God will give him] a glorious [th]rone, [a sacred] crown, and elegan[t] garments. [20][. . . He will put a scepter] in his hand, and he will rule over all the G[enti]les, even Magog [21][and his army . . . al]l the peoples his sword will control. As for the verse that says, "He will not [22][judge only by what his eyes see,] he will not decide only by what his ears hear," this means that [23][he will be advised by the Zadokite priests,] and as they instruct him, so shall he rule, and at their command [24][he shall render decisions; and always] one of the prominent priests shall go out with him, in whose hand shall be the garments of [. . .]

The second surviving Isaiah commentary consists of one large fragment containing portions of three columns. The interpreter apparently did not comment on every verse. The first portion is taken as a prediction of calamity and distress in the Last Days; the second focuses on the "Men of Mockery," that is, the Pharisees.

4Q162 Col. 1 [1][As for the verse that says, "I will remove its hedge so it can be devoured; I will break] down its fence so it can be trampled" (5:5) which [2][. . .] the passage means that he abandoned them [3][. . .] and the verse that says, "Let briar [4][and bramble come up . . ." (5:6) . . .] and the verse [5][that says . . .] the way of [6][. . .] their eyes. [7–10][. . . As for the verse that says, "Five acres of vineyard will produce only five gallons of wine; ten bushels of seed will yield only one of grain" (5:10),] **Col. 2** [1]the passage refers to the Last Days, when the land itself is condemned by sword and famine; so it shall be [2]at the time when the land is punished.

"Woe to those who get up early to hunt for liquor, who stay up late [3]to get drunk on wine, who have lyre, lute, drum, and pipe at their wine parties but [4]take no note of the LORD's work, who can't see the things He has made. Therefore my people are exiled without true knowledge, the masses go hungry, [5]the throngs are parched with thirst. Therefore the underworld has opened its throat wide, its mouth is gaping beyond measure; [6]all her fin-ery and her hubbub will go down there, and the clamor will merrily enter it!" (5:11–14).

These are the Men of Mockery [7]who are in Jerusalem. They are the ones "who have rejected the Law of the LORD, and the word of [8]Israel's Holy One they have cast off. For this reason He became very angry with His people, He stretched out His hand against them and struck them so that [9]the mountains shook and the corpses lay like garbage in the middle of the streets. Even so, His anger [10][has not receded, His hand is still stretched out" (5:24–25).] This is the company of the Men of Mockery who are in Jerusalem.

The third column contains portions of Isaiah 5:29–30. None of the interpretation has been preserved.

The third commentary, written on papyrus, is extremely fragmentary. Of the fifty-seven pieces that remain, most are too small for meaningful translation. Only a few of the others contain both text and interpretation. The references to "Babylon" and the "Gentiles" are particularly reminiscent of that vision of the Last Days that one reads in the War Scroll *literature (text 11).*

4Q163 Frag. 1 [2][. . .] he [. . .] [3][. . .] and He will destroy the way of [. . .] [4][. . . as it stands wr]itten concerning him in Jer[emiah . . .]

Frags. 4–7 [1]["And it shall be] when [the LORD] finishes [all his work on Mount Zion and Jerusalem, he will punish] [2][the heav]y [fruit] of the heart of the king of A[ssyria and the glory of his proud eyes, for he said, By the strength of my hand I have done this] [3][and by] my [wisdom; for I am wise, and have removed the boundaries of the peoples and plundered their treasures" (10:12–13).] [4]The passage refers to the destruction of Babylon [. . .] [5]laws of the Gentiles [. . .] [6]that many should become traitors [. . .] [7]Israel; and the verse that says, ["The number of trees left in the forest will be so few that a child could write them down" (10:19),] [8]this refers to the few remaining people [. . .]

[9][. . .] [10]"At that time, [the remnant of Israel and the refugees of] [11]Jacob's house [will no longer] rel[y on the one who hurts them, but shall rely on the LORD, the Holy One of] [12][Isra]el. Indeed, only a rem[nant will return, a remnant of Jacob, to God Almighty.] [13]For even if your people, O I[srael, were as many as the sand of the sea, only a remnant of it would return" (10:20–22).] [14]This passage is for the Last [Days . . .] [15]they will go into the [. . . and as for the verse that] [16]says, ["Even if your people, O Israel, were as many as the sand of the sea, only a remnant of it would return,"] [17]this refers to the fewness of [. . .]

Frags. 8–10 [1][. . .] against the k[in]g of Babylon [. . . "Even the pine trees] [2][are happy to see you fall,] and the cedars of Lebanon. Since [you died, no one has come up] [3][to cut them] down" (14:8). "The pines" and "the cedars [of Lebanon" are . . .] [4][. . .] and as for the verse that says, "Thi[s is what is planned] [5][against all] the earth, and this is the hand [outstretched against all the Gentiles;] [6][for the LOR]D of Hosts has made [His plan; who will contest it? His hand is stretched out;] [7][who can] make Him [with]draw it?" (14:26–27). This is [. . .] [8][as it stands writ]ten in the book of Zechariah [. . .]

Frag. 21 [1–2]["In a very little while, Lebanon will revert to a grove, and the grove will be] considered [underbrush"] (29:17). "Lebanon" is [. . .] [3][. . .] to "the grove," and they will return [. . .] [4][. . .] by the sword, just as [. . .] [5–6][. . .] the Teacher of [Righteousness . . .]

Frag. 23 Col. 2 [3]"[Fo]r so says the [LO]RD, the Holy One of [I]srael, By repentance and r[epose you will be saved;] [4][in qui]et trust is your power. But you did not agree, and y[ou said,] [5]No, let us flee on horseback. So you shall flee indeed! You said, Let us ride something swift. But [6]your pursuers will also be swift. If a thousand flee [a]t the threat of one, at the threat of [7]five you all will flee, until you are left like a pole on a mountaintop, [8]a flag on a hill. But the LORD is waiting to show you m[erc]y, truly He will rise up [9]to have mercy on you, for the LORD is a God of justice. How happy are all who wait for Him" (30:15–18).

[10]The meaning of this passage is for the Last Days and refers to the company of Flattery-S[eekers] [11]who are in Jerusalem [. . .] [12]in the Law and not [. . .] [13]heart, for to seek [. . .]

Frag. 22 ["Your teachers shall no longer be hidden, but your eyes will see your teachers, and your ears will hear someone behind you if you deviate to right or left, saying, This is the right way to walk in" (30:20–21).]

[1]This passage refers to [. . .] [2][. . .] who sought [. . .] [3][. . .] the Zadokite [priests . . .] [4][. . . as for the verse] that says, "The bread from [your soil will be rich" (30:23) . . .]

Frag. 25 ["The LORD will make His glorious voice heard, He will show the strength of His arm, with a wind of anger and consuming fiery flames, torrents and thunder and hail, for by the voice of the LORD Assyria will be defeated, with His staff He will break them. And it shall be, with every pass of His chastening rod that the LORD will lay on him will be heard the sound of drums and lyres; by brandishing that rod He will fight battles"] (30:30–32).

[1][This refers to . . .] the king of Babylon [. . .] [2][. . .] with drums and with ly[res . . .] [3][. . . "Torrents and] thunder" are weapons of war [. . .]

The following fragment states that at its founding an important component of the Yahad *was the priests.*

4Q164 ["I am putting kohl around your stones, I will make sapphires your foundation" (54:11)].

[1][. . .] all Israel like kohl on the eye. "I will make sap[phires your foundation." This passage means] [2][th]at they founded the party of the *Yahad* on the priests, and the pe[ople . . .] [3]the company of his chosen, like the sapphire among the stones [. . .]

["I will make of rubies] [4]all your posterns" (54:12a).

This refers to the twelve [priests . . .] [5]who make the Urim and the Thummim shine in judgment [. . . and there is nothing] [6]missing from them, like the sun with all its light.

"And all [your gates are shining gems"] (54:12b).

[7]This refers to the chiefs of the tribes of Israel [. . .] [8]his appointed lot, the offices of [. . .]

Only a few fragments from this manuscript remain, and only bits of interpretation with the text. The possible mention of the Teacher of Righteousness is the principal interest.

4Q165 Frags. 1–2 [2][. . .] and Jerusalem [. . .] And as for what is written, ["Like a shepherd he will graze his flock" (40:11)], [3]this refers to [the Teacher of Righteousness, who] has revealed the Law of righ[teousness.]

—E.M.C.

22. A Commentary on Hosea

4Q166–167

The surviving portion of this text, unlike the other commentaries, deals primarily with the fate of "the generation God punished," perhaps Israel before the Exile. It also refers to the "calendar controversy" reflected in many other Dead Sea Scrolls.

4Q166 Col. 1 [1–3][. . .] [4]and they were pleased [. . .] [5–6]they acted deviously [. . .]

[7]["So now I am going to block her passage] with thorns, her paths [8][she cannot find"] (2:6).

[This refers to . . . in madness] and blindness and confusion [9][. . .] and the time they turned traitor did not[10] [. . .] they are the generation [God] punished [11][. . .] from [. . .] [12][. . . to be] gathered in the times of wrath, for [13–14][. . .]

[15]["So she said, I'm going back to my fi]rst [husband], because [16][I was better off then than now."] (2:7).

[This refers to . . .] when the captives [of Israel] returned [17][. . .]

Col. 2 [1]["She was not aware that] it was I who had given her the grain, [the wine,] [2][the oil, and the silver that] I multiplied, and the gold they made [into Baal"] (2:8).

[This meaning is] [3]that [they ate] and were satisfied and forgot God who [gives them the blessings, because] they left behind his [4]commandments that He had sent them [through] [5]his servants, the prophets. Instead they listened to those who deceived them. They honored them [6]and revered them in their blindness as if they were gods.[7]

[8]"So I will again take away my grain in its time, my wine [in its season]. [9]I will withdraw my wool and my flax from covering [her nakedness.] [10]Now I am uncovering her infamy in front of her lo[vers. No one can] [11]rescue her from my power" (2:9–10).

[12]The passage means that He assailed them with famine and nakedness, so that they became a disgr[ace] [13]and a scandal in front of the Gentiles on whom they had relied, but who [14]could not save them from their punishment.

"I will put an end to all of her joy: [15][her] pil[grimages, new] moons, Sabbaths, and all her sacred days" (2:11).

This means that [16][. . .] of the testimony they will bring in on the Gentile sacred days, so that [all] [17][her joy] will be turned into mourning.

The rest of the column contains the text of 2:12, but none of the commentary is preserved.

The few surviving fragments of this portion contain more coded references than the preceding text. As noted in the Introduction, such codes apparently referred to actual historical events and personages, but the meanings of the codes are not always clear to modern scholars. The "Lion of Wrath" is elsewhere the name for Alexander Jannaeus (see A Commentary on Nahum, *text 23).*

4Q167 Frag. 2 [1]["He cannot heal yo]ur sore" (5:13).

This refers [to . . .] [2][. . .] the Lion of Wrath.

"For I am like a panther [to E]ph[rai]m, [a lion to the house of] [3][Judah"] (5:14).

[This refers t]o the last priest, who will stretch forth his hand to smite Ephraim [4][. . .]

[5]["I will go back to my place until] they admit guilt and seek my presence. When it goes badly [6][for them, they seek Me"] (5:15).

[This means that . . .] God [will tur]n his face fr[om them . . .] [7][. . .] and they did not listen [. . .]

Frags. 7–9 [1]["They, like Adam, b]roke the covenant" (6:7).

This means that [. . .] [2][. . .] they abandoned God and followed the laws of [. . .] them in all [. . .]

—E.M.C.

23. A Commentary on Nahum

4Q169

The *Commentary on Nahum* may well be the most important scroll of all for reconstructing the history behind the Dead Sea Scrolls. Unlike the usual enigmatic style of this genre of commentary (see the introduction to *A Commentary on Habakkuk*, text 2), it mentions one identifiable historical figure: Demetrius III Eukairos, the king of Seleucid Syria, who invaded the Holy Land in 88 B.C.E. The story behind this episode is indirectly retold in the commentary.

Alexander Jannaeus ruled over Israel as king and high priest from 103 to 76 B.C.E. Although he expanded the nation's territory to its greatest extent since the reign of Solomon nearly a millennium earlier, some groups deeply detested him for what they claimed was laxity in religious observance. The feeling was very mutual, and Jannaeus had no qualms about suppressing dissent in the most effective manner available: by executing or banishing the dissenters. It is apparent from the writings of Josephus that the Pharisees were leaders of the anti-Jannaeus faction, while Jannaeus was affiliated with the Sadducees and priestly groups. His affiliation with priestly groups, by the way, clearly shows that Jannaeus was not necessarily lax in religious matters.

Eventually the strife between Jannaeus and his enemies became so severe that the latter formed an alliance with Demetrius III of Syria, inviting him to invade Israel and depose the king. Demetrius duly—and, we may presume, eagerly—complied and put Jannaeus to flight in a battle near Shechem. At this point, however, many of the allies of the Pharisees, apparently unwilling to participate in reestablishing Gentile dominance over the Holy Land, deserted the cause and gave aid to Jannaeus and his allies. Demetrius accordingly withdrew his armies.

After reasserting his rule, Jannaeus turned wrathfully against those he considered traitors and banished many of the rebels; others he executed. The most notable of his acts of revenge, according to Josephus, was the crucifixion of eight hundred rebel leaders. He also killed their wives and children while they watched from their crosses.

Jannaeus's enemies had the last laugh. After his death, the Pharisaic faction came into its own, exercising almost unopposed authority through their influence on the king's widow, Queen Salome Alexandra. Now the tide turned, and the Pharisees instituted their own reign of terror against the opposition. It seems likely that the Teacher of Righteousness and his followers formed part of this opposition.

The original setting of the prophecy of Nahum was the imminent downfall of the Assyrian Empire and its capital Nineveh in 612 B.C.E., and it breathes a spirit of unbridled joy at the destruction of Israel's enemies. The writer of the commentary exploits this vengefulness in predicting the overthrow of a group called the "Flattery-Seekers"—clearly the Pharisees, who, at the time of the scroll's writing, must have been in power. The writer, then, belonged to a group that had opposed the Pharisees and, by implication, supported Jannaeus, here called the "Lion of Wrath." Scholars have been reluctant to admit that the *Yahad* may have admired a violent man like Jannaeus; but that this was indeed the case has been confirmed by the recent publication of another scroll manuscript, *In Praise of King Jonathan* (text 114).

The first part of Nahum describes the coming of the Almighty in wrath, a theme still relevant to the commentator. Like the original prophet, the writer believed God would judge the Gentiles.

Frags. 1–2 [1][. . . in storm and tempest He comes, and] clouds a[re the dust of his feet" (1:3b).

This means that . . .] [2]the [. . .] the skies of His heaven, and His earth that [. . .]

[3]"He rebukes the sea, and dries [it up" (1:4a).

The m]eaning of this passage: "the sea" is all the [. . . , and "drying them up" is] [4]to pass judgment on them and to wipe them off the face of [the earth.

"He dries up all the rivers" (1:4b).

This means . . .] [5a] with [all their ru]lers when their rule comes to an end.

[5]["Bashan and] Carmel [have withered;] even the flowers of Lebanon have withered" (1:4c).

[This means that . . .] [6]many will [. . .] in it the height of wickedness, because "Ba[shan" refers to . . . and . . . is called] [7]["Car]mel," and its rulers "Lebanon." "The flowers of Lebanon" are [. . .] [8][the men of their par]ty, and they will perish before [. . .] the chosen of [. . .] [9][all] the inhabitants of the world.

"Moun[tains shake before him, hills crumble;] [10]the land [heaves] because of him, and [the world] before him, with all who live in it. Who can resist his anger? And who can [11][survive] his fierce wrath?" (1:5–6).

[This means that . . .]

The invasion of Demetrius is treated almost incidentally, with the focus on Alexander Jannaeus, the Lion of Wrath, and his severe ways with his enemies.

Frags. 3–4 Col. 1 [1]["Where is the lions' den, the feeding place for the cubs?" (2:11a).

This refers to . . .] a dwelling for the wicked Gentiles.

Jerusalem is a veritable lions' den for the ancient commentator; Gentile lions seek to enter it, and Jewish lions come out of it. The contrast drawn below between the "kings of Greece" and the "rulers of the Kittim" confirms that Kittim is the code name for the Romans.

"Where the old lion goes, there is the lion's whelp [2][without fear" (2:11b).

The "old lion" is Deme]trius, king of Greece, who sought to come to Jerusalem through the counsel of the Flattery-Seekers; [3][but the city never fell into the] power of the kings of Greece from Antiochus until the appearance of the rulers of the Kittim; but afterwards it will be trampled [4][. . .]

"The lion catches enough for his cubs, and strangles prey for his mates" (2:12a).

[5][This refers to . . .] to the Lion of Wrath who would kill some of his nobles and the men of his party [6][. . .]

Although moderns usually consider crucifixion an abhorrent act, the commentator and his community wholly approved of this method of punishing God's enemies; they believed it was prescribed by the Bible (see Deut. 21:23).

[6][. . . "He fills] his cave [with prey], his den with game" (2:12b).

This refers to the Lion of Wrath [7][. . . ven]geance against the Flattery-Seekers, because he used to hang men alive, [8][as it was done] in Israel in former times, for to anyone hanging alive on the tree (Deut. 21:22), [the verse app]lies: "Behold, I am against [you,] [9]sa[ys the LORD of Hosts"] (2:13a).

It is clear that the ruthless "Flattery-Seekers" are the Pharisees, but it is not as clear what the code names "Ephraim" and "Manasseh" stand for. Sometimes Ephraim is associated with the Flattery-Seekers, as it is below; at other times, the writer is hopeful that some of Ephraim will come to see things aright. Manasseh may represent the secular followers of Jannaeus, that is, the aristocrats who have no sincere interest in religious controversy.

["I will burn with smoke you]r [horde], the sword will consume your lions, and [I] will annih[ilate] its [p]rey [from the land.] [10][And your messengers' voice shall] no l[onger be heard" (2:13b).

The meaning of the] passage: "your horde" are the troops of his army [. . .]; "its lions" are his [11]nobles [. . .]; "its prey" is the wealth that [the prie]sts of Jerusalem gathe[red], which [12]they will give t[o . . . E]phraim, Israel will be given to [. . .]. **Col. 2** [1]"His messengers" are his ambassadors, whose voice will no longer be heard among the Gentiles.

"Woe, you murdering city, all [lies] and full of [plun]der!" (3:1a).

[2]The meaning of the passage: this is the city of Ephraim, the Flattery-Seekers in the Last Days, who conduct themselves in deceit and lie[s.]

The "rule of the Flattery-Seekers" is portrayed here as fully equal to the tyrannical domination of the Assyrians of old. It is clear that from the wording of the commentary that the Flattery-Seekers are in power as the book is being written.

[3]"Prey is never absent; the sound of the whip, the sound of rumbling wheels, galloping horses, rattling chariots, rearing chargers, blades, [4]lashing spears, a mass of slain, a horde of corpses, no end of bodies; one trips over the bodies" (3:1b–3).

This refers to the rule of the Flattery-Seekers; [5]never absent from their company will be the sword of the Gentiles, captivity, looting, internal strife, exile for fear of enemies. A mass [6]of criminal carcasses will fall in their days, with no limit to the total of their slain—indeed, because of their criminal purpose they will stumble on the flesh of their corpses!

[7]"All because of the harlot's many fornications. Beautiful is she, a witch indeed, who betrays peoples through fornication, whole clans through sorcery" (3:4).

[8]This refers to the deceivers of Ephraim, who through their deceptive teaching, lying talk, and dishonest speech deceive many: [9]kings, princes, priests, native and resident foreigner. Cities and clans will pass away through

following their principles, nobles and rule[rs] [10]will perish through their [arrog]ant talk.

According to Josephus, Jannaeus had to relinquish power over some of his Transjordanian conquests to buy the neutrality of the Arabians. The reference to "cities of the East" being "stripped" may be to this strategy.

"See, I am against you, says the LORD of H[ost]s. You will strip off [11]your skirts over your face and show the Gentiles [your] nudity, the kingdoms your shame" (3:5).

This refers to [. . .] [12][. . .] the cities of the East, for "the skirts" are [. . .] **Col. 3** [1]the Gentiles in their filth [and in] their abhorrent [i]dols.

"I will throw your abominations at you, I will treat you with scorn, I will make you [2]repulsive, so that everyone who sees you will avoid you" (3:6–7a).

[3]This refers to the Flattery-Seekers. In the Last Time, their bad deeds will be made manifest to all Israel and [4]many will perceive their wrongdoing and reject them and be disgusted with them because of their criminal arrogance; and when the glory of Judah is made manifest, [5]the simple-hearted folk of Ephraim will withdraw from their company, abandon the ones who deceive them, and ally themselves to the [God of] Israel.

"They will say, [6]Nineveh is in ruins. Who will mourn for her? Where can I find people to comfort you?" (3:7b).

This refers to the Flattery-Seekers, [7]whose faction will pass away, and whose assembly will be disbanded. They will no longer deceive [the] congregation and the sim[ple-hearted] [8]will no longer support their party.

"Are you better than Am[on, who lived by] the streams?" (3:8a).

[9]The meaning of "Amon": they are Manasseh, and "the streams" are the nobles of Manasseh, the respectable of [. . .]

[10]"Water surrounds her, her army is the sea, the waters her walls" (3:8b).

[11]The meaning of the passage: they are the men of her army, the warriors for her battle.

The historical reference here is unclear. The "divisive group" may be some of the foreign mercenaries who supported Jannaeus in his struggle; Cush, Egypt, Put, and Libya are Gentile nations.

"Cush [and Egypt] are her [limitless] strength" (3:9a).

[12][The meaning is . . .

"Put and Libya are her allies" (3:9b).]

Col. 4 [1]The meaning of the passage: they are the wicked of [. . .], a divisive group who ally themselves to Manasseh.

"She too w[ent] into exile [a captive,] [2]her infants were smashed at the head of every street. They throw lots for her respectable citizens, all [her] n[ob]les [have been bound] [3]with chains" (3:10).

This refers to Manasseh in the Last Time, for his kingdom shall be brought low in Is[rael . . .] [4]his women, his infants, and his children shall go into captivity; his warriors and his nobles [shall fall] by the sword.

["You too shall drink] [5]and become dazed" (3:11a).

This refers to the wicked of [. . .] [6]whose cup shall come after Manasseh.

[. . ."You too will seek] [7]shelter in the city from the enemy" (3:11b).

This [refers to . . .] [8]their enemies in the city [. . .

"All your fortresses] [9]are fig trees with [their firstfruits . . ." (3:12).

This refers to . . .]

Frag. 5 [1]["Behold, your people are like wo]men [in your midst; the gates of your land are open to your enemies; fire consumes your gate bars" (3:13).]

[2][. . .] all the border of Isra[el] to the sea [. . .]

—E.M.C.

24. Commentaries on Psalms

4Q171, 4Q173, 1Q16

In the Qumran commentaries on the Psalter, the Teacher of Righteousness, the Wicked Priest, and the Man of the Lie are on center stage (see the Introduction for an initial discussion of these figures). The largest surviving fragments of 4Q171 preserve a running commentary on Psalm 37, which deals with the necessity of the righteous to keep faith in God despite the apparent successes of the wicked. God will ensure that both righteous and wicked get their due: for the righteous, a reward for their faithfulness; for the wicked, punishment.

The *Yahad* members and their leader, the Teacher of Righteousness, represent the righteous of the psalms, while their enemies, the Wicked Priest and the Man of the Lie, who have persecuted them, represent the wicked. The psalm and its attendant commentary are shot through with a passionate desire to see the injustices of the world put right, tempered with a recognition that patience is required for the suffering that is inevitable while waiting for God to act. These commentaries, then, have an eschatological fervor that the more historical commentaries, such as *A Commentary on Habakkuk* (text 2) and *A Commentary on Nahum* (text 23) only occasionally display.

The righteous, who belong to the sect, must endure suffering, but may expect that a final judgment will set all accounts right.

4Q171 Frags. 1–2 Col. 1 [12]["He will make your innocence shine like the light, and your justice like] noonday" (37:6).

[13][. . .] the will of [14][. . .] lunatics have chosen [15][. . .] those who love dissolution and lead astray [16][. . .] wickedness through the power of G[o]d.

[17]["Be si]lent before [the LORD and] wait for him, and do not be jealous of the successful man [18][who doe]s wicked deeds" (37:7).

[This refers] to the Man of the Lie who led many people astray with deceitful [19]statements, because they had chosen trivial matters but did not listen to the spokesman for true knowledge, so that **Col. 2** [1]they will perish by sword, famine, and pestilence.

"Renounce your anger and abandon your resentment, don't [2]yearn to do evil, because evildoers will be wiped out" (37:8–9a).

This refers to all who return [3]to the Law and do not hesitate to repent of their sin, because all who refuse [4]to repent of their faults will be wiped out.

"But those who trust in the LORD are the ones who will inherit the earth" (37:9b).

This refers [5]to the company of his chosen, those who do his will.

The sect's eschatological timetable allowed that there would be forty years from the time of their Teacher's death to the final showdown between Good and Evil.

"Very soon there will be no wicked man; [6]I look where he was, he's not there" (37:10).

This refers to all of the wicked at the end of [7]the forty years. When those years are completed, there will no longer be on the earth [8][any w]icked person.

"Then the meek will inherit the earth and enjoy all the abundance that peace brings" (37:11).

This refers to [9]the company of the poor who endure the time of error but are delivered from all the snares of [10]Belial. Afterwards they will enjoy all the [. . .] of the earth and grow fat on every luxury of [11]the flesh.

[12]"The wicked plots against the righteous and gnashes [his teeth against him. But the LO]RD laughs at him, for he knows [13]his day is coming" (37:12–13).

This refers to the cruel Israelites in the house of Judah who [14]plot to destroy those who obey the Law who are in the party of the *Yahad*. But God will not leave them [15]in their power.

Ephraim and Manasseh are already present as code names in the Commentary on Nahum. *They represent the religio-political factions that side with the sect's enemies. The reference to "the Priest" is obscure—is he the same as the Teacher of Righteousness or a different leader?*

"The wicked have drawn a sword, they have bent their bows, to strike down the poor and needy, [16]to slaughter those who live honestly. May their sword pierce themselves, may their bows break!" (37:14–15).

[17]This refers to the wicked of "Ephraim and Manasseh," who will try to attack [18]the Priest and the members of his party during the time of trial that is coming upon them. But God will save them [19]from their power and afterwards hand them over to the cruel Gentiles for judgment.

[20–21]"Better is the little the righteous man has than the great abundance of the wicked" (37:16).

[. . . This refers to] [22]the one who obeys the Law who does not [. . .] [23]for wicked things, for "the arm[s of the wicked will be broken, but supporting the righteous] [24]is the LO[RD]" (37:17).

["The LORD cares about the life of the pure; what belongs to them will last forever" (37:18).]

[This refers to those with whom] [25]He is pleased [. . .]

"Returning from the wilderness" may mean that some of the sect were in exile, or it could refer symbolically to those who have repented of their sins and joined the sect.

[26]"[They will] n[o]t be put to shame in [an evil time"] (37:19a).

[This refers to] **Col. 3** [1]the ones who return from the wilderness, who will live a thousand generations in virtue. To them and their descendants belongs all the heritage of [2]Adam forever.

"In a time of famine, they will hav[e pl]enty, but the wicked [3]will perish" (37:19b–20a).

This means that He will sustain them in famine during the time of e[rro]r, but many [4]will perish from famine and pestilence, all who did not go forth [. . .] to jo[in] [5]the company of His chosen.

"Those who love the LORD are as magnificent as rams" (37:20b).

This refers to [. . .] [5]who shall be leaders and princes, [like leaders of] [6]sheep among their flocks.

[7]"All shall vanish like smoke" (37:20c).

[This] refers to the w[icke]d princes who oppressed his holy people, [8]and who shall perish like the smoke of a bra[nd in the w]ind.

Control over the Temple Mount and the sacrifices made at the Temple was an important ambition of the Qumran group.

"The wicked borrow and do not repay; [9]but the righteous give generously, for those whom God blesses [will in]herit the earth, but those whom He curses [will be exte]rminated" (37:21–22).

[10]This refers to the company of the poor, w[ho will ge]t the possessions of all [. . . , who] [11]will inherit the lofty mount of Is[rael and] enjoy His holy place. ["Those whom He curses] [12]will be exterminated": these are the tyrants of the co[venant, the w]icked of Israel who will be exterminated and destroyed [13]forever.

[14]["A man's path is ordain]ed by the LOR[D]; he delights in all His ways. If he stu[mbles, he shall not] [15]fall, because the L[ORD holds his hand"] (37:23–24).

This refers to the priest, the Teacher of R[ighteousness, whom] [16]God [ch]ose to arise [and] ordained him to form for Him a company [. . .] [17][his w]ay He smoothed for the truth.

"I ha[ve been young], and now I am old, but I have not [seen a righteous man] [18]abandoned and his children begging food. [All the time] he is lending generously, and [his] chil[dren are blessed"] (37:25–26).

[19][This] refers to the Teacher of [Righteousness . . .]

Col. 4 [1]"[. . .] judg[ment, and will not forsake his devotees. For]ever they are protected. But the descendants of the w[icked will be exterminated"] (37:28).

[This refers to] the cruel [2][Israelites . . .] the Law.

"The righteo[us will inherit the earth and dwell for]ever on it" (37:29).

[This refers to . . .] for a thousand [generations].

[3]["The righteous man utters] wisdom, his tongue speaks [4][justice, in his heart is God's Law: that's why his steps are sure" (37:30–31).

This refers to] the truth that the [Teacher] spoke [5][. . .] he declared it to them. [6][. . .]

If "the righteous man" of the following section refers to the Teacher of Righteousness, it may imply that the Teacher was in danger from the Wicked Priest, but still alive, at the time of composition. The writer is confident that the Teacher will live through this time of trial. The mention of the "Law that he (the Teacher) sent to the Priest" is intriguing, and some have suggested that this "Law" may be A Sectarian Manifesto *(text 100) or the* Temple Scroll *(text 155).*

[7]"The wicked man observes the righteous man and seeks [to kill him. But the LO]RD [will not leave him in his power and will not co]ndemn him when he comes to trial" (37:32–33).

[8]This refers to the Wicked [Pri]est who ob[serv]es the Righ[teous Man and seeks] to kill him [. . .] and the Law [9]that he sent to him, but God

will not le[ave him] and will not [condemn him when] he comes to trial. But to the [wicked God will give] his just [de]serts, by putting him [10]into the power of the tyrant[s of] the Gentiles to do with him [what they want].

["Look to the L]ORD and obey his rules; then He will honor you so that you will inherit [11]the earth. You will [look on] while the wicked are exterminated" (37:34).

[This refers to . . .] who will see judgment passed on the wicked and with [the company of] [12]His chosen they will rejoice in a sure heritage [forever].

[13]["I once saw] a wicked man, cruel, and stretched [out like a stately tree. But] when I passed by [. . .], he was gone. I [looked for him] but he was [14][nowhere to be found"] (37:35–36).

[This refers to] the Man of the Lie, [who . . .] against God's ch[osen pe]ople [and sou]ght to put an end to [. . .] [15][. . .] judgment [. . .] he defiantly presumed [16][. . .]

["Take note of the pure, observe] the honest, [for there is a future for the ma]n of peace" (37:37).

This refers to [. . .] [17][. . .] of pea[ce].

"Sinners [18]perish as one, and the futu[re of the wicked will be cut short"] (37:38).

[This refers to . . .] they will perish and be exterminated [19]from the midst of the company of the *Yahad*.

"The [deliverance of the righteous is the LORD's work; He is their stronghold in time of trouble. The LORD helps them and] [20]rescues them and saves them from the wicked [and delivers them because they trusted in Him"] (37:39–40).

[This refers to . . .] [21–22]God will deliver them and save them from the power of the wi[cked . . .]

Since the commentary on Psalm 45 comes immediately after that on Psalm 37 it is evident that the writer did not attempt to comment on every verse of the Psalter.

[23]"To the choirmaster, on [Shoshan]im. [For the sons of Korah, a wisdom psalm, a song of love . . ."] (45:heading).

[This refers to . . . t]hey are the seven divisions of [24]the repentant of Is[rael . . .]

"My h[ear]t is [astir] with a good message: [25][I address my poem to the king"] (45:1a).

[This refers to . . . words spoken through the] holy [spi]rit, for [26][. . .] books of [. . .]

"My tongue is the pen of [27][an adept scribe"] (45:1b).

[This refers to] the Teacher of [Righteousness . . .] God [gave] by an eloquent tongue [. . .]

Frag. 13 [3]"God spoke [in his holiness, I will joyfully divide Shechem] [4][and the valley of Succ]oth I will measure. [Gilead] is mine, [Manasseh is mine, Ephraim is my chief fortress."] (60:6–7).

[5][This refers to Gile]ad and the half-tribe [of Manasseh . . .] [6]they shall be gathered [. . .]

4Q173 Frag. 1 [2]["... vain] for you [to get up early, stay up late, eat your meals in worry, for truly] [3][He gives His friends sleep"] (127:2).

[This refers to those] who seek [. . .] [4][. . . secr]et things of the Teacher of Righteousness [. . .] [5–6][the pr]iest for the ti[me] to come [. . .]

[7]["Now children are a possession from the LORD"] (127:3).

[This refers to] those who inherit the possessions [. . .]

A very fragmentary interpretation of Psalms was found in Cave 1. The few legible pieces speak, like the Commentary on Habakkuk *(text 2), of the "Kittim."*

1Q16 Frags. 3–7 [2][. . .] they had recognized [. . .] [3][. . .] "Kings of great armies flee, [flee away; even the housewife shares the spoil"] (68:12).

[This] refers to] [4][. . . the b]eauty of [. . .] [5][. . .] who will share [the spoil . . .]

Frag. 8 [2][. . . "In the midst maidens beating tambour]ines; in assemblies bless God" (68:25–26).

[3][This refers to . . .] the convocation to bless the Name [. . .]

Frags. 9–10 [1]["From Your temple overlooking Jerusalem, king]s [bring You] tribute" (68:29).

This refers to all the rul[ers of] [2][the Kittim . . .] before him in Jerusalem.

"You have rebuked [the swamp beast,] [3][that herd of bulls, the Gentile heifers; he tramples on bars of] silver" (68:30).

The "s[wamp] beast" refers to [4][. . . the K]ittim [. . .]

—E.M.C.

25. The Last Days: A Commentary on Selected Verses

4Q174

A few years ago many people were agitated about the dawning of a new millennium. Thoughts turned with new urgency to what that change might portend. Similarly, the author of this text thought that events on earth were moving toward a climax, and he wanted to know what was going to happen. He was concerned not just for himself, but also for the group he belonged to (apparently the *Yahad* mentioned in various texts above), which he called the "House of Judah." To find out what the future would bring, he turned to various passages in the Scriptures. For the most part, he considered portions of the Prophets, for among Second Temple Jews it was everywhere and by everyone agreed that prophecy meant predicting the future. Where better to find the answers, then?

Yet some of his selections might seem surprising. Why consult the Psalms, and why certain parts of the book of Genesis? The answer is that our author thought the men he believed wrote those parts of the Bible were prophets. David, to whom he doubtless attributed Psalms, was acknowledged to have been among the prophets (cf. text 151). Moses, also, author of Genesis, had been a prophet—indeed, the preeminent prophet in the history of Israel. Therefore, when David or Moses wrote in the future tense, it was not some indefinite expression of hope or vague musing; it was prophecy, and fair game for the interpretive methods that could crack open a verse and reveal its hidden meaning.

One verse led our author to another, mostly on the basis of analogy. Finding a given word used in one biblical portion, he would then turn to another verse where the same word was used. (How well he knew the Bible!) Comparing the verses, he could then extract more information than just one verse would give him, for he assumed that because of their similar usage the verses were describing the same future person, institution, or situation. This approach is essentially the classical technique of Protestant Christianity: "scripture interprets scripture." The type of rabbinic biblical interpretation known as *midrash* operated by similar methods. The rabbis employed one principle they called *gezerah shawah,* literally "similar injunction." This type of inference by analogy meant that when words of similar or identical meaning occurred in any two given parts of the Law, then both—no matter how different they might seem—would be of identical application.

Applying this sort of analysis, our author grouped verses that he believed spoke of the Last Days. He extracted predictions about his community's enemies. He also discovered that two future heroes should arise from his group's ranks: an inspired interpreter of the Bible, whom he called the "Interpreter of the Law," and a messianic deliverer, scion of Israel's greatest king, the "Shoot of David." He further teased out information about a future temple, the "Temple of Adam." The name derived from a pattern commonly seen in Israel's Prophets: the end shall be like the beginning. (Cf. Isaiah, for example: "The lion will lie down with the lamb.") Some scholars have seen in this temple a reference to the notion of community as temple. This is the idea that the author's group would somehow come to form, as it were, a temple; the apostle Paul speaks of Christians in just such terms in the book of Ephesians. But that notion does not seem to be intended here, though it is found in the scrolls (text 7).

The present text is clearly sectarian in language and concept and aligns with a number of the other biblical commentaries found among the scrolls. Note especially the commentaries on Isaiah, Habakkuk, and Psalms (texts 2, 21, and 24). Its method is different, of course. Rather than commenting on a single biblical book from beginning to end, this text comments on the Bible thematically. For another sectarian work taking the same tack, compare the *Coming of Melchizedek* (text 154).

Quotation and interpretation of Deuteronomy 33, Moses's final blessing upon the Israelites. What remains concerns the blessings of Levi, Benjamin, Zebulun, and Gad.

Col. 1 9["Of Levi he said: Give to Levi Your Thummim, and Your Urim to Your loyal one, whom You tested at Mass]ah, with whom You con[tes]ted at the waters of Meribah; who s[aid] 10[of his father and mother, 'I regard them not'; he ignored his kin, and did not] acknow[ledge his children.] For [they observed Your wo]rd, [and kept Your] covenant. 11[They teach Jacob Your ordinances, and Israel Your law; they place incense] before You, and whole burnt offerings on Your altar. 12[Bless his substance, O LORD, and accept the work of his hands; crush the loins of his adversaries, of those who hate him, so that they never] rise again" (Deut. 33:8–11).

13[. . . The] Urim and the Thummim belong to the man who 14[. . .] For he sai[d] 15[. . . the] land, because [. . .]

16[. . . "And of Benjamin he sa]id: The beloved of the LO[RD] 17[rests in safety—the High God surrounds him all day long—the beloved rests between his shoulders . . ."] (Deut. 33:12).

Col. 2 1And the glory [. . . i]t refers to the righte[ous] sacrifice [. . .] 2the goodness of the la[nd . . .]

[3]"And of Gad he sa[id: Blessed be the enlargement of Gad! Gad lives like a lion; he tears at arm and scalp. He chose the best for himself, for there the allotment] [4]of a commander [was reserved; he came at the head of the people, he executed the justice of the LORD, and His ordinances for Israel . . ."] (Deut. 33:20–21).

[5]concerning the captives, [. . .] the hidden [. . .] [6]to rescue [. . .] everything that He commanded us. They carried out the entire [. . .]

The author describes a time of trial for his community, the House of Judah, to be followed by a glorious era. This time of future glory shall witness heightened purity, triumph over the community's enemies, a new temple, an inspired interpreter of Scripture, and a messiah descended from David.

[12][. . .] who swallow up the offspring of [13][. . . en]raged against them in his zeal [14][. . .] This is the time when Belial shall open his mouth [15][. . . to bring] trials [a]gainst the House of Judah, cultivating animosity against them [16][. . .] and he shall seek with all his might to disperse them [17][. . . th]at he brought them to be.

[18][. . . the House of Ju]dah, but the God of I[sra]el sh[all] [19][be with them, as He said through the prophet: "And I will appoint a place for My people Israel and will plant them, so that they may live in their own place, and be disturbed no more; and] **Col. 3** [1][no] enemy [shall overtake them ag]ain, [nor] evildoer [afflict] them any [mo]re, as formerly, from the time that [2][I appointed judges] over My people Israel" (2 Sam. 7:10–11a). This "place" is the house that [they shall build for Him] in the Last Days, as it is written in the book of [3][Moses: "A temple of] the LORD are you to prepare with your hands; the LORD will reign forever and ever" (Exod. 15:17–18). This passage describes the temple that no [man with a] permanent [fleshly defect] shall enter, [4]nor Ammonite, Moabite, bastard, foreigner or alien, forevermore. Surely His holiness [5]shall be rev[eal]ed there; eternal glory shall ever be apparent there. Strangers shall not again defile it, as they formerly defiled [6]the Temp[le of I]srael through their sins. To that end He has commanded that they build Him a Temple of Adam (*or* Temple of Humankind), and that in it they sacrifice to Him [7]proper sacrifices.

As for what He said to David, "I [will give] you [rest] from all your enemies" (2 Sam. 7:11b), this passage means that He will give them rest from [al]l [8]the children of Belial, who cause them to stumble, seeking to destroy the[m by means of] their [wickedness]. They became party to the plan of Belial in order to cause the S[ons] of [9]Li[ght] to stumble. They plotted wicked schemes against them, [so that they might fall pr]ey to Belial through guilty error.

[10]"Moreover the LORD decl[ares] to you that He will make you a house," and that "I will raise up your offspring after you, and establish the throne of his kingdom [11][fore]ver. I will be a father to him, and he will be My son" (2 Sam. 7:11c, 12b, 13b–14a). This passage refers to the Shoot of David, who is to arise with [12]the Interpreter of the Law, and who will [arise] in Zi[on in the La]st Days, as it is written, "And I shall raise up the booth of David that is fallen" (Amos 9:11). This passage describes the fallen Branch of [13]David, [w]hom He shall raise up to deliver Israel.

The author finds scriptural mention of his community, then turns his mind to the final war against the Gentiles and the time of persecution awaiting the House of Judah.

[14]The interpretation of "Happy are those who do not follow the advice of the wicked" (Ps. 1:1a): The meaning is, [th]ey are those who turn aside from the path of [the wicked], [15]as it is written in the book of Isaiah the prophet in reference to the Last Days, "And it came to pass, while His hand was strong upon me, [that He warned me not to walk in the way of] [16]this people" (Isa. 8:11). These are they about whom it is written in the book of Ezekiel the prophet, namely, "They shall ne[ver again defile themselves with] [17]their idols" (Ezek. 37:23). They are the Sons of Zadok, and the m[e]n of the[i]r council who pu[rsue righ]teousness and follow them to join the *Yahad*.

[18]["Why] do the nations [con]spire, and the peoples plo[t in vain? The kings of the earth s]et themselves, [and the ru]lers take counsel together against the LORD and His [19][anointed" (Ps. 2:1). The m]eaning [is that the na]tions [shall set themselves] and con[spire vainly against] the chosen of Israel in the Last Days. **Col. 4** [1]That will be the time of persecution that is to co[me upon the House of J]udah, to the end of sealing up [the wicked in consuming fire and destroying all the children of] [2]Belial. Then shall be left behind a remnant of [chosen on]es, the pre[des]tined. They shall perform the whole of the Law, [as God commanded through] [3]Moses. This is the [time of whic]h it is written in the book of Daniel the prophet, ["The wicked] will act ever more wicked[ly and shall not understand.] [4a]But the righteous will [be purified, clea]nsed, and refined" (Dan. 12:10). So, the people who know God shall be steadfast. These are [the men of] [4]truth, [who shall instruct many] following the persecution that is to desc[end] upon them [in that time . . .] [5][. . .] in its descent [. . .] [6][ev]il, just as [. . .] to the wicked [. . .] [7][I]srael and Aaron [. . .] **Col. 5** [2]"Listen to the soun[d of my cry, my King and my God, for to You I lift my prayer. O LORD, in the morning You hear my voice" (Ps. 5:2–3a). The] [3]meaning concerns the Last

D[ays . . .] **Col. 6** [1][written in the book of Isa]iah the prop[het, "They shall not build and another inhabit; they shall not plant and another eat;] [2][for like the days of a tree] shall the days of My people be, [and] My ch[osen shall long enjoy the work of their hands. They shall] no[t labor in vain,] [3][or bear children for calam]ity; for [they shall be] offspring [blessed by the LORD" (Isa. 65:22–23). For] they are [. . .]
—M.O.W.

26. A Collection of Messianic Proof Texts

4Q175

When John Allegro first published this text in 1957, he gave it the title "4QTestimonia." By the name *testimonia* he referred to a theory that there circulated among ancient Jews, and even more so among early Christians, collections of passages selected from the Bible for use in disputation. These collections are known as *testimonia*. According to the theory, the collections were often of texts having messianic significance.

But why were these specific passages collected? What does their collocation mean? Many students of the text agree on the significance of the first three passages. They represent respectively the *Yahad*'s expectations for the coming of a prophet like Moses, a royal scion of David to lead in war, and a proper high priest. All three could be considered "messiahs" in the sense that each was to be "anointed" by God (the basic meaning of the Hebrew word *messiah*).

Most problematic is the case of the fourth quotation, from the nonbiblical work *Apocryphal Joshua* (see text 92). Scholars are divided on whether the portion refers to two or to three figures, and whom those figures represent. According to the Standard Model set out in the Introduction, the "cursed man, one belonging to Belial" refers to the Wicked Priest and therefore (according to which subdivision of the Standard Model one follows) either to Jonathan or Simon of the Maccabee family. The son or sons vary accordingly. But if we are correct in adjusting the time of the Teacher later by over fifty years, as we have suggested in the Introduction, then, of course, none of the solutions proposed by adherents of the Standard Model work. What then?

Note that there is no compelling reason to equate the "cursed man" with the Wicked Priest who persecuted the Teacher. He is certainly described in less negative tones than are his sons, whereas the Wicked Priest was public enemy number one for the group. Would they really have described someone else as even worse? The wording "a fowler's net to his people and a source of ruin for all his neighbors" accurately and (more or less) objectively describes Alexander Jannaeus (103–76 B.C.E.). He was a fowler's net to the Jews in that the nation was so divided during his reign that civil war continued for nearly a decade. Certainly Jannaeus was a source of ruin for his neighbors, as he incessantly attacked first one, then another in a series of wars. The text's description of the sons fits Jannaeus's sons Aristobulus and Hyrcanus II from a certain perspective: "they shall work blasphemy in the land, a great uncleanness among the children of Jacob. They shall pour out blood like water upon the bulwark of the daughter of Zion and within the city limits of Jerusalem." The last statement, in particular, is a reasonably straightforward description of what actually happened at the climax of the civil war that turned into war with Rome in the period 67–63 B.C.E. At the end, the Romans broke into the temple where Aristobulus's supporters were holed up and slaughtered many of them. Over twelve thousand Jews died in Jerusalem that day. If this explanation of the fourth passage is correct, then the present work fits into the historical period for the origin of the scrolls that we suggest in the Introduction.

These two passages refer to a prophet like Moses, who was expected to arise. Possibly the author did not collate here two passages from Deuteronomy, but rather quoted a single passage from a reworked Bible. Compare text 18 frag. 6 above.

Col. 1 [1]And the LORD* said to Moses, "I have heard the words of [2]this people, which they have spoken to you; they are right in all that they have spoken. [3]If only they had such a mind as this, to fear Me and to keep all [4]My commandments always, so that it might go well with them and with their children forever!" (Deut. 5:28–29).

[5]"I will raise up for them a prophet like you from among their own people; I will put My words [6]in his mouth, and he shall speak to them everything that I command. Anyone [7]who does not heed the words that the prophet shall speak in my name, I Myself [8]will hold accountable" (Deut. 18:18–19).

This quotation apparently foretells the coming of a royal messiah who would lead in war.

[9]"So he uttered his oracle, saying: 'The oracle of Balaam son of Beor, the oracle of the man [10]who sees clearly, the oracle of one who hears the words of God, and knows the knowledge of the Most High, who [11]sees the vision

*Apparently motivated by piety, the scribe did not write the divine name, but substituted four dots, one for each Hebrew letter. He did the same in l. 19.

of the Almighty, who falls down, but with his eye uncovered: I see him, but not now; [12]I behold him, but not near—a star shall come out of Jacob, and a scepter shall rise out of Israel; it shall crush [13]the borderlands of Moab, and the territory of all the Shethites' " (Num. 24:15–17).

Next the text quotes a portion of Scripture to foretell a future priestly figure. The Thummim and Urim were oracular stones that the high priest carried in a pouch on his breastplate.

[14]"And of Levi he said: Give to Levi Your Thummim, and Your Urim to Your loyal one, whom [15]You tested at Massah, with whom You contended at the waters of Meribah; who said of his father [16]and mother, 'I know them not'; he ignored his kin, and did not acknowledge his children. [17]For he observed Your word, and kept Your covenant. They shall cause Your ordinances to shine for Jacob, [18]Your law for Israel; they place incense before You, and whole burnt offerings on Your altar. [19]Bless his substance, O LORD, and accept the work of his hands; crush the loins of his adversaries, of those who hate him, [20]so that they do not rise again" (Deut. 33:8–11).

Last, the author quotes a portion from Joshua, adding its interpretation from an extrabiblical work, Apocryphal Joshua *(text 92). Clearly he thought these lines foretold the rise of several—perhaps three—wicked figures, but no suggestion for precisely whom he meant to describe has won a scholarly consensus.*

[21]When Joshua finished praying and offering psalms of praise, [22]he said, "Cursed be anyone who tries to rebuild this city! With the help of his firstborn [23]he shall lay its foundation, and with the aid of his youngest he shall set up its gates!" (Josh. 6:26). "Behold, one cursed man, one belonging to Belial, [24]is about to arise to be a fow[ler's n]et to his people and a source of ruin for all his neighbors. Then shall arise [25][so]ns [after him,] the two of them [to b]e instruments of wrongdoing. They shall rebuild [26][this city and s]et up for it a wall and towers, creating a stronghold of evil [27][and a great wickedness] in Israel, a thing of horror in Ephraim and Judah. [28][. . .] They shall [wo]rk blasphemy in the land, a great uncleanness among the children of [29][Jacob. They shall pour out blo]od like water upon the bulwark of the daughter of Zion and within the city limits of [30]Jerusalem" (*Apocryphal Joshua* frag. 22 col. 2).

—M.O.W.

27. A Commentary on Consoling Passages in Scripture

4Q176

Sometimes the words of Scripture needed little or no commentary; they just needed a little rearranging. If more of this commentary remained, no doubt we would find more explanatory comments from the compiler of these passages. Yet the proportion of comment to quotation in the fragments that survive shows that in general these verses from the Old Testament Prophets, all foretelling the future comfort of Israel, were allowed to speak for themselves.

If the following fragments belong at or near the beginning of the scroll itself, they seemed to have introduced the anthology with a commentary on Psalm 79:1–3: "The Gentiles have come into your possession; they have defiled your holy temple; they have made Jerusalem a heap of ruins. They have left the corpses of your servants as food for the birds of the air, the bodies of your devotees for the beasts of the earth. They have poured out their blood like water around Jerusalem, with no one to bury them." The scroll writer felt that the Israel of his day was much in need of the consoling and saving power of God. As in the time of the psalm, something had gone terribly wrong in the conduct of the worship in the sanctuary and priests had been killed.

Frags. 1–2 Col. 1 1So perform Your miracle and do good deeds among Your people and they will be [. . .] 2Your sanctuary, and so contend with kingdoms for the blood of [Your servants . . .] 3Jerusalem, and see the corpses of Your priests [. . .] 4with no one to bury them.

And from the book of Isaiah, words of comfort: [. . . "Comfort, comfort my people], 5says your God. Speak gently to Jerusalem, and pro[claim to her that] her [punishment is over,] for 6her sin is forgiven, that she has received from the LORD a double punishment for all her offenses. A voice cries: 7In the wilderness prepare the way of the LORD, make straight in [the desert] a highway for o[ur] God. Let every valley be filled, 8[every mountain and hi]ll be level, let every rugged place be a [pl]ain, [and the rocky areas a m]eadow. 9The [g]lory of the LORD [will be revealed]" (Isa. 40:1–5). "But you, Israel, are [my] serva[nt, J]ac[o]b [whom I] have chosen. 10[Seed of Abra]ham, my friend, whom I have sustained [from the ends of] the [ea]rth, and from its far reaches 11[I have summoned you, and said] to you, you are my servant; [I have chosen you and not rejected] you" (Isa. 41:8–9). **Col. 2** ["Thus says the LORD, Israel's redeemer, its Holy One, to the despised in spirit, abhorred by Gentiles, slave of rulers: Kings shall see you and rise up; so will princes, and bow down, for the sake of [1]the LORD who is] faithful, the Holy One of Is[rael who chose you" (Isa. 49:7). "Be glad, heavens, exult, earth,] [2]give voice, mountains, for Go[d] has comforted [His people and showed mercy to His afflicted. Although Zion had said,] [3]The LORD has abandoned me, [my Lord has forgotten me, can a woman forget her baby, a parent the child of her womb?] [4]Even if these should forget, [I will never forget you. See, on my palms I have engraved you,] [5]and your walls [are always on my] mi[nd. Your children have hastened, while those who have destroyed and ruined you] [6]shall de[part] from you" (Isa. 49:13–17).

Frag. 3 [1]["And now th]us says the LO[RD, Your creator, O Jacob, and Your maker, O Israel, [2]Do not be afrai]d, for I have redeemed you. [I have called you by your name, you are mine. When you pass] [3][through the water] I am with you, and in the f[loo]d[s, they will not drown you"] (Isa. 43:1–2).

Frags. 4–5 [1][. . . "I ga]ve men in exchan[ge for you, and nations in exchange for your soul.] [2][Do not be] afraid, [for I am with you.] From the East I will brin[g your descendants, and from the West I will gather you.] [3][I will sa]y to the North, [Give them up; and to the South,] Do not retain them, but br[ing back my children from afar, and my daughters from the end of] [4][the ea]rth" (Isa. 43:4–6).

Frags. 6–7 [1]["Thus says] Your [Lord, the LORD] Your G[o]d, [who contends for His people: Behold, I have taken from your hand the] [2][cup that makes you st]agger, [the roun]d cup of [My] wr[ath. You will never again drink of it. I will put it] in the hands of those who trouble you" [. . .] (Isa. 51:22–23).

Frags. 8–11 [2]"Wake up, [wake up, put on your strength,] Zion! Pu[t on your beautiful clothes, J]erusalem, holy city! For [3][the uncircumcised, impure Gentile will never again enter you. So shake off the dust, get u]p, return, Jerusalem. Loosen [4]the bonds of your neck, [dear ca]ptive [Zion! For thus] says [the LORD: You were sold for nothing, so without] money you will be reclaimed" (Isa. 52:1–3). [5]"Do not be afra[id, for] you will not be ashamed. [Do not be mortified f]or you will not be disgraced. Truly the shame of [6]your [youth] you will forget, the [con]tempt of your widowhood [you will] not [remember again,] for your Maker has become your husband, the LORD [7][of Hosts] is His name. Your redeemer is the Holy One of Is[rael; the] G[od of al]l [the ea]rth He is called. For like an abandoned woman [8][downcast] in spirit the LORD has called you. Like a young wife when [she] is rejected—so says the LORD your God. [9][For a] short [moment] I left you alone, but in great mercy I am bringing you back. In raging wrath [I turned away] [10][briefly from] you, but by My eternal grace I had pity on you. So says your Redeemer, the LORD. This is as it was in the time of Noah, when [11][I swore that the waters of] Noah [would not] cov[er] the earth, so I have forsworn My anger forever, and My punishment of you. [12][For the mounta]ins may shift or the hills totter, but My grace will not shift from you [. . .]" (Isa. 54:4–10).

Again the voice of the compiler is heard, buttressing the comforting words of the Bible with consolations of his own.

[13][. . . one could not g]row tired of these words of comfort, for great honor is written in [. . .] [14][. . .] for those who love [Him . . .] never again [. . .] [15][Beli]al to oppress His servants [. . .] [16][. . .] will rejoice [. . .]

Frag. 15 [3]["I will p]ut [one-third in the fire, and refine them as one refines silver; I will test them] as one tests [4][gold. They will call Me by name, and I will answer them. I say,] My people, and he [5][says, The LORD is our God"] (Zech. 13:9).

The author of the scroll may have explained the current tribulation of Israel as having been foreseen, and thus it is part of God's wonderful, though mysterious, plan. Those who continue to trust and obey God can count on sharing in his comfort.

Frag. 16 [1–2][. . .] my secrets. He has cast the lot [. . .] [3][. . .] the sanctuary, and to give human fulfillment to [. . .] [4][. . .] for those who love Him and to those who keep [His] command[ments . . .]

Frags. 19–20 have been recognized as containing parts of the Book of Jubilees *(see text 42).*

—E.M.C.

28. The Last Days: An Interpretation of Selected Verses

4Q177

The burden of making sense of the Qumran commentaries doubles when the already enigmatic text is fragmentary. Such is the case with the present work. It is a commentary on themes chosen because of their supposed relevance to the "Last Days," the time of the final showdown between Light and

Darkness, Righteousness and Evil. The method and theme have much in common with the *Last Days: A Commentary on Selected Verses* (text 25), and it has been argued that the two scrolls are actually two copies of the same work that do not happen to overlap.

This commentary mentions none of the central *dramatis personae* of the story the members of the *Yahad* told about themselves. The Teacher of Righteousness, the Wicked Priest, the Man of the Lie—all are absent. The Flattery-Seekers, however, the sect's archenemies, are mentioned in one passage, as is the *Yahad* itself. Also appearing is the figure known as the Interpreter of the Law, who may be the anointed prophet or priest who was expected to come before the end.

The author sketches the Last Days in general terms: although Belial will make an attempt to destroy the righteous, the children of light, the Angel of Truth will protect them; and in the end, Good will triumph, and Evil will perish.

Frags. 12–13 Col. 1 [6][. . .] "Instruction [will not perish] from the [priest, or advice from the sage, or oracles] from the prophet" (Jer. 18:18).

[7][This refers to] the Last Days, of which David said, "O LORD, do not [rebuke me] in Your anger. [Have mercy on me, for] I am fading. [8][Heal me, O LORD, for my innermost being is tormented.] Yes, my soul is in great torment. But now, O LORD, how long? Have mercy, deliver [my] soul [. . ."] (Ps. 6:1–4).

[This refers to] the Last Days, about [9][the righteous, when] Belial [planned] to destroy them in his fury, so that none would remain of [. . . God will not allow] Belial [10][. . . Abra]ham up to ten righteous in a city, for the Spirit of Truth [. . . for] there is no [11][. . .] and their brothers by the wiles of Belial, and he will strengthen [. . .] [12][. . . but] the angel of God's truth will help all the Children of Light from the power of Belial [. . .] [13][. . .] and to scatter them in a dry and desolate land. This is a time of tribulation that [. . .] [14][. . . but] the righteous are always beloved, and the great power of God is with them, helping them against all the spirits [of darkness . . .] [15][. . . and those who worship] God will hallow His name and come to Zion with joy, and Jerusalem [. . .] [16][. . . but as for] Belial and all those who belong to him, [they shall perish] forever, but all the Children of [Light] will be gathered in [. . .]

Before the end comes, the unrighteous will attack the righteous.

Frags. 5–6 [1][. . .] the boasters who [. . .] come against the men of the *Yah*[*ad* . . .] [2][as it is written in the book of Isaiah the] prophet, "This year eat what grows [by itself, and next year the aftergrowth" (Isa. 37:30). The meaning of] "what grows by itself" is [. . .] [3][. . .] up to the time of purifi[cation that shall come upon them in the Last Days,] and afterwards shall appear [. . .] [4][. . .] for all of them are children [. . .] said the boasters [. . .] [5][. . . that is written] about them in the book of [Isaiah the prophet . . . for] the Law of the [. . .] [6][. . .] it calls them, as [it is written about them in the book of Isaiah the prophet, "He] thinks up plots to [destroy the humble with lying words" (Isa. 32:7). . . .] [7][. . .] to condemn Israel. [. . .]

Those who belong to the sect will go into exile in the face of the enemy persecution.

["To the master singer,] to David. In the LORD [I have taken refuge, so how can You say to me, Flee] [8][to your mountain, little bird, for now the wicked are bending their bow,] and fitting arrows to [the string to shoot in the night at the honest in mind"] (Ps. 11:1–2).

[This means that] the men of [the *Yahad*] shall flee [. . .] [9][. . . like] a bird from its place and be exiled [from their land . . . they are written about] in the book of the [prophet Micah: [10]"Rise and go, this is not the right place to stay, impurity has marred it, it is completely ruined.] It belongs to one who walks [in lies and tells untruths . . ."] (Mic. 2:10–11). [. . .] [11][. . .] which is written about them in the book of [. . .] [12][. . .] "To the master singer, on the [eighth, a psalm of David . . ." (Ps. 12:1).] [13][. . .] for them the eighth season [. . .] [14][. . .] there is no peace, for they [. . .] [15][. . . "There is merriment,] slaying cattle, slaughtering sheep, [dining on meat, drinking wine . . ." (Isa. 22:13). . . .] [16][. . .] of the Law, those who make up the *Yahad* [. . .]

Despite the apparent success of the wicked during this period, the righteous are to regard it as a time when they themselves are tested and purified.

Frags. 10 + 11 + 7 + 9 + 20 + 26 [1]["The words of the LORD are pure, like silver purified in a clay furnace,] refined seven times" (Ps. 12:6). As it is written [2][in the book of the prophet Zechariah, "Here is a stone I have placed before Joshua the priest. Upon this one stone are seven eyes. I am] making an inscription on it, says the LORD" (Zech. 3:9). As it [3][says . . .] concerning them it is written, I will heal [4][. . .] the men of Belial and all the rabble [5][. . .] them the Interpreter of the Law, for there is no [6][. . .] each man on his own rampart when they appear [7][. . .] those who impede the Children of Light [8][. . . "How long, O LORD?] Will You forget [me forever? How long will You turn away] from me? How long will I turn over [9][thoughts] in my mind, [having pain in] my heart [every day]? How long [shall my enemy exult over me? . . ."] (Ps. 13:1–2).

This refers to the inner endurance of the men of [10][. . .] in the Last Days, for [. . .] to test them and to purify them. [11][. . .] them in the spirit and pure and refined [. . .]

The enemies of the righteous are identified as the "Flattery-Seekers." They will join forces with the Gentile forces from nearby Edom and Moab to attack the Children of Light.

[As for the verse that says,] "Lest the enemy say [12][I have overcome him . . ." (Ps. 13:4). . . .] they are the company of the Flattery-Seekers, who [. . .] who seek to destroy [13][. . .] in their zeal and in their hostility [. . . which] is written in the book of the [prophet] Ezekiel, [14]["Because Edom and Moab have said, Behold, the house of] Judah is like all the Gentiles" (Ezek. 25:8).

[This refers to the Last] Days, when [the . . .] will gather together against [them . . .] [15][. . .] with the righteous and the wicked, the fool and the simple[ton . . .] of the men who have served God [. . .] [16][. . .] who have circumcised themselves spiritually in the last generation [. . .] and all that is theirs is unclean [. . .]

Frags. 1 + 4 + 14 + 24 + 31(?) [1][. . .] their words [. . . pra]ises of glory that [Israel] shall utter [2][. . . The LORD shall remove] from you every illness.

Those who are faithful and endure the time of suffering will live to see their vindication, when the true priesthood of God will be revealed and the works of darkness will perish.

"As for the holy [ones that are] in the land, the nobles, in whom is all my pleasure" (Ps. 16:3). [. . .] [3][. . .] has ever happened like this [. . .] "and knocking of knees and trembling in everyone's bowels" (Nah. 2:10). [. . .] [4][. . .] "Hear, [O righteous LORD,] listen to my complaint, give ear to [my prayer . . ." (Ps. 17:1).[. . .] [5][. . .] in the Last Days in the time when He shall seek [. . .] the party of the *Yahad*. He is [. . .] [6]["From You shall flow my judgment" (Ps. 17:2). . . .] The meaning of the verse is that a man shall arise from the children of [. . .] [7][. . .] they will be like a fire on the whole earth. They are the ones of whom it is written in the Last [Days . . .] [8][. . .] he said concerning the company of the light who shall have grief when Be[lial] rules, [but concerning the company of darkness] who shall have grief [. . .] [9][. . .] from him [. . .] mourning, return, O LORD, [. . .] God of mercy and God of Israel [. . .] just deserts [. . .] [10][who have] indulged themselves in the spirits of [Be]lial, but it will be forgiven them forever, and bless them [. . .] again forever and bless them [. . .] their times [. . .] [11][. . .] their ancestors by the tally of [their] full names, one after the other [. . .] and the time of their term of office [. . .] their tongue [. . .] [12][. . .] the descendants of Judah.

All of the events of the Last Days are foreordained, written down on heavenly tablets. Note the reference to the "second book of the Law" that was "rejected." The identity of this book is unknown; some scholars have suggested that it was the Temple Scroll *(text 155), others that it was the* Sectarian Manifesto *(text 100). Just as likely, perhaps, is that the reference is to a work that has not survived. Another possibility is that the author of the* Last Days *was passing on a tradition and did not himself know the identity of the book, in which case his description—which makes the book sound substantial, equivalent to the books of Moses—may not have been very precise.*

Now, behold, all is written in the tablets that [. . .] in order to tell him the tally of [. . .] and he will make [them] inherit [13][. . .] and to his descendants forever. Then he left there to go from Aram. "Blow the horn in Gibeah" (Hos. 5:8). The "horn" is the [first] book of [the Law. "Sound the trumpet in Ramah" (Hos. 5:8). . . .] [14][The "trumpet"] is the second book of the Law that [all the] men of his party rejected, and they advised rebellion against it and they sent [. . .] [15][. . .] great miracles upon [. . .] and Jacob is to stand by the winepresses and he will rejoice when descends [. . .] [16][. . .] is chosen [. . .] the men of his party are "the sword." As for the verse that says [. . .]

—E.M.C.

29. A Lament for Zion

4Q179

The lamentation for a fallen city was a well-known literary genre in the ancient Near East. One of the oldest known is the "Lamentation for the Destruction of Ur," written in Mesopotamia in the twentieth century B.C.E., and several others are known. The biblical exemplar of the form is the book of Lamentations, comprising five laments over the destruction of Jerusalem by the Babylonians in the sixth century B.C.E.

The scroll 4Q179 is clearly modeled after the biblical Lamentations and quotes from it occasionally. It is unclear whether this lament describes a historical incident. Between 586 B.C.E. and 70 C.E., Jerusalem was not completely destroyed, but it suffered many conquests, most notably at the hands of the Syrian king Antiochus IV Epiphanes, who, according to Josephus, robbed the Temple, took thousands captive, pillaged the city, and burned down many of the finest buildings (*Ant.* 12.250–252). This ordeal, which helped to incite the Maccabean war for independence, may well have inspired this lament.

Frag. 1 Col. 1 [1][. . .] all our misdeeds and it is not within our power; for [we] did not obey [. . .] [2][. . .] Judah, that all these things should befall us, by evil [3][. . .] his covenant.

Woe to us [4][. . .] has become burned by fire and overthrown [5][. . .] our distinction, and there is nothing pleasing in it, in the hou[se of . . .] [6][. . .] his holy courts have become [7][. . .] Jerusalem, city of [8][the sanctuary, has become a plac]e for wild animals, and there is none to d[isturb them,] and her avenues [9][. . .] all her fine buildings are desolate [10][. . .] there are no pilgrims in them, all the cities of [11][Judah . . .] our inheritance has become like the desert, a land not [12][cultivated;] we no longer hear re[joi]cing, and [there is none] who seeks [13][God . . . no] one [to heal] our wounds. All our sins [14][. . .] our offenses [. . .] our sins.

Col. 2 [1]Woe to us, for the wrath of God has come upon [. . .] [2]that we should congregate with the dead [3][. . .] like an unloved wife Is[rael . . . neglects] [4]her babies, and my dear people [have become] cruel [. . .] [5]her young men are desolate, the children of [. . . fleeing] [6]from winter, when their hands are weak [. . .] [7]Ash heaps are now the home of the house of I[srael . . .] [8]they ask for water, but there is no attend[ant . . .] [9]those who were worth their weight [in] gold [. . .] [10]there is nothing to delight them in it, those who drew their strength from scarlet [clothing . . .] [11]nor fine gold, their garments bearing jewelry [. . . no longer] [12]do they touch purple stuff and embroidery [. . .] has risen [. . .] [13]the pampered women of Zion with them [. . .]

Frag. 2 [4]["How] lonely [she sits], the city [once full of people!" (Lam. 1:1). . . . Jerusa]lem [. . .] [5][. . .] the princess of all the natio[ns] is as desolate as an abandoned woman, and all her [dau]ghters are likewise abandoned. [6][. . . like a wo]man abandoned and miserable, [whose husband] has left her. All her fine buildings and [walls] [7][are like] a barren woman, all [her] streets are like a woman confined [. . .] like a woman whose life is

bitter [8]and all her daughters are like those in mourning for [their] husba[nds . . .] like those bereft [9]of their only children, Jerusalem keeps on weeping [. . . tears] on her cheek for her children [. . .]
—E.M.C.

30. The Ages of the World

4Q180–181

An important theological tenet of the *Yahad* was the notion of predestination: that from the very beginning, God had foreordained how history would develop, who would inherit eternal life and who was destined for perdition. The *Ages of the World* is apparently a discussion of this notion, proving the idea using examples drawn from the biblical text. In the surviving portions, the example of the ten generations between Shem and Abraham is the centerpiece.

The introduction to the work, which emphasizes God's predetermination of history.

4Q180 Frag. 1 [1]The prophetic interpretation concerning the ages which God made: an age to complete [all that is] [2]and shall be. Before He created them, He established [their] workings [. . .] [3]age by age. And it was engraved upon [eternal] tablets [. . .] [4][. . .] ages of their dominion. This is the rule of the so[ns of Noah to] [5][Abraham un]til he bore Isaac, ten [generations (?) . . .] [6][. . .]

A version of the story of original sin, similar to that known from 1 Enoch 6–11 (text 36) and Jubilees *4–5 (see text 42 and Gen. 6:1–2, 4).*

[7]The prophetic interpretation concerning Azazel and the angels wh[o went in to the daughters of man,] [8][so that] they bore mighty men to them. And concerning Azazel [who taught them] [9][to love] iniquity and to pass on wickedness as an inheritance, all [. . .] [10][. . .] judgments, and the judgment of the council of [. . .]

The fate of Sodom and Gomorrah was foreknown from creation (Gen. 18–19).

Frags. 2–4 Col. 2 [1]that [. . .] He who dwells [. . .] [2]that [this] l[and] was beautiful to Lot [. . .] to inherit [. . .] [3][. . .] three me[n . . .]

4[who appeared to Abra]m at the oaks of Mamre were angels. [And the Lord said,] 5"How g[reat] is the [outc]ry against Sodom and Gomorrah, and their sin, how 6very [grea]t! I must go down and see whether [they ha]ve done altogether according to their outcry that has come 7[to me;] and if not, I will kno[w." . . .] the word [. . . all] 8fle[sh] which [. . .] concerning every [. . .] 9speaks [. . .]. . . and I will see that everything [. . ."] 10[. . .] before He created them He knew [their] design[s. . . .]

God has a predetermined plan for man. This plan includes punishment (ll. 1–2) and rewards (ll. 3–6). For the concept of sitting in the council of the gods, see the "Self-Glorification Hymn," 4Q491 frag. 11 col. 1 (text 11) and 1QH^a col. 26 (text 12).

4Q181 Frag. 1 1[. . .] for the guilt in the *Yahad,* with the coun[cil of . . .], to wa[l]low in the sin of humankind, and for great judgments and evil diseases 2in the flesh, according to the powerful deeds of God, and corresponding to their wickedness, according to their uncleanness caused by the council of the sons of h[eaven] and earth, as a wicked association until 3the end.

Corresponding to the compassion of God, according to His goodness, and the wonder of His glory, He brings some of the sons of the world near, to be reckoned with Him in [the council] 4[of the g]ods as a holy congregation, destined for eternal life and in the lot with His holy ones [. . .] 5[. . .] each one [acco]mplishes according to the lot which falls t[o him . . .] 6[. . .] for e[te]rn[al] life [. . .]

There are sufficient similarities between ll. 1–4 of this fragment and ll. 5–9 of 4Q180 frag. 1 to suggest that the texts are related.

Frag. 2 1[. . . Abraham until he bor]e Isaac, [ten generations. The prophetic interpretation concerning Azazel and the angels who went in to] 2[the daughters] of man, so that [they] bore mighty me[n] to them. [And concerning Azazel . . .] 3[. . .] He satisfied Israel with plenty (*or* Israel, in seventy weeks, He entreated) [. . .] 4and those who love iniquity, and pass on guilt as an inheritance, all [. . .] 5before all those who know Him [. . .] 6and there are no bounds to His goodness [. . .] 7these are the wonders of knowledge [. . .] 8He established them in His truth and [. . .] 9in all their ages [. . .] 10th[eir] creatures [. . .]

—M.G.A.

31. A Commentary on Collected Verses

4Q182

The very fragmentary work before us seems to be the remains of a commentary on selected verses, along the lines of the *Last Days: A Commentary on Selected Verses* (text 25) and the *Last Days: An Interpretation of Selected Verses* (text 28). Alternatively, it may be that this writing was an interpretation of all or parts of the book of Jeremiah. Although the Qumran caches include commentaries on many of Israel's prophets, none on Jeremiah has otherwise survived. His many sharp-edged criticisms of the Israel of his day would have lent themselves nicely to new application in the politics of the late Second Temple period.

Frag. 1 seems to preserve portions of a criticism directed at Israel generally, at the "Flattery-Seekers," or perhaps at another code-named group such as Manasseh. Compare the Commentary on Habakkuk *(text 2).*

Frag. 1 [1][. . . The interpretation applies to] the Last Days, concerning [. . .] [2][. . .] who stiffened their neck [. . .] [3][. . .] and they arrogantly threw off restraint, so as to defile [. . .] [4][. . . as it] is written about them in the book of Jere[miah, "How can I forgive you?] [5]Your [children] have forsaken me, and have swo[rn by those who are no gods"] (Jer. 5:7).

Frag. 2 [1][. . .] in the Last D[ay]s [. . .] [2][. . .] so as to smite them w[ith . . .]

—M.O.W.

32. A Sectarian History

4Q183

This short text clearly derives from a commentary, perhaps a thematic one such as the *Last Days* (text 28). None of the biblical text that was the basis of this commentary has been preserved. What remains is a scrap of history from a sectarian perspective: long ago God delivered the righteous and punished the wicked during the time of tribulation—and he still does. If the restoration suggested by the context in l. 2 is correct, we may have here a reaction to the events of the civil war between Hyrcanus II and Aristobulus and their supporters in 67–65 B.C.E.; for more on this war and its significance for the setting of the scrolls, see the Introduction (pp. 29–33).

Col. 2 [1]their enemies, and they defiled their sanctuary [. . .] [2]from them, and they advanced to war, each [against his brother . . . those who were faithful] [3]to his covenant, God delivered and rescued [. . . those deserving His] [4]good pleasure, and He gave to them a single mind, to wal[k in His ways . . . to avoid all] [5]wicked lucre, and they abstained from the wa[ys of wickedness . . . they withdrew from] [6]those who err in spirit, and with a truthful tongue [. . .] [7]and they satisfied the debt of their sins by [their] sufferings [. . .] [8]their sin. [. . .] And as for the verse that says [. . .]
—E.M.C.

33. Wiles of the Wicked Woman

4Q184

This work, entitled by its first editor, John Allegro, "The Wiles of the Wicked Woman," is another example of wisdom literature (see the introduction to the *Book of Secrets,* text 6). It is typical of wisdom literature to portray life in terms of a contrast between the wise man and the fool and between the wisdom and folly that they live by.

The ancient Israelites personified wisdom itself as a wise woman, Lady Wisdom, who invited all and sundry to come to her house and learn from her (Prov. 8:1–9:6). According to the apocryphal Wisdom of Solomon, king Solomon desired to "marry" Lady Wisdom.

The natural next step would have been a personification of Folly, which appears to be the intent of the present work. "Lady Folly" here is a seductress; she is a more sensational version of the archetypical loose woman depicted in the Bible (Prov. 7:1–27). She seeks to draw men away from the path of truth and lead them to her own house of falsehood.

Folly's evil intent pervades her being.

Frag. 1 [1][Folly] produces nothingness, and in [. . .]. She is always seeking error, she whets the words of [her mouth. With raillery] [2]and jesting she flatters, and adds derision to useless va[nity]. Her heart creates lewdness, and her inner being [. . . Her eyes] [3]are befouled with perversity, her hands grip corruption tight. Her feet come down to do evil, and to walk in the crimes of [. . . Her thighs are] [4]pillars of darkness, a horde of sins is under her hem, her [. . .] blackest night.

Her clothing and dwelling reveal the corruption of wickedness.

Her attire [. . .] [5]her robes are gloom of twilight, while her jewelry is infected with rot. Her bed is a couch of corruption [. . .] [6]pits of hell. Her inns are where darkness lies down, she holds sway at dead of nigh[t]. Among the pillars of gloom [7]she pitches her tent, and settles among the tents of silence, in the middle of perpetual flames. She has no part with any of those [8]illumined by brightness.

Those who follow Lady Folly, like those whom the adulteress seduces, shall be eternally punished ("her house is the way to Hades," Prov. 7:27).

No, she is the beginning of all evil paths: alas for all who take possession of her, and destruction comes to a[ll] [9]who take hold of her, for her ways are deadly, her paths lead to sin, her byways end in [10]evil, her tra[ck]s in criminal wrongdoing. Her gates are the gates of Death, in the entrance of her house she walks. To Ha[des] [11]a[l]l, [without] return! All who take possession of her descend to the pit.

Folly is always on the lookout for new prey; like the adulteress, "she lies in wait at every corner" (Prov. 7:12).

She lies secretly in wait [. . .] [12]all [. . .] in the city streets she hides, in the town gates she takes her stand, and no one will [. . .] [13][. . .] her eyes dart here and there, she flutters her eyelids lewdly, lookin[g fo]r a [14]righteous man to catch, looking for a [st]rong man to trip up, for someone honest to lead astray, for innocent youths [15]to keep from obeying the commandments, for the firm of [purpose] to make empty with lewdness, for those who live honestly to make them break the l[aw]; to cause [16]the humble to rebel from God, and to divert their steps from the ways of righteousness, to put arrogance in their [hearts], so that they do not remain [17]in the paths of integrity. She seeks to make people go wrong in the ways of Hell, and to seduce the sons of men by flattery.

—E.M.C.

34. In Praise of Wisdom

4Q185

Like the *Book of Secrets* (text 6), this is a wisdom instruction. It argues that true wisdom can come only from God and is a unique possession of the chosen people, Israel.

Mortals cannot rank with God and his angels, because their life span is comparatively short. Some of the wording is borrowed from Isaiah 40:6–8.

Frags. 1–2 Col. 1 [4][. . .] pure and holy [. . .] [5][. . .] His [. . .] and His [an]ger [. . .] [6][. . .] up to ten times [. . .] [7][. . .] there is no strength to stand before His anger and no hope [8]before His wrath [. . .] and who can endure to stand before His angels, for as [9]flames of fire [they] mete out judgment [. . .] of His spirits. And you, O mortals, [. . .] for just [10]like gr[as]s man sprouts from the earth, and his virtue blossoms like the flower; but His spirit blows [on it], [11]and [his stalk] dries up, and the wind carries its flower to nothingness, to [. . .] [12]and it is no more, because of the wind. One may seek it, but not find it, and there is no hope for it. [13]He is like a shadow [. . .] upon the lig[ht.]

In view of the brevity of human life, the righteous should devote themselves to learning more about God and his ways.

So now, pray give heed, my people, and learn [14]from me, you who are unlearned. Grow wise by learning about the [gr]eat deeds of our God, and call to mind the miracles He did [15]in Egypt, and His wonders [in the land of Ham.] Let your hearts tremble before His awesomeness **Col. 2** [1]and do [His will . . . Renew] your [sp]irit according to his tender mercies. Seek for yourselves the way [2]of life, the highway [that . . .] something to leave your children after you; why should you give [3]your[self] to futility? [. . . ju]dgment. Listen to me, my children, and do not defy the commandments of the LORD. [4]Do not walk [in wickedness, but in the way He established for] Jacob, and the path He ordained for Isaac. Truly, better is one day [5][in His house] than ten [in the house of fools . . .] His worship, and not to be burdened by fear or the trapper's lure [6][. . .] from His angels, for there is no darkness [7]or fog [. . .] He [. . .] His [. . .]

and His true knowledge. And you, what [8][. . .] calamity comes from Him on every people.

Happiness is only to be found by seeking true wisdom from God.

Happy is the man to whom [wisdom] is given [9][. . .] The wicked should not boast, saying, It is not given [10]to me, and it is not [. . . wisdom was given] to Israel, and He measures it out generously, and He redeems all His people, [11]but kills [those who reject . . . nor should] the braggarts say, Truly we have found it by ourselves. Seek it, [12]and you will find it. Hol[d fa]st to it, and you will own it, and with it [long l]ife and prosperity and joy of heart, rich[es . . .] [13]His eternal mercies and salvation [. . .]

Happy is the man who puts it into practice and does not slander [. . . by means of] [14]cunning one cannot seek it, nor can one hold on to it by flattery. As it is given to his ancestors, so he will obtain it [and hold on to it] [15]with all his mighty strength and with all his [. . .] without limit. Then he can bestow it on his offspring, and his knowledge to [his] people [. . .]

Col. 3 [. . . he knows all the] [12]innermost parts of the belly, and searches out the inner man [. . . He made] [13]the tongue and knows its speech; God made the hands [. . .]

—E.M.C.

35. A Horoscope Written in Code

4Q186

4Q186 is perhaps the closest thing to a scientific treatise that has yet emerged from the caves of Qumran. This writing combines astrology and the ancient "science" of physiognomy in an attempt to determine the character and destiny of given individuals. As the author of the third century B.C.E. pseudo-Aristotelian tractate *Physiognomonica* describes it, "The physiognomist takes his information from movements, shapes, colors, and traits as they appear in the face, from the hair, from the smoothness of the skin, from the voice, from the appearance of the flesh, from the limbs, and from the entire character of the body" (806a). In other words, physiognomy tried to judge a book by its cover, to discover individuals' true character—as opposed to how they might present themselves—from a close examination of every aspect of their outward appearance. By the time of the scrolls this was already an ancient form of divination. Examples many centuries older than our text are known from ancient

Mesopotamia. In the Greco-Roman period, physiognomy was greatly elaborated beyond those Near Eastern forebears, and its practitioners memorized long catalogs of physical traits and the significance assigned to those traits.

Our text uses physiognomy as an adjunct to astrology, the "royal science" and true predictor of destiny. On the basis of a person's appearance, the reader of the text learns how to discover the person's birth sign. Knowing the birth sign enables the text's user to predict what sort of character the person in question possesses and, in a very general way, what sort of future he or she will have. The text describes character as proportions of light and darkness, expressing the proportions as fractions of the number nine. Presumably the number derives from the period of human gestation. The theory would seem to be that for each month in the womb, the embryo takes on one "part." The fetus's crucial first month—the birth sign—would determine whether this allocation got off on the right foot, so to speak.

But how would the proportion of parts express itself in the way someone looked? That is, why was appearance related to astrology? To answer this question we have to read between the lines a bit and recall certain doctrines of Greco-Roman medicine. Our author seems to have believed that the "spirit" (which, as indicated, every human received in certain proportions) moved through the blood and thus to every extremity of the body. Once it reached a given locality in the body its nature would become manifest. For a bad birth sign, one such manifestation could be hairiness, for example. For such a theory the author could find biblical foundations such as Genesis 9:4, "The life is in the blood." A portion of the *Damascus Document* (text 1) explicitly states that spirits move through the blood and have physical outworkings; the *Damascus Document* is explaining skin diseases, but the principle is the same. This whole way of thinking is immediately reminiscent of Greco-Roman medical ideas that came to full expression in the writings of the famous Greek medical writer Galen (ca. 129–199 C.E.). Galen wrote of "humors" circulating in the body and used this idea to explain the observed truths of pseudo-Aristotelian physiognomy.

Two other particular aspects of our author's thinking deserve comment. First is his comparison of the individuals he describes to animals. Such comparisons were a commonplace of Greco-Roman physiognomy. The underlying idea was that if a person resembled a certain animal physically, he or she would also be similar "in soul." Thus if one knew a person's animal, it became possible to make valuable deductions about that person's character. To choose an example that parallels our own text (the second individual below), Pseudo-Aristotle wrote, "Those with a wide and thick neck are bad-tempered; compare bad-tempered bulls" (*Physiognomonica* 811a).

Also notable is our author's statement about the second individual: "This is the birth sign under which such a person shall be born: the haunch of Taurus." The reference to the "haunch" of the sign of Taurus implies the concept of *dodecatmo-*

ria. This Greek word is a name for further subdivision of the zodiac. According to astrological doctrine, each sign occupied 30 degrees of space in the heavens (twelve signs, 360 degrees). But each sign could be further subdivided into twelve parts, a sort of micro-zodiac or "zodiac of the zodiac." To say that someone was born under the haunch of Taurus meant that the person was born when the sun, as observed, had nearly completed its movement through that sign. The "haunch" was the last 2.5 degrees of the sign of Taurus. Taken together with all the other elements of our text, this greater specificity indicates that our author may once have described a large number of individuals, for many unique combinations of these elements are possible. The larger part of this writing is quite likely lost; 4Q186 may have been an entire handbook on physiognomic astrology.

A fragmentary description of the first individual. The reference in col. 2 to "granite" suggests that the text may have incorporated ideas about birthstones.

Frag. 1 Col. 1 [7]Anyone, the ha[ir of whose head] shall be [. . . and whose head and forehead] [8]are broad and curved [. . .] [9]intermediate, but the rest of [his] head is not [. . .] **Col. 2** [1][. . .] unclean [2][. . . his stone is] granite.

The second individual, a person more good than bad. "Fixed eyes" are a regular category in Greco-Roman physiognomy and are generally a bad sign. Note the virtuous significance of long and slender limbs.

[3][And] anyone [whose] eyes are [4][. . . and lo]ng, but th[e]y are fix[e]d, [5]whose thighs are long and slender, whose toes [6]are slender and long, and who was born during the second phase of the moon:* [7]he possesses a spirit with six parts light, but three parts in the House of [8]Darkness. This is the birth sign under which such a person shall be born: [9]the haunch of Taurus. He will be poor. This is his animal: the bull.

The third individual. This person has poor potential for righteousness, being eight-ninths bad. In particular, he has hairy thighs. In Greco-Roman physiognomy, hairy thighs signified one whose animal was the goat; like that animal, he tended to be lustful.

Col. 3 [5]and whose head [. . .], [whose] ey[es] [6]inspire fear [and are . . .], whose teeth protrude (?), whose [7]fingers are thick, whose thighs are

*Literally, "and he derives from the second column/stand." Similar phrasing in Ptolemy's *Tetrabiblos,* where he is describing phases or "stations" of the moon (i.e., the places where it "stands"), suggests the present interpretation.

thick and extremely hairy, [8]and whose toes are thick and short: he possesses a spirit with [ei]ght [9]parts in the House of [Darkness] and one from the House of Light [. . .]

The fourth individual. This person has excellent potential for righteousness, and evidences the "Golden Mean" that was important in Greco-Roman physiognomy: his physical characteristics are extreme in neither direction. Note that he is also relatively hairless.

Frag. 2 Col. 1 [1]regula[r,] whose [e]yes are neither dark n[or] light (?), whose beard [2]is sp[arse] and medium curly, whose voice resonates, whose teeth [3]are fine and regular, who is neither tall [4]nor short but is well built, whose fingers are thin [5]and long, whose thighs are hairless, the soles of whose feet [6][and whose to]es are as they should be: he possesses a spirit [7][. . .] eight parts [from the House of Light] and o[ne] [8][in the House of Darkness. This is the birth sign under which] such a person shall be born [. . .]
—M.O.W.

Introduction to the Enoch Literature

It is fair to say that the patriarch Enoch was as well known to the ancients as he is obscure to modern Bible readers. Besides giving his age (365 years), the book of Genesis says of him only that he "walked with God," and afterwards "he was not, because God had taken him" (5:24). This exalted way of life and mysterious demise made Enoch into a figure of considerable fascination, and a cycle of legends grew up around him.

Many of the legends about Enoch were collected already in ancient times in several long anthologies. The most important such anthology is known simply as the *Book of Enoch,* or *1 Enoch,* over one hundred chapters long in its final form. It still survives in its entirety (although only in the Ethiopic language) and forms an important source for the thought of Judaism in the last few centuries B.C.E. Significantly, the remnants of several copies of *1 Enoch* in Aramaic were found among the Dead Sea Scrolls, and it is clear that whoever collected the scrolls considered it a vitally important text.

1 Enoch, as it survives in the Ethiopic version, is composed of several discrete works:

- *Book of Watchers* (chaps. 1–36)
- *Parables* (or *Similitudes) of Enoch* (chaps. 37–71)

- *Book of the Heavenly Luminaries* (chaps. 72–82)
- *Dream Visions of Enoch* (chaps. 83–90)
- *Apocalypse of Enoch* (chaps. 91–105)
- *Birth of Noah* (chaps. 106–107)
- *Appendix:* "Another Book of Enoch" (chap. 108)

These works likely existed separately before they were combined into the anthology now known as *1 Enoch.* Each smaller work, in turn, was itself composed of other still smaller works that probably circulated separately before being added to the larger work. The *Book of Watchers,* for example, after an introduction that warns of the coming judgment on the wicked (chaps. 1–5), has the story of the fall of the Watchers (angels) and how they brought sin to the earth (chaps. 6–16), and then relates how the angels lifted up Enoch and showed him the entirety of the earth and the underworld (17–36). All these sections were probably once independent works.

Among the Qumran scrolls were found:

- seven fragmentary manuscripts of parts of the *Book of Enoch* that together yield about 20 percent of the original Aramaic text,
- another four manuscripts that form an earlier, longer version of the *Book of the Heavenly Luminaries,* and
- another nine scrolls, extremely fragmentary, that constitute a hitherto little-known story of Enoch that scholars call the *Book of Giants.*

Judging from the Qumran fragments, their "Book of Enoch" was made up of the *Book of Watchers,* the *Dream Visions of Enoch,* the *Apocalypse of Enoch,* the *Birth of Noah,* and possibly the *Book of Giants.*

The *Book of the Heavenly Luminaries,* at least at Qumran, was separate from the rest of the book and was probably not added to the book of Enoch until after the first century C.E. The longer version found at Qumran scholars call *Astronomical Enoch* (text 38).

No trace of the *Parables of Enoch* has been discovered at Qumran, and it is widely considered today to be a composition of the later first century C.E. If a pre-Christian copy of the *Parables* were ever discovered, it would create a sensation, since it is the only text besides the Christian Gospels that uses the title "Son of Man" for the heavenly Savior of Israel.

Clearly the Qumran sect placed a high value on the Enoch literature, which profoundly influenced their conceptions of God, creation, salvation, sin, and the coming judgment. *Astronomical Enoch* contains a detailed description of the heavenly mechanisms of the solar calendar, adherence to which formed a central part of the religious system of the Dead Sea Scrolls. The *Book of Enoch* portrays a world divided between the wicked and the elect of God, who alone would escape the coming judgment in fire. This division between good and evil extended into the world of the angels, who significantly influence human destiny, both for good and for ill. Sin itself is understood to be not the product of the Fall in the Garden of Eden, but the result of malign teaching that entered the world through depraved angels. The only remedy for sinful knowledge was the true teaching from heaven, written down on the heavenly tablets and read by Enoch, the chosen one, who had visited heaven, and whose task it was to bring the teaching to the elect on earth. All these ideas were taken over virtually in their entirety by the sect of the Dead Sea Scrolls. The *Book of Jubilees* (text 42), itself highly prized at Qumran, was also influenced by *Enoch*.

The influence of the *Book of Enoch* was not limited to Qumran. Other groups used it, including early Christians. A quotation from *1 Enoch* 1:9 is found in the Letter of Jude (Jude 9), and several verses from *1 Enoch* 89 are quoted in the second-century Letter of Barnabas as "Scripture"; other early theologians such as Irenaeus and Clement of Alexandria show a knowledge of the legends of Enoch. The early church writer Tertullian regarded the *Book of Enoch* as inspired, although he admitted that "it is not received by some." Over time, the church became less inclined to accept Enoch as scriptural; in his fourth-century *City of God,* Augustine says that the writings circulating under the name of Enoch "are properly judged by prudent men to be not inspired" (15.23). Today it is accepted as canonical only in the church of Ethiopia.

In this book, the Enoch literature is presented in three sections. The first is the *Book of Enoch* proper (text 36) as it was known at Qumran; the second is the *Book of Giants* (text 37); and the third is *Astronomical Enoch* (text 38), the longer, original version of the *Book of the Heavenly Luminaries* (chap. 72–82 of the later *I Enoch*).

36. The Book of Enoch

4Q201–202, 4Q204–207, 4Q212, 1Q19

The Book of Enoch *begins with Enoch's description of the coming judgment, in which God will descend with his angels to bring fiery punishment on the wicked (1 Enoch 1).*

4Q201 Frag. 1 Col. 1 [1][. . . visio]n of Enoch to [the] cho[sen . . .] [2][. . . he took up] his discourse [and s]aid [. . .] [3][. . .] and from the words of [the Watchers] and all the holy ones [. . .] [4][. . . Not for thi]s generation but for a [di]stant gene[ration] do I spe[ak . . .]

[5][The] Holy [G]reat One will come out of [his dwelling . . .] [6][. . .] the [Gr]eat One, and he will shine [in the strength of his] might [. . .] [7][. . . end]s of the earth, and [a]ll the end[s of the earth] shall qu[ake . . .] [8][. . .] hills [. . .]

4Q204 Frag. 1 Col. 1 [15][. . . he will come with myri[ads of his] holy ones [. . .] [16][. . . to judge all f]lesh for [their] works [of . . .] [17][. . .] great and harsh [. . .]

Enoch tells the wicked that, although the created world obeys the laws of its Creator, they have transgressed his laws and will receive his punishment.

4Q201 Frag. 1 Col. 2 [1][. . .] and they do not vio[late] their order. Be[hold] the earth, and con[sid]er the work [2][. . . from first to l]ast, that n[o]th[ing c]hanges, and all [. . .] appears. Behold the signs of [3][summer . . .] upon it, and the signs of winter, that [all] the earth [. . .] [4][. . .] and clouds and rain pour out (water). Behold how all the tre[es] wither [5][. . . except] for fourteen trees whose leaves remain [6][. . .] two or three years [. . .] Behold the signs of [7][summer . . . the sun] burns and you seek shade and shelter from before it [8][. . .] you cannot [t]read on the dust or [o]n the [rock]s because of [. . .] [9][. . .] the leaves of all the trees blossom, covering them with greenery [. . .] [10][. . . for ho]nor and praise [. . .] So consider all these works. [11][. . . he who] lives for all eternity has done these works. Year [12][after year . . . and] all of them follow his command. But you have perverted your works [13][. . . you have spo]ken against him proud and hard words in the time of your impurity. [14][. . .] there shall be no peace for you. Then you will curse your days [and] the years of [15][your life . . . and the year]s of your destruction shall be many because of an [ete]r[nal] cu[rse, and mer]cy [16]you shall not find . . .] for an eternal curse for [. . .] [17][. . .] for all [. . .]

The fall of the angels (1 Enoch 6–8). The chief angel Shemihaza causes two hundred angels to swear an oath that, with him, they will descend to earth, mate with human women, and teach the magical arts among the human race. They do so, binding themselves with a curse, and give rise to the race of wicked giants. The giants, in turn, begin to spread sin and destruction on the earth.

Col. 3 [1]and they all said to him, Let us swe[ar . . .] [2]We will [not] turn away, any of us, from th[is] plan [. . .] [3]all of them together and [they] took an oath [. . .] [4]in the days of Jared on [. . .] [5]who swore and took an oath [. . .] and these [. . .] [6]Shemihaza wh[o . . .] second to him; Ramat[el . . .] [7]to him; Kokaba[el . . . fif]th to him;

Raame[l . . .] [8]Daniel sev[enth to him . . . eigh]th to him; Barakel nint[h to him . . .] [9]Asael tenth [to him . . .] to him; Matarel twelf[th . . .] [10]Ananel thirteenth [to him; Se]tawel [fo]urteenth to him; Shamshi[el fif-] [11]teenth to him; Sahariel [si]xteenth to him; Tummiel seven[teenth to him;] [12]Turiel eighteen[th] to him; Yammiel nine<teenth> to him; [. . .] [13]These are the leaders of the groups [of] ten; th[ey and th]eir [lieu]tenants [. . . they took] [14]women of all that they chose and [. . .] [15]and to teach them sorcery [. . .] [16]and the women became pregnant by them and bo[re . . . and giants] [17]were being born on the earth [. . . they consumed] [18]the labor of all the sons of men and did not [. . .] [19]were conspiring to slay humankind [. . .] [20]against every bird and [beas]ts of [the] earth [. . .] [21][and in] the heavens and to devour the fish of the sea; [their own] flesh [. . .]

The wicked angels begin to teach the arts of sin to the human race.

4Q202 Frag. 1 Col. 2 [26]Asae[l] ta[ug]ht [human]k[ind to] make swords of iron and ar[mor o]f cop[per . . .] [27]to them how [. . .] g[old] to be made into coins, and silver, how to make it into bracelets [. . .] [28][. . .] concerning kohl and eye shado[w . . .]

Col. 3 [1][. . . and they wer]e acting le[wdly . . .]

4Q201 Frag. 1 Col. 4 [1]Shemihaza taught spell[s . . .] [2][m]agic and sorcery and tri[cks . . .] [3][s]pells of the stars; Zikie[l taught . . .]

4Q202 Frag. 1 Col. 3 [4][. . . Ara]takoph taught spell[s of the] earth [. . .]

4Q201 Frag. 1 Col. 4 [4][Sham]shiel taught spells of [the] su[n . . .] mo[on . . .] [5][to revea]l secrets to their wives.

The complaint of the earth and its inhabitants comes before the unfallen angels remaining in heaven (1 Enoch 9).

And as many as perished [. . .] from the earth, [their] vo[ice] [6]went up be[fore heaven . . .] Michael looked out [. . . and] Raphael and Gabri[el] [7]from [the] holy places [. . . and they sa]w much blood being sh[ed on] the [earth], and all [. . .] [8]was filled with w[ickedness and] violence that [was being] committed upon it [. . .] [9]and they said before [. . .] the voice and [. . .] [10][the] gates of heaven [. . . to the holy] ones of he[aven . . . the souls] [11]who cry out [. . .] and [they] s[aid . . .]

The good angels bring the complaint of those suffering on earth to God, who commands them to bind the fallen angels and imprison them.

4Q202 Frag. 1 Col. 3 [14][. . .] our great lord, he is the Eternal Lord [. . .] [15][and the thron]e of your glory endures [for] all generations from eternity [. . .] [16][. . .] and blessing unto al[l ages . . .]

Col. 4 [5][. . . said] the [L]ord: G[o . . .] [6][son]s of the Watchers [. . .] a battle of destruction [. . . and] len[gth of days . . .] [7][. . . liv]e life [eternal . . .] [8][. . . bin[d] [9]Shem[ihaz]a and a[ll] his [companions] who united themselves to [women . . .] [10]their sons perish and [they] se[e the destructi]on [. . .] seventy ge[nerations . . . abysses of] [11]the earth until the Great Day [of Judgment . . .]

God decrees that the giants and those corrupted by them will be destroyed in the Day of Judgment. Afterward the "plant of righteousness," those chosen by God, will inherit a cleansed earth, which will regain and increase its fertility.

4Q204 Frag. 1 Col. 5 [1]And all who are g[uilty . . .] [2][. . .] and the end of [all generations.] Then they will perish for al[l ages . . .] [3][. . .] And destroy evil from [. . .] [4][. . . p]lant of righteousness and it shall be [. . . they shall be plant]ed. [5][. . . all the righ]teous will be saved and they will be [. . . they will beget thou]sands, and all the days of [6][. . . and] old age [will be fulfilled] in peace. [. . .]

[7][. . .] in truth and all of it shall be plant[ed and filled with] blessing, and all the trees [8][. . . the vine that] is planted on it [9][. . . one measure of seed will bear a th]ousand [measures].

The angels reveal the decree of heaven to Enoch, who is commanded to tell the fallen angels what is to come upon them. When he has done this, the fallen angels ask Enoch to intercede for them and petition heaven for forgiveness. But Enoch is taken to heaven, to the very house of God, and given a message of wrath, not forgiveness, for the fallen angels (1 Enoch 12–16).

Col. 6 [1]with [. . .] their [peti]tions for all of their [lives], and for each one separately [. . .] [2][. . .]

And [I wen]t away [. . .] which is to the we[st . . .] [3][. . .] th[eir] petitions [. . . visions upon me fel]l until [. . . I lifted] [4]my eyes to the gates of [heaven . . .] [5]and I saw a vision of the wrath of [rebuke . . . I came] [6]unto them, and all of them were gathered together sitting down and [. . .]

[7]And I spoke before them all [the visions . . . I spoke] [8]the words of truth and the vision, rebuking the Watchers of hea[ven . . .]

[9]The book of the words of truth [. . . the command of] [10][the Holy Grea]t One in the dream that I [dreamed . . .] [11][wh]ich the Great One ga[ve] to the sons of [men] to sp[eak . . .] [12][word]s of knowledge, he formed me and made and created (me) to r[ebuke . . .] [13]and in the vision it [ap]peared to me likewise that [your] petiti[on . . .] [14]and by the decrees [concerning] you that from n[ow on], never [. . .] [15][. . . to bind] you through all the days of et[ernity . . .] [16]their sons and by [. . .] of y[our] loved ones [. . .] [17]destruction, likewise [yo]ur p[etition] for [them . . . even if] [18]you pray and make suppli[cations . . .] [19]from the writing that I have written. [. . . the clouds] [20]were calling to me, and meteors and li[ghtning hastened me . . . the winds brought me] [21]upward and carried me and bro[ugh]t me into [heaven . . .] [22][and tongue]s of fire circling all arou[nd . . .] [23][unti]l I drew near to a gr[eat] house [. . .] [24][. . . its] foundations were made [of] snow [. . .] [25][. . .] all the[ir] walls [. . .] [26][. . . as] snow, and all [. . .] [27][. . .] and [fear] fell [upon me . . .] [28][. . . a house] larger than the first one and all of it [. . .] [29][. . . I am not a]ble to describe to y[ou . . .]

While he is in heaven, the angels show Enoch the entirety of earth and the underworld, including the area usually hidden from humanity (1 Enoch 17–36). Most of this section has not survived in the scrolls.

Enoch is shown the mountain where the souls of the dead are kept. Enoch hears the voice of Abel continuing to cry out against his murderer, Cain (Gen. 4:10).

4Q206 Frag. 1 Col. 22 [1][soul]s of all the sons of men, and behold these are the pits for a place of imprisonment. [2]For this were they made until a day that they are judged, until the very time and day o[f] [3]the Great Judgment that will be passed on them.

There I saw the spirit [4]of a dead man making complaint, [and] its sound(?) rose up to heaven, an outcry and compla[int] [5][. . . to Raphae]l, the Watcher and holy one w[ho . . .]

Fragments survive of Enoch's journey to the far eastern parts of the earth (1 Enoch 30–33).

4Q204 Frag. 1 Col. 12 [23][. . . beyon]d these things, I went far [to the east . . .] [24][. . . of] goodly reeds of spice which [25][. . .] I [saw] the cinnamon spice.

And beyond the valleys [26][. . . and I saw] other [mountain]s, and also in them I saw trees, from which there came out [27][sap . . . galbanu]m. [And be]yond these mountains, I was shown [28][another] mountain [. . .] all the trees [in it . . .] and it was like the bark of al[mond] [29][. . .] from [them] a [swe]et smell when the bark was crushed.

4Q206 Frag. 1 Col. 26 [17][. . .] these, toward the northeast of them I [was sh]own other mountains [18][. . .] fine [n]ard and mastic and cardamom [and pe]pper.

Enoch is taken to the Garden of Eden and shown the Tree of the Knowledge of Good and Evil (1 Enoch 32).

And from there I was carried [19][east]ward of all these mountains, far away from them, to the east of the earth, and [I] was made to pass [20][hig]h above [the] Red [Sea], but I went farther still and was carried abo[ve] [21]the darkness, far away from it. And I was made to come to the Garden of Truth.

Col. 27 [9][This is the tree of knowledge that they ate from, your Ancient Father] [10][and] your Great Mother, and [they] kn[ew . . .] [11]that [they were] naked [. . .]

The next two sections of the Ethiopic Book of Enoch—the Parables of Enoch *(chaps. 37–71) and the* Book of the Heavenly Luminaries *(chaps. 72–82) —are not found in the Qumran scrolls as part of the* Book of Enoch. *In the original Aramaic text, the story of Enoch's journeys to the ends of the earth (1 Enoch 17–36) is followed by a section telling of Enoch's dream visions (1 Enoch 83–90), in which he sees the history of Israel from Adam and Eve to the establishment of the messianic kingdom. All the human figures are portrayed allegorically by means of various animals. This section is sometimes known as the "Animal Apocalypse."*

The fall of the wicked angels (1 Enoch 86). Enoch sees stars fall from heaven among a herd of cows. The stars turn into bulls and begin to mate with the cows.

4Q207 Frag. 1 [1][. . . the heavens] above [and, behold] a star [. . .] [2][. . . it grazed] among them. Then, behold, [I] saw [. . .] [3][. . .] and their sheepfolds [and] t[heir c]alves [. . .] [4][. . .] and, behold, man[y] stars [. . .] [5][. . .] the [bu]lls in [the] mid[st . . .]

The punishment of the fallen angels (1 Enoch 88). The "fallen stars" are bound and cast into pits by the four archangels Michael, Gabriel, Raphael, and Uriel.

4Q206 Frag. 4 Col. 1 [11][. . .] numerous [s]tars [12][. . . bound] all of them hand and foot and threw [13][them into the abyss . . . one of] the four went to one of the bulls [. . .]

The Flood (1 Enoch 89:1–9). One of the "bulls" (Noah) builds a boat and is saved from the deluge.

[14][. . . and he m]ade himself a boat and dwelt within it [15][. . .] with him to the boat, and the boat was coated and covered [16][. . . I was] watching and, behold, seven sluices were pouring out [17][water . . .] and, behold, chambers were opened within the earth, and they began [18][. . . and] while I was watching, the earth was covered with water [19][. . . the water was] standing on the earth, and the bulls sank down, drowning [20][. . .] but the boat sailed on top of the water, and all the bulls [21][. . .] and the elephants and the oxen.

The Flood is ended and the ark comes to rest on a mountaintop.

Col. 2 [1][. . . in] my [dr]eam until [the] s[luices . . .] [2][. . .] the chambers were stopped up [. . . the water was] [3]going down into them until it disappeared [. . . the boat] [4]came aground [o]n the earth [. . .]

The sojourn of Israel in Egypt (1 Enoch 89:10–16). A "ram" (Jacob) brings eleven "sheep" (the sons of Jacob) to dwell among the "wolves" (Egyptians).

[16]And the ram brought [the eleven . . .] [17]among the wolves and [they] mul[tiplied . . .] [18]they began to oppress [the] flock [. . .] [19][to] sink them in the water. T[hen . . .]

The Exodus and Sinai (1 Enoch 89:23–37). The wolves pursue the escaping sheep, but are drowned when the waters of the Red Sea close over them. The sheep who led the flock (Moses) supplies them with water and leads them to a high rock (Mount Sinai).

Col. 3 [14][. . .] the [w]olves were pursuing [the] flock [. . .] [15][. . . and] the waters covered them. And [the] f[lock . . .] [16][. . .] wasteland, a place which [. . .] [17][. . .] and their eyes were opened [. . .] [18][. . .] to them, and he gave to th[em] water [to dr]i[nk . . .] [19][. . . w]ent up to the t[op of] a high r[ock], and [20][. . . and a]ll of [them s]tood [far] off [. . .]

1 Enoch 89:31–37: The sheep are afraid to behold the "lord of the flock," and while their leader (Moses) goes to the top of the rock, the flock goes astray and wishes to return to their old sheepfolds (Egypt). But the leading sheep brings them back, is changed into a human being, and builds a tent for the lord of the flock. All of this is a retelling of the story of Israel at Sinai as given in Exodus 24–34.

4Q204 Frag. 4 [1][. . .] all of them were a[f]ra[i]d [. . . be]fo[re him] [2][. . . the sheep] who was among them, We are not able to sta[nd] before [. . .] [3][. . .] a second time and ascended to the top of that rock; but the flock began to be bl[inded] [4][. . .] them, but the sheep was not aware of them. And the lord of the flock became angry at [. . .] [5][. . .] that [sheep], and he came to the flock and found most of them bl[inded] [6][. . . feared b]efore him and wanted to re[tu]rn to their folds. [7][. . .] all the ones who had strayed, and they began to [. . .] [8][. . .] that sheep brought back all the flock that had strayed to th[eir] folds. [9][. . .] not [to] reveal or confront or oppress he swore [. . .] [10][. . .] this [s]hee[p] was changed and became a man and made a t[ent.]

The last section of the Book of Enoch *(1 Enoch 91–107) is an address of Enoch to his son, Methuselah. It combines visions of the coming divine judgment, moral exhortation, and a prophecy of Israel's story divided into ten "weeks" (called the "Apocalypse of Weeks").*

Enoch foresees the time when the righteous prevail on the earth and every sinner is destroyed (1 Enoch 91).

4Q212 Frag. 1 Col. 2 [13][and] the [righteous . . .] [14][standi]ng and walk[ing . . .] [15]and to him pra[ise . . .] [16]and [the] ear[th] shall have rest [. . .] [17]all the generations of the age[s . . .] [18]ways of righteousness [. . .] [19]so you will know what [will happen . . . the ways of] [20]righteousness, to walk in them [. . .] [21][be]cause he will be destroyed to the uttermost of destruction [. . .]

The introduction to the "Apocalypse of Weeks" (1 Enoch 92–93).

[This is the book] [22][that he wr]ote and gave to Meth[uselah . . .] [23][and] the wisest of men, and [the] chos[en of the] sons of [. . .] [24][his]

sons [and] for future generations, all who [. . .] [25][. . . Be not] in perplexity, you [. . .]. . .

Col. 3 [18][. . . E]noch [took up] his discourse, [19]saying [. . .] from the plant of [20]uprightness [. . .] I am [21]Enoch, I will decl[are . . . from] the utterance of the Watchers and holy ones [22]I have come to know all [. . . I] re[ad and pondere]d.

The first and second weeks: creation, the Fall, and the Flood (1 Enoch 93).

[23]Enoch took up his discourse and said, I [was born] seventh [. . .] [24][in the] first [week], and for me there still was righteousness [. . .] [25][a] second [week], in which deceit and crime shall flourish [. . .]

The seventh week: the election of the righteous.

Col. 4 [12][. . . s]hall be chosen [. . .] to be witnesses of truth from [the] eter[n]al p[lant] [13]of righteousness, to whom shall be given seven[fold] wisdom and knowledge [. . .] [14]And they will uproot the foundations of wrongdoing and the work of deceit, to pass [judgment] on it.

The eighth week: the righteous execute judgment on the wicked.

[15]And after it shall come an eighth week, one of righteousness, in which [a sword] shall be given [16]to all the righteous to execute true judgment on all the wicked, [17]and the wicked will be delivered into their hands. When it is over, they will acquire possessions righteously, [18]and a great temple of [ki]n[g]ship will be built in majestic splendor to endure for eternal generations.

The ninth week: the universal revelation of truth.

[19]And after it shall come a ninth week, and t[ruth . . .] will be revealed [20]to all those on the entire earth, and all the wor[ks of evil shall depart] from all [21]the whole earth, and they will throw [them] into the pit[s . . .] all of them [22]to the way of truth eternal.

The tenth week: the final judgment and the revelation of the new heavens and the new earth.

And af[ter it . . .] [23]eternal judgment, and the time of the Great Judgment [. . .] the [24]former heavens will pass away, and [the new] heavens [. . . lights of] heaven [25][will] s[hin]e and rise forevermo[re . . .] weeks, years [26][. . .] there will be [no] end to [. . . and] they will do [righ]teousness.

Enoch, alone of all humankind, has become the chosen vessel of God's revelation.

Col. 5 [15][. . . who is ab]le to know what is in the mind of [the Lord . . . is there one] [16][wh]o is able to hear the words of the Holy One? [. . .] [17]Or who is he of all humankind who [is able . . .] [18]the splendor of [. . .] [19]to return and to re[late . . .] [20]Or who is he [who . . . is able to know] [21]the length and breadth of the whole earth, or [. . .] [22]and its form? And who is he of all humankind who is ab[le . . . how great is] [23]the height of heaven, or how [its foundations] support [. . .] [24]And now, to you I say, my sons [. . .] [25][the] ways of truth [. . .]

The birth of Noah (1 Enoch 106–107). The grandson of Enoch, Noah, is born with supernatural signs attending his birth: his eyes shine with supernatural radiance, and he is able to speak and praise God from the cradle.

1Q19 Frag. 3 [2][. . . they] were astoun[ded . . .] [3][a] firstborn son has been born, for glorious [is his face . . . It frightened] [4]his father. And when Lamech saw [the child . . .] [5][light filled] the rooms of the house like rays of the sun [. . .] [6][. . .] to frighten [. . .]

Lamech is afraid the child is not his, but the offspring of one of the fallen angels. Methuselah goes to Enoch to find out the truth. (The same story appears in Tales of the Patriarchs, *text 4.) Enoch replies that the child is sent from God as a response to the wickedness of the earth.*

4Q204 Frag. 5 Col. 2 [17][. . .] in the days of Jared [my] fa[ther] [18]they transgressed [. . . sin]ning and trans[gressing . . .] they changed [. . .] [19][. . .] [20][. . . on] the [ear]th [. . . this child] [21]who is born [unto yo]u [. . .] his [three sons] will be sa[ved . . . on the] earth.

[22][. . . and] the earth [will be pur]ified [by] the [g]reat destruction.

[. . .] truly [. . .] [23]the [chi]ld [who is b]or[n . . .] his name [Noah . . .] [24][. . .] he shall be saved [. . .] [25][. . . that] shall be in [his] days.

Enoch knows this because he has read in the heavenly tablets all that is to come. Although wickedness will continue to grow on the earth, even after Noah, a time will come when righteousness will prevail over evil.

[And a]fte[r them shall] come mighty wicked[ness . . .] [26]in [their] d[a]ys, [fo]r I know the mysteries [of] the Holy Ones. They told me and showed me [. . . the tablets of] [27]heaven I have read. And I saw written in them that each generation will be more evil than the last, and will continue being evil [until] [28]the generations of truth [arise], and evil and wickedness will come to an end, and crime will cease from the earth and [. . .] [29]upon them.

So now go to Lamech your [son . . . tell him] [30]that this child is his son in all truth and not in lies [. . .]

—E.M.C.

37. The Book of Giants

4Q203, 4Q530–532, 6Q8, 1Q23, 2Q26

Besides fragments of the previously known *1 Enoch,* fragments of another Enoch story, the *Book of Giants,* were found at Qumran. This book had been known only through scattered allusions and very fragmentary Central Asian manuscripts of a version known and used by the adherents of the Manichean heresy of the third and fourth centuries C.E. The seven fragmentary Qumran scrolls of *Giants* show that the composition is at least five hundred years older than previously thought.

Enoch lived before the Flood, during a time when the world, in ancient imagination, was very different. Human beings lived much longer for one thing; Enoch's son, Methuselah, for instance, attained the age of 969 years. Another difference was that angels and humans interacted freely—so freely, in fact, that some of the angels begot children with human females. This fact is neutrally reported in Genesis (6:1–4), but other stories view this episode as the source of the corruption that made the punishing flood necessary. According to the *Book of Enoch,* the mingling of angel and human was actually the idea of Shemihaza, the leader of the evil angels, who lured two hundred others to cohabit with women. The offspring of these unnatural unions were giants, 450 feet high. The wicked angels and the giants began to oppress the humans and teach them to do evil. For this reason God determined to imprison the angels until the final judgment and to destroy the earth with a flood. Enoch's efforts to intercede with heaven for the fallen angels were unsuccessful (*1 Enoch* 6–16).

The *Book of Giants* retells part of this story and elaborates on the exploits of the giants, especially the two children of Shemihaza, Ohya and Hahya. Since no complete manuscript exists of *Giants,* its exact contents and their order remains a matter of guesswork. Most of the content of the present fragments concerns the giants' ominous dreams and Enoch's efforts to interpret them and to intercede with God on the giants' behalf. Unfortunately, little remains of the independent adventures of the giants, but it is likely that these tales were at least partially derived from ancient Near Eastern mythology. Thus the name of one of the giants is Gilgamesh, the Babylonian hero and subject of a great epic written in the third millennium B.C.E.

A summary statement of the descent of the wicked angels, bringing both knowledge and havoc (cf. Gen. 6:1–2, 4).

1Q23 Frags. 9 + 14 + 15 [2][. . .] they knew the se[crets of . . .] [3][. . . si]n was great in the earth [. . .] [4][. . .] and they killed ma[ny . . .] [5][. . . they begat] giants [. . .]

The angels exploit the fruitfulness of the earth.

4Q531 Frags. 2–3 [2][. . . everything that the] earth produced [. . .] [3][. . .] the gr[ea]t fish [. . .] [4][. . .] all the birds of the sky with all that grew [. . .] [5][. . . and with] plants yielding seed of the earth and all kinds of grain and all the trees [. . .] [6][. . . and with] sheep, small cattle with [. . .] [7][. . . al]l creeping things of the earth and after all [. . .] [8][. . . eve]ry harsh deed and utterance from [. . .] [9][. . .] male and female, and among humans [. . .] [10][. . .] knowledge [. . .] wisdom and [. . .]

The two hundred angels choose animals, including presumably humans, on which to perform unnatural acts.

1Q23 Frags. 1 + 6 + 22 [1][. . . two hundred] [2]donkeys, two hundred asses, two hundr[ed . . . rams of the] [3]flock, two hundred goats, two hundred [. . . beasts of the] [4]field from every animal, and thousands from every [bird . . .] [5][. . .] then [. . .]

The outcome of the demonic corruption was violence, perversion, and a brood of monstrous beings (cf. Gen. 6:4, and the Book of Watchers *from 1 Enoch, text 36).*

4Q531 Frag. 1 [1][. . .] they defiled [. . .] [2][. . . they begot] giants and monsters [. . .] [3][. . .] they begot and, behold, a[ll the earth was corrupted . . .] [4][. . .] with its blood and by the hand of [. . .] [5][giants] which did not suffice for them and [. . .] [6][. . .] and they were seeking to devour many [. . .] [7][. . .] [8][. . .] the monsters [destro]yed it.

4Q532 Frag. 2 [2][. . .] flesh [. . .] [3][. . .] monster[s . . .] [4][. . .] they were stand[ing . . .] [5][. . .] the earth [grew corrupt . . .] [6][. . .] they were considering [. . .] [7][. . .] from the Watchers upon [. . .] [8][. . .] perished and died [. . .] [9][. . .] they caused great corruption in the ea[rth . . .] [10][. . . this did not] suffice to ea[t . . .] [11][. . .] the earth and until [. . .] [12][. . .] in the earth in all [. . .] [13][. . .] great and now not [. . .] [14][. . .] they [pl]aced a stro[ng] bon[d . . .]

The giants begin to be troubled by a series of dreams and visions. Mahway, the titan son of the angel Barakel, reports the first of these dreams to his fellow giants. He sees a tablet being immersed in water. When it emerges, all but three names have been washed away. The dream may symbolize the destruction of all but Noah and his sons by the flood.

2Q26 [1][. . .] they drenched the tablet in the wa[ter . . .] [2][. . .] the waters went up over the [tab]let [. . .] [3][. . .] they lifted out the tablet from the waters, the tablet [. . .]

The giant goes to the others and they discuss the dream.

4Q530 Frag. 1 Col. 1 [2][. . . this vision is for] cursing and sorrow. I am the one who confessed [3][. . .] and all the whole group of the castaways that I shall go to [. . .] [4][. . . the spirits of the sl]ain complaining about their killers and crying out [5][. . .] that we shall die together and be made an end of [6][. . .] much [wra]th, and I will be sleeping, and bread [7][. . .] the vision had shut my eyelids, and moreover [8][. . .] entered into the gathering of the giants [9][. . .]

6Q8 Frag. 1 [2][. . .] Ohya [answered] and he said to Mahway [. . .] [3][. . .] without trembling. Who showed you all this vision, [my] br[other? . . . And Mahway answered] [4][and said to Ohy]a, Barakel, my father, was with me. [. . .] [5][. . . And] Mahway had not [fi]nished [te]lling what [. . . showed him,] [6][and Ohya answered and said to h]im, Now I have heard wonders! If a barr[en woman] gives birth [. . .]

4Q203 Frag. 4 [3][There]upon Ohya said to Ha[hya . . .] [4][. . . to be destroyed] from upon the earth and [. . .] [5][. . . the ea]rth. Wh[en . . .] [6][. . .] they began to weep befo[re the giants . . .]

Frag. 7a [3][. . .] your strength [. . .] [4][. . .] [5]Thereup[on] Ohya [said] to Hahy[a . . . Then he answered, It is not] [6]for us, [but] for Azazel, for he did [. . . the children of angels] [7]are the giants, and the W[atchers] will forget all [their] com[panions . . .]

The giants realize the futility of fighting against the forces of heaven. The first speaker may be Gilgamesh or Hobabish.

4Q531 Frag. 22 [3][. . . I am a] giant, and by the mighty strength of my arm and my own great strength [4][I went up against a]ll mortals, and I have made war against them; but I am not [5][. . .] able to stand against them, for my opponents [6][are angels who] reside in [Heav]en, and they dwell in the holy places. And not [7][. . . they] are stronger than I. [8][. . .] of the wild beast has come, and the wild man they call [me.]

[9][. . .] Then Ohya said to him, My dream disturbed [me] [10][. . . the sle]ep of my eyes [vanished], to let me see a [vis]ion. Now I know that because of [11][the vision I will not] sleep, and I will not hasten to [. . .] [12][And then Gi]lgamesh said: Your [d]ream [. . .]

Ohya's dream vision is of a tree that is uprooted except for three of its roots; the vision's import may be the same as that of the first dream.

6Q8 Frag. 2 [1]three of its roots [. . .] [2][while] I was [watching,] there came [. . . they moved the roots into] [3]this garden, all of it [. . .]

Ohya discusses the vision. The reading of the fragment and the resulting translation is not certain.

4Q530 Frag. 2 Col. 2 [1]concerns the death of our souls. [Then en]tered all his comrades, [and Oh]ya told them what Gilgamesh said to him [2][. . .] and it was said [. . .] concerning his soul, the guilty one has cursed the potentates [3]and the giants were glad concerning him. Then he turned and [. . .] concerning him.

More dreams afflict the giants. The details of this vision are obscure, but it bodes ill for the giants. The dreamers speak first to the monsters, then to the giants.

Thereupon two of them had dreams [4]and the sleep of their eyes fled from them, and [they] a[rose . . . and o]pened their eyes [5]and came to [. . .] and told their dreams, and in the assembly of [their] c[omrades] [6]the monsters [. . . In] my dream I was watching this very night [7][and there was a great garden . . .] gardeners and they were watering [8][every tree in the garden . . . two hundred trees and] large shoots came out of their root [9][. . .] while flames of fire from [10][heaven . . .] in all the waters, and the fire burned in all [11][. . .] the earth when [. . .] [12][. . .] and this was the end of the dream.

[13][. . .] the giants [were not] able to tell him [14][the d]rea[m . . .]

Someone suggests that Enoch be found to interpret the vision.

This [dre]am you should tell [to Eno]ch, the noted scribe, and he will interpret for us [15]the dream. Thereupon his brother Ohya [de]clared and said to the giants, [16]I too had a dream this night, O giants, and, behold, the Ruler of Heaven came down to earth [17]and thrones were set out and the Great Holy One sa[t . . . were] serving him a thousand thousands [18][. . . be]fore him were standing and behold [. . .] were opened and a judgment was uttered and judgment [19][. . . wr]itten and signed with a mark [. . .] all that lived and everything mortal and [20][. . .] that was the end of the dream. [Thereupon] all the giants [and monsters] grew afraid [21]and called Mahway. He came to [them and the] giants sent him to Enoch [22][the noted scribe]. They said to him, Go [. . .] to you that [23][. . .] you have heard his voice. And he said to him, He will tell [y]ou the me[ani]ng of the dreams and that all [. . .] [24][. . .] in truth. Truly they brought [. . .] **Frag. 7 Col. 2** [3]request for mercy of the giants [. . .]

After a cosmic journey, Mahway comes to Enoch and makes his request.

[. . . Mahway mounted up in the air] [4]like strong winds, and flew with his hands like an ea[gle . . . he left behind] [5]the inhabited world and passed over Desolation, the great desert [. . .] [6]and Enoch saw hi[m] and hailed him, and Mahway said to him [. . . I was sent] [7]hither and to [. . .] a second time to you [. . . The giants await] [8]your words, and all the monsters of the earth. If [. . .] has been carried [. . .] [9]from the days of [. . .] their [. . .] and they will be added [. . .] [10][. . .] we would know from you their meaning [. . .] [11][. . . two hundred garden]ers that from heaven [came down . . .]

Enoch sends back a letter on a tablet with a grim message of judgment, but with hope for repentance.

4Q203 Frag. 8 [1]The scribe [Enoch . . .] [2][. . .] [3]a copy of the sec[o]nd tablet of the l[etter . .] [4]in the very handwri[ti]ng of Enoch the noted scribe [. . . In the name of God the great] [5]and holy one, to Shemihaza and all [his] c[ompanions . . .] [6]let it be known to you th[at . . .] [7]and the things you have done, and that your wi[ves . . .] [8]they [and their] sons [and] the [w]ives o[f their sons . . .] [9]by your licentiousness on the earth, and there has been [up]on you [. . . and the land is crying out] [10]and complaining about you [and] the deeds of your sons [. . .] [11]the harm that you have done to it. [. . .] [12]unto Raphael it has reached; and, behold, destruc[tion is coming, a great flood, and it will destroy all living things] [13]and whatever is in the deserts and the seas. And the meaning of [the] matter [. . .] [14]upon you for evil. But now, loosen the bonds [. . .] [15]and pray.

This fragment may possibly belong with Enoch's speech above.

4Q531 Frag. 7 [1][. . .] and to Ahiram [. . .] [2][. . . and to] Anael and to Barake[l and to the mo]nsters [. . .] [3][. . .] and to Naamel and to Ra[ziel] and to Ammiel [. . .] [4][. . . and to] all these giants: What are these sins to you that [you] killed [. . .] [5][. . .] Behold, all of these have gone away through your sword [. . .] [6][. . . blood] like great rivers on [the] ea[rth . . .]

Fragments apparently detailing another vision that Enoch saw.

Frag. 24 [1][. . .] a thousand thousands [were serving] him [2][. . .] not frightened at any king or [. . .] [3][. . . great fear] seized me and I fell on my face; [I] hea[rd] his voice [. . .] [4][. . .] dwelt among human beings but he did not learn from them [. . .]

4Q203 Frag. 9 [2][. . . qu]aking before the splendor of [your] gl[ory . . .] [3][. . .] because [you] kno[w] all mysteries [. . .] [4][. . .] and nothing is too hard for you [. . .] [5][. . . be]fore you and now [. . .] [6][. . .] the kingdom of your greatness [. . .]

—E.M.C.

38. Astronomical Enoch

4Q208–211

As noted in the "Introduction to the Enoch Literature" above, the work known as *1 Enoch* contains seven discrete works, all of which presumably once circulated separately. The third division in the Ethiopic tradition, chapters 72–82, bears the Ethiopic title "Book of the Revolution of the Heavenly Luminaries." Four Aramaic manuscripts among the Dead Sea Scrolls contain a substantially longer form of this part of *1 Enoch,* and these manuscripts are collectively called *Astronomical Enoch* to differentiate them from the "*Reader's Digest*" form that has come down in Ethiopic. None of the Qumran manuscripts of *Astronomical Enoch* preserve any of the other six divisions of *1 Enoch,* so it appears that *Astronomical Enoch* did indeed circulate separately from the other Enochic literature.

It is even possible that *Astronomical Enoch* is itself a composite work, since of the four Dead Sea Scroll manuscripts assigned to it, one of them (4Q208) contains nothing but the "synchronistic calendar" (see text 72), while 4Q210–211 contain only material from the second part of *Astronomical Enoch* (the part that roughly corresponds to *1 Enoch* 76–78; 82). 4Q209 alone bridges the gap and includes material from both subdivisions.

In a nutshell, the synchronistic calendar tabulates aspects of the movements of the sun and the moon. Using repetitive and stereotyped phrases the author describes the waxing and waning of the moon. He conceives of the moon's light as divided into fourteen parts, though he describes those parts in terms of the holy number seven: each seventh is divided in half, and the waxing and waning proceeds one-half seventh per day. He synchronizes the conjunctions and oppositions of the sun and moon as well, conceiving of their movements in terms of entry and exit into any of six "gates" of heaven. The gates stand at the two horizons, east and west. All of this discussion is highly technical and, frankly, for most people exceedingly boring. Furthermore, the material is poorly suited to verbal description; what is needed is a table or illustration. For these reasons and possibly others the motivation to abbreviate the synchronistic calendar must have been considerable, and the form known in *Astronomical Enoch* survived in neither Greek nor Ethiopic. It did have considerable influence on Jewish thought in the time of the scrolls, and in particular on the circles whose calendrical materials are represented in this book. Note especially the *Phases of the Moon* (text 69) for further development of the synchronistic calendar.

1 Enoch 76–78 and 82 contain materials of a different character from the synchronistic calendar. These materials too concern heavenly movements and gates and the relations between the things of heaven and their observable earthly effects. The Qumran materials that correspond to these chapters are somewhat longer and frequently slightly different in their conceptions. They make clear that the Greek-Ethiopic tradition was interpretive and did not always clearly understand the Aramaic; or else, as is also possible, the Aramaic tradition itself was somewhat variegated and what we find in the scrolls is only one form of what circulated among the Jews.

This fragment probably fits either in the third or fourth month of the synchronistic calendar.

4Q208 Frag. 1 [1][and a] ha[l]f [sevenths.] And the moon shines on [the eleventh night of this month] [2]at five and a hal[f] sevenths strength. [Then it sets and enters the] [3]first gate, and it is dark the rest [of this night . . .]

Because this portion is broken at crucial points, no certain placement is possible. It can belong to any one of six months of the year: the second, third, fourth, eighth, ninth, or tenth.

Frags. 19 + 21 [1]fiv[e]. [And the moon's light equals five-sevenths strength. Then it exits and rules] [2]over the rest of this day [with two-sevenths strength. It shines on the tenth night of this month with] [3]five-[sevenths strength.] Then it [se]ts [and] enters [gate x and is dark the rest of] [4]this night at two-sevenths darkness. And [it increases during this day to five] [5]and one-half [sevenths] strength. Its light equals [. . .]

This portion may tentatively be restored as representing portions of days 6–11 of the third or fourth month of the synchronistic calendar.

4Q209 Frag. 1 Col. 1 [1][. . . And the moon's light shines on the sixth night of this month at three-sevenths strength. T]hen it set[s and enters the fourth gate] [2][and is dark the rest of this night at four-sevenths darkness. It increases during this day to three and one-half sevenths strength, so] its light [equals] three and [one-hal]f sevenths. [3][Then it exits from the fourth gate and rules over the rest of this day at three and one-half sevenths strength. And the moon's light shines] on the [se]venth night of this month at three and one-half sevenths strength. [4][Then it sets and enters the third gate and is dark the rest of this night at three and one-half sevenths darkness. It increas]es during this day to four-sevenths strength, so its [light] equals [5][four-sevenths strength. Then it exits from the third gate and rules over the rest of this day at three-sevenths strength.] And it shines on the eighth night of this month at [four]-sevenths strength. [6][Then it sets and enters and is dark during the rest of this night at three-sevenths darkness. It increases during this day to] four-[seve]nths and one-half, so its light equals [7][four and one-half sevenths strength. Then it exits and rules over the rest of this day at two and one-half sevenths strength. And] it shines on the ninth night of this month at [four and one-half]-sevenths strength. [8][Then it sets and enters the second gate and is dark during the rest of this night at two and one-half sevenths darkness. It increases during] this [day] to five-sevenths strength, [9][so its light equals five-sevenths strength. Then it exits from the second gate and reigns over the rest of this day at two-sevenths strength. It shines on the tenth night of this month at five-sevenths strength.] [10][Then it sets and enters and is dark during the rest of this night at two-sevenths darkness. It increases during this day to five and one-half sevenths strength, so its light equals] [11][five and one-half sevenths strength. Then it exits and rules over the rest of this day at one and one-half sevenths strength. Then it shines on] the eleventh [nigh]t of this month [at five] [12][and one-half sevenths strength. Then it sets and enters and is dark during the rest of this night at one and one-half sevenths darkness. It increases during this day to] six-[sevenths strength, so its light equals six-s[evenths . . .]

This is the description of a twenty-nine-day month. The ancients reworked the scheme of the synchronistic calendar in various ways, one of which reveals itself in l. 9, where one would expect "six-sevenths," not "six and one-half sevenths."

Frag. 2 Col. 2 [2][And the moon's light shines on] the twelfth [night] of this month at [three-se]ve[nths strength. Then it sets and enters and is dark during the rest of this night at one-seventh darkness.] [3][And it increases during] this [da]y up to six and one-half sevenths strength, so [its light] equals [six and one-half sevenths. Then it exits and rules over the rest of this day] [4][at a strength of one-]half seventh. And it shines on the thir[teenth] night [of this month at six and one-half sevenths strength. Then it sets and enters and is dark during the rest of] [5]this [night] at one-seventh darkness. It increases this entire day, becoming full. [. . .] [6]And the moon shines on the entire fourteenth night of [this] mon[th as full . . .] [7]On the fifteenth ni[gh]t of this month it is one-seventh covered, one-seventh being subtra[cted from its light. Then it exits and shines] [8]during the rest of [th]is ni[gh]t at six-sevenths strength. The moon's darkening increases during [this] day [to one-seventh darkness. Then it sets and enters and is covered during the rest of] [9]this day to six and one-half sevenths strength. On [the sixteenth] ni[ght of this month it is covered up to one-seventh darkness,] one-[se]venth [being subtracted from its light.] [10]Then it exits and shines during the [re]st of [th]is night [at six-sevenths strength. It increases during this day to one and one-half sevenths, then] [11][sets and] enters and is covered during the rest of this day at [five and one-half] seve[nths darkness . . .]

This fragment most probably describes days 2–4 of the eleventh month.

Frag. 3 [2][And the moon's light shines on] the seco[nd night] of this month at one-seventh strength. [Then it sets and enters the second gate, and is dark during the rest of this night at six-sevenths darkness.] [3][It increases] during the day to one and one-half sev[enths] strength, so [its light] equals [one and one-half sevenths. Then it exits from the second gate and rules over the rest of] [4][this day] at five and one-half [sev]enths strength. [And the moon shines on the third night of this month at one and one-half sevenths. Then it sets, enters and is dark] [5][during the rest of this night] at fiv[e and one-half] sevenths strength. [It increases during this day to two-sevenths, so its light equals two-sevenths strength. Then it exits] [6][and rules over the rest of] this [d]ay [at five-sevenths strength. And it shines on the fourth night of this month at two-sevenths strength, then] [7][sets and] enters the thir[d gate. It is dark during the rest of this night at five-sevenths darkness, then increases during this day to two and one-half sevenths strength, so its light equals] [8]two and one-half [sevenths.] And [then it exits from the third gate . . .]

This fragment concerns either days 22–23 of a twenty-nine-day month or days 23–24 of a thirty-day month.

Frag. 4 [1][four. Then the moon exits and shines during the rest of] this [night at three-s]ev[enths strength. Its darkness increases during this day up to four and one-half sevenths,] [2][then it sets and enters and is covered the rest of] this [day] at [two and] one-half sevenths. [3][On the twenty-fourth night of this month the moon is covered at] four [and] one-half [seve]nths, [four and one-half sevenths] being subtracted [from its light.] [4][Then it exits and shines during the rest] of this [night] at [two and] one-half seventh[s. It increases during this day to five-sevenths . . .]

The calculations that appear in this description of a thirty-day month are incorrect; l. 2 should read not "two-sevenths" but "one and one-half sevenths." This sort of error makes clear the difficulty of transcribing technical material as well as the fact that ancient scribes did not always understand what they copied. It was very easy to make mistakes, and they were often difficult to detect at a quick reading.

Frag. 5 [1][fi]ve and one-half [sevenths. And on the eighteenth night of this month the moon is covered at two-sevenths. Subtracted from its light are] [2]two-[seventh]s. Then [it exits and shines during the rest of this night at five and one-half sevenths. It increases during] [3]this [day] to two-sevenths strength, then s[ets and enters and is covered during the rest of this day at five-sevenths darkness.] [4]On the nineteenth night of this month it is cov[ered at two-sevenths, two-sevenths being subtracted from its light. Then] [5]it exits and shines during the rest of this night at [five-]sevenths strength. [It increases during this day to two and one-half sevenths, then] [6][sets and en]ters. [It is covered during the r]est of this day at [four and one-half] seventh[s. On the twentieth night of this month the moon is covered at two and one-half sevenths,] [7][two and one-half sevenths being subtracted from] its [li]ght. [Then it exits . . .]

This portion concerns the last days of a thirty-day month, but it cannot be the ninth month since frag. 7, col. 2 (below) contains that description.

Frag. 6 [4][five and one-half sevenths. Then the moon exits and shines during the rest of this night at one and one-ha]lf [sevenths strength.] Darkness increases during this day to [six-]seven[ths. Then] [5][the moon sets and enters and is covered during the rest of this day at one-seventh. On the twe]nty-[seventh] night of this month it is six-sevenths covered, there [being subtra]cted from its li[g]ht [6][six-sevenths. Then it exits and shines during the rest of this night at one-seventh strength. Darkness increases during] this [d]ay to six and one-half sevenths. Then the moon se[ts] [7][and enters and is covered during the rest of this day at one-half of a seventh. On the] twenty-eighth [night] of this month the moon is covered at six and one-half sevenths darkness, there being subtracted from [its li]ght [8][six and one-half sevenths. Then it exits and shines] during the rest of this night with one-half of a seventh. Darkness increases during this day, becoming complete. Then the moon sets and enters [9][the *x* gate. It is completely dark during the rest] of this da[y]. The rest of its light is removed and its disk exits, empty of all light, hidden by [the] s[un . . .]

Days 24–27 of the ninth month.

Frag. 7 Col. 2 [2][and darkness increases during this day to four and one-half sevenths. Then the moon sets and enters and is covered during the rest of] this day at [two and one-half] sevenths. [3][On the twent]y-[fourth night] of this month, the moon is covered at four and one-half sevenths. Subtracted from its light are [4][four and one-half sevenths. T]hen it exits and shines during the rest of this night at two and one-half sevenths strength. Darkness increases [5][during] this [d]ay to five-sevenths, then it sets and enters. It is covered during the rest of this day at two-sevenths. [6]On the twenty-fifth night of this month the moon is covered at five-sevenths, five-sevenths being subtracted from its light. [7]Then it exits and shines during the rest of this night at two-sevenths strength. Darkness increases during this day to five and one-half sevenths. [8]Then the moon sets [and] enters the second gate and is covered during the rest of this day at one and one-half sevenths. [9]On the twenty-sixth night of this month it is covered at five and one-half sevenths darkness; subtracted from its light are five [10]and one-half sevenths. Then the moon exits from the second gate and shines during the rest of this night at one and one-half sevenths strength. Darkness increases during this day [11]to six-sevenths. Then the moon sets and enters and is covered during the rest of this day at one-seventh. On the [tw]enty-seventh night [12]of this month the moon is covered at six-sevenths, [six]-sev[enths] being subtracted from its light. [Then it exits and shines] [13][during the re]st of this night at one-seventh strength. Darkness increases during this day [to six and one-half sevenths. Then the moon sets and enters . . .]

Partial description of the tenth lunar month. This fragment also provides the key to the system of the synchronistic calendar found in 4Q208–209. The statements in ll. 1–2 and 5–6 allow one to deduce that we have here detailed the end of the ninth solar month and beginning of the tenth, since the first day of the tenth solar month in a 364-day calendar equates with the tenth day of the tenth lunar month in a 354-day lunar calendar (i.e., 10/1 solar = 10/10 lunar).

Col. 3 [1][And the moon shines on the eighth night] of this month at four-[s]ev[enths] strength. Then it sets and enters. During this night the sun compl[etes] [2]its traversal of all the sections of the first gate, and begins to traverse and exit its sections yet again. [The moon] [3]sets and enters and grows dark during the rest of this night to three-sevenths darkness. Its light increases during this day to four and [one-half] sevenths. [Then] [4]the moon exits and rules over the rest of this day at two and one-h[al]f-sevenths darkness. On the ninth night of [this month] the moon shines [5]at four and one-half [sevenths] strength. Then the moon sets and enters. During this night the sun begins once more to traverse [its] section[s and to set] [6]in them. Then the [moo]n sets and enters the fifth gate, and is dark during the rest of the night at [two-] [7]and one-half seve[nths.] Its light increases during th[is] day to five-[sevenths] and is exactly equivalent to five-sevenths. [Then the moon exits] [8]from the [f]if[th] gate [and rules over the rest of this day at two-sevenths darkness. The moons shines on the tenth night of this month] [9][at five-sevenths strength. Then it sets and enters and is dark during the rest of this night at two-sevenths. Its light increases during this day to] [10][five and one-half] sev[enths . . .]

One may tentatively place these fragments as belonging to the tenth month.

Frags. 15–16 [1][. . . Then the moon exits and shines during the rest of this night at four and one-half seven]ths strength. [Darkness increases] [2][during this day to three-sevenths. Then the moon sets and enters] the third gate [and is covered the rest] [3][of this day at four-sevenths. On the tw]enty-[first night] of this month the moon is covered [at four-sevenths, there being subtracted] [4][from its light] three-[sevenths]. Then it exi[ts from] the third [gate] and shin[es during the rest of this night] [5][at four-sevenths strength].

Darkness increases during [this] day [to three] and one-hal[f sevenths. Then the moon sets and enters] [6][the *x* gate and] is cov[ered the] re[st of this day at three and one-half sevenths . . .]

The verbal tables of the synchronistic calendar completed, Enoch explains to his son, Methuselah, other sorts of heavenly mysteries. For additional conversation between these two men, compare Tales of the Patriarchs *(text 4). The equations with 1 Enoch, given before the lines they reference, are only approximate as the wording is somewhat different.*

4Q210 Frag. 1 Col. 2 [1]And three gates after those, on the north, [and three gates after those, on the west. (76:4) Through four of these exit the winds that] [2]will serve to heal the earth and to bring it back to life. And [through eight of these gates exit damaging winds when they are sent to destroy all the earth,] [3]the waters, and all that is in them that grows, sprouts, and creep[s in the waters and upon dry ground, and all humankind who dwells in it. (76:5) First,] [4]the east wind exits through the first gate that is in the [east facing south. Destruction, drought, heat, and desolation exit from it too.] (76:6) [5]Through the second gate exits the east-ea[st] wind—[the gate in the middle: rain, fruitfulness, revival, and dew. And through the third gate exits the] [6]northeast wind, that is near the north[ern] quarter: [cold and drought. And after them, from the three gates of the heavens that face south,] [7]exit first, through the first gate, [a south wind that is in the south and faces west: a hot wind. And through the second gate exits a south wind] [8]that they call "South": dew [and rain, health and revival. And through the third gate exits a southwest wind: dew and rain and locusts and destruction. (76:10) [9][And] after it exits a [north wind . . .] [10][And des]truction [. . .]

Note in this portion the interesting etymologies Enoch offers for the names of the four directions.

4Q209 Frag. 23 + 4Q210 Frag. 1 Col. 2 [1][. . .] (76:14) so completing [2]the twelve gates of the four quarters of heaven. [I ha]ve shown you their fullness and explanation, [Methuselah, my son.] (77:1) [3][They call the first quarter "East" (*qedim*)] because it is first (*qadmay*). They call the south "South" (*derom*) because the Great One dwells (*dar*) there. And th[ere . . .] [4][. . . fr]om eternity. (77:2) The great quarter they call "West" (*maarav*) because there [5]the [st]ars of heaven [go,] hundreds setting (*mein aravin*) and hundreds entering, all of them stars. Accordingly, they call it "West." (77:3) [6][The north is "North" (*tsippun*)] because all the ships of heaven hide (*tsepan*) and gather and make their circuits there, traveling to the eastern heaven. [7][The east is "Ea]st" (*madnah*) because there the vessels of heaven rise (*denah*), and it is also "East" (*mizrah*) because the vessels shine (*zerah*). [8][And I saw the three . . .] of the earth; one of them for humankind to live in, and one of them [for . . .] [9][. . . and one of them] for the deserts and for the Se[v]en [and] for the [Parad]ise of righteousness. (77:4) [10][And I saw se]ven mou[ntains higher than al]l [the mountains on ear]th. Upon them [des]cends the snow [. . .]

Here Enoch discusses general principles of the moon's movement and the waxing and waning of its light.

4Q210 Frag. 1 Col. 3 [3][. . . (78:6) And when the moon rises, one-half of one-seventh of its light sh]ines in the heavens, so as to be se[en upon the earth.] [4][. . . and the portions of light become more fu]ll each day until the fourteenth day, [5][when all its light is made fu]ll. (78:7) And its light increases by one-fifteenth, being made more complete day by day until day] fifteen, when all its light is made full. [6][. . .] and it directs the moon's phases by halves of sevenths. (78:8) [7][And during its waning the moon's light decreases: on the first day, one-fourte]enth; on the second day, one-thi[rteenth;] [8][on the third day, one-twelfth; on the four]th [day,] one-elev[enth . . .]

The single surviving fragment of 4Q210 above belongs to the conclusion to Astronomical Enoch. *The conclusion was once fuller than the form that has come down in the Ethiopic version, and this portion was a part of that fuller conclusion.*

4Q211 Frag. 1 [2][(After 82:20) . . . the clouds that make dew] and rain to fall upon the earth, and seed [3][. . .] herbs of the earth and tree. And [the sun] falls and enters [4][. . .] and winter comes, and the foliage of all the trees [5][withers and falls, except for four]teen trees for which such is not natural [6][. . .] their leaves [re]m[ain . . .]

Frag. 2 [2]this from its measure [. . .] [3]one-tenth of o[ne-]ninth [. . .] [4][. . . one-tenth of] one-ninth. And the stars move through the fir[st gates] of heaven, [then] exit. [5]On the first day, [one-]tenth [by] one-[six]th; on the second day, one-fifteenth [6]by [o]ne-sixth; [and] on the third day, on[e-]thirtieth [b]y one-sixth.

Frag. 3 [4]On the [fif]te[enth day [. . .] [5]only [in] this night from [. . .] a [t]hird part of one-ninth. And fiv[e . . .] [6]and one-tenth of one-ninth.

—M.O.W.

39. The Words of Levi

4Q213, 4Q213a–b, 4Q214, 4Q214a–b, 4Q540–541, 1Q21, Geniza Fragments, Mt. Athos Greek Text

A prominent form of religious literature in ancient Judaism and Christianity was the "testament," containing the edifying teaching and prophetic words that bygone heroes of the faith were feigned to have uttered before their deaths. One of the most popular collections of testaments was the *Testaments of the Twelve Patriarchs,* composed of the imagined last words of the sons of Jacob, the forefathers of the twelve tribes of Israel. Although parts of the collection contain Christian ideas added by later copyists, these testaments were originally Jewish works composed during the same period as the Dead Sea Scrolls. They are preserved only in Greek, but most now agree that the testaments were modeled after Aramaic or Hebrew originals. This fact is particularly clear in the case of the *Testament of Levi*. Although the Greek *Testament of Levi* was not found at Qumran, scholars did discover the present work, an Aramaic composition that seems to have influenced it.

Jacob's twelve sons were the ancestors of the twelve tribes of Israel. Since Levi, the third of the twelve sons of Jacob, was the forefather of the priestly tribe, the *Words of Levi* stresses the duties and prerogatives of the priests. The ideal priest, to judge from this text, would have been a combination of a zealous warrior for God, a punctilious observer of ritual purity, an inspiring teacher, and a recipient of divine revelation through dreams and prophecy.

Testaments often begin with reflections by the "author" on his life, then move into ethical exhortations, and conclude with prophecy, as the hero looks beyond his death to foretell the "future"—generally the time when the text was actually composed and for whose readers it was really intended.*

*The *Words of Levi* survives in three different forms. Like the *Damascus Document,* portions were found in the Cairo Geniza in the late nineteenth century and first published in 1906–7. (The Geniza fragments are divided between the libraries of Oxford and Cambridge.) The identification of fragments from seven (possibly nine) scrolls of the same document in Caves 1 and 4 at Qumran confirmed its great antiquity. Finally, certain passages inserted into a manuscript of the Greek *Testament of Levi* from the Mt. Athos monastery in Koutloumous, Greece, are translated directly from the *Words of Levi*. The present translation combines the texts from all these sources.

The prayer of Levi. According to the Words of Levi, *Levi was the most righteous and zealous of all the sons of Jacob. His desire to please God is embodied in his prayer for righteousness. The prayer of Levi is partially preserved in 4Q213a and completely in the Mt. Athos manuscript, which has been used to restore any missing text below. (The line numbers are for the Qumran fragment only.)*

4Q213a Frag. 1 Col. 1 [6][Then] I [washed my clothing and purified them with clean water,] [7][and] I bath[ed all over in fresh water, so making] all [8][my ways correct. Then] I raised my eyes [and face] to heaven, [9][I opened my mouth and spoke,] and my fingers and hands [10][I spread out properly in front of the holy angels. So I prayed and] said:

"Lord, You [11][know all hearts, all the thoughts of the mind] You alone understand. [12][Now my brothers <**Mt. Athos** MS.: sons> are with me, so entrust to me] the right ways. Remove [13][from me, O Lord, the immoral spirit,] rid me of wicked [thoughts] and unchastity. [14][Reveal to me, Lord, the holy spirit; counsel and] wisdom and knowledge and strength [15][grant me so I can do what pleases You and] find favor with You, [16][praising Your words with me, O Lord, doing] what is proper and right in Your eyes. [17]Let no demonic adversary have power over me, [18][making me wander from Your path. Have mercy] on me, O Lord, and draw me near to be Your [servant . . .] **Mt. Athos** MS. . . . and to worship You properly. May Your wall of peace be around me, may the shelter of Your might protect me from all harm. Purify my heart, O Lord, from all impurity, that I myself may be lifted up to You. Do not hide Your face from the son of Your servant Jacob. **Col. 2**[5][. . . You], [6]O Lord, have b[lessed my great-grandfather Abraham and my great-grandmother Sarah, and commanded that they be granted] [7]r[ighteous] descendants [forever blessed. So hear also] [8]the prayer of [Your] ser[vant Levi, that he may draw near to You. Let me share Your words, so as to render] [9]proper judgment for[ever, yes, my sons and I, for all generations. So do not reject] [10]Your servant's son from [Your presence for all eternity." And I began to pray silently.]

Levi's first vision. After Levi's prayer, he is granted a vision of the heavens, in the course of which God reveals to him that he has been chosen to be the priest of Israel.

[11]Then I went on [. . .] [12]to my father Jacob, and whe[n . . .] [13]from Abel-Main. Then [. . . where] [14]I lay down. And I remained o[n . . .] [15]Then I was shown visions [. . .] [16]in the appearance of a vision, and I saw heav[en . . . and a mountain] [17]under me so high it reached heave[n . . . and they opened] [18]for me the gates of heaven and an angel [. . .]

Revenge on Shechem and Hamor. Genesis 34 relates how Levi and Simeon kill Hamor and his son Shechem, who had raped Jacob's daughter, Dinah. In the Words, *Levi apparently resists the suggestion of Jacob and Reuben that Hamor and Shechem be brought into the family by circumcision. The fragments (preserved only in the Geniza texts from Cambridge) do not preserve the narrative of the actual killing. What does remain is often difficult to follow.*

Cambridge Geniza Text Col. A [15][. . .] region of Is[rael . . .] [16]so that all [. . .] [17]to act in this way against [. . .] [18]Jacob my father and Reu[ben my brother . . .] [19]and we said to them [. . . If] [20]you want our daughter, so that we all would become br[others] [21]and partners, you must circumcise the flesh of your foreskin, [22]so that you may appear li[ke us] and become sealed [23]like us with the [tru]e circumcision. Then we will be yo[ur . . .]

Col. B [15][. . .] my brothers always [16][. . .] who were in Shechem [17][. . .] my brothers and his brothers. This is [18][. . .] in Shechem, and whatever [19][. . . weapons for committing] crimes. So [20]Judah told them that I and Simeon [21]my brother had gone to [. . .] to Reuben [22]our brother, who [. . .] [23]and Judah jumped forward [to l]eave the flock.

Levi's second vision. After Levi had further displayed his zeal for God in the slaughter of the Shechemites, seven messengers from God visit him in a dream to confirm his appointment to the priesthood. No notion of this vision appears in the Bible. In the vision, only the end of which is preserved, the seven tell him some of the rights and responsibilities of his new office.

Oxford Geniza Text Col. A (+ 1Q21, 4Q213b) [1][. . .] peace, and the choicest firstfruits of the [2]whole land to eat. But during the reign of the sword there is only strife, [3]war, slaughter, toil, [4]hardship, killing, and famine. Sometimes you will eat, [5]sometimes you will hunger; sometimes you will toil, sometimes [6]you will rest; sometimes you will sleep, sometimes [7]sleep will evade you. See now how we have magnified you (**4Q213b**: I have favored you) [8]more than anyone (**4Q213b**: more than all humanity), and how we have given you the anointing of [9]peace eternal.

Then these seven left me, [10]and I woke up from my sleep. [11]I said, This is a vision, and because I was [12]astonished that <I> (MS.: he) should have had a vision, I kept [13]this one too to myself, revealing it to no one.

Levi installed as priest by his father, Jacob.

[14]So we went to my father Isaac, and he too blessed me. [15]Then when Jacob my father was tithing [16]everything he had in accordance with his vow,

[17][. . .] I ranked first, at the head of [18][the priesthood]; and to me, of all his sons, he gave the gift of [19]a ti[the] to God, and he dressed me in priestly vestments, and [20]officially appointed me as priest to God Eternal. [21]I offered all his sacrifices and blessed my father [22]for life and also my brothers. Then all of them [23]blessed me, and my father too blessed me. When I finished **Col. B** [1]offering the sacrifices in Bethel, we left [2]Bethel and lived in our great-grandfather Abraham's palace [3]with Isaac our grandfather.

Instructions from Isaac. Levi's grandfather Isaac instructs Levi in the practical and moral duties of the priesthood.

When [4]Isaac our grandfather saw us all, he greeted us [5]joyfully. When he recognized that I had become priest to God [6]Most High, the Lord of Heaven, he began [7]to teach me authoritatively the [8]priestly way of life.

He said to me, Levi, carefully avoid, [9]my son, all ritual impurity and every kind of [10]sin. Your way of life is to be more strict than all [11]other humans. So now, my son, I will show you [12]the proper way for you to live, not withholding [13]from you any thing you need to know about the [14]priestly way of life.

First, carefully avoid, [15]my son, all impure lewdness and every kind of [16]improper sexual act. You must marry [17]a woman from my clan, so as not to defile your seed with harlots, [18]because you are a holy seed, and holy is [19]your seed as the holy temple, and because [20]you are considered a holy priest to all the seed of [21]Abraham. You are close to God and close to [22]all his holy angels. So purify [23]your flesh from every impurity of any man.

Col. C (+ 4Q214b) [1]When you rise to enter the house of God, [2]bathe first in water, then put on [3]the priestly vestments. When you are dressed, [4]once more wash your hands [5]and your feet before you come near the altar. [6]When you begin to sacrifice [7]whatever is fitting to place on the altar, [8]once again wash your hands and feet.

[9]When you sacrifice split logs, examine [10]them first for any worms [11]and then place them on the altar, for [12]I saw my father Abraham taking care to do this. [13]He told me that any of twelve kinds of wood [14]are fitting to place on the altar, [15]because the odor of their smoke is sweet-smelling [16]as it ascends. These are their names: cedar, juniper, [17]mastic, pine, small pine, aduna, [18]cypress, thekaka, [bay,] [19][tama]risk, myrtle, and camel's-thorn. These are [20]the ones he told me were suitable to place [21]under the whole burnt offering on the altar.

[22]When [you have placed] any of these kinds of wood on [23]the altar and the fire begins to kindle **Col. D (+ 4Q214, 4Q214b)** [1]in them, at that moment you should begin to sprinkle the blood [2]on the sides of the altar. Then once more wash off your hands [3]and feet from the blood and begin to put

on the salted pieces. [4]Put the head on first, [5]and cover it with the fatty portions, so that none of the blood [6]from the slaughtering of the bull is showing. After that, the neck, [7]and after the neck, the forefeet; after the forefeet, [8]the breast with the side; after them, [9]the thighs with the lower spine; [10]after the thighs, the hind feet rinsed [11]with the entrails. All these are to be salted with [12]the right amount of salt proper to each. After this, fine flour [13]mixed with oil, and after all of this, the libation wine. [14]Then burn incense on them.

Let [all] [15]your actions be done in order and all your sacrifices [will be acceptable] [16]as a sweet-smelling savor to God Most High; [and] [17]as you do [everything] in order, observe [the proper measures] [18]and weights. Don't add anything that does not [belong], [19]but don't lessen the proper amount, either!

The proper amount of wood [20]suitable to bring for whatever is sacrificed on the altar is as follows: [21]for a large bull: a talent* of wood is a proper weight for it; [22]but if the fat alone is sacrificed, six [23]minas (about ten pounds).

If a second bull is offered [. . .]**Mt. Athos** MS.: fifty minas, but for its fat alone, five minas. For an unblemished calf, forty minas. If the sacrifice is a ram from the flock or a male goat, thirty minas, and for the fat alone, three minas. If it is a lamb of the flock or a kid, twenty minas; for the fat alone, two minas. If it is an unblemished one-year-old lamb or kid, fifteen minas; for the fat alone, one and a half minas.

Bring salt for the large bull to salt its flesh and place it on the altar. One seah [about eleven quart jars] of salt is the proper amount for the bull. Salt the skin with the salt that remains. For the second bull, five-sixths seah; for the calf, half seah; for the ram or the male goat, half seah; for the lamb and the kid, one-third seah.

The amount of fine flour proper to them: for the large bull and the second bull and the calf, one seah; for the ram and the goat, two-thirds seah; for the lamb and the kid, one-third seah.

As for the oil, one-fourth seah for the bull, mingled with the fine flour; for the ram, one-sixth seah; for the lamb and kid, one-eighth seah.

As for the wine, pour out a libation on the bull, ram, and kid in the same amount as the oil.

Use six shekels of incense for the bull, half that for the ram, a third of it for the kid.

As for the mixed fine flour, if you offer it alone, not on the fat, pour out two shekels of incense on it.

*About seventy-five pounds.

The third of a seah is the third of an ephah, and two parts of a bath measure and the weight of the mina is fifty shekels; as for the shekels, the fourth of a shekel weighs four thermoi; therefore the whole shekel weighs about sixteen thermoi.

So now, my son, hear my words and pay heed to my commandments. Never forget my words, for you are a priest holy to the Lord, and all your descendants will be priests. Bid your descendants to live according to the priestly way of life as I have shown it to you, for so my father Abraham commanded me to do and to bid my children to do.

So now, my son, I rejoice that you have been chosen for the holy priesthood, to offer sacrifice to God Most High in the way that has been decreed to be fitting. When you offer a sacrifice from anyone to the Lord, receive from them the amount of wood, salt, flour, wine, and incense that I have instructed you along with whatever animal is to be sacrificed. You must wash your hands and feet every time you approach the altar, and whenever you leave the holy things, no blood must be touching your garments. Do not light a fire on it on that day.

You must constantly wash any flesh off your hands and feet. No blood or flesh must appear on you, for the blood is the soul in the flesh. Whenever you have meat to eat in the house, cover the blood in the ground first, before you eat the meat, so that you will not be eating with blood around. Thus my father Abraham commanded me, because he found it written so in the book of Noah concerning blood.

So now also I say to you, my beloved son, you are dear to your father and holy to God Most High; and dearer you shall be than any of your brothers. Your descendants shall be blessed in the land and placed in the book of the memorial of life forever, so that your name and your descendants' names will never be forgotten.

So now, Levi my son, may your descendants be blessed on the earth for all the ages of the world!

Levi's children and later life.

Now when four weeks of years in my life had passed, when I was twenty-eight, I took a wife from the stock of my great-grandfather Abraham: Milkah, daughter of Bathuel, the son of Laban, my mother's brother. She became pregnant by me and bore a first son, and I called his name Gershom, for I said, My descendants shall be homeless in the land where they are born; and indeed we are considered homeless in this land today. And concerning this child I saw in my vision that both he and his descendants would be removed from the high-priesthood. I was thirty years old when he was born; it was in the tenth month, <on the . . . day,> toward sunset.

Once again she conceived by me at the proper time fitting for women, and I called his name Kohath. **Cambridge Geniza Text Col. C** [5]I called his name [Kohath. I saw] that [6]all [the people would] gather to him, and that [7]the high-priesthood [over all Is]rael would be his. [8]In the [thir]ty-fou[rth] year of my life [9]he was born, in the fir[st] month, on the [fi]rst day of [the] mon[th], [10]towards sunrise.

Once [11]again I was with [her] and she bore me a [12]third son, and I called his name Merari, because [13]his birth was very distressing (*mar*) to me, for when he was born, [14]he was dying, and it was very bitter (*marir*) to me [15]indeed that he should die, so I appealed and prayed [16]for him, and it was a bitter (*merar*) experience. [17]In the fortieth year of my life he was born, in the third month.

[18]Once again I was with her and she conceived [19]and bore me a daughter, I gave her the name [20]Jochebed. I [sa]id when she was born to me, For glory [21]she is born to me, for the honor of Israel. [22]In the sixty-fourth year of my life was she born, [23]on the first day of the seventh month, after **Col. D** [1][we had] en[tered] Egypt.

In the sixteenth [2]year, He brought us into the land of Egypt. [3]At that time the daughters of my brothers [were given] to my sons, when considered [4]worthy, [to bear] them children.

The names of the sons of [5]Gershon: [Libni and] Shimei.

The names of the sons of [6]Ko[hath: Amra]m, Izhar, Hebron, and Uzziel.

[7][The names of] the sons of Merari: Mahli and Mushai.

[8]Now Amram took a wife, my daughter Jochebed, [9]while I was alive, in the ninety-four[th] year [10]of my life; I had called him Amram when [11]he was born, because when he was born I said, [12]This one [shall bring] the people out of the lan[d of Eg]ypt, [13]and so s[hall be call]ed "Exalted [People"] (*amma rama*). [14]On one day were born [both he and] Jochebed [15]my daughter.

When I was eighteen, I was brought [16][into the l]and of Canaan, and I was [ei]ghteen [17]when I killed She[chem] and eliminated [18]those who commit crimes.

I was nineteen [19]years old when I became a priest, and I was twenty-[20]eight when I took a wife for myself, and [21]I was forty-eight when [22]God brought us into the land of Egypt. [23]I lived eighty-nine years in Egypt. **Col. E** [1]In all I lived 137 [2]years and I saw my descendants to the t[hird] generation before [3]I died.

Levi's teaching in praise of wisdom. After a long life serving God, Levi passes on to his sons the duty to pursue wisdom. Levi's praise of wisdom echoes similar themes in other Jewish literature, particularly the poem commending wisdom in Sirach 51: 13–30.

(Col. E + 4Q213): In the one hundred and eighteenth year [4]of my life, the y[ear] that [5]my brother Joseph died, I called together my s[ons and] their sons [6]and I began to command them everything that was [7]in my mind. I raised my voice and said to [my] sons,

[Listen] [8]to your father Levi's speech, pay heed to the precepts of [9]God's friend. I will instruct you, my sons, I [10]will tell you what is right, my dears. The whole [11]of your actions must be right, [12]so may goodness remain forever with you, [13]and the right [. . .] [14]a blessed yield. Whoever sows [15]goodness will reap goodness; but whoever sows [16]evil, his seed will return to him.

[17]So now, my sons, teach writing and discipline [18]and wisdom to your children, so that [19]wisdom may be their perpetual glory, [20]for the one who learns wisdom shall have glory [21]through it. But whoever disdains wisdom becomes an object of scorn (**4Q213** adds: and contempt). [22]Consider, my sons, my brother Joseph, [23]who teaches writing and wise discipline (**4Q213** adds: for glory and majesty); and [he advises] kings [. . .]).

Col. F (+ 4Q213) [1–5][. . .] Do not ignore the learning of wisdom, [for] every man who learns wisdom, his days [will be long], [6]and [his reputation] will grow in every lan[d] [7]and nation [that he goes] to. He will be like a brother there, [8]and will be recognized, and will [not] seem like [9]a foreigner or [10]a half-breed, for all of them will give [11]him honor, because all will want [12]to learn from his wisdom. [13]His friends will be many, his well-wishers numerous, [14]and they will make him sit in the chair of honor [15]to hear his words of wisdom. [16]So wisdom is a great treasure of honor (**4Q213** adds: for those who know it), and a fine [17]trove for all who possess it.

If [18]mighty kings come with many people, [19]and an army, horsemen, and many chariots [20]with them, and if they seize the wealth of lands and [21]nations, plundering everything in them, [22]they still could not plunder the storehouses of wisdom, [23]nor could they find its hidden riches. **4Q213 Frag. 1, Col. 2** [1]they could not enter its gates, nor could they [. . .] [2]could not overrun its walls [. . .] nor [. . .] [3]would they see her treasure, the treasure [. . .] [4]for there is no price equal to it [. . . he who] [5]seeks wisdom, [will find] wisdom . . . and nothing will be] [6]hidden from him [. . .] [7][he will] lack nothing [. . .] [8]in truth [. . .] from all who seek [9]wisdom [. . .] **4Q213 Frag. 2** [5]reading and discipline [6][. . .] you will inherit them [7][. . .] great [honor] you shall give [8][. . .] honor. [9]Tr[uth . . .] also in the books [10][. . .] rulers and judges [11][. . .] and servants [12][. . .] priests and kings [13][. . .] your kingdom [14][. . .] there shall be no end [15][. . . the priesthood shall never] pass from you until all [16] [. . .] in great honor.

The prophecy of Levi. Along with edifying narrative and moral exhortation, prophecies of future woes and blessings are typical ingredients of the testament genre. Levi's prophecy is specially concerned with the fate of the priesthood and of the high priests of Israel. Only disconnected portions of Levi's prophecy survive among the scrolls. Occasionally there are indications of a conversation between two parties, either between Levi and his sons or between a messenger angel and Levi.

4Q213 Frags. 3–4 [1][. . . to] you all the peoples [2][. . . the] moon and stars [3][. . . for]ever [4][. . .] to the moon [5][. . .] you will grow dark [in your thoughts . . .] [6][. . .] truly [En]och had received [. . .] [7][. . .] So on whom will the guilt rest? [. . .] [8][. . .] Is it not on me and you, my sons, for they will know it [. . .] [9][. . .] you shall leave the ways of truth, and all the paths of [10][goodness] you will give up, and you will walk in d[arkness . . .] [11][. . .] da[rk]ness will come upon you, and you will be handed over [12][. . .]

Now sometimes you will be abject [. . .]

The placement of this fragment is uncertain, but it seems to be an admonition about sexual immorality.

4Q213a Frags. 3–4 [3][. . .] as wife. She will profane her name and her father's name [4][and the name of] her husband [. . .] and shame. Every [5][vir]gin who has corrupted her reputation and the reputation of her ancestors, and brought shame to her brothers [6][. . .] her father. The name of her disgrace will never be erased from all her people [7][. . .] for all generations [. . .] the holy ones of the people [8][. . .] tithe of holy things an offering for teaching [. . .]

Possibly from the same prophetic section are two scrolls describing the fate of certain high priests of Israel. The first (4Q540) describes a priest who will lose his possessions.

4Q540 [1][. . .] Again tribulation will come upon him, and the lesser will lack possessions [. . .] [2][. . .] Again privation will come upon him and he will lack possessions [. . .] [3][. . .] He will not be [like] a man who lacks possessions, but on the Great Sea [. . .] [4][. . .] The house he was born in he shall depart, and another home [. . .] [5][. . .] the servant [. . .] temple [. . .]

Another scroll (4Q541), unfortunately very fragmentary, also preserves parts of Levi's prophecy about his descendants. The numbering of the fragments does not necessarily reflect their original order.

4Q541 Frag. 1 [1][. . .] everything. Meditate on [. . .] [2]false gods shall fall [. . .] [3]and all the[ir] souls [. . .]

Frag. 2 Col. 1 [5][. . . w]ords he [shall] speak and according to the will of [6][God . . . he showed] me another writing [7][. . .] it spoke about him in riddles [8][. . .] was [not] near to me but far away from me [9][. . .] shall be [. . .] a vision. And I said, The fruits [. . .] **Col. 2** [1]was suspended, because [. . .] [2]from God [. . .] [3]you shall receive a blow [. . .] [4]I will bless you. The burnt offering [. . .] [5]your spirit, and you shall rejoice [. . .] [6]because [he is] wise [. . .] [7]comely [words . . .] [8]he persecuted him and sought [to kill him . . .]

Frags. 3–4 Col. 1 [2][. . . upon] them the suffering of your peace [. . .] [3]I shall t[ake] up a parable against you [. . .] [4][. . .] and he will ponder deep things and he will speak riddles [. . .] [5][. . .] shall come to you, for you are possessed by zeal, and the fowl [6][for sacrifice . . .] to consume. For you will greatly re[joice, and greatly [. . .]

Frag. 6 [1][. . .] wounds upon w[ounds . . .] [2][. . . you will be found innocent in your] case, and you will not be guil[ty . . .] [3][. . .] the tracks of your wounds th[at . . .] [4][. . .] what has been entrusted to you and all [. . .] [5][. . .] your heart from [. . .]

A large fragment of 4Q541 describes a priest who is to appear in the future, whose righteous teaching brings light to his generation, but who also arouses fierce opposition. Like Jesus, he is a "light for revelation," but also "a sign to be spoken against" (Luke 2:32, 34).

Frag. 9 Col. 1 [2][. . .] his wisdom. And he shall make atonement for all those of his generation, and he shall be sent to all the children of his [3][peo]ple. His command is like the command of Heaven, and his teaching is like the will of God. The Sun everlasting will shine [4]and its fire will give warmth to all the ends of the earth. It will shine on darkness; then will darkness vanish [5][fr]om the earth, and mist from the land.

They will speak many words against him, and many [6][falsehood]s; they will concoct lies and speak all kinds of slander against him. His generation is evil and perverse; [7][. . .] will be; his term of office will be marked by lies and violence [and] the people will go astray in his days and be confounded. **Col. 2**[5][. . .] seven rams are fitt[ing . . .] [6]some of his children shall go [. . .] [7]and they shall be added to [. . .]

Another brief fragment apparently speaks of the same priest's great wisdom and insight and mentions his power over the "great sea," recalling Jesus's power to calm the winds and seas (cf. Mark 4:39–41).

Frag. 7 [1]The hid[den mysteries] he shall reveal [. . .] [2][for the one] who does not understand he shall write [. . .] [3]the Great Sea shall be quiet because of him [. . .] [4]Then the books of wis[dom] shall be opened [. . .] [5]his command; and like [. . . his] wis[dom . . .] [6][his t]eaching [. . .]

The final fragment speaks of books or scrolls entrusted to the descendants of Levi through which the reader may find joy and wisdom in "the light of the world" (cf. John 8:12).

Frag. 24 [2]Do not mourn [for him . . .] [3]God will prepare many [books? scrolls? . . .] many revelations and [. . .] [4]Examine them and seek and know what will befall you. But do not damage them by erasure or [we]ar like [. . .] [5]Do not touch the priestly headplate.

Thus you will keep up a good reputation for your father and you will become a sound foundation for your brothers. [6]You will grow and understand and be glad in the light of the world; you will not be a disowned vessel [. . .]

—E.M.C.

40. The Last Words of Naphtali

4Q215

This work is another example of the testament genre. As seen in the *Words of Levi,* testaments often have similar outline: an autobiographical sketch of the speaker, followed by a heavy dose of moral exhortation, and concluding with a prophetic glimpse into the future. Only part of the biography survives in the present fragment of *Naphtali*.

What remains of Naphtali's autobiography mainly has to do with his mother, Bilhah. The twelve sons of Jacob were borne by four different mothers: two of them were Jacob's wives, Rachel and Leah, and two were the wives' handmaidens, Bilhah and Zilpah (Gen. 29–30). Naphtali was the fifth son of

Jacob, and plays little role in the Bible beyond the narrative of his birth in Genesis 30:7–8, which is retold below.

Frags. 1–3 [1]Bilhah [my mother] was with my father's sisters. [. . .] Deborah who had nursed Re[bekah . . .]. [2]He had been taken captive, but Laban sent and redeemed him, and gave him for a wife Hannah, one of [his] maidservants.

[. . .] first, [3]Zilpah. He called her Zilpah after the name of the city where he had been captured.

[He again lay with her] [4]and she conceived and gave birth to my mother Bilhah. Hannah named her Bilhah, because when she was born [. . . she] [5]was eager to suckle, and she said, "How eager my daughter is!" So from then on she was called Bilhah [. . .]

[6]When my father Jacob came to Laban fleeing from his brother Esau and when [. . .] [7]father of my mother Bilhah, then Laban led forth my grandmother Hannah and her two daughters [and gave one to Leah] [8][as a servant] and one to Rachel.

When Rachel continued not to bear children, [she asked her servant to bear children] [9][in her place for] my father [Jaco]b. She gave to him my mother Bilhah and she gave birth to Dan [my] brother.

[She conceived again and gave birth a second time] [10][. . . that] I have borne after him the name Naphtali [. . .]

—E.M.C.

41. The Time of Righteousness

4Q215a

This prophecy, formerly considered to be part of the *Last Words of Naphtali,* contains themes very typical of the Dead Sea sect, particularly the division of history into "eras" predetermined by the plan of God.

Frag. 1 Col. 2 [2][. . . "how much more the] heart of man" (Prov. 15:11) and [. . .] iniquity [. . .] "furnace of [miser]y" (Isa. 48:10), [3]and the affliction of the oppressor and the ordeal of the pit; and they will be purified by these things for the chosen ones of righteousness; and He will efface all their wickedness [4]for the sake of those who are devoted to him; for the era of wickedness is complete, and all iniquity [. . . For] [5]the time of righteousness is coming, and the land is full of true knowledge and the praise of God in [. . .] [6]the era of peace is coming, and the reliable statutes and the proper times, making wise [everyone] [7]in the ways of God, and in His powerful deeds [from this time and] for the eternal ages. Every tongue [8]shall bless Him, and every person shall bow down to Him, [and He will make] their he[art] on[e], for He [prepared] [9]their actions before they were created; and the right way of worship He apportioned, their borders [. . .] [10]in their generations, for the dominion of Good is coming and the [holy] throne will be exalted [. . .] [11]and strength, majesty, wisdom, insight, and perception are tested by [His] holy pur[pose . . .] [12][. . .]

Frag. 2 [1]His holiness. He founded them for [. . .] [2]He created them for [. . .] [3]His waters and darkness [. . .] [4]to its appointed time [. . .] darkness [. . .] [5]for appointed times before [. . .] [6][. . .] ho[st . . .]

Frag. 3 [1][. . .] to proscribe earth [by] His wrath and to renew [. . .] [2][. . . sp]ring of their knowledge [. . .]

—E.M.C.

42. The Book of Jubilees

1Q17–18, 2Q19–20, 3Q5, 4Q176b, 4Q216–224, 11Q12

The *Book of Jubilees* is a fascinating ancient Jewish work unfamiliar to most modern readers. Containing an account of things revealed by an angel to Moses on Mt. Sinai that he was ordered to keep secret, *Jubilees* presents an overview of the history of humankind and of God's chosen people until Moses's time. Usually categorized as rewritten Bible, the book may be divided into seven sections:

- An introduction (chap. 1), in which God describes the apostasy of his people and their future restoration
- A primeval history (chaps. 2–4), dealing with the creation and Adam
- Stories about Noah (chaps. 5–10)
- Stories about Abraham (11:1–23:8)
- Thoughts on Abraham's death (23:9–32)
- Stories about Jacob and his family (chaps. 24–45)
- Stories about Moses (chaps. 46–50)

The author follows the general outline of Genesis and the early part of Exodus, but in the process of retelling the biblical narratives, he frequently omits, condenses, expands, supplements, or otherwise alters the biblical accounts. For example, the long account of the plagues in Exodus 7–10 receives only a few verses in *Jubilees* (48:4–11), whereas the account of Reuben's apparent incest (Gen. 35:22) is expanded to become *Jubilees* 33:2–20. The author is also very concerned to date precisely—in terms of years, "weeks of years," and jubilee periods—as many of the biblical events as possible. This use of jubilee periods for dating is what gives the book its modern name.

Before the discovery of the Dead Sea Scrolls, *Jubilees* was known to scholars from Greek, Syriac, Latin, and Ethiopic translations and was part of the most ancient canon of the Ethiopic church. The discovery of a large number of *Jubilees* manuscripts at Qumran surprised many and has aroused considerable interest. Some fifteen *Jubilees* scrolls were found in five caves: two each in Caves 1 and 2, one in Cave 3, nine in Cave 4, and one in Cave 11. (The actual total of these frequently fragmentary manuscripts is not certain and may be as low as thirteen or as high as sixteen.) All of them are written in Hebrew, and one on papyrus.

From the perspective of the scrolls, *Jubilees* is especially significant in view of its relationship to several sectarian texts. Prominent shared elements include the 364-day calendar, division of the course of history into 49-year jubilee periods, and the practice of dating covenants to the third month (especially the fifteenth day of that month). This last element of *Jubilees* may have inspired the sectarian practice of renewing the covenant annually on the Festival of Weeks.

Three factors point to the conclusion that the writers of many of the Qumran texts considered *Jubilees* to be Scripture. First, a variety of writings quote the work as though it were authoritative. Thus *Work with a Citation of Jubilees* (text 46) seems to refer to *Jubilees* by its Hebrew title, "The Divisions of the Times," and later introduces the first word of the title by a citation formula commonly used for biblical books: "For thus it is written in the Divisions (of the Times)." Similarly, CD (*Damascus Document,* text 1) 16:2–4 cites *Jubilees* as the source of information concerning the times when Israel would be blind to the Law of Moses, while CD 10:7–10 may well be based on *Jubilees* 23:11, referring to people's loss of knowledge in their old age.

Second, *Jubilees* claims to be divine revelation; its contents are given by an angel of God, inscribed on heavenly tablets. It seems likely that at least some readers believed these intrinsic claims just as they believed other things the book says. Third, the comparatively large number of copies shows that *Jubilees* was as popular as almost any biblical book, and so most likely considered authoritative. Only five of the traditional twenty-four biblical (Old Testament) writings—Psalms, Deuteronomy, Isaiah, Exodus, and Genesis—can lay claim to a greater number of manuscripts at Qumran.

The chapter and verse notations in the following translation, which precede the lines they reference in parentheses, are according to the traditional form of the book.

Prologue.

4Q216 Col. 1 [3][. . . Sinai, when he went up to] re[ceive the tablets of stone, the law and the commandment,] by the word of the LORD [as He had told] [4][him, "Come up] to the summit of the moun[tain."

Moses is summoned to go up onto the mountain (Exod. 31:18; 32:15; Deut. 9:11).

(1:1) And on the first year] of the exodus of [the Israel]ites [5][from Egypt, in] the thi[rd mon]th, [on the sixteenth of t]his [month,] the LORD spoke t[o] [6][Moses, saying, "Come up to Me on] the mountain [and I will give you] the [two tablets of] stone, the law [7][and the commandment which I have written so that you might t]ea[ch them." (1:2) So Moses went up to the mountain of the LORD and the g]lory of the LOR[D settled] [8][on Mount Sinai, and the cloud covered it for six days.

(1:3) And He called to Moses from the cloud on the seventh day,] [9][and he saw the glory of the LORD as a fire blazing on the mountaintop. (1:4) Moses remained] [10][on the mountain for forty days and forty nights while the LORD told him of the first and] [11][the last things and what was to come. He told him of the di]visions of [the ti]mes, for the la[w] [12][and for the testimony.

Moses is instructed to write a book documenting the future transgressions of his people (Exod. 34:27).

(1:5) He said to him: "Pay attention to all the wor]ds which I tell you [13][on this mountain. Write them in a book so that] their generations [might kno]w that I have not abandoned them [14][because of all the evil that they have done, breaking the covenant that] I am making between Me and you today [15][for all their generations on Mount Sinai. (1:6) So when] all of [these] things [happe]n to t[hem] [16][they will understand that I have been more faithful than they in all] their [judgments] and [in all] their curses. [They] will understand [17][that I have truly been with them.

(1:7) Now write for yourself al]l these [wor]ds **Col. 2** [1][which I am telling you today, because I know their rebelliousness and their stubbornness before I bring them] [2]into the l[an]d [that I swore to their fathers, Abraham, Isaac, and Ja]c[ob,] [3]saying, "To [your] offspring [I will give a land flowing with milk and hone]y." They will eat and be satisfied [(1:8) and will turn] [4]after oth[er] gods [who will not save them from any dis]tresses. And the [testimony] will answer [to] [5]this testimony. (1:9) F[or they will forget all my commandments, everything that I shall] command you, and they will wa[lk after] [6][the nat]ions, [their dis]g[race, and] their [shame.] And they will serve [their] g[ods and they will become for them an offense,] [7]a distress, [an affliction,] and a [snare. (1:10) Man]y [will be destroyed] and will be captured and will fall [into the hand of the enemy because] [8][they have abandoned] My statutes, [My commandments, the festival]s of My covenant, [My Sabbaths, My holy things] [9]which they have consecrated for Me am[ong themselves, My tabernacle, and My] temple [that I consecrated for Myself in the midst of] [10]the land to set [My name] on it [so that it would dwell there.

(1:11) They will make for themselves high places, Asherahs, and idols,] [11]and they will worship a[ll the wor]ks of [their] delusion. [And they will sacrifice their children to demons and to all the works of the delusion of their heart.] [12](1:12) I will send witnesses to [them] to [warn them, but they will not listen and will kill the witnesses.] [13]The[y] will persecute those who seek [the] law [and will change everything so as to do what is evil] [14]in My eyes. (1:13) I will hid[e] my [face] from them, and [I] will ha[nd them over to the nation]s for cap[tivity,] [15][de]vastations, [and devouring. I will remove them from the midst of the land, and] I will scatter them among all the nation[s.] [16][(1:14) Then they will forget all My statutes, all My commandments,] and all My instruction, and [they] will forg[et month, Sabbath,] [17][festival, jubilee, and covenant.

(1:15) Afterwards they will return] to Me from among the nation[s with all their heart, . . .]

The second command to write is directed to the "angel of the presence."

Col. 4 [3][(1:26) . . . the first and the] last thing[s] [4][and that which will come about during all the divisions of the times for the la]w and the testi[mony] [5][and for the weeks of the jubilees forever, until I come down] and dwell w[ith them] [6][for all the ages of eternity.

(1:27) And He told the angel of the] presence to write [7][for Moses about the period from the beginning of the creation unti]l My sanctuary is built [8][in their midst for all eternity. (1:28) The LORD will appear in the sight of] all, and [all] will know [9][that I am the God of Israel, father of all J]acob's [children,] and king [10][on Mount Zion for all eternity. Then Zion and Jerusa]l[em will be holy . . .]

The description of the six days of creation (Gen. 1).

Col. 5 [1][(2:1) The angel of the presence said to Moses by the word of the LORD, "Write all the wor]ds of the creation, ho[w] [2][on the sixth day the LORD God completed all His works and everything that He had created] and then rested on the [seventh] day. [3]He consecrated it for all ages and appointed it as a sign for all] His works.

[4][(2:2) For on the first day He created the] highest [heaven]s, the ear[th,] [5][the waters, and all the spirits who minister before Him: the angels of] the presence; the angels of ho[liness]; [6]the a[ngels of the spirits of fire; the angels of the winds that blo]w; the angels of the spirits of the [clouds], [7]of dar[kness, hailstones, frost, dew, snow, hail, and i]ce; the angels of the thunde[r]; [8]the angels of the winds; [the angels of the spirits of cold and] heat, of winter and summer; [and of all] [9]the spirits of His creatures [which He made in heaven, which He made on ear]th, and in every place, the dept[hs], [10]darkness, dawn, [light, and evening, which He determined by] His [know]ledge. (2:3) Then we saw His works and [blessed Him] [11]for all His [wo]rks, and [we praised Him because He] had d[one seven] great works [on the first day].

[12]On the [second] da[y He made the expanse betwee]n th[e water]s, [and the waters were divided on that day. Half of them] [13]went up abo[ve the expanse, and half of them went down below the expanse that is in the midst above] [14]the [whole] earth.[. . .]

Col. 6 [2][(2:7) . . . and the poo]ls, all the d[ew of the earth,] [3][seed-bearing plants, all that sprouts, fruit trees, the] forests, and the Garden of E[de]n [in Eden] [4][for enjoyment and for food. These four great types] He made {He made} on the thi[rd] day.

[5][(2:8) On the fourth day the LORD made the s]un, the moon, and the stars. [And He placed] [6][them in the expanse of the heavens to give light over the whole earth,] to rule the day and the night, and to di[vide] [7][light from darkness. (2:9) He appointed the sun as a gre]at [sign over the earth] for day[s], for [Sab]baths, for [months,] [8][for festivals, for years, for the weeks of years, . . . for jubi]lees, and for all the sea[sons of the years.] [9][(2:10) It divides the light from the darkness and brings healing so that everything that] sprouts and grows on the ea[rth may prosper.] [10][These three kinds He made on the fourth day.]

[11][(2:11) On the fifth day He created the gre]at [sea monsters] in the m[idst of the depth]s of the wa[ters, for these] [12][were the first works of flesh from His hands, everything that swarms in the] waters, fish, [and] all {and al[l} the birds] [13][that fly, and all their kinds. (2:12) The sun shone on them that they might] prosper and o[n everything] that was on the ea[rth, everything] [14][that sprouts from the earth, all fruit trees, and all flesh. These] thr[ee] gr[eat kind]s [15][He made on the fifth day.]

Col. 7 [1][(2:13) On the] sixth [da]y <He made> all [the land] ani[mals, all the cattle, and everything that creeps about on the earth. (2:14) After all these things] [2]He made humankind, male and fem[ale He made them. He made him rule over everything on the earth, in the seas, and over everything that flies,] [3]over the animals, over all the creeping things that cre[ep about on the earth, over the cattle, and over the entire earth. Over all these He made him rule.] These [four] [4]kinds He made on the [sixth day.

(2:15) In all there were twenty-two kinds. (2:16) He finished all His works on the sixth day, everything] [5]that was in the heavens, on the earth, [in the seas, in the depths, in the light, and in the darkness, in every place.

The Sabbath day (Gen. 2:1–2).

(2:17) He gave us as a great sign, the] [6]Sabbath [day,] on [which] He rested [. . .] [7]were made in six days [. . .] [8]and we should rest on the se[venth] day [from all our work. (2:18) For we, with all the angels of the presence and all the angels of holiness—] [9]these [two] kinds—He to[ld us to keep Sabbath with Him in heaven and on earth. (2:19) He said to us, "I am separating for myself] [10]a people from among My nations. And [they shall keep the Sabbath. I will consecrate them as My people, and I will bless them. They will be my people and I will be their God.] [11](2:20) And {He} <I> chose the offspring of Jacob from among [all of those whom I have seen. I have recorded him as my firstborn son and have consecrated him for Myself] [12]forever and ever. [I will tell them about] the [seventh] day [so that they might rest on it from everything," (2:21) as He blessed them and consecrated them for Himself as a special people] [13]out of all the nations that [they] might [rest] together [with us. (2:22) He offered up His commands as a sweet savor, acceptable before Him] [14]for all time.

[(2:23) There were twenty-two heads of humankind] [15]from Adam until him (Jacob); and twenty-two k[inds of work were made until the seventh day. This is blessed and holy and that is blessed] [16]and holy. Both were made together for holiness [and blessing. (2:24) It was given to this one (Jacob and his seed) to be for all time the blessed and holy ones.] [17]This is the testimony and the fir[st] law [. . .]

Sabbath laws (Exod. 20:8; 31:13).

4Q218 Frag. 1 [1][(2:26) . . .] to con[secrate it, not to do any work on it, and not to defile it, for] [2]it is holier [than] all the other days. (2:27) Anyone [who profanes it shall surely die,] [3][and any]one who does work on it will be cut off [fore]v[e]r [so] t[h]at [the Israelites may obser]ve [4]thi[s] day [throughout] their [generatio]ns and not be cut off from the ea[rth].

The murder of Abel (Gen. 4:1–14).

11Q12 Frag. 1 [1][(4:6) . . .] we [make known,] when [we] co[me] [2][before the LORD our God, all the sins] which are done in [heaven] [3][and on earth, and in the light and in the darkness and everywhere.]

The descendants of Adam (Gen. 4:17–5:12).

[(4:7) And] Adam and his wife [mourn]ed [4][four weeks for Abel. And] in the fourth year of the f[ifth] week [5][they rejoiced. And Adam knew his wife once again] and she bore him a son, and he named [him Seth] [6][for he said, "The LORD has granted us] another [child on] the earth in place of Abel, since [Cain] killed him." [7][(4:8) In the sixth week he fathered Azu]ra his daughter. (4:9) And Cain took [his] sister [8][Awan as his wife, and she bore him Enoch at the end of the] fourth [jubi]lee.

[9][And in the first year of the first week of the fif]th [jubilee,] houses were built on the ear[th.] [10][And Cain built a city and named it after] his [so]n Enoch.

(4:10) And Ada[m] [11][knew Eve his wife, and she bore nine more children. (4:11) And in] the f[ifth wee]k [. . .]

Frag. 2 [1][(4:13) . . . Enosh took his sister Noam as his wife, and she bore him a s]on in the [third] y[ear] [2][of the fifth week and he named him Qenan. (4:14) And] at the end of the [eighth] ju[bilee] [3][Qenan took a wife for himself, his sister Muhallelet] as a wife. [And she bore] [4][him a son in the ninth jubilee, in the first week, in the thi]rd year of [the week . . .]

The birth of Enoch (Gen. 4:17).

Frag. 3 [1][(4:16) . . . in the fourth week of the jubilee. And she bore him a son in the f]ifth [week, in the fourth year] [2][of the jubilee, and he called him Enoch.]

(4:17) He was the firs[t . . .] **Frag. 4** [1][And he wrote down in a book the signs of the sky, according to the order of their months, tha]t [men] might know [2][the seasons of the years, according to the orders of all their months.] (4:18) H[e was the fir]st [3][to write a testimony, and he testified to the sons of men among the generations of the earth. The weeks of] the [jubilees . . .]

The life of Adam just short of a thousand years (2 Pet. 3:8).

Frag. 5 [1][(4:29) . . . he was the first to be bu]ried in [the ground. (4:30) He lacked seventy years of one thousand] [2][years, for] a thousand

[y]ears [are one day in the testimony of heaven. Therefore] [3][it is written about the tre]e of knowledge: "For on [the day you eat from it, you shall die." Therefore] [4][he did not complete] the years of [this] day [because he died during it. (4:31) At the end of this jubilee . . .]

Abel's death is avenged.

Frag. 6 [1][(4:31) . . . Cain was killed] after him [in the same year. His house fell on him, and he died in his house,] [2][and he was killed by] its [stone]s for [with a stone he had killed Abel . . .]

The union of angels and humans (Gen. 6:1–5; 1 Enoch 6–11 [text 36]).

Frag. 7 [1][(5:1) . . . they bore them, and these are the g]i[ant]s. (5:2) And [violence] increased [on the earth, and all flesh corrupted] [2][its way, alike men and] animals, and b[easts and birds and everything that creeps] [3][on the earth, and they all c]orrupted their way and [their] or[ders, and they began to eat one] [4][another. And violence increased on the earth, and al]l [. . .]

Noah's sacrifice (Gen. 8:20).

Frag. 7a [1][. . . (7:4?) And he put some of its blood upo]n the flesh of [the sacrificial offering that is on the altar . . .] [2][and] he shall of[fer al]l their [burnt o]ff[ering]s [upon the altar . . .] [3][(7:5?) . . . and] their [food offer]ing and their sacrificial offering [were offered] as an ac[ceptable sacrifice before the LORD his (?) God . . .]

Abram's night watch.

Frag. 8 [1]and [. . . (12:15) . . .] [2]with [Terah his father in Haran for two weeks of years.]

[(12:16) And in the sixth week] [3]in [its] fifth year [Abram sat up through the night on the first day of the seventh month to observe] [4]the star[s from the evening to the morning in order to see what kind of year it would be in respect to the rains. And while] [5]he [was sitting alone and observing, (12:17) a word came to his heart that said: "All the signs] [6]of the sta[rs . . .]

Terah's blessing on Abram's departure for Canaan.

Frag. 9 [2][. . .] (12:28) And in the sev[enth year of the sixth week] [3][he spoke with his father and told him that] he was going to leave [Haran to go to the land of] [4][Canaan to see it, and that he would return to him. (12:29) And] Terah [his] f[ather said] to him: ["Go in peace.] [5][May the eternal God make your way straight, may the LORD be wit]h you and pro[tect you from all evil,] [6][and may no man have power over you to d]o you evil. [Go in peace." . . .]

The testament of Abraham and the length of his life (Gen. 25:5, 7).

4Q219 Col. 1 [10][. . . (21:1) And in the sixth year,] [11][in] the seventh [week] of [this jubilee, Abraham called his son Isaac,] [12]and he commanded him, saying, "I am ol[d but do not know the day of my death, though I have reached] [13]a ripe old age. (21:2) I am now [one hundred seventy-]two [years old. Throughout my life I have remembered] [14]our [G]od alwa[ys] and sought [Him with all my heart . . .] [15][. . .]

Continuation of the testament of Abraham (Lev. 3:7–11; reconstructed with the aid of 4Q219 1:32–38).

4Q220 Frag. 1 [1][(21:5) . . . observe His statutes, His] commandments, [and His judgments, and do not go a]fter idols, [images, or] [2][molten images.] (21:6) And do not [eat any blo]od of an animal, cattle, or any bird that [flies in the sky.]

[3][(21:7) If you sa]crifice a well-be[ing] as a burnt offering, o[f]fer it in such a way that it is acceptable: you are to sprinkle the blood on the alt[ar,] [4][and all] the meat of the burnt offering you are to bu[r]n on the al[tar] with the flour of its offering mixed with [o]i[l,] [5][with its libation. You shall] burn all of it on the altar as an offering by fire, a sweet savor before God. (21:8) The fat of [6][the sacrifice of wel]l[-bei]ng you are to burn up on the fire which is on the altar, and the fat [that is upon] [7][the entrails,] the [f]at that is above the entrails, the kidneys [and] the [fat that is on them,] [8][and that which is on the loins] and the appendage of the liver you are to remove, together with the kidneys. [(21:9) You shall burn] [9][all of it as a sweet savor before G]od with its offering and its libation as a sw[eet savor, a food offering by fire] [10][to God. (21:10) Eat its meat on] that [day] and on the next; but do no[t] let [the sun] s[et on it] [11][on the next day until it is eaten. It is not to be left to the th]i[rd day . . .]

Continuation of the testament of Abraham (Lev. 17:13–16; reconstructed with the aid of 4Q221 frag. 1:1–9).

4Q219 Col. 2 [7][(21:12) . . . olive wood, myrtle, bay wood, j]uniper-ceda[r, and balsam.

(21:13) From these kinds of wood] [8][you shall place under the offering on the] altar [those which are tested as to their appearance. Do not place any split wood . . .] [9–10][. . .] [11][. . . (21:14) . . . their fragrance goes up to] heaven.

(21:15) Ke[ep] [12][this commandment and do it, my son, that you might be up]right in all your deeds. [13][(21:16) And at all times be pure in your flesh and wash in water before you] go to burn [14–16][. . .]

[17][(21:18) And you shall no longer eat blood] for the blood is [life; and you shall not eat any blood. (21:19) You shall not take] [18][a bribe for any] human [blood] that will be shed [in vain without judgment, for the blood which is shed] [19][pollutes the earth, and the] earth cannot [be purified from human blood except through the blood] [20][of the one who shed it. (21:20) You shall not take a br]ibe or a ransom f[or human blood, it must be blood for blood, and then it will be acceptable] [21][before the LOR]D God Most High. His protection will be ov[er the good and that you may keep yourself from every] [22][evil and to del]iver you [from] every pestilence. [. . .]

[23][(21:21) I see, my son, that all] the de[eds of human]kind [are sin and wickedness, and all] [24][their deeds are impurity, disgrac]e, and perversion, and there is no truth among them. (21:22) Take [care lest you walk] [25][in their ways, and] tread in their paths, and commit a sin leading to death [before God Most High] [26][and He hide His face] from you, give you into the power of your transgressions, and cut you off [from the earth] [27][and your seed from] under heaven. And your name and your memory will perish from [the] wh[ole earth.] [28][(21:23) Turn aside from all] their [de]eds and from all their abominations, and [ke]ep the oblig[ations of] [29][God Most High, and do] His will so that you might be successful in everything. (21:24) He will bless you in all your deeds, [and will raise up] [30][from you the plant] of truth on the earth for all the generations of the earth. Then He will not bring an end to [my name and your name] [31][unde]r heaven throughout all the days.

(21:25) Make your way straight, my son, in pea[ce,] [32][that the God Mo]st High [might strengthen you,] my God and your God, to do His will and to [bless your seed] [33]and the [remnant of] your [see]d for all the generations forever, with all the blessing[s of the truth, so that you may be] [34]a blessing [in all the ea]rth. (21:26) And he departed from Him rejoicing. [. . .]

[35][(22:1) And it came abou]t in the first week of the fo[rty-]third [jubilee, in the second year] [36][of it, that is] the year in which Abraham died, [Isaac and Ishmael] cam[e] [37][from Beersheba to celebrate th]e feast of [we]e[k]s, the festi[val of the firstfruits of the harvest . . .]

Abraham's blessing on Jacob.

4Q221 Frag. 2 Col. 1 [1][(22:22) . . . there is no] hope [for th]em in the land [2][of the living. For they will descend into Sheol and will go into the place of judgment. There will be no remem]brance of them all on the earth. [3][Just as the Sodomites were destroyed from the eart]h, so all [who serve idols] will be destroyed.

The burial of Abraham (Gen. 25:8–10).

3Q5 Frag. 3 [1][(23:6) And a voice] was heard [in the house of Abraham,] [2][and Ishmael his son arose and] went to A[braham his father, and wept over Abraham his father,] [3][he and all the me]n of the house of A[braham, and they wept bitterly.] **2Q19 Frag. 1** [1][(23:7) His sons, Isaac and Ishmael, buried him in the cave of Ma]chpelah ne[ar Sarah, his wife.] [2][They mourned him] for forty days, all the men [of his house, and Isaac and Ishmael, and all their sons, and all] [3][the sons of Keturah in their places.]

[4][And the days of mourning for Abra]ham [were completed.] (23:8) And he lived three jubilees and fo[ur weeks of years, one hundred and seventy-five] [5][years, and completed the days of his life,] being old and full of days [. . .]

The decline in longevity (reconstructed with the aid of 3Q5 frag. 1).

4Q221 Frag. 3 [1][(23:10) . . . justly all the days of his life, but even he did not complete four jubilees in] his life until h[e] [2][had grown old because of wickedness and came to an end of his days.

(23:11) All the generations which will arise from n]ow until the d[a]y [3][of Great Judgment will grow old quickly . . . before they complete tw]o jubilees. [4][And their knowledge will abandon them because of their advanced age, and all their knowledge will be lost. (23:12) In] those [day]s, [5][if a man lives for a full jubilee and one-half they will say about him: "He has lived long, but] the better part of his days [6][are pain, trouble, and distress without peace. (23:13) For there is blow upon blow and turmoil upo]n [turmoil] **3Q5 Frag. 1**[3][distress upon distress, and evil report upon [evil] report [. . ."]

The future evil generation.

4Q176b Frags. 19–20 [1][(23:21) . . . and they will name the great name, but not in trut]h nor in righteousness [2][and they shall defile the holy of holies with impur]ity and the cor[ruption of their abominations.] (23:22)

And there will be great anger against the deeds of [that] generation [3][from the LORD. And He will hand th]em [over] to the sword and to judgment and [to captivity] and for plunder and for devouring. [(23:23) And] He will rouse against them [4][the wicked ones of the gentiles who have neither mercy nor com]passion, and [who shall] resp[ect] n[o one,] nor [. . .]

4Q176b Frag. 21 [1](23:30) And [those who] h[ate them] shall see [all their judgment] [2]in all [their] curse. [(23:31) And their bones shall rest on the earth,] [3]and their spirits sh[all rejoice greatly, and they shall know that] [4]there is a God who executes [judgment and shows mercy] [5]to [thousand]s and to te[ns of thousands, to all that love Him.]

Jacob responds to his mother's instruction regarding marriage (Gen. 28:1).

4Q222 Frag. 1 [1][(25:9) ". . . all] the days of my life [I will] not [take a wife for myself from any of the daughters of Canaan and I will not act wickedly as] [2]my brother Esau [has done.] (25:10) Fear not, my mother. Be assured [that I will do your will and will walk uprightly] [3][and] will [no]t ever corrupt my ways."

(25:11) Then she lifted [her face to heaven, spread the fingers] [4][of] her [hand]s, opened her mouth, and blessed God Most High, c[reator of heaven and earth, and she gave Him] [5][tha]nks and praise. (25:12) And she said, "Blessed is LORD Go[d, and blessed is His name forever] [6][and ev]er who has given me J[a]c[ob, a pure son and holy seed. For he is Yours] [7]and Yours [shall be his seed . . ."]

Jacob directed to go to Haran.

Frag. 2 [1][(27:5) ". . . evil in his eyes, be]cause [I] leave [him and depart from you, and my father would become angry and curse] [2][me.] (27:6) I will [n]ot go unless h[e sends me; then I will go."

(27:7) And Rebekah said to Jacob,] [3]["I will go in] and I will [spe]ak to him. [Then he will send you . . ."]

Jacob's dream at Bethel (Gen. 28:10–11).

1Q17 Frag. 1 [2][(27:19) Jacob went from the Beersheba to] go to Haran on the first [year of the second week in the forty-fourth jubilee.] [3][He came to Luz wh]ich is on the mountain, that is, Bethel, [on the first of the first month of this week.] [4][He came to] the pl[ace when it was even]ing and turned from the way to the we[st that night: and he slept there, for the sun had set.] [5][(27:20) He to]ok one of the stones of [that] place [and l]ai[d it at his head under the oak, and he lay down there,] [6][for he] was journeying by himself [. . .]

4Q223–224 Unit 1 Col. 1 [1][(32:18) . . . and] the earth. I will make you fruitful [and multiply you exceedingly, and kings shall come forth from you,] [2][and ru]le in every place where the sole [of human foot shall tread. (32:19) I shall give to your offspring all the land] [3][under heaven, and] they shall rule over all the [nations as they please. Afterward, they will take all the earth and possess it as an inheritance forever."] [4](32:20) [And he finished spea]king with him and went up [from him. Jacob watched until he ascended to heaven. (32:21) He saw in a vision] [5][of the nig]ht that an an[gel . . .]

Incest laws (Deut. 22:30).

4Q221 Frag. 4 [1][(33:12) Again it is wri]tt[en] a second time: ["Cursed is one who lies with] his father's [wife,] for he has uncov[ered] [2]his father's skirt." [And all the holy ones of the LORD said, "Ame]n, amen." (33:13) And as for you, [3]command the [Israel]ites [to keep thi]s [word.] For [4]it is a death sentence [and] a disgra[ce. There is no atonement to co]ver [5]the man who will com[mit this wickedness, forever. Bu]t [6]he shall be put to death by sto[ning; he shall be stoned and cut off from the people.] [7][(33:14) For no one] shall live even [{one] day} [one day in the land] [8][wh]o commits such a thing in Israel, [for it is an abomination and a disgrace.]

[9](33:15) Let them [not] say, "Reuben was granted [life and atonement after he lay] [10][with the concubi]ne of his father, [Jacob," for . . .]

Rebekah warns Jacob about Esau.

4Q223–224 Unit 2 + 1Q18 Frags. 1–2 Col. 1 [4][(34:4) . . . who were living in] the forest in the land of [5][Canaan. (34:5) They informed Jacob, saying, "The kings of the Amorites have surrounded your sons and] your flocks [. . .]

[45][(35:7) . . .] sickness [46][had not touched her all the days of her life. (35:8) And Jacob spoke to her, saying, "I would be blessed, mother,] if [the years of my life should even approach those] of your[s;] [47][would that my strength would be such as yours. You will not die, for you speak lightly wi]th me regarding your death."

Rebekah warns Isaac about Esau while praising Jacob, and Isaac's reply.

(35:9) She went [to Isa]ac [48]and said to him: "One petitio]n I make to you. Make Esau swear that he will n[ot] injure Jacob, his brother, [49][nor pursue him] with enmity. For you kn[ow] the inclination of Esau, that it has been evil from his youth. He lacks upright character, for [50][he wants to kill him after you die. (35:10) You know all that he has d]one with us from the day his brother, [J]acob, [51]went [to Haran until this day. He wholeheartedly abandoned us and afflict]ed us. He led your flocks away and [52][stole your possessions from you. (35:11) When we sought to ask him for what was ours, he act]ed treacherously [yet ag]ain, only pretending to take [53][pity on us. (35:12) He is embittered against you because you blessed Jacob, your perfect and upright son, in whom is n]o evil [54][but only good. From the day he came from Haran until] this day [he has not denied us] the least thing, [but] **Col. 2**[1][brings us everything in its proper time every day, rejoicing with his whole heart when we take it from his hands; and he blesses us, and has not separated from us] [2][from the day when he came from Haran until this day. Instead, he lives with us in our home always and gives us honor." (35:13)

And Isaac replied to her,] [3]"I too kno[w and see Jacob's behavior, that he is with us wholeheartedly,] [4]honoring us and carrying out our wishes. [At first I loved] Esau much more [than Jacob, just after he was born.] [5]But now I love Jacob more than [Esau, because] he has done so much evil, and [there is no truth in him; instead,] [6][al]l his ways are viol[en]ce and evil, and there is [truth] n[either in him, nor around hi]m. (35:14) Now [my] heart [is broken by his deeds; neither he] [7][nor his offspring should be rescued; they should be exterminated from the earth, cut off from under heaven, since he] [8][has abandoned the God of Abraham. He and his sons have pursued the impurity of the wo]men and the error of the wo[men. (35:15) You have said] [9][to me that I should make him swear not to kill his brother, Ja]c[ob.] Even if he swears, he will not keep the oath, nor do [10][good, but rather evil. (35:16) But if he seeks to kill Jacob,] his brother, he will be given into Jacob's power [11][and will not escape from it, but will descend into his power. (35:17) As for] you, do not worry [about Jaco]b, for He who guards Ja[co]b is greater, more powerful, [12][more honored, and more praised than he who guards Es]au. Like dust befo[re the wind,] so are all the guardians of Esau before the God [13][of Abraham, the God of Isaac, and the God of J]acob, [my perfect and hon]orable son. But I lov[e the one who carries o]ut our wishes [14][. . .] my sister, in peace."

Rebekah sends for Esau, and he makes her grand promises.

(35:18) Then Re[bekah] summoned [15][Esau, and he came to her. She said to him, "I have something to ask of you, my son. Tell me that you will do it." [16](35:19) And] he replied, "I will do what [you ask me; I will not refuse your request." (35:20) So she] said, "I [17][would ask of you that on the day I die, you bring me and bury me next to Sarah, your father's mother, and that you] [18][and Ja]cob love one an[other and not seek one another's harm, but rather love each other. Then you will prosper,] [19][my sons, and be honored in the land. Your enemies will not rejoice over you; you will become a blessing and compassion itself] [20][in the eyes of every fr]iend." (35:21) And he repl[ied, "I will do all that you ask. I will bury you on the day] [21][you die next to Sarah, my father's mother, just as you have desired; surely her bones will lie near yours.] [22](35:22) [I will] love [Jacob my brother] above [all flesh; I will have no brother in all the land but him alone. It is not . . ."]

Remaining portions of Isaac's final testament to Jacob and Esau. Isaac makes his sons swear to love one another and threatens judgment for disobedience.

4Q223–224 Unit 2 Col. 2 (36:7) (. . . the Name glorious and honored) [48]and gr[eat who created the heavens and the earth,] and all things to[gether, in order that you fear Him and serve] [49]Hi[m. (36:8) And let each man love his brother with compassion and ri]ghteousness, and not [seek evil for his brother] [50]from no[w on, forever, all the days of your lives. Then you will prosper in] all your deeds and no[t perish. (36:9) But if] [51]a man [seeks harm for his brother, know henceforth that anyone who] seeks ha[rm] for his friend [will fall into that man's] power [and be cut off from the land of] [52]the liv[ing, and his descendants will perish from under heaven. (36:10) Moreover, on the day] of wrath, in [a]ng[er,] malice and ra[ge, and by a burning and devouring flame,] [53]as [they] bu[rned Sodom, so shall his land be burned, together with his] cities [and everything he owns. He will be erased from the Book of Human Instruction] [54][and enter not the Book of Life, but destruction. He will pass over to an eternal curse, so that for all the days] **Col. 3** [1][their judgment will be renewed with hatred, a curse and eternal sickness. (36:11) I speak and testify against you, my sons, according to the judgment that] [2][will come against the man who seeks to work evil against his brother. (36:12) Then he divided all his possessions between the two of them, on that day,] [3][and he gave the greater portion to the firstborn, together with the fortress and a]ll [its] environs, [and all that] [4][Abraham had acquired in Beersheba. (36:13) And he said, "I will grant the greater portion to the firstborn] man." (36:14) [5][But Esau said, "I sold everything to Jacob, and gave my rights as firstborn to Jacob.] Let it be given [to him;] [6][I will make no claim on it, for it has become his." (36:15) Then Isaac spoke: "May a blessing rest upon you, my sons, and upon your descendants] [7][on this day, for you have set me at rest so that I have no anxiety about the right of the firstborn;] evil [shall not be done] [8][concerning it. (36:16) May the LORD Most High bless that man who acts uprightly—him and his descendants, for]e[ver." (36:17) He finished] [9][comm]an[ding them] and bl[essing them, and they ate and drank together in his presence. He rejoiced at the peace] between them. Then [they went out from] [10]h[im and rested and slept on that] da[y. (36:18) And Isaac slept in his bed] that [da]y; he rejoiced, then slept [an eternal] sl[eep.] [11]Thus [he died, aged one hundred] and eight[y years; he completed t]wenty-[five] weeks of years [and five] years. [12]And [they] bu[ried him, his two sons, Esau and Jacob.]

The brothers leave and go their separate ways. After a long and upright life, Leah dies. The exalted praise of her that follows this notice is nowhere found in the Bible.

(36:19) [Then] Esau [went] to the land of [Mount] Seir and dwelt [13]ther[e. (36:20) In turn Jacob settled in the mountains of Hebron, in the fortress] in the land of Canaan, in the lan[d of A]braham [his forefather. [14]And [he served God wholeheartedly according to the commandments that had been revealed,] acc[ording to the divisions of] the days [of his birth.] [15](36:21) [Then Leah, the wife of Jacob, died, in the fourth year of the second week of the forty-fifth jubilee.] [16]And he buried [her in the Cave of Machpelah next to Rebekah his mother, on the left of the grave of Sarah, the mother of] his father. [17](36:22) [All his daughters and sons] cam[e to weep for Leah his wife with him and to comfort him about her, because he was mourning] [18]he[r. (36:23) For he had loved her very, very much since the death of Rachel,] her [sis]ter, for she was per[fect] [19][and upright in all her ways. She had honored Jacob, and during all the d]ays of her life [with him never . . .]

Esau approaches to do battle with Jacob (Gen. 32:6).

4Q221 Frag. 5 [1][. . . (37:11) They said to] their [father, "Go, lead them out. And if not, we will kill you." (37:12) And Esau was filled with anger and wrath] [2]when he saw that his sons were intending to for[ce him to lead them out against his brother. (37:13) Afterward he remembered] [3]all the wicked things which we[re hidden in his heart against Jacob, his brother,] [4]but he did not remember the oath that [he had sworn to his father and his mother that he would never seek any wickedness] [5]against Jacob. (37:14) And in all this [Jacob] did not kno[w that they were coming against him for war. He] [6]was mourning for his wife until [they came against him near the fortress with four thousand] [7]men of war. [The men of Hebron] sent t[o him saying, "Your brother has come against you to do battle . . ."]

After Jacob rebukes Esau for the assault in contravention of their earlier oath and while he was in mourning for Leah, Esau replies in harsh poetry that they are no brothers and that oaths are made to be broken. In the Bible (Gen. 33), on the other hand, the two brothers make peace; the change probably reflects warfare between the Jews and the Nabatean Arabs (descendants of Esau, according to the Bible) at the time Jubilees *was composed.*

4Q223–224 Unit 2 Col. 4 [2][. . . (37:17) "Yo]u have [sinned] against the oat[h.] [3][Indeed, at the very time that you swore to your father, you were judged." (37:18) Esau answered immediately and said to him,] "Neither human b[eings] [4][nor sn]akes possess an in[violable oath that they actually swear for perpetuity. No, every day, th]ese against those, [they seek] [5]ev[il: how they may murder, each ma[n his enemy or rival. (37:19) As for you, you hate me and] my children, al[ways] [6]w[ill.] It is impossible to practice [brotherhood] with yo[u. (37:20) Hear these words of mine that I hereby de]clare to you: [7][If] a boar [could] change [its] sk[in or make its bristles] soft [like wool,] if it could grow [ho]rns on [its] he[ad] like those of a r[am] [8][or shee]p, then could I practice [brotherhood] with you. [The breasts might as well have separated from their mother; surely] you have been [n]o brother [of mine. (37:21) Or if] [9][wolv]es could make peace with lambs, n[ot to eat them or oppress them, if] their hearts were inclined [toward them] for [good,] [10]then would there be [peace] in my heart [toward you. (37:22) If a lion could be] friend and trustee [to] an ox, [if he could be paired] [11][with him to] plow jointly yoked, the[n would I make peace with you. (37:23) If yet] ravens [could blanch] like a peli[can, then] know that [12][I mig]h[t love you and ma]ke [peace with you. Be cut off, you; and] may your children be [cut] off, so that [yo]u hav[e] no peace." [13](37:24) [When Jacob saw that Esau meant evil against him with all his heart, and intended with all his spirit] to slay him, [and] came charging [14][like a boar rushing upon a spear that pierces and kills it, yet without falling back] from it—(37:25) only th[en] did he order his sons [15][and his servants to fall upon him and all his allies.]

The battle, resulting in the defeat of Esau and his forces.

(+ 4Q221 Frag. 6) (38:1) [After that Judah spoke to Jac]ob his father [16][and said to him, "Draw back your bow, father, and let fl]y your arrow. [Fell the adversary, slay the fo]e. May [17][you have the power, since we shall not kill your brother:] he i[s] your brother, [and resembles you], and is like you [18][in our esteem." (38:2) Immediately Jacob drew back] his [bo]w and let fly [the first arrow; it smote] Esau [19][his brother in the right breast and killed him. (38:3) Then he sh]ot a seco[nd] arrow [and struck Adurim the A]ramaean in [20][the left breast, throwing him backward and killing him. (38:4) At that] Jacob's sons [sallied forth, they and their servants, form]ing four companies, one for [21][each side of the fortress. (38:5) Judah went] first, and Naphtali and Gad [beside, their fifty men with] them, to the south of [22][the fortress, killing all they encountered. Not one] escaped them. (38:6) [Levi,] Dan, and Asher [23][sallied to the east of the fortress, toge]ther with [their fifty. They slew the wa[rriors] of Moa[b and Ammon.] (38:7) Reuben,[24][Issachar, and Zebulun] sallied [to the north of the fortress, their fifty wi]th them. And [they] kil[led] the warriors] of Philistia. [25](38:8) [Simeon, Benjamin, and Enoch,] the son of Reub[en, sallied] to the [west of the fortress, their fifty beside, and] slew of the Edom[ites] [26][and Horites four hundred heroic warriors, while six hundred fled. Fou]r [sons of] [27][Esau fled with them, leaving their father dead, splayed upon the hill that is] in Adurim. [28](38:9) [The sons of Jacob pursued them as far as Mount Seir while Jacob buried his brother on the hill that is] [29][in A]dur[im and returned to the fortress. (38:10) The sons of Jacob besieged Esau's sons on Mount Seir and] [30][sub]dued them, making them [suppliant to themselves. (38:11) Then they sent word to their father asking if they should make peace with them] [31][or kill th]em. (38:12) [Jacob] sent back [to his sons that they should make peace with them, and they did.] [32][But they put the yoke of servitude upon them,] to pa[y tribute to Jacob and his sons in perpetuity. (38:13) So they were] [33][paying tribute to Jacob until the da]y they went down [to Egypt . . .]

Joseph in Potiphar's house (Gen. 39:1–10).

4Q221 Frag. 7 [1][(39:4) The Egyptian] committed [everything to Joseph, for he recognized that the LORD was with him and everything that he did] [2]God made successful.

[(39:5) Now Joseph was well built and handsome.] [3]And his master's [w]ife [took notice] of [Joseph and fell in love with him. She asked him] [4][t]o lie [with her. (39:6) But he did not give in to her and remembered God] [5][and] the words [which Jacob, his father, used to read from the words of Abraham, that] [6][no man should fornicate with a woman who has a husband. For a death penalty has been established] [7][on such a one in heave]n [before God Most High. The sin shall be recorded against him on the eternal tablets] [8][for al]l tim[e before the LORD. (39:7) Joseph remembered this reading and] [9]did [not] d[esi]re to li[e with her. (39:8) She asked him for one year and then a second, but he refused to listen. Then she brought] [10]a deceitful plan against him. [(39:9) She grabbed him, but he left his garment in] her hand. Then h[e closed th]e gate [and fled] out[side away from her.] **4Q223–224 Unit 2 Col. 5** [2][(39:10) When that woman saw that he would not] lie with her, [she lied ab]out him to [his] mas[ter, saying,] [3]["Your Hebrew servant came to me, the one wh]om [you] lov[e, to harass] me, to lie wi[th me. When] [4][I raised a shout, he fled outside,] le[aving his garment in my hand] in the moment when I g[rabbed] [5][him by it, and he secur]ed the exi[t." (39:11) The Egyptian saw Joseph's garment, and the exit secured,] [6][so he believed] his [w]ife and put [Joseph in the prison, the place where the prisoners] [7][of the king were confined.

(39:12) And so he was ther]e, in the pris[on. But the LORD gave him favor with the captain of the prison,] [8][and kindness from him too be]cause [the man] saw [that the LORD was with him, and that the LORD gave success to everything he] [9][was doing. (39:13) So he committed everything to Joseph; the captain of the prison oversaw nothing,] [10][but Joseph was doing it all, and the LORD was giving success. So he lived there two years. (39:14) At th]at [time] [11][Pharaoh, the king of Egypt, grew angry with his two courtiers, the chief butler and the chief of] [12]the [cooks, and he put them in prison, in the house of the captain of the guard, the prison where Joseph] [13][was] con[fined. (39:15) And the captain of the prison assigned Joseph to serve them, which he did. (39:16) Then each of them] [14][had a dream, the chief butler and the chief cook, and told it to Joseph. (39:17) And just as he interpreted] [15][to them, so it came to pass. As for the chief butler, the Pharaoh restored him] to off[ice; as for the chief] [16][cook, he hanged him, just as Joseph had interpreted to him. (39:18) Yet the chief] butler [forgot Joseph in the prison,] [17][though he had told him what was to come. He forgot to tell Pharao]h wh[at Joseph had told him;] [18][he simply forgot.]

[(40:1) In those days Pharaoh dream]t t[wo dreams in a] si[ngle] [19][night, about the matter of the famine that would b]e over al[l the land. He awoke from his sleep and summoned] [20][all the magicians of Egypt, and the wise men, and] recounted [his dreams to them. But they were unable] [21][to explain. (40:2) Only then did the chief bu]tl[er remember Joseph. He] reported concerning [him to the king, who brought him out of the] [22][prison and told him about the] dreams. (40:3) And [he interpret]ed them befo[re Pharaoh, that the two dreams] [23][were actually just one. He said to him, "Seven years of plenty are coming ov]er all the land of [Egypt, then seven] [24][years of famine a]fter[ward, the like of which has never been in all the la]nd. (40:4) And now, let [25][Pharaoh appoint of]ficer[s in all the land of Egypt, and let them gather food for each] cit[y during the years of] [26][plenty. Let that] be fo[od for the seven years of famine, so that the land will] not [be cut off because of the famine, since] [27][it will be severe." (40:5) And] Go[d] gav[e Joseph favor and kindness] from Pharaoh. [Pharaoh said to his servants,] [28]["Will we find a m]an who under[stands and is wise like this man? Surely a spirit of the g]ods is [in him." (40:6). And he appointed him second in all] [29][his kingdom, and gave him to rule] over all the land of Egypt, and placed him in the [second] chariot [to] [30][Pharaoh's own. (40:7) He dressed] him in garment[s of linen and hung a golden necklace about his throat. He had heralds proclaim before him:] [31]["El, El, and Abirel."] And he placed [the signet ring upon his hand, and gave him to rule over all his house, exalting him.] [32][And he said, "I will not be exalted above] you, except [. . ."]

Surviving portions of the story of Tamar and Judah (Gen. 38).

Unit 3 Col. 2 [1][(41:7) . . . thi]s (week). (41:8) [In its sixth year Judah went up to shear his sheep in Timnah, and it was reported to Tamar, "Your father-in-law is going up to shear] [2][his] shee[p in Timnah." (41:9) So she removed her widow's garments, assumed a veil, beautified herself, and sat down by the gate on the road entering Timnah. (41:10) When] [3]Ju[dah] came along [. . .]

The death of Joseph (Gen. 50:26).

2Q20 Frag. 1 [0][. . . (46:1) They increased] [1][exceedingly, ten] wee[ks] of years, a[ll the days of the life of Joseph.] [2][(46:2) There was no Satan or anything evil] all the days of the life of Joseph wh[ich he lived after] [3][his father, Jacob. For all of the Egyptians] were giving ho[nor to the children of Israel] [4][all the days of the life of Joseph. (46:3) Joseph died] at one hundred and [ten years of age.]

The plagues on Egypt (Exod. 7–11).

4Q222 Frag. 3 [1][. . .] [2][(48:5) . . . he destroyed everything] that sprouted [. . . and by locusts which devoured that which was left to them from the hail;] [3][and by darkness and by the firstborn of] humankind and [cattle . . .]

—M.G.A., M.O.W.

43. A Paraphrase of Genesis and Exodus

4Q225

Like *An Annotated Law of Moses* (text 84) and other examples of rewritten Bible among the scrolls, *A Paraphrase of Genesis and Exodus* interprets the Bible by retelling selected portions. The most interesting of the fragmentary remains concern the story of the "binding of Isaac," a theme that was richly developed in later Judaism and continues to generate profound reflection up to the present day.

In the text before us, the story of the binding reads much like that of the biblical Job: a man of transcendent righteousness undergoes sore testing because Satan (here called Mastemah) has received permission from God to bring trials upon him. The Jobian parallels are, of course, absent from the passages in Genesis that recount the tale of Isaac nearly being sacrificed upon God's command. Yet the rationale for their introduction is compelling, for the biblical story does present a difficult problem: how could God command Abraham to sacrifice his own son? If God did not really intend Abraham to go through with it, was God being deceitful? Why would God act as described? Our author urges an interesting solution to the problem by introducing the figure of Mastemah and rooting the entire episode in evil that God merely countenances, but does not originate—just as in Job.

This fragment evidently discussed the period of bondage in Egypt, suggesting that God appointed Moses to rescue Israel out of God's own faithfulness to his covenant with Abraham.

Frag. 1 [1][. . .] because of the sin of fornication [. . .] [2][. . .] he [. . .] [3][. . .] so He struck them with [. . .] [4][. . . the covenant that] was made with Abraham. And he circumcised [. . .] [5][. . .] Egypt, and God sold them [. . .] [6][. . .]

And you, Moses, when I spoke wi[th you . . .] [7][. . .] the creation, until the day of creation [. . .] [8][. . .] standing, and he arose (*or* he avenged) [. . .] [9][. . .] and in the day that [. . .] [10][. . . Israel saw the Egyptians dead up]on the shore [of the sea . . .]

Abraham and Sarah are childless.

Frag. 2 Col. 1 [1][. . .] that pe[rson] shall be cut off [2][from the midst of] his [peop]le [. . . and he li]ved in Haran for twen[t]y [y]ears. [3][. . . and Ab]raham [said] to God. "Lord, behold, I continue to be ch[ild]less and Eli[ezer] [4]is [a child of my house;] he shall be my heir" (Gen. 15:2).

God promises Abraham a descendant, and he believes.

[5][So Go]d [said] to A[b]raham, "Look up at the stars and see [6][and count] the sand which is upon the shore of the sea and the dust of the earth, for if [7]these [are countab]le, and if not, thus your seed shall be" (Gen. 15:5). And [Abraham] be[lieved] [8][in] Go[d] and it was reckoned to him as righteousness (Gen. 15:6).

Isaac is born and the Prince of Malevolence (Mastemah) conspires to destroy him (Gen. 21:1–3; 22:2–4; Jubilees *17:15–18:13).*

And af[ter] this a son was born [9][to Abraha]m and he named him Isaac. Now the Prince of Malevolence (Mastemah) approached [10][G]od and displayed his anger against Abraham on account of Isaac. And [G]od said [11][to Abra]ham, "Take your son, Isaac, [your] only one, [whom] [12][yo]u [love,] and offer him up to [Me] as a burnt offering upon one of the [high] mountains [13][which I will point out] to you" (Gen. 22:2). So he r[ose and we]n[t] from the wells to M[ount Moriah] [14][. . .][. . .] And Ab[raham] lifted **Col. 2** [1][his ey]e[s and there was] fire, and [he s]et [the wood on Isaac and they walked on together.]

The plot of the Prince of Malevolence (Mastemah) is foiled because of Abraham's obedience (Gen. 22:7–12). See Commentaries on Genesis *frag. 1 col. 3 (text 53).*

[2]Then Isaac said to Abraham [his father, "Here is the fire and the wood, but where is the lamb] [3]for the burnt offering?" And Abraham said to [Isaac his son, "God will supply the lamb] [4]for Himself" (Gen. 22:7–8). Isaac said to his father, "T[ie me well . . .] [5]Holy angels stood weeping above [the altar . . .] [6]his sons from the earth. And the angels of ma[levolence (Mastemah) . . . they] [7]were rejoicing and saying, "Now he shall perish." And [by all of this the Prince of Malevolence (Mastemah) was testing to determine whether] [8]he should be found to be deceitful, and if not, that A[braham] might be found trustworthy [before God. And God said,] [9]"Abraham, Abraham!" And he said, "Here I am!" And He said, "N[ow I know that . . . (Gen. 22:12) . . .] [10]you shall not be loving." Then God the LORD blessed Is[aac all the days of his life. And he bore] [11]Jacob. And Jacob bore Levi, a [third] gen[eration.]

[And all] [12]the days of Abraham, Isaac, Jacob, and Lev[i were . . . years.] [13]And the Prince of Malevolence (Mastemah) was bound (?) be[cause of them. The holy angels were . . .] [14]Prince of Male[vo]lence (Mastemah). And Belial listened to [the Prince of Malevolence (Mastemah) . . .]
—M.G.A.

44. Israel and the Holy Land

4Q226

The present work paraphrases biblical episodes in the tradition of the *Book of Jubilees* (text 42) and the many other examples of rewritten Bible found among the scrolls. Surviving portions correspond to passages in Genesis, Exodus, and Joshua. Although the work is so fragmentary that analysis is hazardous, the mention of "jubilees" is notable and suggests that the author may have been wrestling with chronological concerns. The connection of jubilees and Joshua also appears in *Apocryphal Joshua* (text 92). For a fuller explanation of the role of jubilees in the scrolls, see the introduction to the *Calendar of the Heavenly Signs* (text 71).

God appears to Moses (?) and commissions him to rescue Israel from bondage (Exod. 3:1–12).

Frag. 1 [2][. . .] in a flame of fire from the midst of [. . .] [3][. . . commanding] you to go down to Egypt and to bring ou[t . . .] [4][. . .] the signs I have [g]iven to you, that you might dwell (*or* return) [. . .] [5][. . .] years you have made from the week [. . .] [6][. . .] this jubilee, for it is holy [. . .] [7][. . .] holy [fo]rever [. . .]

Moses is forbidden entrance to the land of Canaan (Deut. 3:27, 31:2).

Frag. 3 [1][. . .] when [you (?)] do [. . .] [2][. . .] you shall do and [. . .] [3][. . . this] wilderness [. . .] [4][. . .] and you shall not cro[ss over . . .] [5][. . .] to the land of Canaa[n . . .]

Joshua instead of Moses shall lead Israel into the promised land (Deut. 31:3).

Frag. 4 [1][. . . for Joshua the s]on of Nun, he will cross over befo[re you . . .] [2][. . .] deed and set for [yourself (?) . . .] [3][. . .] for yourself all [. . .]

Joshua prepares the people to cross the Jordan (Josh. 3:1–2).

Frag. 6 [2][. . .] until three [. . .] [3][. . .] since th[eir] coming [. . .] [4][. . .] from the day they cross the [Jordan . . .] [5][. . .] these under [. . .] [6][. . .] in order that they may cross [the Jordan . . .] [7][. . .] exce[pt . . .] [8][. . . wh]o said [. . .]

Abraham is faithful. See text 43 for a possible overlap.

Frag. 7 [1][. . .] Abraham was recognized as faithful to [G]o[d . . .] [2]for acceptance. And the LORD blessed [Isaac all the days of] [3]his life, and he bore Ja[cob and Jacob bore] [4]Levi, the thi[rd] generation.

[And all the days of] [5]Abraham, Isaac and Ja[cob and Levi were . . . years.] [6]And the [holy] angels [. . . And Belial listened] [7]to the prince, "Fast here [. . .]

—M.G.A.

45. Enoch and the Watchers

4Q227

This fragmentary manuscript is similar to portions of the *Book of Jubilees* (text 42), an important writing of Second Temple Judaism that survived only among Christian readers and that has long been known to us from versions in Greek and Ethiopic. Among Ethiopian Christians *Jubilees* was so treasured that it actually became a part of the Old Testament. Fifteen fragmentary exemplars of *Jubilees* have turned up among the scrolls, establishing the work as one of the most common among those caches, and clearly testifying to its importance for those who hid the texts. Like the Ethiopian Christians, they may have considered the book a part of the canon of Holy Writ.

In that light, the present work seems to be a retelling of *Jubilees,* and it may be that we should consider it an example of rewritten Bible, the interpretive phenomenon we encounter so often in the scrolls. Surviving fragments of 4Q227 relate to *Jubilees* 4:17–24, but give the material in a different order. *Jubilees* 4:18 reports that the angels taught Enoch the calendar, which seems to be the subject of our frag. 2, l. 1. *Jubilees* 4:22 says that Enoch testified against the Watchers, or fallen angels, who had taken human wives and whose progeny were the giants (Gen. 6:1–2; cf. the *Book of Giants,* text 37). Our author also relates this story, in frag. 2, l. 4, and apparently goes on to connect it, under the influence of *Jubilees* 4:23, to the judgment of the entire world.

This fragment concerns Enoch's training at the hands of the angels. See Jubilees *4:21 (text 42) and* Tales of the Patriarchs *2:21 (text 4).*

Frag. 2 [1][. . . E]noch, after we taught him [2][. . . he was with the angels of God] six full jubilees [3][. . . the la]nd into the midst of the sons of man and he testified against them all [4][. . .] and also against the Watchers. And he wrote all [5][. . .] heavens and the ways of their hosts and [ho]ly ones [6][. . . so th]at the ri[ghteous ones] shall not commit error [. . .]
—M.G.A.

46. Work with a Citation of Jubilees

4Q228

In *Jubilees* 1:26 (text 42), God reveals to Moses the entire scope of the world's existence, "what was in the beginning and what will be at the end," and commands him to write it down. This fragmentary manuscript echoes this command and the overarching outline of what follows: judgment for the wicked and eternal life for the righteous.

Frag. 1 Col. 1 [2][. . . the]m [the divi]s[ion]s of the times, [3][for the law and for the testimony . . . and I tol]d you that you may know [4][. . . and I rela]ted to him the division of His/its time and all [5][. . .] in the judgment of times of injustice [6][. . .] a burning fire, devouring the council of wickedness [7][. . .] in the division of its time he will find it [8][. . . deliver . . . from all] the snares of the pit, and the angel of His peace [9][. . . lif]e everlasting. For thus is it written in the divisions of [10][the times (?) . . .] they will walk. And you [. . .] all [11][. . .] He will strengthen you (?) in [. . .] [12][. . .] and He will cause [. . .] to inherit [. . .] [13][. . .] and in the day[s . . .]
—M.G.A.

47. The Healing of King Nabonidus

4Q242

Nabonidus was the last king of the Neo-Babylonian Empire, reigning from 556 to 539 B.C.E. Beset by political problems and economic difficulties in Babylonia, Nabonidus decided to appoint his son Belsharusur as regent ("King Belshazzar" in the Bible: Dan. 5:22; 7:1; 8:1), while he himself moved west to Teima, an oasis in northwest Arabia. By removing to this locality, the king hoped to secure the trade routes from southern Arabia and thereby to ameliorate his money problems. He remained in Teima for a full decade, establishing garrisons and planting colonies to the south of his base of operations. Among these colonies were five oases that, at the time of Muhammad a millennium later, were occupied by Jews. Almost certainly, then, Nabonidus had a strong contingent of Jews among his colonists, whether drawn from those in exile in Babylonia or from those left behind in Judah. The presence of "a Jew, a member of the community of exiles" in the scroll here translated may be an accurate memory of this historical situation.

The king's ten-year absence from the capital city is probably the basis for the tale our scroll recounts. In turn, the correspondences between the scroll and the story told in Daniel 4 about the much more famous King Nebuchadnezzar are systematic and striking. These similarities have convinced most scholars that in some fashion the present story lies behind the biblical episode. If that theory is right, it would mean that we have discovered in this scroll a previously unknown source for the Bible. The story in this scroll would then antedate 200 B.C.E., and it could be a century or two older. The change of names, from Nabonidus to Nebuchadnezzar, was done, not to protect the innocent, but to implicate the guilty. Nebuchadnezzar, of course, was the Neo-Babylonian king who had sacked Jerusalem, burned the Temple, and carried the people into exile in 586 B.C.E. Likewise, the change from Nabonidus's "inflammation" to Nebuchadnezzar's lupine madness in Daniel 4 represents a raising of the stakes: an increase in the tension the storyteller hoped to create.

Eventually, King Nabonidus returned to Babylonia, but was overthrown by the forces of the Persian empire builder Cyrus. A form of that story appears in our Bibles in Daniel 5.

The actions of the Jewish exorcist described in our scroll accord exceedingly well with what we read about the figure of Daniel in the biblical book of the same name. Scholars have convincingly suggested that there once existed a "Daniel cycle" that included more stories—possibly quite a few more—than have survived in our Bibles. This would be one of them, as would the *Vision of Daniel* (text 48) and, perhaps, the *Vision of the Four Trees* (text 142). Further, bearing in mind the many New Testament parallels, the exorcism described here may profitably be compared with that carried out by Abraham in the *Tales of the Patriarchs* (text 4) and the actual wording of an exorcism preserved in text 146.

Nabonidus confesses his sins and explains how he was healed.

Frags. 1–3 [1]The words of the pra[y]er of Nabonidus, king of [Ba]bylon, [the great] kin[g, when he was smitten] [2]with a severe inflammation at the command of G[o]d, in Teima.

[I, Nabonidus,] was smitten [with a severe inflammation] [3]lasting seven years. Beca[use] I was thus changed, [becoming like a beast, I prayed to the Most High,] [4]and He forgave my sins. An exorcist—a Jew, in fact, a mem[ber of the community of exiles—came to me and said,] [5]"Declare and write down this story, and so ascribe glory and gre[at]ness to the name of G[od Most High." Accordingly, I have myself written it down:] [6]I was smitten with a severe inflammation while in Teima, [by the command of God Most High. Then] [7]for seven years I continued praying [to] the gods made of silver and gold, [bronze, iron,] [8]wood, stone, and clay, for I [used to th]ink that th[ey] really were gods.

—M.O.W.

48. The Vision of Daniel

4Q243–244

"An excellent spirit, along with knowledge and insight sufficient for interpreting dreams and explaining riddles and solving problems are found in this Daniel" (Dan. 5:12). Such was the judgment of the queen of Babylon, and her endorsement reflected the common image of Daniel in the last few centuries B.C.E. Like Enoch (text 36), Daniel was made into the hero of a cycle of stories, most of which are now lost. The biblical book of Daniel is part of this literature. The ancient Greek translation of the Old Testament contributes more stories about Daniel, and the Qumran caches offer even more. The *Healing of Nabonidus* (text 47) is one; this text is another.

Unfortunately, the *Vision of Daniel* is so fragmentary that not even an incomplete story can be recovered from it. It is clear only that Daniel is relating a vision (as he does several times in the biblical book, chaps. 7–12) that relates to the history of Israel.

These fragments may give the setting: Daniel is speaking to Belshazzar, as in Daniel 5. A writing of some kind is mentioned.

4Q243 Frag. 2 [1][. . .] Daniel befo[re . . .] [2][. . . King] Belshazzar [. . .] [3][. . .]

4Q244 Frags. 1–3 [1]before the princes of the king and the Assyrians [. . .]

4Q243 Frag. 1 [1]He asked Daniel, saying, Bec[au]se [. . .] [2]your God, and whence [. . .] [3]let him pray [. . .]

Frag. 6 [2][. . . a book was brought] and in it was written [. . .] [3][. . .] Daniel, who [. . .] [4][. . .] was found writt[en . . .]

Daniel gives an account of the history of Israel, beginning apparently with the story of Noah and the Flood (Gen. 6–9).

4Q244 Frag. 8 [2][. . .] after the flood [. . .] [3][. . . N]oah from [Mount] Lubar [. . .] [4][. . . built] a city [. . .]

The story of the Tower of Babel (Gen. 11).

Frag. 9 [2][. . .] a tower, [its] he[ight reached the heavens . . .]

4Q243 Frag. 10 [2][. . . agai]nst the tower and He sent [angels . . .] [3][. . . to] inspect the building [. . .]

The prediction to Abraham of the Egyptian captivity (Gen. 15:13).

4Q244 Frag. 12 [1][. . . fo]ur hundred [years . . .]

The Exodus is predicted (Gen. 15:14; Exod. 15–16). Note the division of history into jubilees (cf. text 95 for such a method).

[2][. . .] their [oppressi]on and they shall come out of [3][Egypt . . . the day] they cross the Jordan is the [*x*]th jubilee [. . .]

The Israelite apostasy is described in terms borrowed from the Old Testament.

Frag. 13 [1][. . .] the children of Israel [hi]d their face from [the presence of God] [2][and were "sacrific]ing their children to the demons [of idols" (Ps. 106:37). "So God grew angry with them" (Ps. 106:40) [3]["and commanded that they] be given into the power" (Ps. 106:41) of Nebu[chadnezzar] **Frag. 12** [3][king of Ba]bylon and that their land be destroyed from them, because [. . .] [4][. . .] children of exile [. . .]

The punishment of the Exile is limited to seventy years, and then God will bring the Israelites back.

Frag. 16 [1][. . . seve]nty (*or* [for]ty) years [. . .] [2][. . . he delivered them by] His mighty [ha]nd and saved th[em . . .] [3][. . .] mighty [. . .] but the kingdoms of the Gen[tiles . . .] [4][. . .] that is the fi[rst] kingdom [. . .]

Daniel describes a succession of kingdoms to come after Babylon. The text apparently gives the names of some of the kings. "Balakros" is known as a satrap under Alexander the Great.

Frag. 19 [1][. . . he will reign for *x*] years [. . .] [2][. . .] RHWS son of [. . .] [3][. . .]WS th[irty years . . .] [4][. . .] they will speak [slanderous lies . . .]

Frag. 20 [1][. . .]S son of [. . .] [2][. . .] twenty-[*x* yea]rs [. . .]

Frag. 21 [1][. . .] he will reign for [*x*] years [. . .] [2][. . .] Balakros [. . .]

A gathering of some kind is foretold, perhaps for the final battle.

Frag. 24 [2][. . . in that time] those who are called [by name] shall be gathered [. . .] [3][. . . from among] the Gentiles, and it shall be, from [that] day [. . .] [4][. . . the ho]ly ones, and the kings of the Gentiles [. . .] [5][. . .] servants unto [this] day [. . .]

Frag. 25 [2][. . .] unto Is[rael . . .] [3][. . .] and [the] l[and] shall be filled [. . .] [4][. . .] all [their] corpses [. . .]

—E.M.C.

49. A Second Vision of Daniel

4Q245

The writer of this fragmentary Aramaic work chose to compose in the name of the famous seer Daniel and so to attach to that veracious figure his own vision of the truth. He wrote after the fact, but presented his work as prophecy to intensify the impact; also, of course, if Daniel, now long dead, were really the author, then the only possibility for his describing events occurring around 100 B.C.E. was through prophecy. In the narrative Daniel appears at the court of a foreign monarch and during a discussion, now mostly lost, is handed a book of some sort. Reading from it, Daniel recites the names of all the kings of Judah and of many of the high priests yet to come. The list of high priests is really the centerpiece of this *Second Vision,* since the kings lived long before our author's time. The high priests continued right down to his day, and his point is that when the last named priest appears or shortly thereafter—when time known beforehand and designated by the list runs out—the kingdom of God shall come.

In ll. 10–11 the work enumerates the Hasmonean high priests from Judah the Maccabee (not considered a true high priest by all historical sources, but making the grade according to our author) down to a second Judah, better known to history as Aristobulus I. This man reigned for just one year and then died in 103 B.C.E. At that point Alexander Jannaeus took over the high-priesthood and soon declared himself a king as well. This is the time when our author lived. The structure of the vision that he attributes to Daniel completely separates kings and high priests. That there are two lists censors as illegitimate the claim to be king and high priest simultaneously; this, the separation declares, is a breach of God's eternal laws. When this unthinkable breach comes to pass, Daniel is made to say, the end is at hand and God's kingdom is right around the corner.

Other Jews disputed Alexander's claim to the monarchy as well, and a coalition that included the Pharisees actually fomented a civil war in 96 B.C.E. that lasted nearly a decade. Josephus tells us that fifty thousand Jews lost their lives during those years of warfare. Overcoming all such opposition, Alexander continued in power another dozen years (for more details on this period and other scrolls that concern it, see the Introduction).

Col. 1 1[. . . the priests and] the [king]s 2[. . .] and when 3[. . .] Daniel 4[. . . and Daniel read in] a book that was given 5[to him the names of all of the men. He said, "The priests are Lev]i, Kohath, 6[Amram, Aaron, Eleazar, Phineas, Abishua,] Bukki, Uzzi, 7[Eli, Ahitub, Ahijah, Ahitub, Abimelech, Zado]k, Abiathar, 8[Azariah, Amariah, Ahitub, Zadok, Shallum,] Hi[l]kiah, 9[Azariah, Seraiah, Jehozadak; and after him Sim]o[n] and Onias, 10[Jeshua, Onias, Eliakim, Judah, Jon]athan, Simon, 11[Johanan, and Judah. And the kings: Saul] and David, Solomon, 12[Rehoboam, Abijah, Asa, Jehoshaphat, Joram,] Ahazia[h, Jo]ash, 13[Amaziah, Azariah, Jotham, Ahaz, Hezekiah, Man]asse[h, Amon,] 14[Josiah, Joahaz, Jehoiakim, Jehoiakin,] and Ze[dekiah. In all,] 15[the kings number twenty-two] prior to [the time] for the cessation of evil. 16[In all,] the [priests] number thirty-five. [Of these men,] some [will walk] in blindness, error, 17[and wickedness, s]ome [in truth and uprightness.] Then shall arise 18[the Elect of God, and they shall receive the h]oly [kingdom], and restore [. . .]

—M.O.W.

50. A Vision of the Son of God

4Q246

This small text ignited a controversy when a portion of it was published in 1974. It speaks of a powerful figure who shall appear in a time of tribulation and be called the "son of God" and "son of the Most High" and whom all nations obey. The expressions irresistibly recall the language that the Gospels use of Jesus, especially in the episode describing the angel's message to Mary that she would bear a son: "He will be great, and will be called the Son of the Most High . . . and of his kingdom there will be no end" (Luke 1:32–33).

At the time, some scholars argued that the published portion proved an important idea: that an earthly king destined to come and bring peace (i.e., the messiah) would also be called by Second Temple Jews the "Son of God." Certain biblical texts could be taken to support this idea (e.g., 2 Sam. 7:14), and if true, it would shed substantial light on the New Testament's portrayal of Jesus. Others scholars, however, understood the text's "Son of God" as a villain, one who usurps the place of God but is subsequently overthrown by the "people of God," who have God on their side. Now that the entire work has finally become available, a careful reading confirms this second, "Antichrist," option.

The historical background of this text may well be the persecution of the Jews under the Syrian tyrant Antiochus IV in the period 170–164 B.C.E. This ruler's chosen second name, "Epiphanes" (Greek for "appearance"), encapsulated the notion of a human king as God manifest. Such human pretensions to deity have never been welcome in Judaism and were condemned out of hand in the prophecies of Isaiah (14:12–21) and Ezekiel (28:1–10). Jesus's claims to more-than-human status were likewise rejected by his contemporaries: "We would stone you for blasphemy, because you, though you are a man, are making yourself God" (John 10:33). A similar distaste for claims to divinity seems to animate this fragmentary prophecy.

The seer receives the power to interpret the king's vision.

Col. 1 [1][. . . a spirit from God] rested upon him, he fell before the throne.

The beginning of the interpretation. War and slaughter are imminent. This tribulation will culminate in the accession to power of a cruel tyrant.

[2][. . . O ki]ng, wrath is coming to the world, and your years [3][shall be shortened . . . such] is your vision, and all of it is about to come unto the world. [4][. . . Amid] great [signs], tribulation is coming upon the land. [5][. . . After much killing] and slaughter, a prince of nations [6][will arise . . .] the king of Assyria and Egypt [7][. . .] he will be ruler over the land [8][. . .] will be subject to him and all will obey [9][him.]

The tyrant's son will succeed him and begin to accrue to himself the honor due only to God. Yet the reign of father and son will be brief.

[Also his son] will be called The Great, and be designated by his name. **Col. 2** [1]He will be called the Son of God, they will call him the son of the Most High. But like the meteors [2]that you saw in your vision, so will be their kingdom. They will reign only a few years over [3]the land, while people tramples people and nation tramples nation.

Deliverance from distress finally comes when the people of God arise, bringing peace and prosperity. God is working through them and in them and his rule shall finally prevail.

[4]Until the people of God arise; then all will have rest from warfare. [5]Their kingdom will be an eternal kingdom, and all their paths will be righteous. They will judge [6]the land justly, and all nations will make peace. Warfare will cease from the land, [7]and all the nations shall do obeisance to them. The great God will be their help, [8]He Himself will fight for them, putting peoples into their power, [9]overthrowing them all before them. God's rule will be an eternal rule and all the depths of [10][the earth are His].
—E.M.C.

51. The Acts of a King

4Q248

Using biblical imagery and cast in the form of a prophecy, this one surviving fragment of a larger apocalyptic writing seems to concern events connected to the Syrian king Antiochus IV Epiphanes, who as the "Little Horn" so exercised the author of the book of Daniel. It particularly resembles Daniel 11:21–45. As reconstructed, the extant portions read chronologically and cover approximately 170–168 B.C.E., during which Antiochus invaded

Egypt twice and also besieged and sacked Jerusalem. The author evidently expected (and so prophesied) that after Antiochus finished his second invasion of Egypt, the Jews would repent, the chaotic situation in Jerusalem would settle down, and life could return to normal. In point of fact, however, this was not what happened. Many trials yet awaited the Jews at the hands of Antiochus, as detailed in Daniel and 1–2 Maccabees. Accordingly, it seems that the author must have written in 168 B.C.E., or at any rate before the end of 167 B.C.E., when Antiochus forced the Jews to cease worshiping God and sacrifice instead to "Zeus in the Highest." His actions immediately precipitated the revolt led by the Maccabees, which began as a guerrilla action and ended by freeing the Jews from Syrian rule.

Frag. 1 [2][. . . he shall rule] Egypt and Greece while exalt[ing] himself against [3][the greatest Go]d. Accordingly, they shall consume [4][the flesh of their own s]ons and daught[e]rs during the siege of [Alexandria.] [5][Then] the LORD shall cause a spirit to pass through their lands, and the king shall turn [back from Alexandria] [6][and] come to Egypt, selling her land. Then he shall com[e] [7]to the Temple City and seize it, together with a[ll its treasure stores.] [8]He shall overthrow some of the Gentile nations, then return to Egyp[t. With the final] [9]shattering of the Ho[ly] People's power, [then . . .] [10]all these things [shall be complete]; the children [of Israel] shall return [to the LORD . . .]

—M.O.W.

52. A Commentary on the Law of Moses

4Q251

This work is a collection of legal dicta, including among other things laws about the proper observance of the Sabbath, the tithing of agricultural produce, what portions of produce priests were to receive from the laity, proper sacrifice, and marriage. These laws are extremely revealing for anyone interested in the late Second Temple period and Palestine in the time of Jesus, for they are a window into certain segments of society, revealing how people of the time actually lived their lives.

Whereas portions of the commentary do little more than quote relevant biblical texts, others legislate for situations not explicitly recognized by the authors of the Bible. We learn here, for example, that if a priest had a daughter who turned to prostitution, she could no longer eat at his table. We learn that in the author's system, priests were to receive the fourth-year fruit from newly planted fruit trees, a requirement that contrasts with rabbinic law, in which the grower took the fruit to Jerusalem and ate it there before God. The commentary agrees with the stipulation on the same topic in the *Sectarian Manifesto* (text 100); further, the *Temple Scroll* (text 155, col. 60), the *Damascus Document* (text 1), and the book of *Jubilees* (text 42, 7:36) all agree with the position of the commentary.

So this law serves well to illustrate two general principles that apply to the legal materials among the scrolls: (1) the laws tend to be stricter than those of the rabbis where the same topics are addressed and, as the rabbinic laws go back in some cases to the Pharisees, the laws here are presumably part of a system stricter than that of the contemporary Pharisees; and (2) the legal materials of the scrolls seem to represent a single school of thought. That is to say, whenever different Dead Sea Scrolls address the same or similar topics, they take the identical general approach, one particularly favorable to the interests of the priesthood. Although the different scroll writers sometimes disagree among themselves, their disagreement is incidental, not systematic. The Dead Sea Scrolls therefore represent a school of legal thought different from and competing with the Pharisaic approach. That such should be the case is hardly surprising given the attitudes toward the Pharisees manifested in non-legal, historical writings among the scrolls. As discussed in the Introduction, for the movement behind the scrolls, the Pharisees were public enemy number one.

Sabbath laws (cf. Damascus Document, *Geniza text col. 10, text 1).*

Frags. 1–2 [1][. . . f]ive [. . .] [2][. . .] all [. . .] [3][. . .] an animal and to draw water from a cistern, [4][. . .] the drawing [. . . Let no] man take anything out of his place for the entire Sabbath, [5][neither from outside into the house] nor from the house to the ou[tsi]de [. . .] to expound or to read a book aloud on [the Sabba]th [6][. . . to] profane [. . .] impurity, his ski[n] on [the] Sabbath day [7][. . .] on the sixth d[a]y, ba[re] skin [. . .]

Laws concerning personal injury.

Frags. 4–7 [1][. . .] holy, for [. . .] [2][. . . "I]f m[en] quarrel [3][and one stri]kes [the other with a stone or with a fist and he does not] di[e but remains] in his b[ed;] [4][if he gets up] and wa[lks about outside, the one that str]uck him [shall be innocent,] except [he shall pay for his] loss of ti[me] and see to [his complete] recovery.

[5][If someone strikes his male or female servant] with a rod [. . .]" (Exod. 21:18–20).

Frag. 8 [1][“If a man strikes his male or female servant] in the eye [and destroys it, or if he knocks out the tooth] [2][of his male or female servant, he shall set hi]m [free] and he shall compensate for [his] loss of time [and assure his full] recovery [3][on account of the eye or the tooth” (Exod. 21:26–27).]

Laws concerning damage done by beasts.

[“If a bull gores a man or] a woman, then the bull shall be put to death; they shall stone it. [4][And the meat shall not be eaten, but the owner of the ox is not responsible. If the ox] has been accustomed to gore in the past [5][and its owner was warned but did not guard it and it kills a ma]n or a woman, [6][then the ox shall be stoned and its owner put to death as well. If a ransom is appointed for him, a ma]n [shall pay . . .” (Exod. 21:28–30).]

Laws concerning the firstfruits of agricultural produce (Exod. 22:29).

Frag. 9 [1][Let no man eat grain, and fresh wi]ne and fresh oil, unless [the priest has waved] [2]the choicest, the firstfruits, and the full crop. Let no man delay, for [fresh wine (?)] [3]is the choicest of the full crop, [and] grain is the offering (for the priests?) [. . . And the bread] [4]of the firstfruits is the leavened bread which they shall bring [on the d]ay of the [firstfruits;] [5]these are the firstfruits. Let no m[a]n eat the new wheat [. . .] [6]until the day the bread of the firstfruits comes to [the . . .]

Laws concerning the redemption of the firstborn, human and animal (Num. 18:15, 17), and first harvest of the fruit trees (Lev. 19:23–25).

Frag. 10 [1][. . . whether much or] little[. . .] [2][. . . f]ew. Let no [man] decre[ase . . .] [3][. . .] the tenth part for [. . .] [4][. . . m]an and the unclea[n and clean] animal [. . .] [5][. . . but] the firstborn of man and the unclean animal [6][. . . but the firstborn of the o]x [and] the sheep. And the one who sanctifies from [. . .] [7][. . . i]t is as the firstborn, and the produce of a tree [8][and every fruit tree, the fig, the pome]granate and the olive, in the fourth year [9][all its fruit shall be holy offering of praise, like a] contribution. Every devoted thing [shall belong] to the priest.

Laws concerning the proper slaughter and sacrifice of beasts (Exod. 22:29–30; Lev. 7:24; 22:8; Deut. 14:21).

Frag. 12 [1][. . .] an ox, a lamb, or a goat that has not completed [seven days . . .] [2][. . . whic]h is in the wom[b] of its mother. And let no man eat its flesh because [. . .] [3][. . .] is [. . .], let no man eat the flesh of an animal.

[. . .][4][. . . carca]sses or that torn by beasts, that which is not alive, for [. . .] [5][. . .] to the foreigner, and [use] its fat to ma[ke . . .] [6][. . .] and to [sa]crifice it (the fat?) from it, he [shall certainly] be c[ut off from his people . . .] [7][. . . wa]sh in [. . .]

Laws concerning unclean animals (Lev. 27:11) and devoted fields (Lev. 27:28).

Frag. 14 [1][. . .] the unclean animal that [. . .] [2][. . . they shall not offer it, they shall] redeem it. And the devoted field shall be the property of [the priest . . .] [3][. . .] himself to [. . .]

Laws concerning property set aside for the priests (Lev. 27:21).

Frag. 15 [1][. . .] it is [most ho]ly and it shall b[e . . .] [2][. . . and] they shall dedicate it to the priest to pass it [. . .] [3][. . . and it shall be] for him, for the priest. And the man wh[o . . .] [4][. . . Let no] man eat [. . .]

Laws concerning those who might eat the priest's portion (Lev. 21:7–9, 14).

Frag. 16 [1][. . . and when a woman is married to a priest,] she [shall eat] her husband's food [2][. . . a woman who is purchased or born into his household] shall eat his food. Only a prostitute [3][or one defiled may not eat the holy food. . . . And] any treachery which [a man] might practice [4][against God . . .] to eat, for [it is] an abomination [5][to God. . . .] master who has no redeemer [. . .]

Laws concerning proper marriage (Lev. 18:6–19; 20:11, 17, 19; Deut. 23:1). Note the ruling on niece marriage in l. 3; such marriages were encouraged by the Pharisees. Compare these lines to col. 66 of the Temple Scroll *(text 155).*

Frag. 17 [1]Concerning prohibited relationships: [. . .] [2]Let no man take the w[ife of his father, let him not uncover the skirt of his father. Let no one take] [3]his brother's daughter or the daughter of [his] si[ster . . . Let no] man [uncover] [4]the nakedness of the sister of [his] mo[ther or his father; it is wickedness. And no woman shall be the wife of the brother of] [5]her father or the brother of her mother [. . .] [6]Let no man uncover the nakedness of [. . .] [7]Let no man marry his un[married] daughter [to a layman . . .]

Laws concerning expiation for the unknown murderer (Deut. 21:1–9). The elders of the nearest town were to sacrifice a heifer to bear the bloodguilt that would otherwise attach to the town.

Frag. 18 [1][. . . a ma]n with his neighbor [. . .] [2][. . .] the land to defile it [. . .] [3][. . . if] a corpse [is found] fallen in [a field . . .] [4][. . . and they shall break the heife]r['s neck there] in [the wad]i in return for the life [of the slain . . .] [5][. . .] it is a substitution, anything which is cut off on a[ccount of him . . .] [6][. . .] everything that has no breath of life within it is dead, [it must be buried] in a g[rave . . .]
—M.G.A.

53. Commentaries on Genesis

4Q252–254a

The *Commentaries on Genesis* share characteristics with the sectarian biblical commentaries on Habakkuk, Hosea, and Psalms (texts 2, 22, and 24, respectively), on the one hand, and with the *Annotated Law of Moses* (text 84) and similar writings, on the other; yet they have a character distinctly their own.

The *Commentaries on Genesis* have in common with the other commentaries certain techniques of interpreting the Bible, notably the use of *pesher* method (for an explanation of this method see the introduction to the *Commentary on Habakkuk*). But unlike the other commentaries, the purpose here is not to discover current fulfillments of biblical prophecies, but to give selected passages a particular spin, to show how they support the authors' ideas. Indeed, unlike the other commentaries, here the authors recognize that only some of the chosen passages are prophetic.

Like the *Annotated Law,* the present works excerpt and amplify Scripture, but they do not do so verse by verse. Rather, these writings skip from passage to passage, having no discernible overarching purpose or thematic link.

Whether the *Commentaries on Genesis* represent one work or several is unclear. Of the four manuscripts, 4Q252 is the best preserved; its six columns cover Genesis 5:32–49:21. The tiny fragments of 4Q253 (see MS.) are taken as the remains of a commentary on Genesis, but the matter is tenuous. (The word "ark" found in frag. 1 is only suggestive.) 4Q254a appears to be an intentional alteration of 4Q252 frag. 1, cols. 1–2.

Col. 1 and the first lines of col. 2 are a retelling of the Flood story (Gen. 6:3–8:18) that becomes a clear polemic for the 364-day sectarian calendar. After charting the major events of the year-long flood by month and day of the week, the writer concludes that Noah went out of the ark "at the end of . . . three hundred and sixty-four days."

4Q252 Frag. 1 Col. 1 [1][In the] four hundred and eightieth year of Noah's life, he came to the end of them and God [2]said, "My spirit shall not dwell with man forever, their days shall be determined to be one hundred and twenty [3]years until the waters of the flood come." And the waters of the flood came upon the earth in the six hundredth year of [4]Noah's life, in the second month, on Sunday, the seventeenth. On that day [5]all the fountains of the great deep were rent and the windows of the heavens were opened. And the rain fell upon [6]the earth forty days and forty nights until the twenty-sixth day of the third month, [7]on Thursday. The waters prevailed upon the earth one hundred and fifty days [8]until the fourteenth day of the seventh month, on Tuesday. And at the end of one hundred and fifty [9]days, the waters decreased for two days—Wednesday and Thursday—and on [10]Friday the ark came to rest upon Mount Ararat. T[his was] the seventeenth day of the seventh month. [11]And the waters continued to abate until the tenth month. On the first of the month, on Wednesday, [12]the tops of the mountains appeared. At the end of forty days, at the appearance of the tops of [13]the mountain[s], Noah [op]ened the window of the ark. It was Monday, the tenth [14]of the ele[venth] month. He sent out the dove to see if the waters had subsided, but [15]it found no roosting place and came back to him [to] the ark. He waited a[nother] seven days [16]and again sent it out, and it came to him and in its beak was a freshly plucked olive leaf. [This was the twenty]-fourth [day] [17]of the eleventh month, on Sunday. [So Noah knew that the waters had subsided] [18]from the earth. At the end of anoth[er] seven days [he sent out] the [dove and it did not] [19]return to him again. This was the f[irst] day [of the twelfth] month, [on Sunday.] [20]And at the end of thirt[y-one days from the sending of the dov]e which had not [21]returned again, the wat[ers] were dried up [from the earth, and] Noah removed the covering of the ark [22]and looked, and behold, [the surface of the ground was dry, on Wednesda]y, the first day of the first month.

Col. 2 [1]In the six hundred and first year of Noah's life, on the seventeenth day of the second month, [2]the earth was dry, on Sunday. On that day Noah went out from the ark, at the end of an exact year, [3]three hundred and sixty four days, on a Sunday. On the seventh, [4]one and six (a scribal error has confused the text here), Noah [went out] from the ark, to the day, [5]after a complete year.

The curse on Canaan, the grandson of Noah (Gen. 9:24–27).

And Noah awoke from his wine and knew what [6]his youngest son had done to him, he said, "Cursed be Canaan, the lowest of slaves shall he be to his brothers." And he did not [7]curse Ham, but rather Ham's son, because God had already blessed the sons of Noah. "And let him live in the tents of Shem."

The chronology of Genesis 11:31–12:4. The age of Terah agrees with the Masoretic Text (205 years) rather than the Samaritan Pentateuch (145 years).

[8]He gave the land to Abraham His beloved.

Terah was one hundred and forty years old when he left [9]Ur of the Chaldees and went to Haran and Ab[ram was s]eventy years old. And Abram dwelt five years [10]in Haran. Then [Terah died] six[ty years after Abram] went out [to] the land of Canaan [. . .] [11]the heifer, the ram, and the go[at . . .] Abram to (*or* did not) [. . .] [12]the fire when it passed [. . .] he took for himself [. . .] [13]for Ab[ram] to go out [to the land of] Canaan to [. . .]

Sodom (Gen. 18:16–33).

Col. 3 [1]just as it is written [. . .] twelve [2]men [. . . Gomor]rah, and also [3]this city [. . .] righteous [4]I [will] not [destroy . . .] these only shall be destroyed. [5]And if [ten (?)] are not found there [. . . and everything] which is found in it, its spoil, [6]its children, and the rest of [. . .] forever.

The binding of Isaac (Gen. 22:10–12). See also A Paraphrase of Genesis and Exodus, *frag. 2 (text 43).*

And Abraham reached out [7]his hand [and took the knife to kill his son. But the angel of the LORD called to him from heav]en [8]and said to him, "Now I know that you fear God, since you have not withheld your son,] [9]your only son, fr[om me." . . .]

This portion may parallel the biblical blessing on Jacob (Gen. 28:3).

[12]El Shaddai will b[less you and make you fruitful . . .] [13]the blessing of your father [Abraham, to you and to your descendants with you . . .] [14][. . .] shall be [. . .]

An account of the descendants of Esau, which ends with the curse on Amalek (Gen. 36:12; Exod. 17:14; Deut. 25:19).

Col. 4 [1]Timna was a concubine of Eliphaz, Esau's son; she bore Amalek to him, he whom Saul def[eated.]

[2]Just as he said to Moses, "In the Last Days, you will blot out the remembrance of Amalek [3]from under heaven."

Jacob's prophecy concerning Reuben (Gen. 49:2–4).

The Blessings of Jacob: Reuben, you are my firstborn, and the firstfruits of my vigor, [4]excelling in rank and excelling in power. You are unstable as water, so you shall no longer excel. You went up [5]onto your father's bed; then you defiled it—he went up onto his couch!

Its interpretation is: He rebuked him because [6]he lay with Bilhah, his concubine, so he [s]aid, "Reuben, you are my firstborn," [. . .] Reuben was [7]the first of [. . .]

The prophecy concerning Judah is interpreted as fulfilled in the Messiah of David (Gen. 49:10).

Col. 5 [1][. . .] a ruler shall [no]t depart from the tribe of Judah while Israel has dominion. [2][And] the one who sits on the throne of David [shall never] be cut off, because the "ruler's staff" is the covenant of the kingdom, [3][and the thous]ands of Israel are "the feet," until the Righteous Messiah, the Branch of David, has come. [4]For to him and to his seed the covenant of the kingdom of His people has been given for the eternal generations, because [5]he has kept [. . .] the Law with the men of the *Yahad*. For [6][. . . the "obedience of the people]s" is the assembly of the men of [7][. . .] he gave . . .

The prophecies concerning Asher and Naphtali (Gen. 49:20–21).

Col. 6 [Asher's food shall be rich] [1]he shall provide [royal] delicacies [. . . Naphtali is a doe let loose that bears] [2]lovely [fawns . . .] [3]the [. . .]

The curse on Canaan, the grandson of Noah (Gen. 9:24–25).

4Q254 Frag. 1 [1] [. . .] who said [. . .] [2]upon the doorways and the [. . . When Noah awoke from his wine] [3]and knew wha[t his youngest son had done to him, he said, "Cursed be Canaan;] [4]lowest of slaves [shall he be to his brothers."]

This portion is a commentary on the two anointed ones of Zechariah 4:14; it may be part of the blessing on Judah (Gen. 49:8–12).

Frag. 4 [1][. . .] to them [. . .] [2][. . . "These are] the two anointed sons who [stand by the Lord of the whole earth." . . .] [3][. . .] those who keep the commandments of God [. . .] [4][. . .] for they are the men of the *Yahad* [. . .]

Jacob's prophecy concerning Issachar and Dan (Gen. 49:15–17).

Frags. 5–6 [1]So he bowed [his shoulder to the burden and became a] slave [at forced labor.]

[. . .] [2]which [. . .] the great ones [. . .] [3]servant [. . . Dan shall judge] his [peo]ple as on[e] of the t[ribes of Israel.] [4]And Dan shall be as a sna[ke by the roadside, a vi]per along the w[ay that bites] [5]the horse's heel[s . . .] [6]Isra[el . . .]

Jacob's prophecy concerning Joseph (Gen. 49:24–26).

Frag. 7 [2][. . . Yet his] bow [remai]ned taut, [and his arms were made agile by the hands of the Mighty One of Jacob,] [3][by the name of the Shepher]d, the Rock of Israel [by the God of your father, who will help you by the Almighty, who will bless you] [4][with blessings of heaven] ab[o]ve [. . .] [5][. . . th]an [the] bl[essings . . .]

As in 4Q252 cols. 1–2 the Flood is reckoned at exactly one year (l. 2). These fragments of 4Q254a record the dimensions of the ark (Gen. 6:15) and continue with the sending of the birds (Gen. 8:7–8).

4Q254a Frags. 1–2 [1][Then he sent out] the dove [. . .] [2]And this is the account of the construction of the [ark: three hundred cubits shall be the leng]th of the ark, and fif[ty cubits] [3]the width, and thirty [cubits its height . . .] [4]and the measurement of the ark [. . .]

Frag. 3 [1][. . . In the six hundredth year of Noah's life, on the] seventeenth day of the [second] month [2][. . .] Noah went out from the ark exactly one year later. [3][. . .]

[4][And he sent out the ra]ven; and it went to and fro and returned in order to make known to the l[ast] generations [5][. . .] before him, for the ra[ven] went to and fro and re[turned.]

—M.G.A.

54. A Commentary on Malachi

4Q253a

This fragment was originally assigned with 4Q253, one of the *Commentaries on Genesis* (text 53), due to similarities in handwriting. The first four lines of the fragment contain Malachi 3:16–18. The extant words in l. 5 are not found in the traditional text of Malachi and are assumed to be the beginning of a comment on the biblical text.

Frag. 1 Col. 1 1[. . . Then those who feared the LORD spoke to one another,] and [the LORD] gave attention 2[and listened, and a book of remembrance was written before him, for those who feared the LORD and took account of His name.] "They shall be mine, 3[a special possession," said the LORD of hosts, "on the day I am preparing. And I will have compassion o]n them just as 4[a man has compassion for a son who serves him. And you shall once again see the difference] between the righteous and the wicked 5[between the one who serves God, and the one who does not serve him" (Mal. 3:16–18) . . .] the righteous and upon [. . .]

Col. 2 1and any Israelite who shall e[at . . .] 2shall bring its blood to [. . .] 3that [man (?) . . .]

—M.G.A.

55. Portions of Sectarian Law

4Q265

Portions of Sectarian Law is a medley composed from other legal texts found among the Dead Sea Scrolls. The work may be an *ekloge,* the technical term used to refer to a writing that gathers extracts from various works. Often such selections were made by ancient scholars for private study; in other cases "authors" made extracts in order to pirate the work of more gifted writers and claim it for themselves. By this method many anthologies arose in the ancient world. An author's work might appear in extended or truncated form, combined with extracts from other authors, while ironically no one read his original book. Apparently this was what happened to the Greek writer Menander (ca. 341–293 B.C.E.), for example; much of what we know of his work we know only through anthologies.

Portions bears a particularly close relationship to the *Damascus Document* (text 1) and the *Charter of Jewish Sectarian Association* (text 7). The present author has sometimes changed the penalty clauses of the laws his work has in common with those others, however, indicating a certain process of development among those who consulted these writings.

A biblical quotation.

Frag. 1 [1][. . .] [2][. . . ju]st as it is written [in the book . . .] [3][. . .] it is written in the b[ook] of Isaiah the prophet, [4]["Sing, O barren one who did not bear; burst into song and] shout, you who have not been in labor! For the children of the desolate will be more [5][than the children of her that is married, says the LORD.] Enlarge the site of [your] ten[t] [6][and stretch out the curtains of your dwelling; do not hold back" (Isa. 54:1–2). Its interpretation conce]rns [. . .]

Proscriptions concerning the Passover.

Frag. 3 [1][. . . "Have we not all one father? Has not one God] [2]created us? W[h]y then are we faithless to one [a]nother?" (Mal. 2:10). [3][Let not] a young boy or a woman eat [the] Passover [sacrifi]ce [. . .]

*Punishments for various transgressions. See CD 14:21–22 (*Damascus Document, *text 1) and 1QS 6–7 (text 7). In 2:4–9 are rules for the entrance into the group, rules that vary from those of text 7.*

Frag. 4 Col. 1 [2][. . . and he shall be banned for thirty] [3][days and he shall be punished for t]en d[a]ys.

[Anyone who . . .] [4][and he shall be set apart for] thirty days. [The one who raises his voice in foolish laughter shall be fined] [5]with half rations for fift[een days.]

[Anyone who . . .] [6]he shall be punished for three months wi[th half rations.]

[Anyone who speaks preceding] [7]his comrade who is his superior, they shall set [him] apart [from the community meal six months and he shall be punished] [8]in them with half rations.

Anyone who rev[iles his comrade shall be punished] [9]for thirty days.

Anyone who deceives [his] f[riend shall be set apart for six] [10]months and fined in them with half rations.

[Anyone who lies] [11]consciously in any matter, shall be punished for thirty days.

[Anyone who lies concerning property] [12]conscio[usly, they shall] set him apart for six months.[. . .]

Col. 2 [1][Anyone who sleep]s in the assembly of the general member[ship] shall be punished thirty [days. And when they sit to read] [2][from] the book [he shall] fall asleep up to three times, and if [he leaves he shall be punished for ten days.] [3][Anyo]ne who enters to [joi]n the party of t[he *Yah*]*ad* [shall be examined by the Overseer] [4][of] the general membership. If his [und]erstanding fails him, he shall examine him for [one] year, [and when he stands] [5]b[ef]ore the general membership and they shall be consulted [concerning] him, and if he is not found [to be ignorant, the man] [6]who oversees the *Yahad* [shall instruct him] in [the works] of the law, and he shall not [touch the drink of the general membership] [7][y]et a full year. [And when] the year of [his inquiry is complet]ed, [they shall hand over his property into] [8][the hand of the ma]n who oversees the general membership [. . .] if [. . .] [9][. . .] he himself will enter [. . .]

Laws concerning the Sabbath. Note the extreme severity: an animal that has fallen into water on the Sabbath must be left to drown; a man can only be drawn out with a garment, not an implement, since the use of an implement would be "work," and work on the Sabbath was forbidden. Presumably, if no garment were available, the man must be allowed to drown. Contrast the dictum of Jesus as given in the Gospels: "The Sabbath was made for humankind, not humankind for the Sabbath" (Mark 2:27).

Frag. 6 [1] [. . .] the Sa[bbath [. . .] [2]on the Sabbath day, let no [one wear] dirty [garment]s. [3]Let no one [we]ar garments wh[ich] have dust or [lint] on them [4]on the day of the Sabbath.

Let no one ta[ke] a vessel or foo[d out] from his tent [5]on the day of the Sabbath.

Let no one raise up an animal which has fallen [6]into the water on the Sabbath day. But if it is a man who falls into the water [7][on] the Sabbath [day,] one shall extend his garment to him to pull him out with it, but he shall not carry an implement [8][to pull him out on the] Sabbath [day.] And if an army [. . .]

Frag. 7 [1][. . .] on the [Sabbath] day. [. . .] [2][. . . on] the Sabbath [day.] And not [. . .] [3][Let n]o one from the seed of Aaron sprinkle the wa[ter for cleansing . . . And they shall not bathe or] [4][laund]er [on a] great day, and fast on the Day of [Atonement. The one who walks outside his city to graze] [5][his] animal may walk two thousand cubits. [No man shall eat the flesh of an ox or lamb near] [6][the Sa]nctuary, thirty ris (i.e., four miles). Let not [the priest who is expert in the Book of Hagi] dep[art where there are ten men of the community.] [7]When there are fifte[en men] in the party of the *Yahad* [as God presaged by means of his servants] [8][the pr]ophets, then shall the party of the *Yah*[*ad* truly] be established [as an eternal planting, true witnesses, and the elect of] [9]God's will, and a soothing aroma to atone for the [l]and, an of[fering . . .] [10]and times of unrighteousness shall end in judgment and the [. . .]

The author indicates that Adam was not brought into the Garden of Eden immediately after his creation, but had to wait to be purified from ceremonial uncleanness. He then appears to suggest an inference concerning the purification of women after giving birth (Lev. 12:2–5).

[11]In the firs[t] week [Adam was created but he had no holiness] [12][un]til he was brought to the Garden of Eden. And a bone [from his bones was taken for the woman, but] [13]she [h]ad no [holiness] until she was brought t[o him in the Garden of Eden after eighty days] [14][because] the Garden of Eden is holy, and every growing thing in its midst is holy. [Therefore a woman who bears a male child] [15]she shall be unclean for seven days; as at the time of her menstruation she shall be unclean. And [she shall remain for thirty-three days in the blood] [16]of her p[u]rification.

And if she bears a female child, then she shall be unclean [for two weeks, as in her menstruation; and for sixty-six days] [17][she shall rema]in in the blood of her purification. [N]o holy thing [shall she touch, nor come into the sanctuary, until the days of her purification are completed.]

—M.G.A.

56. Ritual Purity Laws Concerning Liquids

4Q274

According to Numbers 5:2, there were three areas of ritual uncleanness with which the nation Israel had to be concerned: leprosy, bodily discharges of any kind, and contact with the dead. Each of these types of uncleanness rendered a person ritually unfit. This concept differed from sin, for it required no confession or forgiveness, but it was similar to sin in that it created a barrier between the individual and God. In the Bible, the man or woman who was unclean had to separate for a stated period from the Israelite camp in which God dwelled. The period's length varied according to the type of uncleanness.

For Jews of Second Temple times, determining the proper time period was sometimes a problem, but the main difficulty was the meaning of "camp." Did biblical laws concerning the camp now apply only to the Temple environs? Or did they apply to all of Jerusalem, the holy city? Or, more broadly yet, were they meant to regulate life throughout the Holy Land? The present author casts his vote for the third alternative and here seeks to interpret certain biblical laws of uncleanness in a way that will guarantee the purity of the "holy ones of Israel," who live in "camps" all through the land.

Preserved portions mostly echo Leviticus 15 and are thereby concerned with bodily discharges—that is, the menstrual blood of the woman and the seminal discharge of the man. What we consider very private areas of life were a public concern for these ancients, since one unclean person could "infect" everybody, with the result that an unknowingly unclean person might touch holy things or, worse yet, enter the Temple—an abomination according to biblical law. An important principle of laws on discharges was that liquids were thought to transmit uncleanness like an electrical cord transmits a charge. Accordingly, frag. 2 explicates ritual problems that might be caused by handling different kinds of liquids.

Frag. 1 Col. 1 0[Let him not] 1begin to reduce his suppli[cati]on. He shall lie down on a bed of sorrow, and in a seat of sighing he shall sit. He shall sit apart from all those who are unclean and at a distance 2of twelve cubits from the purity when he speaks to them. He shall dwell to the northwest of any habitation at a distance of the same measurement.

3Anyone of the unclean [wh]o [touches] him, shall bathe in water and wash his clothes and then he may eat. For as it says, "Unclean, unclean" (Lev. 13:45), 4he shall cry all the days which [he] has [the afflic]tion. And she who has a flow of blood, for seven days let her not touch the man who has a discharge or any vessel [t]hat he touches or that he has lain 5upon or sat upon. And if she has touched anything, she shall wash her clothes and bathe and then she may eat. She must make every effort [no]t to mingle during her seven 6days that she might n[o]t defile the camps of the hol[y ones of] Israel. Nor may she touch any woman [who has had a dischar]ge of blood lasting man[y] days. 7And the one who is counting (the seven days), whether male or female, may not tou[ch one who has an uncle]an [flow] or a menstruating woman during her impurity, unless she was purified from her i[mpuri]ty. For, behold, the blood 8of menstruation is considered as a discharge and that which touches it. And if [a man ha]s a flow of semen contact with him is defiling. A [man who to]uches any one of [9]these unclean people during the seven days of [his] impu[rity, le]t him [n]ot eat; just as if he had been defiled by [a human] corp[se and he shall b]athe and wash and the[n] **Col. 2** [1]he may e[at. . . .]

Frag. 2 Col. 1 [1][. . . just a]s they sprinkle on him [the] f[ir]st time, then he shall bathe and wash before [2][he eats. And if] for him the seventh [f]alls on the Sabbath, let him not sprinkle on the Sabbath because [3][He said, "Keep] the Sabbath" (Deut. 5:12).] However, let him not touch the pure food until he repeats. [4][Whatev]er touches a discharge of semen, whether it be a person or any vessel, he shall immerse it, and the one who carries it [5][shall imme]rse and he shall immerse the garment which it is on and the vessel which carries it [6][in wate]r. And if there is a man in the camp who does not have the means, he shall bat[he] [7][and wear an]y garment which has not touched it. However, let him not touch his food with it. And the one who touc[hes] [8][the b]e[d or the se]at, if [his] g[arment] has not touched it, [he shall bathe] in water, but if [9][his garment touched it] then he shall launder. And concerning all the holy things, he shall wash in water **Col. 2** [1]his flesh. And thus [. . .]

Liquids are conductors of uncleanness.

Frag. 3 Col. 1 [1][. . . when] God uncovers the pupil of his eye and he calls o[ut . . .] [2][. . .] b[efor]e them and every statute [. . .] [3][. . .] for the one who eats [. . .] [4][. . .] [5][. . .] and it is unclean [. . .] [6][If] its juice [has not oozed out] he may consume it in purity and any [7][that] are pressed so that their juice oozes out, no one may eat them. [8][If] an unclean person touches them [and] also the vegetables [. . .] [9][. . .] or ripe cucumber, and a person who [. . .]

More on uncleanness that is transferred by liquids.

Col. 2 [2][. . .] unclean of days [. . .] [3]and any (vessel) which has a seal [. . .] [4]for a very clean person. Any greens [which have no] [5]moisture of dew [on them] may be eaten. But if [it is] n[ot eaten, let him immerse it] [6]in the water. For if a man [puts it upon] [7]the ground and w[ater] wets it [when] [8]the rain [falls] upon it, and if an u[nclean person] touches it [let him take] extreme care [not to eat it] [9]in the field during the period of [his purification . . .] [10]any clay vessel [into] which [any creeping thing] fal[l]s, [11]that which is in it [becomes unclean . . . any] [12]liquid be[comes unclean . . .]

—M.G.A.

57. Rule of Initiation

4Q275

The "official" catalogues of the Dead Sea Scrolls classify the *Rule* as a work concerned with ritual purity, but it lacks the themes common to such writings (cf., for example, *Ritual Purity Laws Concerning Liquids,* text 56, or the *Ashes of the Red Heifer,* text 58). Therefore, the older, original classification is probably more accurate, and we have adopted it. The writer appears to be discussing initiation and membership procedures. The liturgical expression, "he shall say in response" (frag. 1, l. 4) and the curses on the unrighteous or disobedient (frag. 3, l. 4) suggest a relationship to the *Charter of a Sectarian Jewish Association* (text 7, 1:16–2:18).

Frag. 1 [1][. . . those who wal]k the paths of the [. . .] [2][. . . the elect of Israe]l, those who are called by name [. . .] [3][. . .] in the third month.[. . .] [4][. . .] and he shall say in response [. . .] [5][. . .] peoples and nations in the lan[d . . .]

Frag. 2 [1][. . . judgme]nt and they shall discipline themselves until the [seventh] week [. . .] [2][. . .] they [shall pos]sess their inheritance, for He is a [faithful] God[. . .] [3][. . . me]n of truth and those who hate of unjust gain [. . .] [4][. . .] they [vo]wed not to kill a man [. . .] [5][. . .] the [da]y of judgment [. . .] [6][. . .] to the place [. . .] [7][. . .] if he was [. . .]

Frag. 3 [1]and the elders with him, until [. . .] [2]they shall enter by genealogy [. . .] [3]And the Overseer sha[ll . . . without] [4]mercy, "Curs[ed are you . . .] [5]from His inheritance fore[ver . . .] [6]when He visits destruc[tion . . .]

—M.G.A.

58. The Ashes of the Red Heifer

4Q276–277

Today, among certain groups in Israel, plans go forward for the building of a Third Temple. Since the destruction of Herod's Temple, the so-called Second Temple, by the Romans in 70 C.E., there has been no Jewish Temple in

Jerusalem. But plans are under way to change that two-thousand-year-old fact. Priestly garments are being woven, guided by the laws preserved in the Bible and in rabbinic literature; molten silver and gold is being poured into molds to produce the many necessary Temple accoutrements—ladles, bowls, sprinklers, and so forth. A great deal of preparation is required.

Perhaps the most daunting task is the quest for a red heifer. According to Numbers 19, the ashes of a red heifer were a primary ingredient in the "water of impurity," a solution that restored the purity of those unclean because they had touched a corpse. The water of impurity is an indispensable element of Temple life, for the impure cannot enter the Temple and only this water can render them pure again. The impurity does not otherwise grow weaker or disappear with time; it never goes away.

The writing before us describes how to prepare a red heifer once you have one—it is not exactly your run-of-the-mill cow. But the procedure described is contrary to what rabbinic literature stipulates (*Mishnah Parah* 3:7). The rabbis required that the priest who was to burn the red heifer be rendered unclean before the procedure began. The procedure our author recommends is the one, according to the Mishnah, the Sadducees endorsed. See the Introduction for further discussion of Sadducean connections with the scrolls.

4Q276 Frag. 1 [1][. . . And the priest shall put on garments] which he has not worn to serve in the holy place [2][. . .] and he shall gird up (?) his garments and slaug[hter] [3][the] heifer [be]fore him and he shall collect its blood in an earthen vessel that [4][was sanctif]ied by the altar. He shall then sprinkle some of the blood with [his] finger seven [5][times to]ward the front of the t[e]nt of meeting. And he shall throw the cedar bough and [6]the hyssop and the crimson [material] into the midst of its burning. [7][And a man who is pure from uncleanness which lasts until evening shall gath]er the ashes of the heifer [8][. . . and they shall st]ore it for safekeeping [9][. . . And] the priest shall put on [. . .]

4Q277 Frag. 1 Col. 2 [1][And he shall throw the cedar bough] and the hyssop and the [crimson material into the midst of the burning of the heifer.] [2][Then] a man who is pure from uncleanness which lasts until evening [shall gather the ashes of the heifer and give them] [3][to] the priest who makes atonement with the blood of the heifer. And anyone [who touches the ash or carries] [4][the] clay [vessels by whic]h they made atonement according to the ordinance of [the sin offering, shall bathe] [5]with water. [And he shall be unc]lean until the [eveni]ng. The one who touches [the] moisture of the water for cleansing shall be un[clean.] [6][And no] man [shall sprinkle] the water for cleansing upon those defiled by a c[orpse.] Only a clean priest [shall sprinkle] [7][upo]n them fo[r] he [shall] make atonement for the unclean. One who is negligent (*or* a child) may not sprinkle on the unclean. And tho[se who receive] [8][the] water for [cl]eansing shall enter the water and shall be cleansed from [human (?)] corpse uncleanness [and from any] [9]other [uncleanness] when [the pr]iest [shall sp]lash the water for cleansing upon them to cleanse [them, for] [10][they shall not be sanctified] unless they [ar]e cleansed and their flesh shall be c[lean.] And anyone who is touched [11][by a man with] a bodily discharge [. . .] and [his] ha[nds] were [no]t rins[ed] in water shall be unclean. [12][. . .] his [b]ed and [his] sea[t . . .] they have touched his discharge, it is as an unclean affliction, [13][and he shall be un]clean until [the] evening. The one who carries his [ga]rments shall [bat]he and be unclean until the [ev]ening.

—M.G.A.

59. Ritual Purity Laws Concerning Menstruation

4Q278

This small fragment is related to the *Ritual Purity Laws Concerning Liquids* (text 56) and *Ritual of Purification for Festival Days* (text 61). *A Liturgy of Ritual Washings* (text 104) appears to be a "handbook" containing prayers for the ritual accompanying the cleansing. The author here interprets Leviticus 15:19–24.

Frag. 1 [1][. . . and he shall] rinse [2][in water . . .]

[3][. . . Le]t no one lie [4][with a woman . . .] that she shall sit [5][upon . . . And] if he has not touched it, [6][. . . on the th]ird [day,] when he touches [7][. . .] contact with the bed is [like co]rpse [uncleanness] [8][. . .] in the place [. . .]

—M.G.A.

60. Laws Concerning Lots

4Q279

Ordinarily, when the Hebrew term translated "lot" appears in the scrolls, it refers to the two groups into which all humanity is divided. In the language of the *War Scroll* (text 11), these groups are the Sons of Light and the Sons of Darkness. In this small fragment, however, the word "lot" appears to mean something different. It seems to refer to a literal division of wealth or rank. Four groups are involved, of which two are clearly identifiable. The first group consists of the sons of Aaron (priests), and the fourth group consists of proselytes, or converts to Judaism. A passage in the *Damascus Document* (text 1, Geniza 14:3–4), may shed light on the situation and on the identity of the two groups whose names are missing: "All shall be mustered by their names: the priests first, the Levites second, the children of Israel third, the proselytes fourth."

Frag. 1 ^{2}[. . .] his [fello]w who was recorded after [him . . .] ^{3}[. . .] and greatness of pedigree upon him, and t[hu]s [. . .] ^{4}[. . . for the pries]ts, the sons of Aaron, the [first] lot shall go [. . .] ^{5}[. . .] each man according to his disposition. And the [second] lo[t . . .] ^{6}[. . . and] the fourth lot is for the pro[selytes . . .]

—M.G.A.

61. Ritual of Purification for Festival Days

4Q284

This text is a good example of how greatly an interpretation can evolve in the editing process. The change in a single word has caused this transformation. The word once translated "impurities" (frag. 1 1:6), suggesting the title "Rule of (Sexual) Impurities," is now read "thanksgivings." The composition now appears to guide the purification with the sprinkling of water on various festival days and most closely resembles *A Liturgy of Ritual Washings* (text 104).

The references to Sabbaths, months, and seasons provide the calendar for the purification rites that follow.

Frag. 1 Col. 1 ^{3}[. . . Sab]bath for each of the weeks of ^{4}[. . . the year and] its twelve months ^{5}[. . . the four seas]ons of the year on the days of ^{6}[. . .] the "Rule of Thanksgivings" for Israel ^{7}[. . .] water of cleansing to [sancti]fy themselves ^{8}[. . .] semen ^{9}[. . .] to him [. . .] ^{10}[. . .] that [. . .]

The seven-day period followed by washing for purification is found in Leviticus 14:8; 15:13 and is reflected in several scrolls: Ritual Purity Laws Concerning Liquids *frag. 1 (text 56),* A Liturgy of Ritual Washings *frag. 11 (text 104), and the* Temple Scroll *col. 45 (text 155).*

Frag. 2 Col. 1 [1][. . .] he shall not eat [2][from the holy food . . .] anything which touched [him (?) . . .] with the waters of [3][sprinkling . . . and when] his seven [days] have been completed, [. . .] [4][. . .] he shall bathe [his] bo[dy in water and shall be clean . . .]

Ritual Purity Laws Concerning Liquids *frag. 1 (text 56) stipulates that no food may be eaten until the purification process has begun. On subsequent days meals must follow bathing.*

Col. 2 [1]They left [him] in the impurity of [. . .] [2]holy and no[t . . .] [3]from food the seven [days of uncleanness . . . after the setting of] [4]the sun on the seventh day [. . . and he shall say in response,] [5]"Blessed are You, O God of Israel [. . .] [6]seasons of pea[ce] for the fee[ble . . .]

The reference to the sun setting on the seventh day is likely an echo of a legal battle with the Pharisees concerning the state of purity after washing on the seventh day. The Pharisees had established an intermediate state called tevul yom *("one who is immersed on that day") that allowed a return to some activities after washing. The sectarians waited until the setting of the sun. See the* Temple Scroll *col. 50 (text 155).*

Frag. 3 [1][. . .] its fixed times [. . .] [2][. . .] when the sun sets on the [seventh] day [. . .] [3][. . . water of] cleansing. And he shall say in response, "Blessed are Yo[u, O God of Israel . . .] [4][. . . and Yo]u inscribed a true purification for Your people, for [. . .] [5][. . . to be] cleansed with them from all their uncle[anness] to [. . .]

Laws concerning uncleanness from a corpse (Num. 19:14).

Frag. 4 [2] [. . .] to the children of Your covenant [. . .] [3]in Your t[rue] lot for [. . .] [4]and pure before You in [. . .] [5]concerning the person who dies in [. . .] [6]And it shall be at the time of the affliction [that . . .]
—M.G.A.

62. Laws About Liquids and Gleaning

4Q284a

This fragment, like the *Ritual Purity Laws Concerning Liquids* (text 56), deals with the kinds of uncleanness transferred by liquids contained in food. The food the community eats must be carefully prepared in a state of ritual purity.

Frag. 1 [2][. . . the ba]sket [. . . no unclean person] shall glean them [and everyone] [3][who] may not touch the drink of the general membership, for these [will defile] [4][the] basket and the figs and the pomegranates, [if] [5]their [liquids] come out wh[en pre]ssed, all of them, or they are gleaned by [6][a man] who has not been brough[t into the cov]enant, and if they crush [olives] [7][in the pr]ess, he may not defile them in [. . .] to leave them open until he empt[ies them . . .] [8][let] them [be cru]shed in purity, and [when] their preparation [is complete], [they can] eat [. . .]

Frag. 2 [2][. . . all of] them may glean in purit[y . . .] [3][. . .] and ea[ch] will glean [. . .] [4]any of the [men of] the *Yaha[d* . . .] [5][. . . p]urity [. . .] [6][. . .] clean [. . .] [7][. . .] unless [. . .]
—E.M.C.

63. The War of the Messiah

4Q285, 11Q14

"Rediscovered" among the unpublished fragments of the scrolls when they first became available late in 1991, 4Q285 frag. 7 of the *War of the Messiah* created a flurry of excitement and generated front-page headlines all over the world. Line 4 of the fragment is ambiguous in the original Hebrew, which is written without vowels. According to the vowels mentally supplied by the Hebrew reader, l. 4 could say either "they (the enemy) will put the Leader of the congregation to death" or "the Leader of the congregation will have him (the enemy leader) put to death." The Leader of the congregation is a messianic figure known from other Dead Sea Scrolls (see *Priestly Blessings for the Last Days,* text 9, and *Commentaries on Isaiah,* text 21). Thus, following the first option, frag. 7 appeared to be describing the execution of a messiah, and the obvious parallels to Jesus of Nazareth were drawn.

The excitement has since died down. After a whirlwind of research activity and a number of critical assessments, scholarly consensus has rejected the first option and settled on the second. Even the primary exponent of the "dying messiah" interpretation, Robert Eisenman, has publicly recanted, saying that in fact he never really believed it in the first place. Scholars have concluded in favor of the second option largely because of parallels between frag. 7 and other Dead Sea Scrolls. They argue that the Leader of the congregation is elsewhere always a victorious deliverer, a son of David raised up to lead Israel back to primacy at the head of the nations. The context of the fragment itself commends a victorious messiah, beginning as it does with a quote from Isaiah 11, which continues "He shall strike the earth with the rod of his mouth, and with the breath of his lips shall he slay the wicked" (v. 4). Frag. 7, according to current consensus, describes a particularly important instance of messianic slaughter of the wicked: the messiah kills the enemy leader.

The *War of the Messiah* is an important find for another reason, for it may preserve the missing end of the *War Scroll* (text 11). The text might be arranged to give the following description of the final battle: the high priest takes his stand before the troops and blesses them before the seventh and final foray against the Sons of Darkness. This blessing reflects the imminent age of peace and prosperity that lies on the horizon (frag. 8). Frag. 4 describes a battle that begins in the mountains of Israel and concludes on the Mediterranean Sea. The forces of the Sons of Darkness are routed with the aid of the angelic forces (frag. 1), and the wicked leader is brought before the royal messiah (the Leader) for judgment. Fulfilling Isaiah 10:33–11:5, the wicked leader is slain. The people of Israel then rejoice with dancing and song. Finally, the high priest orders the troops to cleanse the land from the corpses of the Kittim (frags. 7 and 10).

A Cave 11 manuscript, 11Q14, has been determined to coincide with frag. 8 of 4Q285, so the caves apparently housed two copies of this extraordinary writing.

Angelic forces fight on the side of the Sons of Light (1QM 9:15–16).

4Q285 Frag. 1 [1][. . .] and upon [. . .] [2][. . .] for the sake of His name and [. . .] [3][. . .] Michael, G[abrie]l, [Sariel, and Raphael . . .] [4][. . .] and with the chosen [of heaven (?) . . .]

The battle is fought on land and sea and ends with the leader of the forces of evil standing in judgment before the Leader of the congregation.

Frag. 4 [1][. . . in three lots] evil shall be smitten [. . .] [2][. . . Lead]er of the Congregation and all Isr[ael . . .] [3][. . . just as it wa]s written [in the book of Ezekiel the prophet, "And I will strike your bow from your left hand] [4][and bring down your arrows from your right. You shall fall] upon the mountains of I[srael, you and all your troops and the peoples that are with you" (Ezek. 39:3–4) . . .] [5][. . . King of the] Kittim and [. . .] [6][. . . and the Le]ader of the Congregation [pursued them] to the [Mediterranean] Sea [. . .] [7][. . . And they shall flee] from Israel at that time [. . .] [8][. . . And] he shall stand before them and they shall arrange themselves against them [. . .] [9][. . .] and they shall return back to the dry land at th[at] time [. . .] [10][. . .] then they shall bring him before the Leader of [the Congregation . . .]

As it is written in Isaiah 10:34–11:1, the forces of evil are cut down by the messianic "shoot of Jesse." The shoot, who is the Leader, condemns the leader of the forces of evil to death and the chosen of Israel rejoice.

Frag. 7 + 11Q14 Frag. 1 Col. 1 [1][. . . just as it is written in the book of] Isaiah the prophet, "And [the thickets of the forest] shall be cut down [2][with an ax, and Lebanon with its majestic trees wil]l fall. A shoot shall come out from the stump of Jesse [3][and a branch shall grow out of his roots" (Isa. 10:34–11:1). This is the] Branch of David. Then [all forces of Belial] shall be judged, [4][and the king of the Kittim shall stand for judgment] and the Leader of the congregation—the Bra[nch of David]—will have him put to death. [5][Then all Israel shall come out with timbrel]s and dancers, and the [high] priest shall order [6][them to cleanse their bodies from the guilty blood of the c]orpse[s of] the Kittim. [Then all the people shall . . .]

The last (?) address of the high priest before the final and victorious battle against the Kittim.

Frag. 8 + 11Q14 Frag. 1 Col. 2 [. . . And he blessed them] before Israel [and said in response, ". . .] [1][. . . Israel, Blessed are you in the name of G]od Most [High who . . .] [2][and blessed is His holy name f]orever and ever [and blessed are His true works and blessed] [3][are all His holy angels. May] God Mos[t High bless] you, [and shine His face upon you and open] [4][His] good [treasure for you whic]h is in heaven to [bring down upon your land showers] [5][of blessing, dew and] rain—both early and late—in their season to give [you bountiful fruit, grain,] [6][fresh wine and] oil abundantly. And let the earth [pro]duce for yo[u delicacies, and you shall eat] [7][and become fat] and there will be no barren woman [in your la]nd and no [sickness. Smut or mildew] [8]shall not appear in [its] produce, [and n]o stum[bling block in your congregation. Wild animals shall cease] [9]from the land, nor shall there be any plagu[e in yo]ur [land.] For God is w[ith you and His holy angels shall take their stand in your congregation, and] [10]His holy name shall be called u[pon you . . .] [11]together."

And before you engage [in battle, the priest shall come forward and speak to the troops. . . .]

In the aftermath of the battle, the soldiers dig graves and cleanse the land of the dead.

Frag. 10 2[. . . He shall separate them] from the midst of the congregation [. . .] 3[. . . leave the] unjust gain and profit [for them . . .] 4[. . .] and you shall eat [the spoil of your enemy . . .] 5[. . . And they shall dig] grave[s] for them [. . .] 6[. . . and you shall cleanse yourselves from al]l their corpses [. . .] 7[. . . and afterwar]ds they shall return [. . .] 8[. . .] water (?)[. . .] 9[. . .] God (*or* to) [. . .]
—M.G.A.

64. A Liturgy of Blessing and Cursing

4Q280, 4Q286–289

Moses never lived to enter the promised land, the Bible says; but that did not keep him from issuing detailed commands for what was to happen once Israel did enter Canaan. "On the day that you cross over the Jordan into the land that the LORD your God is about to give you . . . these shall stand on Mount Gerizim for the blessing of the people: Simeon, Levi, Judah, Issachar, Joseph, and Benjamin. And these shall stand on Mount Ebal for the curse: Reuben, Gad, Asher, Zebulun, Dan, and Naphtali" (Deut. 27:2–13). The antiphonal blessings and curses that followed were a defining element in God's covenant with Israel.

The members of the *Yahad* took this unique biblical ceremony extremely seriously. They incorporated its pattern into both their initiation ceremony (*Charter of a Jewish Sectarian Association* 2:1–18, text 7) and their battle liturgy (the *War Scroll* 13:1–4, text 11). Furthermore, the present work takes over the structure of the biblical ceremony wholesale. The writer details first blessings upon God and his holy angels, then curses upon Satan—here called Belial and Melkiresha'—and his attendant evil spirits. Clearly this work represents a liturgy, as witnessed by the repeated introductory formula "they shall say in response." Each blessing or curse ends with the *Yahad*'s characteristic twofold "Amen," which is rare in the Bible (it occurs only in Neh. 5:22; 8:6). In Deuteronomy 27 and elsewhere in the Old and New Testaments the "Amen" is never repeated twice—except, of course, for the twofold "Amen" with which Jesus is said to preface his most sober pronouncements.

Origin of and curse on Melkiresha'. 4Q280 has been given the designation 4QCurses in the official publication despite the fact that it is clearly related to the covenant renewal of 1QS and the 4QBerakhot manuscripts (4Q286–289). The lack of the twofold "Amen" and blessings is to be explained by the fragmentary nature of the manuscript: one seven-line fragment and two smaller fragments (not translated here) that add a total of six readable words.

4Q280 Frag. 2 [1][And God shall set him apart] for evil from the midst of the Sons of Li[ght because of his apostasy from Him.]

[And they shall continue] [2][saying, "Cur]sed are you, O Melkiresha', for all the sch[emes of your sinful desires. May] God [appoint you] [3]as an object of terror in the hands of those who wreak vengeance. May God not be gracious to you when you call out, [and may He lift up His angry face] [4]against you in indignation, so that there might be no peac[e] for you in the mouth of all who make interces[sion. Cursed are you] [5]without remnant. You are damned, without survivor. And cursed are all who carry o[ut their wicked schemes] [6][and tho]se who establish evil plans in their heart, to plot against the covenant of God [. . . against the Law and against] [7][the word]s of all those who see [His] tru[th. And ev]eryone who refuses to enter [into the covenant of God, walking in the stubbornness of his heart . . .]

In praise of God.

4Q286 Frag. 1 Col. 2 [1][. . .] Your honored seat and Your glorious footstools are in the [he]ights where You stand, even Your holy walkway. [2]And Your glorious chariots, with their cherubim and their wheels and all [their] foundations: [3]bases of fire, flames of bright light, majestic brightness, lights of fire, wondrous luminaries, [4]splendor and majesty, glorious height, a holy foundation, a [sh]ining fou[nt], splendorous height, w[onder of] [5][prais]e, a reservoir of powers, a majesty of praises, greatness of fears, and heali[ngs . . .] [6]wondrous works, wise counsel, a pattern for knowledge, a fount of understanding, a fount of discernment, [7]a holy council, a true foundation, a storehouse of understanding, structures of righteousness, and dwellings of integr[ity; abounding in] [8]mercies, genuine humility, true loving-kindness, and eternal mercies. And won[drous] mysteries [9]when [the]y app[ear:] holy weeks according to their plan, divisions of the months [. . . ,] [10][beginnings of the year]s in their seasons, glorious festivals at [their] appointed times [. . .] [11][. . .] and the sabbath years for the earth in [their] divis[ions and appointed] times of liber[ty . . .] [12][. . .] eternal [li]berties and [. . .] [13][. . .] light and darkne[ss . . .]

Blessing to God for giving the land as an inheritance to Israel.

Frag. 5 [1][. . .] the earth and all [th]at is [upon it, the world and all] those who dwell in it, the land and all of its designs, . . .] [2][. . . the earth and eve]ry living thing, [the mountains and al]l the hill[s], the valleys, and all the ravines, the deser[ts . . .] [3][. . . c]edar, the shady forests, and all the wastelan[ds . . .] [4][. . .] and its lack of form, and the foundations of its structure, the islands, and [. . .] [5][. . .] th[eir] fruit, tall trees, and all the cedars of Leban[on . . .] [6][. . . grain, fr]esh wine and fresh oil, and all the produce [of . . .] [7][. . .] and all the wave offerings of the world in the tw[elve] months [. . .] [8][. . .] Your word. Amen. Amen. [. . .]

[9][. . .] and the boundary of the seas, the springs of the deep [. . .] [10][. . .] and all the wadis, the currents of the depths [. . .] [11][. . .] their [. . .] seas [. . .] [12][. . . a]ll their councils (*or* foundations) [. . .] [13][. . .] Your [. . .]

Blessing to God for his protection.

Frag. 7 Col. 1 [1][. . .] the lands [2][. . . and al]l of their elect [3][. . .] and all who [under]stand them in psalms of [4][. . .] and true blessings at f[estival] times [. . .] [5][. . .] Your [. . .] and Your kingdom is exalted among the p[eople]s [6][. . . the cou]ncil of the pure divine beings with all those who know how to prai[se] eternally, [7][and to ble]ss Your glorious name through all [the times of eterni]t[y.] Amen. Amen.

[8][And] they shall continue to bless the God of [. . . a]ll the [. . . of] His truth. [9][. . .]

Col. 2 (with **4Q287 Frag. 6**) [1]The Party of the *Yahad* shall say, all of them in unison, "Amen, Amen."

Curse on Belial and the spirits of his lot.

Then [t]he[y] shall denounce Belial [2]and all his guilty lot. And they shall say in response: "Cursed is [B]elial because of his malevolent [pu]rposes, [3]and he is damned for his guilty dominion. Cursed are all the spirits of his [lo]t for their wicked purpose, [4]and they are damned for their filthy [un]clean purposes. For they are the l[o]t of darkness and their punishment [5]is the eternal pit. Amen. Amen."

Belial and his sons are destined for annihilation.

Cursed is the wick[ed one in all of the ages of] his dominions, and damned [6]are all the sons of Beli[al] for all the iniquities of their office, until their annihilation [forever. Ame]n. Amen.

Curse on the angel of the pit and the spirits of perdition.

[7]Then [they shall continue and say, "Cursed are you, O ange]l of the pit, O spir[it of Aba]ddon, for al[l] the purposes of your guilty desire, [8][and for all your abomina]ble [purposes] and [your] wicked counsel, [and da]mned are you for [your unjust domi]n[ion] [9][and your guilty] and [wicked] authority with all [the] de[filements of Sheo]l and w[ith the reproaches of the pi]t, [10][with the disgra]ces of destruction wi[thout remnant and without] forgiveness by the fierce anger of [Go]d [for all eternit]y. Amen. A[men.] [11][Cursed are a]ll who carry out their [wick]ed [schemes] and those who establish their evil plan [in their heart, plotting evil] [12][against the covenant of G]od and [. . . the words of the seers of] His [tru]th and exchanging the judgments of [the law . . .]

Blessing to God and his angels.

4Q287 Frag. 2 [1][. . .] their [. . .] and [. . .] their basins [. . .] [2][. . .] their [. . .] their splendid [patt]erns [. . .] [3][. . . the walls of] their glorious [hal]ls, their wondrous gates [. . .] [4][. . .] their [. . .] angels of fire and spirits of cloud [. . .] [5][. . . shin]ing, variegated patterns of the spirits of the utterly hol[y . . .] [6][. . .] and the holy expanse [. . .] [7][. . . the utterly] holy [spirits will sing for joy] in all the fixed time[s . . .] [8][. . . they will bless] the glorious name of Your divinity [. . .] [9][. . .] their [. . .] and all the h[oly] ministers [. . .] [10][. . .] in the perfection of th[eir] works [. . .] [11][. . .] in the palaces of [Your] d[ominion . . . wond]ers of [12][. . .] all [Your] minister[s in] their [glorious] splendor, the angels of [13][. . .] Your holy [spirits] in [their glorious] dwel[lings,] Your righteous [a]ngels [. . .]

Frag. 3 [1][. . . in] their [awesom]e deeds, and they will bless Your holy name with blessings [. . . the utterly holy ones . . .] [2][. . .] all creatures of flesh, all of them that [You] created [shall ble]ss You [. . .] [3][. . . b]easts and birds and creeping things, and fish of [the s]eas and all [. . .] [4][. . . Y]ou created all of them anew [. . .]

Blessings to God.

Frag. 5 [8][. . . the wealth of a mu]ltitude of nations, to giv[e . . .] [9][. . .] their families in [. . .] [10][. . .] in Your righteous truth when [Your kingdom] is exalt[ed . . .] [11][. . . and] all of them [shall bless] You together. Amen. A[men.]

[. . .] [12][. . .] those who dra[w] near to You and the see[d . . .] [13][. . . all] the families of the land, to be [. . .]

4Q288 Frag. 1 (with **4Q286 Frag. 20**) [1][. . . me]n of the *Yahad* [. . .] [2][. . . wo]rks of deceit [. . .] [3][. . .] his works from all [sin . . .] [4][. . . let no one avenge] himself, for any matter, for [. . .] [5][. . .] and let no one deliver hi[mself . . .] [6][. . .] in anger or with a jealous sp[irit . . .] [7][. . .] and burning anger and rebelling without justice [. . .]

Curse on Belial.

4Q289 Frag. 1 [1][. . . and the co]uncil of wickedness[. . .] their [ser]vice is in [. . .] [2][. . . and] etern[al] condemnations [in] complete [reproach . . . Amen. Amen.]

Liturgical instructions in preparation for blessing God.

[. . .] [3][. . .] for the truth of God and to bless His name and [. . .] [4][. . .] then the priest, [the Ov]erseer at the head of [the general membership,] shall [. . .] [5][. . . for] the holy [angels] are in the midst of all [their congregation . . .] [6][. . . and to give than]ks before Him. [And they shall say in response,] "Blessed [are You, O God of Israel . . .] [7][. . .] all [. . .]

Blessing for God the creator.

Frag. 2 [1][. . . You] created the [heavens and the earth . . .] [2][. . .] all of them and al[l . . .] [3][. . . the prie]sts, those who enter [the covenant . . .] [4][. . .] Amen. Ame[n. . . .]

—M.G.A.

65. The Sage to the "Children of Dawn"

4Q298

The *Sage to the "Children of Dawn"* is one of a handful of texts found in Cave 4 that were written in a Cryptic Script A, the secret form of writing discussed in the Introduction. This form of writing used a secret symbol for each letter of the Hebrew alphabet, making it impossible for the uninitiated to read works so inscribed. The decision to encrypt the present work suggests that only those instructed in the mysteries of the group were supposed to read its contents, although what remains may not seem particularly remarkable compared to other scrolls.

The addressees of this exhortation are called the "Children of Dawn" (initiates?), a mysterious title found nowhere else among the scrolls. The writer speaks in the first person and calls himself the "Instructor" or "Sage," an office of leadership and instruction within the *Yahad*. This work is a wisdom instruction comparable to the *Book of Secrets* (text 6) and the *Secret of the Way Things Are* (text 105). For further discussion of the characteristics of wisdom writings, refer to those texts.

Introduction exhorting the initiates to listen to the words of the Instructor.

Frags. 1–2 Col. 1 [1]The [word]s of the Instructor which he spoke to all the Sons of Dawn: "Hear[ken unto me, a]ll you men of understanding. [2][You who purs]ue righteousness, unders[ta]nd my words. You who seek faithfulness, l[iste]n to my words, all [3][that com]es out of [my] lips. [For those who k]now have sou[gh]t [th]ese things and turne[d to the way of] life. O m[en of] [4]His [wil]l, and eterna[l righteousness (*or* light) which cannot be] searched out [. . .]

Fellowship to be established on wisdom and law (?).

Col. 2 [1] its roots went [out . . .] [2]in the deep be[neath . . .] [3]consider [. . .]

Doing justice and walking humbly with God (Mic. 6:8) bring understanding. The notion of "appointed days" in l. 8 of col. 2 reflects the Yahad*'s doctrine that God has not merely foreseen, but actively willed, all of history.*

Frags. 3–4 Col. 1 [1][. . .] lofty dwelling [2][. . .] and in them (*or* by what) [3][. . .] dust [4][. . .] God gave [5][. . .] in all the earth [6][. . .] He measured their plan [7][. . . un]derneath He placed [8][. . .] their [p]lan to walk [9][. . .] storehouse of understanding [10][. . .] my [w]ord and that [. . .]

Col. 2[1][. . .] and the number of its borders [2][. . .] without being raised up [3]from [its] p[lan . . .] its border. And now [4]heark[en, O wise ones,] and those of you who know, listen! And you men of [5]understanding, i[ncrease learnin]g, and those who requi[re] justice, walk [6]humbly. [Those of you who] kn[ow the way,] increase strength, and you men of [7]truth, purs[ue righteousness] and love kindness, increase [8]humility and in[crease your know]ledge of the *appointed [da]ys* whose [9]interpretation [I shall recoun]t so

that you might understand the end [10]of the eternal ages and examine the ancient things to know [. . .]
—M.G.A.

66. The Parable of the Bountiful Tree

4Q302

In his classic work the *Parables of Jesus,* Joachim Jeremias wrote in 1954: "Jesus' parables are something entirely new. In all the rabbinic literature, not one single parable has come down to us from the period before Jesus."* This is a strong statement, and not all scholars have affirmed it. Many are inclined to see the use of parables for teaching as reasonably widespread in Second Temple Judaism. These scholars argue that Jesus drew from a common fund of popular stories or that his themes, at least, came from such a fund. Nevertheless, their view has, until now, relied more upon inference than evidence. Concrete proof was just not to be found.

Rabbinic literature abounds with parables similar to those of Jesus, but those writings are, as Jeremias implied, uniformly later than the time of Jesus. Thus they cannot safely be used to prove that parables were a common teaching device when Jesus walked the shores of the Sea of Galilee. Further, no parables appear in the Apocrypha or the pseudepigraphical writings that have come down to us. Nor was it known, before the release of the unpublished Dead Sea Scrolls in 1991, that parables survived among the materials from Qumran. The text before us is therefore of great interest and importance, for it is manifestly a parable.

Unfortunately, the work is very fragmentary, but enough survives to reveal parallels with New Testament parables. The introductory address, "Please consider this, you who are wise," reminds one immediately of Gospel statements framing Jesus's teaching: "Let anyone with ears to hear, listen!" (e.g., Mark 4:9). Our author's choice of a tree as the parable's metaphor also resonates with Gospel parables, including the budding fig tree (Mark 13:28–32), the good and bad trees (Matt. 7:16–20), and Luke's story of the barren fig tree (Luke 13:6–9).

*Joachim Jeremias, *The Parables of Jesus,* 2d rev. ed. (New York: Scribner, 1954), 12.

A parable of a fine tree and its owner's prudent concern for its welfare.

Frag. 2 Col. 2 [2]Please consider this, you who are wise: If a man has [3]a fine tree, which grows high, all the way to heaven [. . .] [4][. . .] of the lands, and it [pr]oduces succulent fruit [. . .] [5]the autumn rains and the spring rains, in scorching heat and in thirst, [6]will he not [love] it [. . .] and guard it [7][. . .] to multiply the boughs (?) of [8][. . .] from its shoot, to increase [9][. . .] and its mass of branches [. . .]

Whether the parable of the tree continues in this fragment is uncertain. The contents might be seen as an interpretation of the parable, in which the people of Israel represent the tree. God's treatment of them is analogous to the careful cultivation of a tree.

Frag. 3 Col. 2 [2][. . .] your God [3][. . .] [4][. . .] your hearts [. . .] [5][. . .] with a willing spirit. [6][. . .] Shall [not] God take vengeance against your rebellion, [7][against your evil] intentions? Will He not confront you, to reprove [8]you and reply to your complaint? [9][. . .] As for God, His dwelling is in heaven, and [His king]dom [10]embraces the lands, the seas [and all that is] in them [. . .]

—M.O.W.

67. A Meditation on Creation

4Q303

This is a fragmentary exhortation inspired by the creation narratives (Gen. 1:1–2:25).

Creation of the waters, the heavenly lights, and their realms.

Col. 1 [1][. . . All] you who possess understanding, listen and [. . .] [2][. . .] the waters and they caused to cease from upon a[ll . . .] [3][. . .] the wonders of God, wh[o . . .] [4][. . .] for an eternal light and pur[e] heavens [. . .] [5][. . . ligh]t in a place formless and vo[id . . .] [6][. . .] all their works to the end that [. . .] [7][. . . ove]r whom he reigned, and for all of them [. . .]

Creation of Adam and Eve.

[8][. . .] and the understanding of good and evil [. . .] [9][. . . the

earth,] taking Adam from it. All [. . .] ^{10}[. . .] and He made for him a helper as [his partner . . .] ^{11}[. . .] "Woman," for [she was taken] from him [. . .]

—M.O.W.

68. The People Who Err

4Q306

This fragmentary work seems to describe a situation also mentioned in the *Damascus Document* (text 1). The phrase "groping for the way" occurs both here and in that very important work related to the *Yahad.* In the *Damascus Document,* the phrase describes a period in the history of the group when a definite understanding of the Law and how it ought to be obeyed had not yet crystallized. The second fragment of the present text may be describing the same period. The first fragment seems to speak in a predictive strain of disobedience to the law. With its mention of dogs and the Temple court, the work is perhaps referencing the need to ban dogs from the Temple, also described in the *Sectarian Manifesto* (text 100).

Frag. 1 ^{1}the descendants who will stray and fail to observe the [commandments . . .] ^{2}For they will transgress [from day] to day and from month to mon[th . . .] ^{3}it, all that is in the covenant with I[srael . . .] ^{4}will rend its flesh and spit out [. . .] ^{5}and He will be stirred to wrath, while the dogs are eating [bones in the courtyard . . .] ^{6}to bring it out of the courtyard, the [do]gs and the [. . .] ^{7}concerning days in which they se[r]ve [. . .] ^{8}the [. . .] and the new oil [. . .]

Frag. 2 ^{1}[and] they sought the Law and the [commandment . . . with all their heart] ^{2}and with all their soul; they were as those groping for the w[ay . . . who have no] ^{3}eyes; the Law continues to [. . .] ^{4}[ag]ain, until their eyes are opened and they perceive [the ways of God . . .]

—M.O.W.

A Reader's Guide to the Qumran Calendar Texts

We in the modern world are obsessed with time. We tell time, keep time, mark time, fill time, kill time—some even do time. We have alarm clocks, atomic clocks, cuckoo clocks, pocket watches, and stopwatches. We consult chronicles, registries, annals, journals, time sheets, time cards, logs, date books, date slips, and timetables. Time obsesses us, time possesses us. It was not so for the ancients.

Inhabitants of the ancient world generally did without the chronometric cycles that structure our lives. Farmers for the most part, they were concerned with little more than the seasons and the changing weather the seasons brought with them. Though it seems incredible to us, ancient testimony shows that the average person often did not know what year it was. Longer spans of time were utterly beyond normal comprehension. Peasants appearing before the Spanish Inquisition (for which ample documentation exists) could not say, when asked, how old they were. Most members of ancient society just did not think measuring time was very important.

But there were two groups for whom it was important: astronomers and priests. In antiquity the two were often one and the same. Priests were interested in time for different reasons than we are. Our interest in timekeeping usually springs from economic concerns ("Time is money"). Ancient priests kept track of it as a way of serving God. For them, time was sacred. The astronomical bodies by which time was measured had been created by God; consequently, its measurement was a sacred priestly task. This task gave rise to festival calendars. Alongside all our other concerns with time, we still follow such festival calendars, we who celebrate Passover or Easter.

Calendars, or writings that presuppose them, comprise a very substantial percentage of the Dead Sea caches. Indeed, as stated in the Introduction, adherence to a peculiar calendar is the thread that runs through hundreds of the Dead Sea Scrolls. More than any other single element, the calendar binds these works together. It is the calendar that makes the scrolls a collection. The calendar is the intentional element. No matter who wrote the scrolls or put them in the caves, the manuscripts do, in some sense, form a library, because they all embrace one particular type of solar calendar and its ancillary developments. Therefore, if we want to understand the Dead Sea Scrolls, we must come to terms with their system for measuring sacred time. Understanding this system can be demanding, as matters get technical; the best approach is to read the next few pages once over, to get a rough idea of what's involved, and then, when reading the calendars themselves, return to this discussion as needed.

The authors and readers of the scrolls differed from most Jews of their day in the importance they ascribed to the sun. The sun's annual journey through the heavens was the basis for their calendar. Most Jews, in contrast, embraced a lunar calendar that was the primitive ancestor of the modern Jewish calendar. The difference in outlook was not absolute, but rather a matter of degree. The writers of the scrolls were interested in the moon; the other side perforce kept an eye on the sun. The lunar calendar of most Jews employed a system of intercalation (intermittent adding of months) based on the solar cycle. The dispute—and it was a bitter dispute, to judge from the polemics we read in the scrolls—was really about which heavenly body was more important. Logically, the more important body should rule, should govern sacred time. Would the sun and its cycle govern the festivals of Israel's sacred year, or would the moon have pride of place? The authors of the scrolls cast their vote for the sun.

The calendar of the scrolls proposed a 364-day solar year. The moon, as a secondary body, was sometimes considered, and when it was, its movements were described in terms of the sun. The movements of the moon are inherently much more complicated than those of the sun, and the scroll writers knew this fact. Their struggles to describe those movements are evident in erasures and marginal comments on the scrolls. In fact, despite the pleasing symmetry of their solar system, these calendrical works were not very accurate in the long term. Their solar year fell behind the astronomical year by more than a day each time the earth revolved around the sun. Likewise, their lunar calendars lost nearly half an hour a month. These differences might be relatively insignificant for a few years, but eventually the seasons would begin to wander through the year, and the phases of the moon would not correspond to what was expected. Inaccuracy would become a major problem. Yet so far scholars have been unable to identify any system of intercalation that the writers would have used to make the differences good. How did the calendars actually function in real life?

For they did function; these writings were not mere abstract theory. We know that from the *Commentary on Habakkuk*, which describes a Day of Atonement on which the Teacher of Righteousness and his followers were attacked by the Wicked Priest (see text 2, 11:4–8). As Shemaryahu Talmon has shown,* this attack was only possible because the Teacher was following one calendar, the Wicked Priest another. For the Teacher, it was the Day of Atonement. Battle, as a type of work, was forbidden. For the Priest, it was an ordinary day and a perfect opportunity to strike. At least in this instance, people were actually trying to live by the Qumran calendar. Did they keep doing so long enough to perceive an incipient inaccuracy, and did they try to fix it?

Logic would suggest they did, but we must be wary of assuming our logic was that of the ancients. Perhaps no system of intercalation ever did develop. A passage in *1 Enoch* points to this possibility, as Roger Beckwith has noted.‡ *1 Enoch* was a work that embraced the solar calendar; indeed, nearly a dozen

*Shemaryahu Talmon, "Yom Hakippurim in the Habakkuk Scroll," *Biblica* 32 (1951): 549–63.

‡Roger Beckwith, "The Modern Attempt to Reconcile the Qumran Calendar with the True Solar Year," *Revue de Qumran* 7 (1969-71): 379–96.

copies of this work were found among the scrolls. *1 Enoch* 80:2–4 contains a prophecy couched in literary fiction: "In the days of the sinners the years shall be shortened, and their seed shall be tardy on their lands and fields, and all things on the earth shall alter, and not appear in their time. . . . The moon shall alter her order, and not appear at her time." These lines seem to describe the seasonal and lunar drift that would arise without intercalation of the Qumran calendar. The author's explanation is noteworthy: "Many chiefs of the stars shall transgress the order" (80:6). Seasonal drift was not, in his view, the result of an imperfect calendrical system; no, it stemmed from angelic sin. Yet given his presuppositions, this was a logical move. The problem could not be with the calendar, for that had been divinely revealed and was therefore perfect. The *Damascus Document* argues that God revealed to his chosen "things hidden, in which all Israel had gone wrong: His holy Sabbaths, His glorious festivals, His righteous laws, His reliable ways" (text 1, 3:14–15). The revelations about the Sabbaths and festivals involved the solar calendar, which the author of the *Damascus Document* knew most Jews did not follow. He blamed that fact on ignorance. Other scrolls show that followers of the solar calendar found support for their ideas in the creation narratives and, explicitly, in time references in the story of Noah and the Flood (Gen. 6–8; see *Commentaries on Genesis,* text 53).

Beyond the problem of intercalation, another basic area of ignorance hindering complete understanding of the calendars involves the meaning of the recurrent Hebrew term *duq*.* This word, describing one of the phases of the moon, occurs frequently in the *Synchronistic Calendars* (text 72). The system of lunar observation associated with the term clearly underlies other texts as well, even though they don't mention *duq*. Before the discovery of the scrolls, scholars had never encountered this word. (Knowledge of ancient Hebrew is far from perfect; quite a bit of lost vocabulary has been recovered from the scrolls.) Reasoning from etymology, *duq* most likely means "carefully examined." But what is being examined?

Given the context in which *duq* occurs, the options are just two: the first crescent or the full moon. Either understanding implies that the scroll writers once again differed from other Jews. Not only did they support a solar calendar, but they evidently also used an unorthodox lunar calendar. As with the modern Jewish calendar, for most ancient Jews the lunar month began with the first sighting of the moon's crescent. But if *duq* refers to the observation of the first crescent, then the lunar month of the scrolls must have begun with a full moon. If, on the other hand, *duq* refers to observation of the full moon,

*The lack of vowels in Hebrew would also allow for the word to be pronounced *daveq*.

then the lunar month of the scrolls must have begun with a "dark day," i.e., with the (invisible) astronomical new moon, as in modern astronomy. For both options analogs exist.

The medieval writer Albiruni spoke of a Jewish sect called the "cave dwellers" (the *Yahad* or its descendants?). This group followed a lunar calendar in which the month began with a full moon. Albiruni wrote that their practice stood "in opposition to the custom of the majority of the Jews, and to the prescriptions of [the Law]."* Perhaps the lunar practice of the Qumran calendars lived on among the "cave dwellers," and Albiruni is our key to understanding them.

On the other hand, the ancient Egyptians held to a lunar calendar based upon the astronomical new moon. Moreover, so did a Jewish sect, the Samaritans, who were contemporary with the scrolls. For both peoples, the month began with a dark day.

In short, scholars are still debating the options for *duq,* and a reasonable case can be made for either approach. The authors of this book do not themselves agree on what it means but have decided to translate according to the full-moon option. Hence, we will take *duq* to refer to observation of the first crescent.

The calendars of the Dead Sea Scrolls plot time using five different cycles. None of the calendars uses them all, but frequently more than one cycle appears in the same work. These cycles are as follows, beginning with the shortest:

(1) The 364-day year. Some writers further divide the year into four equal quarters of thirteen weeks each (ninety-one days). *Priestly Service as the Seasons Change* (text 77) is an example of such a work. Each quarter comprises three solar months—thirty, thirty, and thirty-one days long, respectively. The year begins in the spring, and New Year's Day—day one of month seven—is always on a Wednesday. The reason is that the writers understood time to begin only with the fourth day of creation week, Wednesday, when God made the sun, moon, and stars. The *Sabbaths and Festivals of the Year* (text 99) is an example of a one-year calendar.

(2) A three-year lunar cycle. Lunar months (as opposed to the solar months above) alternate between twenty-nine and thirty days long (the cycle always beginning with a twenty-nine-day month). After thirty-six lunar months the moon is exactly thirty days behind the solar calendar. Then a thirty-day "leap month" is added to synchronize sun and moon once again. The three-year lunar cycle is the subject of *Calendar of the Heavenly Signs* (text 71).

*C. E. Sachau, ed., *The Chronology of Ancient Nations: An English Version of the Arabic Text of the Athar-ul-Bakiya of Albiruni* (London: Wm. H. Allen, 1879), 278.

(3) A six-year cycle of priestly service in the Temple. Twenty-four priestly divisions, or courses, took turns serving in the Temple. Each division would serve for a week, then rotate out as a new division arrived. Because there were twenty-four divisions for the fifty-two weeks of the solar calendar, each division would serve twice a year, and four divisions would serve a third week. Six years were needed to equalize the courses; that is, only after six years would all have served the same number of weeks. This six-year cycle is very important for the Scroll writers. They name years and other periods of time according to the priestly division in service at the point in question. The names of the priestly divisions are those we know from 1 Chronicles 24:7–18. *Synchronistic Calendars* (text 72) is a good example of a calendar employing the priestly cycle.

(4) A forty-nine-year cycle, called a jubilee. *Calendar of the Heavenly Signs* (text 71) relies heavily upon this cycle; see the introduction to that work for more on jubilees.

(5) A 294-year cycle of six jubilees. This is the cycle that plots a rare occurrence: the service of the first priestly division, named Gamul, on New Year's Day at the beginning of a jubilee period. Two hundred and ninety-four years would pass between occurrences. The scroll writers believed that this situation reprised that of the fourth day of creation. The only text that mentions this cycle is *Calendar of the Heavenly Signs* (text 71).

In the Western world we take the calendar for granted, but this is the first century in history in which all major cultures use the same calendar. Even quite recently, travel across certain borders in Europe entailed a thirteen-day shift in the date. Only in 1923 did Greece embrace the current Gregorian calendar; France, Italy, Spain, Portugal, and Luxembourg had adopted it in 1582. The Russian Orthodox church and several Middle Eastern Christian groups still reckon by the old Julian calendar, now fallen nearly fourteen days behind the Gregorian. These differences are not something we really fight about anymore, but we once did. History is replete with Christian imbroglios over the date of Easter. Essentially these were calendar controversies. Medieval rabbinic Jews likewise fought neighboring Karaite Jews about which of two calendars ought to regulate life. This was the climate in which the Dead Sea Scrolls were written.

Calendar wars can be vicious, and they are irresistibly divisive. How can people compromise on whether today or two days from now is the Day of Atonement? Easter may be this week or two weeks away, but one cannot split the difference and celebrate it next week. So calendars are polarizing documents. When the belief that time is sacred is factored in—well, people have always fought wars to defend their beliefs about God. That is the historical and philosophic context in which to read the Qumran calendar writings. Technicalities aside, these works set forth inherently divisive ideas that must, at times, have set neighbor against neighbor.

The man on the ancient street may not have cared about time or known what year it was, but the Qumran calendar texts shine a light on a different corner of the ancient world. Their priestly authors were perhaps even more obsessed with time than we are.

69. The Phases of the Moon

4Q317

Phases of the Moon is unique among the Dead Sea calendrical writings in that it deals solely with the moon and its phases. The author makes no mention of priestly divisions, festival days, or Sabbaths; rather, with an almost mind-numbing regular cadence, he plots the lunar phases according to the solar calendar, day after day after day. The system that he uses to describe the moon may strike the reader as peculiar. It's really not so much peculiar as theological—certainly "biblical" in the eyes of its adherents. The writer conceives of the lunar month in terms of the moon's being "obscured" or "revealed." When the moon is more and more "obscured," the writer means that the moon is in the process of waning; when it is progressively "revealed," he means that the moon is waxing. Each stage of movement he describes as fractions of fourteen: for example, when the moon is one-fourteenth "revealed," the crescent is just barely visible. This system is, as noted, only very roughly accurate, but it enjoyed a certain popularity in the Second Temple period. The same basic fourteen-stage progression underlies a Qumran liturgical work *Daily Prayers* (text 126) and appears in *Astronomical Enoch* (text 38) and *1 Enoch* 78:7–9.

The largest surviving portion of *Phases,* frag. 1, plots days 4–25 of a certain month. Just which month—and indeed, which year of the six-year cycle—is uncertain and debatable. The answer to these questions depends on how one understands the Hebrew term *duq* (on which, see "A Reader's Guide to the Qumran Calendar Texts" above). According to the understanding that we are following here, the text records the movement of the moon on days 4–25 of month twelve, year one of the cycle.*

Frag. 1 Col. 2 [1][On the fourth of the month, eleve]n parts [are obscured. And thus the moon enters the day.] [2][On the f]ifth of the month,

*If *duq* denotes the full moon, the calendar would indicate days 4–25 of year three, month six. A series of errors, only partially corrected, creates problems for either interpretation.

[tw]elve [parts are obscured.] [3]And thus [the moon enters the day. On the sixth of the month,] [4]thir[teen] parts are obscured. [And thus the moon enters the day.] [5]On the seventh of the month, [fourteen parts] are obscur[ed. And thus] [6]the moon enters the day. [. . .]

[7]On the eighth of the month, the moon [rules all the day in the midst] [8]of the sky [, fourteen and one-half (?) parts being obscured. And when the sun sets,] its light [ceases] [9]to be obscured, [and thus the moon begins to be revealed] [10]on the first day of the week.

[On the ninth of the month,] [11]on[e] part [is revealed. And thus the moon enters the night.]

[12]On the tenth of the month, [two parts] are r[evealed. And thus the moon enters] [13]the night.

On the ele[venth of the month, three parts are revealed.] [14]And thus the moon enters the night. [. . .]

[15]On the twelfth of the month, [four parts] are reve[aled. And thus] [16]the moon enters the night.

On the t[hirteenth of the month,] [17]five parts are revealed. And thus the moon enter[s the night.]

[18]On the {thirteenth} <fourteenth> of the month, [six parts] are reveal[ed. And thus the moon enters the night.]

[19][On the fi]fteenth [of the month, seven parts are revealed. And thus the moon enters] [20]the night.

On the s[ixteenth of the month,] eight [parts are revealed.] [21]And thus [the moon enters the night.]

[22][On the s]ev[en]teenth [of the month, nine parts are revealed. And thus the moon enters the night.] [23][On the eighteenth of the month, ten parts are revealed. And thus the moon enters the night.] [24]On the {eighteenth} <ni[n]ete[enth> of the month, eleven parts are revealed. And thus the moon enters the night.] [25]On the {nineteenth} <twentieth> [of the month, twelve parts are revealed. And thus the moon enters the night.] [26]On the {twentieth} <twenty-first> of the month, [thirteen parts are revealed. And thus the moon enters the night.] [27]On the {twenty-first} <twenty-second> [of the month, the moon rules all the night in the midst of the sky,] [28]fourt[een and one-half (?) parts being revealed.] And when [the sun] sets, [its light ceases to be revealed,] [29]and thus the moon begins to be [obscured on the first day of the week (the twenty-second of the month).]

[30]On the {twe[nty-seco]nd} <tw[enty]-third> [of the month, one part is obscured. And thus] [31]the moon [en]ters the day. [. . .]

[32]On the {twenty-third} <twenty-fourth> [of the month, two parts are obscured. And thus the moon enters the day.] [33]On the twenty-fifth [of the month, three parts are obscured. And thus the moon enters the day.]

—M.G.A.

70. A Divination Text (Brontologion)

4Q318

The scroll 4Q318, of which two large fragments remain, is an example of ancient Jewish astrological lore, like *A Horoscope in Code* (text 35) and *An Aramaic Horoscope* (text 147). But instead of predicting human behavior through analysis of physical traits as those texts do, this writing belongs to the ancient genre of *brontologia* (from Greek *brontos,* "thunder," and *logion,* "discourse"), which relied upon thunder to foretell the future. The ancient Mesopotamians had much earlier exploited thunder for this purpose. One such early example reads, "When Rammanu thunders in the great gate of the Moon, there will be a slaying of Elamite troops with the sword; the goods of the land will be gathered into another land."*

The technique was refined to a greater degree of complexity in the Greco-Roman period, particularly in Alexandria, Egypt. In connecting thunder to both the moon and the zodiac, the present work manifests one such refinement. According to the system of our text, the occurrence of thunder when the moon was in a particular sign of the zodiac portended definite events.

The Qumran brontologion consists of two parts. The first is a list of the days of the Jewish months according to the lunar position in the zodiac. 4Q318 is almost alone among the Qumran calendrical scrolls in giving the names, rather than the numbers, of the Jewish months. Moreover, this writing contains the earliest list of zodiacal signs ever discovered in Aramaic. By and large, they are the names familiar to use from modern astrology and newspaper columns; thus we begin to see astrological doctrines take on recognizably modern dress. In earlier Mesopotamian form, the number and names of the signs had been different. The signs are the Ram (Aries), the Ox (Taurus), the Twins (Gemini), the Crab (Cancer), the Lion (Leo), the Virgin (Virgo), the Scales (Libra), the Scorpion (Scorpio), the Archer (Sagittarius), the Kid (Capricorn), the Drawer (Aquarius), and the Fish (Pisces).

The text introduces one particularly crucial innovation into the genre: the Jewish seven-day week, in which the zodiac is structured by a pattern of two, two, and three days. In this way the moon could "rest" on the Sabbath (the extra day in the pattern).

*In R. Campbell Thompson, *The Reports of the Magicians and Astrologers of Nineveh and Babylon* 2 vols. (London: Luzac, 1900), 2:lxxx (no. 256a).

The first part of the text gives the days of the month in which the moon was to be found in a given sign of the zodiac. Originally, the text gave this information for all the days of a 364-day year.

Col. 4 [5][. . .] 13th and 1[4th,] [6][. . . on the 1]9th and on the 20th and on the 2[1st] [7][. . . on the] 27th and on the 28th [8][. . .] [9][. . . on the 7th], the Kid; on the 8th [. . .]

Cols. 5–6 are lost.

Col. 7 [1]and on the 13th and on the 14th, the Crab; on the 15th and on the 16th, the Lion; on the 17th and on the 18th, [2]the Virgin; on the 19th and on the 20th and on the 21st, the Scales; on the 2[2nd and the 2]3rd, the Scorpion; on the 24th [3]and on the 25th, the Ar[cher]; on the 26th and on the 27th and on the 28th, the [Kid]; on the [2]9th [4]and on the 30th, [the] Drawer.

Shebat. On the 1st and on the 2nd, the [Fishes]; on the [3rd and on the] 4th, [5][the Ram; on the] 5th and on the [6th and on the] 7th, the Ox; on the 8[th and on the 9th, the Twins]; on the 10th [6][and on the 11th], the Crab; on the 12th [and on the] 13th and on the 14th, the Lion; [on the 15th and on the 16th, the Virgin;] [7]on the 17th and on the 18th, the Scales; on the 19th and on the [20th and on the 21st, the S]corpion; on the 22nd [8]and the 23rd the Archer; on the 24th and on the 25th, the Kid; on the 2[6th and on the] 27th and on the 28th, [9]the Drawer; on the 29th and on the 30th, the Fishes.

Col. 8 [1]Adar. On the 1st and on the 2nd, the Ram; on the 3rd and on the 4th, the Ox; on the [5th and on the 6th and on the 7th, the Twins;] [2]on the 8th and on the 9th, the Crab; [on the 10th and on the 11th, the [L]ion; on the 12th and on the [13th and on the 14th,] [3]the Vir[gin]; on the 15th and on the [16th, the Scales; on the 1]7th, on the 1[8th, the Scorpion;] [4]on the [1]9th and on the 20th, 21st, the Ar[cher; on the 22nd] and on the 2[3rd], the [K]id; [on the 24th and on the 25th,] [5]the Drawer; on the 26th and on the 2[7th and on the 28th, the] Fi[shes]; on the 2[9th and on the 30th,] [6]the Ram.

The second part of the scroll is a list of the omens that the thunder portends. Unfortunately little of this section remains. The reference to "Arabs" is probably to the kingdom of the Nabateans, directly east of Palestine across the Jordan River.

[If] it thunders [in the Ox], a siege against [the city . . .] [7][and] trouble for the nation and violence [in the co]urt of the king, and among the nations in [. . .] [8]there shall be; and as for the Arabs, [. . .] famine, and they

will plunder each oth[er . . .] [9]If it thunders in the Twins, panic and sickness due to foreigners and [. . .]
—E.M.C.

71. Calendar of the Heavenly Signs

4Q319

Today the contents of this text would be presented as a table in an almanac. In ancient Judea, however, tables of that sort did not yet exist. So our author presents his ideas in prose form, and they do not make for easy reading. (Those who are mathematically challenged, be advised: proceed at your own risk!)

Essentially, the writer wants to track the relationships between three elements: jubilee periods, the phenomenon he calls in Hebrew *'ot,* and sabbatical years. In order to calculate these relationships, he employs a sort of algorithm that he never explains. He expected his specialized audience to be familiar with it already. This algorithm is the correspondence between the solar and lunar calendars (see text 72). So, to follow this text, we must bear in mind a total of five items: the three elements that the author wants to track and the two components that function in the algorithm.

The first element is the jubilee period. In a modern table, the jubilees would be in the first column. Although the Bible defines the jubilee as the fiftieth year (Lev. 25:11), the Qumran calendar uses the term to bracket a forty-nine-year period. Counting inclusively, the fiftieth year is then the last year of one jubilee and the first year of the next. The calendar before us tabulates by forty-nine-year periods. The work covers six such jubilees.

The "second column's" element, *'ot,* refers to the fairly uncommon appearance of the full moon* on the first day of the solar year. More generally, *'ot* means "sign," so our author took this conjunction as a sort of sign from God. He believed that this conjunction had first occurred on the fourth day of creation week. That day was significant because on it the sun and the moon were created, and time reckoning depended on their movement. (Thus, the first three days of creation were, in a sense, "outside time"—long before modern physics, black holes, and such.) The biblical passage that provided the mandate for an interest

*Or possibly the conjunction of the astronomical new moon and the first day of the solar year. This and other issues regarding the calendrical texts are discussed in "A Reader's Guide to the Qumran Calendar Texts" above.

in the conjunction was Genesis 1:14: "God said, 'Let there be lights in the expanse of the heavens to distinguish the day from the night, and let them be for *signs* and for seasons and years.' " The author designates each new conjunction with a name. In every case the name is that of the priestly division that would be in service at the time. Because of the peculiarities of the rotation of priests, the names of the conjunctions are always the same, alternating between the priestly families of Gamul and Shecaniah.

According to our author's understanding, the *'ot* recurred every three years. To figure out this fact he needed to know solar and lunar correspondences. So we must understand his algorithm, the motor that made his conceptual machine run. The equation for the solar calendar covering three years is: 364-day solar year × 3 years = 1092 days. This solar period then had to be correlated with lunar movement. In the Qumran calendar, the lunar month alternates between twenty-nine and thirty days, beginning with twenty-nine. Accordingly, twelve lunar months equal 354 days; each year the lunar calendar falls ten days behind the solar calendar. At the end of three lunar years, with the two calendars now thirty days out of kilter, the difference is made good. An additional thirty-day month is added. (What would have been expected, according to the pattern of alternation described above, is a twenty-nine-day month. But thirty days are added, in order to force the desired conjunction on New Year's Day of year four.) In sum, the equation for the lunar calendar is: 354-day lunar year × 3 years = 1062 days + 30-day month = 1092 days.

The author thus calculates the number of conjunctions using this method. He goes on to tabulate the conjunctions that fall on sabbatical years, the third element he is tracking. That would be the third column of a modern table. As their name implies, on analogy with the weekly Sabbath, sabbatical years occurred once every seven years. Among other things, biblical laws required that in the sabbatical year the land must lie fallow. A good deal of planning was therefore necessary to avoid starvation in these years.

Since 4Q319 covers a period of six jubilees, it reveals the longest cycle of the Qumran calendars, 294 years (6 × 49). In year 295 the cycle returns to the beginning. A mystery of the cycle is that the author reckons the year of creation as the beginning of the second jubilee, not the first. That is, the jubilees are counted as two through seven, not one through six. We still do not understand the reason. Perhaps it is simply that a completed 294-year cycle thus coincides with the end of the *seventh* jubilee. The number seven was regarded as a holy number.

A Cave 4 copy (4Q259) of the Charter of a Jewish Sectarian Association *(text 7) preceded the* Calendar of the Heavenly Signs. *In essence, this calendar replaces the hymn concerning times of prayer found in cols. 10–11 of the* Charter.

The lunar-solar conjunctions of the second jubilee.

Frag. 1 Col. 4 [9][. . .] blessed [. . .] [10][. . .] its light on the fourth day of the wee[k . . .] [11][. . . the] creation on the fourth day of (the priestly course of) G[amul; the conjunction of Shecaniah in the fourth year; the conjunction of Gamul in the Sabbath year;] [12][the conjunction of Shecaniah in the thi]rd year; the c[onjunction of Gamu]l in the sixth year; the conjunction of [Shecaniah in the second year; the conjunction of Gamul] [13][in the fifth year; the conjunct]ion of Shecaniah in the year after the Sabbath year (first year); the conjunction of Gamu[l in the fourth year; the conjunction of Shecaniah] [14][in the Sabbath year; the conjunct]ion of Gamul in the third year; the conjunction of Shecaniah [in the sixth year; the conjunction of Gamul] [15][in the second year; the conjunct]ion of Sh[ecaniah] in the [fi]fth year; the conjunction of Gamu[l in the year after the Sabba]th year (first year); the conjunction of [16][Shecaniah in the fo]urth year; the conjunction of Gamul in the Sabbath year; the conjunction of the e[nd of the jubilee. The conjunctions of the second j]ubilee [17]are seventeen, of which [three] are in sabbatical years. [. . .] the creation [18][. . .]

The lunar-solar conjunctions of the third jubilee.

(The conjunction of) Sheca[ni]ah in the third year; the conjunction of Gamu[l in the sixth year; the con]junction of Shecaniah [19][in the second year; the conjunction of G]amul in the fifth year; the conjunction of Shecaniah in the year after the Sa[bbath year (first year); the conjunction of Ga]mul **Col. 5** [1][in the fourth year; the conjunction of Shecaniah in the Sabbath year; the conjunction of Gamul in the third year; the conjunction of Shecaniah] [2][in the sixth year; the conjunction of Gamul in the secon]d year; the con[junction of Shecaniah in the fi]fth year; [the conjunction of Gamul] [3][in the year after the Sabba]th year (first year); the conjunction of Shecaniah in the fo[urth year; the conjunction of] Gam[ul in the Sabbath year; the conjunction] [4][of Shecaniah in the thi]rd year; the conjunction of Gamul in the si[xth year; the conjunction of] Shecania[h is the end of] [5]the thi[r]d jubilee. The conjunctions of [the third] jubilee are [seven]teen, of which [6]two are in sabbatical years.

The lunar-solar conjunctions of the fourth jubilee.

(The conjunction of) Shecaniah [in the second year; the conjunction of Gamu]l in the fifth year; the conjunction of Shecaniah [7]in the year after the Sabbath year (first year); the conjunct[ion of Gamul in the fourth year; the conjunction] of Shecaniah in the Sabbath year; the conjunction of [8][Ga]mul in the third year; the conjunction of [Shecaniah in the sixth year; the conjunction of Ga]mul in the second year; the conjunction of [9]Shecaniah in the fifth year; the conjunction of [Gamul in the year after] the Sabbath year (first year); the conjunction of Shecaniah [10]in the fourth year; the conjunction of Gamul [in the Sabbath year; the conjunction] of Shecaniah in the third year; the conjunction of Gamul [11]in the sixth year; the conjunction of Sheca[niah in the second year; the conjunction of] Gamul in the fifth year; the conjunction of Shecaniah [12]in the year after the Sabbath year (first year); this con[junction is the end of the fourth jubilee. The conjunctions of the fou]rth jubilee are seventeen, [13]of which two are in sabbatical years.

The lunar-solar conjunctions of the fifth jubilee.

(The conjunction of) G[amul] in the fourth year; the conjunction of Shecaniah [14][in the Sa]bbath year; the conjunction of Gamul in the [third year; the conjunction of Shecaniah in the sixth year; the conjunction of Gamul] [15]in the second year; the conjunction of Shecaniah in the fi[fth year; the conjunction of Gamul in the year after the Sabbath year (first year); the conjunction of Shecaniah] [16]in the fourth year; the conjunction of [Ga]mul in the [Sabbath year; the conjunction of Shecaniah in the third year; the conjunction of Gamul] [17]in the six[th year; the con]junction of She[caniah in the second year; the conjunction of Gamul in the fifth year; the conjunction of Shecaniah] [18][in the year after the] Sabbath year (first year); the conjunction of G[amul in the fourth year; the conjunction of Shecaniah in the Sabbath year; the conjunction of the end of] [19][the fif]th [jubilee is] in Jeshebeab. [The conjunctions of the fifth jubilee are sixteen, of which] **Col. 6** [1][three are in sabbatical years.]

The lunar-solar conjunctions of the sixth jubilee.

[The conjunction of Gamul in the third year; the conjunction of Shecaniah in the sixth year; the conjunction] [2][of Gamul in the] second year; the con[junction of] Shecaniah in the [fifth year; the conju]nction of Gam[ul in the year after the Sab]bath year (first year); [3][the conjunct]ion of Shecaniah in the fourth year; the conjunction of Gamul in the [Sab]bath year; [the conjunction of Shecaniah] in the third year; [4]the conjunction of Gamul in the sixth year; the conjunction of Shecaniah [in the second year; the conjunction of] Gamul [5]in the f[if]th year; the conjunction of Shecaniah in the year after [the] S[abbath year (first year);] the conjunction of [6]Gamul in the fo[u]rth year; the conjunction of Shecaniah in the Sab[bath year; the conjunction of Gamul in the] third year; [7]the conjunction of [Shecaniah in the si]xth year; the conjunction of the end of [the sixth jubilee. The conjunctions of] [8][the sixth] jubilee are [six]teen, of which two are in [sabbatical years.] [9]the fi[fth . . .]in the Jubi[lee . . .] [10]and for the jubi[lee.]

The lunar-solar conjunctions of the seventh jubilee.

[(The conjunction of Gamul) in the second year; the conjunction of Shecaniah in the fifth year; the conjunction of Gamul in the year after] [11]the Sabba[th] year (first year); [the conjunction of Shecaniah in the four]th year; the conjunction of Gam[ul in the] Sabba[th year;] [12][the conjunction of Shecaniah in the third year; the conjunction of] Gamul in the sixth year; the conjunct[ion of Shecaniah] [13][in the] second year; the con[junction of Gamul] in the fifth year; the conjunction of Shecaniah in the year [after] [14]the Sabbath year (first year); [the conjunction of Ga]mul in the fourth year; the conjunction of Shecaniah in the Sa[bbath year; the conjunction of] [15]Gamul [in the thir]d year; the conjunction of <Shecaniah> (MS.: year) in the sixth year; the <conjunction> (MS.: end) of [Gamul] [16]in the se[cond year; the conjunction of Shecaniah] in the fifth year; the conjunction of the end of the jubilee.

[17][The conjunctions of the] seventh [jubilee] are sixteen, of which [18][two are] in sa[bbati]cal years. [. . .] sign of the j[u]bilees, the [ye]ar of the jubilees, according to the da[ys holiness.] [19][In Gamul the first, in Jedaiah the] secon[d,] in Mijamin the third, [in Shecaniah . . .]

Col. 7 of the Calendar of the Heavenly Signs *continued with a roster of the courses serving at the beginning of each of the four yearly quarters. A similar table is also found in* Priestly Service as the Seasons Change *(text 77).*

—M.G.A.

72. Synchronistic Calendars

4Q320–4Q321a

The three Dead Sea Scrolls manuscripts grouped together here have one purpose in common: to synchronize the 354-day lunar calendar with the 364-day solar calendar.* In addition, two of these writings, 4Q320 and 4Q321,

*For a fuller discussion see "A Reader's Guide to the Qumran Calendar Texts," above. As discussed more fully there, the following translations follow the assumption that at the creation, the moon was full, and that the word *duq,* which occurs frequently in 4Q321–321a, means the first crescent.

record the beginnings of the solar months and the festivals. The third, 4Q321a, may have done so as well, but the relevant portion of the text has perished. All of these texts designate dates by the name of the priestly rotation in service at the time in question. Twenty-four courses of priests served altogether, rotating into service for a week at a time. The names of the courses follow the biblical list of 1 Chronicles 24:7–18.

4Q320 Mishmerot A

Frag. 1, cols. 1–2, and frag. 2 tabulate the dates of the full moon through three years of the calendar. Although the dates of this phenomenon would begin to recycle at this point (year four being the same as year one), the priestly divisions do not begin to repeat until year seven. Therefore it must be assumed that three additional columns of this fragment have been lost.

Frags. 3 and 4 record the priestly divisions serving in the sanctuary at the beginning of each of the solar months, followed by a table of the festivals. These calendars record a complete six-year cycle. Note that 4Q321 below records these two tables together.

Calendar of full moons for the first year. The "courses" were the priestly families who rotated into service in the Temple at Jerusalem.

Frag. 1 Col. 1 [1][. . .] to show itself from the east [2][and] to shine forth [in] the center of the sky at the base of [3][the . . .], from evening to morning on the fourth day of the week [4][of G]amul, in the first month of the [5][firs]t year.

[6][On the fifth day of Jeda]iah is the twenty-ninth day (of the lunar month), on the thirtieth day of the (first solar) month. [7][On the Sabbath of Ha]kkoz is the thirtieth day (of the lunar month), on the thirtieth day of the second (solar month). [8][On the first day of Elia]shib is the twenty-ninth day (of the lunar month), on the twenty-ninth day of the third (solar month). [9][On the third day of Bilga]h is the thirtieth day (of the lunar month), on the twenty-eighth day of the fourth (solar month). [10][On the fourth day of Petha]hiah is the twenty-ninth day (of the lunar month), on the twenty-seventh day of the fifth (solar month). [11][On the sixth day of Delaiah] is the thirtieth day (of the lunar month), on the twenty-seventh day of the sixth (solar month). [12][On the Sabbath of Seori]m is the twenty-ninth day (of the lunar month), on the twenty-fifth day of the seventh (solar month). [13][On the second day of Abijah is the thirtieth day (of the lunar month),] on the twenty-fifth day of the eighth

(solar month). 14[On the third day of Jakim is the] twenty-[ninth day (of the lunar month,)] on the twenty-fourth day of the ninth (solar month). **Col. 2** 1On the fifth day of Immer is the thirtieth day (of the lunar month), on the twenty-third day of the tenth (solar month). 2On the sixth day of Jehezkel is the twenty-ninth day (of the lunar month), on the twenty-second day of the eleventh (solar month). 3On the first day of Jehoiarib is the thirtieth day (of the lunar month), on the twenty-second day of the twelfth (solar month).

The remainder of col. 2 and frag. 2 record the calendar of full moons for the second and third years.

Introduction to the calendar of the solar months.

Frag. 3 Col. 1 9[. . .] the second [day.] The holy 10[. . . the] creation. Holy 11[. . . on] the fourth day of, 12[Gamu]l, at the beginning of all the years 13[. . . conjunctio]ns of the second jubilee 14[. . . seventeen conjunction]s . . .

A list of the solar months of the first year.

Col. 2 8[. . .] 9with the sacrifice[s . . .] 10days [. . .] 11holy. [The first month has thirty days and begins in Gamul.] 12The second month has thirty days [and begins in Jedaiah.] 13The third month has thirty [one days and begins in Hakkoz.] 14The fourth month has thirty days [and begins in Eliashib.]

Solar months of the fifth year.

Frag. 4 Col. 1 11[The ninth month has thirty-one days] and begins in Jehoiari[b.] 12[The tenth month has thirty days] and begins in Malchijah. 13[The eleventh month has thirty days] and begins in [J]eshua. 14[The twelfth month has thirty-one days] and begins in Jeshebeab.

Conclusion of the calendar of solar months and introduction to the calendar of festivals.

Col. 2 10the days, and for the Sabbaths; 11for the months, 12[for] the years, for sabbatical years, 13and for jubilees. On the fourth day 14of the week of the sons of Gamul [. . .]

Festivals of the first year.

Col. 3 [1]The festivals of the first year: [2]On the third day of the week of the sons of Maaziah is the Passover. [3]On the first day [of] Jeda[iah] is the Waving of the [Omer.] [4]On the fifth day of Seorim is the [Second] Passover. [5]On the first day of Jeshua is the Feast of Weeks. [6]On the fourth day of Maaziah is the Day of Remembrance. [7][On the] sixth day of Jehoiarib is the Day of Atonement, [8][On the tenth day of the] seventh (month), [9][on the fourth day of Jeda]iah is the Feast of Booths.

The festivals of the second through sixth years are detailed in the remainder of cols. 3–6.

4Q321–321a Mishmerot B and C

These two manuscripts record the same calendar. The original work appears to have tabulated a complete six-year cycle of full and first crescent moons, followed by a calendar that listed the first day of each solar month and each festival.

Lunar calendar for the first year (months two through five).

4Q321a Frag. 1 Col. 1 [1][. . .] [2][The first year: (the full moon is) on the fourth day of Gamul, on the first day of the first month. On the fifth day] [3][of Jedaiah, on the thirtieth day of the month, is the second (full moon), and the first crescent is on the sixth day of Maaziah, on the seventeenth of the month.] [4][(The full moon is on the) Sabbath of Koz, on the thirtieth day of the second month, and the first crescent is on the first day of Malchijah, on the seventeenth] of the month. [5][(The full moon is) on the first day of Eliashib, on the twenty-ninth day of the third month, and the first crescent] is on the second day of Jeshua, on the [sixteenth] [6][of the month. (The full moon is) on the third day of Bilgah, on the] twenty-[eig]hth day of the fourth month, [7][and the first crescent is on the fourth day of Huppah, on the fifteenth of the month.]

[8][(The full moon is) on the fourth day of Pethahiah, on the twenty-seventh day of the fifth month, and the first crescent is on the fifth day of Hezi]r, [9][on the fourteenth of the month.]

Lunar calendar for the first year (months seven through twelve).

4Q321 Col. 1 [1][. . . and the first crescent is on the first day of Jedaiah on the twe]lfth of the (seventh) month. (The full moon is) on the second day of Abija[h, on the] twe[nty-fifth day of the eighth month, and the first crescent is on the third day] [2][of Mijamin, on the twelfth] of the month. (The full moon is) on the third day of Jakim, on the [twenty-]fou[rth day of the ninth month, and the first crescent is on the fourth day] [3][of Shecaniah, on the elev]enth of the month. (The full moon is) on the fifth day of Immer, on the tw[en]ty-third day of the ten[th month, and the first crescent is on the sixth day of Je]shebeab, [4][on the tenth of the mo]nth. (The full moon is) on the [si]xth day of Jehezkel, on the twenty-second day of the eleventh month, and [the first crescent is on the Sabbath of] Pethahiah, [5][on the ninth of the month.] (The full moon is) on the first day of Jehoiarib, on the twenty-second day of the twelfth month, and [the first crescent is on the secon]d day of Delaiah, [6][on the ninth of the month.]

The continuation of cols. 1.6–4.7 tabulates the second through the sixth year of the lunar calendar.

Solar months and festivals of the first year.

4Q321 Col. 4 [8][The fi]rst [year:] the [firs]t mon[th] begins in G[amul. On the thi]rd day of Maa[ziah] is [the Passover.] [9][The Waving of the Omer is in Jedaiah. The second month begins in Jedaiah. The Second Passover is in] Seorim. [The third month begins in Koz.] **Col. 5** [1]The Feast of Week[s] is in Jeshua. [The fo]u[rth month begins in E]liashib. The fifth month begins in [Bilgah. The sixth month begins in Jehe]zkel. The sev[enth month begins in Maaziah.] [2]The Day of Remembrance is in Maaziah. The Day of Atonement is in Jehoiarib. [The Feast of] Booths is in Jedaiah. The eighth month begins [in Seorim.] [3]The ninth month begins in Jeshua. The tenth month begins in Huppah. The eleventh month begins in Hezir. The twelfth month begins in Gamul.

The continuation of cols. 2–4 records years two through six of the solar months and festivals.

—M.G.A.

73. Priestly Service: Sabbath Entrance

4Q322–324a

These fragments were originally thought to be part of an annalistic calendar that plotted historical events on the 364-day calendar in conjunction with the priestly rotation. That type of writing is evident in *Fragmentary Historical Writings* (text 74). If the present organization is correct, these four manuscripts are concerned solely with plotting the date of the entrance of the twenty-four priestly courses as they began their week of Temple service on the Sabbath.

This text pertains to the eighth and the beginning of the ninth months of year two in the six-year cycle of the courses. The reference in l. 2a to some important event or remembrance on the second day of Jakim's service is obscure. Indeed, the scribe wrote this note above the line, and it is unclear how to integrate it into the remaining text.

4Q322 [1][. . . of the eigh]th; on the nint[h of the eighth month is the entrance] [2][of the course of Shecaniah.] On [. . . in] the course of Shecaniah, which is [2a]on the second day in the course of Jakim (?) [3][On the twenty-thi]rd of the month is the entrance of the course of Jakim, and on the fo[urth day of Jakim . . .] [3a][. . .] second [da]y of the course of Huppah, which is [the second day of the ninth month . . .]

This text presents portions concerning the tenth and eleventh months of year two in the cycle of courses.

4Q323 [1][. . . the fou]rth [day] of Hez[i]r is the [fi]rst day of the t[enth month . . .] [2][on the fourth of the month is the entrance of the course of Pi]zzez. On the ele[v]enth of the month is [the entrance of the priestly course of Pethahiah.] [3][On the eighteenth of the month is the entran]ce of the course of Jehezkel. On the twent[y-fifth of the month is the entrance] [4][of the course of Jachin . . .] [5][. . . On the second of the eleventh month] is the entrance of [the course of Gamul . . .]

The cycle of priestly courses in the fifth through seventh months of the fifth year. The reference to covenants in ll. 3 and 7 remains unexplained.

4Q324 Frag. 1 [1][the entrance of Shecaniah. On the twenty-third of the fifth month is the entrance of the course of Eliashib. On the thirtieth of the fifth month] [2][is the entrance of the course of Jakim. The first day of Jakim is the fir]st day of the si[xth month. On the seventh of the sixth month is the entrance of the course of Huppah.] [3][. . . On the four]teenth of the fifth month is [the entrance of the course of Jeshebeab:] a covenant (?). On the tw[enty-] [4][first of the fifth month is the entrance of the course of Bilga]h. On the twenty-[eighth of the fifth mo]nth is the entrance of the course of Imm[er.] [5][The fourth day of the course of Immer is the fi]rst day of the seventh month. On the fo[u]rth of the seventh month is the entrance of the course of H[ezir.] [6][The sixth day of] the course of Hezir, which is the tenth day of the seventh month, is the Day [7][of Atonement, it is] as a covenant (?). On the eleventh of the seventh month is the entrance of [the course of Pizzez . . .]

The cycle from the middle of the ninth to the middle of the tenth month of the fifth year.

4Q324a Frag. 1 Col. 2 [1]day [. . .] On the fou[rteenth of the ninth month is the entrance of the course of Ha]r[im. On the] twe[nty-first day] [2][of the mon]th is the entrance of the course of S[eor]im. On the twenty-eighth of the month is the entrance of the course of Malchi[jah.] [3]The fourth day [of] Malchijah is the first day of the tenth month.

[4]On the fourth day of the tenth month is the entrance of the course of Mija[m]in. On the eleventh of the month is the entrance of the course of K[oz.]

—M.O.W.

74. Fragmentary Historical Writings

4Q322a, 4Q331–333, 4Q468e, 4Q578

Among the Qumran texts very few are what we moderns would consider to be historical writings. Even those that mention historical events generally do so while interpreting Scripture or in the context of an apocalyptic vision. This predilection among the scrolls seems to reflect Jewish sensibilities of the time more generally, for with few exceptions (1 Maccabees, Josephus) the Jews of these years did not compose history in the manner fashionable in the broader Greco-Roman world. The writings gathered here may represent the exceptions that help prove that rule, for these works do seem to be historical writings in the proper sense. Of course, given their fragmentary character, such a judgment must be ventured very cautiously.

Arguably all of the persons mentioned fit into the period 135–30 B.C.E., a time of tremendous upheaval in Jewish society. Several of the most clearly identifiable persons can be dated even more narrowly to the years 76–50 B.C.E. First, Alexandra (called in these texts Shelamzion, her Hebrew name) came to the throne and gave the Pharisees carte blanche in the nation's affairs, thereby sounding the starter's gun for a persecution of the ruling coalition that had functioned under her husband and predecessor, the anti-Pharisaic Alexander Jannaeus. Then when Alexandra died in 67 B.C.E., her son Hyrcanus II, who figures at several points below, took the throne. He soon abdicated his rights to his brother, Aristobulus II, another figure in this collection. Under the goading of several self-serving advisers—including the Idumean Antipater, father of Herod the Great—Hyrcanus had second thoughts and tried to take power back from Aristobulus. The result was that from 67 to 63 B.C.E., the nation was wracked by civil war. In the latter stages of that conflict, the Roman Pompey decided to inject himself into the situation and seek Rome's advantage. The Romans ultimately sided with Hyrcanus, and events climaxed with the siege of Aristobulus's priestly supporters in the Temple at Jerusalem in 63 B.C.E. After several months, the Romans broke through; they surged into the Temple environs and put to the sword everyone they encountered. Josephus reports that a total of twelve thousand Jews lost their lives, many of them priests. Along with the king himself, large numbers of Aristobulus's supporters who survived the massacre ended up being taken to Rome as prisoners and slaves. In all of these Roman actions, a leading general of Pompey's, M. Aemilius Scaurus, played a decisive role. He too is named in the writings below, where he seems to be credited with the Temple massacre.

After the Roman triumph, Palestine for some thirty years remained a simmering caldron of tensions. Conflict between the parties of Hyrcanus and Aristobulus continued into the next generation, occasionally erupting into violence and only settling down when the Romans enabled Herod the Great to take the throne as a client (read, "puppet") king in 37 B.C.E.

The texts here are arranged in approximate chronological order.

Between 305 and 30 B.C.E., no fewer than fourteen men who bore the name Ptolemy ruled Egypt. Many had some doings with the Jews of Palestine, so it is impossible to determine with certainty which figures find mention in the present fragmentary scroll. Paleographical analysis has suggested to one scholar that the text was copied about 125 B.C.E. This suggestion would limit the number of possible men to seven or eight, but precise dating by the method is hardly reliable even when one has a substantial sample of the scribe's handwriting. Here we have almost nothing. We must be content with the conclusion that the text describes events that probably occurred in the first or second centuries B.C.E.

4Q578 [2][. . .] Ptolemy [. . .] [3][. . . Ptole]my his son [. . .] [4][. . .] Ptole[my . . .]

An undated event involving one Yohanan. The reference is probably to John Hyrcanus I, 134–104 B.C.E., *but it is also possible that the author had in mind John Hyrcanus II, with whom Aristobulus fought for the kingdom in the civil war of 67–63* B.C.E. *The reason to favor the first option is that Hyrcanus II is elsewhere referenced by the name "Hyrcanus," not "Yohanan" (4Q332 frag. 2).*

4Q331 Frag. 1 Col. 1 [6][. . . the high] priest, [7][. . .] Yohanan, to bring to [. . .]

An undated event involving Shelamzion (Salome Alexandra, 76–67 B.C.E.*).*

Col. 2 [5]a man [. . .] [6]the [. . .] [7]Shelamzion [. . .]

An undated event possibly involving an act against Aristobulus II (67–63 B.C.E.*).*

4Q322a Frag. 1 [5][. . .] men [of . . .] [6][. . .] and against Ar[istobulus . . .] [7][. . .] they said [. . .] [8][. . .] seventy [. . .] [9]that he [. . .]

Opaque references to an unknown person and to the eighth month, Marheshvan, the latter perhaps an element in a dating formula.

Frag. 2 [1][. . .] subdued [. . .] [4][. . .] a man [. . .] [5][. . .] from Ma[rhe]shvan [. . .] [6][. . .] eighty [. . .]

Frag. 1 lists a number of historical events impossible to identify specifically, but they involve military conflict generating prisoners, and some of the forces are apparently Roman.

4Q332 Frag. 1 [1][. . .] on the tent[h of the sixth month . . .] [2][on the fourteenth of the month is the entran]ce of the course of Jedaiah, on the sixteen[th of the month . . .] [3][on the twenty-]seventh of the [seventh] month [. . .] [4][. . .] he settled [. . .] [5][. . . Gen]tiles (*or* Kit]tim) and also [. . .] [6][. . .] those who are [bi]tter of spirit [. . .] [7][. . .] prisoners [. . .]

Line 1 records an undated event connected with gaining honor among the Nabateans. This may be a reference to Hyrcanus II and his flight to seek asylum in that kingdom early in the civil war. Line 2 makes some reference to the eleventh month of the Jewish calendar, Shevat. Line 4 records an undated event involving Shelamzion. Line 6 records a rebellion involving Hyrcanus, perhaps referring to the outbreak of the civil war. The statement that "Hyrcanus rebelled" implies the author's sympathy with Aristobulus, since no partisan of Hyrcanus would describe his attempt to regain his birthright and return to power as rebellion.

Frag. 2 [1][. . . to] give him honor among the Nabate[ans . . .] [2][. . . on the n]inth [day] of Shevat, this is [. . .] [3][. . .] that is the twentieth of the month [. . .] [4][. . .] Shelamzion secretly came [. . .] [5][. . .] to confront the [. . .] [6][. . .] Hyrcanus rebelled [against Aristobolus . . .] [7][. . .] to confront [. . .]

An undated murder or massacre.

Frag. 3 [2][. . . the leader of the Gen]tiles (*or* Kit]tim) murdered [. . .] [3][. . .] on the fifth [day] of the course of Jedaiah, this is [. . .]

This fragment describes certain slayings by M. Aemilius Scaurus, one of the leading Roman generals involved in the Roman capture of Jerusalem in 63 B.C.E.

4Q333 Frag. 1 [1][. . . On the] twenty [2][-first day of the month is the entrance of the course of Pethahiah. On the twenty-eig]hth day [3][of the month is the entrance of the course of Jehezkel. On the first (*or* second, *or* third) day of Je]hezkel, which is [4][the twenty-ninth (*or* thirtieth, *or* thirty-first) day of the sixth month,] Aemilius killed [5][. . . The fourth day of Jehezkel is the first of the] seventh [mont]h. [6][On the fourth of the month is the entrance of the course of Jachin. On the eleventh of the month is the en]tr[ance of] the course of Gamul. [7][. . . The fourth day of Gamul, which] is [8][the fifteenth day of the seventh month, is the Feast of Booths. On this day] Aemilius killed [. . .]

Frag. 2 [1][. . .] a Judean man [. . .]

This fragment seems to describe a massacre or battle involving Peitholaus, a Jewish general who was a party to warfare and violent massacres in the years 55–51 B.C.E. according to Josephus. Peitholaus first aligned himself with the Romans and helped punish Jewish rebels who supported Aristobulus's wing of the Hasmoneans.

Later, he switched sides and became an ally of those same partisans. In this role he took part in a battle with the Romans in which many Jews lost their lives. Shortly thereafter, having been captured, Peitholaus was executed by the Romans.

4Q468e [2][. . . to k]ill many of the me[n . . .] [3][. . .] Peitholaus and the people who [. . .]
—M.O.W.

75. Priestly Service: Sabbath, Month, and Festival—Year One

4Q325

The work before us records the Sabbaths, first days of the months, and the festivals by priestly division and according to the solar calendar. All that remains of the composition is part of the record for the first year of the six-year cycle. The Festival of Wood Offering in frag. 2 is striking, for this was a controversial festival. Not even all the adherents of the solar calendar so ubiquitous among the scrolls held that there should be such a festival. Most of the calendars found in the Qumran caves do not include it. Josephus seems to indicate that in his time no such regular week of bringing wood existed. Instead, people would supply wood to the temple at regular intervals throughout the year.

Sabbaths, solar months, and festivals of the first year (months one through three). The Barley Festival, mentioned in l. 3, is elsewhere called the Waving of the Omer.

Frag. 1 [1][. . . the Passover is on the fourteenth of the month on the thi]rd [day.] On the eighteenth of the month is the Sabbath o[f Jehoiarib. Passover ends] [2][on the third day] in the evening. On the twenty-fifth of the month is the Sabbath of Jedaiah, its responsibility [includes] [3]the Barley [Festiva]l on the twenty-sixth of the month, on the day after the Sabbath. The beginning of the se[cond month is] [4][on the si]xth [day of the week] of Jedaiah. On the second of the month is the Sabbath of Harim. On the ninth of the month is the Sabbath of [5][Seorim.] On the sixteenth of the month is the Sabbath of Malchijah. On the twenty-third of the [month] [6][is the Sabbath of Mija]min. On the thirtieth of the month is the Sabbath of Hakkoz.

The beginning of the third month [7]the day after the Sabbath [. . .]

Sabbaths, solar months, and festivals of the first year (months five and six). In addition to the wood offering, two firstfruits festivals—wine and oil—are dated here. Each of them falls seven weeks (fifty days counted inclusive of the start) after the previous, echoing the pentecostal count to the Feast of Weeks. See The Sabbaths and Festivals of the Year *(text 99).*

Frag. 2 [1][The beginning of the fifth month is on the sixth day of the week of Bilgah. On the second of the month is the Sabbath of I]mmer. On the th[i]rd of the month [2][is the Wine Festival, the day after the Sabbath of Immer. On the] ninth of the month is the Sabbath of Hezir. [3][On the sixteenth of the month is the Sabbath of Happizzez. On the twent]y-third of the month is the Sabbath of [4][Pethahiah. On the thirtieth of the month is the Sabbath of Jehezkel. The beginn]ing of the sixth month [5][is on the day after the Sabbath of Jehezkel. On the seventh of the month is the Sabbath of Jachin. On the fou]rteenth [6][of the month is the Sabbath of Gamul. On the twenty-first of the month is the Sabbath of Delaiah. On the twenty]-second [7][of the month, is the Oil Festival, on the day after the Sabbath of Delaiah. On the following day is the Wo]od [Offering.]

—M.G.A.

76. Priestly Service: Sabbath, Month, and Festival—Year Four

4Q326

4Q326 records the Sabbaths, first days of the solar months, and the festivals, apparently for the fourth year of the six-year cycle familiar from other calendrical works. The remains preserve the names of none of the priestly divisions, but frag. 1, l. 1, "In the first month: on the fourt[h of the month is a Sabbath. . . .]" suggests some connection to the priestly cycle.

Sabbaths were the only holy days on which the Jews of this period might have been in at least partial agreement, since the Sabbath always fell on a seventh day. All the other holy days, attached as they were by biblical mandate to dates rather than to days of the week, turned into matters of controversy. The Sabbaths might have been different. In fact, however, even the Sabbaths were not days of rest from controversy. As this text illustrates, the Qumran calendars attached the Sabbath, like all the other festivals, to a specific date. Thus even the

Sabbaths, which might have offered a moment's peace, instead became battlegrounds for the calendar wars.

The Barley Festival, mentioned in l. 4, is elsewhere called the Waving of the Omer.

Frag. 1 [1]In the first month: on the fourt[h of the month is a Sabbath. . . .] [2]On the eleventh of the month is a Sabba[th. On the fourteenth of the month is the Passover, on the third day of the week. On the fifteenth of the month] [3]is the Feast of Unleavened Bread, on the fou[rth day of the week. On the twenty-fifth of the month is] [4]a Sabbath. On the twenty-sixth of the month is the B[arley] Festival, [on the day after the Sabbath. The first month] [5]has thirty days. On the second of the [(second) month is a Sabbath. On the ninth of the month is a Sabbath. On the sixteenth . . .]
—M.G.A.

77. Priestly Service as the Seasons Change

4Q328

The first line of this fragmentary work lists the priestly families, or courses, that begin each year of the six-year cycle. Lines 2–6 list the course that begins each quarter of the year. Apparently our author held to the view, known from *Jubilees* and the *Charter of a Jewish Sectarian Association* (text 7, col. 10), that the year comprised four three-month seasons, each of which began with a sort of New Year's Day.

[1][At the beginning of the first year Gamul is serving; in the second is Jedaiah, in the third is Mijamin, in the fourth is Shecaniah, in the fifth is Jeshebe]ab, and in the sixth is Happizzez. These are the heads of the years: [2][In] the first [year,] Gamul, Eliash[ib,] Maaziah, [3][and Huppah. In the] second, Jedaiah, Bilgah, Se[o]rim, and He[zir.] [4][In the third, Mija]m[in,] Pethahiah, Abi[jah, and Jachin.] [5][In the fourth, Shecaniah, De]laiah, Jakim, and Jeh[oiarib. In the fifth,] [6][Jeshebeab, Harim, Immer,] and Malchijah. In the si[xth, Happizzez, Hakkoz, Jehezkel, and Jeshua.]
—M.G.A.

78. Priestly Rotation on the Sabbath

4Q329

The first fragment of this calendar is a listing of the twenty-four priestly courses recorded in 1 Chronicles 24:7–18. Then, like the preceding work, the first several lines of frag. 2 tabulate the name of the priestly course that is serving when each new quarter of the year begins. The fragment begins in year two. The author goes on to list the name of the priestly division that begins to serve in the Temple for each Sabbath of the year.

In this and other calendrical works among the scrolls, we see clearly illustrated the priestly concern for taxonomy, or classification. Life was to be described; life was to be orderly, its phases so regular that they could be compiled in lists. By such classification, the priests did not actually *describe* reality, of course, so much as *create* it. At the heart of what may strike modern readers as a dull and repetitive list, then, lies the desire to create a reality. And that desire is nothing but a will to power. So when we read the many calendrical works among the scrolls, we are reading the record of a struggle for authority among Second Temple Jews.

Frag. 1 [1][Gamul, Delaiah, Maaziah, Jehoiarib,] Jedaiah, Harim, and Seo[rim, Malchijah, Mijamin,] [2][Hakkoz, Abijah, Jeshua, Shecaniah,] Eliashib, Jakim, and Huppah, [Jeshebeab, Bilgah, Immer,] [3][Hezir, Happizzez, Pethahiah, Jehez]kel, Jac[hin . . .] [4][. . .]

Frag. 2 [1]Seorim, [and Hezir. The third year. Mijamin, Pethahiah, Abijah, and Jachin.] [2]The {third} <fourth> year: [Shecaniah, Delaiah, Jaki]m, and Jehoiarib. [The fifth year: Jeshebeab,] [3][Ha]rim, Immer, [and Malchijah. The sixth year:] Happizzez, Hakko[z, Jehezkel, and Jeshua.] [4]The first year in the [first] mo[nth: Gamul, Delaiah, Maaz]iah, and Jehoiarib. In the [second: Jedaiah,] [5][Harim, Seorim, Malchijah, and Mijamin. In the] third month: Ha[kkoz Abijah, Jeshua, and Shecaniah.]

—M.G.A.

79. Priestly Service on the Passover

4Q329a

This calendar records the priestly course whose duty it was to sacrifice the lamb for Passover for the first five years of the six-year cycle. Passover was, and is, perhaps the most important of the Jewish festivals, for it celebrates the deliverance of the Jews from servitude in Egypt and their coming to live in the Holy Land as free people. The Passover occurs each year in March or April by the modern Western calendar.

1[The festivals of the first year:] on th[e third of the] week 2[of Maaziah falls the Passover.] The f[estival]s [of the secon]d (year): [on the th]ird 3[of Seorim falls the Passover.] The festivals [of the thir]d (year): on the third 4[of Abijah falls the Passov]er. The festivals of the fourth (year): 5[on the third of Jakim falls the Pa]ssover. The festivals of the fifth (year): 6on the third of Imm[er falls the Passover. The festivals of the sixth (year) . . .]

—M.G.A.

80. Priestly Service on New Year's Day

4Q330

The first portion of the present work records the name of the priestly course serving in the Temple on New Year's Day. New Year's Day, according to the Qumran calendars, fell on the first day of Nisan, which equates to about March 20 or 21 in modern terms. This was the day of the vernal equinox. Even the proper accounting of New Year's Day was a matter of strife among Second Temple Jews, for some held that the year should begin on the first day of Tishri, that is, the seventh month.

The beginning of l. 2, "in the sixth week," does not fit the New Year pattern, so additional information must have been included, but we can only guess what it might have been.

Frag. 1 [In the third year,] **Col. 2** 1Mijamin on the first of the f[irst] month [. . .] 2in the sixth week. In the [fourth] year, [Shecaniah on the

first of the first month . . .] [3]In the {second year} f[ifth] year, Jeshebeab on the [first of the first month . . .]
—M.G.A.

81. A Liturgical Calendar

4Q334

Basic to any calendar is the idea of order. Because there is order in the universe—because the sun, moon, and stars move on orderly and more or less predictable paths—a calendar is possible. Such an orderly creation calls for an orderly response, and that is what this text represents. Even what might seem the least orderly and, by nature the most spontaneous type of human expression—praise—here has order imposed upon it.

This intriguing and orderly liturgical writing records the number of "songs" (Hebrew *shirot*) and "words of praise" (Hebrew *divre tishbuhot*) for each of two daily services. In the following reconstruction the letter "*x*" indicates an unknown number, either the date or the number of songs or praises, according to context. The *Liturgical Calendar* is clearly a methodical work, but only one aspect of the method is still apparent: the number of "words of praise" that are sung during the day is double the date of the month (note particularly frag. 2, ll. 4–5).

An undated fragment.

Frag. 1 [1][. . . On the *x*th] of the month, in the evening, [eight songs . . .] [2][. . . and *x* w]ords of prais[e . . .]

Record for the eighth, ninth, and tenth days of an unknown month.

Frags. 2–4 [1][On the eighth of the month, in the evening, e]ight [s]ongs, and forty-[*x* w]ords of prai[se.] [2][During the day, *x* songs, and] sixtee[n wor]ds of [praise. On the nint]h of the month, in the evening, [3][eight songs] and fort[y-tw]o words of praise. [During the d]ay, [*x*] songs, [4][and eighteen words of praise.] On the tenth of the [month,] in the evening, eight songs [5][and forty-*x* words of praise. During the day, *x* songs,] and twent[y] wor[ds of p]raise.

A fragment whose dates have been lost.

Frag. 5 [1][On the *x*th of the month, in the evening, eight songs and *x*-] teen [words of praise.] During the d[ay, *x* songs, and *x* words of praise.] [2][. . .] twenty-[*x* words of praise.]

Record for the sixteenth, seventeenth, and eighteenth of an unknown month.

Frags. 6–7 [1]On the sixt[eenth of the month, in the evening, *x* songs and *x* words of praise.] [2]During the day, [*x*] s[ongs, and thirty-two words of praise. On the sevente]enth of the month, [3][in the evening, *x* songs and *x* words of praise. During the d]ay, [*x*] songs, [4][and *x* words of praise. On the eighteenth] of the month, [5][in the evening, *x* songs and *x* words of praise. During the day, *x* song]s [. . .]

—M.G.A.

82. False Prophets in Israel

4Q339

Inscribed on this small scrap of skin are the names of seven or eight false prophets. Except perhaps for the last, all are known biblical figures. Why would anyone want to compile a list of biblical figures in this way? The reason for composing the work probably hinges on the identity of the last—the seventh or eighth—false prophet. Maddeningly, the name is damaged and cannot be read with certainty. Not to be deterred, however, Alexander Rofe and Elisha Qimron initially suggested that it should be read as "John son of Simon," and this striking possibility does fit what remains of the letters. Later, however, Qimron rethought his suggestion and offered a different reconstruction of the last line of the text. This second reconstruction was adopted for the text's official publication.

Yet the first option remains possible. If it is correct, then the purpose of this work immediately becomes apparent, for John—more precisely, John Hyrcanus I—was a king and high priest of Israel in the late second century B.C.E. He was a controversial leader who early in his reign allied himself with the Pharisees, but later broke with them and went over to the Sadducees. Josephus presents a remarkable evaluation of the man: "He was accounted by God worthy of three of the greatest privileges: the rule of the nation, the office of high priest, and the gift of prophecy" (*Ant.*13.299–300). John's reputation for prophecy echoes in a later work known as *Targum Pseudo-Jonathan* (a targum is a translation of the Bible from Hebrew into Aramaic). In translating Deuteronomy 33:11, this targum says, "O Lord, bless the sacrifices of the house of Levi, who give the tithe, and receive with pleasure the offering from Elijah the priest, which he offered on Mount Carmel. Shatter the loins of Ahab, his enemy, and the neck of the false prophets who opposed him. And may the enemies of the high priest John have no leg to stand on." The targum's interpretive translation equates Elijah with John, and as Elijah was a true prophet famously opposed by false ones, John implicitly receives an endorsement as a true prophet.

By listing John Hyrcanus among the false prophets of Israel, of course, our text makes its own, opposite evaluation of Hyrcanus's prophetic gifts. The purpose of making the list may simply have been to put John in it. What that might mean for the author's own politics is not certain, for John was first under the influence of the Pharisees, then the Sadducees. If our author wrote when the king was following the Pharisees, he might well have made a different evaluation later in John's reign.

On the other suggestion for reconstructing the damaged last line, the text's purpose simply becomes a list of biblical content, perhaps for study or exposition in a homily.

The heading for the list, written in Aramaic. Remaining undamaged portions are in Hebrew.

Col. 1 [1][F]alse prophets who have arisen in I[srael:]

Balaam was a Midianite induced by the king of Moab to curse the Israelites as they passed through during the Exodus heading for the promised land. He did not succeed in cursing them, however, according to the Bible, for God prevented that. Israel's subsequent apostasy was considered his fault.

[2]Balaam [son of] Beor;

The prophet from Bethel, nameless in the Bible, appears in 1 Kings 13:11–34. He persuaded a true prophet to deviate from what God had told him, leading to the true prophet's death in a lion attack. Zedekiah son of Chenaanah appears in 1 Kings 22:11.

[3][The] old man from Bethel; [4][Zede]kiah son of Che[na]anah;

These three false prophets opposed the prophet Jeremiah (cf. Jer. 29:21; 29:24). According to the biblical text, Ahab and Zedekiah were delivered to the Babylonians to be executed for "prophesying a lie"; Shemaiah was likewise to be punished, but not in the same way. His line was to die out before seeing "the good" that God was to do for his people in the future.

5[Aha]b son of K[ol]aiah; 6[Zede]kiah son of Ma[a]seiah; 7[Shemaiah the Ne]helamite;

In Jeremiah 28, Hananiah son of Azzur appears as a prophet opposing Jeremiah. Declared by God a false prophet, Hananiah was dead within the year.

8[Hananiah son of Az]zur;

This reference may be to the Maccabean high priest and member of the Hasmonean family John Hyrcanus I (reigned 134–104 B.C.E.). Although several ancient sources remark on John's reputation for prophecy, only this work considers that prophecy false.

9[John son of Sim]on.

The alternative reconstruction of the last line refers back to the Hananiah of l. 8 and gives his origin. If this reconstruction is correct, then the text provides more information about this man than about any of the other false prophets, suggesting that he may have been the focal point of the list.

9[the prophet who was from Gib]eon.

—M.O.W.

83. A List of Temple Servants

4Q340

This list of people called *netinim* (Hebrew for "given ones," referring to their being attached or "given" to the Temple for service) is intriguing and puzzling. What was its purpose? The given were a category of Temple servants who lived on Mt. Ophel near the Temple and constituted the less important personnel of the sanctuary in Jerusalem. Many of the names of those mentioned in the Bible suggest that they were foreigners, for their names are not Hebrew. The same can be said for those in our list; indeed, apart from Ithra (and the uncertain Tobiah), none of the names is known to us, so the suggested pronunciations are little more than guesses. The biblical Ithra was definitely a foreigner, an Ishmaelite.

Ezekiel 44:7–9 rebukes the Israelites for introducing foreigners into the sanctuary and giving them duties there. Presumably this rebuke would embrace many of the *netinim;* it was a common practice in the ancient Near East to attach foreign slaves to temples, and it happened in Israel as well. Already at the time of Ezekiel, however (about 550 B.C.E.), some were objecting to the practice. Many of the Dead Sea Scrolls betray an animus against foreign involvement in the Temple. Accordingly, this list may be a catalogue of people whose service in the Temple our author opposed. Alternatively, Magen Broshi and Ada Yardeni have suggested that the list comprises blemished people unfit for marriage to upright people, a sort of "negative genealogy."

Col. 1 [1]These are the temple servant[s] [2]who are given an epithet, listed by na[me:] [3]Ithra and Aqum (?) [. . .] [4]"The Nail" [and . . .] [5]Hartu (?) [and . . .] [6]Kawik (?) and To[biah . . .]

—M.O.W.

84. An Annotated Law of Moses

4Q364–365

The ancient Jews had many ways of explaining their sacred texts. One way was the simple commentary, in which a passage of text is explained or interpreted; the Dead Sea group likewise had its commentaries (see the introduction to the *Commentary on Habakkuk,* text 2). Sometimes it was easier just to rewrite a story with added details, as in *Tales of the Patriarchs* (text 4), or to clear up knotty turns of phrase in translation, as in *An Aramaic Translation of the Book of Job* (text 152).

Yet another strategy occurs in the writings before us. Both of these scrolls, to judge from the scant fragments that remain, must originally have contained virtually the entire Pentateuch (Genesis through Deuteronomy, the Law of Moses). When intact, they would have been the longest of all the Dead Sea Scrolls. But they also contain many short—and a few long—additions inserted into the Law (as in text 18). In other cases verses are dropped, drastically shortened, or rearranged. Whether these devices represent something like annotations to the Pentateuch or indicate a "wild," hitherto unknown, version of the

Pentateuch we do not know. If it is the latter case, then some of the verses below may represent not a reworking of the Law of Moses, but the original reading—making the "received" version of the Law of Moses as translated in our Bibles the later, reworked text!

The surviving text begins with the story of Isaac's family.

4Q364 Frag. 1 [1][". . .] as you [go] toward Ash[ur. He settled down opposite all his brothers. Now these are the generations of] [2][I]saac son of Abraham. Abraham [was the father of Isaac" (Gen. 25:18–19)] [3]whom Sarah [his] wife [bore] to him.

When Jacob leaves the Holy Land for Aram, his mother worries about his safety on the journey in an addition paralleled elsewhere only in Jubilees *27:13–18.*

Frag. 3 Col. 2 [1]him you shall see [. . .] [2]you shall see him in good health [. . . before] [3]your death, and unto [your] eyes [he will appear . . .] [4]both of you and [Isaac] called [Rebekah . . . he told] [5]her all [these] thi[ngs . . . her spirit yearned] [6]after Jacob her son [and she wept. . . .] [7]"Then Esau saw that [Isaac had blessed Jacob and sent him away] [8]to Pa[dan] Aram to find him th[ere a wife . . ." (Gen. 28:6).]

The addition to Exodus may have summarized the revelation God gave to Moses on the mountain.

Frag. 15 [1][" . . .] Moses [went] in[to the cloud [2]and ascended the mountain. Moses was on the mountain] forty days and for[ty [3]nights . . ." (Exod. 24:18).] He told him everything a[bout . . .] [4][. . .] to him he had done at the time for summoning [. . .] [5]["And the LORD said to Moses], Speak to the children of Is[rael . . ." (Exod. 25:1–2).]

The next several fragments add short, explanatory phrases to the known words of the biblical text.

Frags. 21a–k [1]["Do not show favoritism] in judgment. You should h[ear] the small along with the great. [Do not be afraid of anyone,] for judg[ment [2]belongs to God . . ." (Deut. 1:17).] Do not ta[ke a bribe . . .]

4Q365 Frag. 3 [1]["It will be a] powder over a[ll the land of Egypt, and on man and beast it will turn into oozing sores,] that is, [2]severe [blisters] on man and beast [in all the land of Egypt" (Exod. 9:9–10).]

Frag. 5 [1][. . .] and they looked "and there were Egyptians coming after them [and they were very afraid . . ." (Exod. 14:10)] [2]two thousand horses and six hundred cha[riots . . .]

Frag. 6a Col. 2 + Frag. 6c [1]with an olive branch [. . .] [2]for the pridefulness [. . .] [3]You are great, O deliverer [. . .] [4]the enemy's hope has perished [. . .] [5]they have perished in the mighty waters, the enemy [. . .] [6]Praise him in the heights, you have given salvation [. . .] [7][who has] done glorious things [. . .] (Exod. 15:22–26 follows.)

This addition mentions the Festival of Oil and the Festival of Wood. For more on these festivals, see the Temple Scroll *(text 155).*

Frag. 23 [1]["In sh]elters you shall dwell seven days; every citizen of Israel should dwell in shelters, so that [your] de[scendants may know] [2]that I made your ancestors live [in sh]elters when I brought them out of the land of Egy[p]t. I am the LORD your God.

[3]"Then Moses spoke of the festivals of the LORD to the children of Israel. [4]The LORD spoke to Moses, saying, Command the children of Israel, saying" (Lev. 23:42–24:2), When you come to the land that [5]I am about to give you as an inheritance, and where you shall dwell securely, bring wood for the whole burnt offering and for all the work of [6][the h]ouse that you shall build for Me in the land, arranging the wood on the altar holding the burnt offering; [and] the calves [and also the wood . . .] [7]for Passover sacrifices and for communion offerings and for thank offerings and for freewill offerings and for whole burnt offerings, the portion of each day [. . .] [8][. . .] and for the do[o]rs and for all the work of the house they will br[ing . . . after] [9][the fes]tival of new oil, let them bring the wood two [by two in their tribes . . .] [10][. . .] those who bring offerings on the first day: Levi [and Judah; on the second day, Benjamin [11]and Joseph; on the third day, Reu]ben and Simeon; [on the] fou[rth] day, [Issachar and Zebulun; on the [12]fifth day, Gad and Asher; and on the sixth day, Dan and Naphtali.]

The text moves directly from the end of Numbers 4 to the beginning of Numbers 7. Probably chaps. 5–6 were placed elsewhere in the book; rearrangement was an allowed editorial device for Bible texts in this time period.

Frag. 28 [1][". . . everyone] who comes to perform the work of service and the [work of carrying in the tent of meeting. Their] [2]number was eight thousand, five hundred and sixty. A[t the command of the LORD he numbered them by] [3–4][Mo]ses each to his work and to his carrying; the numbering was what [the LORD commanded Moses].

[5]["And it came about on the d]ay Moses finished setting up the t[ent, he anointed it and sanctified it and . . ." (Num. 4:47–49; 7:1).]

Another case of topical rearrangement, combining Numbers 27 and 36. Numbers 27 deals with inheritance by daughters, while Numbers 36 concerns the marriage of female heirs. The ancient editor moved chap. 27 to precede chap. 36 so that the related topics would be treated in sequence.

Frag. 36 [1]["If his father has] no [brothers, you shall give his inheritance to his nearest kin from his clan,] [2]and he shall inherit [it. This shall be a perpetual law for the children of Israel, just as the LORD commanded] [3]Moses" (Num. 27:11). "Then drew near [the leaders of the ancestors' clans for the children of Gilead son of Machir son of Manasseh, of the families] [4]of the children of Joseph before [Moses and before the leaders, the leaders of the ancestral houses of the children] [5]of Israel, and they said, [The LORD commanded my lord to give the land in inheritance] [6]by lot to [the children of Israel . . ." (Num. 36:1–2).]

—E.M.C.

85. An Apocryphal Law of Moses

4Q368

Like the *Annotated Law of Moses* (text 84), the *Apocryphal Law of Moses* appears to be a version of the Pentateuch with hitherto unknown additions.

Frags. 1–2 contain the text of Exodus 33:11–13; 34:11–24.

An expanded paraphrase of Numbers 20:25–26.

Frag. 5 [2][. . .] leaders of the tr[ibes and] all their [ju]dges [3][. . .] according to the number of all their ancestral houses [4][. . .] and you shall go up, you and Aaron [5][with you . . .] for Aaron and Eleazar his son, and you shall strip the garments [6][from Aaron . . .]

Moses (?) exhorts the people to remain faithful to the Lord, who will reward them.

Frag. 9 [1][. . .] they mingled with [other] gods [2][. . .] the command of the LORD your God. Honor Him and be in awe be[fore Him] [3][. . .]

their midst and their heart, honor, and greatness [. . .] and life [. . .] 4[. . .] the LORD God will give honor to you, His glorious words [. . .] 5[. . .] and Mose[s . . .]

A passage that hymns the knowledge and greatness of God.

Frag. 10 Col. 1 4[. . . the eyes of the LORD,] in Heaven they go about [. . .] 5[. . .] they enter into the innermost being for the knowledge of thoug[hts . . .] 6[. . .] while they are on their beds. What can one offer, and you [. . .] He performed 7great and amazing [won]ders before your eyes in the land of [Egypt,] 8severe diseases, great afflictions, and [incurable] plagues [. . .]

Possibly a prophetic hint of the punishment to come for apostasy: the desolation of the land.

Col. 2 1–4[. . .] 5for thorn and thistle, and he will not restore the weary [. . .] 6and for beasts of the field and for the one who passes and returns [. . .] 7animals, and fat beasts trampled without [mercy . . .] 8for brutes, and thistles, and [. . .]

—E.M.C.

86. The Inheritance of the Firstborn, the Messiah of David

4Q369

Psalm 89:27 says, "I also shall make him the firstborn, the highest of the kings of the earth." The Psalmist is speaking of David, the most famous king of ancient Israel, but in Second Temple times this and similar biblical statements began to be understood as speaking not of David himself, but of a figure yet to come, a new David, a son of David. People began to think they were reading about a messiah. This understanding of the idea of the "Son of God" eventually helped to turn the world upside down.

The author of the New Testament book of Hebrews took this approach when he quoted Psalm 89:27. Hebrews 1:6, part of a chain of biblical quotations and interpretations, alludes to the psalm in saying "And again, when he brings his firstborn into the world . . ." In the new context of Hebrews, the psalmic term "firstborn" was now being given messianic import. The author of Hebrews went on to argue that Jesus was this firstborn and thus the messiah.

But the author of Hebrews did not write in a vacuum, and Jesus was not necessarily the only—or the first—messianic figure to whom people had applied the metaphor of sonship. By the time of Jesus, and certainly by the time of the writer of Hebrews, the idea had been a part of the intellectual world of the Jews for several generations. The present text proves as much (although we have other evidence from the scrolls as well). The author of *Inheritance* writes "You appointed him as your firstborn son." He goes on to say that this figure will be "prince and ruler in all the earth" and that God gave "him righteous statutes, as a father gives a son." The text says, then, that there will someday arise a Jewish leader who will conquer the world and that he is to be God's son. Further, he will be God's *firstborn* son, a reference to the special privileges that the firstborn got under biblical laws of inheritance. According to the Bible, the firstborn son was to receive twice the inheritance of the other sons (and daughters generally got nothing but their dowry). In *Inheritance,* the designation "firstborn" is, of course, as metaphorical as the term "son." By it the author means to say that this messiah will be specially endowed with God's blessing and all else that God can give.

Inheritance is one of three works to emerge from the caves near Qumran that refer to a messiah as begotten of God, or as God's son.* As Craig Evans has written: "These texts do not indicate that a miraculous birth was expected of a Messiah. But they do help us understand why the evangelists Matthew and Luke would be interested in presenting Jesus's birth in such a light."‡

*This may be the final judgment as revealed to Enoch (*Jubilees *4:19).*

Frag. 1 Col. 1 1[. . .] to all 2[. . .] for the mysteries [. . . the angel of] Your peace 3[. . .] understand [. . . until] they acknowledge their guilt 4[and seek My face (Hos. 5:15?) . . .] of all their fest[ivals] at their times 5[. . .] Your wonder, for from of old You decreed them 6[. . .] His judgment until the determined time of judgment 7[. . .] in all the appointed times until 8[. . .]

9[Now Kenan was the fourth generation and Mahalalel was] his [son.] And Mahalalel was the fifth generation 10[and Jared was his son. And Jared

*For the others, see the *Charter for Israel in the Last Days* 2:11–12 (text 8) and *The Last Days: An Interpretation of Selected Verses* 3:10–11 (text 28).

‡Craig Evans, "A Note on the 'First-born Son' of 4Q369," *Dead Sea Discoveries* 2 (1995): 200.

was the sixth generation and Enoch was] his son. And Enoch was the seventh generation [. . .]

The eternal inheritance of the Messiah, the firstborn son of God. This notion of sonship is especially interesting in light of the genealogical list of col. 1, to which this material in col. 2 presumably bears some relation. All the "sons" of col. 1 are literally sons; thus the juxtaposition with col. 2 tends to make the sonship of the messiah all the more concrete.

Col. 2 [1][. . .] Your name. You assigned his inheritance in order that You might establish Your name there [. . .] [2]it is the glory of Your inhabited world and upon it [. . .] [3]Your eye is upon it, and Your glory appears there for [. . .] [4]for his offspring throughout their generations, an eternal possession. And al[l . . .] [5]and You chose Your good judgments for him to [. . .] [6]in everlasting light, and You appointed him as Your firstbo[rn] son. [There is none] [7]like him, as a prince and ruler in all Your inhabited world [. . .] [8]the c[rown of the] heavens and glory of the clouds You have laid [on him . . .] [9][. . .] and the angel of Your peace in his congregation. And h[e . . .] [10][. . . You gave] him righteous statutes, as a father [gives] a so[n . . .] [11][. . .] his love. Your soul holds fast to [. . .] [12][. . .] for in them Y[ou set] Your glory [. . .]

This fragment concerns either the retribution in store for the wicked or the rewards awaiting the just.

Frag. 2 [1][. . .] and the protection of the angel of intercession [. . .] [2][. . .] Your [stre]ngth, and to fight against all the la[nds . . .] [3][. . .] among them Your retributions [. . .] [4][. . .] and Your [ju]dgments [You] make ma[rvelous] among them [. . .] [5][. . . concern]ing [a]ll Your works [. . .]

—M.G.A.

87. A Sermon on the Flood

4Q370

This intriguing work is a sermon or homily drawing on the biblical account of the Flood (Gen. 6–9). The first column describes the Flood, and so is, in a sense, the body of the sermon. The second column makes the sermon's application or admonition. Unfortunately this column is fragmentary—it would have been interesting to see precisely where the author went.

The text gives us no clue concerning either the audience for whom the sermon was intended or the "preacher" who may have delivered it. We can say, however, that our author knew two other extrabiblical writings that have come forth from the caves near Qumran. 4Q370 1:1–2 alludes to the "Hymn to God the Creator" (l. 13) from the *Apocryphal Psalms of David* (text 151). 4Q370 2:1–5 is closely related to a portion of *In Praise of Wisdom* (1:13–2:3; text 34). In some sense, these works may have been authoritative for our writer, and in the case of the *Apocryphal Psalms of David* in particular he may have thought of himself as quoting Scripture.

One of the sermon's main points is that the sheer abundance present at the creation had a corrupting influence. This idea is not in the Bible and represents an interesting approach to the curse God inflicted upon Adam in consequence of his sin. Because of it Adam, of course, had to work, earning his bread by the sweat of his brow. By implication our author finds a silver lining in this curse: true, humankind now must work, but at least it keeps people from sinning still more. The notion that abundance breeds sin also appears in rabbinic literature. For instance, *Genesis Rabbah,* commenting on Genesis 8:22, notes: "Rabbi Isaac said, 'What was responsible for their rebelling against Me? Was it not because they sowed without having to reap?' " This same sentiment is a commonplace in our own society, of course, a holdover from the past merely rotated one hundred eighty degrees: "An idle mind is the devil's playground."

The Lord speaks of the bounty of creation and humankind's rebellion.

Col. 1 [1]So He decked out the mountains with fo[od, heap]ing up sustenance upon them, satisfying everyone with succulent fruit. "All who do My will may eat and be satisfied," says the L[O]RD, [2]" Then shall they bless My [holy] name." "But thereafter they did what I regard as evil," says the LORD. They rebelled against God in their d[esig]ns.

A description of the Flood.

[3]So the LORD judged them according to a[l]l their practices, according to the designs arising from their [evil] hearts. He thundered against them in [His] might, [so that] the [4]very foundations of the ear[th] were shaken. [Wa]ter burst forth from the depths, all the windows of heaven were thrown open; the depth[s] poured out their awful waters, [5]the windows of heaven em[ptied th]emselves of their rain. [So] He destroyed them in the flood, every one of them [perishing in the w]ater—[for] they had disobeyed [the

commandments of the LO]RD. 6Therefore all on [dr]y ground were blott[ed out,] humanity [and beast,] bird and winged creature—all died; not even the gi[an]ts escaped [. . .]

God's mercy in judgment, at the time of the Flood and also now. Col. 2, ll. 2–4 can be partially reconstructed using 4Q185 (text 34).

7But God established [a sign of the covenant,] He set His bow [in the clouds,] so that He would remember His covenant 8[that He had made with humanity and all that lives: no more] would flood waters destroy, [never again] ravaging waters [be loos]ed [. . .] **Col. 2** 1Because of their guilt, they shall seek [. . .] 2The LORD will justify [. . .] 3He will cleanse them of their transgression [. . .] 4their evil, in knowing [the difference between good and evil . . . For like a nettle] 5they spring up, but their days [on the earth] are as a shadow. [And now, hear me, O my people; let me make you wise, simple ones. For from eternity] 6and forevermore shall He be merciful [to those faithful to His covenant; His tender mercies are upon all who remember His commandments, to do them. Grow wise with] 7the greatness of the LORD, remember the won[ders that He worked in the land of Ham. Let your heart be strengthened] 8through awe of Him, let [your] spiri[t] rejoice [according to His good mercies . . .] 9those who follow after you. Do not rebel at the word[s of the LORD . . .]
—M.O.W.

88. Stories About the Tribes of Israel

2Q22, 4Q371–373

The present scrolls are something of an enigma. They may represent four copies of the same literary work, but there are only a few overlaps and many portions of a particular scroll do not overlap with any of the others. We cannot rule out the possibility, therefore, that these four scrolls do not contain a single literary work, but rather various unconnected episodes or excerpts from other works. In that light, the difficulty of characterizing the great variety of what we read in them is perhaps understandable. The scrolls were once designated "Apocryphal Joseph" texts, but much of what they say has nothing to do with either Joseph the son of Jacob or his eponymous tribes. Joseph is indeed the major figure, but we also have here at least one story about David and Goliath and one or more psalms, one mentioning Zimri son of Salu, a character of the Exodus. Thus the title adopted here is more descriptive of the actual contents.

During the late Second Temple period intense interest arose in the story of David and Goliath. This interest was only natural, because the Jews suffered under the heel of first one, then another powerful foreign nation. The famous biblical story (1 Sam. 17) naturally lent itself to the situation: it was a paradigm of the weak defeating the powerful. Accordingly, 1 Maccabees 4:30 depicts Judas Maccabaeus (the hero of the revolt against Syrian rule in about 167 B.C.E.) as praying, "You are blessed, Savior of Israel, who smashed the attack of the mighty warrior by the hand of Your servant David." Other texts of that general period also invoked the image of the shepherd boy felling the giant, including the Dead Sea work known as the *War Scroll* (text 11; see 11:1–2 of the Cave 1 scroll).

A second notable aspect of the present work(s) is the clear polemic against the Samaritans. The Samaritans were a group who lived to the north of Judah in the former territory of the ten lost tribes of the Northern Kingdom, Israel. Like the Jews, they worshiped the God of Israel. When pressed, the rabbis admitted that the Samaritans were in essence Jews. Yet they did not worship God in acceptable ways and, most important, they did not worship God in the accepted temple at Jerusalem. The Samaritans had built their own temple at Mt. Gerizim, probably in the fourth century B.C.E., and established their own priesthood and sacrifices. They held only to the Torah, the first five books of the Bible, which they modified at points to support their own claims. They did not accept the books of the Prophets, presumably because the Prophets were so centered on the worship in Jerusalem, which the Samaritans contested. To them, Jerusalem was not central; Gerizim was. Part of the legitimation the Samaritans offered for themselves and their temple was the claim that they were descended from the Joseph tribes, Ephraim and Manasseh. Josephus spoke of this claim: "[The Samaritans] alter their attitude according to the situation. When they see that the Jews are doing well, they call them kinsmen, claiming to be descended from Joseph and so related to the Jews through their origin from him. Yet when they see the Jews stumble, they say they have nothing at all in common with them" (*Ant.* 9.291). The polemic between the Jews and Samaritans thus focused in part on the question of who could claim to be the true descendants of Joseph. We see this argument reflected in 4Q372 frag. 1 below, and so glimpse an aspect of Jewish politics and propaganda in the Second Temple period.

A story about David and Goliath, apparently comparing Goliath's size with that of the giant king Og of Bashan, who is mentioned in the book of Joshua.

4Q373 Frag. 1 (with **2Q22** and **4Q372 Frag. 19**) [2]All his servants with Og [. . . six] [3]and a half cubits was his height, two [cubits his breadth

. . . He had] a spear like a cedar, [4]a shield like a tower. He who has quick feet [. . . The Israelite forces] [5]were at a mile's remove. [I] did not stand [far off . . .] [6]and I did not repeat it, for the Lord our God vanquished him; [I struck him] with the edge of [the sword . . .] [7]I had prepared murderous slings, together with bows, and [did] not [. . .] [8]For t[his] was a war to capture walled cities and to strike terror [. . .]

This fragment also seems to be related to the story of David and Goliath.

4Q372 Frag. 2 [2][. . .] the Lord in heaven [. . .] [3][. . .] in the depths, and in all of Abaddo[n . . .] [4][. . . He Who t]rains his hand for warfare, He Who avenges [. . .] [5][. . . He Who g]ives him acumen, so as to discern how to build [. . .] [6][. . . to d]o that which delights Him forever, according to the greatness of [His . . .] [7][. . .] time. Surely He has given you strength to preva[il . . .] [8][. . .] and He gave them into His people's power with judgme[nts . . .] [9][. . . Mou]nt Bashan did [they] van[quish,] together with all [its] cities [. . .] [10][. . .] he was clothed with [. . .] [11][. . .] He Who gives His people confidence in [. . .] [12][. . . the enemy of Is]rael, for he has been vanquished before him [. . .] [13][. . . smiting] his head with a wound[ing] stone [. . .]

The introduction of the Joseph tribes, Ephraim and Manasseh, two of the lost ten northern tribes of Israel. It begins with their exile for idol worship.

Frag. 1 (with **4Q371 Frags. 1–2)** [2]He who does [. . . they followed] strangers [3]and the false priests, and they honored those who craft [idols . . . they abandoned God] [4]Most High, so He gave them into the power of the nations, to [. . . and He scattered] [5]them among all the lands, and among all [the nations] did He disperse them [. . .] they did not come [. . .] [6]Israel, and He eliminated them from the land of [. . .], from the place [. . .] The nations left them [7]no remnant in the Valley of the Vision. They [plowed] Zion [into a field,] and they made [. . .] they turned [8]Jerusalem to ruins, the mountain of my God into wood[ed] high places [. . .] the laws of [9]God, and Judah with him as well. He stood at the crossroads, whether to d[o . . .] [10]to be with his two brothers.

The settling of the Samaritans in the lands formerly belonging to the Joseph tribes. Line 12 apparently refers to the construction of the Samaritan temple on Mt. Gerizim. This temple competed with that in Jerusalem for several centuries, until it was destroyed by the Jewish king Hyrcanus I in about 113 B.C.E. The author's hatred of the Samaritans is manifest.

Moreover, Joseph was carried off into lands he had not kn[own . . .] [11]among a foreign nation, dispersed into all the world. All their mountains were desolate of them, [. . .] and fools [were liv]ing [in their land,] [12]fashioning for themselves a high place upon the high mountain, so as to arouse Israel's jealousy. They spoke [insulting] wor[ds against] [13]the sons of Jacob, saying horrifying things, even blaspheming the tent of Zion. They told lies against them, [14]spoke every sort of untruth, intending to enrage Levi, Judah, and Benjamin with their words.

In exile, the Joseph tribes come to repentance. "Joseph" cries out to God in a lengthy prayer.

Worse, Joseph [had been given] [15]into the power of foreigners, who drained his strength and shattered all his bones, until he was about to perish. At that point he cried out, [16]calling upon the mighty God to save him from their power. He said,

"O Father, my God, leave me not forsaken, in the power of the nations. [17]Render me justice, that the poor and oppressed should not perish. You need no nation or people—[18]need not the slightest help. Your mere finger is bigger, stronger than anything on earth. Surely You prove what is true; [19]no wrongdoing resides with You. Your mercies are many, Your faithfulness great to all those who seek You. My land [has been taken] from me, from all my brothers who [20]have joined me. An enemy people dwells in it, sp[eaking horrifying things, taunting, blas]pheming, reviling [21]all who love You, even Jacob. They anger Le[vi, Judah, and Benjamin with their lying words . . .] [22]The time when You shall exterminate them from the entire earth, when they shall be given [. . .] [23]Then shall I arise to work justice and righteous[ness . . . To do] [24]what pleases my Creator, to offer the sacrifices [of thanksgiving . . . I shall praise] [25]My God, tell of His lovingkindne[ss . . .] [26]I shall praise You, O LORD my God, I shall bless You for all [. . .] [27][the former things.] I shall teach the rebellious Your statutes, all who have abandoned You, [Your] La[w . . . I shall distinguish good] [28]from evil, that Your testimonies not reproach me, so to declare [Your] righteous words. [. . .] [29]Surely God is great, holy, mighty and fearsome, terrible and wondrous [. . . His glory inhabits heaven] [30]and earth, even the depths of the abyss. Honor and [glory . . .] [31]I know and understand [. . .]

This fragment comprises one or perhaps two psalms. The first four lines make some remarkable claims for the authority of the speaker, but we do not know who he may be. The later lines describe God's promise to fight for Israel and to destroy its enemies. Zimri son of Salu is mentioned in Numbers 25:14; he was among those destroyed for apostasy.

Frag. 3 ^{4}[. . .] I shall praise the LO[RD, that] my meditation [might] be pleasing to Him [. . .] ^{5}[and] a heart to teach understanding, a mouth [to rela]te judgment, for my words are [swee]ter than honey, [my] ton[gue] more pleasing than wine. [Every word that I speak] ^{6}is truth, every utterance of my mouth, righ[teousness.] None of these testimonies shall fail, none of these fine promises perish, for all of them [. . .] ^{7}The LORD has opened my mouth, the words that I speak come from Him. His word is in me, so as to declare [. . . To us belong] ^{8}His mercies; He shall not grant His laws to another nation; neither shall He adorn any stranger with them. Surely [. . .] ^{9}their [s]ons, for He made a covenant with Jacob to be with him for all etern[ity . . . He promised that any enemy of] ^{10}[I]srael should come to an end, to exterminate using the nations all who should touch the inheritan[ce of His beloved . . .] ^{11}[. . .] He would seek their shed blood from their hand. See what he did to Midian, e[nemy of Israel, for the LORD is our God,] ^{12}He alone. Zimri son of Salu and five kings of Midian were slain [. . .]

—M.O.W.

89. A Discourse on the Exodus and Conquest

4Q374

The surviving portions of this writing describe the Exodus from Egypt and the conquest of the promised land. Because the work is so fragmentary, we cannot discover how its ideas developed, but a few points are clear. The fear and helplessness of Israel's enemies as God's people battled for Canaan is a dominant theme. In contrast, the author emphasizes God's compassion and support for Israel, even when the people became discouraged. Note the allusion to Exodus 7:1 as the writer calls Moses "a god over the mighty."

Line 8 is striking because it juxtaposes healing with a quotation from the so-called priestly blessing of Numbers 6:24–26. An amulet with precisely these verses inscribed upon it dating to the late sixth century B.C.E.—centuries older than our scroll—has recently surfaced in excavations in Ketef Hinnom in Jerusalem. The fact that the verses were inscribed upon an amulet suggests their early use for magical purposes, and the present Dead Sea Scroll tends to confirm that possibility with its explicit reference "for healing." The connection of the priestly blessing with healing—as a magical incantation—was clearly a long-standing and durable tradition, and in passing our writer refers to the popular conception of the blessing's divine power.

Frag. 2 Col. 2 [1]together and [. . .] [2]So the nations were lifted up in anger [. . .] [3]through their actions and the polluted deeds of [. . .] [4]so that th[ey] have neither remnant nor survivor. As for their offspring, [. . .] [5]He planted His chosen in a land desirable above all others, in [. . .] [6]He made him as a god over the mighty, as a compa[ss] for Pharaoh; His serv[ant Moses . . .] [7]So they melted and their hearts trembled, and th[ei]r insides turned to liquid. Yet He had compassion upon al[l His chosen ones . . .] [8]"When He caused His face to shine upon them" (Num. 6:25) for healing, they were made strong once again, and at the time of [. . .] [9]All who had not known You melted and trem[bl]ed. They staggered at the sou[nd of . . .]
—M.O.W.

90. The Test of a True Prophet

4Q375

In his apology on behalf of Judaism, *Against Apion,* Josephus wrote, "From the time of Artaxerxes until our own day a full history has been recorded, but it is not regarded as equally trustworthy with earlier records because of uncertainty about the *exact succession of the prophets*" (*Ag. Ap.* 1.41; emphasis mine). From this statement we may infer that Josephus believed that prophecy continued to his own day; it was the exact succession of the prophets that had ended, not the phenomenon of prophecy itself. In other words, from about 350 B.C.E. to 90 C.E. there had been a succession, but people argued about whether this or that claimant to the office was credible, was in fact a prophet. Prophets continued to arise, but now there was much uncertainty about which ones were true, which ones false.

The present text illustrates some of the social dimensions of this situation. The text takes as its point of departure a famous passage on prophecy in Deuteronomy 18:18–22, where a false prophet is defined as one who declares something that does not come true. Our author, speaking as Moses, presupposes a situation in which two groups disagree about whether a prophet has spoken truly. The matter is cast in terms of apostasy, but in Second Temple times that might easily connote biblical interpretation with which one did not agree. How was God's revelation to be applied? One group's following God was ipso facto another group's apostasy.

Our author conceives an elaborate ceremonial trial of sorts involving the "anointed priest" (i.e., the high priest) and the Ark of the Testimony. He seems to believe that secret laws, unknown to the generality of Israel, are kept in or near the Ark. Therefore the priest retires there and studies to determine whether the prophet is true or false. In this way he will determine God's verdict. We may imagine, then, that our author belonged to a group that had reason to want to add the stated nuances to the biblical commands. This modification could hardly be done in the name of any but Moses. It would seem reasonable that the person or group who gave birth to this text wished to support someone who had been accused of being a false prophet.

Consideration of a true prophet who, all agree, speaks for God.

Frag. 1 Col. 1 [1](You shall perform) [all that] your God shall command you by the prophet, and you shall observe [2][all] these [sta]tutes. You shall return to the LORD your God with all [3][your heart and with al]l your soul; then your God will Himself turn from His furious anger [4][to save you] from all your dire straits.

The prophet whom some call false, others true.

But any prophet who arises to urge you [5][to apostasy, to turn] you from following your God, must be put to death. Yet if the tribe to [which] he belongs [6]comes forward and argues, "He must not be executed, for he is a righteous man, he is [7]a [trus]tworthy prophet," then you are to come with that tribe and your elders and judges [8][t]o the place that your God shall choose in one of the territories of your tribes. You are to come before [9][the pr]iest who has been anointed, upon whose head has been poured the anointing oil.

The procedure to be followed by the anointed priest in order to determine whether the prophet must die. In ll. 3–6 the ceremony is similar to what the Bible prescribes for the Day of Atonement (Lev. 16).

Col. 2 [3]and he shall take [one young bull from the herd, and one ram . . . he shall take some of its blood] [4]upon [his] fing[er and sprinkle it on the four corners of the altar of burnt offerings . . .] [5]the flesh of the ra[m . . . one] ma[le] goat [6]for a sin offering. Let him ta[ke the goat and ato]ne with it on behalf of the entire assembly. Afterwards, [he is to sprinkle some of the blood] [7]before the curtain [of the veil, then dra]w near to the Ark of the Testimony. There he shall study [all the commandments of] [8]the LORD, comparing all the [laws] that have been ke[pt sec]ret from you. Finally he shall emerge into the presence of a[ll the leaders of the] [9]assembly. This, then, [. . .]

—M.O.W.

91. A Moses Apocryphon

4Q377

Moses wrote many more books than the five in the Bible traditionally credited to him. Or at least so it was claimed. Among the Dead Sea Scrolls are nearly a dozen different works that do not appear in our Bibles, but assert, by one device or another, that Moses was their author. These include *Jubilees,* the *Words of Moses* (text 5), rewritten Bible texts (texts 18 and 84), the *Test of a True Prophet* (text 90), the *Temple Scroll* (text 155), and the present work. In addition, the *Discourse on the Exodus and Conquest* (text 89) may be such a Mosaic writing. The sheer number of these writings testifies to the overwhelming importance of Moses as the legitimator of religious ideas in Second Temple times. If the Bible did not say what you thought it should, what you were convinced God would have said through Moses but somehow neglected to say, then you took reed in hand and, as it were, wrote for Moses.

The present writing is one such apocryphal Moses work, but unfortunately, fragmentary as it is, we can no longer see precisely what its author wanted to ground in Mosaic authority. Noteworthy is our author's description of Moses as an "anointed one" (l. 5, Hebrew *messiah*). Nowhere does the Bible use this term of the famous lawgiver, though it is certainly appropriate in terms of the Hebrew word's connotations. In the same vein the writer calls Moses a "herald of glad tidings." Again, nowhere does the Bible use that term of Moses. These two designations refer to Moses's investiture in the role of prophet and herald (cf. Isa. 61:1–5). We may speculate that one point of this writing was simply to apply these terms to the greatest figure in Israel's history.

The people's reaction on hearing God's commandments from Sinai.

Frag. 2 Col. 2 [3]And Eliba (?) responded, "Hea[r], O congregation of the LORD, and lend an ear, all who are here gathered: [. . .] [4][. . .] Cursed be the man who fails to preserve and car[ry out] [5]all the command[ments of the L]ORD as spoken by Moses His anointed, and who fails to follow the LORD, the God of our fathers, He Who has command[ed] [6]us from Mount Sinai.

For He has spoken wi[th] the congregation of Israel face to face, as a man might speak [7]with his friend; and as a man might allow his friend to see, He has let us peer within a consuming flame above the heavens. [8]On the earth He has stood upon the mountain to teach that there is no God but Him, and no Rock like Him." All [9]the congregation answered, but they were seized with trembling in the presence of God's glory and the wondrous thundering. [10]So they stood at a distance.

Moses the man of God.

Meanwhile Moses, the man of God, was with God in the cloud. The cloud [11]would cover him, for [. . .] as he was sanctified. God would speak through his mouth as though he were an angel; indeed, what herald of glad tidings was ever like him? [. . .] [12]He was a man of piety and [. . .] such as were never created before, and who forever [. . .]

—M.O.W.

92. Apocryphal Joshua

4Q378–379

Joshua the son of Nun was second to none—as a minister to Moses, that is. According to the Bible, he served Moses faithfully and then, when Moses died before entering the promised land, Joshua led the people across the Jordan and into their inheritance. The Bible describes the subsequent conquest and division of the land in the book of Joshua. *Apocryphal Joshua* serves as a kind of second to the biblical book. It belongs to the category of rewritten Bible, expanding upon those aspects of the biblical book that most interested its author. Before characterizing the work any further, however, we should note that we cannot be certain the two manuscripts grouped here are two copies of a single literary work. They do not overlap. They are thought to be two copies of the same work because of their content, style, use of divine names, and method of adapting Scripture.

Assuming this unity, the work seems to have followed the order of events in the biblical book of Joshua more or less faithfully in retelling the story of the conquest (and the fragments below are arranged accordingly). In contrast to the biblical book, however, *Apocryphal Joshua* contains many speeches, prayers, and hymns. Moreover, the author manifests a greater interest in chronology than one finds in the biblical book. 4Q379 frag. 12 presupposes a system of timekeeping by forty-nine-year periods, or jubilees, known from the book of *Jubilees* and various Dead Sea Scrolls writings. The author is also especially interested in the priesthood. For that reason he focuses attention on Levi, the son of Jacob who was to give rise to the priesthood, and singles out Eleazar and Ithamar, the priestly sons of Aaron.

4Q379 frag. 22 is particularly noteworthy because another Dead Sea Scroll, *A Collection of Messianic Proof Texts* (text 26), quotes it as though it were Scripture. The *Collection* quotes the portion right after various other selections taken from the Bible. This juxtaposition implies that all the portions were viewed as more or less equally authoritative and thus raises the question of canon. By the term "canon" we refer to the collection of books that are considered inspired and uniquely authoritative and that eventually came to be the Bible. In the period of the Dead Sea Scrolls, the canon seems not yet to have been closed. In fact, evidence indicates that various groups among the Jews held different ideas about just what books were authoritative. It seems that all agreed on the authority of the books of Moses (Genesis through Deuteronomy) and the Prophets, but that is where agreement ceased. *Apocryphal Joshua* was presumably taken at face value: that is, it represents itself as a work written by Joshua, and people believed the claim. If this inference is correct, then for some Jews at any rate it was no less "biblical" than the book of Joshua familiar to us.

This is a rather mysterious portion, drawing phrases from the Balaam episode of Numbers 24. Perhaps a final prayer of Moses, uttered just before his death, is in view here.

4Q378 Frag. 26 1[. . . a man] who kno[ws] the knowledge of the Most High, who [sees] the vis[ion of the Almighty . . .] 2[. . . kee]p faith with us, O man of God, because [. . .] 3[. . .] and the Council of the Most High h[ea]rd the voice of M[oses . . .] 4[. . .] God Most High [. . .] 5[. . . and] mighty portents. By anger were restrained [. . .] 6[. . .] a pio[u]s [m]an, and remember forever and ever [. . .]

The people mourn the death of Moses. Line 5 refers to the Canaanites' fear of the people of Israel as the conquest began.

Frag. 14 1[. . .] So the children [of Israel] wept [for Moses in the plains of Moab,] 2[at the Jordan near] Jericho, in Beth-jeshimoth [by Abel-shittim—thirty days altogether. They completed] 3[the days of weeping] and mourning for Moses, and the children of Is[rael . . .] [4][. . . the covenant t]hat the LORD had made with him. [And the LORD said, "This day] [5][I am beginning to put the dr]ead of you and fear of you [upon the peoples . . ."]

This portion seems to warn the nation against future apostasy in a fashion reminiscent of Deuteronomy 28–29. The people are warned that if they are unfaithful to God, terrible curses shall fall upon them. Among these curses, according to l. 5, shall be an increase of predatory animals who will eat the people.

Frag. 3 Col. 1 [1][. . .] to render them impure and to [. . .] [2][. . .] your [f]athers to their sons. [3][. . .] many trials shall seek you out and all [4][. . . Moses the ma]n of God [5][. . .] from you, and you shall become something for it to eat [6][. . . from one corner of the] land to the other, and [the LORD] shall make you to wander [7][. . .] to the point of extinction, to the point of rebellion [8][against the LORD . . . the L]ORD your God. They shall come upon you [9][. . . a]ll the nations who [10][. . .] as you have done [11][. . . who] have ruled over you.

An address to the nation in which Joshua recalls the words Moses spoke to him prior to crossing the Jordan (cf. Josh. 1:10–18).

Frag. 3 Col. 2 + Frag. 4 [3]and he brought forth [. . .] [4]And now, [this] very day [. . .] [5]For we have listened to Moses [. . .] [6]a great and upright man [. . . to appoint commanders over groups of one thousand, groups of] [7]one hundred, groups of fif[ty and groups of ten . . . as well as judges] [8]and officials [. . .] [9]he shall listen and not [. . . Fear not,] [10]and do not be afraid. Rather, be strong and cour[ageous, for you shall give this people their inheritance . . . The LORD shall neither] [11]leave you nor forsake [you. Let your hands be strong . . . Arise] [12]to lead [this people] on their journey [. . .]

A speech in which Joshua apparently addresses Israel and refers to an earlier prayer on the people's behalf, perhaps one offered by Moses. A possible context would be the day before the people cross the Jordan. Joshua mentions the fate of the several people who had arisen to oppose Moses, implicitly warning that a similar fate awaits those who oppose himself, God's new leader.

Frag. 6 Col. 1 [4][. . . Acce]pt a prayer concerning our sins [5][. . .] Do not be like those brothers who [de]scended [6][into the pit . . . Make] such a man's evil deeds [known] forever, for all ages (?) [7][. . .] your [gu]ilt. My brothers shall oppose you [. . .]

A similar prayer, perhaps offered by Caleb or Eleazar the priest.

Frag. 22 Col. 1 [1][. . . Because] Moses [prayed,] O My God, You did not destroy them for their sins [2][. . .] with You by the agency of Joshua, the assistant of Moses, Your servant [3][. . .] by means of an oracle to Joshua, for the sake of Your people [4][. . . the coven]ant that You m[ade] with Abraham [5][. . . a God showing] compassion to thousands.

A description of the promised land (cf. Deut. 8:7–9).

Frag. 11 [1][. . .] For the LORD [yo]ur [God] is speaking [2][. . .] to confirm the words that He spoke [3][. . .] that He swore to Abraham to give [4][us and to bring us into a] good and expansive [land], a land with flowing streams, [5][with springs and underground waters welling up in va]lleys and hills, a land of wheat and barley, [6][of vines and fig trees and pomegranates, of olive trees and] honey. Surely it is a land flowing with milk and honey [7][where you will lack nothing, a land] whose st[one]s are iron and from whose hills [you may mine] copper. [8][. . .] to explore. [Israel] shall inherit [. . .]

The crossing of the Jordan River. The reference to the jubilee year reflects a chronological system known from many Dead Sea Scrolls.

4Q379 Frag. 12 [1][. . . the waters] flowing downstream [. . .] [2][. . . the waters] flowing downstream stood still, standing in a single [3][heap . . . The children of Israel cr]ossed over on dry ground in the first [4][mon]th, in the for[ty-fir]st year of their exodus from the lan[d] of [5]Egypt. That was the jubilee year, falling at the beginning of their entry into the land of [6]Canaan. Now the Jordan overfl[o]ws its banks and floods with [7][w]ater from the fo[ur]th month until the month of the wheat harvest.

Two portions apparently praising God after the crossing. The prominence of Levi in the first fragment is notable, for he is listed first though he was not the firstborn.

Frag. 1 [1][. . . Jacob,] and You made him rejoice with tw[elve sons . . .] [2]forever: Levi, the beloved of [. . .] [3][. . . and] Reuben and

Ju[dah and . . .] [4][. . . and] Gad and Dan and [. . .] [5][. . .] the twelve tribes of [Israel . . .]

Frag. 17 [2][. . .] and blessing [. . .] [3]with his words, and he was faithful to the Law [. . .] [4][. . . You gave the covenant You made] with Abraham, Isaac, and Jacob to Moses [5][. . . Aaron, E]leazar and Ithamar. I shall rejoice [. . .]

This fragment preserves a portion quoted in A Collection of Messianic Proof Texts *(text 26). Whatever its interpretation may be in that text, here the portion supplements Joshua 6 and refers mainly to the destruction of Jericho that is recounted by that chapter of the Bible. A "fowler's net" (l. 10) was used to capture birds for eating.*

Frag. 22 Col. 2 [5]Blessed is the LORD, the God of I[srael . . .] [6][. . .] [7]When Josh[ua] fi[ni]shed pra[ying and offe]ring psalms of praise, [he said,] [8]"Cur[sed be any]one who tries to reb[ui]ld this [c]ity! With the help of [his] firstborn he shall lay its foundation, [9]and with the aid of [his young]est [he shall] set up its gates!" (Josh. 6:26). Behold, [one cu]rsed man, [one belonging to Belial,] [10][is about to arise] to be a fowler's net to his people and a source of ruin for all his neighbors. Then shall ari[se] [11][son]s [after him,] the two of them to be instruments of wrongdoing. They shall rebuild [12]this [city] and set up for it a wall and towers, creating [a stronghold of evil] [13][in the land,] a great wickedness in Israel, a thing of horror in Ephraim [and Judah.] [14][They shall work blasphemy] in the land, a great uncleanness among the children of Jacob. They shall po[ur out blood like water upon the bulwark of the daughter of Zion and within the city limits of Jerusalem.]
—M.O.W.

93. A Collection of Royal Psalms

4Q380–381

The 150 poems contained in the biblical book of Psalms do not exhaust the inventory of Israel's hymns. Undoubtedly there were thousands more, and Jews continued to write them long after the biblical period. A number of these previously unknown psalms have turned up in the Qumran caches (see texts 17 and 151). Some of them represent imitations of the biblical genre with a sectarian twist; others would not be out of place within the biblical Psalter itself.

The hymns of praise in this group of scrolls belong to the latter group. They are particularly pure examples of the songs of Israel, although their wording is often derived from biblical expressions. Occasionally verbatim excerpts from the Old Testament occur.

The biblical psalms are generally of two kinds, the "lament" and the "praise." Both kinds may be either personal or communal. The lament focuses on a crisis or calamity suffered by the psalmist or the nation as a whole and usually includes a prayer for deliverance from the affliction. The praise emphasizes the greatness of God and what he has done for the psalmist or for the nation.

The psalms translated here are credited by literary fiction to some of the kings of Judah. Since the king embodies in his person the nation's fate, these hymns have both personal and communal characteristics.

Scholars refer to some of the biblical praise psalms as "songs of Zion," because they emphasize God's choice of Jerusalem in which to place his king and temple (e.g., Pss. 48; 87). The following is another song of Zion.

4Q380 Col. 1 1[. . .] 2[. . . Jeru]salem is 3[the city that the] LO[RD chose] from everlasting to 4[everlasting . . .] holy, 5[for the na]me of the LORD is invoked on it. 6[His glory] is visible on Jerusalem 7[and] Zion. Who can tell the name of 8the LORD, and proclaim all [His] praise? 9The LORD [called him to] mind in His good will, and took care of him, 10showing him what is good [. . .] **Col. 2** 1[for] he gave You a man [. . .] 2for he is the one who kept [His] utterances [. . .] 3which belong to all the children of Israel [. . . will] 4your hand save you? Indeed the power of God [. . .] 5those who do good, and hate evil, until [. . .] 6do you dare to do evil, lest [. . .] perish [. . .] 7[. . .]

Some of the biblical psalms are attributed to figures from Israel's history, principally David, but also King Solomon (Pss. 72; 127) and Moses (Ps. 90). The Qumran collection had a psalm credited to the prophet Obadiah, but little of it remains.

8A psalm of Obadiah. God [. . .] 9truth in it, and grace [. . .]

The "man of God" credited with this psalm is probably King David, since it contains extracts from Psalm 18, also credited to him. (David is called the "man of God" in Neh. 12:24.)

4Q381 Frag. 24 4A psalm of the man of God. O LORD God [. . .] 5free Judah from every enemy, and from Ephraim [. . .] 6generation. And they will praise him for his grace, and they will say, Rise, O God [. . .] 7"Your name is my deliverance, my rock, my fortress, my deliverer" (Ps.

18:2), [O LORD . . .] "on the day [of my] disaster [8]I cry out to the LORD" (18:6), for my God will answer me. My help [. . .] my enemies, and he will say, [9]Indeed [. . .] to the people, "and I [. . . my cry] to Him shall enter His ears [10]and [my] voice [He will hear in His temple" (18:6). "Then] the earth [shall tremble and shake, and the pillars holding up the mountains will quiver . . ." (18:7)]

Although the heading is missing, this psalm too may once have been attributed to David. It quotes from Psalm 86, credited to David, and Psalm 89, which, although credited to "Ethan the Ezrahite," focuses on God's choice of the family of David for royal honors, and the psalmist refers to himself (l. 7) as "your anointed." To be called by God's name (l. 9) means to be especially identified with God's purpose, as was David.

Frag. 15 [1][. . .] You shall renew my heart [. . .] [2]"[. . .turn to me and be gracious to me, and give Your strength to Your servant] and deliver Your maidservant's son" (Ps. 86:16). "Show me [3][a good omen, so that my enemies will be afraid and draw back, for You,] my God, have helped me" (86:17). So let me lay my case to You, my God [4][. . . "You rule over the] tall sea waves, and You quiet its breakers" (89:14), "You [5][crushed the primeval dragon like a corpse, with Your strong arm You have scattered Your enemies" (89:10). "The world] and everything in it You created" (89:11). "You have an arm of [6][power, Your hand is strong, Your right hand is lifted high" (89:13). "Who in heaven can compare to You,] my God, and which of the divine beings in the whole [7][holy council" (89:6). . . . for You] are its glorious splendor. And I, Your anointed one, have come to understand [8][. . . I will tell others] about You, for You have given me knowledge, and indeed You have endowed me with great insight [9][. . .] for I am called by Your name, my God, and for Your deliverance [10][. . .] they will put on [knowledge] like a robe, and a garment of [. . .]

A subcategory of psalm is the wisdom poem, which addresses the listener/reader instead of God. More reflective, it shares some of the expressions and perspective of wisdom literature (see the Book of Secrets, *text 6). A biblical example is Psalm 49. This example from Qumran moves from wisdom themes to a meditation on God's greatness displayed in the created world.*

Frag. 1 [1][. . .] I have declared, and of his marvels I will speak. And Wisdom will teach me what is right [. . .] [2]my mouth, and to the simple, so that they will understand, and to the ignorant, that they may gain knowledge. O LORD, how great [. . .] [3]miracles are, in the day He made heaven and earth, and by the word of His mouth [. . .] [4]He perfected the watercourses, its lakes and pools, and every body of water [. . .] [5]night, and the stars, and constellations [. . .] [6]trees, and every fr[uit of the vine]yard, and all the produce of the field, and by the utterance of His words [. . .] all [. . . the man] [7]with his wife, and by his spirit He appointed them as rulers over all these things on the earth, and over all [. . .] [8]month by month, festival by festival, day by day, to eat its fruit [. . .] [9][. . .] and birds, and everything that is theirs to eat [. . .] all and also [. . .] [10][. . .] in them and all his armies and [His] angels [. . .] [11][. . .] to serve Adam and to minister to him and [. . .] **Frag. 14** [2][. . .] thick clouds, snow [. . .] and hail and all [. . .] [3][. . .] will never transgress his command. The four winds [. . .] **Frags. 76–77** [1][. . .] to me beasts and birds, be gathered [. . .] [2][. . .] to human beings according to the inclination of [their] thou[ghts . . .] [3–6][. . .]

The following section may belong to a different psalm than the wisdom psalm it follows, though it shares some of the same themes, including the greatness of God in his ordering of the world, but it also considers God's historical acts on behalf of Israel.

[7][. . . the com]pany of the Most Holy Place, those who belong to the King of Kings [. . .] [8][. . . hear] my words, and You will be enlightened, hear the wisdom that comes from my mouth, and You will understand [. . .] [9][. . .] and a reliable judge, and a faithful witness, if there is in You the strength to answer me [. . .] [10][. . .] who among You can give an answer, and stand in controversy wi[th Him . . .] [11][. . .] though You have many judges, and witnesses without number, except [. . .] [12][. . .] the LORD will sit in your courts to judge truly, and none will arise [. . .] [13][. . . He will send His seven] spirits to give you reliable decisions. Is there understanding? Then learn [. . .] [14][. . .] Lord of Lords, mighty and marvelous, and there is none like Him. He has chosen [you . . .] [15][. . . from] many [peoples] and out of great nations to be His people, to rule over all [. . .] [16][. . . hea]ven and earth and to be supreme over all the nations of the earth and to [. . .] **Frag. 69** [1][. . .] when He saw that the people of the land committed heinous acts [2][. . .] the whole land [became] doubly filthy through impurity, though from the beginning He did marvelous deeds [3][. . .] He decided in his heart to eradicate them from the land, and to put a [different] people on it [4][. . .] to you, and He gave you prophets in His spirit to enlighten you and teach you [5a][. . .] came down from heaven, and spoke with you to enlighten you and to keep you from the deeds of the [former] inhabitants [5][. . . He gave] laws, instructions, and commandments, He established a covenant

through [Moses . . .] [6][. . .] dwell in the land, then it will be pure; and He [said . . .] [7][. . .] to enlighten you, if you will be His or [not . . .] [8][. . .] to violate the covenant He made for you, and to be estranged and [. . .] [9][. . .] for wickedness, and to pervert the words of his mouth [. . .]

A fragment of a personal lament.

Frag. 33 [2]And You have made me a sign and a [. . .] Rise up, O LORD and God, [be exalted in Your strength] [3]and we will praise Your power, for it is without limit [. . .] You place me, and Your rebuke will turn to [joy . . .] [4]eternal, and to exalt You, for my sins have become too many for me [. . .] and You are my God, send Your [spirit . . .] [5]to Your maidservant's son, and Your mercy to Your servant [. . .] I will sing and rejoice in You while my enemies watch, for [. . .] [6]Your servants in Your righteousness, and in accordance with Your grace [. . .] to deliver [. . .] to You. Selah.

King Manasseh was portrayed in 2 Kings as an infamous idolater whose sins were alone sufficient to bring destruction and exile on Judah (21:1–18). An alternate version of his story describes how the wicked king, when captured by the Assyrians, saw the error of his ways and prayed to God for deliverance, which was granted (2 Chron. 33:10–13). Pious Jews of a much later time wrote the Prayer of Manasseh, which, in Greek translation, became a popular work and is included in the apocryphal/deuterocanonical collection. The Qumran group also possessed a "prayer of Manasseh," unrelated to the Greek text, but reflecting the same desire to supply a suitable prayer of repentance for the wicked king. Here its form reflects the usual style of the personal lament.

[8]The prayer of Manasseh, king of Judah, when the king of Assyria imprisoned him. [. . .] my God [. . .] is near, my deliverance is before Your eyes. [. . .] [9]For the deliverance Your presence brings I wait, and I shrink before You because of [my sins,] for You have been very [merciful,] while I have increased my guilt, and so [. . .] [10]from enduring joy, but my spirit will not experience goodness for [. . .] You lift me up, high over the Gentile [. . .] [11]though I did not remember You [. . .] **Frag. 45** [1][. . .] I am in awe of You, and I have been cleansed [2]of the abominations I destroyed. I made my soul to submit to You [. . .] they increased its sin, and plot against me [3]to lock me up; but I have trusted in You [. . .] [4]do not give me over to be tried, with You, O my God [. . .] [5]they are conspiring against me, they tell lies [. . .] [6]to me deeds of [. . .]

No heading survives for this royal psalm that gives thanks for God's help in winning a military victory.

Frag. 46 [2][. . .] Your great mercy [. . .] and a victory has been given to me [. . .] [3][. . .] fools [despise] Your laws and Your glory and Your splendor [. . .] [4]and like clouds they are spread out on [the surface of the earth . . .] to clouds they scatter abroad [. . .] [5]a mere human will not be bold or lift up [himself . . . You] have tested all and the chosen You purify like an offering to You, but the enemies [. . .] [6]You despise like filth. A storm wind [. . .] their deeds, but those who worship You are always before You, their horns are horns of [7]iron so they can gore many, and they will gore [. . .] and their hooves You will make out of bronze. Sinners like dung [8]on the soil they trample [. . .] will be scattered before [. . .] **Frag. 31** [1][. . .] in the trap that they set [. . .] I will sing to [the LORD, for He helped me . . .] [2][. . .] I will tell of Your miracles, for a God of [. . .] before You [. . .] You deliver me and bring me up from the abode of Death and [. . .] [3][. . . a]ll His ways shall come [. . .] in His holy place. Selah.

Another royal psalm, this one a personal lament, with an expression of confidence in God.

[4][Prayer of . . . , k]ing of Judah. Hear, [my] God [. . .] I shall recount before those who worship You [. . .] [5][. . .] Your thoughts, who can understand them. Truly my enemies have increased while You watch, and You are aware of them, and those who hate me are before Your [eyes . . .] [6][. . .] You will destroy the enemies of the wise and insightful, and You will sweep them away. O God, my salvation, my days are hid with You, and what can mere humanity do to me? Here I am [. . .] [7][. . .] by the sword on the day of wrath. But those who speak truth have woven a garland for my head, for the splendor of [. . .] is their glory [. . .]

—E.M.C.

94. An Apocryphon of Elijah

4Q382

My father, my father! The chariots of Israel and its horsemen!" With this astonished cry, as the Bible says (2 Kings 2:12), the disciple Elisha witnessed the departure of his master, Elijah, "the Tishbite of the inhabitants of

Gilead." Elijah, like Enoch, was believed to have ascended to heaven while still alive. He was a prophet of the ninth century B.C.E. whom the Bible describes as working many miracles, but Elijah is perhaps best remembered for his duel with the prophets of Baal on Mt. Carmel, and for his opposition to King Ahab and his wicked queen, Jezebel. Malachi 4:5–6 says that before the Day of the Lord, Elijah will return to reconcile fathers and sons. Because of his miracles and ascension, the prophet became a figure of great mystery and appears in many texts of ancient Judaism, playing very diverse roles.

Such texts include Sirach (ca. 180 B.C.E.), which calls Elijah a prophet like fire who shall come to restore Jacob (48:1–12). Fourth Ezra (ca. 100 C.E.) includes Elijah when predicting the apocalyptic return of the three men who rose to heaven without tasting death (the other two being Enoch and, according to Jewish legend but not the Bible, Moses). Two portions of the rabbinic Mishnah (compiled ca. 200 C.E., but including much earlier materials) ascribe surpassing importance to Elijah's return. They declare that when he returns he will act as a judge to settle all remaining disputes and resurrect the dead (*Eduyyoth* 8:7; *Sotah* 9:15).

In the Gospels, several texts speak of John the Baptist as Elijah. In Matthew 11:14 Jesus explicitly says of John, "If you are willing to accept it, he is Elijah who is to come." Yet in the Gospel of John, when the Baptist is asked, "Are you Elijah?" he replies "I am not" (John 1:21). Jesus himself was also associated with Elijah. He compared his ministry with the career of the prophet in Luke 4:25–26, and according to Mark 6:15 some of the populace thought Jesus was Elijah. The ominous rumor reached Herod. It was ominous because potentates like Herod, fearful of popular uprisings catalyzed by prophets, generally moved to erase rumored threat before it became a reality. That had been the Baptist's fate. In any event, who should be identified with Elijah may have been open to discussion, but it was being discussed. In that light we note that the present, unfortunately very badly damaged, text could be interpreted to refer to his return (frag. 31).

Obadiah, the official in charge of Ahab's palace, hides prophets when the wicked queen Jezebel begins to seek their lives. Later, Obadiah meets Elijah, who asks him to arrange a meeting with Ahab (cf. 1 Kings 18).

Frag. 1 [2][. . .] And he hid them fif[ty to a cave, and provided them with bread and water . . .] [3][. . .] He feared Jezebel and Ahab the ki[ng of Israel . . .] [4][. . . O]badiah in the la[nd] of Israel [. . .]

Frag. 2 [2][So Obadiah went to meet] Ahab, and tol[d him; and Ahab went to meet Elijah.] [3][When Ahab saw] Elijah, [Ahab said to him, "Is it you, you troubler of Israel?"]

Elijah and his disciple, Elisha, at the time that Elijah was about to ascend to heaven in a whirlwind (cf. 2 Kings 2).

Frag. 9 [5][And the sons of the prophets said to Elisha, "Do you kn]ow that today the LORD* will take [your master away from you?" He replied,] [6]["I know." Elij]ah said to Elisha, "Stay here, [my] son; [for the Lord has sent me as far as Bethel." But] [7][Elisha said, "As the Lord lives, and as you] yourself [live,] I will not leave you." [So they went down to Bethel . . .]

A prophecy. The reference to a future "mighty man" is intriguing and may reflect the belief in Elijah's return at the time of the Last Days.

Frag. 31 [2][. . . g]reat, to give them into the power of all the nations [. . .] [3][. . .] at the end shall arise a mighty man [. . .] [4][. . .] for to all the spirits [. . .] [5][. . . the p]rophets [. . .]

A prayer. The fragment fits well with the overview of history that we find in frag. 31 above.

Frag. 104 [1][. . . not to turn away] from Your words, to hold fast to Your covenant so that their hearts may be sanctified [. . . You sent forth] [2]Your hands to make them Yours, and Yourself theirs, and justified [. . .] [3]Surely You are as the bestower of an inheritance; You have become their master, their father [. . . Yet You] [4]have left them in the power of the[ir] kings, and will make them stumble among the nat[ions . . .] [7][. . .] your life. (?) Did You give them [the Law] by the hand of Moses [. . .] [8][. . .] Your judgment, taking the sin of Your people upon [his] he[ad (?) . . .] [9][. . .] Your patience and abundant forgiveness [. . .]

—M.O.W.

95. A Jeremiah Apocryphon

4Q384, 4Q385a, 4Q387, 4Q388a, 4Q389–390

This important new text and the next, *An Ezekiel Apocryphon,* are perhaps best categorized as prophecy by literary fiction. Although their original editor, John Strugnell, concluded they were a single composition,

*The scribe wrote this divine name with four dots, each dot representing one consonant of the Hebrew.

recent discussion has more or less agreed on separating the fragments according to their relationship to the two prophets. We have followed suit.

Reading *A Jeremiah Apocryphon,* one is often reminded of the latter chapters of Daniel. For example, the second copy of the work (4Q387) recounts ten complete jubilees of unfaithfulness (490 years). At the end of this period the kingdom of Israel was to be destroyed and one called Gadfan (Hebrew for "the Blasphemer") was to rule over it. Daniel, of course, takes a very similar tack, prophesying that after a period of 490 years, at the climax of an unprecedented period of apostasy, there would arise a foreign ruler "speaking blasphemy" (Dan. 7:8, 11, 20). He would be the mightiest ruler yet, but would eventually give way before the kingdom of God, which was to be ruled by righteous Jews who had not, in the midst of general apostasy, turned their backs on God. The *Apocryphon*'s figure Gadfan is probably to be identified with Daniel's blasphemous ruler.

According to most scholars, Daniel is describing the Syrian king Antiochus IV Epiphanes. About 168 B.C.E. Antiochus IV initiated a terrible persecution of the Jews and tried to turn them to Greek ways of worship, which gave rise to the Maccabean revolt. After a number of years, the Jews succeeded in throwing off Antiochus's forced changes, and at his death in 164 B.C.E. the threat evaporated. Antiochus portrayed himself as a divinity, which may explain both Daniel's description and the Syrian's label as Gadfan here. The Jews did not take kindly to human beings claiming divinity—that was ultimate blasphemy. However, this proposal is not without its problems and the programmatic nature of the *Apocryphon* (ten jubilees) makes it just as likely that Gadfan is to be compared with Ezekiel's Gog and Revelation's Beast—a purposefully open-ended description of the desperate evils of the Last Days.

Although there is very little overlap evident between the six manuscripts that make up this work, Devorah Dimant, the official editor, has discerned a rather sweeping story line. According to her reconstruction, the composition is situated in Babylon twenty-five years after the fall of Jerusalem in 586 B.C.E. From this vantage point a full historical review can be reconstructed from the fragments beginning in the biblical period and stretching into the eschatological era.

The original scroll would have stretched some forty columns, about half the size of biblical Jeremiah. We have followed Dimant's outline below. Other outlines may be possible, but this organization at least allows readers to imagine how the pieces *might* have fit together.

Introduction

The circumstances of Jeremiah's final days are not known. The church fathers knew of a tradition that reports he was stoned at Tahpanhes. Jewish tradition (Seder Olam

Rabah 26) suggests that he and Baruch were taken to Babylon, where he died. This fragment may preserve an early witness to the rabbinic story.

4Q389 Frag. 1 [2][. . .] in the land of J[udah . . .] [3][. . .] and they sought for a[ll . . .] [4][. . . and] everyone who remains in the land of E[gypt . . .] [5][. . . Je]remiah, the son of Hilkiah [. . .] from the land of Egy[pt . . .] [6][thir]ty-sixth year of the exile of Israel they read the[se] words [before] [7]a[ll the children of I]srael upon the River Sur at the place of [. . .]

Biblical Period

God promises that a remnant shall return from the Babylonian exile just as he brought the sons of Israel out of Egypt.

4Q388a Frag. 2 [1][. . .] to them [. . .] [2][. . .] in curtains of goat [hair . . .] [3][. . . fort]y years, and when [. . .] [4][. . . and th]ey turned after [. . .] [5][. . .] them [. . .]

4Q389 Frag. 2 [1][. . . you have] sought Me, I was [. . .] [2][. . . I shall] raise up your heads when I bring y[ou] out [from the land of Egypt . . .] [3][. . .] to them and that which they repaid Me. For I carried them [as a man carries his son until] [4][they came to] Kadesh-barnea, and I spoke to them [. . .] [5][. . .] upon them and I swore by [. . .] [6][. . .] and their sons I brought to the [land . . .] [7][. . .] and I walked with them in [. . .] [8][. . .] forty years. And it came to pass [. . .]

Entrance into the land of Canaan?

Frag. 4 [1][. . .] and you ca[me . . .] [2][. . .] the land [. . .]

A fragment echoing 1 Samuel 8:6.

Frag. 5 [2][. . . when] they said, "Give us a king who [. . .] [3][. . . Samue]l, [son of E]lkanah for [. . .]

The era of David and Solomon.

4Q385a Frags. 1a–b Col. 2 [1][. . . And I] raised up [. . .] [2][. . .] his enemy [. . .] [3][. . .] his enemy and I turned [aside . . .] [4]when he sought My face, and he did not exalt himself above Me [. . .] [5]and his days were completed, and Solomon sat [. . .] [6]and I delivered the life of his enemies into his hand [. . .] [7]and I took an offer[ing] from his hand [. . .]

The Temple is defiled as the people wander from God

Frags. 3a–c (with **4Q388a Frag. 3** and **4Q387 Frag. 1**) 2[. . . when] you [were wal]king in [error before Me . . .] 3[. . . th]ose called by name [. . .] 4[. . . a]s I said to Jac[ob . . .] 5[. . .] and [you said,] "You have forsaken u[s, O God," and you despised My statutes,] 6[you forgot] the festivals of My covenant, and you pro[faned My name and My holy things,] 7[you defiled] My Temple, and you offered [your sacrifices to the] goat-demons and [. . .] 8[. . .] the [. . .] in the mystery [. . .] 9[. . .] and you broke everything arr[oga]ntly 10[. . . and I looked for faith but I] did not 11[find . . .]

4Q387 Frag. 1 (with **4Q389 Frags. 6** and **7**) 7[. . . and I delivered] you into the hand of your ene[my] and I made [your land] desolate 8[. . . and the land] made amends for its sa[bba]ths by being desolated [. . .] 9[. . .] in the land[s] of [you]r enemies until [the] sabbath of [. . .] 10[. . . t]o your land [. . . to ap]point [. . .]

4Q388a Frag. 4 2[. . .] sabbaths of the y[ears . . .]

Frag. 5 1[. . .] they forsook Me [. . .]

Frag. 6 2[. . . and I] hid My face from [them . . .] 3[. . . a]ll [. . .] 4[. . .] evi[ls . . .]

Second Temple Period

Israel will forsake God in the seventh jubilee. In the judgment that follows, God promises to preserve a remnant .

4Q390 Frag. 1 2[. . . and] befo[re me, and I shall] again [deliver them] into the hand the sons of Aar[on . . .] seventy years [. . .] 3The sons of Aaron shall rule over them, but they will not walk [in] My [wa]ys which I am commanding you, so that 4you must warn them. And they also shall do evil before Me like all that Israel did 5in the former days of their kingdom, except for those who were the first to go up from the land of their exile to rebuild 6the Temple. But I will speak with them and send them a commandment and they will understand all that 7they and their fathers have forsaken. But at the end of that generation, in the seventh jubilee 8after the destruction of the land, they shall forget law, festival, Sabbath, and covenant and shall bring an end to everything; they shall destroy everything and commit 9evil before Me. So I shall hide my face from them, give them into the hand of their enemies, and hand [them] over 10to the sword. But I shall cause a remnant from them to escape in order that [t]he[y might] not [be complet]ely des[troyed] in my wrath [and] when [My] f[ace] is hidden 11from them. And the angels of Mas[t]emah shall rule over them and [I] will r[eject them . . . and they] shall again [12]do evil before [Me] and walk in the s[tubbornness of their heart . . .]

This is the prophecy of the Gadfan ("Blasphemer") who is to come ten full jubilees after the destruction of the Temple (586 B.C.E.). Although a literal reckoning would suggest a date of 96 B.C.E. and place the prophecy's fulfillment during the reign of Alexander Jannaeus (103–76 B.C.E.), the title Gadfan is more appropriate for the Syrian king Antiochus IV Epiphanes, who initiated a persecution of the Jews in 168 B.C.E. and portrayed himself as divine (thereby committing blasphemy). However, the schematic basis of the prophecy suggests that the character may be intentionally ambiguous, pointing mainly to the hopeless nature—apart from God's intervention—of the Last Days.

4Q387 Frag. 2 (with **4Q385a Frag. 4, 4Q388a Frag. 7 Col. 2,** and **4Q389 Frag. 8 Col. 2** [with some variation]) **Col. 2** [1][. . .] and you will determine to serve Me with all your heart [2]and with a[ll your soul. And they shall see]k [M]y f[ace] in their distress. But I will not care for them [3]because of their treachery [th]at [they] committed ag[ainst Me,] until the completion of ten [4]full jubilees. You will walk about in m[adness,] blindness, and confusion of [5]heart. At the end of that generation I [shall remove] the kingdom from the hand of those who possess [6]it and [e]stablish strangers from another people over it. And [7][arr]ogance shall rule in all the land. And the kingdom of Israel shall be destroyed. In those days [8][there will] b[e a king, and h]e will be a blasphemer. He shall commit abominations and I shall remove [9][his] kingd[om and] that [king] for the destroyers. And My face will be hidden from Israel [10][. . . shall be returned] to many nations. Then the children of Israel will cry out [11][because of the heavy yoke in the lands of their exile and yet there will be no one to deliv]er them [12][because they have certainly rejected My statutes and they have despised My laws. Th]er[efore I have hidden] **4Q389 Frag. 8 Col. 2** [5]My face from [them un]til they finish their iniquity.

And this shall be a sign for them that they have finished [6]their iniquity [for] I have abandoned the land because they acted haughtily toward Me and because they did not recognize [7][tha]t [I have rejected them and] they will turn away and do evil. The ev[il] is g[rea]ter than before. [8][They shall break the covenant which I made] with Abraha[m] and [I]saac and [9][Jacob. In] those [days] a king shall rise up for the Gentiles, a blasphemer, and he shall commit evil and [. . .] [10][And in his days I shall remove Israe]l from being a people. [In his days] I shall shatter t[he k]ingdom of [11][Egypt . . . Egypt, and I shall cut off Israe]l [and hand her over to the sword . . .] **4Q387 Frag. 2 Col. 3** [3][and] I [shall lay was]te t[he la]nd and remove man far away [and shall abandon] [4]the land to the hand of the angels of Mastemah and I shall hide [My face] [5][from Is]rael.

And this shall be a sign for them in the day that I forsake the land [in desolation] [6][and] the priests of Jerusalem [will return] to serve other gods [and to act] [7][in accordance with the abomin]ations of the [nations . . .] **4Q388a Frag. 7 Col. 2** [8]three which shall reign [. . .] [9]the most holy [. . .] [10][. . .] and those who justify [. . .]

An additional (?) episode of disobedience committed by the priests is again linked to a specific jubilee—the number of which has been lost—and precipitates another round of God's judgment.

4Q390 Frag. 2 Col. 1 [2][. . . and My] house, [My altar, and] the sanctuary [. . .] [3]it was done thus [. . .] for these things shall come upon them [. . .] and [4]the rule of Belial [shall] be over them in order to hand them over to the sword for a week of years [. . . and] on that jubilee they will be [5]violating all My statutes and all My commandments which I shall command t[hem, those sent by the han]d of My servants the prophets.

[6]And [t]he[y] will [be]gin to contend with one another for seventy years, from the day of the violation of the [oath and the] covenant that they will violate. Then I shall give them [7][into the hand of the ang]els of Mastemah and these shall rule over them. And they will not know nor understand that I was angry with them for their unfaithfulness [8][by which] they have [fors]aken Me and committed evil before Me. In that which I have not taken pleasure, they have chosen to enrich themselves by ill-gotten wealth, illegal profit, [9][and violence, eac]h robbing that which belongs to his ne[ighbor] and oppressing one another. They will defile My Temple, [10][profane my Sabbaths,] f[orget] My [fest]ivals, and with [foreign]ers [they will] profane [their] see[d.] Their priests will commit violence [11][. . .] and the [12][. . .] their sons [. . .]

Col. 2 [4]from it [. . .] [5]and with the word [. . .] [6]we [. . .] [7]they will know. And I sent [. . .] [8]and with spears to see[k . . .] [9]in the midst of the land upon [. . .] [10]their [pos]session, and they sacrificed [. . .] [11]they [will pro]fane in it and [th]e alta[r . . .]

The prophecy of the three apostate priests.

4Q385a Frags. 5a–b (with **4Q387 Frag. 3**) [1][. . .] God [. . .] [2][. . .] a number of priests [. . .] [3][. . .] others [. . .] [4][. . .] the altar [. . .] [5][. . . those who have fal]l[en by the sword . . .] [6][. . . defi]led [. . .] [7][. . . three priests] who shall not walk in the c[ustoms of the priests, according to the name of the God of] [8][Is]rael shall be called. [And in their days] shall be brought down [the pride of those who violate the] [9][covenan]t [and the serv]ants of that which is foreign. An[d Israel shall be torn asunder in that generation,] **4Q387 Frag. 3** [7]fighting against one another [8]because of the law and because of the covenant. "Then I shall send a famine i[n the lan]d but not of [9]b[re]ad, a drought but n[ot] of water" (Amos 8:11), [but] rather for [hearing the words of God . . .]

Eschatological Era

God's judgment upon Gog (Ezek. 38:22) and the apostasy of the sons of Israel.

4Q387 Frag. 4 Col. 1 [1][. . .] in the lot according to th[eir] tribes [. . .] [2][. . .] the kings of the north, years [. . .] [3][. . .] and the children of Israel [shall cr]y out to God [. . .] [4][. . . flooding rain, h]a[il s]ton[es,] fire, and brimstone (Ezek. 38:22) [. . .] [5][. . .] with (*or* people of) the [. . .]

The demise of Greece.

4Q385a Frags. 16a–b [1][. . . the]y rema[in (?) . . .] [2][. . .] people to the flocks of [. . .] [3][. . .] and seed and he will turn [to] his people and [. . .] [4][. . . and] I [will take] possession of Greece [. . .] [5][. . . and] I [will release] wild beasts against you [. . .] [6][. . . the mount]ain and Lebanon they will inherit [. . .] [7][. . .] they [will see]k the LORD saying [. . .] [8][. . .] Jacob [. . .]

Frags. 17a–e Col. 1 [4][. . .] the rivers of [5][. . .] will [be] subdue[d . . .]

The righteous (?) rest in the shade of the Tree of Life; the demise of Egypt.

Col. 2 [1][. . .] the part and [. . .] [2][. . .] the days of their life [. . .] [3]in the foliage of the Tree of Life. [. . .]

[4]Where is your portion, O Amon, that [s]its by the Nile? [5]Water surrounds you, [your] ra[mpart] is the sea, and water is [your] wall. [6]Cush, Egyp[t is your might, and] there is no end to [your] bar[s.] [7]Libya is your help, and she shall go into exile, into ca[ptivity] [8]and her children shall be da[she]d on [mountain]tops and for [9][her nobles] lots [will be cast] and all her [great one]s in fet[ters . . . (Nah. 3:8–10).]

Conclusion

Jeremiah charges the sons of Israel to keep the covenant of their fathers while in exile in Babylon.

4Q385a Frags. 18a–b Col. 1 [2][. . . And] Jeremiah, the prophet, [went out] from before the LORD [3][and went with the] captives who were taken captive from the land of Jerusalem and went [4][to Riblah, to] the king of Babylon, when Nebuzaradan, the captain of the guard, struck [5][. . .] and took all the utensils of the House of God, the priests, [6][the nobles,] and the children of Israel and brought them to Babylon. Jeremiah the prophet went [7][with them as far as] the river. And he commanded them what they should do in the land of [their] captivity, [8][that they should listen] to the voice of Jeremiah concerning the things which God had commanded him [9][to do,] that they should keep the covenant of the God of their fathers in the land [10][of Babylon, and that they should not do] as they had done, they themselves, their kings, their priests, [11][and their princes . . . for they had] profaned [the nam]e of God so as to [defile . . .]

Jeremiah and the Jews of Tahpanhes.

Frag. 18 Col. 2 [1][. . .] in Tahpanhes w[hich is in the land of Egypt . . .] [2]And they said to him, "Inquire [on our behalf of G]od [. . . But] [3]Jeremi[ah did not listen] to them, not inquiring of Go[d] for them, [nor lifting up] [4]a song of rejoicing and a prayer. Jeremiah lamented [. . . laments] [5][ov]er Jerusalem.

[And the word of the LORD came to] [6]Jeremiah in the land of Tahpanhes, which is in the land of Eg[ypt, saying, "Speak to] [7]the children of Israel and to the children of Judah and Benjamin, [thus you shall say to them,] [8]'Seek My statutes every day and ke[ep] My commandments [and do not go] [9]after the i[d]ols of the Gentiles after which [your fathers] w[ent, for] [10][they] shall not sav[e you . . .] not [. . .]

—M.G.A.

96. An Ezekiel Apocryphon

4Q385, 4Q385b, 4Q386, 4Q388

The book of Ezekiel is the inspiration for the important composition *An Ezekiel Apocryphon*. The biblical text is at turns quoted, rewritten, and explained. Indeed, explanations of Ezekiel have provided the ancients and now moderns with a veritable industry of commentaries, novels, movies, and even whole lecture series. Who of the boomer generation can forget Erich Von Daniken's *Chariots of the Gods*? His book is still in print after thirty-five years, fueled in the main by our desire to understand the prophecies of Ezekiel.

This ancient best-seller—there were four well-thumbed copies in Cave 4—focused on questions concerning Ezekiel's visions. Several are preserved among the fragments: the Merkabah vision (a chariot of the gods!) from Ezekiel 1, a vision of Egypt and Babylon modeled after Ezekiel 29–32, and the vision of the dry bones from Ezekiel 37. It is the last that is preserved most completely in the fragments translated below. It is clear that the ancient writer understood this vision to refer to a literal resurrection of the righteous. To the details of the biblical text the commentator adds, "And a great many people [revi]ved. And they blessed the LORD of hosts wh[o had revived them]" (4Q385 frag. 2, ll. 8–9). This statement, seeming perhaps rather obvious to many Christians and Jews who read Ezekiel today, is quite astounding nonetheless. It is the oldest known reference to a bodily resurrection, a doctrine that became a keynote for both Judaism and Christianity.

Prophecy of God's judgment of Egypt and its cities.

4Q385b Frag. 1 [1][These are the wor]ds of Ezekiel. And the word of the LORD came to [me, saying, "Son of] [2][man, prophe]sy, and say, 'Behold, the day of the destruction of the Gentiles is coming [. . .] [3][. . . Eg]ypt, and there shall be anguish in Put, and a sword in E[gypt] [4][. . . s]hall shake, Cush, [Pu]l, the mighty ones of Arabia, also some of the ch[ildren of] [5][the covenant, and] Arabia shall fall at the gate[s of] Egypt. And [. . .] shall perish [. . .] [6][. . .] by the sword of Egy[pt . . .] will be devastated [. . .]

Prophecy of the dry bones (Ezek. 37).

4Q388 Frag. 7 [2][. . .] you will not di[e . . .]

4Q385 Frag. 2 (with **4Q388 Frag. 7** and **4Q386 Frag. 1 Col. 1)** [1][“For I am the LORD,] who redeems My people, giving the covenant to them.”

[2][And I said, “O LORD,] I have seen many from Israel who have loved Your name and have walked [3]in the ways [of Your heart. So,] when will [th]ese things come to pass? And how will their faithfulness be rewarded?” And the LORD said [4]to me, “I see the children of Israel, and they shall know that I am the LORD.”

[5][And He said,] “Son of man, prophesy over these bones, and say, ‘Come together, bone to its bone and joint [6][to its joint.’ ” And it wa]s s[o.] And He said a second time, “Prophesy, and let sinews come upon them and let skin cover [7][them.” And it was so.] And He s[ai]d, “Again prophesy to the four winds of the heavens, and a let them blow [8][upon the slain.” And it was so.] And a great many people [revi]ved (Ezek. 37:4–10). And they blessed the LORD of hosts wh[o] [9][had revived them.

And] I said, “O LORD, when will [th]ese things come to pass?” And the LORD said to [me, “Until] [10][. . . and after many] days a tree shall bend, and it shall stand up [. . .”]

God’s assurance that Israel would once again possess the land.

Frag. 3 [1][. . .] and [. . .] [2][. . .] LORD. And all the people arose and st[ood] on [their feet to give thanks . . .] [3][and to prai]se the LORD of Hosts and I, too, sp[oke] with them [. . .] [4][. . .]

And the LORD said to me, “Son [of man, sa]y to them [. . .] [5][. . . in the place of] their [bur]ial they will lie until [. . .] [6][. . . from] your [grav]es and from the earth [. . .] [7][. . .] that [the yok]e of Eg[ypt . . .]

God promises to preserve a remnant from the oppressions of Belial.

4Q386 Frag. 1 Col. 2 [1][“. . . lan]d, and they shall know that I am the LORD.”

And He said to me, “Look, [2]son of man, at the land of Israel.” And he said, “I have seen, O LORD, and behold it is a wasteland; [3]when will You gather them together?” And the LORD said, “A son of Belial will plan to oppress My people [4]but I shall not allow him. His dominion shall not come to pass. From the impure, no seed shall survive, [5]nor from the caperbush shall come new wine, nor shall a hornet make honey [. . .] and [6]I will slay the wicked in Memphis. But I shall bring My children out of Memphis, and upon their re[mn]ant I will turn. [7]As they shall say, 'There was peace and quiet,' they shall say, 'The land shall be [8]as it was in the days of [. . .] old.' Therefore, I shall arouse wra[th] u[pon] them [9]f[rom the fo]ur winds of the hea[vens . . .] [10][like a] burning [fi]re a[s . . ."]

God promises to judge Babylon for Nebuchadnezzar's act against the poor of Jerusalem.

Col. 3 [1]and the poor He will show no mercy, but He will bring them to Babylon. And Babylon is but a cup in the hand of the LORD, in [her] time [2]He shall cast her away [. . .] [3]in Babylon and it shall be [. . .] [4]a dwelling place for demons [. . .] [5]desolation [and. . .will] pasture [. . .] [6]to Bab[ylon . . .]

4Q385 Frag. 4 [1][. . .] instead of my grief [2]make my soul rejoice and let the days hasten quickly until men say, [3]"Are not the days hastening quickly so that the children of Israel might take possession?" [4]And the LORD said to me, "I shall not t[ur]n you away, Ezekiel. Be[ho]ld, I am cutting short [5]the days and the year[s . . .] [6]a few, just you said to [. . .] [7][For] the mouth of the LORD has spoken these things. [. . .]

Ezekiel's vision (Ezek. 1) of divine glory—the chariot of God.

Frag. 6 [1]And my people shall be [. . .] [2]with a cheerful heart and with [a willing] s[oul . . .] [3]and hide a little whi[le . . .] [4]and from the breaches [. . .] [5]the vision which Ezek[iel] saw [. . .] [6]the chariot shone, and the four living creatures, a living creature [. . . and as they moved they did not turn] [7]back; upon two wheels each creature moved, and [its] two leg[s . . .] [8][up]on [. . .] in [on]e there was breath. And their faces were one beside the o[ther. And the appearance of] [9]the fa[ces, one of a lion, on]e of an eagle, one of a calf, and one of a man. And [the hand] [10]of a man wa[s] joined at the backs of the creatures and attached to [their wings . . .] and the w[hee]l[s . . .] [11]wheel joined to wheel when they moved, and from the two sides of the w[heels were streams of fire] [12]and living creatures were among the coals, like flaming coals, [. . .] [13]and the wheels, the living creatures and the wheels. Now there was [. . . ove]r [their heads an expanse, like] [14][an] aweso[me gleam of crystal. And] a voice [c]ame [from above the expanse . . .]

—M.G.A.

97. God the Creator

4Q392

In a style reminiscent of the *Thanksgiving Hymns* (text 12), *God the Creator* is remarkable for its theological ruminations on the first lines of the biblical creation narrative. The author speculates that on the first day of creation God created light and darkness for himself, not merely as a preliminary stage to further work of creation and distinction as you might think when reading Genesis 1. The writer goes on to assert that light and darkness are simultaneously present with God, a paradox beyond human comprehension. Only for humankind's sake did God distinguish between darkness and light by means of the various heavenly bodies created on the fourth day.

A meditation on creation (Gen. 1). With God, light and darkness can coexist, but for humankind they must be separated into day and night.

Frag. 1 [1][. . .] and dominions [. . .] [2][. . .] that each one might be joined to God and not turn aside from a[ll . . .] [3]and your soul shall hold fast to His covenant, to [se]ek the words of [Hi]s mouth—[for the Lor]d is Go[d in] heaven [4]above—and to search out the ways of the sons of man, for there is no place to hide from His presence. He created darkness [and li]ght for Himself [5]and in His dwelling place is the most perfect light and all deep darkness is at rest in His presence. He has no need to distinguish between light and [6]darkness, but for the sons [of ma]n He has distinguished them as the li[ght of] day, with the sun, and night, with the moon and stars. [7]He has a light which cannot be searched out, nor can [its end] be known [. . .] for all the works of God are wondrous. We [8]are flesh, should we not seek to understand why he does wonders and miracles without number? [9][For on] high [He has made wi]nds and lightning [His messengers and mi]nisters of the inner sanct[uary. And] the lig[hts] went out from his presence [. . .]

Exodus themes are present in this small fragment. For signs and wonders, see Exodus 7:3. A portion of Exodus 15:5 is quoted in l. 5.

Frag. 2 [1][. . .] His [he]art [. . .] [2][. . . they did not listen] to the signs and wonders [. . .] [3][. . . an]y kingdom until this very day, and

[. . .] [4][. . .] cannot be searched out. In raging water a walkway burst fo[rth . . .] [5][. . . and He made] him [sin]k in the depths as a sto[ne . . .]

God's compassion is contrasted with his judgment in ll. 1–2. His care of the Israelites in the wilderness—reflecting Deuteronomy 32:10–11—appears to form the basis of the second half of the fragment.

Frags. 6–9 [1][. . . God of forgive]ness and compassionate [. . .] [2][. . .] ground and He shall destr[oy . . .] [3][co]nsume from the earth and [. . .] our [father]s to give [to us . . .] [4][. . .] which like it [there has] not [been from] of old. [And] in a l[and of wilderness] and desert [He has sustained us] [5][as a fat]her [sustains] his son, and as a bird [with the] yo[ung of] its nest, [He has gath]ered [our] disp[ersed] which [are] not [. . .] [6][. . .] He shall fly [. . .] there is none like Him [. . .] every ear [. . .] [7][like an eagl]e He will fly, s[preading His wings . . .]
—M.G.A.

98. Prayers for Forgiveness

4Q393

The prayers in *Prayers for Forgiveness* are composed following the pattern of Psalm 51, but they have features in common with other prayers of the late biblical period as well. Thus they recall Ezra's supplication about mixed marriages (Ezra 9:6–15) and the communal confession of sins in Nehemiah 9:5–38.

Frags. 1–2 Col. 2 [2]And I ha[ve done] what is evil [in Your eyes] so that You are just in Your word[s,] [3]You are b[lameless . . . when] You [judg]e (Ps. 51:4). Behold, w[e] were formed in our iniquities, [4]in i[mpurity . . . <we were b]irth[ed> . . . st]iff-necked. O, our God, hide [5]Your face from o[ur] si[ns and] blot out [al]l our iniquities, and create a new spirit [6]in us and establish a faithful inclination within us. And to transgressors (teach, O God,) Your ways, [7]and return sinners to Yourself (51:13). Do n[ot] thrust a broken [spir]it from before You because [8]Your people have fainted on account of [Your gre]at an[ger,] and they [have trusted] continually in [Your] forgiv[eness.] [9]Nations and kingdoms shall s[ay . . .] [10]and in their words [. . .] [11]for Your peoples on account of [. . .]

A mosaic of biblical passages.

Frag. 3 [1][. . .] for [. . .You are] [2][Go]d, the faithful God who maintai[ns] covenant loyalty with [those] who love [You and keep Your commandments (Deut. 7:9), as] [3][You spoke] to Moses. Do not forsake Your people [and] Your [inh]eritance. Do not (forsake) each one that he might walk in the stubbornness of his [ev]il heart (Jer. 11:8). [4]In accordance to Your will, O my God, this ha[s come t]o pass; You have fo[rsa]ken Your people and Your inheritance. But do not (forsake) each one to walk [5]in the stubbornness of his evil heart. Gird on strength! Upon whom shall You make Your face to shine if they have not purified themselves, (nor) sanctified themselves, [6]but have exalted themselves above everything? You are the LORD, You chose our fathers long ago [7]and You appointed us as their remnant to give us (what) you established for Abraham and Israel, to drive out [8]be[for]e them [great nations,] valiant warriors, and those of great strength in order to give us houses filled [9][with all sorts of goods, hewn cisterns, pool]s of water, vineyards, and olive groves (Deut. 6:11), an inheritance of a people [. . .]

—M.G.A.

99. The Sabbaths and Festivals of the Year

4Q394 Section A

The present work plots the Sabbaths and festivals for one complete solar year, but without concording by priestly divisions. This is one of the few calendars that designates the extrabiblical Festival of Oil, which fell on the twenty-second day of the sixth month. The structure of the work makes it likely that two more extrabiblical festivals were originally listed as well: the Wine Festival and the Festival of Wood Offering. Among the Dead Sea Scrolls, only the *Temple Scroll* (text 155) agrees in recognizing all three festivals. Clearly, then, although the Qumran calendrical writings share much in common, they do not march in lockstep. The notable differences show that we are reading the works of a particular school in these calendars, not those of a single small sect.

Some scholars believe that 4Q394 Section A frags. 1–2 was not actually a separate and distinct work. They argue that instead it originally attached to the beginning of one copy of *A Sectarian Manifesto* (text 100). In favor of this suggestion is the handwriting: the same scribe has written both 4Q394 Section A and the copy of the *Manifesto.* Yet certain technical aspects of the reconstruction of the *Manifesto* create problems for this suggestion. As long as the matter remains uncertain, it seems best to present 4Q394 Section A frags. 1–2 as a separate work.

Sabbaths and festivals for months two through six.

Frags. 1–2 Col. 1 [1][On the sixteenth] [2][of the month is a Sabbath.] [3]On the twenty- [4]third [5]of the month is a Sabbath. [6][On the] thir[tie]th [7][of the month is a Sabbath.]

[8][On the seventh] [9][of the third (month)] [10][is a Sabbath.] [11][On the fourteenth] [12][of the month is a Sabbath.] [13][On the fifteenth] [14][of the month is the Festival] [15][of Weeks.] [16][On the twenty-] **Col. 2** [1][fi]rs[t] [2][of the] month is a Sabbath. [3][On the] twenty- [4]eighth [5]of [the month] is a Sabbath. [6](The month) continues (with the day) after [7]the Sabbath, [8]the second day, [9][and an additional day.] [10][This completes] [11][the season,] [12][ninety-] [13][one] [14][days.]

[15][On the fourth] [16][of the fourth (month)] **Col. 3** [1][is a Sa]bb[ath.] [2]On the el[eventh] [3]of the month is a Sabbath. [4]On the eigh- [5]teenth of the month is a Sabbath. [6]On the twenty- [7]fifth [8]of the month is a Sabbath.

[9]On the second [10]of the fi[f]t[h (month)] [11][is a Sa]b[bath.] [12][On the third] [13][of the month is the Festival of] [14][Wine] [15][(the day) after] [16][the Sabbath.] **Col. 4** [1][On the ninth] [2][of the month is a Sabbath.] [3][On the] sixteenth [4]of the month is a Sabbath. [5]On the twenty- [6]third [7]of the month is a Sabbath. [8][On the th]irtieth [9][of the month is a Sabbath.]

[10][On the seventh] [11][of the sixth (month)] [12][is a Sabbath.] [13][On the four-] [14][teenth] [15][of the month is a Sabbath.] [16][On the twenty-] **Col. 5** [1][firs]t [2]of the month is a Sabbath. [3]On the twenty- [4]second [5]of the month is the Festival of [6]Oil, [7](on the day) aft[er the Sab]bath. [8]Aft[er it] [9]is the [wood] offer[ing.] [10][On the twenty-] [11][eighth] [12][of the month is a Sabbath.]

To follow those scholars who have determined that 4Q394 Section A frags. 1–2 is part of the introduction of the Sectarian Manifesto, *continue reading in the next text (100).*

—M.G.A.

100. A Sectarian Manifesto

4QMMT: 4Q394–399

In all of antiquity, only the *Sectarian Manifesto* and Paul's Letters to the Galatians and Romans discuss the connection between works and righteousness. For that reason alone, this writing is of immense interest and importance. But the *Manifesto* has additional significance. Although the sectarian documents found in the caves at Qumran fairly bristle with legal discussions on a variety of issues, only this work, commonly known as 4QMMT (an acronym from the Hebrew words meaning "some of the works of the Law"), directly challenges the position of another religious group. Because of the potentially defining character of such a response, scholars have hoped to find in the *Manifesto* a basis for a definitive identification of the group behind the sectarian scrolls.

Of course, when one expects to find something, one usually does, and so it is here. Seen as pregnant with significance, the *Manifesto* has given birth to a new theory. Based on legal arguments in the first section of the *Manifesto,* this theory suggests that the *Yahad* were Sadducees—not, however, the Sadducees as we know them from Josephus or the New Testament. Rather, the theory holds, these are Sadducees with Essene theological tendencies. Thus, those who have embraced this new theory have as yet seen little reason to jettison the Standard Model (see the Introduction).

The identities of the author and his addressee are not preserved, and have been topics of intense scholarly interest and speculation. Section C, l. 7, "you know that we have separated from the majority of the people," has suggested to some that the author was none other than the Teacher of Righteousness; if so, it follows that the addressee was the high priest in Jerusalem. But this is a conjectural interpretation; other interpretive options are equally attractive. For example, the *Manifesto* may be a record of an intramural debate that caused a split in the *Yahad* itself. The conciliatory tone of the letter supports this understanding.

As reconstructed by Elisha Qimron and John Strugnell, the *Manifesto* presents a well-reasoned argument couched in a homily, complete with applications, illustrations, and exhortations. Following a thesis statement that identifies the central problem—the impure are being allowed to mix with the pure (the profane with the holy)—the author lists some two dozen examples to prove his point (B, l. 3–C, l. 4). The addressee (and secondarily, the reader) is then encouraged to follow the author: separate from those who practice such things.

The author invokes Deuteronomy 30 as evidence that disobedience will bring down the curses of the Mosaic covenant, while obedience will issue in God's blessing. Solomon was blessed for his obedience, he notes, whereas both Judah and Israel were led into exile because of disobedience.

A second round of warnings follows, illustrated by a challenge to remember how the works of the kings of Israel were rewarded: the obedient were blessed, the disobedient, cursed. David is presented as the ideal. A pious man, he was delivered from his trials and forgiven his sins. The final exhortation presses home the author's true point: to be accounted righteous, one must obey the Law as interpreted in the *Manifesto.*

This final exhortation is of great importance for a fuller understanding of statements the apostle Paul makes about works and righteousness in his Letter to the Galatians. The author of the *Manifesto,* probably thinking of Psalm 106:30–31 (where the *works* of Phinehas were "reckoned to him as righteousness"), is engaged, as it were, in a rhetorical duel with the ideas of the apostle. Paul appeals to Genesis 15:6 to show that it was the *faith* of Abraham that was "reckoned to him as righteousness" (Gal. 3:6), and goes on to state categorically that "by the works of the law shall no flesh be justified" (2:16). Probably the "false brethren" (2:4) that Paul opposed held a doctrine on justification much like that of the present writing.

See text 99 for the rest of 4Q394. The translation follows the composite text of Elisha Qimron and John Strugnell.

Section A

Sabbaths and festivals for the twelfth month and summation of the year. As detailed in the introduction to the preceding text, some scholars have determined that Section A frags. 3–7 is a continuation of the Sabbaths and Festivals of the Year *(text 99).*

4Q394 Frags. 3–7 Col. 1 [1][On the twenty-eighth of the month] is a Sabbath. (The month) continues (with the day) after [the] S[abbath, the second day (Monday),] [2][and an additio]nal [day.] The year is complete: three hundred s[ixty-four] [3]days. [. . .]

Section B

I. Legal Body: Do not mix the holy with the profane.

4Q394 Frags. 3–7 Cols. 1–2 (with **4Q395 Frag. 1)** [1]These are some of our pronouncements [concerning the law of Go]d; specifically, s[ome of the pronouncements concerning] [2]works (of the law) which w[e have determined. . .and al]l of them concern [defiling mixtures] [3]and the purity of [the sanctuary . . .]

1. Ban on offerings using Gentile grain (Mishnah Parah 2:1).

[Concerning the offering of] the [gentile gr]ain [that they are . . .] [4]and allowing their [. . .] to touch it and [become] def[iled. No one should eat] [5]from [Gent]ile grain [nor] bring it into the sanctuary [. . .]

2. Ban on sin offerings boiled in (Gentile? copper?) vessels (Mishnah Zebahim 11:6–8).

[Concerning the] sacrif[ice of the sin offering] [6]that they are boiling in vessels of [bronze and] thus [defiling] [7]the flesh of their sacrifices as well as [boil]ing them in the [Temple] court [and defiling] it [8]with the broth of their sacrifice.

3. Ban on sacrifices by Gentiles (Mishnah Parah 2:1?).

Concerning the Gentile sacrifice, [we have determined that they are] sacrifici[ng] [9]to the [. . .] which is [like a woman] who has fornicated with him.

4. Ban on eating peace offerings on fourth day (Lev. 7:11–18).

[Concerning the cereal offering of the] sacrifice [10]of well-b[eing,] they are to set it aside daily. Indeed, [it is written . . .] [11]that the cerea[l offering is to be ea]ten with the fat and the flesh on the day that [they] are sacrifi[ced. For the sons of] [12]the priest[s] are responsible to take care of this matter so as not [to] [13]bring guilt upon the people.

5. Ruling on the purity of those who prepare the red heifer (Num. 19:2–10; Mishnah Parah 3:7; 4:4; text 58, the Ashes of the Red Heifer*).*

Concerning the purity of the heifer of the sin offering, [14]the one who slaughters it, the one who burns it, the one who gathers its ashes, and the one who sprinkles the [water of] [15]purification—for all of these, the sun must se[t] for them to be pure—[16]so that the pure might sprinkle (the water of purification) on the unclean. For the sons of [17]Aaron are responsible to [care for this matter . . .]

6. Ban on bringing skins of cattle and sheep into the Temple (Mishnah Hullin 9:2; Temple Scroll, *text 155, 47:7–18).*

[Concerning] [18]the hides of cat[tle and sheep which they are . . . and fashioning from] [19]their [hide]s vessel[s . . . no one is allowed to] [20][bring] them into the sanctu[ary . . .] [21][. . .]

7. Ruling on skins and bones of unclean animals (Mishnah Yadaim 4:6).

4Q397 Frags. 1–2 (with **4Q398 Frags. 1–3**) Concerning the hid[es and bones of unclean animals, one is not allowed to make] [22]handles for v[essels from their bones] or their h[ides.]

8. Ban on Temple entrance after contact with skins of a carcass (Lev. 11:25, 39).

[Concerning the hi]de from the carcass of [23]a clean [animal, the] one who carries this carcass [must not to]uch the [sacred] pure food [24][. . .]

9. Ruling on who is fit to eat of the holy gifts (Lev. 22:10–16).

4Q394 Frags. 3–7 Col. 2 (with **4Q397 Frag. 3**) [Conc]erning the [. . .] which ar[e . . .] [25][. . . for the sons of] [26]the pri[es]ts are responsible [to c]a[re for] all these matters [so as not to] [27]bring guilt upon the people.

10. Ruling on place of sacrifice (Lev. 17:3–9; Temple Scroll, *text 155, 52:13–21).*

[Concer]ning that which it is written: [anyone who slaughters in the camp or] [28]outside the camp an ox, a lamb, or a goat, for [. . . to the nor]th of the camp. [29]We have determined that the sanctuary [is the "tabernacle of the tent of meeting," that Je]rusale[m] [30]is the "camp," and that outside the camp [is "outside of Jerusalem,"] in other words, the "camp of [31]their citie[s.]" Outside the c[amp . . . the sin offe]ring, [and] they take out the ashes [32]of [the] altar and bur[n the sin offering there. For Jerusalem] is the place that [33][He chose] from all the tri[bes of Israel to make His name to dwell . . .] [34][. . .] [35][. . . Concerning the . . . which] they [are no]t sacrificing in the sanctuary.

11. Ruling on the sacrifice of pregnant animals (Lev. 22:27–28).

4Q396 Frags. 1–2 Col. 1 (with **4Q394 Frag. 8 Col. 3** and **4Q397 Frags. 4–5**) [36][Concerning pregnant animals, w]e have de[termined that one must not sacrifice] the mother and the fetus on the same day. [37][. . .]

12. Ruling on the eating of a fetus (Lev. 22:27–28; Mishnah Hullin 4:1–5).

[Concerning] one who eats [of the fetus, w]e have determined that a person might eat the fetus 38[which is found in the womb of its mother after it has been sacrificed. You know that thi]s is correct, for the matter is written: a pregnant animal.

13. Ban on the inclusion of unfit into the congregation of Israel (Deut. 23:1–4; Mishnah Yebamoth 8:2–3).

4Q394 Frag. 8 Cols. 3–4 (with **4Q396 Frags. 1–2 Cols. 1–2** and **4Q397 Frag. 5)** 39[Concerning the Ammo]nite, the Moabite, the bastard, the one whose t[esticles are crushed, or whose] penis is [cut of]f who enter 40the congregation [. . . and] take [wives,] that they [might become] one flesh 41[and entering the sanctuary . . .] 42[. . .] unclean. We have also determined 43[that there is not . . . one must not have intercour]se with them 44[. . . and one] must not unite with them so as to make them 45[one flesh . . . and one must not brin]g them 46[into the sanctuary. . . . And you know that s]ome of the people 47[and . . . are uni]ting. 48[For all the sons of Israel are responsible to guard themselves] against any defiling union 49and to show reverence for the sanctuary.

14. Ban on the entrance of the blind into the Temple (Lev. 21:17–23).

[Concer]ning the blind, 50who are not able to guard themselves from any defiling mi[xture.] 51They cannot see the defilement of the [g]uilt offering.

15. Ban on the entrance of the deaf into the Temple (Lev. 21:17–23; Mishnah Hullin 1:1).

Col. 4 (with **4Q396 Frags. 1–2 Cols. 2–3** and **4Q397 Frags. 6–13)** 52Concerning the deaf, who have not heard the statute, the judgment, and the purity ruling, who have not 53heard the comman[dments belonging to] Israel. For the one who has not seen or has not heard does not 54know how to perform (according to the law). They may, however, participate in the pure food of the sanctuary.

16. Ruling on poured liquids (Lev. 11:34–38?; Mishnah Yadaim 4:7)

55Concerning streams of liquid, we have determined that they are not intrinsically 56[p]ure. Indeed, streams of liquid do not form a barrier between the impure [57]and the pure. For the liquid of the stream and that in its receptacle become as [58]one liquid.

17. Ban on dogs in the Temple (Mishnah Toharoth 4:3?).

(Concerning dogs,) one may not bring dogs into the holy camp because they [59]may eat some of the [b]ones from the sanc[tuary and] the meat which is still on them. For [60]Jerusalem is the holy camp. It is the place [61]that He chose from all the tribes of Israel, for Jerusalem is the foremost of [62]the camps of Israel.

18. Ruling on offerings assigned to the priests (Lev. 19:23–24; 27:32)

4Q396 Frags. 1–2 Cols. 3–4 (with **4Q394 Frag. 8 Col. 4** and **4Q397 Frags. 6–13**) Concerning the cultivation of fruit trees which are planted [63]in the land of Israel, (their produce is to be considered) as firstfruits belonging to the priests. Also the tithe of the cattle [64]and sheep belong to the priest.

19. Ruling on the cleansing of lepers; intentional and unintentional sins (Lev. 14:2–9; Num. 15:30).

Concerning lepers, we [65]h[ave determined that they may not] enter (any place) containing the sacred pure food, for [66]they [shall] be kept apart, [outside the house (*or* city).] Indeed it is written that from the time that he shaves and washes he [must] remain outside [67][his tent (*or* his house) for seven d]ays. But now, while they are still unclean, [68]l[epers are entering] a house [wit]h sacred pure food. And you know [69][that the one who unknowingly breaks a commandment,] and the matter escapes his notice, he must bring [70]a sin offering. But as [for the one who intentionally sins, it is writ]ten that he is a despiser and a blasphemer. [71][Indeed, while th]e[y are yet l]epro[us,] they may not eat from the ho[l]y food [72]until sunset on the eighth day.

20. Ruling on what constitutes contact with the dead (Num. 19:16–19; Mishnah Yadaim 4:6).

Col. 4 (with **4Q397 Frags. 6–13**) Concerning [the impurity] [73]of the dead, we have determined that every bone, whether [a piece] [74]or the whole, is considered according to the commandment of the dead or the slain. [. . .]

21. Ruling on unlawful sexual unions: any Israelite, even one of an improper union—priest and laity—is holy (Num. 36:6?).

[75]Concerning the fornication (*or* illegal marriage) which is practiced among the people, although they are ch[ildren of] the holy [seed,] [76]as it is written, "Israel is holy" (Jer. 2:3).

22. Ruling on crossbreeding animals (Lev. 19:19).

Concerning [a clea]n ani[mal of an Israelite,] [77]it is written that it is not (lawful) to breed it with another species.

23. Ruling on the intermarriage of the priests and the people (Lev. 19:19; 21:7?; Num. 36:6).

Concerning the clothing [of an Israelite, it is written that] it must [not] [78]be of mixed substances. And he must not sow his field or [his orchard with two species of plant]s, [79]because they are holy and the sons of Aaron are [most] h[oly.] [80][But y]ou know that some of the priests and the [people are intermarrying.] [81][They are] uniting and defilin[g the hol]y seed [as well as] [82]their [own] with forbidden marriage partners. F[or the sons of Aaron must . . .]

Section C

4Q397 Frags. 14–21 (with **4Q398 Frags. 14–17 Col. 1**) [1][. . .] [2][. . .] that [they] shall come [. . .] [3]And who will [. . .] he will [. . .]

24. Ban on polygamous priestly marriages (?) (Deut. 17:17; 21:15–16).

[4]Concerning the wom[en. . .the violen]ce and the unfaithfulness [. . .]

II. First Warning.

1. Transgression of these rulings brings destruction.

[5]For in these [matters (?) . . . because of] the violence and the fornication, [some] [6]places have been destroyed. [Indeed,] it is writt[en in the book of Moses that] "You shall [no]t bring an abomination i[nto your house" (Deut. 7:26). For] [7]an abomination is hated (by God).

2. Thus we have separated ourselves from the violators.

[But you know that] we have separated from the majority of the peo[ple and from all their uncleanness] [8][and] from being party to these matters or going along w[ith them] in these things. And you k[now that no] [9]unfaithfulness, deception, or evil are found in our hands, for we give [some thought (?)] to [these issues.]

III. First Exhortation: Separate yourself, for judgment is sure.

[Indeed,] [10]we [have written] to you so that you might understand the book of Moses, the book[s of the Pr]ophets, and Davi[d . . .] [11][the events of] the generations. In the book of Moses it is written [. . .] not [12][and] you[r] days of old [. . .] It is also written that you "will [turn] from the pa[t]h and evil will befall you" (Deut. 31:29). And it is writ[ten,] [13]"that when [14][al]l these thing[s happ]en to you in the Last Days, the blessing [15][and] the curse, [that you call them] to m[ind] and return to Him with all your heart [16]and with [al]l [your] soul" (Deut. 4:30; 30:1–2), [. . .] at the end of [the age,] then [you shall] l[ive . . .]

IV. First Illustration: The blessings and the curses.

1. Solomon obeyed, and Israel received the blessings.

4Q398 Frags. 11–13 (with **4Q397 Frags. 14–21** and **4Q397 Frag. 22)** [17][It is also written in the book of] Moses and in the b[ooks of the prophet]s that [the blessings and curses] shall come [upon you . . .] [18][the bles]sin[gs] came [. . .] in the days of Solomon the son of David.

2. Jeroboam disobeyed, and Israel received the curses.

Indeed, the curses [19][which] came in the days of [Jer]oboam the son of Nebat until the ex[i]le of Jerusalem and Zedekiah the king of Juda[h] [20][when] He sent them to B[abylon . . .] And so we see that some of the blessings and curses have already come [21]that are written in the b[ook of Mo]ses.

V. Second Warning.

Now this is the Last Days: when those of Israel shall return [22]to the L[aw of Moses with all their heart] and will never turn aw[ay] again. But the wicked will incr[ease in] wicked[ness] and [. . .] [23]And the [. . .]

VI. Second Illustration: The blessings and the curses.

1. Remember the kings of Israel.

[Now] remember the kings of Israe[l] and consider their works carefully. For he who [24]feared [the La]w was delivered from his troubles. These were the se[ek]ers of the Law, [25][those whose] sins [were forgiv]en.

2. Remember David.

Frags. 14–17 Col. 2 (with **4Q397 Frag. 23** and **4Q399 Frag. 1 Cols. 1–2)** Remember David, he was a pious man, [and] indeed [26]he was delivered from many troubles and forgiven.

VII. Second Exhortation: Keep away from the counsel of Belial.

Now, we have written to you [27]some of the works of the Law, those which we determined would be beneficial for you and your people, because we have seen that [28]you possess insight and knowledge of the Law. Understand all these things and beseech Him to set [29]your counsel straight and so keep you away from evil thoughts and the counsel of Belial. [30]Then you shall rejoice at the end time when you find the essence of our words to be true. [31]And it will be reckoned to you as righteousness, in that you have done what is right and good before Him, to your own benefit [32]and to that of Israel.

—M.G.A.

101. The Songs of the Sabbath Sacrifice

4Q400–407, 11Q17, Mas1k

Luke 1:10 reads, "Now at the time of the incense offering, the whole assembly of the people was praying outside." The author of Luke thus offhandedly represents what was probably a widespread belief in the late Second Temple period. The time when the Sabbath sacrifice was offered was a sort of divine window of opportunity, a time when prayers were especially effective. The *Songs of the Sabbath Sacrifice* presupposes this notion. The songs were probably recited as a liturgy to accompany the burnt offering the Bible requires for each Sabbath. The work consists of songs for thirteen Sabbaths arranged according to the Qumran calendar. Accordingly, it covers one-fourth of the year (thirteen being one-fourth of fifty-two, the invariable number of weeks in the year of the Qumran calendar). The songs may have been recycled, so that worshipers worked their way through them four times per year, but that possibility remains uncertain. Except for the third, parts of all the Sabbath songs are clearly identifiable in one or more of the damaged manuscripts that have survived.

The author starts by leading worshipers to consider the mysteries of an angelic priesthood. Then an almost mantric recital focusing on the holy number seven progresses to a climax on the seventh Sabbath, following which the community contemplates the elements of a living spiritual temple. Here the focus is particularly on the living holy chariots of God. In the original Hebrew, the syllables and long, drawn-out phrases tumble over one another in an almost hypnotic cadence. We encounter a constant rotation of synonyms that follow one another to numbing effect. Many long phrases consist almost entirely of nouns. Verbs are hard to find. The effect is highly abstract, and the images are blurred about the edges. Precisely what the author means to say is seldom clear. That is only appropriate, of course. The mysteries of heaven cannot be put into words; approximation is the best a seer can offer.

The Sabbath songs intend to unite the worshiper with the angels worshiping in heaven. What happens on earth is but a pale reflection of that greater, ultimate, reality. What, then, could be more desirable than to join that worship in mystic fashion? The variety of heavenly beings who play a role is dizzying. The apostle Paul wrote of "the tongues of men and of angels" (1 Cor. 13:1), and indeed, our author supplies the angels with different languages, each endowed with its own particular character, each singularly specialized to praise God.

The biblical sources of our work are in the main Ezekiel 1 and 10, which describe the chariot-throne, and Ezekiel 40–48, which depict a future temple. *Songs* is fundamental for the study of later Jewish mysticism. It is especially useful as illuminating the history of that species of mysticism known as Merkabah mysticism. *Merkabah* is Hebrew for "chariot." This variety sought to induce ecstatic experience by focusing thought on the heavenly chariot.

Although *Songs* is a sectarian writing linked with the *Yahad,* it was clearly of broader appeal. Other groups of Jews liked this work. One evidence of this fact is the discovery of a copy (designated Mas1k) at Masada, the site of the last stand made by Jewish freedom fighters in the first revolt against Rome (66–73/74 C.E.). The work may also have tickled the ears of Jewish Christian groups. Dale Allison has noted that the notion of an animate temple (an aspect of *Songs* that strikes us as most peculiar) also appears in the New Testament book of Revelation. In Revelation 9:13 we read: "I heard a voice from the four horns of the golden altar." The altar speaks. Just as in *Songs,* the architecture is alive. At its core Revelation is a Jewish Christian composition whose author knew either the *Songs of the Sabbath Sacrifice* or similar traditions. If it was the latter, those traditions have not otherwise survived.

Further suggesting that *Songs* circulated among Jewish Christians is the conundrum of the "Colossian heresy." The Letter of Paul to the church of the Colossians describes what some scholars have considered to be incipient Gnosticism. Precisely what was the deviation from Pauline teaching we cannot discern, for Paul mentions only certain incidental facts. He naturally presupposes that the recipients are familiar with their own situation. We do know that the heresy involved "matters of food and drink, observing festivals, new moons [and] Sabbaths" (Col. 2:16). Judging from the elements listed, many scholars have concluded that at Colossae, as elsewhere, the Pauline gospel faced the challenge of Jewish Christians who had a different idea of what it meant to be Christian. With that said, we can turn to Colossians 2:18. The verse is notoriously difficult to translate, but Fred Francis, among others, has suggested that it speaks of mystical experiences: the worshiper sought to share in angelic worship in heaven. He renders the verse, "Let no one disqualify you, being bent upon humility and religion of angels, which he has seen upon entering visions." Apart from *Songs* we have no early writing advocating such worship. It is perhaps possible that Jewish Christians had come to Colossae bringing with them a copy of *Songs,* whose mystical elements they found congenial, and proceeded to teach it to the young church there. Certainly *Songs,* which probably dates to the first century B.C.E., is more ancient than Paul's Letter to the Colossians.

The song for the first Sabbath, focusing on the heavenly priesthood and the praise of its angelic princes. Apparently the songs were actually chanted in worship.

4Q400 Frag. 1 Col. 1 [1][A text belonging to the Instructor. The song accompanying the sacrifice on the] first [Sabbath,] sung on the fourth of the first month.

Praise [2][the God of . . . ,] you godlike beings of utter holiness; [rejoice] in his divine [3][kingdom. For He has established] utter holiness among the eternally holy, that they might become for Him priests [4][of the inner sanctum in His royal temple,] ministers of the Presence in His glorious innermost chamber. In the congregation of all the [wise] godlike beings, [5][and in the councils of all the] divine [spirits,] He has engraved His precepts to govern all spiritual works, and His [glorious] laws [6][for all the] wise [divine beings,] that sage congregation honored by God, those who draw near to knowledge.

[7][. . .] eternal, and from the font of holiness to the temple of utter [8][holiness . . .] priests who draw near, ministers of the Presence of the ut-

terly [holy] King [9][. . .] His glory. Precept by precept they shall grow strong, to be seven [10][eternal councils; for He] established them for Himself to be the most hol[y of those who minister in the H]oly of Holies. [11][. . .] They shall become mighty thereby in accordance with the council [. . .] [12][. . .] the Holy of Holies, pr[iests of . . . the]se are the princes of [13][. . . who take thei]r stand in the temples of the King [. . .] in their realm or within their inheritance [14][. . .]

They tolerate none who trans[gress] the true Way, nor is t[her]e any unclean in their holy ranks. [15][The precepts governing the hol]y ones has He inscribed for them, that all the eternally holy might thereby be sanctified. He has purified the pure [16][who belong to the light, that they may recom]pense all those who transgress the true Way, and make atonement for those who repent of sin, obtaining for them His good pleasure.

[17][He has given tongues of] knowledge to the priests who draw near, so that from their mouths issue the teachings governing all the holy ones, together with the precepts [18][concerning His glory . . .] His [lov]ing-kindness for eternal forgiveness is rooted in compassion, but in the vengeance of His zeal [19][. . .] He established for Himself priests who draw near, the utterly holy ones [20][. . . di]vi[ne] godlike beings, priests of the highest heaven who [dra]w near [. . .]

Col. 2 [1][Your] lofty kingdom [. . .] [2]exalted [. . .] [3]the glory of Your kingdom [. . .] [4]in the gates of the highest heaven [. . .] [5][. . .] the spirit of all [. . .] [6]the holy ones of utter holiness [. . .] [7]the King of the divine beings who inhabit the seven [holy] t[emples . . .] [8]the glory of the King. [. . .] [9]His glory in the council of the god[like beings . . .] [10]for the seven paths [. . .] [11]for the precepts governing stillness in the [. . .] [12]for eternity. [. . .] [13]they shall exalt His glory [. . .] [14]the King of the princes of [. . .] [15]holy ones [. . .] [16]holy ones of [. . .] [17]godlike beings and [. . .] [18]righteousness. [. . .] [19]the priestho[od of . . .] [20]the loving-kindness of G[od . . .] [21]to sanctify themselves in [. . .]

A portion of the song for the second Sabbath, containing a description of the elite priestly angels and deprecating human worship in comparison with that of the angels.

Frag. 2 [1]wonderfully to praise Your glory among the wise divine beings, extolling Your kingdom among the utterly h[oly.] [2]They are honored in all the camps of the godlike beings and feared by those who direct human affairs, won[drous] [3]beyond other divine beings and humans alike. They tell of His royal splendor as they truly know it, and exalt [His glory in all] [4]the heavens of His rule. [They sing] wonderful psalms according to [their insight] throughout the highest heaven, and declare [the surpassing] [5]glory of the King of the godlike beings in the stations of their habitation. [. . .]

[6]How shall we be reckoned among them? As what our priesthood in their habitations? [How shall our holi]ness [compare with their utter] [7]holiness? [What] is the praise of our mortal tongue alongside their div[ine] knowledge? [. . .]

Fragments of the song for the fourth Sabbath. The themes of this song can no longer be discerned. The first portion preserves the beginning of the song, the second stood near the end.

4Q401 Frags. 1–2 [1]A text belonging to the Instructor. The so[ng accompanying the sacrifice on the fourth Sabbath, sung on] the twenty-[fifth] of [the first mo]nth.

[2]Praise the Go[d of . . .] [3][. . .] who stand before [. . .] [4]the king[dom of . . .] with all the ch[iefs of . . .] [5]the King of the god[like beings . . .]

4Q402 Frag. 1 [2][. . .] when they come with the godlike beings of [3][. . .] together for all of their assemblies [4][. . .] their mi[ght] for all the powerful warriors [5][. . .] for all the rebellious councils [. . .]

The end of the fifth Sabbath's song. Themes include angelic warfare, presumably in the Last Days, and God's predestination of all events in creation (cf. cols. 3–4 of text 7).

***Frags. 3–4** [5]They shall be judged [. . .] and they shall not come to the *Yahad* [. . .] [6]without [. . . those who pro]vide the plan[s] and the knowledge of the utt[erly holy . . .] [7]light and insigh[t . . .] the war of the godlike beings in the [. . .] [8]removing [. . .] Surely the [weap]ons of war[f]ar[e] belong to the God of divine beings [. . . the armies] [9]of heaven and the won[ders of all the] divine [spirits] shall run at [His] command, while the voice of tumult [. . . with] [10]His might, ar[mies of] divine [spirits] at war in the clouds. But [the victory] shall belong [to the God of divine beings.]

[11]God [by His knowledge has created] wonderful new works. All these has He wondrously created; none can comprehend His glorious plan. [12]To the King of the [wise] godlike beings belong all matters of knowledge; indeed, the God of knowledge causes all that happens forever. Through His

*I follow Qimron's suggested joining of 4Q402 frags. 3 and 4; further reconstruction comes from Mas1k frag. 1.

knowledge [13]and by means of His glorious plan all the eternal seasons have come to be. He has created the former things at their times, and the latter things [14]at the time appointed for them. None among those who are knowledgeable—those to whom revelation has come—can grasp these things before He does them; even when He brings them into existence, none can truly comprehend them. None of the divine beings [15]understands what He has designed, for these things are part of His glorious creation, and were [part] of His [plan] before ever they came to be.

The song for the sixth Sabbath. Each of the seven chief princes recites a psalm; then in order each of the same seven beings offers a blessing.

Mas1k Frag. 1 [8][A text belonging to the Instructor. The son]g accompanying the sacrifice on the sixth Sabbath, sung on the ninth of the [second] month.

[9][Bless the Go]d of the godlike beings, you who inhabit the highest heaven [10][. . .] Holy of Holies, and exalt His glory [11][. . .] knowledge of the eternal godlike beings. [12][. . .] those called to the highest of heights [. . .]

Frag. 2 [A psalm of blessing will be spoken in the language of the first chief prince] [1]to the [eternal] God, [incorporating his language's seven wondrous blessings. Then he will bless] [2]the Kin[g of all the eternally holy seven times with seven] [3][wondrous words of blessing. A psalm of exaltation will be spoken in the language of the second chief prince to the King] [4]of truth and [righteousness, incorporating his language's seven wondrous exaltations. Then he will magnify the God] [5]of all the div[ine beings who are appointed for righteousness seven times with seven words of] [6][wondrous] exaltation. [A psalm of glorification will be spoken in the language of the] **4Q403 Frag. 1 Col. 1** (with **Mas1k Frag. 2, 4Q404 Frags. 1–2,** and **4Q405 Frag. 3 Col. 2)** [1]third chief prince, a glorification of His faithfulness directed to the King of the angels, incorporating his language's seven wondrous glorifications. Then he will glorify the God of the exalted angels seven times with seven words of wondrous glorification.

[2]A psalm of praise will be spoken in the language of the four[th] to the Warrior who is over all the godlike beings, incorporating his language's seven wondrous warrior utterances. Then he will praise the God of [3]warrior power seven times with seve[n] words of [wondrous] prai[se. A ps]alm of thanksgiving will be spoken in the language of the fifth to the glorious [K]in[g,] [4]incorporating his language's seven wondrous tha[nk]sgivings. Then he will thank the glorified God seven times [with sev]en [wo]rds of wondrous thanksgiving. [A psa]lm of rejoicing [5]will be spoken in the language of the

sixth to the God of goodness, incorporating his language's seven cries of [wondrous] rejoicing. Then he will cry out with rejoicing to the King of goodness seven times with s[even words of] wondrous rejoicing.

[6]A psalm of musical praise will be spoken in the language of the seventh [chief] pri[nce,] a powerful musical praise to the God of holiness incorporating his language's seven wond[erful praise elements.] [7]Then he will sing praise to the King of holiness seven times with [seven] wondrous words of musical [praise,] together with seven psalms of blessing to Him, seven [8]psalms of exaltation of His righteousness, seven psalms of glorification of His kingdom, seven psalms of pra[ise of His glory,] seven psalms of thanksgiving for His wondrous doings, [9]seven psa[lms of re]joicing for His might and seven psalms of musical praise of His holiness. The generations of [. . .] seven times with seven [10]wondrous words, words of [. . .]

[Then] in the name of the glory of God [the first of] the ch[ief] princes [will bl]ess [all the . . . and all] the wise [with seven] wondrous [w]ords, [11]blessing all th[ei]r councils in [His holy] temple [with se]ven wondr[ous] wo[r]ds, [and ble]ssing those who know eternal things. [In the name of] His truth [the second] [12][chief prince will bless] all [their] stati[ons with] sev[en] wondrous words. Indeed, he shall bless with seven [marvelous] words. [13][He will also bless all who exalt the] King with seven words of His marvelous glory, and he will bless all who are eternally pure. [14][In the name of] His exalted kingdom the th[ird of the chief princes will bless] all who are exalted in knowledge with seven words of exaltation, blessing all [the divine beings] [16]wise [in His truth.] Indeed, he shall bless with seven marvelous words. He will also bless all those [appointed for] righteousness with sev[en] marvelous [w]ords.

In the name of the majes[tic ki]ng [the fourth] [17]of the chief princes will bless all who wal[k upri]ght with [sev]en maj[estic] words. He will also bless those who establish majesty with seven [18][wondrous w]ords, blessing all the divine beings [who draw] near to [His] verit[able] truth with seven righteous words, so that they can gain [His glor]ious compassion. In the name of His [majestic] wonders the fifth [19][chief prin]ce will bless all who comprehend the mysteries of pure [insight] with seven w[ords] of [His] exalted [20]truth. [He will also bless] all who are quick to do His will with seven [wondrous words,] blessing those who confess Him with seven majestic [wo]rds comprising [21]a wondrous thanksgiving. In the name of the warrior deeds of the divine beings the sixth chief prince will bless all who are insightful warriors with seven [22]wondrous words of His warrior power. He will also bless all who are perfect in the Way with seven wondrous words, that they might continue forever in the company of all the [eter]nal [23]beings. Yet again will he bless all who wait for Him with seven wondrous words, that His compassionate loving-kindness might return to them.

In the name of His holiness the [sev]enth chief priest [24]will bless all the holy who establish knowledge with seven words of [His] wondrous holiness. He will also bless all who exalt [25]His laws with se[ven] wondrous [wo]rds that act as mighty shields. Yet again will he bless all who are prede[stined] for righteous[ness,] they who praise His glorious kingdom [forever and] ever, [26]with seven wondrous words that lead to eternal peace.

Then in [the name of His holiness] all the [chief] princes [will bless in unis]on the God of divine beings with all [27][their] sevenfold appointed words of blessing. They will also bless those predestined for righteousness and all those blessed of [. . .] the eternally [bless]ed [. . .] [28]to them, saying "Blessed be [the] Lord, the Kin[g of] all, exalted above every blessing and pr[aise, He who blesses all the ho]ly who bless [Him] and those [who declare His righteous]ness [29]in the name of His glory, [He who] blesses all who receive blessing, forever."

The seventh and central Sabbath song. The angels addressed are probably the members of the seven angelic councils. Toward the end of the song, the animate architectural elements of the heavenly temple are called upon to praise.

[30]A text belonging to the Instructor. The song accompanying the sacrifice on the seventh Sabbath, sung on the sixteenth of the (second) month.

Praise the most high God, you who are exalted among all [31]the wise divine beings.

Let those who are holy among the godlike sanctify the glorious King, He who sanctifies by His holiness each of His holy ones.

You princes of praise [32]among all the godlike, praise the God of majestic [pr]aise. Surely the glory of His kingdom resides in praiseworthy splendor; therein are held the praises of all [33]the godlike, together with the splendor of [His] entire rea[lm.]

Lift His exaltation on high, you godlike among the exalted divine beings—His glorious divinity above [34]all the highest heavens. Surely He [is the utterly divine] over all the exalted princes, King of king[s] over all the eternal councils. By the wise will—[35]through the words of His mouth—shall come into being all [the exalted godlike]; at the utterance of His lips all the eternal spirits shall exist. All the actions of His creatures are but what His wise [36]will allows.

Rejoice, you who exult in [knowing Him, with] a song of rejoicing among the wondrous godlike. Hymn His glory with the tongue of all who hymn to His wondrous, joy-filled knowledge, [37]with the mouth of all who chant [to Him. Surely He] is God of all who rejoice in eternal wisdom, and mighty Judge over all perceptive spirits.

[38]Laud, all you confessing divine beings, the King of praise; surely all the wise divine shall laud His glory, and all the righteous spirits His truth. [39]Through the precepts of His mouth is their knowledge found acceptable, at the return of His warrior hand to dispense judgment is their praise perfected.

Sing praises to the mighty God, [40]make the choicest spiritual offering; make me[lod]y in the joy of God, and rejoice among the holy ones through wondrous melodies, in everl[asting] joy.

[41]With such songs shall all the [foundations of the hol]y of holies offer praise, and the pillars bearing the most exalted abode, even all the corners of the temple's structure. Hy[mn] [42]the G[od a]wesome in power, [all you] wise [spirits] of light; together laud the utterly brilliant firmament that girds [His] holy temple. [43][Praise] Him, godli[ke] spirits, laud[ing] eternally the firmament of the uttermost heaven, all [its bea]ms and walls, all [44]its [stru]cture and crafted desi[gn.]

The utterly holy spirits, living divinities, eternally holy spirits above [45]all the hol[y ones . . .] wondrous and wonderful, majesty and splendor and marvel. Glory abides in the perfected light of knowledge [46][. . . in a]ll the wondrous temples, divine spirits surrounding the abode of the righteous and true King. All its walls [. . .]

Col. 2 (with **4Q404 Frag. 6** and **4Q405 Frags. 8–9)** [1]perfect light, a weaving of an utterly holy spiritual substance [. . .] [2]raised places of knowledge. At the footstool of his feet, [. . .] [3]appearance of the glorious bodies belonging to the princes of the spiritual kingdom [. . .] [4]His glory; and with all their turning back, the gates of [. . .] [5]the flashing of the [lig]htning [. . .] to the chief of the godlike beings of [. . .] [6]running between them are god[li]ke beings having the appearance of [glowing] coals [. . .] [7]walking to and fro. The utterly holy spirits [. . .] [8]the utterly holy, divine spirits, an ete[rnal] vision [. . .] [9]and divine spirits, fiery shapes round about the [. . .] [10]wondrous spirits. And the most exalted tabernacle, the glory of His kingdom, innermost sanctuary of [. . .] [11]and He consecrates the seven lofty holy places.

A voice of blessing issues forth from the princes of His innermost sanctuary [. . .] [12]and the voice of blessing is glorious in the hearing of the divine beings and those who establish [. . .] [13]the blessing. All the crafted furnishings of the innermost sanctum shall hasten to take part in the wondrous psalms in the innermost sanctum. [. . .] [14]of wonder, sanctum to sanctum with the sound of thronging holy ones. All the crafted furnishings [. . .] [15]The chariots of His innermost sanctum shall offer praise as one, and their Cherubim and wheel-beings shall marvelously bless [. . .] [16]the chiefs of the divine building. They shall praise Him in His holy innermost sanctum.

The eighth Sabbath song, containing an account of the blessings offered by the seven deputy princes.

[18]A text belonging to the Instructor. The song accompanying the sacrifice on the eighth Sabbath, sung on the t[wenty-]third [of the second month.]

Praise the God of all the highe[st heavens, al]l you who are [eter]nally holy, [19]deputies among the priests who draw near, the second council in the wondrous habitation among the seven [priesthoods, . . .] among those knowledgeable of [20]eternal things. Exalt Him, princes who rule, with His portion, His wonders. Praise [the God of the godlike,] you seven priest[hoods] who draw near to Him . . . highest] [21]heaven, seven wondrous realms set out by the precepts governing His temples. [. . .] the temples of the realm of the [22]sevenfold priest[hood,] in the wondrous temple belonging to the seven holy councils [. . .] [23]the prince, the angels of the King in the wondrous habitations. The perceptive knowledge of the seven [. . .] [24]princes, the High Priest of the inner sanctum, and the leaders of the King's council in a gathering [. . .] [25]and exalted praises to the glorious King, magnifying the Go[d of . . .] [26]to the God of the godlike, the King of purity.

The exaltation coming from their tongues [. . .] [27]seven mysteries of knowledge in the wondrous mystery attached to the seven utterly holy realms [. . . The tongue of the first deputy prince shall sound seven times louder when joined by that of the second; the tongue] of the second shall sound [28]seven times louder when joined by that of the third; the tongue of the third shall sound seven times louder when joined by that of the [fourth; the tongue of] the fourth shall sound seven times louder when joined by that of the fifth; the tongue of the fifth shall sound sev[en times louder when joined by the tongue of] [29]the sixth; the tongue of the sixth shall sound seven times louder when joined by that of the se[ve]nth; and the tongue of the seventh shall so[und . . .]

A portion of the song for the ninth Sabbath, which would fall on the thirtieth of the second month. What remains describes the vestibules of the multiple heavenly sanctuaries, particularly the vestibule through which God enters.

4Q405 Frags. 14–15 Col. 1 [2][. . . From] the wondrous spiritual likeness, utterly holy and engrav[ed . . . , issues a to]ngue of blessing, and from the [divine] image [3]issues [a vo]ice of blessing to the King of the exalted angels. Their wondrous praise extols the God of the godlike [. . .] their embroidered [. . .], and they sing joyously [4][. . .] the vestibules of their entryways, utterly holy spirits who draw near in [. . .] eternally. [5][The like]ness of living divine beings is carved on the walls of the vestibules by which the King enters, luminous spiritual figures [in the innermost sanctums of the K]ing, figures of glorious li[ght,] wondrous spirits. [6][In] the midst of the glorious spirits stand wondrous embroidered works, figures of living divine beings [. . . in the] glorious [in]nermost sanctums that belong to the structure of [7]the utterly ho[ly temple,] in the innermost sanctums of the King are div[ine] figure[s; and from] the likeness of [. . .]

A fragment of the song for the tenth Sabbath. Like the song for the ninth Sabbath, the central theme here is apparently description of the heavenly temples.

Frag. 15 Col. 2 + Frag. 16 [1]The fringed edge [. . .] [2]and rivers of fire [. . .] [3]appearing as fiery flames [. . . be]autiful upon the veil of the King's innermost sanctum [. . .] [4]in the innermost sanctum of His Presence, an embroidered work [. . .] everything that is engraved upon the [. . .], divine figures [. . .] [5]glory issuing from both sides of them [. . .] the veils of the wondrous innermost sanctums. They bless the [. . .] [6]sides of them, declaring [. . .] wondrous, inside the innermost sanctum [. . .] [7][. . . They ex]tol the glorious king with a joyous cry [. . .]

Portions from the middle and end of the eleventh Sabbath song. Description of the heavenly temples and architecture continues, focusing here on the innermost sanctuaries, the chariot-thrones, and attendant priestly angels.

Frags. 19a–d (with **11Q17 Frags. 12–15)** [2]Then the divine figures, the ut[terly holy] spirits, shall praise Him [. . .] the glorious figures, the floor [3]of the wondrous innermost sanctuaries, the spirits of the perpetual divine beings—all [. . .] the fig[ures of the inner]most sanctuary of the King, spir[it]ual handiwork of the wondrous firmament [4]made utterly pure, [spi]rits of knowledge, truth and righteousness in the Holy of [H]olies, [f]orms of the living godlike beings, luminous spiritual forms—[5]all these h[ol]y handiworks are wondrously connected to each other. Embroidered [spirits,] figures of the godlike beings, are engraved [6]all around the [gl]orious bricks; these are glorious figures, handiwork belonging to the splendid and majest[ic bri]cks. All these handiworks are living godlike beings [7]and their figures are holy angels. From beneath the marvelous inn[ermost sanctums] is heard the quiet voice of god[like] beings praising [. . .]

Frag. 20 Col. 2 + Frags. 21–22 (with **11Q17 Frags. 3–6**) 1[They do not hesitate when they arise . . . the innermost sanc]tums of all the priests who draw near [. . .] 2In obedience to the ordinance they are steadfast, serving [. . .] a seat similar to His royal throne in His glorious innermost sanctums. They do not sit [. . .] 3His glorious chariots [. . .] holy Cherubim, luminous wheel-beings in the inner[most sanctum . . .] godlike spirits of [. . .] purity [. . .] 4of holiness; the handiwork of its corners [. . .] royal; the glorious chario[t] seats [. . .] knowledgeable wings [. . .] wondrous works of warrior power [. . .] 5perpetual truth and righteousness [. . .] when His glorious chariots move to the [. . .] they do not turn to this side or that [. . . rather,] they go straight ahead [. . .]

The twelfth Sabbath song. Remaining portions contain a description of God's chariot-throne and its praise. The text then moves to an account of praise given by the angels, who are assembled military-style in camps and units. The latter part of the song focuses on the ceremonial angelic worship taking place in the heavenly temple.

6A text belonging to the Instructor. The song accompanying [the sacrifice] on the twelfth Sabbath, sung on the [twenty-first of the third month.]

[Praise the God of . . .] 7[. . .] Exalt Him, [. . .] the glory in the tabernacl[e of the God of] knowledge. The [Cheru]bim fall before Him and bless Him; as they arise, the quiet voice of God 8[is heard], followed by a tumult of joyous praise. As they unfold their wings, God's q[uiet] voice is heard again. The Cherubim bless the image of the chariot-throne that appears above the firmament, 9[then] they joyously acclaim the [splend]or of the luminous firmament that spreads beneath His glorious seat. As the wheel-beings advance, holy angels come and go. Between 10His chariot-throne's glorious [w]heels appears something like an utterly holy spiritual fire. All around are what appear to be streams of fire, resembling electrum, and [sh]ining handiwork 11comprising wondrous colors embroidered together, pure and glorious. The spirits of the living [go]dlike beings move to and fro perpetually, following the glory of the [wo]ndrous chariots. 12A quiet voice of blessing accompanies the tumult of their movement, and they bless the Holy One each time they retrace their steps. When they rise up, they do so wondrously, and when they settle down, 13they [sta]nd still. The sound of joyous rejoicing falls silent, and the qui[et] blessing of God spreads through all the camps of the divine beings. The sound of prais[es]

[. . .][14][. . .] coming out of each of their divisions on [both] sides, and each of the mustered troops rejoices, one by one in order of rank [. . .]

11Q17 Frags. 5–6 [1][. . .] wondrous, knowledge and insigh[t . . .] wondr[ous] firmaments [. . .] [2][. . .] in the essence of light, a splendor of [. . .] every form of wond[rous] spirits [. . .] [3][. . .] godlike beings, fearfully powerful, all [. . .] their [utt]erly wondrous acts by the power of the God of [. . .] [4][per]petual, exalting the warrior acts of the Go[d of . . .] from the four foundations of the wondrous firmament [5]they ann[oun]ce when they hear the sound of praise lifted up to God, [. . .] blessing and praising the God of [6]the godlike. A tumu[lt . . .] the highest [heaven . . .] the glorious King [. . .] of the wondrous foundations, [7]lifting up praise [. . .] of the God of [. . .] and all their foundations [. . .] utterly [8]hol[y . . .] praise lifted up [. . .] their [w]ings, ex[alting . . . over] their heads, [9]and they cal[l] out [. . .]

4Q405 Frag. 23 Col. 1 [1][. . .] when they lift up praise [. . .] [2][. . .] When they stand still, [. . .] [3][. . .] His glorious royal thrones, and the entire congregation of the ministers of [4][. . .] wondrous; the [wondrous] godlike beings shall not be shaken, forever; [5][. . . to rem]ain steadfast in every task, for the godlike beings in charge of His whole offering [6][. . .] His whole offering. The godlike beings praise Him [when fir]st they take their positions, while all the sp[irits of] the splendid firma[m]ents [7]continuously rejoice in His glory. A voice of blessing comes from all of His divisions, telling of His glorious firmaments, and His gates praise [8]with a joyful noise. When the wise divine beings enter through glorious portals, and when the holy angels go forth to their realms, [9]the portals through which they enter and the gates through which they exit declare the glory of the King, blessing and praising all the godlike [10]spirits each time they exit or enter through the holy ga[t]es. None of them omits a precept or fails to acknowledge anything [11]the King says. They neither run from the Way nor reverence anything not a part of it; they consider themselves neither too exalted for His realm nor [12]too humble for His commissions.

He shall have no compassion when His furious annihilat[ing] anger reigns, yet He will not punish those from whom His glorious anger was removed. [13]Awesome fear of the King of the godlike beings grips a[ll] of the godlike [when He sends them forth] on all of His commissions according to His veri[ta]ble order, and they go [. . .]

The thirteenth Sabbath song. Portions of this selection concern the clothing worn by the ministering spirits.

11Q17 Frags. 7–8 [1][. . .] good favor [. . .] all th[eir] works [2][. . .] for the sacrifices of the holy ones [. . .] the smell of their offerings [. . .] [3][. . .] and the sm[el]l of their drink offerings, according to the num[ber of . . .] of purity in a spirit of holine[ss] [4][. . .] perpetual in [splendor and] majesty for [. . .] the wondrous [. . .] and the form of the breastplates of [5][. . . be]auty [. . . spirits] clothed with embroidery, a sort of wo[ven handiwork . . .] splendidly purified dyed garments [. . .]

4Q405 Frag. 23 Col. 2 [7]their holy places. At their wondrous stations are spirits, clothed with embroidery, a sort of woven handiwork, engraved with splendid figures. [8]In the midst of what looks like glorious scarlet and colors of utterly holy spiritual light, the spirits take up their holy stand in the presence of [9]the [K]ing—[splendidly] colored spirits surrounded by the appearance of whiteness. This latter glorious spiritual substance is like golden handiwork, shimmering in [10][the lig]ht. All their crafted garments are splendidly purified, crafted by the weaver's art. These spirits are the leaders of those who are wondrously clothed for service, [11]the leaders of each and every holy kingdom belonging to the holy King, who serve in all the exalted temples of His glorious realm.

[12]The leaders of the exaltation possess tongues of knowledge [so as] to bless the God of knowledge for all His glorious works. [In] His insightful knowledge and [glo]rious acumen [He has inscribed the ord]inances governing their military units in all the hol[y inn]er [sanctums.]

11Q17 Frags. 2 + 1 + 9 [1][. . . His] glorious heights [. . .] His [gl]ory with [. . .] [2]His [rec]ompense by judgments of [. . .] His compassion with the gl[orious] honor of [. . .] His [s]easons [3][and] all the blessings of [His] peace [. . . the gl]ory of His works, and in the ligh[t of . . .] and with the splendor of [4]the praise given Him in all the firmam[ents of . . .] light and darkness and the figures of [. . .] the glorious [ho]liness of the King [5]for all [His] veritable works [. . .] for the angels of knowledge in all [their] king[doms . . .] His [cam]p, holy exaltations [6]for His glorious thrones and the footstool of [His] f[eet and all] His majestic [ch]ariots and [His] ho[ly] inner sanctums [. . .] and for the portals of [the Kin]g's entrance, [7]together with all the exits of [. . . the cor]ners of its str[uc]ture and all the [. . .] for His glorious temples and the firmaments of [. . .]

—M.O.W.

102. A Liturgy

4Q409

This manuscript contains the remnant of a hymn praising God for the festivals of the holy year. The calendar followed is a subspecies of the solar version known from other Dead Sea Scrolls. This variant on the theme adds several festivals the Bible never explicitly mentions. These additions are particularly important when trying to get a clear picture of the Qumran calendrical writings as a whole, since most of them do not include the new festivals. Just a few other calendrical works among the scrolls seem to support them (note in particular the *Sabbaths and Festivals of the Year,* text 99, and the *Temple Scroll,* text 155). Thus, in respect to these extra festivals, the scrolls are at odds, pointing to the complexity of the historical situation in which they arose.

The beginning of the calendrical recital is missing. Preserved portions include or imply the following festivals: the Feast of Weeks, or Pentecost, which falls on the fifteenth day of the third month; the Feast of Firstfruits of Wine, the third day of the fifth month; the Feast of Oil, the twenty-second day of the sixth month; the Feast of Wood Offering, the twenty-third day of the sixth month; the Day of Memorial, the first day of the seventh month; the Day of Atonement, the tenth day of the seventh month (presumably; the relevant lines are damaged and reconstruction is uncertain); and the Feast of Booths, the fifteenth day of the seventh month. Of these festivals, the Firstfruits of Wine, the Feast of Oil, and the Feast of Wood Offering do not appear in the Bible, at least not clearly (Neh. 10:34 alludes to the wood offering, but not to a full-blown festival for it). These, then, were the controversial entries—objects of heated debate, no doubt, because of their extrabiblical nature.

Frag. 1 Col. 1 [1][. . . Praise and bless on the da]ys of the fi[rstfruits:] [2][of wheat, of new wine and fresh oil, with the] new [cer]eal offering, [3][and bless His holy name. Prai]se and bless on the days of [4][the festival of woods, with the offering of] woods as a burnt offering, [5][and bless His name. Praise and bless] on the day of remembrance with a blast [6][on the ram's horn. Bless the Lor]d of all. Praise [7][and bless . . . and bles]s His holy name. [8][. . . and bles]s the Lord of all [9][. . . Praise and bless] on these days [10][. . .] Praise and bless and give thanks [11][. . . Praise and bless and] give thanks with tree branches.

—M.G.A.

103. An Unknown Prophecy

4Q410

This fragmentary text is addressed to a person or group ("you") who has committed sin (l. 2), incurred "curse after curse" (l. 4), and is fated to be without peace (l. 5). The speaker then declares that he has seen a vision (l. 7) concerning a certain "house" (l. 9)—possibly the Temple—and speaks of violations of God's law (l. 10). The phrases that survive in the fragment are reminiscent of the words of the biblical prophets.

4Q410 Frag. 1 [1][. . .] which [. . .] [2][. . .] you transgress any of [. . .] [3][. . .] which you will die not [. . .] [4][. . .] curse after curse will cling to you [5][. . .] upon you and you will not have any peace there [. . .] [6][. . .] what is truly good and what [is truly] evil [. . .] [7][. . .] all the days of eternity. And now, I, with [the help of the Lord] in the spirit [. . .] [8][. . .] he will not l[ie . . .] [9][. . .], the oracle, and about the house of [. . . the] vision, for I have seen [. . .] [10][. . .] and h[e] broke the l[aw of God . . .]

—E.M.C.

104. A Liturgy of Ritual Washings

4Q414, 4Q512

This present work, found in two copies, was intended to govern a ritual of ablutions. A sectarian text by virtue of its mention of the *Yahad,* this liturgy or something similar might have been used for the ritual washings mentioned in the *Charter* (see text 7, 3:4–9; 4:21; 5:13b–14). For additional discussion of the importance of purity laws for Second Temple Jews, see the introduction to *Ordinances* (text 19) and *Ritual Purity Laws Concerning Liquids* (text 56).

The *Liturgy*'s distinctive formula, "and He shall bless and say in response, Blessed are You . . . ," (4Q414 Frags. 1–2 2:1) establishes a clear relationship between this work and other purification texts among the scrolls, such as the *Ritual of Purification for Festival Days* (text 61). And as 4Q512 col. 4 evidences, the washings of the present text may also have been related to the festival calendar.

It is of special note that 4Q512 was inscribed on the reverse side of the fragments of *Daily Prayers* (text 126). This suggests that this scroll was a private copy, as opisthographs—two-sided scrolls—did not circulate in the normal book market. The combination of these two texts produces a practical handbook.

A blessing for "those purified for His appointed time," perhaps the Sabbath.

4Q414 Frags. 1–2 Col. 2 [1][. . . and he shall bless and] say [in response,] Blessed [2][are You, God of Israel, . . .] those purified for His appointed time, [3]Your light [. . .] Your [. . .] and to make atonement for us [4]by Your will [. . . to be] pure before You [5]alw[ay]s [. . .] I have [not known (*or* touched)] anything [6][. . .] to purify oneself prior to [7][. . .] You made us [. . .]

The setting for this blessing is evidently "the first, the third and the seventh (days)." This would parallel the washings described in IIQT[a] 49.7–20 (text 155) and would suggest that purpose of the blessing is corpse uncleanness.

Frags. 2–4 Col. 2 (with **4Q512 Frags. 42–44 Col. 2)** [1]And You shall purify us for [Your] holy statutes[. . .] [2]for the first, the third, and the se[venth . . .] [3]in the truth of Your covenant [. . .] [4]to purify oneself from the impurity of [. . .] [5]and afterwards he shall enter the water [and wash himself and bless] [6]and say in response, Blessed are Y[ou, God of Israel, . . .] [7]for by what comes from Your mouth [the purification of all things is] de[termined so as to be separated from all] [8]impure people in accordance with [their] g[uilt, they shall not be purified by ritual bathing . . . .] [9][the w]ays of [Your] will [. . . and I] [10]shall praise Your name [. . .]

Frag. 7 [1]s[ou]l [. . .] [2]that [. . .] [3]to Yourself as a pu[re] people [. . .] [4]And I also [. . .] [5]the day that [. . .] [6]at the appointed times of purity [. . .] [7]the *Yahad* (*or* together).

[. . .] [8]by the purification of Israel, to e[at and to drink . . . in the cities] [9][where they re]side, [and to be a holy people . . .] [10]And it will happen on [that] day [. . .] [11]female and the menstruant [. . .]

Frag. 13 [1]For You made me [. . .] [2]Your will is that we purify ourselves befo[re You . . .] [3]and He established for Himself a statute of atonement [. . .] [4]and to be in rig[hteous] purity [. . .] [5]and he shall ba[t]he in water and sprinkle u[pon . . .] [6][. . .] and afterward he shall return [. . .] [7]purifying His people in the waters of bathing [. . .] [8][. . .] second time upon his station. And he shall [say] in re[sponse, Blessed are You, God of Israel] [9][tha]t You purified in Yo[ur] glory [. . .] [10][. . .] eternally. And today [. . .]

Frags. 27–28 [1][But when] a m[an or a woman approaches . . . then he will bless and say in response,] [2]Blessed are Y[ou, God of Israel, who . . . and You shall distinguish for us] [3][between] impure and p[ure . . . in the purity of] [4]righteousness [. . .]

A fragment that mentions the cryptic "secret of men." The Damascus Document *(text 1, 14:10) stipulates that the Overseer of the camps was to be an expert in the details of this secret.*

4Q512 Col. 3 (Frags. 36–38) [11][. . .] his clothes and [. . .] [12][. . .] all tongues [. . .] [13][. . .] for You, the secret of me[n . . .] [14][. . .]

[15–16][. . .] [17][. . .] Your [. . .] from every impurity [of] our flesh for [. . .]

The four feasts of the year, mentioned only here among the scrolls (l. 2), may be celebrations at the beginning of the first, fourth, seventh, and tenth months, the demarcations of the solar calendar's seasons.

Col. 4 (Frags. 33, 35) [1][. . .] and for the appointed time of the Sabbath, for the Sabbaths of all the weeks of [2][. . . and the] appoint[ed time of . . . and] the four seasons of [3][the year on the days of. . . and] the season of the ha[rve]st, the end of see[d time] and of grass [4][. . .]

[5][. . .] in water [. . .] to consecrate oneself [6][. . .] he shall [bless] and shall say [in response,] Blessed are You, [7][O God of Israel . . .] to have compassion [on us . . .] Your [. . .] [8][. . .] and I [. . .] [9][. . .] in impuri[ty . . .] [10][. . .] purity [. . .]

Burnt offering for the atonement of sin.

Col. 7 (Frags. 29–32) [1][. . .] Blessed are Y[ou, O God of Israel . . .] [2][. . .] holy people [. . .] [3][. . .] leads astray [. . .] [4][. . . in] water and [. . .] [5][. . .] and he shall bless [the God of Israel] there [and say in response, Blessed are You, O] [6][God of Israel. I am standing] before You at the appointed ti[me . . .] [7][. . .] You [. . .] me for the purification of [. . .] [8][. . .] and his burnt offering. And he shall bless and say in respon[se,] Blessed are You, [O God of Israel,] [9][You delivered me from al]l my transgressions, cleansed me from filthy shame, and atoned for me that I might enter [. . .] [10][. . .] purity, the blood of the burnt offering that You desire, and a memorial, a pleasing aro[ma . . .] [11][. . .] Your holy and sweet smelling incense that You desire [. . .] [12–18][. . .] my sin

[. . .] [19][. . .] righteousness and [. . .] [20][. . .] You shall leave unpunished until [the] judgment [of . . . Is]rael whi[ch . . .] [21][. . . Blessed are] You, O God of Is[rael . . .] for atonement [. . .]

The seven days of purification.

Col. 10 (Frag. 11) [1][. . .] [2][and when] he [has completed] the seven days of [his] puri[fication . . .] [3][. . . then] he shall wash his clothes in w[ater and bathe his body . . .] [4]and he shall cover (his nakedness) with his clothes and kneel up[on his knees . . . And he shall say in response, Blessed are You,] [5]O God of Isr[ae]l [. . .]

A man with a seminal discharge is cleansed and renewed to fellowship.

Col. 11 (Frags. 7–9) [1]all [these] th[ings the man with a discharge shall perform . . .] [2]when he is cleansed from [his] f[low . . . pu]rification of Isr[ael,] [3]to eat and to d[rink . . . in their] inhabited [ci]ties, [4]to be a [holy] people [. . .]

Liturgical response for the washing of the third day (Num. 19:12, 19).

Col. 12 (Frags. 1–6) [1]On the third day [. . . And he shall ble]ss and sa[y] in response, [Blessed are] [2][Yo]u, O God of Israel, [You commanded . . .] to cleanse themselves from [the impurity of] [3][. . .] soul in the atonem[ent that You desire . . .] holy ash [. . .] [4][. . .] in purify[ing] waters [. . .] on the eternal tablets, [5]and waters of washing for cleansing appropriate for each time [. . .] his clothes. And then [they (?) shall sprinkle on him] [6]the waters for sp[rin]kling so as to cleanse him and all [. . .] [7]And aft[er] he has been [s]prinkled with water[s of sprinkling, he shall say in response, Blessed are You,] [8]O Go[d of Israe]l, for You gave [us . . .] [9]and from the filth of uncleanness. And today [. . .] [10]impurity, to consecrate oneself for You and [. . . e]tern[al,] for [11][. . .] impurity and no one shall be abl[e . . . all] the [d]ays of Your glory [12]and the co[venant (?) of] the forefathers and [. . .] their guilt and upon [. . .] [13]all [. . .] and You consecrated him [in the] [14]atoneme[nt which] You desire [. . .] and You abhorred them for [. . .] [15][. . .] their works and [. . .] [16][. . .] with the onset of impurity so as to be separated [from] [17][. . .] banished [. . .]

Praise for the distinction between the clean and the unclean (Lev. 20:25).

Col. 14 (?) (Frags. 40–41) [1][. . .] that by [which] is unclean. [2][But] when a [ma]n or a woman approaches, [. . . Then he shall bless] and say in response, [3][Bl]essed are You, O God of Isr[ael. . . and You shall di]stinguish for us between [4]the impure and the pure [. . . to ser]ve You [5][in the] purity of righteousness [. . .] and Your [6][goo]d pleasure [. . .]

God is praised for commands that allow for the cleansing of all things.

Frags. 42–44 Col. 2 (with **4Q414 Frags. 2–4 Col. 2)** [2]And afterwards he shall enter [the water and wash himself and bless and] say [3][in response,] Blessed are [Y]ou, [O God of I]s[rael, . . . for by what comes from] [4]Your mouth the purification of all [things] is determined [so as to be separated from all impure people in accordance with their guilt,] [5]they shall not be purified by ritual bath[ing . . .] And [to]d[a]y I [. . .] [6][. . .] the [sp]reading of the hand[s,] then to [. . .]

Cleansing is completed when the sun sets.

Frags. 48–50 [1][. . . Then he shall bless] [2]and [say] in response, [Blessed are You, O God of Israel . . .] [3]a hol[y] people [. . .] [4]And who is the one who [(*or* And waters of [) . . .]

[5]And after [the] sun [sets] on the [. . .] day [. . .] [6]just as You [took] us for Yourself as a people [. . .]

God's command to separate from uncleanness is a key to understanding the Yahad*'s emphasis on ritual purity (Lev. 15:31).*

Frag. 69 [2]And You commanded us to separate ourselves from [. . .]
—M.G.A.

105. The Secret of the Way Things Are

4Q415–418, 1Q26, 4Q423

The *Secret of the Way Things Are* represents a further development of the wisdom instruction (cf. the *Book of Secrets,* text 6), in which a sage delivers his teaching to his disciples, addressed as his children. This text has the same kind of framework, but the content goes beyond the usual contrasts of wisdom and folly. As in the *Book of Secrets,* the teacher appeals to "the secret of the way things are" (Hebrew, *raz nihyeh)*—that is, knowledge of the inflexible purposes of God acquired by study of Scripture and the laws of the sect.

Again and again the teacher returns to the theme of poverty and the importance of being satisfied with what God has provided. The biblical book of Proverbs usually portrays poverty as the unwelcome result of foolish behavior (e.g., 28:19). Here, in contrast, poverty is the natural circumstance of the ideal disciple—a motif that anticipates the high view of poverty in early Christianity: "Blessed are you poor" (Luke 6:20). The *Secret* seeks to motivate by appeal to the judgment to come and the eternal damnation of the wicked—another new theme that foreshadows the importance of the Last Days for early Christianity.

The manuscripts assigned to this work are all fragmentary in varying degrees, and the order of the fragments is hypothetical; nor is it certain that all the pieces originally belonged to one composition. One large subsection in particular is addressed to "farmers" and uses agricultural language extensively. It may originally have formed a separate work. Nevertheless, a single perspective is at work here, finding expression in a number of themes. The nearest analog once again is in early Christianity: the collection of sayings called the Sermon on the Mount (Matt. 5–7) is the same type of genre, that is, ethical instruction under threat of impending judgment.

Given the nature of the work, no references to the greater world of war and politics appear. Hence, we cannot date its composition or infer as much as we would like about its original setting. Did it serve a purpose within the *Yahad*? Some scholars now believe that the *Secret of the Way Things Are* originated outside the Qumran community. Nevertheless, two clues suggest that it was a sectarian work. In 4Q418 Frags. 81 + 81a, l. 17, the disciple is urged to obey the "Instructors" (*maskilim*). That was a technical term designating an official of the sect according to the *Charter of a Jewish Sectarian Association* (text 7). Second, we encounter here a "Vision of Insight" (4Q417 frag. 1 1:16). The same expression appears in the *Damascus Document* (text 1) and in the *Charter for Israel in the Last Days* (text 8), in both cases representing a body of knowledge whose mastery is incumbent upon the members of the community. Accordingly, the *Secret of the Way Things Are* may be an introductory course of study for new or probationary initiates into the *Yahad*.

The stars, the "host of heaven," communicate (through astrological knowledge?) the ways of God.

4Q416 Frag. 1 [1]every spirit [. . .] [2]and to measure His will [. . .] [3]time by time [. . .] [4]according to their host, for [every dominion . . . kingdom by] [5]kingdom, na[tion by nation, man by man . . .] [6]according to the need of their host [. . .] [7]and the host of heaven He has established [. . . lights] [8]for omens for them and signs for [their festivals . . .] [9]one to the other and all their number [. . .] they counted [. . .]

In the Last Days, God will punish evil and reward the good.

[10]From heaven He will judge the work of wickedness, but all those who belong to the truth will gain favor [. . .] [11]its time, and all who have indulged in wickedness will be afraid and cry aloud, for Heaven sees [. . .] [12]seas and abysses were afraid, and every mortal spirit overwhelmed, and the members of the heavenly retinue [. . .] [13][He ju]dges it, and every evil act will perish, until the era of truth is complete [. . .] [14]in all the eras of eternity, for He is the God of truth, and of old the years of [. . .] [15]to establish justice between good and evil (**4Q418**: that the righteous may distinguish between good and evil) [. . .] every judgm[ent . . .] [16]it is the impulse of flesh, and understanding [. . .]

The initiate into this teaching will acquire comprehensive knowledge of God's purposes and of good and evil.

4Q417 Frag. 1 Col. 1 [1][. . .] you, enlightened one [. . .] [2][. . .] behold, [and you will understand the awesome] secrets of the wonders [of God . . .] [3][. . .] and behold [the secret of the way things are, and the deeds of old, why they came to be and what they were . . .] [4][. . . why] [5][things are and why they continue to be . . .] every deed [. . .] [6][day and night meditate on the secret] of the way things are and investigate it at all times, and then you will know truth and evil, wisdom, [7][and falsehood . . .] in all their ways, with their punishments throughout the world eras and the eternal punishment [8]and then you will know the difference between [goo]d [and [evil according to their] deeds, for the God of knowledge is the counsel of Truth, and in the secret of the way things are [9]He has made plain its basis [and its actions . . . with all wis]dom and with all cleverness, its nature and the governing principle of its deeds [10]with all [. . . He has m]ade plain to their minds, with every d[ee]d, how to live by [11][the nature of] their understanding; and He has made plain [. . .] and with the faculty of understanding [the sec]rets of His purpose [are made known], [12]with blameless conduct [in all] His deeds. Inquire into these things at all times, give careful thought [to al]l [13]their effects, and then you will know the glory of [. . . wi]th His wonderful secrets and His mighty deeds.

In early Judaism there was a legend that Seth, the son of Adam, wrote out many revelations on stone tablets, which could be read only by the righteous (Josephus Ant. *1.68–71). A later Gnostic sect called the Sethians used the myth of the tablets of Seth to support its own ideas, as did Christians in the later apocalyptic Testament of Adam. In the following passage, the tablets of Seth are identified with the "Vision of Insight," in which all the secrets of God are revealed.*

And you, [14]enlightened one, the entirety of your reward is in the (book of) remembrance of [. . . , for] the decree is engraved, and inscribed is every time of punishment, [15]for that which is decreed is engraved before God, over all [. . .] the children of Seth. A book of remembrance stands written before Him [16]for those who keep His words; and that is the "Vision of Insight," the book of remembrance, and He bequeathed it to Enosh with a spiritual people, because [17]his nature was patterned after the holy angels. But "Insight" he did not again give to carnal spirits, for they did not know the difference between [18]good and evil according to the judgment of His spirit.

And you, O enlightened son, look on the secret of the way things are and know [19][the ways] of all that is living and their manner of behavior. He will watch over [. . .] [20][. . .] between much and little and in your intimacy [with . . .] [21][. . .] by the secret of the way things are [. . .] [22][. . .] all the vision of [know]ledge and in all [. . .] [23]So always be strong, do not grow weary; in injustice [. . . He who acts] [24]by it will not be held guiltless; according to his inheritance in it [. . .] [25]for the man of insight has carefully considered your secrets and [your deeds . . .] [26]his [foun]dations in you [. . .] with the reward of [. . . As it is said,] [27]"Do not follow after your heart or your eyes, [which led you to fornication" (Num. 15:39) . . .]

Col. 2 [2][. . .] [3]by the secret of the way things are [. . .] [4]comforted [. . .] [5]walk blame[lessly . . .] [6]bless His name [. . .] [7]by your joy [. . .] [8]great are the mercies of G[od . . .] [9]praise God, and for every plague bless [. . .] [10]by His will they have come to pass, and He understands [. . .] [11]He will guard all your ways [. . .] [12]Do not let a thought from the evil impulse deceive you [. . .] [13]seek the truth, do not let [. . .] deceive you [. . .] [14]without a command from God; do not let carnal understanding make you err [. . .] [15]you think [. . .] do not say [. . .] [16]Thus [. . .]

The wise man is advised to avoid unnecessary conflict with the powerful. The wrath of kings is a common theme of the wisdom literature as in Proverbs 16:14–20.

Frag. 2 Col. 1 [1][Speak gently to a ruler] at all times, lest he adjure you; and speak to him in accordance with his mood, lest [he . . .] [2]without reproach. Be wise, pass by him; but when it is forbidden [stay away . . .] [3]Moreover do not trouble his spirit, because you speak gently, [. . .] [4]quickly recount his rebuke, but do not pass over your sins [. . .] [5]and he is righteous as you are, for he is a prince [. . . what he wants,] [6]he will do, for he is incomparable in every deed, without [. . .]

An admonition not to give this teaching to the wicked.

[7]Do not consider an evil man a helper, nor any enemy [. . .] [8]the wickedness of his deeds with his punishment. Therefore know how to conduct yourself with him [. . .]

Poverty is no barrier to acquiring wisdom. True wisdom is more important than riches.

[God's commandment] [9]must not depart from your heart; do not enlarge for yourself alone [. . . by your poverty . . .] [10]For what is more lowly than a poor man? So do not rejoice when you should mourn, lest you toil pointlessly in your life. [Consider the secret of] [11]the way things are, and learn about the causes of well-being, and know who will acquire honor or harm. For indeed [. . .] [12]and for their mourners, eternal joy. Be an advocate for your affairs, without [. . .] [13]all your offenses. Argue your case like a righteous governor; do not [. . .] [14]and do not pass over your [si]ns. Be like a humble man in your dispute; his judgment [. . .] [15]learn of it. And then God will see and his anger will cease and he will pass over your sins, for before [his anger] [16]none will stand; and who will be acquitted in his judgment? And without forgiveness [. . .] [17]needy.

God will take care of those who are faithful to him. "Seek first the kingdom of God and its righteousness and all these things will be given to you" (Matt. 6:33).

Now if you have need, the food you desire and more besides [He will supply . . . And if] [18]you have something left over, bring it to the city He delights in. Accept your legacy from Him, but do not continue to [. . .] [19]but if you have need, your need is not due to lack of wealth, for [His] storehouse lacks nothing. [. . .] [20][from] His mouth all things shall come to pass; so whatever He feeds you, eat, and do not continue in [. . .] [21]your life. If you borrow the wealth of men in your time of need, [you will have] no [quietness] [22]day or night, and no rest for your soul [until] you restore to the moneylender [what you owe;] do not deceive [23]him; why should you bear guilt and even insult [. . . do not entrust yourself any]more to his friend, [24]who, in your time of need will close up his hand, like a hook [. . . and like him, a borrower; so know . . .] [25]if some affliction befalls you, then hasten [. . . do not hide from . . .] [26]behold, he will reveal [. . . rules him, and then] [27]he will not strike him with a rod [. . .] [28]anymore. And you too [. . .]

The angels in heaven, like the true disciples, are followers of God's wisdom.

4Q418 Frag. 55 [3][. . .] in toil will we dig her paths, we shall have rest [4][. . .] and vigilance shall be in our hearts [at all times] and He will make all our paths secure [. . .] [5][. . .] true knowledge, but they did not seek [enlightenment] and they did not choose [to do God's will.] Indeed the God of knowledge [6][. . .] for truth to establish all [their ways.] Insight He has allotted to those who inherit truth [7][. . .] vigilance in [. . .] action, indeed peace and quiet [8][. . .] or have you not heard that the holy angels [. . .] in heaven [9][. . .] truth and they traced back all the causes of insight, and they were vigilant concerning [10][. . . according to] their knowledge a man is honored more than his fellow, and his honor will increase according to his intelligence [11][. . . are the angels] like mortals, who are slothful? Are they like humans, who cease to be? Indeed [12][. . .] they obtain an eternal inheritance. Have you not seen [. . .]

Frag. 77 [2][. . .] the secret of the way things are, and learn the nature of man and gaze at the faculties [. . .] [3][. . . the punishment for] his deeds. Then you will understand the nature of mortal man and the weight of [. . .] [4][the utterance of his lips according to] his spirit, and learn the secret of the way things are, with the weight of eras and the measure of [. . .]

The disciple is again encouraged to seek everything from the hand of God, from whom everything comes.

4Q416 Frag. 2 (with **4Q417** and **4Q418 Frag. 8) Col. 1** [21][. . .] If you are in a hurry [22][to avoid sending . . . from him you should] ask your food, for he **Col. 2** [1]has opened up his generos[ity . . . to fill up] all that is la[cking from his kindness, giving food] [2]to everything that has life, without [. . . if] he should close his hand, [the spirit of everything] [3]mortal would [be withdrawn.] Do not ac[cept . . .] In the time of [our] reproach, cover your face, and in [his] folly [4]imprisonment (?) [. . .]

Be wary when borrowing money or delaying repayment for a long time.

[. . . As for money . . . if you borrow,] repay [quickly!] Then you will be equal to the lender, for otherwise your purse [5]with all its treasures you have [effectively left with him. As for someone who lends you money for your friend, you have giv]en him your entire life; quickly give him what is his, [6]and get back [your] purse. [In such dealings do not degrade] yourself; do not exchange your holy spirit for any amount of money, [7]for there is no price adequate [for your spirit.]

Various precepts on serving God and doing his will.

[. . .] Let no man turn you aside [from worshiping God.] In His favor seek His presence, and according to His way of speaking [8]you should speak, and then you will find what you truly desire. [. . .] Do not be lax in your regulations, and be careful with the secrets you have learned.

[9][. . .] if he assigns you a task [do not allow rest to your soul or] sleep to your eyes until you perform [10][his] com[mand . . .] If there is anything to set [aside . . .] do not let any money be left over for him without [11][. . . lest he should say, He has defrauded me, and . . .] and behold how powerful is [12][human] jealousy, and "deceitful is the heart above all things" (Jer. 17:9) [. . .] so by His favor be strong in His service and in the wisdom of His goodness.

[13][. . .] you will consult with Him [and you will be] to Him like a firstborn son and he will feel for you as a man does for his only child [14][. . . for you are His servant and] His [chosen.] So do not be too credulous, lest you err inadvertently; and yet do not be over-anxious of your pride. [15][And you, be like a wise servant for Him.] Do not lower yourself to whatever is not worthy of you; then you will be [16][a servant . . .] Do not touch anything for which your strength is not equal, lest you falter and you are terribly embarrassed.

[17]Do not sell your soul for money; it is good for you to be a servant in spirit, and to serve your overseers freely.

[18]Do not sell your honor for any price, and do not barter away your inheritance, lest you bring ruin on your body.

Do not overindulge yourself with bread [19]when there is no clothing. Do not drink wine when there is no food. Do not seek luxuries when you [20]lack bread.

Do not pride yourself on your need when you are poor, lest [21]you despise your life, and moreover, do not disdain your wife, your closest companion.

More admonitions on the danger of money.

Col. 3 [2]Remember that you are poor [. . .] and your poverty [3]you will not find, and when you violate a promise [. . . If someone] leaves something valuable with you, [4]do not touch it, lest you be burned and your body consumed by its fire. As you have taken it, so return it, [5]and joy will be yours if you are innocent with regard to it. Also, do not take money from anyone you do not know, [6]lest he add to your poverty. But if he forces it on you with the threat of death, deposit it safely, and do not corrupt your soul [7]with it. Then you shall lie down to die with the truth, and when you expire, your memory will blossom for[ever], and your posterity will inherit [8]joy.

The poor disciple should be content with whatever God gives. Serving God is the truly noble way of life.

Yes, you are needy. Do not crave anything except your inheritance, and do not be consumed by it, lest you cross [9]the boundaries of the Law. If He should return you to an honorable position, conduct yourself accordingly, and, knowing the secret of the way things are, seek its causes; then you will know [10]His true inheritance, and you will live righteously, for God will make His face shine in all your ways. Give honor to those who pay you honor [11]and praise His name always, for your head is taller than the mountaintops, and He has made you sit among the nobility, and [12]he has made you master of a glorious inheritance. Seek His will always.

Yes, you are needy. Do not say, "Since I am poor, [13]I cannot seek true knowledge." Apply yourself to every kind of discipline and in every [. . .] refine your heart, and your thoughts will be characterized by great insight. [14]Seek the secret of the way things are, and give careful thought to all the ways of truth, look long at the roots of wickedness. [15]Then you will know what is bitter for someone and what is sweet for a man.

True wisdom entails honoring parents.

Honor your father by your poverty, [16]and your mother in your ways, for a man's father is like God to him, his mother is like his master. For [17]they are the crucible of your conception, and since He gave them authority over you and thus formed the spirit, so serve them. And since He [18]has revealed to you by the secret of the way things are, honor them for your own honor's sake, and in [. . .] honor their presence [19]for the sake of your life and the length of your days. Even if you are as poor as [. . .] [20]without the law.

The disciple may take a wife, if she too is a disciple. God has given him authority over her.

If you would marry a wife in your poverty, learn the causes of [. . .]

[21]from the secret of the way things are. When you are united, live together with your fleshly helper [. . . For as the verse says, "A man should leave] **Col. 4** [1]his father and his mother [and adhere to his wife and they will become one flesh" (Gen. 2:24).] [2]He has made you ruler over her, so [. . .] [3]He did not give [her father] authority over her, He has separated her from her mother, and unto you [He has given authority . . . He has made your wife] [4]and you into one flesh. He will take your daughter away and give her to another, and your sons [. . .] [5]But you, live together with the wife of your bosom, for she is the kin of [. . .] [6]Whosoever governs her besides you has "shifted the boundary" of his life [. . .] [7]He has made you ruler over her, for her to live the way you want her to, not adding any vows or offerings [. . .] [8]Turn her spirit to your will, and every binding oath, every vow [. . .] [9]annulling the utterance of your mouth, and forbidding the doing of your will [. . .] [10]your lips, forgive her, for your sake do not [. . .] [11]your honor in your inheritance [. . .] [12]in your inheritance lest [. . .] [13]the wife of your bosom and shame [. . .]

A wise man should use his wisdom in the marketplace, not allowing himself to be cheated; he should do the same when contemplating taking a wife. He should consider a prospective mate's spirit as well as her physical beauty.

4Q418 Frags. 167a–b [1][. . .] its proportion in al[l . . .] [2][. . .] in them, for by accur[ate] scales [. . .] [3][. . .] shall be [. . .] this will outweigh that [. . .] [4][. . .] which is not [by two different] ephahs or two different omers [. . .] [5][. . .] which are not together [. . .] by the beauty of her appearance [. . . understanding that according to spirits he measures . . .] [6]you have measured together their spirit . . . al]l her defects tell him and in [her] bo[dy examine . . . lest] [7][it be for him] a stumbling block before [him . . .] stumbled in the dark and [. . .]

A further discourse on the punishment of evil in the Last Days.

Frag. 69 Col. 2 [4]And now, O foolish of heart, what is goodness without [5][. . . what] good is tranquillity for what has not come to pass? What good is justice for what has not been established? And how can the dead groan for [. . .] [6][. . .] you were created; and you will return to eternal destruction, for [. . .] your sin [. . .] [7][. . .] In darkness they will wail for your judgment. But that which exists eternally, those who seek truth, will awaken to give judgment [. . .] [8]they will destroy those who are foolish of heart, and the children of evil will no longer exist, and all who cling to wickedness will be bewildered [. . .] [9]at your judgment the pillars of the sky-dome will be shattered, and all the [host of heaven] will thunder [. . .]

The disciple must not grow tired of his learning; an eternal reward awaits him.

[10]But you, O chosen of truth, who earnestly follow [. . .] seek[ers of insight. . .and] the watchful [11]for all knowledge. How can you say, We are weary of insight, and we have been careful to pursue true knowledge [. . .] [12]and untiring in all the years of eternity. Indeed he will take delight in truth forever and knowledge [eternally] will serve him; and [the sons of] [13]heaven, whose inheritance is eternal life, will they truly say, We are weary of deeds of truth, we worked hard [. . .] [14]of every era. Indeed, in eternal light they will wa[lk . . .] glory and great honor you [. . .] [15]in the sky [. . .] council of the divinities all [. . .]

But you, O [enlightened] son [. . .]

The poverty of the student is a constant theme. It is probably both a literal poverty and a spiritual poverty, in that all are poor compared to God.

4Q415 Frag. 6 [1][. . .] the secret of men [. . .] [2]You are needy, and [. . .] [3]your poverty in your counsel [. . .] [4]Test these things by the secret of the way things are [. . .] [5]from the place of [origins] and by the weight [. . .]

This exhortation uses expressions evoking the duties of the priesthood. The disciple is separated from the general run of humanity; he receives God himself as his inheritance, as do the Levites (Num. 18:20); he is consecrated to God.

4Q418 Frag. 81+81a [1]Open your lips as a spring to bless the holy ones, and give praise like an eternal spring [. . .] He has separated you from every [2]carnal spirit; so you, be separate from everything He hates, and abstain from every abomination of the soul, for He made everything [3]and bestowed on each his inheritance. And He Himself is "your portion and inheritance" (Num. 18:20) among the human race, and He made you ruler over His inheritance. So [4]honor Him by this when you consecrate yourself for Him, just as he has made you a Holy of Holies [for all] the world, and among [di]vin[ities] [5]He has cast your lot and greatly increased your honor and has made you like a firstborn son for Him [. . .] [6]I will give to you my goodness, and you, is my goodness not for you? So in my faith walk always [. . .] [7]your deeds and you should seek His judgments at the hand of every opponent [. . .]

More about the priesthood of the disciple.

[8]Love Him and in kindness everlasting and mercy toward all those who keep His words and with zeal [. . .] [9]And He has opened knowledge for you and made you ruler over His storehouse and given the authority to determine a reliable measure [to you . . .] [10]are with you, and it is in your power to turn away wrath from those whom God favors and to number [. . .] [11]with you. Before you take your inheritance from His hand honor His holy ones, and be[fore . . .] [12]He has opened a [sp]ring for all His holy ones, and all who have been called by His name are holy [. . .] [13]for all times His glory and His beauty are for the eter[nal] plantation [of His chosen . . .] [14][. . .] the world, in it all those who inherit the earth shall walk, for in hea[ven . . .]

[15]You, O enlightened one, if He has made you rule by the skill of your hands, then know [. . .] [16]goodness for all humans who pass by, and from there you will attend to your food [. . .] [17]consider well and add to your learning by listening to all your Instructors [. . .] [18]show your poverty to all who seek pleasure and then you will establish [. . .] [19]you will be filled, and satisfied by abundant goodness and by the skill of your hands [. . .] [20]for God has distributed an inheritance to every [living thing] and all those who are wise at heart will have success [. . .]

Frag. 88 [1]you will establish all your pleasures [. . .] [2]in your life He will make you complete a multitude of years [. . .] [3]be careful of yourself lest you mingle [. . .] [4]you will judge an evil man and by the strength of your hands [. . .] [5]He will close his hand against your poverty [. . .] [6]to the sole of your foot, for God seeks among [. . .] [7]by your hand to live and you will be gathered in [. . .] [8]and your inheritance will be full in truth, and you will become [. . .]

Frag. 102 [1][. . .] in corruption [. . .] [2][. . .] pleasure, and righteous truth all his deeds [. . .] [3][. . . And you,] O one enlightened by truth, from every skill of your hands [. . .] [4][. . .] your movement (?), and then He will seek your pleasure with all who seek Him [. . .] [5][. . . from] abominable sin you will be clean and in the joy of truth you will [. . .]

The disciple is also like a farmer, who knows how to plant crops properly and not to mix different crops, as forbidden in Leviticus 19:19.

Frag. 103 [2][. . .] farmers until all [. . .] [3][. . .] put in your baskets and in your granaries all [. . .] [4]he will compare one time with another, study them and do not be silent [. . .] [5][. . .] for all of them will study at the right time, and each one according to his desire [. . .] your [. . .] will be found [. . .] [6]like a spring of living water that contains go[odn]ess

[. . . from] your merchandise do not mingle [. . .] [7]lest it become a case of "forbidden mixtures" (Lev. 19:19; Deut. 22:9), like the mule, and you will become like a garment [of linsey-woolsey], of wool and flax mingled; or your work might be like one who plows [8]with an ox yoked to a donkey; or your produce might be [to you] like one who sows improper mixtures, of which the seed and the full yield and the produce of [9][the vineyard] should be holy [. . .] your money with your body and [even] your life, all will perish together, and in your life you will not find it [. . .]

Frag. 107 [1][. . . se]ek and then you will fin[d . . .] [2][. . .] above [. . .] [3][. . .] for your need [. . .] [4][. . .] your merchandise and your wages in the things of [. . .] [5][. . .] with all the plants of the soil, for all of [them] shall [they] seek [. . .] [6][. . .] herbs with [. . .] root [. . .] [7][. . .] their vineyard (?) with [. . .]

The section concerning former disciples cautions them against offending the God-ordained authorities. Line 1 refers to the bad example of Korah, who rebelled against Moses (Num. 16).

4Q423 Frag. 5 [1][. . .] the judgment passed on Korah, and because He has opened your ear [2][to the secret of the way things are . . . the he]ad of [your] clans [. . .] and the Leader of your people [3][. . .] He has assigned the inheritance of all those who exercise authority and the purpose of every[thing that is done] is in His power, and He [has . . .] the actions of [. . .] [4][. . . judging] all of them in truth, and He has appointed duties to fathers and sons to [. . .] with all the native-born and spoken [5][. . . for] those who till the soil He has appointed the summer festivals and the gathering of your crops at the proper time. The change of [6][seasons] you must closely observe for all your crops and be wise in your business [. . .] the good with the bad [. . .] [7][. . . Is there] insight with the foolish man? [. . .] thus the man [8][. . .] all [. . .] shall say [. . . the abun]dance of his insight [9][. . . the secret of the way] things are in all his [way . . .] without [. . .]

4Q418 Frag. 123 [2]when years begin and when eras end [. . .] [3]everything that has happened in it, why it was and what will be in [. . .] [4]His era that God opened the ears of those who understand by the secret of the way things are [. . .] [5][And] you, O enlightened one, when you observe all these things [. . .] [6][. . .] weigh your deeds with the era [. . .] [7][. . .] Whatever is left with you, guard carefully [. . .] [8][. . . jud]ge iniquity [. . .]

God has divided the good and the evil from before creation.

Frag. 126 [1][. . .] not a single one of all their host shall be lacking [. . .] [2][. . .] in truth from all the kindness of men [. . .] [3][. . .] a reliable [measure] and an accurate weight God has measured out; all [. . .] [4]He distinguished them in truth, He made them and for their needs He seeks [. . .] [5]the secret place of everything, and indeed nothing has happened apart from His will and from [His wisdom . . .] [6]judgment to wreak vengeance on evildoers and the punishment [. . .] [7]to lock up the wicked and to show favor to the weak [. . .] [8]by eternal glory and perpetual peace and the spirit of life to separate [. . .] [9]all the children of life and in God's strength and the abundance of His glory with His goodness [. . .] [10]and of His faithfulness they will speak all the day, they will constantly praise His name [. . .]

The disciple belongs to those foreordained for God's favor.

[11]And you shall walk in truth with all those who seek [Him . . .] [12]and by your hand His kindness; and from your basket he will seek his pleasure, and you [. . .] [13]and if his hand is not sufficient for your need and the need of his kindness [. . .] [14][. . .] and God will arrange it by his pleasure, for God [. . .] [15][. . .] your hand for plenty, and your livestock will increase [. . .] [16][. . .] forever and not [. . .]

The grim fate in store for those who reject God.

Frag. 127 [1][. . .] your source and your need you will not find; and your spirit will grow faint unto death, deprived of all goodness [. . .] [2][. . .] all the day, and your spirit will yearn to enter her gates and you will bury and cover [. . .] [3][. . .] your body and you will become food between the teeth of wild animals and you will be consumed by pestilence (cf. Deut. 32:24) before [. . .] [4][. . . those who seek what they] desire, you have oppressed them in their life, and also you [. . .] [5][. . .] to you, for God has done whatever He wanted in kindness, and apportioned them in the truth [. . .] [6][. . .] He weighed their character in the scales of righteousness and in the truth [. . .]

4Q423 Frags. 1–2 [1][. . .] every fruit of the crops and every pleasant tree "that is desirable to make one wise" (Gen. 3:6), is it not the garden [. . .] [2][. . . desirable] to make one [very] wise, and he made you ruler over it to till it and keep it.

[. . .] [3][. . . "the land] will sprout thorns and thistles for you" (Gen. 3:18), and "it will not yield its strength to you" (4:12) [. . .] [4][. . .] when you fall away.

[. . .] [5][. . .] begotten, and all the wombs of [. . .] all your kindness [6][. . .] in all your needs, for it shall grow all [. . .] always not [7][. . .] and when you plant [. . . rejecting] evil, knowing the good [8][. . .] his way and the way of [9][. . .] bread [. . .]

Frag. 3 [1][. . .] in vain [your] stren[gth . . .] [2][. . . by the secret of] the way things are, and so comport yourself, and [all your] c[rops . . .] [3][. . . pos]session of the land; and at His command it has conceived all [. . .] [4][. . . with] the first yield of your womb and the firstborn of all [your livestock . . .] [5][. . .] saying, I have sanctified [. . .]

Frag. 4 (1Q26 Frag. 1) [1][. . . wat]ch [yourself lest] you glorify yourself from it and [. . .] [2][. . . and you become accursed in a]ll [your] crops [and guilty] in all your deeds [. . .] [3a][. . . your case and by] His [hand] he put [judgment . . . and He said to him, I am your portion] [3][and your inheritance among the children of men . . . I will exalt] you bef[ore all . . .]

—E.M.C.

106. An Instruction

4Q419

Once thought to be part of the *Secret of the Way Things Are* (text 105), this text seems instead to be an independent example of the genre of wisdom instruction.

Learners are exhorted to accept the authority of the priests and their interpretation of the Law.

Frag. 1 [1]which you should do according to all the rulin[gs . . .] [2]unto you through Moses and that should be done [. . .] [3]through his priests for they are loyal to the coven[ant . . .] [4]he will make known that which is [His] and what is g[ood . . .] [5]He chose the seed of Aaron to [. . .] [6]His [w]ays and to bring to sacrifice the savory [. . .] [7]and He gave them [. . .] which to all His people and [. . .] [8]and He commanded [. . .] [9]the throne exalted in glory [. . .] [10]He lives forever and His glory is eter[nal . . .] [11]you shall diligently seek, but the filthy abomination [. . .] [12]you have loved and they fouled themselves in all the [ways . . .]

The teacher teaches the ways of God from the nature of creation.

Frag. 8 Col. 2 [1]they delighted [. . .] [2]and in His words [. . .] [3]in [. . .] and he numbered them [. . .] [4]from them their ways with the number[ing. . .between light] [5]and darkness; and from his storehouse [. . . he will give] [6]a harvest for all the times of eternity [. . .] [7]If He should close His hand, the spirit of everything [mortal] would be withdrawn [8][. . . un]to their soil they will return [. . .]
—E.M.C.

107. A Commentary on Genesis and Exodus

4Q422

A Commentary on Genesis and Exodus is yet another example of that method of biblical interpretation so popular in Second Temple Judaism (at least in certain circles): the rewritten Bible. This type of writing varies widely with respect to just how freely the Bible gets rewritten, and the point of the rewriting is sometimes obscure. Other examples in this book include texts 4, 5, 18, 20, 43, 44, 45, 53, 84, 91, 94, 143, and 155—the length of the list demonstrates just how important this type of writing was.

Genesis 1–4, the creation and rebellion of humankind.

Col. 1 [6][. . .] He made [the heavens and the earth and all] their host by [His] word [. . .] [7][. . . And he rested on the seventh day from all the work whi]ch He had done, and [His] holy spirit [. . .] [8][. . . and He appointed man to rule over every] living [creatur]e and creeping thin[g upon the earth . . .] [9][. . . He set man upon the ear]th; He gave him permission to eat the frui[t of the earth . . .] [10][. . .] not to eat from the tree of the kn[owledge of good and evil . . .] [11][. . . and] he arose against Him and they forgot [His statutes . . .] [12][. . .] with an evil inclination, and for work[s of wickedness . . .] [13][. . .] peace [. . .]

Genesis 6–9, the Flood.

Col. 2 [1][. . . and God saw that (?)] great and [. . . the evil of man on the earth] [2][. . .] the [. . .] [2a][. . . righteous in] his generation up[on the earth . . .] to a beast [. . .] [3][. . .] they were delivered upon [. . . up]on the earth, for [. . .] [4][. . . to deliver Noah] and his sons,

[his] w[ife and the wives of his sons from] the waters of the flood and [. . .] [5]and he who d[oes . . . and] God [cl]osed it behind them [. . .] and He placed [. . .] upon it (*or* him) [. . .] [6]that G[od] chose [. . .] the windows of heav[en] ope[n]ed [. . .] upon the earth [7]under the heaven[s . . . that] the water might come up upon the ear[th . . . forty] days and for[ty] [8]nights the [rain] was up[on the earth . . . the wat]er prev[ailed] upon [the earth . . .] in order [9]to know the glory of the Most [High . . .] He set [. . .] before him [10]and it shone upon [the] he[avens . . . the ea]rth and [. . .] a sign for the genera[tions] [11]eternally, after [. . . and there shall never again] be a flood [to destroy the earth . . .] [12]the se[t tim]es of day and night [shall not cease . . . lights to shine upo]n the heavens and the ear[th . . .] [13][the earth and] its [fu]ll[nes]s [. . .] He gave [everythi]ng [. . .]

Exodus 1–11, the plagues on Egypt.

Col. 3 [1][. . .] and not [. . .] [2]the [t]wo midwiv[es . . . and they cast] [3]their [so]ns into the Nil[e . . . t]hem, [4][and] He sent Mo[ses] to them [. . . and He appeared] in the vision of [the burning bush . . .] [5]in signs and wonders [. . .] they take hold and [. . .] [6]and He sent them to Pharaoh [. . .] plagues [. . .] wo[nd]ers for the Egyptians [. . .] and they brought His word [7]to Pharaoh to let [their people] go, [but] He hardened [his] heart [to] sin so that the pe[ople of Isra]el might know it throughout their gener[ations.] Then He changed their [water] to blood. [8]The frogs were in all [their] land and gnats were throughout all of [their] territory; swarms of flies were [in] their [ho]uses, and [they came up]on all their [. . .] And He struck with pestilen[ce all] [9]their livestock and animals; He delivered them up to [dea]th. He appoi[nted dar]kness on their land and gloom [in] their [houses] so that they could not see one another. [And He smote] [10]their land with hail and [their] earth [with] frost so as to d[estroy al]l their edib[le] fruit. Then He brought the locust so as to cover the surface of the l[and,] a locust infestation in all their territory, [11]so that they ate every green plant in [their] l[and . . .] And God h[ardened] the heart of [Pharao]h that he might not let [them go] and that He might multiply His wonders. [12][And He smote their firstborn,] ever[y one of their] first [progeny . . .]

—M.G.A.

108. A Collection of Proverbs

4Q424

Unlike the exalted exhortations of the *Book of Secrets* (text 6) and the *Secret of the Way Things Are* (text 105), this wisdom text remains very much in the tradition of homespun prudence that generally characterizes the biblical book of Proverbs. From what survives, it seems to be a simple collection, not organized into an instruction like the other wisdom compositions among the scrolls. Nothing in this work is overtly sectarian.

The first (fragmentary) proverb is reminiscent of Jesus's description of the foolish man whose house, built on sand, later fell apart during a rainstorm (Matt. 7:27).

Frag. 1 [2][. . .] with the winepress [. . .] [3][. . .] when he chooses to build a partition, and coats his wall with plaster, also he [. . .] [4][it will fa]ll apart during a downpour.

Various maxims on using wisdom in associating with certain types of people.

Do not accept a legal decision from a cheater, and with a capricious man do not [5]enter a fiery ordeal, for he will melt like lead and will not be steady in the flames.

[6]Do not give an important task to a lazy man, for he will not be careful with your assignment; and do not send him to get anything, [7]for he will not keep straight on any of your paths.

Do not [trust] a complainer [. . .] [8]to get money for your needs.

Do not trust a man known for devious speech [. . .] [9]your cause he will surely pervert with his speech, for he takes no pleasure in truth. [. . .] [10]by the fruit of his lips.

Do not give a stingy man responsibility for mon[ey . . .] [11]he will measure out your surplus for your needs [. . .] whatever is left over [. . .] [12]and in the time of harvest he will be found godless.

The impatie[nt . . .] [13]fools, for he will surely destroy them.

A man [. . .]

This fragment may speak of the punishment awaiting the wicked man.

Frag. 2 [2][. . .] from the guilt of the judgment of G[od,] and from [. . .] [3][. . .]

Do not make a pledge for him among the hum[ble . . .] [4][. . .] and the only son of an oppressor [. . .] a man [. . .] [5][. . . nee]dy do not [. . .] him [. . .] [6][. . .] is no[t] to be done [. . .]

More maxims concerning those whom it is unwise to trust.

Frag. 3 [1][. . .] he does not do his work by measure.

Someone who passes judgment before investigating or who believes before [examining the evidence] [2]should not be given authority over those who pursue true knowledge, for he will not understand their case, acquitting the innocent and condemning the g[uilty.] [3]So he too is liable to become an object of scorn.

Do not send a man with blurred eyes to perceive the upright, for [. . .]

[4]Do not send a man hard of hearing to seek justice, for he will not weigh the dispute between men properly, like one who scatters to the wind [seed] [5]that has not been cleansed.

The same is true when one speaks to an ear that does not hear, or recounts a tale to one who is fast asleep in the spirit [. . .]

[6]Do not send a thick-headed man on a job requiring deep thought, because his mind's abilities are hidden and he does not govern [his spirit, and] [7]he cannot use the skill of his hands.

The text moves from the negative examples of folly to positive traits of the wise and righteous man.

A man of insight will receive under[standing,] a man of knowledge can recognize wisdom [. . .]

[8]An honest man will take pleasure in good judgment.

A man of truth [. . .] a strong man will be zealous for [. . .] [9][and h]e disputes with those who would shift the boundaries.

A man of compa[ssion does] good to the poor [. . .] [10][. . .] concern for all those who lack money, the children of the righteous [. . .] [11][. . .] in all money of [. . .]

—E.M.C.

109. Thanksgivings

4Q433a

Four papyrus fragments—three of which are presented here—are all that remains of a collection of thanksgiving psalms inscribed on papyrus. The themes are similar to those of the *Thanksgiving Hymns* (text 12). This work was not assigned a separate numerical designation until 1996, a reflection of the fact that it has but recently been recognized as a discrete literary work. *Thanksgivings* was written on the other side of a copy (4Q255) of the *Charter of a Jewish Sectarian Association* (text 7).

Songs and praises calls to mind A Liturgical Calendar *(text 81) and the two daily services.*

Frag. 1 2 [. . . thank]sgivings [. . .] 3[. . .]in [His] return, [and] He produced [. . .] 4[. . . He] appointed His songs as holy for [. . .] 5[. . .] and praises in the mouth of the migh[ty . . .] 6[. . .] new wine, then God shall rejoice [. . .]

As in Thanksgiving Hymns *(text 12, 20:7) or often in the* Songs of the Sabbath Sacrifice *(text 101), this fragment preserves a psalm for the Instructor. In this instance it concerns the elect of Israel, who thrive as a delightful plant (Isa. 5:7).*

Frag. 2 1[. . .] for the everlasting sea[sons].

2For the Instructor: a p[ara]ble concerning the glory of [. . .] 3He planted a delightful plant in His gard[en] and in His vineyard [. . .] 4its vines, and its branches brought forth fruit and multiplied in [. . .] 5and its branches are over the lofty supports of the heavens and it offered itself willingly [. . .] 6branch throughout the eternal generations and to produce the frui[t of . . .] 7to all those who taste it, and among its fruit no worthless fruit shall appear [. . .] 8its foliage and its leaves and its shoots shall be on it [. . . con]tinually [. . .] 9from its roots, it shall not be pulled up from its aromatic bed, for [. . .]

*Thanks to God for deliverance from the torments of enemies (*Thanksgiving Hymns *12:20–37).*

Frag. 3 [1][. . .] burning for [. . .] [2][. . .] poured out [. . .] upon [. . .] [3][. . .] those who [b]low [. . . to] permit a shattering [. . .] [4a][. . .] and He was indignant [. . .] [4][. . .] thus [. . .] His anger for all the [. . .] [5][. . .] it shall burn [. . .] with flaming fire [. . .] [6][. . .] flames of [fire] in the shee[p]folds [. . .] [7][. . .] those who trample the flock (*or* scornful tramplers) tra[mple . . .] [8][. . .] with coals, and those who gird on flam[es of fire . . .] [9][. . .] rivers of pitch consuming [. . .] [10][. . .] throughout the generation[s . . .]
—M.G.A.

110. In Praise of God's Grace (*Barki Nafshi*)

4Q434, 4Q436–437, 4Q439

Unlike *A Collection of Royal Psalms* (text 93), these hymns are almost wholly devoted to the descriptive praise of God's goodness as shown to the righteous in Israel. This group includes no examples of the other main type of psalm, the individual or communal lament. As with the *Royal Psalms,* the songs of *In Praise of God's Grace* are outstanding imitations of the biblical psalms. Like them, they occasionally quote verbatim from the books of the Old Testament.

These praise hymns contain no clear indication of the time of composition. The official editors of this collection refer to it by the title *Barki Nafshi,* a Hebrew phrase meaning "Bless, O my soul . . . ," which occurs several times in the poems.

This hymn extols God for his goodness to the righteous in Israel.

4Q434 Frag. 1 Col. 1 (= 4Q437 Frag. 1) [1]Bless, O my soul, the Lord, for all His wonderful deeds forever, and blessed be His name, "for He has saved the life of the poor" (Jer. 20:13) and the [2]humble He has not spurned, and He has not overlooked the needy in trouble, He has kept his eyes on the weak, and paid attention to the cry of orphans for help. He has inclined His ears to [3]their cry, and because of His abundant mercies, has shown favor to the meek. He has opened their eyes to see His ways and their ears to hear [4]His teaching. "He has circumcised their hearts' foreskin" (Deut. 10:16), and delivered them for the sake of His kindness. He has set their feet firmly on the path, and has not abandoned them in their great distress. [5]He has not given them into the power of cruel tyrants, nor judged them with the wicked, nor aroused his anger against them, nor destroyed them all [6]in His wrath. His fierce wrath has not blazed out against all, and He has not judged them in the fire of His zeal. [7]No, He has judged them by His abundant mercies, sent grievous judgments only for the sake of testing them. Multiplying [his] mercies, He hid them among the Gentiles; [from the power of] [8]mortals He has saved them, nor has He judged them by a mass of Gentiles. He has not [abandoned] them within the nations, and hidden them in [. . .] [9]"He made dark places light in front of them, and He made rough places smooth" (Isa. 42:16). He revealed to them laws of peace and truth. [He created] [10]their spirit by measure, He apportioned their words by the proper weight, and made them sing like flutes, He gave them a different mind, so they could walk in [the ways of peace.] [11]He also brought them near to His heart's path, for they had pledged their spirit to Him. So He wove a protective hedge around them, and commanded that no plague should [smite them], [12]"His angel camped around them" (Ps. 34:7) for protection, lest [Belial] attack them [through] [13]their enemies. [The fire of] his wrath burned [. . .], His anger [. . .] in them [. . .] [14][. . .] **Col. 2** [1]in [their] trouble and [distress], and You [delivered] them [from] every danger. [Miracles] [2]You have performed for them while humanity watches, and You delivered them for Your sake. [. . .] [3]so that they make amends for their sins and their ancestors' sins, and atone for them [. . .] [4]by Your statutes, and to the path that You have shown [. . .]

This hymn praises God for the deliverance he will bring to Israel in the future, not for what he has already done. Since the focus is on Jerusalem, this is another example of the songs of Zion (see the first psalm in A Collection of Royal Psalms, *text 93).*

Frag. 2 [1][. . .] that the poor woman might be comforted in her mourning [. . .] [2]the Gentiles unto destruction and the nations will be exterminated and the wicked [. . .] renew [3]the activity of heaven and earth and they will rejoice and His glory fills [all the earth . . .] their [guilt] [4]He will forgive, and He will console them with abundant goodness, the goodness of the [. . .] to eat [5]its fruit and its goodness.

[6]Like one whose mother comforts him, so He will comfort them in Jerusalem [as a bridegroom] does his bride. [7]His [presence] will rest upon it forever, for His throne will last forever and ever, and His glory [. . .] and all the Gentiles [8][. . .] to Him and the host [of heaven] will be in it and [. . .] its delight [9][. . .] for beauty [. . .] I will bless the [10][. . .]

Blessed is the name of the Most High [. . .] [11][. . .] Bless, [O my soul], Your mercies upon me [12][. . .] You have established it on the Law [13][. . .] the book of Your statutes [. . .]

This fragment once belonged to a psalm that emphasized God's goodness to Israel in historical-biblical terms.

Frag. 7b [2][. . . He changed] their lodgings from there in the wilderness to a "door of hope" (Hos. 2:15) and "He made a covenant" for their welfare "with the birds of [3]the air and the beasts of the field" (2:18). He made their enemies like dung and dust, and he ground Edom and Moab to powder.

The poem above praises God for his mercy to Israel as a whole; the following hymn describes his grace to the pious individual.

4Q436 Frag. 1 Col. 1 [1][. . .] understanding to strengthen the "repentant heart" (Ps. 51:17), to give it perpetual relief, to console the weak in their time of distress, to lift up the hands of the fallen, [2]to make tools of knowledge to give true knowledge to the wise, that the honest may increase learning, to comprehend [3]Your great deeds that You have done in years of old and throughout every generation.

A perpetual knowledge that [4][. . .] before me. You preserved Your Law before me, and Your covenant You have ratified for me, You strengthened the heart [. . .] [5][. . .] to walk in Your ways, You have commanded my heart and trained my mind not to forget Your rules [. . .] [6][. . .] You have [. . .] Your Law, and You have opened up my mind and strengthened me to pursue Your way. [7][. . .] Your [. . .] and You have made my mouth like a sharp sword, my tongue You have unbound to speak holy words, and You put [8][on my lips] a chain lest they babble of the deeds of the man whose utterances are corrupt.

My feet You have strengthened [9][. . .] with Your hand You have taken my right hand, and You have sent me [. . .] [10][. . . impure thoughts] You have driven from me, and put a pure heart in their place. You have kept the evil impulse from me [. . .] **Col. 2** [1][and a hol]y [spirit] You have placed in my heart. You have removed lustful eyes from me, and gazed [. . .] [2][. . .]. You have sent away stubbornness from me, and put humility there instead. Also You have removed hostility [from me, and given me] [3][a spirit of] patience. You have made me forget haughtiness and pride [. . .] [4][. . .] you have given me [. . .]

Another individual hymn of praise that recalls God's deliverance in time of need.

4Q437 Frag. 2 Col. 1 [1][. . .] from the company of those who seek [. . .] [2][. . . a net] they have set to catch me and pursued [my] so[ul . . .] [3][. . . "may] their [swo]rd [enter] their own heart, and may their bows shatter" (Ps. 37:15) [. . .] [4][for all] this I will bless Your name during my life, for You have delivered me from [. . .] [5][. . .] and Your kindnesses are a shield around me and You protected my life among the Gentiles [. . .] [6][. . .] You have [not] put to shame those who love me. I did not forget Your laws when my soul was in distress. [7][. . .] You did not hide Your face from my supplications; You looked pityingly on all my suffering. My sins [8][. . .] my spirit grows weak. When I was in distress You heard my voice. "In Your quiver You [hid me, under the shadow of your hand] [9][you concealed] me, You made me a polished arrow" (Isa. 49:2). You hid me in the shelter of Your palms and [. . .] [10][from the river] You saved me from drowning, from a stream of Gentiles, lest it overwhelm me [. . .] [11][. . .] You brought me up out of the grave, You set new life [before me,] [12][men of] good omen [you have seated] before me and You comforted me through the offspring of righteousness. With the cord of j[ustic]e you have gladdened [13][my soul, and with a] righteous [measure] you have renewed my spirit.

I will bless the Lord with [all my soul]. [14][I will praise] His [go]odness with the joy of my heart. Lord, I remember You, my heart is firm b[efore yo]u, my hope [15][is for Your deliverance . . . Your goodness] I call to mind that my heart may exult in You. You have given me [victory. "My soul] thirsts [16][for you, my] soul [c]lings [to] you" (Ps. 63:1, 8). I speak always of Your great deeds, "I call You to mind on [my bed] in the watches [of the night" (63:6). . . .]

The last fragment seems more like a lament; the author (a prophet or leader) seems to be in present distress. Therefore this piece may not truly belong to the same collection.

4Q439 Frag. 1 [1][. . .] to gather the righ[teous] with me, and to raise a road [2]of life [. . .] into Your covenant those who are closest to me, and all those of (my) zodiacal sign [3]and [. . .] possess my inheritance. Therefore my eye has become a spring of water [4][. . .] discipline, and those who stand behind them that [5][. . .] and now my whole city has turned into thorns [6][. . .] all my judges are found to be foo[ls . . .] [7][. . .] my righteous ones have become simpletons [. . .] [8][. . .] traitors [. . .]

—E.M.C.

111. A Meditation on the Fourth Day of Creation

4Q440

These fragments once stood near the end of a poetical work similar to the *Thanksgiving Hymns* (text 12). As extant, the work begins with a consideration of the fourth day of creation with special reference to Genesis 1:16–18: "God made the two great lights—the greater light to rule the day and the lesser light to rule the night—and the stars. God set them in the dome of the sky to give light upon the earth, to rule over the day and over the night, and to separate the light from the darkness." The author apparently conceived of some scheme whereby light and darkness were described as "portions" and each ruled for certain "ages." Unfortunately, the fragmentary remains preclude a fuller understanding of this fascinating scheme, which seems clearly to be related to the astronomical and calendrical concerns that appear in many other Dead Sea Scrolls. The author then turns to a praise of God with mention of God's "mysteries," presumably an allusion to the creation.

Frag. 1 [1][. . . On the] fourth [day] You opened a great light in the rea[lm of . . .] [2][. . .] forty-[n]ine portions of light, seven [. . .] [3][. . .] for the three ages of darkness. Seventy [. . .] [4][. . .] for all the days of its dominion. [. . .] [5][. . .] ages to shine forth sev[enfold . . .]

Frag. 3 Col. 1 [16][. . .] and to proclaim the glad tidings of et[ern]al peace. [18][. . . for eve]ry spirit, and Your insight for every [19][. . .] Your [g]lory to every living creature [20][. . . Blessed are] You, my God, the Just among all [21][. . .] all of us at our creation. Surely [22][. . . th]ese and in Your goodness You established [23][. . . the dep]th of Your fearsome mysteries [24][. . .] Your glorious [pl]an. [You] are blessed, [25][my God, . . .] and until the latter times [You] will not [. . .]

—M.O.W.

112. Hymns of Thanksgiving

4Q443

Exodus 15:2 proclaims, "The Lord is my strength and my song." The Hebrew term for song, echoed elsewhere in the Bible (Isa. 12:2; 51:3; Ps. 118:14), occurs among the scrolls only in this manuscript and the *Songs of the*

Sabbath Sacrifice (text 101). In frag. 1, l. 8, the author calls his congregation "the sons of the council," a nonbiblical term that occurs elsewhere only in the *Charter* (see text 7, 2:25). One may suspect, therefore, that *Hymns of Thanksgiving* belongs among the sectarian scrolls rather than among the nonsectarian.

Frag. 1 [2][. . .] song of praise [. . .] [3][. . .] please extend [. . .] [4][. . . to] you from [my] youth [. . .] [5][. . .] God of [. . .] [6][. . .] and we will stand toget[her . . .] [7][. . .] and violence, You [. . .] [8][. . .] and from the sons of the council of [. . .] [9][. . .] Your [. . .] and the fruit upon [. . .] [10][. . .] for to Your words [. . .] [11][. . .] to rule, and [t]he[y] shall dest[roy . . .] [12][. . .] Your [sa]lvation and in [Your] righteous[ness . . .] [13][. . .] and You opened my mouth [. . .] [14][. . .] faithless [. . .] [15][. . . You] forgive iniquity because [. . .] [16][. . .] they [. . .] You and [t]he[y] violated [. . .] [17][. . . Ja]cob (*or* dec]eitful) and [. . .]

Frag. 2 [2][. . .] You were not pleased and [. . .] [3][. . .] his [witnes]ses and ever triumphant [. . .] [4][. . .] in my mouth, You will not put to the test [. . .] [5][. . .] Your mouth, and You show me [Your] cou[nsel . . .] [6][. . .] until You cause me to stand for judgment [. . .] [7][. . .] and I have a dispute, and his witnesses shall testify against [me . . .] [8][. . .] to You, I have understood all [. . .] [9][. . .] as my judgment and there is nothing [. . .]

—M.G.A.

113. Incantation of the Sage

4Q444

These fragments are what remains of an incantation intended to ward off evil spirits and spoken by a sage who claims to speak for God. He describes spiritual warfare, a battle within himself between good and evil, in which good has triumphed by means of God's statutes and truth. The speaker now urges the same truth upon others so that they too can stand against the devil's wiles. Note the connection he draws between evil spirits and thievery, a connection found as well in *An Exorcism* (text 146, 1:5). Also, the author seems to mention the dominion of Belial—that is, Satan—in l. 7; this dominion is described more fully in other Dead Sea texts.

Frags. 1–5 Col. 1 [1]As for me, I am the Dread of God. He opened my mouth with the knowledge of His truth, and [. . .] empowered by His holy spirit. [. . .] [2]truth for all [thes]e, and they became contentious spirits in my bodily frame; [God's] statute[s . . .] [3][. . . in] the blood vessels. God has placed a spirit of knowledge and understanding, truth and righteousness in [my] hea[rt . . .] [4][. . . in order to . . .], fortify yourself with the statutes of God, and in order to battle evil spirits, and so as not [to . . .] [5][. . .] its judgments. Cursed is [6][. . .] of truth and justice [7][. . .] until its dominion is complete. [8][. . . ba]stards and the unclean spirit [9][. . .] and thiev[es . . .] [10][. . . the ri]ghteous. Curs[ed is . . .] [11][. . .] and abominat[ion . . .]

—M.O.W.

114. In Praise of King Jonathan

4Q448

In Praise of King Jonathan is a composition whose importance is out of all proportion to its size, for this small and fragmentary text is pivotal for the question of the origin of the Dead Sea Scrolls. Since the work evidently praises Alexander Jannaeus, a Hasmonean who reigned as king from 103 to 76 B.C.E., its very existence raises profound difficulties for the Standard Model. According to the model, the Hasmoneans were supposed to be sworn enemies of the group behind the scrolls. How could the latter have composed or treasured a paean favoring perhaps the worst villain of that family?

Contrary to the stand taken by proponents of the Standard Model, we believe this text must be integrated into—not dismissed from—discussion of the origins of the scrolls. It must be allowed to cast doubt on the Standard Model, if that is what it does. (For further discussion, see the Introduction.)

Alexander also appears in the *Commentary on Nahum* (text 23), where he is described as the "Lion of Wrath."

Lines 7–10 of this fragment incorporate a portion (vv. 16–20) of a noncanonical psalm commonly entitled Psalm 154. Known from a tenth-century C.E. Syriac manuscript, this composition is also found in the Apocryphal Psalms of David *(text 151, col. 18).*

Col. 1 [1]Praise the LORD! A psal[m,] a song of [. . .] [2]You loved as a fa[ther . . .] [3]to rule over [. . .]

[4][. . .] [5]Tho[se who] hat[e You] shall fear [. . .] [6][in the] general [assembly] procl[aim His splendor; bind your soul to the good] [7]and blameless

ones [to glorify the Most High. Behold the eyes of the LORD show compassion upon the good,] [8]and upon those who glorify Him H[e increases His loving-kindness. The Redeemer shall deliver their soul from the evil time,] [9]the afflicted from the power of their oppressors, [and delivers the blameless from the hand of the wicked. He desires] [10]His dwelling in Zion, [He] ch[ooses Jerusalem forever.]

Col. 2 [1]Awake, O Holy One, [2]for Jonathan, the king, [3]and all the congregation of Your people [4]Israel [5]that is (dispersed) to the four [6]winds of the heavens, [7]let peace be on all of them [8]and Your kingdom. [9]May Your name be blessed. **Col. 3** [1]In Your love [. . .] [2]in the day until evening. [. . .] [3]to draw near so as to be [. . .] [4]Remember them in blessing [. . .] [5]by Your name that is called [. . .] [6]kingdom to be blessed [. . .] [7]for the day of war and [. . .] [8]for Jonathan, the kin[g . . .] [9][. . .]

—M.G.A.

115. A Fragmentary Narrative

4Q458

There is not enough remaining in these fragments to piece together a coherent narrative, but the phrases that are legible are tantalizing. The first fragment seems to refer to the judgment on Adam and Eve in the Garden of Eden, with its mention of the "evil tree" and the "sword of destruction." The other fragments seem to speak of a war against the Gentiles ("the uncircumcised") and one who is "anointed" (*mashiach*) with the oil of kingship—possibly a messianic reference.

Frag. 1 [1][. . .] to the friend [. . .] [2][. . .] the friend [. . .] [3][. . .] in the tent [. . .] [4][. . .] they did not know [. . .] [5][. . .] flames of fire [. . .] [6][. . .] they will stand with him [. . .] [7][. . . sa]id to the first, saying [. . .] [8][. . .] for life; let the first angel pour out [9][. . . swor]d of destruction, and he struck the evil tree [10][. . . E]gypt, for spoil [. . .]

Frag. 2 Col. 1 [2][. . . mo]on and the stars [3][. . .] a second time [4][. . .] [5][. . .] the unclean [6][. . .] the fornication [. . .] **Col. 2** [3]and he destroyed him and his army [. . .] [4]and it swallowed up all the uncircumcised [. . .] [5]and they were justified and went against [. . .] [6]anointed with the oil of kingship of [. . .]

—E.M.C.

116. Fragment of a Lost Apocryphon

4Q460

The nature and extent of this work is unclear, but it may form part of a "testament" (see texts 136 and 137). The overall thrust of the work is to counsel endurance and faith in God during a time of national unrest and violence.

An exhortation to stand firm during tribulation. The reference to Judah is obscure. Is it directed against the fusion of kingship and priesthood in the Hasmonean dynasty?

Frag. 7 [3][. . .] but He did not choose [. . .] [4][. . .] and He named him [. . .] [5][. . . he did (not) choose J]udah to be a prie[st] for him [. . .] [6][. . .] do [no]t worry about the unrest [. . .] [7][. . .] about the afflictions and distress [. . .] [8][. . .] and the distress when they beset you [. . .] [9][. . .] do not be afraid or [discouraged . . .] [10][. . .] come to you and you will seize [. . .] [11][. . .] for a time of tribula[tion . . .]

Readers are reminded that God has chosen a certain group (the priests?) for a particular task and reward.

Frag. 5 [1][. . .] and He blessed him and [said . . .] [2][. . .] and is giving you a[ll . . .] [3][. . .] to y[o]u and to [your] se[ed . . .]

Frag. 3 [2][. . .] for in heaven [. . .] [3][. . .] and His pure priests [. . .]

A plea to God to judge the wicked in Israel. It is noteworthy that God is addressed as "my Father"; the notion that God may be addressed as the father of the pious individual (rather than of the nation as a whole) is rare in Jewish literature of this period.

Frag. 9 Col. 1 [2][. . .] and before You I am in awe, for in the fear of God are the pla[ns] [3][. . .] for unrest in Israel and for scandal in Ephraim [4][. . . full is] the land of shameful deeds to the highest heaven, because for a generation [5][. . . f]or You have not abandoned Your servant [6][. . .] my Father and my Lord [. . .]

The writer turns to unrepentant Israel, asserting that its troubles are due to its own sin.

[7][. . .] miraculous deeds, for He will rebuke the arrogant, and who [8][. . .] reproof when you abandon your God, O Israel, and who [. . .] [9][. . .] and the idols of Baal, for not one in Ephraim will be taken [. . .] [10][. . .] the LORD [will . . .] the words of your mouth, and all your plots He will turn aside to [. . .] [11][. . .] crimes of Ephraim, and Israel is plundered for her by a cruel people [. . .] [12][. . . st]and before you, O Israel, for you have greatly angered [your] G[od.]

The nation should not look to kings or armies for help, but to God alone.

Frag. 8 [2][. . .] in the land "let the warriors not boast [of their strength" (Jer. 9:23) . . .] [3][. . .] of their power, nor kings of their mighty prowess, nor princes [. . .] [4][. . .] of their weapons of war, or their strong fortresses [. . .] [5][. . . there is no one as majes]tic as He, and none as glorious [. . .] [6][. . .] glorious to help us and a w[all around us . . .] [7][. . .] and our God [. . .]

—E.M.C.

117. Fragment of a Lost Narrative

4Q461

One can do little more than guess about the nature and purpose of the fragmentary work before us. It seems to deal with the history of Israel and is reminiscent of the "creedal" confession in Deuteronomy 26 and the historical summary found in the *Damascus Document* (text 1): Israel sins, becomes subject to foreign rulers, repents and seeks God, and, chastened, devotes itself to following God's Law.

Frag. 1 [1][. . .] to slay him [. . .] [2][. . .] in them, and he put them into the power of [. . .] [3][. . .] with "harsh labor" (Deut. 26:6) and they put upon [. . .] [4][. . .] up to its end, and "he made them a desolation" (2 Chron. 30:7) [. . .] [5][. . .] "they sought him and they found him" (15:4) [. . .] [6][. . .] to become obedient, and a wise man [. . .] [7][. . . the pil]lars of the earth [. . .] [8][. . . to] do His will and to keep His laws [. . .] [9][. . .] to bring [Israel] back to the LORD their God [. . .] [10][. . .] and the LORD will see their repentance [. . .]

—E.M.C.

118. A Meditation on Israel's History

4Q462

To the Jew first and also to the Gentile," wrote the apostle Paul, attempting to define the ideal audience for his gospel (Rom. 1:16). His Jewish contemporaries would have agreed that the Jew comes first, but there would have been significant differences of opinion about Gentiles, who were clearly outside of the faith of Israel but had to play some part in God's plan. Were they simply there to provide a hapless foil for the chosen people, to be eliminated or subdued when God redeemed Israel? Or could they somehow be incorporated into Israel through conversion and enjoy some of the blessings of Israel?

Both points of view could claim support from the Bible. The prophetic books are full of vitriolic denunciations of the Gentile powers, whose occasional downfall was greeted with open glee (as in the prophecy of Nahum). On the other hand, even the loathsome Assyrians could be imagined as repentant sinners (as in the book of Jonah). Gentile armies could be mythologized as the dreadful legions of Gog and Magog (Ezek. 38–39), destined only for slaughter, but Gentiles could also be imagined to say, "Let us go to the LORD's mountain, that he may teach us his ways" (Isa. 2:3).

The same ambivalence is reflected in the Dead Sea Scrolls. In the *War Scroll* (text 11), the Children of Light wage the final battle against Gentile armies, without any suggestion that the latter might conceivably have an interest in learning of the Lord's ways. But the *Priestly Blessings for Israel in the Last Days* points out that the Gentile nations will finally come to serve the Leader of the Nation (text 9, 5:28–29), and the *Damascus Document* allows for the presence of converts to Judaism in the community (text 1, Geniza text 14:5), although they will rank lowest of all. The *Temple Scroll,* though legislating for an ideal Israel generally devoid of Gentiles, allows for their entrance into the outermost Temple court after conversion to Judaism (see text 155).

The present text is the only one of the scrolls that seems to speak of Gentiles with any sympathy—although that sympathy is limited to a certain rueful regret that they did not recognize God's plan for his people. It is possible that the unnamed Gentiles are Edomites, if l. 5 is properly understood. Rekem was the ancient name for Petra, a famous city located in biblical Edomite territory. If so, then the historical setting may be the forced conversion of the Idumeans (Edomites) to Judaism in the time of the Hasmonean ruler John Hyrcanus I (134–104 B.C.E.).

The human families descended from Noah's three sons disperse; Israel inherits the Holy Land, while the Edomites(?) must be content with their territory to the south and east of Palestine.

Frag. 1 [2][. . . Shem and] Ham and Japeth [. . .] [3][. . .] to Jacob, and he [said . . .] and remembered [. . .] [4][. . .] to Israel [. . .] Then [they] shall say [. . .] [5][. . .] to Rekem we went, for [*x*] was taken [. . .] [6][. . .] to slaves for Jacob in love [. . .] [7][. . . he will] give it as a possession to many.

In the time to come, the Gentiles will recognize the greatness of God, their own sin, and the special status of Israel.

The LORD,* ruler of all [. . .] [8][. . .] His glory, which all at once will fill the waters and the earth [. . .] [9][. . . he gave to Israe]l the dominion alone; they were His people. The light was with them, but on us was [the darkness . . .] [10][. . . the e]ra of darkness [has passed] and the era of light has come, and they will rule forever. Therefore they shall say [. . .] [11][. . .] to [I]srael, for in our midst is the beloved people, Jac[ob . . .]

Israel's endurance during domination by foreign powers and the judgment that later came on the oppressors are remembered.

[12][. . .] they toiled and endured and cried out to the LORD and [. . .] [13][. . .] now, see, they were put in the power of Egypt a second time in the age of the monarchy, and they endu[red . . .] [14][. . . the inha]bitants of Philistia, and Egypt became booty and a ruin and her pillars [. . .] [15][. . .] to exalt the wicked man so that she will become im[pure . . .] [16][. . .] her bold face will be changed, in her splendor and adornments and garments [. . .] [17][. . .] and what she did to her, thus the impurity of [. . .] [18][. . .] rejected just as she was before being built [. . .] [19][. . .] and he will remember Jerusalem [. . .]

—E.M.C.

*The scribe wrote this divine name with four dots, each dot representing one consonant of the Hebrew.

119. Lives of the Patriarchs

4Q464

The remnants of this fragmentary manuscript expound the lives of the patriarchs Abraham, Isaac, and Jacob. *Lives* does not discover fulfillments of biblical prophecies as does the *Commentary on Habakkuk* (text 2), but rather appears to select passages that support the author's ideas in a way similar to *Commentaries on Genesis* (text 53).

Line 9 of this fragment quotes Zephaniah 3:9, which refers to the conversion of the Gentile nations in the Last Days. The remains of l. 8 suggest that this verse was taken to mean that everyone would speak Hebrew at that time. The phrase "holy language" is also found in Midrash Tanhuma *(a rabbinic commentary edited by S. Buber, §28), in reference to Genesis 11:7, which* Tanhuma *interpreted as meaning that all the world was created speaking the holy language, which God then confused at the Tower of Babel. The midrash follows with a quote of Zephaniah 3:9 to show that a day is yet to come when God will again make the people "pure of speech" so that they might serve him as one.*

Frag. 3 Col. 1 [3][. . .] servant [4][. . .] on the first (*or* in one) [5][. . .] confused of [6][. . .] to Abraham [7][. . .] forever, for he [8][. . . re]ad the holy language [9][. . . "For I will give] purified lips to the people" (Zeph. 3:9).

The Egyptian bondage is foretold with a prophetic interpretation (pesher).

Col. 2 [2]the judgment [. . .] [3]just as He said to Abrah[am, "Indeed you know that your offspring shall be strangers in a land that is not their own] [4]and they shall serve them and they shall oppress [them for four hundred years" (Gen. 15:13). . . .] [5]and he shall sleep with [his fathers . . .] [6][. . .] [7]The prophetic interpretation o[f . . .]

The binding of Isaac (Gen. 22:12). See also A Paraphrase of Genesis and Exodus, *frag. 2 (text 43) and* Commentaries on Genesis *frag. 1, col. 3 (text 53).*

Frag. 6 [2][. . .] his hand and not [. . .] [3][. . . do not lay] your hand on the lad and [do] no[thing to him . . .] [4][. . .] make it an offering [. . .]

Jacob's departure for Haran (Gen. 28:10).

Frag. 7 [1][. . . and] they shall be fifteen [years] old [. . .] [2][. . . and Jacob went out from Beer]sheba to go to Haran and E[sau . . .] [3][. . . just a]s He promised to give him t[he land . . .]
—M.G.A.

120. The Archangel Michael and King Zedekiah

4Q470

Zedekiah (597–586 B.C.E.) was the last king of Judah, the monarch at the time that the city fell to the forces of Nebuchadnezzar, king of Babylonia. Zedekiah was himself taken captive when Jerusalem fell and, after his sons had been killed before his eyes, he was blinded and taken into exile in Babylon. There he died some years later. On several occasions the Bible records that Zedekiah "did evil in the eyes of the LORD" (2 Kings 24:19), and on the whole the Bible portrays him as a weak-willed ruler whom his nobles were able to manipulate.

In later Jewish literature this negative portrait of Zedekiah begins to take on more positive overtones. The Talmud says at one point, "The Holy One, blessed be He, planned to turn the world back to chaos and formlessness because of the generation of Zedekiah. Taking a closer look at Zedekiah, however, His anger calmed" (*b. Arakin* 17a). Josephus also calls Zedekiah "by nature kind and just" (*Ant.* 6.213). The present scroll fragment appears to be another witness to the notion of a good king Zedekiah. Here he is portrayed entering a covenant instituted by the archangel Michael, in which he evidently agrees both to live uprightly himself and to use his royal power to encourage others to do the same. The idea that angels mediate covenants also appears in the New Testament (Acts 7:53; Gal. 3:19; Heb. 2:2). Thus the assignment of this role to angels was probably a commonplace in the Judaism of this period.

For further adventures of Michael, note especially the *Words of the Archangel Michael* (text 132).

Frag. 1 [2][. . .] Michael [. . .] [3]On [th]at day, Zedekiah [shall en]ter a co[ven]ant [4][. . .] to live by the whole Law, and to cause others to do so [5][. . . At] that time, M[ich]ael shall say to Zedekiah [6][. . .] "I will make a [cove]na[nt] with you witnessed by the entire congregation." [7][. . . to d]o and [. . .]
—M.O.W.

121. Assorted Manuscripts

4Q471–471a, 4Q471c

In the fragments catalogued as 4Q471 we once again face the question of whether certain fragments have been properly assigned to their original scroll. Because of similar handwriting and a presumed connection with the *War Scroll* (text 11), the original editor grouped together eight small fragments and called them a text—4Q471. Scroll scholars now agree this was a mistake. These fragments do not belong to one manuscript, but rather to four. Moreover, none of the fragments is directly related to the *War Scroll*. The four works are respectively (1) a discussion of the (messianic?) king's royal bodyguard (4Q471 frag. 1) and an exhortation to keep God's covenant (4Q471 frag. 2), (2) a condemnation of a war not blessed by God (4Q471a frag. 1), (3) the boast of a man claiming to be reckoned among the gods (4Q471b), and (4) a hymn praising God (4Q471c frag. 1).

Two explanations have been suggested for frag. 1. The first suggests a relationship to the first lines of col. 2 of the War Scroll *(text 11) detailing the various groups that served in the Temple or its precincts during the sabbatical year (E. and H. Eshel, 1992). The reconstruction below echoes the* Temple Scroll *57:5–11 (text 155). This passage reveals the makeup of the king's royal guard.*

4Q471 Frag. 1 [1][. . .] from all tha[t . . .] [2][. . . And from the priests, twelve,] each man from among his brothers, the sons of [3][Aaron. . . .] and they shall be with him continually, and k[eep] [4][him from any sort of sin. And twelve commanders from] each tribe, a man [5][per household. They shall be with him continually, sele]ct [men.] And from [the] Levites tw[elve] [6][. . . and they shall b]e sit[ting with hi]m continually for [7][judgment and Torah . . . in] order that they might be teaching [him . . .] [8][. . .] division[s . . .]

Keep the covenant of God: reject evil and choose good.

Frag. 2 [1][. . .] [2][. . .] so as to keep the testimonies of our (?) covenant [. . .] [3][. . . the One who has gua]rded all of their armies with patien[ce . . .] [4][. . .] and to restrain their heart from every wo[rk . . .] [5][. . . se]rvants of darkness. For [righteous] judgments [. . .] [6][. . .] in his guilty lot [. . .] [7][. . . to reject goo]d and to choose evil and to [. . .] 8[. . . but rather to reject everything which] God hates. And He established [. . .] 9[. . .] all the good which [God has given you . . .] 10[. . .] vengeful wrath [. . .]

This fragment warns against engaging in a war not blessed by God. This theme reveals a possible relation to Numbers 14:40–45.

4Q471a Frag. 1 1[. . .] from the time You command them not to 2[engage in war. . . .] you have proved false to His covenant 3[. . . and yo]u said, "Let us fight His battles, for He has redeemed us 4[from the hand of our enemy . . .". . . .] your [mighty me]n shall be humiliated for they do not know that [the Lord] has rejected 5[you . . .] you presume to make war. And as for you, you are regarded 6[with the men of injustice. "You have staggered as a drunkard] in his vomit" (Isa. 19:14).

You seek righteous judgment and [true] service 7[. . . but] you exalt yourselves.

He has chosen [them . . .] for the cry 8[. . .] "And you have substituted [bitter for sweet] and sweet 9[for bitter" (Isa. 5:20). . . .]

The fragments that comprise 4Q471b have been recognized as an additional copy (4Q431) of the Thanksgiving Hymns *(text 12) and play an important role in the reconstruction of col. 26.*

This scrap of a hymnic or liturgical text praises God for righteous judgment and the forgiveness of sins.

4Q471c Frag. 1 1[. . .] God, and [. . .] 2[. . .] eternal [. . .]. And He appointed us [. . .] 3[. . . He jud]ges His people with justice and [. . .] 4[. . . and to give th]em [understanding] in all the statutes of [God . . .] 5[. . .] to us in [our] sins [. . .] 6[. . .] Belial [. . .]
—M.G.A.

122. The Two Ways

4Q473

In Deuteronomy 11:26–28, Moses, speaking as God's intermediary, says to the people: "See, I am setting before you today a blessing and a curse: the blessing, if you obey the commandments of the LORD your God that I am commanding you today; and the curse, if you do not obey the commandments of the LORD your God, but turn from the way that I am commanding you today." This metaphor picturing life as a choice between two paths appears in a more elaborated form in the present Dead Sea Scroll.

The Gospels depict Jesus as setting forth a similar metaphor: "Enter through the narrow gate; for the gate is wide and the road is easy that leads to destruction, and there are many who take it. For the gate is narrow and the road is hard that leads to life, and there are few who find it" (Matt. 7:13–14).

The Qumran writing finds a further analog in the early Christian book known as the *Didache,* or *Teaching of the Twelve Apostles.* The original core of this manual of instruction for the early church may well go back to the first century C.E. and is thus nearly as old as our scroll. The *Didache* treats worship, baptism, fasting, Communion, and other topics, but the first section, entitled "The Two Ways," is a statement of the principles of Christian conduct. Thus the *Didache* begins with a line immediately reminiscent of our scroll: "There are two ways, one of life and one of death, and there is a great difference between the two ways."

Frag. 2 [2][. . .] and He is setting [before you a blessing and a curse . . . These are] [3]t[wo] ways, one goo[d and one evil. If you walk in the good way, He will watch over] [4]and bless you. But if you walk in the [evil] way, [He will curse and maledict you,] [5]and bring [evil] against you. He will exterminate you, [smiting you and the product of your toil with blight] [6]and mildew, snow, ice and hai[l . . .] [7]together with all the angel[s of destruction . . .]

—M.O.W.

123. A Record of Disciplinary Action

4Q477

A Record of Disciplinary Action reflects an attempt to obey Leviticus 19:17: "You must certainly rebuke your neighbor, and thus not bear any sin because of him." We know that reproof was an important element of life in the *Yahad* from the *Charter of a Jewish Sectarian Association* (text 7). There we read, "The Instructor must not reprove the Men of the Pit, nor argue with them about proper biblical understanding. Quite the contrary: he should conceal his own insight into the Law when among perverse men. He shall save reproof—itself founded on true knowledge and righteous judgment—for those who have chosen the Way, treating each as his spiritual qualities and the precepts of the era require" (9:16–18). According to the *Charter* 5:24–6:1, this reproof had to be done humbly and for the purpose of restitution. Matthew 18:15–17 is a notable New Testament counterpart, demonstrating the importance of reproof among early Christians as well.

This is the only known work among the scrolls that records actual names of members of the *Yahad.*

Perhaps 1.2 should be reconstructed ". . . is to reprove his fellow in truth, humility and lovingkindness" (Charter *5:24–25).*

Frag. 2 Col. 1 [1][. . .] the men of the [*Yahad* . . .] [2][. . .] their soul and to reprove [. . .] [3][. . .] the meeting of the assembly concerning [. . .]

This passage records the names of the guilty parties along with their crimes. One Johanan is convicted of transgressions the apostle Paul would later classify as "deeds of the flesh" (Gal. 5:19–21; see Prov. 14:17; 28:22). Another member of the Yahad *(Joseph?) apparently transgressed the command prohibiting sexual intercourse with next of kin (Lev. 18:6).*

Col. 2 [2]that [he . . . and also wh]o was treating [. . .] badly [. . .] [3]the assembly [. . . And they reproved] Johanan ben Ar[(?) . . . because] [4]he has a quick temper [. . .] with him [. . .] his iniquity remains and he is also still vainglorious [. . .] [5][. . .] he [. . .] that [. . .]

And they reproved Hananyah Nothos because he [. . .] [6][to tr]ouble the spirit of the *Yah*[*ad* and] also to be involved wi[th . . .] to [. . .] [7][. . . Jose]ph (?) they rep[rov]ed because evil [. . .] with him and also does not [. . .] [8][. . .] and he also loves his blood relation [and they did not reprove . . .] [9][. . .]

And Hananyah ben Sim[on they reproved . . .] [10][because he . . . and al]so he loves the good [life . . .]

—M.G.A.

124. A Prayer for Deliverance

4Q501

This communal prayer asks God for deliverance from persecution at the hands of unfaithful Israelites, who surround the righteous covenant keepers "with their false tongue" (l. 4).

[1][. . .] do not give our inheritance to strangers, nor our produce to foreigners. Remember that [2][we are the enslaved] of Your people, the forsaken of Your inheritance. Remember the members of Your covenant, the desolate [3][. . . Yo]ur [. . .] those who are committed are wandering astray, and there is no one to return them, wounded with no one to bind their wounds, [4][bowed down with no one to ra]ise them up. The scoundrels of Your people have surrounded us with their false tongue. Let them be overturned.

[5][. . . You]r [. . .] and Your beauty to one born of a woman. Look and see the shame of the members of [6][Your community, for] our skin [. . .]. Horrors have seized us because of the tongue of their reviling. Do not [7][. . .] Your commandments, let their seed not be included with the members of the covenant. [8][. . .] against them with the abundance of Your strength, and execute vengeance on them [9][for . . .] Your [. . .] they have no regard for You, and they have overrun the poor and oppressed. —M.G.A.

125. A Liturgy of Thanksgiving

4Q502

This extremely fragmentary text comprises a liturgy of thanksgivings for various blessings of life. The frequent mention of "adults" may indicate that the liturgy was intended to accompany the entrance of youths into the *Yahad* when they came of age. The *Charter for Israel in the Last Days* (text 8) mentions such a ceremony.

This passage has been interpreted as part of a wedding ceremony, but it is more likely a liturgy of offering produce and other goods to God.

Frags. 1–3 [1][. . . a m]an who acknowledges [. . .] when [God] adds [. . .] [2][. . .] the ordinance of God [. . .] to one who lacks [. . .] [3][. . . the man] and his wife for [. . .] [4][. . .] to produce seed [. . .] these [. . .] [5][. . .] who has pur[posed to offer holy sac]rifices, giving thanks to God [. . .] [6][. . .] from being hol[y . . . bring] to him a reliable bath measure, and [. . .] [7][. . .] his spouse who [. . .] intelligence and insight within [. . .] [8][. . .] *Yahad* to be [. . .] [9][. . .] season of [new] o[il . . .] and atoning [. . .] [10][. . .] for the children of ri[ghteousness . . .] on this day [. . .] [11][. . . A]aron [. . .]

This larger passage contains words of thanks for the blessings of the natural world, of Israel's religious festivals, and of the community of faith.

Frags. 6–10 [0a][. . .] Is[rael . . .] [0b][. . .] give thanks [. . .] [1][. . .] mutual [jo]y [. . .] [2][. . . He will bless the] God of Israel and raise his voice and s[ay,] [3][Blessed is the God of Israel who has brought us to this ti]me of joy to praise His name [4][. . .] adults and youths [5][. . .] their [beasts, r]ams and go[ats . . .] with our flocks and from the creeping things [6][. . .] in our shelter and the birds [that fly in] our [sky] and our soil and all its produce [7][. . . and al]l the fruit of its trees and our water [. . .] and the waters of its deeps, all of us [8][. . . blessing] the name of the God of Israel w[ho has given us this fes]tival for our joy and also [9][. . .] season of th[anksgiving . . .] among the righteous adults [10][. . .] in peace [. . .] giving thanks to God and praising [11][. . .] brothers to me, elders [12][and youths, . . . ble]ssed among us [13][. . .] holy [. . .] elders of the Most [Ho]ly Place [14][. . . t]oday I am [. . . blessing] the God of Israel [. . .] [15][. . . e]lders of k[nowledge . . .] [16][. . .] we [rejoi]ce in the sea[son of . . .] to be [. . .] [17][. . .]

This fragment seems to speak of someone's entry into the community or into the leadership of the community.

Frag. 19 [1]So let him dwell with him in the council of the h[oly ones . . .] [2]descendants of blessing, elder men and wo[men . . . young men] [3]and virgins, boys and gi[rls . . .] [4]with all of us together and I [. . .] [5]and afterwar[ds] the men of [holy perfection] shall say [. . .] [6][and raise their voice] and say, Blessed is the [Go]d [of Israel who . . .] [7][. . .] their [s]ins [. . .]

This fragment indicates that women also took active part in the liturgy of thanksgiving.

Frag. 24 [1][. . .] all the festivals [. . .] [2][. . .] the woman [shall raise her voice and say] the thanksgivings: Blessed is the God of Israel who has helped [His handmaid . . .] [3][. . . in]crease of your life in the midst of the people who endure foreve[r . . .] [4][. . . and] she shall stand in the council of the elder m[en] and wome[n . . .] [5][. . .] your days in peace [. . .] [6][. . . a]mong the el[ders . . .]

—E.M.C.

126. Daily Prayers

4Q503

This work is an extremely fragmentary collection of paired prayers that once comprised no fewer than thirteen columns, and possibly many more. Because the work is so fragmentary, we provide only the best-preserved portions. The first prayer in each pairing is recited in the evening, the second in the morning as the sun rises. This order seems to agree with the mainstream Jewish calendar of the time, which began the day in the evening, and so to conflict with the Qumran calendar, which began each day in the morning, but one cannot be sure how such matters may have been rationalized.

The author of these prayers adopted a curious system known (in various slightly different forms) from *Astronomical Enoch* (text 38) and the *Phases of the Moon* (text 69). Using proportions of the number fourteen, the writer characterized each day of the month in terms of light and darkness on the moon's surface. Thus, the first day of the month would have fourteen parts darkness and no light, the second day thirteen parts darkness and one part light, and so on. The fifteenth day of the month would have no darkness and fourteen parts light; this would be the day of the full moon. As the moon waned, the proportions would reverse. The work also mentions "gates" of light, whose number is always the same as the date of the month, and makes puzzling references to "flags." The flags are associated sometimes with light, sometimes with darkness, so that the precise meaning of the term remains mysterious.

Prayers for the fourteenth and fifteenth of a month. Note the possible pun on "Passover" in l. 5, perhaps indicating that this portion was recited in the first month, Nisan, when Passover occurred.

Col. 3 (Frags. 1–6) [1]When [the sun] rises [out of] the firmament of heav[e]n, they shall offer praise. They shall re[spond,] [2]"Blessed is the G[od of Israel, who has . . .] This day [You] have renewed [. . .] [3]in four[teen gates of light . . .] for us the dominion [of light . . .] [4]ten fla[gs of . . .] the heat of the [sun . . .] [5]when the sun passes over [. . . by the mig]ht of [Your] powerful hand [. . . Peace be upon you,] [6]O Israel."

On the fift[eenth of the month, in the ev]ening, they shall offer praise. They shall say, "Blessed is the Go[d of Israel,] [7]who conceals [. . .] before Him in every division of His glory. [This] evening, [. . .] [8][. . . e]ternally, and to praise Him. Our redemption is at the beginni[ng of . . .] [9][. . .] the cycles of the light-giving orbs. [. . .] Today, the fourte[enth] [10][day of the month, we have celebrated the rule of] the light of day. Pe[ace] be [upon] you, O Israel."

[12][When the sun r]ise[s . . .] to shed light upon the earth, they shall give praise. They shall respo[nd . . .] [13]"the numb[er . . . ele]ven [days] for joyous pilgrimages and glor[ious] festivals. [14]for [that] d[a]y [in f]ifteen gate[s of light . . .] [15]glor[ious] festival [. . .] by the portions of the evening [. . .]

Prayers for the sixteenth through eighteenth of a month.

Col. 8 (Frags. 29–32) [2]On the six[teenth of the month, in the evening, they shall offer praise. They shall say, "Blessed is the God of Israel Who] [3]has sanctified for Himself [. . .] [4]and now this evening, [. . .] with [. . .] [5][. . . pr]ecious to us. Pe[a]ce [. . .] [6][. . .] God shall bless Jeshur[un . . ."]

[7][When the sun rises to shed light up]on [the ea]rth, they shall give praise. [They shall respond, "Blessed is the God of Israel] [8][Who . . .] light." They shall rejoice in [. . . "We] [9][pra]ise Your name, O God of the heavenly ligh[t]s, for You have renewed [. . . six-] [10][teen] gates of light, and with [u]s in the joyous praise of Your glory, in the [. . .] [11][fl]ags of night. May the peace of God be [up]on you, O Israel, at the ris[ing of the sun."]

[12][On the se]venteenth of the mon[th, in the] evening, they shall offer praise. They shall say, ["Blessed is the God of Israel, who] [13][. . .] to [pr]aise the [Go]d of [. . .] [14–16][. . .]

[17][When the sun rises to shed light upon the earth, they shall give praise. They shall respond, "Blessed is the God of Israel, Who] [18][. . .] You have made [us gl]ad [. . .] [19][. . .] flags of night. [. . .] [20][. . .] Tod[ay] we [. . .] [21][. . . May the peace of God be upon you, O Is]rael, at all the app[ointed times of eternity."]

[22]On the eig[hteenth of the month, in the evening,] they shall give praise. They shall say, "Bl[essed is the God of Israel, Who] [23][. . . the Holy of Ho]lies. Now, this evening [. . .]

—M.O.W.

127. The Words of the Heavenly Lights

4Q504–506

This collection of prayers is one of the few Dead Sea Scrolls whose ancient title, the *Words of the Heavenly Lights,* is known, for it was inscribed on the outside of the scroll. But although we may know the ancient title, understanding it is another matter: nothing in this writing clearly relates to celestial bodies or their imagined praise of God. The most plausible explanation is M. Baillet's suggestion that the title is a metaphor referring to the priests as luminaries—those through whom the "light of God" was made manifest.

A few preserved headings show that this collection of prayers was arranged by the days of the week, one or two being recited each day. In addition, several marginal notations can be made out, written in one of the secret scripts known from the scrolls, Cryptic Script A. The notations apparently give directions for using the prayers in public worship. One such notation, an "m," may have been an abbreviation whose placement cued the participation of the *maskil* (the Hebrew word used in some of the scrolls to mean "Instructor"). Alternatively, the "m" may have been an abbreviation for the Hebrew word *mizmor,* a technical term that also appears in the headings of many biblical psalms. We do not know precisely what the biblical term meant, but it almost certainly had something to do with musical accompaniment.

A prayer of forgiveness.

4Q504 Col. 2 [7]Please, Lord, act as is Your character, by the measure of Your great power. Fo[r] You [for]gave [8]our fathers when they rebelled against Your command, though You were so angry at them that You might have destroyed them. Still, You had pity [9]on them because of Your love, and because of Your covenant (indeed, Moses had atoned [10]for their sin), and also so that Your great power and abundant compassion might be known [11]to generations to come, forever.

May Your anger and fury at all [their] sin[s] turn back from Your people Israel. Remember [12]the wonders that You performed while the nations looked on—surely we have been called by Your name. [13][These things were done] that we might [repe]nt with all our heart and all our soul, to plant

Your law in our hearts [14][that we turn not from it, straying] either to the right or the left. Surely You will heal us from such madness, blindness, and confusion. [15][. . . Behold,] we were sold [as the price] of our [in]iquity, yet despite our rebellion You have called us. [16][. . .] Deliver us from sinning against You, [17][. . .] give us to understand the seasons [18][of Your compassion . . .]

A prayer celebrating God's choice of Israel.

Col. 3 [2][. . .] Behold, [3]all the nations are [as not]hing compared to You; [they] are counted [as] naught, as a mere specter in Your presence. [4]In Your name alone have we boasted, for we were created for Your glory. You have adopted [5]us in the sight of all the nations; indeed, You have called [6][I]srael "My son, My firstborn" (Exod. 4:22), and You have chastened us as a man chastens [7]his child.

You have raised us through the years of our generations, [8][disciplining us] with terrible disease, famine, thirst, even plague and the sword—[9][every reproa]ch of Your covenant. For You have chosen us as Your own, [10][as Your people from all] the earth. That is why You have poured out Your fury upon us, [11][Your ze]al, the full wrath of Your anger. That is why You have caused [the scourge] [12][of Your plagues] to cleave to us, that of which Moses and Your servants [13]the prophets wrote: You [wou]ld send evil ag[ain]st us in the Last [14]Days [. . .]

A prayer celebrating the glorious future of Israel and Jerusalem.

Col. 4 [2]Your tabernacle [. . .] a place of rest [3]in Jerusa[lem, the city that You ch]ose out of all the earth, [4]that Your [name] should dwell there forever. Surely You love [5]Israel more than all the other peoples; more narrowly, You chose the tribe of [6]Judah. You have established Your covenant with David, making him [7]a princely shepherd over Your people, that he sit before You upon the throne of Israel [8]eternally.

Having seen Your glory—[9]inasmuch as You have displayed Your majesty in the midst of Your people Israel, for the sake of Your great [10]name—all the nations shall bring their offerings: silver, gold, and gems, [11]even every precious thing of their lands, whereby to glorify Your people and [12]Zion, Your holy city, as well as Your glorious temple, "there is neither adversary [13]nor misfortune" (1 Kings 5:18). No, rather peace and blessing [. . . Israel] [14]shall eat until satisfied, shall even grow fat [. . .]

A prayer celebrating God's faithfulness.

Col. 5 [1][. . . They abandoned] [2]the fount of living water [. . .] [3]and served a foreign god in their land. Further, their land [4]became a wasteland thanks to their enemies. For Your wrath was [pou]red out [5]and Your burning anger was a zealous flame, leaving the land desolate, [6]so that no one went to and fro.

Nevertheless, You did not reject [7]the seed of Jacob nor spew Israel out, [8]making an end of them and voiding Your covenant with them. Surely You [9]alone are the living God; beside You is none other. You have remembered Your covenant [10]whereby You brought us forth from Egypt while the nations looked on. You have not abandoned us [11]among the nations; rather, You have shown covenant mercies to Your people Israel in all [12][the] lands to which You have exiled them. You have again placed it [13]on their hearts to return to You, to obey Your voice [14][according] to all that You have commanded through Your servant Moses. [15][In]deed, You have poured out Your holy spirit upon us, [16][br]inging Your blessings to us. You have caused us to seek You in our time of tribulation, [17][that we might po]ur out a prayer when Your chastening was upon us. We have entered into tribulation, [18][cha]stisement and trials because of the wrath of the oppressor.

Surely we ourselves [19][have tr]ied God by our iniquities, wearying the Rock through [our] si[ns.] [20][Yet] You have [not] compelled us to serve You, to take a [pa]th more profitable [21][than that] in which [we have walked, though] we have not harkened t[o Your commandments.]

A prayer for forgiveness and help. Judging by its relation in the scroll to what follows, this prayer was recited on Friday, the traditional day for confessing sins.

Col. 6 [2][. . . You have hurl]ed all ou[r] transgressions fro[m] us, and pu[ri]fied us [3]from our sins for Your own sake. Justice is Yours alone, O Lord, for [4]it is You who has done all these things. And now, on this day, [5]with humble heart we seek atonement for our iniquities and the iniquity of [6]our fathers, for our rebellion and continued hostility to You.

Yet we have not refused [7]Your trials, nor has our spirit loathed Your chastisement, so as to break [8]our covenant with You, despite all our distress of soul when You sent our enemies against us. Surely it is You [9]who has given us strength of heart, to the end that we recount Your mighty deeds for all the generations of [10]eternity.

Please, O Lord, just as You work wonders from everlasting to [11]everlasting, let Your anger, and especially Your fury, turn back from upon us. Look upon [our] aff[liction,] [12]toil and oppression, and rescue Your people Isr[ael from all] 13the lands, near and far, to wh[ich You have banished them—] 14each one who is written in the Book of Life. [. . .] 15to serve You and praise [Your holy name . . . Rescue them] 16from all those who are hostile toward them [. . .] **Col. 7** 2Who has rescued us from every distress. Amen! [Amen!]

The title preserved indicates that these are prayers for the Sabbath, traditionally a day to praise God. "Holy ones" is here, as often in the scrolls, a synonym for angels. Abaddon is essentially hell.

4Praises for the Sabbath day. Give thanks to [the Lord, bless] 5His holy name forever with a [holy] so[ng. Praise Him,] 6all the angels of the holy firmament, and [all the Holy Ones above] 7the heavens, the earth and all its handiwork; [. . . the great] 8Abyss, Abaddon, the waters and all that is in [them. Let] 9all His creatures [bless Him] continuously, forever and [ever. Amen! Amen!]

10[Bless] His holy name, sing joyously to the awe[some] God [. . .]

A prayer of praise and confession.

Frag. 4 (with **4Q506 Frags. 131–132**) 3[. . . the] earth and the work of all the [. . . have] You [given to him,] 4[together with the j]oy of [his] hear[t. Sure]ly You are the God of knowledge, [and] every though[t of our hearts] 5lies open be[fore Y]ou. We know these things because You have graciously granted us [Your] h[oly] spirit.

[Take pity on us,] 6and [rem]ember not to hold against us the iniquities of our forebears with all their wick[ed] deeds, [those] 7who were stiff-necked. Redeem us, and [please] forgive our iniquities and si[ns.] 8[. . .] the Law that [You] commanded through Mos[es Your servant . . .]

A prayer extolling God's special care of Israel.

Frag. 6 6[. . . Re]member, please, that all of us are Your people. You have "borne us miracu[lous]ly 7[on] eagles' [wings] and brought us to Yourself" (Exod. 19:4). "As an eagle stirs up its nest, [and] 8hovers [over its young;] as it spreads its wings, takes them up and bears them aloft on its [pinions" (Deut. 32:11).] 9[So we] dwell apart and are not reckoned among the nations. [. . .] 10[O Lord,] it is You who is in our midst in a pillar of fire, who [appears to us] as a cloud; 11Your [hol]iness goes before us, Your glory [dwells] among [us.]

A prayer recalling God's dealings with the father of all humanity, Adam.

Frag. 8 [1][. . . Re]member, O L[o]r[d,] that [. . .] [2][. . .] and it is You who lives for[ever . . .] [3][. . . You have done] wonders of old, and awesome deeds [long ago.] [4]You fashioned [Adam,] our [fa]ther, in the image of [Your] glory; You breathed [5][the breath of life] into his nostrils, [and filled him] with understanding and knowledge. [6]Y[ou] set him to rule [over the Gar]den of Eden that You had planted. [7][. . .] and to walk about in a glorious land [. . .] [8][. . .] he guarded it. You enjoined him not to turn as[ide from Your commands.] [9][. . .] flesh is he, and to dust h[e shall return.] [10][. . .] It is You who knows [. . .] [11][. . .] for the generations of eternity [. . .] [12][. . .] the living God, and Your hand [. . .] humankind in the ways of [. . .] [14][. . . to fill the] earth with [wro]ngdoing and to she[d innocent blood . . .]

—M.O.W.

128. The Songs of the Sage for Protection Against Evil Spirits

4Q510–511

According to *Jubilees* 10:1–14, in the days following the Flood powerful evil spirits began to trouble Noah's children. Noah prayed to God and received assurance that these spirits would be bound and held for judgment. But then Mastemah, the chief of the evil spirits, complained that he would be unable to carry out his task of corrupting humanity, so God compromised and allowed him to keep one-tenth of the spirits. The *Songs of the Sage* contains incantations to help protect the faithful against the power of these spirits. It bears comparison with *An Exorcism* (text 146) and *Songs to Disperse Demons* (text 153). Unlike those works, however, this writing is almost certainly sectarian, for it uses the technical term "Instructor," the name of one of the officials of the *Yahad*.

God's dominion over all is established (ll. 1–4a) and he is called upon by the Instructor to terrify (ll. 4b–9) the demons who were leading men astray.

4Q510 Frag. 1 [1][. . .] praises.

Ble[ssings to the K]ing of Glory. Words of thanksgiving in psalms of [. . .] [2][. . .] to the God of knowledge, splendor of s[treng]th, the God of gods, Lord of all the holy ones. [His] domini[on] [3]is over all the mighty, strong ones, and by the power of His streng[th] all will be dismayed and scattered, running hurriedly from the majesty of the dwe[lling] [4]of His royal glory.

And I, the Instructor, proclaim His glorious splendor so as to frighten and to te[rrify] [5]all the spirits of the destroying angels, spirits of the bastards, demons, Lilith, howlers, and [desert dwellers . . .] [6]and those which fall upon men without warning to lead them astray from a spirit of understanding and to make their heart and their [. . .] desolate during the present dominion of [7]wickedness and predetermined time of humiliations for the sons of lig[ht], by the guilt of the ages of [those] smitten by iniquity—not for eternal destruction, [8][bu]t for an era of humiliation for transgression. [. . .]

Sing for joy, O righteous ones, for the God of Wonder. [9]My psalms are for the upright. And [. . . let] all those who are blameless exalt Him!

4Q511 Frag. 10 [8]With the lyre of salvation [9]they [shall ope]n their mouths for God's compassion. They shall seek His manna.

Save me, O Go[d,] [10][He who preserves loving-kindne]ss in truth for all His works and judges in righteous[ness] those who exist forever [11][unt]il eternity. He judges in the council of gods and men. [12]In the height of heaven is His rebuke, and in all the foundations of the earth, the judgments of the LORD [. . .]

Thanks to God for freedom from demonic activity.

Frag. 1 [1][. . . their d]ominions [2][. . .] and al[l . . . on the e]arth and with all [3]the spirits of its domain, [let them] continually b[less] Him in their times, [4]the seas and every creature. Let them proclaim [. . .]. the splendor of [5]it all. Let them rejoice before the righteous God, with sho[uts of joy for] salvation [6]for the[re is no] destroyer within their borders [7]nor do wicked spirits walk among them. For the glory of the God of knowledge has shone forth [8]through His words, and none of the sons of injustice shall be sustained.

To protect his own, God promised Jacob an inheritance, ordered the camps of Israel in the wilderness, established festivals, and gave dominion to the Yahad.

Frag. 2 Col. 1 [1]For the Instructor: [. . .] song [. . . Praise the name of] [2]His holiness. Let all who know [righteousness] exalt Him. [3]And He put a stop to the head of the dominions without [. . .] [4]eternal [joy] and life everlasting, making the light shine [. . .] [5]His lot is the firstfruits in Jacob, the inheritance of God [. . .] Israe[l . . .] [6][those who kee]p the way of God and His [h]oly highw[ay] for the holy ones of His people. By the discerning knowledge of [7][Go]d, he placed Israel [in t]welve camps [. . .] for

Himself [8][. . .] the lot of God with the ange[ls of] His glorious lights. In His name the praises of [9]their [. . .] He established as the festivals of the year, [and the d]ominion of the *Yahad,* to walk [in] the lot [10][of God] according to [His] glory [and] to serve Him in the lot of the people of His throne. For the God of [. . .]

The second song of incantation.

Frag. 8 [1][. . .] [2][. . .] they shall rejoice in God [. . .] [3][. . .]

[4][For the Instructor:] the second [so]ng so as to frighten those who terrify [. . .] [5][. . .] his straying through humiliations but not for [eternal] destructi[on . . .] [6][. . .] God in the secret of the Almighty (Shaddai) [. . .]

The Instructor acknowledges that God has given him understanding.

Frag. 18 [1–2][. . .] [3][. . .] in His [s]trength [4][. . .]

[5][Is there any foolishness] in my words? There is none. Or [in] the utterance of my lips? There is no worthlessness [6][. . .] and the spirit of my understanding and [. . .] work of wickedness, for [7]G[o]d is concerned with me. And I have hated all the works of impurity, for [8]God has shined the knowledge of understanding in my heart. Righteous instructors [9]correct my sins, and faithful judges correct all my guilty transgressions. For God is my judge and in the hand of a stranger [He shall] not [. . .]

The Instructor acknowledges that he is but a humble mortal.

Frags. 28–29 [1][. . .]. [2][. . .] they [shall] rejoice in God with joy. And a[s for me, I shall thank Yo]u that, for the sake of Your glory, [3]You [pl]aced knowledge in my frame of dust in order that I might p[raise You.] And I was formed of spittle (?). [4]I was molded [of clay] and [my] format[ion] was in darkness [. . .] and injustice is in the filth of my flesh [5][. . .]

The Instructor speaks of God's infinite power.

Frag. 30 [1]You sealed [. . . l]and [. . .] [2]and they are deep [. . . the] heavens and the deeps and the dar[k places of the earth . . .] [3]You, my God, have sealed all of them forever, and there is none to open. And to who[m . . .] [4]Shall the abundant waters be measured by the hollow of a man's hand? [Shall the heavens be measured] by a span? [Who with a measure] [5]can calculate the dust of the earth or weigh the mountains in a balance or the hills with scale[s?" (Isa. 40:12 modified). . . .] [6]Man did not make these things. [How then] can a man measure the spirit [of God?]

God will judge wickedness and preserve his righteous people.

Frag. 35 [. . .] [1]G[o]d with all flesh, and a judgment of vengeance to wipe out wickedness and by the fierce [2]anger of God among those who have been refined sevenfold. But God will consecrate some of the holy ones [3]for Himself as an eternal sanctuary; a refining among those who are purified. And they shall be [4]priests, His righteous people, His army, and ministers, His glorious angels. [5]They shall praise Him for His awe-inspiring wonders.

[6]And I am pouring out the fear of God to the ends of my generations, to exalt the Name [. . . to frighten] [7]by His strength al[l] the spirits of the bastards, to subdue them by [His] fear [. . .]

The Instructor acknowledges that God has given him knowledge of God's purpose.

Frags. 48–49, 51 [1]in the council of God, for [. . .] His knowledge he put [in my] hear[t . . .] [2]the praises of His righteousness, and [. . .] and by His mouth he frightens [all the spirits] [3]of the bastards to subdue [. . .] uncleanness. For in the filth of [4]my flesh is the foundation of [. . . and in] my body are conflicts. The statutes of [5]God are in my heart, and I prof[it] from all the wonders of humankind. The works of [6]guilt I condemn [. . .]

God is gracious and righteous in his judgment.

Frags. 52, 54–55, 57–59 [1][. . .] their [. . .] And You, my God, [are a merciful and gracious God,] slow to anger, abounding in steadfast love, the foundation of tr[uth . . .] [2][. . .] for Adam and for [his] son[s . . .] the [s]ource of purity, the reservoirs of glory, great in righteousn[ess . . .]

The Instructor proclaims the wonders of God.

Frag. 63 Col. 2 + Frag. 64 [2][. . .] I will bless Your name. And in my appointed times I shall relate [3]Your wonders. I shall engrave them, the statutes of thanksgiving for Your glory. The beginning of every purpose of the heart [4]is knowledge and the beginning of every blessed utterance is righteous lips and in being prepared for every true service.

The song of the tongue set free.

Frag. 63 Col. 3 1And as for me, my tongue shall sing out Your righteousness, for You set it free. You placed on my lips a fountain 2of praise and on my heart the secret of the origin of all the works of humankind, and the fulfillment of the deeds 3of the blameless, the judgments for all the toil of their works, in order to justify 4the righteous one in Your truth and to condemn the wicked one in his guilt, to proclaim peace 5to all the men of the covenant and to e[xal]t with a terrifying voice, "Woe to all who break it!"

The Instructor's concluding praise.

Frag. 63 Col. 4 1Let them bless all Your works 2continually, and blessed be Your name 3forever and ever. Amen, amen.
—M.G.A.

129. Redemption and Resurrection

4Q521

The Gospel of Matthew tells of an occasion on which John the Baptist sent word to Jesus, asking, "Are you the one who is coming, or are we to look for another?" Jesus is said to have answered, "Go and report to John what you hear and see: the blind have regained their sight, the lame walk, lepers are cleansed, the deaf hear, the dead are raised, and the poor have the good news preached to them" (Matt. 11:2–5).

This account of Jesus's response to the Baptist (see also Luke 7:22) parallels the Dead Sea Scrolls' *Redemption and Resurrection* in a remarkable way. Both the Gospels and this scroll presuppose that during the age of the messiah, the dead will be resurrected, either by God himself or through his messianic agent. Yet nowhere in the Old Testament do we clearly read of this belief. This fact suggests that the Gospel writers may have known *Redemption and Resurrection*—or at least been familiar with the traditions it contains. Thus Jesus's response to John's disciples was "Yes, I am he." His works reflected the messianic expectation.

Precisely how the first two paragraphs of frags. 2–4 col. 2 of our work once related is no longer clear. Too much of the scroll has been lost. But if it is correct to read them as part of a continuous description of activity during the messianic era, then the figure before us is unique among the scrolls. Notably lacking are the characteristics of the royal messiah seen so clearly in the *War of the Messiah* (text 63, especially frag. 7) and the *Commentaries on Genesis* (text 53, frag. 1, col. 5). It may be, as John Collins has suggested, that an anointed prophet of the Last Days is in view here. Elijah, for example, was an anointed prophet, and we know from many sources of the time of the scrolls that some Jews expected him to return. *An Apocryphon of Elijah* (text 94) is another text that incorporates this notion.

Frags. 2 + 4 Col. 2 [1][. . . For the hea]vens and the earth shall listen to His Messiah [2][and all w]hich is in them shall not turn away from the commandments of the holy ones. [3]Strengthen yourselves, O you who seek the Lord, in His service.

[4]Will you not find the Lord in this, all those who hope in their heart? [5]For the Lord attends to the pious and calls the righteous by name. [6]Over the humble His spirit hovers, and He renews the faithful in His strength. [7]For He will honor the pious upon the th[ro]ne of His eternal kingdom, [8]setting prisoners free, opening the eyes of the blind, raising up those who are bo[wed down. (Ps. 146:7–8)] [9]And for[ev]er I shall hold fast [to] those [who h]ope and in His faithfulness sh[all . . .] [10]and the frui[t of] good [dee]ds shall not be delayed for anyone [11]and the Lord shall do glorious things which have not been done, just as He said. [12]For He shall heal the critically wounded, He shall revive the dead, He shall send good news to the afflicted (Isa. 61:1), [13]He shall sati[sfy the poo]r, He shall guide the uprooted, He shall make the hungry rich, [14]and [. . .] disc[erning ones . . .] and all of them as the ho[ly ones . . .] [15]and [. . .]

The theme of a final judgment is clear in this fragment. A review of God's creative power is given in ll. 1–3. The second paragraph (ll. 4–6) capitalizes on the biblical picture of curses and blessing (Deut. 27–28)—the cursed are destined to die, whereas the blessed are to be resurrected (Deut. 30:19, Matt. 22:30–32; 1 Cor. 15:12ff.; Rev. 20:4–6).

Frags. 7 + 5 Col. 2 [1][. . .] see all t[hat the Lord has made,] [2][the eart]h and all that is on it, the seas [and all] [3][that is in them,] and every lake and stream.

[4][. . . al]l [of you] who have done good before the Lor[d] [5][bless and no]t as those who curse. They shall b[e] destined to die, [when] [6]the Reviver [rai]ses the dead of His people.

[7]Then we shall [giv]e thanks and relate to you the righteous acts of the Lord which [. . .] [8]thos[e destined to d]ie. And He shall open [the graves . . .] [9]and o[pen . . .] [10]and [. . .] [11]and a valley of death [. . .] [12]and a bridge of de[eps . . .] [13]the accursed shall languish (?) [. . .] [14]and the heavens shall advance [. . .] [15][and a]ll the angels [. . .]

The term "messiah" is used in this fragment in the plural (l. 9) in probable reference to the priests, as tabernacle utensils are mentioned (l. 8).

Frag. 8 [1][. . .] a wall be[twe]en [2–4][. . .] [5][. . .] they shall shine forth [6][. . .] Adam [7][. . . bl]essings of Jacob [8][. . . the temp]le and all its holy vessels [9][. . . the priestho]od and all its anointed ones [10][. . .] t[o be sanctified,] and the word of the Lord, and [they] shall sa[y . . .] [11][. . . Ble]ss the Lord [12][. . .] the eyes of [. . .]

Frag. 9 [1][. . .] you sh[all] not [. . .] [2][. . .] and by [the se]rvant of the L[ord . . .] [3][. . .] you have left in the hand of the me[ssiah (*or* an[ointed one) . . .] [4][. . .]

—M.G.A.

130. A Tale of Joshua

4Q522

The legible fragments of the present work concern strikingly different subjects. The first fragment comprises a simple list of geographical names, while the second praises God's choice of Mt. Zion for the building of the Temple. The thread that seems to bind the two parts together is that God has specially blessed the land of Israel as a whole and Jerusalem in particular. The list of city names, as a genre, has something in common with the description of the apportionment of the Holy Land in Joshua 13–21. Some of the cities are unknown; others are mentioned in the Bible.

From the narrator's perspective, Jerusalem is still in the hands of the Amorites, and Eleazar son of Aaron is the officiating priest (Josh. 14:1). These items, plus the similarity of the first column to the geographical lists of Joshua, make it likely that the scroll originally contained a hitherto unknown narrative about Joshua and his times.

A list of cities in Canaan and the tribes to which they are assigned.

Frag. 8 [1][. . . Jud]ah and Sime[o]n, [the hill country and] the Neg[ev (Josh. 10:40) . . .] [2][. . .] shall be theirs; but Dan also did not defeat the [. . .] [3][. . .] and Issachar: Beth Shean (17:11); and Asher: [. . .] [4][. . . Si]don (Judg. 1:31) and Cab[u]l (Josh. 19:27) [. . .]

Frag. 9 Col. 1 [2][. . .] and En-qober, and Beth- [3][. . .] Biqah and Beth-zippor and [4][. . .] the whole valley of Mizpah and [5][. . .] Hekalim, Jaaphor, and [6][. . .] and Mano, and En-kobed [7][. . .] Garim, Haditha, and

Oshel [8][. . . Ek]ron (Josh. 13:3) of [9][. . .] and Ashkelon (13:3) [10][. . . Ga]lilee and two [in the lowlan]d of the Sharon (Isa. 33:9) [11][. . .] Judah: Beer-sheba (Josh. 15:28), Baaloth (15:24) [12][. . .] Keilah (15:44), Adullam (15:35) and [13][. . .] Gezer (21:21), Timni (15:57), Gimzon (2 Chron. 28:18), and [14][. . .] Heker, and Kitr[on] (Judg. 1:30), and Ephronaim, and Sekut (1 Sam. 19:22) [15][. . .] Up[per] and Lower Beth-horon (1 Chron. 7:24), and [16][. . .] Upper and L[owe]r Giloh (Josh. 15:51)

God reveals the time when the Temple will be built.

Col. 2 [2]He will not [. . . abandon Zi]on, to set up there the Tent of Me[eting. . . to the end] [3]of time, for, look, a son is born to Jesse son of Peretz son of Ju[dah . . . he will choose] [4]the rock of Zion and drive out from there all the Amorites from Jeru[salem . . .] [5]to build the temple for the LORD God of Israel; gold and silver [. . .] [6]cedar and pine shall he bring [from] Lebanon to build it; and his younger son [shall build the temple. . . and Zadok] [7]shall serve as priest there first [. . .] [8][. . .] from heave[n . . .] the beloved of the LOR[D] will dwell there securely [. . . for a long] [9]time [and] His people will dwell forever. But now, the Amorite is there, and the Canaani[te and the Jebusite and all the] [10]inhabitants who have committed sin, whom I have not sought [. . .] [11]from you. As for the Shilonites, I have made them servants [. . .] [12]And now, let us [s]et up the T[ent of Mee]ting far from [. . .] [13]Eleazar [and Josh]ua the T[ent of Me]eting from Beth[el . . .]

—E.M.C.

131. The Blessings of the Wise

4Q525

Blessed is the man who attains wisdom, and walks in the law of the Most High." With these words and others like them, the *Blessings of the Wise* could almost come right out of the pages of the New Testament—so great is the occasional similarity of form and ideas to those of the famous Beatitudes of Matthew 5:3–10. Striking similarities aside, the *Blessings* is another example of wisdom literature, comparable to the *Book of Secrets* (text 6) and the *Secret of the Way Things Are* (text 105). In keeping with wisdom literature as a whole, the author contrasts the nature and behavior of the righteous with those of the wicked; the recommended course of behavior becomes obvious. Just in case particularly thick-headed ancient readers did not see the obvious, near the end of the work our author hits them between the eyes with a graphic description of hell, replete with fire, brimstone, and venomous serpents (frag. 15).

The possible thematic statement, "to know wisdom and discipline, to understand" echoes Proverbs 1:1–6.

Frag. 1 [1][. . . which he spok]e in the wisdom which God gave to him [. . .] [2][. . . to kno]w wisdom and disc[ipline,] to understand [. . .] [3][. . .] to increase [. . .]

This portion of the manuscript reveals distinct similarities to the beatitude form of Sirach 14:20–15:1 and Matthew 5:3–10. Although wisdom is clearly exalted here, it is important to note that the pronoun "it" finds its antecedent in the law as well (see ll. 3–4). Wisdom and law are viewed as inseparable.

Frags. 2–3 Col. 2 [Blessed is the one who . . .] [1]with a pure heart and does not slander with his tongue (Ps. 15:3). Blessed are those who hold fast to its statutes and do not hold fast [2]to the ways of injustice. Ble[ssed] are those who rejoice in it, and do not exult in paths of folly. Blessed are those who seek it [3]with pure hands, and do not search for it with a deceitful [hea]rt. Blessed is the man who attains wisdom, and walks [4]in the law of the Most High: establishes his heart in its ways, restrains himself by its corrections, is continually satisfied with its punishments, [5]does not forsake it in the face of [his] trials, at the time of distress he does not abandon it, does not forget it [in the day of] terror, [6]and in the humility of his soul he does not abhor [it.] But he meditates on it continually, and in his trial he reflects [on it, and with al]l [7]his being [he gains understanding] in it, [and he establishes it] before his eyes so as not to walk in the ways [of wickedness . . .] [8][. . . and . . .] together, and kept his heart fixed on it, [and . . .] [9][. . . and You place a crown of gold upon] his [hea]d, and with kings You shall se[at him, and . . .] [10][. . . by] His [sc]epter up with eq[uity and amon]g brothers He shall scatt[er . . .] [11][. . .]

[12][And] now my sons, li[sten to me and do n]ot turn aside [from the words of my mouth.]

The incomparable nature of wisdom/law.

Col. 3 [1]he shall dwell in it continually (*or* it is like [him] continually) [. . .] [2]It cannot be obtained with gold o[r silver . . . or] [3]with precious stones [. . .] [4]by the form of his face he resembl[es . . .] [5]and purple flowers with [. . .] [6]crimson, with all the garments of [. . .] [7]and with gold and jewels [. . .]

Those who walk in perfection turn aside injustice and do not reject wisdom's demands or the law's punishments.

Frag. 5 [2][. . . do not abandon i]t in a time of tr[ou]b[le . . .] [3][. . .] its testing, and [. . .] [4][. . .]

[5][And now my sons, listen to me . . .] w[alk in pu]rity [. . .] [6][. . .] tr[uly] do n[ot] seek it with an ev[il] heart [. . .] [7][. . .] its ways [. . .] do not [see]k it with a deceitful heart but in the st[atutes of . . . do not] [8]abandon your [portio]n to s[trangers] or your allotment to foreigners, for [the] wise [. . .] [9][they] instruct in sweetness. [For] those who fear God keep its ways and walk in [. . .] [10]its statutes and they do not reject its chastisements. Those who discern obtain [. . .] [11]those who walk in perfection turn aside injustice and do not reject its reproofs [. . .] [12]they are laden. The shrewd uncover its ways and its depths they [. . .] [13]they gaze. Those who love God walk humbly in it and in [the] wa[ys of . . .]

A description of the unjust/unwise (see frags. 10, 13).

Frag. 6 Col. 2 [1][. . . without] resp[on]se and jealous without [. . .] [2]that he might not understand because of an erra[nt] spirit [. . . that he might not] [3]know because of a perverted spirit [. . .] [4]with weakness and causes stumbling witho[ut . . . without] [5]certainty and sends away without [. . . without] [6]pride and exalts without [. . .]

An exhortation to be upright.

Frag. 10 [1][. . .] from a book and there is no [. . .] [2][. . .]

[3][. . . And now,] pay attention to me, all you sons of [. . .] [4][. . .] meekness, and uprightness, for sin and for i[nnocence . . .] [5][. . . ordinanc]e of the enemy and the friend. But may God not justify all flesh [. . .] [6][. . . I]f you do well, He shall prosper you, b[ut if] you do n[ot] repent [. . .] [7][. . .] all [Israe]l, wickedness of [humankind . . .]

The lot of the just/wise.

Frags. 11–12 [1][. . .] bountiful peace [wit]h all the blessings of [. . .] [2][. . . with] a robe of honor to a[l]l who hold fast to Me [. . .] [3][. . .

to all who walk] blameless in all My paths, and to a[ll . . .] [4][. . .]with all the spirit[s of . . .]

Frag. 13 [1][. . .] and from their mouths [. . .] [2][. . . you shall inhe]rit among the miserly, you shall give t[hem . . .] [3][. . .] they bear a grudge to shed blood among [. . .] [4][. . .] you shall inherit pride and in its bowels [. . .] [5][. . . and] all who inherit it [. . .] [6][. . . And now li]sten to me a[l]l [. . .]

A description of the just/wise teacher.

Frag. 14 Col. 2 [1][. . .] your [inher]itance among [. . .] [2]upon a throne of injustice and upon the heights of [their] asse[mbly . . .] [3]with their heart and they will raise up your head [. . .] [4]you shall p[rais]e, and because of your word [t]he[y] pr[evailed . . .] [5]with a[l]l majesty and desirable with a[ll . . .] [6]he has drawn near your paths, you shall not be shaken [. . .] [7]you shall be blessed. In the time of your reeling you shall find s[upport . . .] [8]the reproach of the enemy shall not overtake you a[nd . . .] [9]together, and your enemies shall lie at the threshold [. . .] [10]your heart, and you shall delight in G[od] while [they] defile [. . . and he shall bring you] [11]to a spacious place, and you shall tread upon the heights of your [en]emies a[nd you shall love God with all your heart and with all] [12]your soul. And He shall deliver you from every evil, and terror shall not overtake you [. . .] [13]He gives you to possess. He shall fill your days with good, and you shall [enjoy] bountiful peace [. . .] [14]you shall inherit honor. And when you are swept away to eternal rest, they shall inherit [. . .] [15]and all those who know you shall walk together in your teaching [. . .] [16]they shall be lost together. But they shall remember you in your ways, and you shall be g[ood . . .]

An exhortation—most likely from the Instructor—to righteous humility.

[18]And now, O discerning one, listen to me, and devote your heart to [the] w[ords of My mouth . . .] [19]obtain knowledge for your innermost part and with [your] bo[dy] meditate [. . .] [20]with righteous humility utter [your] words. Do [no]t give [. . . Do not] [21]be turned aside by words of your companion, lest he [gi]ve you [. . .] [22]answer as is worthy in accordance to what you hear. Take ca[re . . . do not] [23]utter a complaint before you hear their words, p[ay attention . . .] [24]exceedingly. First, hear their explanation, and then answer wi[th words of . . .] [25]patiently bring them out. Answer with certainty in the midst of princes and [. . .] [26]with your lips.

Be very careful of an offense with the tongue in [. . .] [27]lest you be entrapped by your lips [and] likewise [ens]nared with [your] ton[gue . . .] [28]insolent words w[hich . . .] from me and they become entangled [. . .]

A description of hell, the lot of the unwise/unjust.

Frag. 15 [1][. . . grea]t darkness [. . .] gather poverty and in stor[ehouses . . .] [2][. . .] vipers in [. . . and yo]u shall go to it. You shall enter [. . .] [3][. . .] poisonous snake, and with trem[bling] a viper shall be suspended on hig[h . . .] [4][. . .] they shall take their stand. Eternal curses and the venom of serpents [. . .] [5][. . .] adder. And in it the flame[s of] death shall fly about, at its entrance [. . .] [6][. . . da]rkness [. . .] flaming brimstone is its footing, and its foundation is f[ire . . .] [7][. . .] its [door]s are shameful reproaches and its locks are the snares of perdition [. . .] [8][. . .] they shall not attain the paths of life. You shall en[ter . . .] [9][. . .] those injured by the poisonous [snake shall] be put to death [. . .]

Frag. 16 [2]have you have released [. . .] [3]discerning men go astray in it [. . .] [4]and [they] h[id] snares [. . .] [5]bloodshed [. . .] put to dea[th . . .] [6]with unfaithfulness and oppression [. . .] [7]house and doo[rs . . .]

Frag. 17 [2][. . .] its [. . .] coals [. . .] [3][. . .] they are full of lie[s . . .] [4][. . . ve]nom of serpents mel[ted . . .] [5][. . .] strong [ ] around [. . .] [6][. . .] in the brightness [of li]ght and [. . .]

Frag. 21 [1][. . .] dark places, and I shall be hea[led (?) . . .] [2][. . .] those cursed of God [. . .] [3][. . . the wi]cked you pro[claim . . .] [4][. . .] you choose depravity [. . .] [5][. . .] they shall exalt themselves in it and walk [. . .] [6][. . .] those who roll in the muck [. . .] [7][. . .] its source, [the] source of [. . .] [8][. . . to] gather wrath and pat[iently (?) . . .] [9][. . .] certain, and indignation [. . .]

Frag. 22 [2][. . .] come to Me, [O doe]rs of wickedness [. . .] [3][. . .] they remained together and [. . .] [4][. . . wickednes]s they shall wallow. Is it n[ot . . .] [5][. . . against] his magnificences I will gather my anger [. . .] [6][. . .] they shall return and in [. . .]

Divination by the examination of entrails (hepatoscopy) is condemned.

Frag. 23 [1]they held my entrails before G[od (?) . . .] [2]I flee. And on the day designated [. . .] [3]so as to go down to the depths of the pit and to [. . .] [4]in the fiery furnace.

An exhortation to spurn unrighteousness.

For I am wi[se . . .just as] [5]God commanded men of cunning [. . .] [6]on behalf of them, from the knowledge of wisdom [. . .] [7]he turned about, lest they meditate on the words [. . .] [8]I have abhorred, and with mockers [. . .] [9]righteousness, and as a rock of st[umbling . . .] [10]For Go[d] has denounced me [. . .] [11][. . . and the wo]rd of [. . .]

The lot of those who attain the paths of wisdom.

Frag. 24 Col. 2 [1][and unders]tanding you utter its word [. . .] [2]heart, listen to Me and de[ceit . . . that] [3]I established and they shall drink water [of the well. . .for] [4]My house is a house of [prayer . . .] [5]My house. The one who dwells in [. . .] [6]forever. And they walk [. . .] [7]those that gather it shall asse[mble . . .] [8]burning and whoever drinks [. . .] [9]the well from the waters of the sp[ring . . .]

—M.G.A.

132. The Words of the Archangel Michael

4Q529

According to Daniel 12:1, the archangel Michael is the "protector of Israel," and the *War Scroll* (text 11) speaks of "the glorious angel, the dominion of Michael in light eternal" (17:6). He plays a prominent role in the Jewish literature of this period and for centuries thereafter as the chief of the angels; the New Testament refers to "Michael and his angels" (Rev. 12:7). For this reason he is often imagined as God's chief messenger or revealer. (For other appearances of Michael in the Dead Sea Scrolls, see text 120).

The *Words of the Archangel Michael* is unique in portraying Michael as speaking to the other angels, and not to a human being, and as receiving a vision from Gabriel. The genre of the text is uncertain, as is its sense. The key to the meaning is the restoration at the end of l. 9. In the city spoken of, will "evil be done" or "[nothing] evil be done"? If it is the former, then the city may be Babylon or even Rome (K. Beyer); but if the latter, then it may be Jerusalem (Eisenman and Wise). The similarity to *A Tale of Joshua* (text 130) and the nameless "man" who will come requiring "silver and gold" makes one think more of Jerusalem and of David, who will amass materials for the building of the Temple.

If this understanding is correct, then Michael may be telling the angels about seeing angelic troops permanently quartered on Mt. Zion and asking for an explanation. Gabriel shows him that in the future a great city is to be built there for the worship of God.

[1]The words of the book that Michael said to the angels [. . .] [2]he said,
I found there fiery troops [. . .] [3][. . .] nine mountains, two to the east,
[two to the west, two to the north and two[4] to the] south. There I saw the
angel Gabriel [. . .] [5][. . .] he showed me a vision and said to me
[. . .] [6]in my book of the Great One, Eternal Lord it is written [. . .]
[7]the children of Ham and the children of Shem, and behold, the Great One,
Eternal Lord [. . .] [8]when tears flow freely [. . .] [9]and, behold, a city is
to be built to the name of the Great One, [Eternal Lord . . . and there
nothing] [10]evil shall be done before the Great One, [Eternal] Lord [. . .]
[11]and the Great One, Eternal Lord, will call His creation to mind [. . .]
[12]mercy belongs to the Great One, Eternal Lord, and also [. . .] [13]in the
distant lands there will be a man [. . .] [14]is he, and he will say to him, This
one is [my holy mountain . . .] [15]to me silver and gold [. . .]
—E.M.C.

133. The Birth of the Chosen One

4Q534–536

That all things happen according to the divine plan is a characteristic theme of the Dead Sea Scrolls. If someone belonged to the Qumran sect, that was not simply good fortune, but the outcome of a divine decision, and the Qumran sect sometimes referred to itself as the "chosen of heaven" (*A Commentary on Habakkuk* 10:13, text 2; the *War Scroll* 12:5, text 11; and so on).

This text, however, speaks of a particular person as the "chosen one"—chosen, it is clear, to be a revealer of God's secrets to others. When the first part of the text was published, scholars surmised that the "chosen one" was the Messiah; later, following a suggestion of J. A. Fitzmyer's, scholars began to attribute the text to a lost *Book of Noah* and to understand the "chosen one" as Noah.

In fact, it is not clear that one should assign the text to a *Book of Noah,* although Noah's birth was taken to be miraculous (see *Tales of the Patriarchs,* text 4). With the full release of all the unpublished scrolls, it seems possible that the initial impulse was correct: the "chosen one" is *a* messiah, if not *the* Messiah. Particularly striking are the parallels to the scroll 4Q541, the latter part of the *Words of Levi* (text 39). There a prophecy is given of a mighty priest who will arise and "reveal hidden mysteries" and whose "teaching is like the will of God"—much like the "chosen one" of this text who "will reveal secrets like the Most High" (4Q536, l. 8) and whose "wisdom shall come to all peoples" (4Q534 1:8).

The coming priest of the *Words of Levi,* then, may well be the "chosen one" of this text, that is, the priestly messiah, who, with the "Leader of the Nation," the royal messiah, shall rule Israel in the Last Days. The *Birth of the Chosen One* relates some of the distinguishing physical characteristics of this important person and describes the greatness and success of his ministry.

The "chosen one" may be recognized by certain telltale physical traits.

4Q534 Frag. 1 Col. 1 [. . .] [1]of the hand [and] his two knees. [And on his head str]ipes of a mark. Red will be [2][his] hair, [and] moles will be on [. . .] [3]and tiny marks on his thighs, and they will be different from each other.

The education and future greatness of the "chosen one."

And knowledge will [be] in his heart. [4]In his youth, he will be adept [and like a m]an who does not know anything until [5]he knows the three books.

[6]Then he will be wise and will know the [. . .] visions to come to him on his knees, [7]and through his father and his forefathers [long] life and old age shall be his, and prudence and wisdom, [8][and] he will know the secrets of men, and his wisdom shall come to all peoples, and he will know the secrets of living things. [9][Al]l their designs against him will fail, and the array (?) of all living things will be great [10][. . .] his purposes, because he is the chosen one of God. His birth and the spirit of his breath [11][. . .] his purposes will last forever [. . .]

This section seems to speak of the eschatological time of peace.

Col. 2 [. . .] [12]and nations wi[ll be . . .] and virgins will dwell with no [. . .] [13]and they will destroy [. . .] the idol altars will be destroyed, all these shall go [. . .] [14]water shall end [. . .] [15][. . .] enclos[ur]es shall be built, its work will be like the Watchers [16][. . .] they will lay its foundation on it; its sin and iniquity [17]instead of a curse [. . .] a holy one and suffering [. . . as] the word of [18][. . .] of joy [. . .] they said about him.

More on the circumstances of his birth. The details are obscure.

4Q535 Frag. 3 (= 4Q536 Frag. 1) [1][. . . is] born and they are [. . .] together [. . .] [2][. . .] is born at night and comes out who[le

. . .] [3][. . . at a] weight of three hundred and fi[fty] shekels [. . .] [4][. . . in the da]ys he sleeps until half his days [are done and . . .] [5][. . .] in the daytime until the completion of [eight yea]rs [. . .] [6][. . .] shall be removed from him; and after [*x*] ye[ars . . .]

The sublimity of the chosen one's teaching. This fragment makes clear in l. 13 that the revelation of the chosen one is being given to a seer.

4Q536 Frag. 2 Col. 1 + Frag. 3 [1][. . .] will be [. . .] [2][. . .] he will call to mind the [h]oly [angels . . .] [3][. . .] the lig[hts] will be revealed to him [4][. . .] all of his teaching, spl[endor . . .] [5][. . . wi]sdom of humanity and all [the] wise [6][. . .] in mortality; and he will be great [7][. . .] humanity will be [t]roubled [8][. . .] he will reveal secrets like the Most High [9][. . .] and with the perception of the mysteries of [10][. . .] [11][. . .] like the dust [12][. . .] first [. . . he ap]portioned the secret [13][. . .] which he transmitted to me among the numbers of the remnant [. . .] and his portion [. . .]

The seer continues his utterance with moral exhortation and the wish that his words be preserved in a book.

Col. 2 [9][. . .] for you are concerned about it. For every man [. . .] [10]his clothing; with a sword I will be mightier than your fortresses (?). Blessed is every m[an . . .] [11]and he will not die in the days of evil. Woe to you, O fool, for your mouth will deceive you [. . .] [12]a sin deserving death. Would that someone would write these words of mine in a writing that would not wear out, and th[is] utterance of mine [keep in a scroll that will never] [13]pass away! Behold, the time of the wicked will be snuffed out forever. Any man who [. . .] your servants [. . .]

—E.M.C.

134. The Vision of Jacob

4Q537

When the patriarch Jacob came of age to marry, his father, Isaac, sent him to his uncle Laban to get a wife. While en route, Jacob spent a night at a "certain place," as Genesis 28:11 describes it. Falling asleep, he had a dream in which he saw a ladder reaching to heaven, with angels ascending and descending.

He heard God speak to him, promising land, numberless descendants, and blessing. When he awoke, Jacob set up a stone, poured out a libation upon it, and named the place Bethel, meaning "House of God."

The extrabiblical book *Jubilees* elaborates on this vision of Jacob. The author of *Jubilees* is concerned with explaining why Bethel—despite this promising beginning and its portentous name—was not the place God ultimately chose for his Temple. Indeed, *Jubilees* goes the Bible one better and portrays Jacob as having every intention of sanctifying Bethel as a cultic site: "Jacob planned to build up that place and to build a wall around the court and to sanctify it" (32:16). To forestall this intention, God appeared to Jacob in a second vision—about which the Bible, of course, says nothing.

The portion of *Jubilees* that narrates the second vision is clearly related to the text before us. Indeed, at points there is a manifest verbal connection. But the present work is not simply an Aramaic version of this portion of *Jubilees,* for the story here is told in the first person, whereas in *Jubilees* an angel is telling Moses about the events. Furthermore, our author outdoes *Jubilees* in some of the details he provides.

Jacob receives some heavenly tablets on which he reads about the future and learns that no temple should be built at Bethel. The reconstruction in l. 5 follows from Jubilees *32:22.*

Frag. 1 01–02(Then I saw in a vision of the night and behold, an angel of God descended from heaven with seven tablets in his hands. He said to me, "God Most High has blessed you, you and) 1your progeny. All the righteous and upright shall be a remnant. [. . . No longer will] 2evil [be done;] lying shall no longer be found. [. . .] 3Now, take the tablets and read all [that is written on them." So I took the tablets and read. Written on them were all my sufferings] 4and oppression, indeed, everything that would happen to [me during the hundred and forty-sev]en years of my life. [Again he said to me, "Take] the tablet from my hand." [. . .] 5[So] I took this tablet from his hands, [and . . . I read all of it.] I saw inscribed on it that [no sanctuary was to be built in this place,] 6[and that,] "You are to leave it, and on the [eighth] day, [your offers will not be] unavailing before [God Most High. . . ."]

Jacob sees the city and temple, presumably the new Jerusalem. The city is apparently divided into numerous squares (compare the description in A Vision of the New Jerusalem, *text 143).*

Frag. 12 1[I saw . . .] and how the structure should be built [. . . and how] their [priests] were to be dressed and [their hands] purified, [2][and how] they were to offer up sacrifices on the altar, and h[ow in ev]ery [la]nd they were to consume as food some of their sacrifices, [3][and how they were to drink water] that would be exiting the city, underneath its walls. Then, behold, [much water] will be pou[red out . . .] [5][Then I looked and, behold,] before me was an area divided into squares, two and fo[rty (?) in number . . .]

—M.O.W.

135. An Apocryphon of Judah

4Q538

In Genesis 37–50 the Bible narrates the famous story of Joseph. Beginning life as a mere shepherd in Canaan, Joseph goes on to become the vizier of Egypt, second only to Pharaoh in the world's most powerful kingdom. Along the way he has many adventures and numerous close calls; the Joseph novella has all the elements of great literature. Several of the episodes in Joseph's life center on conflict with his brothers. Except for Benjamin, Joseph is Jacob's youngest son and evidently his father's favorite. Through the jealousy of his older brothers, the young Joseph is sold into slavery in Egypt. Yet ultimately they all meet again. Famine in Canaan forces Joseph's brothers to come to Egypt to buy grain, not once, but twice. On those occasions they come face-to-face with Joseph, now vizier. Although he recognizes them, they do not know him for who he is. The fragments before us seem to tell the story of the second dramatic meeting between Joseph and his brothers, corresponding to Genesis 44:1–45:10.

Judah narrates the meeting in Egypt between Joseph and his brothers. Judah presents himself as observing from a distance, perhaps reflecting his earlier disagreement with the brothers' plot against Joseph. They had planned to kill Joseph, but Judah persuaded them to sell the youth into slavery (Gen. 37:26–27).

Frags. 1–2 [1][. . .] Then he conceived a scheme agai[nst his brothers . . .] [2][. . .] they [ent]ered, and if they had [an evil spirit] in their hea[rt] against hi[m]. When I was br[ou]ght and entered, [3][before him,] they [dr]ew near as one and entered with me, (bringing) their pa[cks] together with [their gifts, silver at] the mou[th of] their packs. [They all] [4][fell down] before Joseph and prostrated themselves [to him.] Then he realized that there

was no evil [sp]irit [in their hearts,] and was no longer able [5][to suspect evil in their he]ar[ts] because of him. Able to con[trol himself] no longer, he had a great [mea]l brought to his brothers. [6][Then Joseph made himself known to them; and f]a[lling up]on my neck, he kissed me and wep[t copiously, because I had] feared [. . .]
—M.O.W.

136. The Last Words of Joseph

4Q539

The biblical story of Joseph (Gen. 37–50) was—and still is—an immensely rich lode for later Jewish and Christian interpreters interested in mining moralisms. Among such interpreters was the early Christian author of the *Testament of Joseph,* which comprises a series of chapters in the larger work known as the *Testaments of the Twelve Patriarchs.* As we have noted above, many of the Christian testaments incorporated earlier Jewish writings like those we find in the scrolls, and that seems to be the case here as well. The very fragmentary remains of the present Qumran scroll appear to lie behind the later *Testament of Joseph* 15–17. The *Testament of Joseph* does not, then, derive from the Bible without mediation. It relies upon other early writings as well. Particularly striking is the apparent relationship of ll. 5–6 below with the *Testament of Joseph* 17:1, which reads, "See, children, how much I endured . . . that I not put my brothers to shame." The wording of the rest of the fragment is only broadly similar to that of the Christian writing, so we must conclude that a free reworking of the *Last Words* took place in Christian circles.

Joseph addresses his children, relating the story of his sale to Ishmaelite slave traders and drawing moral principles from the events. The money in l. 4 apparently refers to the price for which Joseph was sold. According to the Testament of Joseph *16:5, the price was eighty pieces of gold.*

Frags. 2–3 [1][. . . For on]e [year], Jacob we[pt over Joseph.]

[2][And now, li]sten, my children, [to the word of Joseph your father, and pa]y attention to me, my beloved, [and I will tell you the truth.] [3][When the s]ons of my great-uncle, [Ish]ma[el, sold me in Egypt, he,] my father, Ja[cob,] held a mourning fe[ast] for me. [Memphis sent a eunuch] [4][to pay e]i[gh]ty talents and [to fetch] a slav[e. He paid] eighty talents using pieces of [gold shekels, and they agreed] [5][on the pri]ce. If you [. . .] notifying the mess[enger . . .] [6][See, my children,] this [story], how I was en[during it

so as not] to shame my brothers by announcing [that I was a slave] [7][. . .] lov[e . . . h]uman [. . .]
—M.O.W.

137. The Last Words of Kohath

4Q542

The *Last Words of Kohath* is another example of a testament (see the introduction to the *Words of Levi,* text 39). In fact, since Kohath was Levi's eldest son, this text forms a sequel to the *Words of Levi* and was itself succeeded by the *Vision of Amram* (text 138).

The Bible says of Kohath only that he was the son of Levi (Gen. 46:11). According to the *Words of Levi,* Levi saw in a vision that "all the people would gather to him, and that the high priesthood over all Israel would be his" (Cambridge C:6–7). As the ancestor of high priests, Kohath, like Levi and Abraham before him, is portrayed as one who encouraged his sons to be faithful to their calling and to perform their duties with care and reverence.

We do not know when the *Last Words of Kohath* may have been composed. Kohath's warning to his sons in 1:5–6 of the danger of giving the priestly inheritance to "strangers" and the inheritance to "assimilationists" may be an allusion to the religious crisis under the high priest Jason (174–171 B.C.E.). According to 2 Maccabees, "There was such an extreme of hellenization and increase in the adoption of foreign ways because of the surpassing wickedness of Jason, who was ungodly and no high priest, that the priests were no longer intent upon their service at the altar. . . . For this reason heavy disaster overtook them, and those whose ways of living they admired and wished to imitate completely became their enemies and punished them" (4:13–14, 16). *Kohath* may have been composed in part to encourage the assimilating priests to resist temptation.

Since the beginning and end of the text is lacking, we do not know whether this work, like other testaments, contained any narrative or prophetic vision.

Kohath blesses his sons and descendants.

Col. 1 [1][May you receive the blessing of] the greatest of all gods forever, and may he shine his light upon you, and tell you his great name [2]so that you may truly know him. For he is the God of the ages, and Lord of everything that is done, and ruler [3]of all people, doing with them whatever he pleases. May he give you happiness, and to your descendants joy, in the generations of [4]truth forever.

Kohath commands future priests to protect their office from contamination and make their ancestors proud. In this way they will defeat the wicked.

And now, my sons, be careful with the inheritance that has been entrusted to you, [5]and which your ancestors have bequeathed to you. Do not give your inheritance away to strangers, nor your inheritance to [6]assimilationists, lest you become low and degraded in their eyes, and they despise you; for then [7]they will be alien to you and become your rulers.

So hold firm to the command of Jacob [8]your ancestor, grasp tightly the judgments of Abraham and the good deeds of Levi and myself, and be holy and pure [9]from all intermingling, holding firm to the truth, walking in integrity and not with a divided heart, [10]but with a pure heart, and with an honest and good spirit. Then you will have among them a good reputation, and happiness will come [11]to Levi, joy to Jacob, celebration to Isaac, and praise to Abraham, because you have kept [12]and passed on the inheritance that your ancestors left you: truth, good deeds, honesty, [13]perfection, purity, holiness, and priesthood, according to everything that I have commanded you and according to everything **Col. 2** [1]I have taught you reliably, from this time forth and forever. All [. . .] [2]all the reliable utterances shall come true for you [. . .] [3]Eternal blessings shall rest on you and [. . .] [4]endures for eternal generations, and you shall no longer [. . .] [5]from your sufferings, and you shall stand up to give judgment on [. . .] [6]to behold the sins of the sinners of the ages [. . . they shall be punished] [7]by fire and in the abysses and in all the infernal caverns, terrifying [. . .] [8]in the generations of the truth, but all the wicked shall pass away. [. . .]

Kohath commands Amram, the father of Moses, to protect the sacred priestly writings and to pass them down to his descendants.

[9]Now, to you, Amram my son, I command [. . .] [10][. . .] you, and to their descendants I command [. . . to guard the sacred writings that they left behind] [11]and gave to my father Levi, and that my father Levi gave to me. [. . .] [12]all my writings as a testimony that you should be careful with [. . .] [13]to you. In them is great merit when you carry them along with you [. . .]

—E.M.C.

138. The Vision of Amram

4Q543–548

The *Vision of Amram* is the last testament in a series that began with the *Words of Levi* (text 39) and continued with the *Last Words of Kohath* (text 137; Kohath was Levi's son and Amram's father).

This scroll alone of the Qumran discoveries preserves its opening paragraph containing the ancient title.

4Q543 Frag. 1 Col. 1 [1]A copy of the book "The Words of the Vision of Amram [son of Kohath, son of Levi." It contains everything that] [2]he told his sons and everything that he commanded them on [the day he died, in the one hundred and] [3]thirty-sixth year, that is the year of [his death, in the one-hundred] [4]and fifty-second year of the e[xile of I]s[ra]el in E[gyp]t [. . .]

According to the Bible, Amram married his own aunt, Jochebed (Exod. 6:20). According to this text, he similarly gave in marriage his daughter Miriam, Moses's sister, to his own brother Uzziel. The practice of aunt-nephew marriage is condemned in the Bible (Lev. 18:12–13) and uncle-niece marriage is condemned in the Damascus Document (text 1, A 4:7–11). The inconsistency among these texts is still unexplained.

4Q545 Frag. 1a Col. 1 [4][When he settled in the land] [5]he called to Uzziel his younger brother [and gav]e him Mir[ia]m his daughter [6]in marriage when she was thirty years old. Then he gave a feast lasting seven [day]s [7]and he ate and drank at the feast and rejoiced.

In this cycle of priestly literature, Amram's claim to fame is not as the father of Moses, but as the father of Aaron, who was the ancestor of all rightful priests and the high priest par excellence. It is not clear in these fragments who is the subject of the prophecy, but it is possible that Amram here foretells Aaron's elevated status as the spokesman for God. It is also possible that the prophecy speaks of Moses under the name Malachijah ("angel of the LORD").

4Q545 Frag. 1a (= 4Q543 Frags. 1–2) Then when [8]the [d]ays of the feast were over, he sent and called for Aaron his son, [who] was [twenty(?)]

years old [9][and he said] to him, "Summon me Malachijah, my son." [. . .] from the house of [10][. . . when he c]ame to him, he called out to him [11][. . .] I am [comm]anding [12][. . .] his father [13][. . .] from [14][. . .] your command [15][and we will give you . . . generations of eter]nity [16][and we will give you wisdom . . .] will be added [17][to you . . . chosen (?) of God you will be, and the an]gel of God [18][you will be called . . . you shall do in] this [lan]d [19][and justice for the pious . . . and if] your name is [his] to [al]l [. . .]

The following paragraph relates that Kohath and Amram returned with a group to Canaan from Egypt in order to build tombs for their forebears who had died during the Egyptian sojourn. While in Canaan the threat of war brought Kohath back to Egypt, but he left Amram in Canaan to finish the work. When war finally broke out between Egypt, Canaan, and Philistia, Amram was unable to return to Egypt and to his wife and family for forty-one years.

Frags. 1a–b Col. 2 [11]in this land and I went up to [. . .] [12]to bury our fathers and I went up [to Hebron . . . with . . . and also my father Kohath there] [13]to remain and to live and to build t[ombs . . . and there went up with us] [14]many [men] of my cousins togeth[er . . . every man and from] [15]our servants, ve[ry m]any, [while] the dead [were being bur]ied. [In the first year of my authority, when there was] [16]a frightening rumor of war, our [gro]up longed [for] the land of E[gypt; so I went up to bury them] [17]quickly but they had not bu[ilt the tom]bs of their fathers; so [my wife Jochebed and my father Kohath] left [me to stay] [18]and to build and to take to th[em al]l [their needs fr]om the land of Canaan; [and we dwelt in Hebron] while [19]we were building. And [there was] war [between] the Philistines and Egypt [and the king of Philistia] defeated [the king of Egypt . . .]

4Q544 Frag. 1 [5]and the b[orders] of Egypt were closed and it was no longer possible [for Jochebed to come from Egypt . . .] [6]forty-one years and we were not able to [return to Egypt [. . .] therefore [. . . war] [7]between Egypt and Canaan and Philistia. [During] this [time] Jochebed [my wi]fe [. . . was far away from me in the land of Egypt . . . and with me] [8]she was not. I [did not] take ano[ther] wife [. . .] [9]everything, for I would return to Egypt safely and see my wife's face [. . .]

As is typical in this genre of literature, the hero of the story is granted a prophetic vision (as, for instance, in the Words of Levi, *text 39). Amram's vision expresses the strong dualism of light and darkness that is central to many of the Qumran documents, particularly the idea that a good angel of light and an evil angel of darkness contend for control of human destiny (see the* Charter of a Jewish Sectarian Association *3:13–24, text 7).*

[. . . and I saw in a dream, and beheld] [10]in my vision, the vision of the dream, and there were two figures arguing over me, and saying [. . .] [11]and holding a great dispute over me. So I asked them, "How is it that you have [authority over me?" They said, "We] [12][r]ule and have authority over all the human race." And they said to me, "Which one of us do you [seek to be ruled by?" And behold, I lifted my eyes and saw] [13][one] of them, whose appearance was hostile and [fright]ening; [his cloth]ing was multicolored and very dark [14][. . . and I saw another and] behold, [he was pleasant] in his appearance, and his face was smiling [and he was covered in . . .]

Apparently Amram chooses to follow the angel of light and begins to question him about the meaning of the vision. The angel of darkness is named Malki-Resha, and the angel of light, we may presume, is called Melchizedek, ruler of righteousness. Melchizedek as an angelic figure also figures in the Coming of Melchizedek *(text 154).*

4Q545 Frag. 2 Col. 3 [11][. . . r]ules over you [. . .] [12][. . .] who is this one? He said to me, "Now this one [. . .] [13][. . . His name is] Malki-Resha (ruler of wickedness)." And I said, "My lord, what is the do[minion of . . .] [14][. . .] all his deeds are da[rk]ness, and he l[eads] into darkness [. . .] [15][. . .] sees, and he rules over all darkness, while I [am Melchizedek . . .] [16][. . . from the] height to the depths, I am ruler over all light and al[l . . .]

Frag. 3 Col. 4 [1]["\. . .] I have been made ruler." And I asked him [. . .] [2][He answered and s]aid, "Three name[s . . ."]

Melchizedek tells Amram the fates of those who follow the light or darkness.

4Q548 Frag. 1 Col. 2. [2][. . . hea]ling to them and all the ways of [. . .] [3][. . .] them from their healer [. . .] [4][. . .] them from death and from de[struction . . .] [5][. . . u]pon you, sons of the blessing and j[oy . . .] [6][. . . for] all the generations of Israel, for all [eternity . . .] [7][. . . the zeal of] my [Lo]rd burned in me, for the sons of ri[ghteousness . . .] [8][. . . if you do wrong,] your name [shall be] sons of deceit and not son[s of truth . . .] [9][. . .] I t[ell] to [you] truly, I make known to [you that all the children of light] [10]shall be light [and all the children of] darkness shall be dark [. . .] [11]in all their knowledge [. . .] they shall be and the children of darkness will pass away [. . .] [12]Indeed, every fool and wic[ked man is dar]k and every [wise] and honest man is light [. . . all the children of light] [13]are destined for light and [. . .] and [shall receive a just] judgment while all the children of dark[ness are destined for darkness . . .] [14]and shall go to destruction [. . .] to the people illumination. I shall tell [. . .] [15]and make known [. . .] away from darkness for all [. . .] [16]the children [. . .] and all the children of light [. . .]

As part of the vision, Amram's angelic mentor speaks of the future of the priestly clan, of Moses and Aaron, and predicts the coming of a great high priest.

4Q545 Frag. 4 [14][. . .] I shall tell you the names [. . .] [15][. . . was] written in the land for him: "Moses." And also concerning the o[ther one . . .] [16][I] shall tell you the secret of his work: he is a holy priest [. . .] [17]Ho[l]y to God shall be all his descendants for all the generations of e[ternity . . .] [18]seventh among those whom [God] favors [he] shall be called, and it will be said [that he is chosen of God, for] [19]he will be chosen as a priest forever.

4Q547 Frag. 9 [2][. . .] delivered [. . .] [3][. . .] on Mount Sinai [. . .] [4][. . .] your great [cattle?] on the bronze altar [. . .] [5][. . .] his son shall be exalted as priest over all the children of the world. [. . .] [6][. . .] and his sons after him for all the eternal generations [. . .] [7][. . .]

Amram commits the vision to writing and eventually returns to Egypt to give the writing to his family.

Then I awoke from the sleep of my eyes and [I] wrote down the vision [. . .] [8][. . .] from the land of Canaan and it so happened to me, that when he said [. . .] [9][. . .] Miriam and afterw[ards] to Kohath [. . .]

4Q546 Frag. 14 [1]And now, my son, I [. . .] [2]to your people; [and] you shall kno[w . . .] [3]to the entrance of your house u[pon] them [. . .] [4]And now, my sons, hear what [I am commanding you . . .]

—E.M.C.

139. Hur and Miriam

4Q549

Two small fragments are all that remain of an Aramaic work that may have retold the stories of Exodus in the same way that *Tales of the Patriarchs* (text 4) retells those of Genesis. The first part of frag. 2 tells of the death of an unknown individual—perhaps the first husband of Miriam, older sister of Moses and Aaron. After a paragraph break, further details about her family follow, including the mention of a cousin, Sithri.

Next the author turns to Hur. He apparently combines two biblical figures who may originally have been distinct: the Hur who was the hero of the battle against Amalek (Exod. 17:10, 12) and the Hur of Exodus 31:2, who was the father of Uri (in our work's l. 10, spelled "Ur") and grandfather of the famed craftsman Bezalel. Josephus (*Ant.* 3.54) knew of a tradition that made Hur the husband of Miriam, and our author may have seen things the same way. That would be the reason for his mentioning Hur at this juncture. Given the text's fragmentary character, however, this line of interpretation is a bit speculative, and other ways of understanding the work may be possible.

Frag. 2 [1][. . . H]ur, and he shall eat, he and hi[s] sons [and . . . and Jochebed his wife, when] [2]eternal sleep [ca]me to her [. . . they came] [3]unto him and they found hi[m . . .] [4]his sons and the sons of h[is] brother [. . .] [5]they returned immediately [. . . After this, Amram] [6]departed to his eternal home [just as it was] written [in the writing of the words of the vision.]

[7]And fr[om the wedding feast of Uzziel were] [8]ten [months.] And with Miriam he fathered a people[, three sons, Mishael and Elizaphan] [9]and Sithri.

Then Hur took [as a wife . . . daughter of . . .] [10]and with her fathered Ur; and Aaro[n took as a wife Elizabeth and he fathered] [11]four sons with her, [Nadab, Abihu, Eleazar, and Ithamar . . .]

—M.G.A.

140. The Tale of Patireza and Bagasraw

4Q550, 4Q550a–d

Although the Israelites' ideal place was the Holy Land, they were forced to spend time outside it, most notably during the time of bondage in Egypt and the exile in Babylon. Both periods served as the settings for what scholars call "court stories," tales set within the royal court of a foreign land in which members of a despised ethnic group (usually the ones telling the story) prove their worth or cleverness. Such is the tale of Joseph in the court of Pharaoh (Gen. 38–50) and also the stories about Daniel and his friends in the time of Nebuchadnezzar and his successors (Dan. 1–6; ca. 600–540 B.C.E.). The entire book of Esther is devoted to the story of how the pious Esther and her uncle Mordecai foil the plans of the evil Haman and save the Jews from genocidal destruction in the court of Ahasuerus (Xerxes) in the time of the Persian Empire (fifth century B.C.E.).

These tales do not exhaust the supply of court stories from the ancient Near East; other cultures had them too. But it also appears that Jews produced more tales of this sort than are preserved in the Bible, and one of them is the *Tale of Patireza and Bagasraw.* It takes place, like Esther, in the Persian court, and the king whose court provides the setting is also Xerxes. But what exactly happens in this tale is not clear. Two main figures appear, Patireza and Bagasraw. Both names are Persian, and both men are rewarded by the Persian king for unspecified services, but it is not clear what their relationship is or even whether they belong to the same story. However, the following summary, though largely hypothetical, is consistent with the extant fragments and resembles the kind of plot that is normal in the court story.

Patireza was in charge of making the royal garments for King Darius; at some point, Patireza was able to help Darius in some way, and the king recorded this favor in his records. When his son Xerxes learned of the episode, he decided to show favor to Patireza's son.

A certain Bagoshi had adopted or employed the Jew Bagasraw, who may in fact have been Patireza's son and who rejected (or received) the riches of Bagoshi. In some unspecified way, Bagasraw, either with or against Bagoshi's wishes, comes to the attention of the king and receives the royal acclamation. The king commands all to honor Bagasraw and to revere his God.

Bagasraw hears about his father, Patireza.

4Q550 [1][. . . everyone] would obey Patireza your father [. . .] [2]and among those who make the royal garments [. . .] to do [3]the business of the king, according to everything that [. . .].

The Persian king discovers the service Patireza performed for his father.

At that very time [4]the king was patient [and read all the re]cords of his father. They were read before him, and among [5]the books was found a scroll [seal]ed with seven seal[s] with the signet of Darius his father. On the outside it said [6][. . . "Dar]ius the king to those who exercise authority in the land, greeting." It was opened and read, and the following was found written in it: "Darius the king [8][to the kings who] will reign after me and to those who exercise authority, gr[eet]ing. Let it be known to you that all oppression and deceit [. . ."]

The king decides to reward the family of Patireza. "Ushai king of Tamar" is not known elsewhere, but the name Ushai appears in several ancient inscriptions.

4Q550a [. . .] [1]a man, therefore the king knows if there is [. . .] [2]and his good name will not perish [and his] loyalty [will be rewarded . . .] [3]the king [asked], "Does Patireza have a son?" And [they said . . .] [4]the fear of the house of [. . .] fell on him [. . .] [5]Ushai king of Tam[ar] and it will be given [. . .] [6]my house and my possessions to whatever may be [given . . .] [7]are you able to take upon yourself your father's business? [. . .]

4Q550b [1][. . .] [U]shai king of Tamar to Sharhata his [wife . . .] [2][. . .] Patireza [your] father from the day that he stood over [the] work [from] before the king [. . .] [3][. . .] with [him and] he served honestly and relia[bly be]fore him [. . .] [4][. . .] and Ushai said [. . .] [5][. . . clothe] him in pur[ple . . .]

Bagasraw promises to serve Bagoshi. A story of some kind of procession of gifts follows. In the end, Bagasraw receives all the benefits that were rightfully his.

4Q550c Col. 1 [1]For you know [. . .] in the sins of my fathers [2]that they committed before you [. . .] and I spent a long time [. . .] a man, [3]a Jew, from the princes of the k[ingdom . . .], standing before him and asking [. . .] a good [deed] [4]the good man has done [. . .] what shall I do for you, since you know [. . . What is] possib[le] [5]for a man like me to answer [a man] like you, standing in the place where you stand? [. . .] [6]Ho[we]ver, whatever you w[an]t, command me, and when [you d]ie, I will bury you [. . .] [7]dwelling in everything, it may be that you would bri[ng] my work be[fore . . . al]l that [. . .] **Col. 2** [1][. . .] decreed [. . .] and the se[con]d ones passed [. . .] [2][. . . the] plag[ues, and the t]hird ones passed [. . .] in the clothing of [the kingdom . . .] [3][. . .] a crown of gol[d on] his [he]ad; and the fifth ones passe[d . . .] [4][. . .] he alone [. . . and the s]ixth ones passed [. . .] [5][. . . all si]lver and all gold, [all the posses]sions that [belong]ed to Bagoshi, in double measure [. . .] [6]and the seve[nth ones passed . . . then] Bagasraw came in pe[a]ce to the court of the king [. . .] [7][. . .] Bagosh[i . . . was ki]lled, then [Ba]gasraw entered the co[u]rt of the king [. . .] [8]so he took him by [the] hand [. . .] on [his] head [. . .] and he kissed him. He raised his voice and said, "Ba[gas]raw, Bagasraw, from [. . ."]

The king recommends to his court and people the worship and respect of Bagasraw's God.

Col. 3 [1][. . .] the Most High that you all revere and [wo]rship; He rules over [all the ear]th. All who will, draw near in honor to [. . .] [2][. . .] everyone who says anything [ba]d about Bagasraw [. . .] shall be killed, so that there may be no [. . .] [3][. . .] I for[ev]er [. . . everything] that is proper [. . .] twice. And the king said, "Let it be writ[ten . . .] [4][. . . r]ule[r . . .] they are in the great court of the king [. . .] [5][. . . those] who arise after Bagasr[aw] will read in thi[s] book [. . .] [6][. . . who says anything b]ad, the bad shall come upon his [head . . .]

—E.M.C.

141. Aramaic Fragments

4Q551, 4Q569

These texts are too fragmentary in context to understand fully, but enough remains to show that they bear some similarities to texts contained in the Hebrew Bible.

The wording of this text seems to be from the story of the murdered concubine in Judges 19:22–30.

4Q551 [2][. . . t]hen an old man [. . .] he was from [3][Ephraim, named . . .] son of Jonathan son of [Jo]shua son of Ishmael son of [. . . there is no fear of God] in this place [4][. . .] And all the men of the city gather around the house, and say to him, Bring out [the man . . .] God, and they say [5][. . . sai]d to them, My brothers, do not act wickedly [. . .] here [6][. . . up]on [. . .] peace [. . .] peace to them [7][. . .] [8][. . . because of] this [. . .]

This text, although containing only fragments of sentences, seems to be of the genre of proverbial wisdom.

4Q569 Frag. 1 [2]let him acquire a physician [. . .] [3][. . .] [4]and do not be humbled [. . . if you are exalted] [5]and you become like a ruler [. . .] [6]if your master loves [. . .] [7]to kill you [. . .] [8]remember the poor in [. . .] [9]teach your sons [. . .]
—E.M.C.

142. The Vision of the Four Trees

4Q552–553

The book of Daniel on two occasions foretells the fate of four kingdoms to come: once with the metaphor of a great statue made of four different materials (Dan. 2) and once through a vision of four beasts (Dan. 7). The "four kingdom" motif goes back to ancient Near Eastern tradition, and there are examples of the pattern in Roman and Persian texts as well.

In Daniel, the four kingdoms are Babylon, Media, Persia, and Greece. After the fall of the Greek kingdoms to Roman power, Daniel's four kingdoms were reinterpreted to refer to Babylon, Media-Persia, Greece, and Rome, and this interpretation lasted as long as the Roman (and Byzantine) Empire itself. It entered into Jewish tradition, and later exegetes of the Bible found the same four kingdoms in other texts. For example, the phrase "a great and frightful darkness fell upon Abraham" (Gen. 15:12) is paraphrased in a later Aramaic translation as follows: "Four kingdoms are going to subdue the children of Abraham. Frightful is Babylon; darkness is Media; great is Greece; and fell is Edom [= Rome], which is going to fall, never to rise again" (*Targum Pseudo-Jonathan*).

Along with the four-kingdom tradition is a common metaphor of trees standing for kings or kingdoms. The parable of the trees in Judges (9:7–15) represents different trees as types of rulers. The king of Egypt is compared to a great tree cut down (Ezek. 31), as is Nebuchadnezzar (Dan. 4).

The *Vision of the Four Trees* combines both these motifs. It probably belongs to the cycle of stories about Daniel; angels are mentioned, and so is a king, and it is not clear whether Daniel or the king has seen a vision. In any case, the vision is of four trees that symbolize four kingdoms. But which four? The only identification that survives is of the first tree, which has a double identification. It is Babylon, but it also "rules over Persia." If this is a device to combine kingdoms, then the first kingdom would be Babylon-Persia, the second Greece, the third Rome, and the fourth tree-kingdom may represent the kingdom of God.

The setting of the vision: present are angels, a king, and a seer who speaks in the first person.

4Q552 Frag. 2 Col. 1 [5][. . . the li]ght of the angels who were [6][. . .] he said to them, "All of it will be [7][. . . lan]d of the south is this [. . .] [8]and the king said to me, Because of this [9][. . .] how all this came to pass. They were standing [. . .] [10][. . .] he said will happen, and explaining to them openly [11][. . .] their lords and [. . .] one of them [12][. . .] **Col. 2** [. . . on them] [1]the brightness was resting, and four trees [. . .]

The first tree, which represents Babylon-Persia.

[The] [2]tree rose and the other trees were far away from it.

He said [. . . "Do you see] [3]the form?"

And I said, "Yes, I see it and I am lo[okin]g at [it." . . .] [4]the tree that I should pay [attention to . . .] [5]and I asked him, "What is your name?" And he said to me, "Babylon."

[And I said to him,] [6]"[Yo]u are the one who rules over Persia."

The second tree (Greece?).

And [I saw] [7][another tr]ee [and] I looked to the West, to [. . .] and he said [8]to [. . .], and I asked him, "What is [your] name?" [And he said to me . . .] [9]And I said to him, "You are the one wh[o rules over all . . .] [10]the strongholds of the sea and over the harbor [. . ."]

The third tree may represent the power of Rome.

[And I saw] [11]the third tree [and] I said to [him . . .]

The fourth tree is not explicitly mentioned in the remaining sections. It may be referred to in these fragments.

4Q553 Frag. 8 Col. 1 [1][. . .] by itself [2][. . .] from Moses [3][. . .] the place which [4][. . .] its [ru]ler to be called [5][. . .] by the name of [. . .] **Col. 2** [1]its appearance and [. . .] [2]mighty of power [. . .] [3]from among them [. . .] [4]to me [the] third one [said . . .]

Frag. 9 [. . .] [1]beauty in the heavens to rul[e . . .]

Frag. 10 [2][the] ruler of the tre[es . . .]

—E.M.C.

143. A Vision of the New Jerusalem

4Q554–555, 5Q15, 11Q18, 1Q32, 2Q24

In the year 586 B.C.E., the armies of Nebuchadnezzar, king of Babylon, destroyed the Temple of the Lord that King Solomon had built in Jerusalem. Some of the best religious thinkers in ancient Israel, such as the prophet Jeremiah, saw in this event the welcome judgment of God on a nation that had placed too much reliance on external worship and not enough on the religion of the heart. Others equally pious, such as Ezekiel, agreed, but longed for the day when the God of Israel would restore to his people all that had been lost, giving them a new temple and temple city. Ezekiel himself contributed to this longing with a vision of a new temple and a new Jerusalem (Ezek. 40–48), but he was not alone. The book of Isaiah speaks of a new Jerusalem encrusted with jewels (54:11–12), and the book of Tobit speaks of a time when "Jerusalem and the temple of God will be rebuilt in splendor, just as the prophets have said" (14:6–7).

The new Temple built after the Israelites returned from exile in the fifth century B.C.E. was only a modest substitute for these dreams, and those who remembered the first Temple wept when they saw the foundation laid for the new one (Ezra 3:12). There were still dreams of another, greater temple. In the first century B.C.E., Herod the Great doubtless depended on widespread fascination with such a dream to provide popular support for his building programs within Jerusalem, including a new, magnificent Temple.

The Qumran texts testify to this continuing fascination of the idea of a new Jerusalem with two examples: The *Temple Scroll* (text 155) and the present text. *A Vision of the New Jerusalem,* reconstructed from several scrolls, is a detailed description of a Jerusalem-to-be given by an angel to an unknown recipient quite in the manner of Ezekiel's vision, but differing in many details. No description of the temple itself survives in the fragments, but the temple is mentioned several times.

The dimensions of the visionary city and buildings are too large to be realistic. The city, for example, measures 140 *stades* on the east and the west and 100 *stades* on the north and south. In modern terms these dimensions would be 18.67 miles by 13.33 miles (a *stade* is 2/15 of a mile). This new Jerusalem would have been larger than any ancient city and could only have been built by divine intervention, like the even larger city beheld by a later visionary in the New Testament book of Revelation (21:9–27).

The description of the twelve gates of the city, each named for one of the twelve tribes, as in Ezekiel's prophecy (48:30–35) and the vision of Revelation (21:12–13).

4Q554 Frag. 2 Col. 1 [9][. . .] sixteen [. . .] [10][. . .] and all of them each facing [11][the other . . . he measured from the] northeastern [corner] [12][to the south, to the first gate], thirty-five stades, and the name [13][of this gate is called the gate of] Simeon.

From [this gate to] the middle gate [14][he measured thirty-five stades] and the name of this gate is [call]ed the gate of [15][Levi.

From this gate he measured to the] south, thirty-five stades, [16][and the name of this gate is called the gate of Judah.

From] this gate he measured to the [17][southeastern] corner, [thirty-five stades,] and he measured from this corner westwards [18][twenty-five stades and the name of this gate] is called the gate of Joseph.

[19][He measured from this gate to the middle gate,] 25 [stades] and the name [20][of this gate is called Benjamin.

From] this gate he measured to the [west] gate [21][twenty-five stades and the name of this gate is called] the gate of Reuben.

[From] this [ga]te [22][he measured to the southwestern corner twenty-five stades] and from this corner he measured to **Col. 2 (=2Q24, 5Q15)** [1][the north, thirty-five stades, and the name of this gate is called the [2]gate of Issachar.

He measured from this gate to the middle gate, [3]thirty-five stades, and the name of] this [gate] is called the gate of Zebulun.

From this gate [4][he measured to the north gate, thirty-five stades, and the name of this gate is] [5][called the gate of Gad.

From this gate he measured to the northwest corner] [6][thirty-five stades and from this corner] he measured [to the east,] [7]25 stades, and the name [of this gate is called the gate of Dan.

He measured] from this gate [to the] middle [gate] [8][twenty-five] stades [and the name of] this [gate is] c[all]ed the gate of Naphtali.

From this [9]gate he measured to the [east] gate, 25 stades, and the name of this gate is called [10]the gate of Asher.

He measu[red from] this [ga]te to the eastern corner [11]25 stades.

The city itself was divided into square blocks like a checkerboard. Each block was surrounded by a spacious street, and the city as a whole was divided by larger streets, three passing from east to west, two passing from north to south.

[12]Then he brought me into the city, and mea[sured all the] city blocks. Length and breadth, they measured [13]51 staffs by 51 staffs, making a square a[ll around], 350 cubits, [14]7 cubits to each side. Each block had a sidewalk around it, bordering the street, [15]three staffs, that is, 21 cubits.

So he showed me the mea[su]rement of all the blocks: between each block was [16]a street six staffs in width, that is, 42 cu[bits.] The main streets that passed [17]from east to west were ten [staffs]. The width of the street was [18]70 cubits, for two of them. A third street, which was on the [north] of the temple, he measured at [19]18 staffs in width, that is, 1[2]6 cubits.

The width of [20]the streets that go from sou[th to north, for two of them,] nine staffs, [21]with 4 cubits to each street, making [sixty-seven] cubits. He measured [the middle street in the] middle [22]of the city. Its width was [thirteen staffs and one cubit, that is nine[ty-two cubits.]

[23]And every street and the city itself [was paved in white stone.]

The angelic guide now shows the visionary the structure of the outer walls, its gates, towers, and the stairs providing access to the towers.

5Q15 Frag. 1 Col. 1 [7][. . .] marble and onyx [8][and he showed me the measurements of the e]ighty [portals. Their] width was two staffs, [fourteen cubits . . .] [9][. . .] Every gate had two doors of stone. Their width was [one] staff, [seven cubits . . .] [10][He showed me the measurements of the] twelve [. . .] The width of their gates was three staffs, [twenty-one] cubit[s. . . . Every] [11][gate had two doors]. The width of [the] doors was one and a half staffs, [t]en and a half cubit[s . . .]

[12][Two tow]ers [flanked each gate], one o[n the r]ight and one on the l[ef]t. Their breadth and length [was the same, five by five staffs,] [13][that is, thirty-five cubits. The stairs that went up next to] the gate on the inner side, to the [righ]t of the towers, is of the same height as the to[wers. Their width is five cubits. The towers [14]and the stairs were five by five staffs, plus five cu]bits, [f]orty [cubits] for each side of [the] door.

The description now moves to give more detail about the structure of the city blocks.

4Q554 Frag. 2 Col. 3 [12][He then showed me the measurements of the gates of the city blocks. Their width was two] staffs, [fourteen cubits,] [13]and the width of the [. . .] s, its measurement [. . .] cubits. [He then measured] the width [of each atrium: [14]t[wo] staf[fs], fourteen [c]ubits, and the ceiling, one cubit.

[Then he measured over each] at[rium] [15]its doors. Then he measured inside the atrium: its length was 13 cubits, and its width ten cubits.

[16]He brought me into the atrium and there was another atrium. The gate by the inner wall on the right side [17]had the same measurements as the outer gate. Its width was four cubits. Its height was 7 cubits. It had two doors, and in fr[ont of] [18]this g[a]te was an entranceway. Its width was one staff, seven cubits, and its length, passing inward, two staffs, [19]14 cu[bits;] and its height, two staffs, 14 cubits.

Now a gate opposite the gate opened into the bloc[k] [20]and its measurements were like those of the outer gate. On the left of this entrance he showed me a spiral staircase go[ing u]p: its w[idth] [21]and its length was a single measurement, two staffs by two, fourteen cubits; and g[ates opposite the gates] [22]were of a like measurement.

There was a pillar [in the very center] that the stairs ascended around. Its w[idth and its length] **5Q15 Frag. 1 Col. 2** [4][were six cubits by six,] [5]square. The stairs that went up around it were four cubits wide and they spiraled up[wards to] a height of t[wo staf]fs until [. . .]

A description of the houses within each block.

[6]Then he brought me [within] the city block and showed me the houses in it. From gate to ga[te there were fifteen houses, eigh]t in on[e direction to the corner] [7][and se]ven from the c[o]rner to the other gate. Such was their width. The length of [the] hous[es was three staffs, twenty[-one cubits, and their width] [8]was two [staff]s, fourteen cubits. The rooms likewise were [t]wo [staffs high,] fourteen c[ubit]s, [9][and their middle gate] was t[w]o

staffs, fourte[en] cubits [wide. And he measured the width of the mid]dle of the house and the interior of [the] r[ooms; four] [10][cubits. It was one staff, seven cubits, in length and height.

And he showed me the measurement of the houses of] dining. The site was [ninet]een cubits [long] [11]and twe[lve cubits wide.] A house of [t]wenty-t[w]o beds [and el]even closed windows above the [beds] [12][and next to it an outer gutter. And he measured] the window two [cu]bits high [its width . . .] and the thickness of the width of the [first] wall [. . .] [13][cubits . . . bor]ders of [the] platforms was nineteen [cubits long] and [twelve cubits] wide [14][. . .] open [windows, two staffs, [15]fourteen cubits . . .]

Additional description of the city towers.

4Q554 Frag. 3 Col. 2 [13][. . .] its foundation. It was two staffs [wid]e, [14]four[teen] cu[bi]ts, and it was seven staffs high, forty-nine cubits. All of it was [15]built of elec[trum] and sapphire and chalcedony; and its beams were of gold, and its towers numbered one thousand [16][four hun]dred and thirty-two. Their length and width were the same measurement [17][. . .] and their height was ten staffs, [18][seventy cubits . . . two staffs,] 14 [cubits . . .]

The visionary also sees the priests at their work in the temple. The fragments that follow combine regulation—what the priests ought to do—with narrative—what the visionary saw the priests doing.

A description of the change of priestly courses. This text may reflect a tradition of twenty-six priestly courses instead of twenty-four, as in the War Scroll *(text 11; see also "A Reader's Guide to the Qumran Calendar Texts.")*

11Q18 Frag. 15 [1][. . . he shall not serve in] the course again, unless there shall be [. . .] [2][. . .] and all who will be finishing their weeks [of service . . .] [3][. . .] their brothers will enter in their place, four hundred [. . .] [4][. . .] He said to me, For twenty-six [. . .] [5][. . . Ho]ly of Holies and not [. . .]

A description of part of the clothing of the high priest.

Frag. 14 Col. 2 [. . . the likeness of the leaves of a] [1]vine when it separates from [the] branches [. . .] [2]when they are planted. The fif[th] crown [. . . likeness of the] [3]interior of the henna flower; and the sixth crown

[. . .] [4]the seventh crown, as the likeness of the rose blossom [. . .] [5]the high priest shall wear [. . .]

Details of the sacrificial ritual.

Frag. 13 [1][. . .] with its four feet and he flayed the bull [. . .] [2][he wa]shed its feet and its entrails and he salted all of it [. . .] [3][he] placed it on the fire and brought the purest fine flour [. . .] [4][a fo]urth of a seah and he placed it on the altar, all of it [. . .] [5][a fou]rth of a seah and he poured a libation into [the] channels [. . .] [6][. . .] and the meat mixed together [. . .] [7][. . . every] side.

Further details of the priestly activities.

2Q24 Frag. 4 (+ 11Q18 Frag. 13) [1]their meat [. . .] [2][. . .] for an offering acceptable [to the Lord . . .] [3][then] they will enter the temple [. . .] [4]eight seahs, fine flou[r . . .] [5]then they shall carry the bread [. . .] [6]first upon the al[tar . . . then they shall put the bread in two] [7]rows on the ta[ble . . .] [8]two rows of br[ead . . .] [9]of the bread, and they shall take [the] bread [outside the temple to the south-] [10]west, and [the bread] shall be divided [. . . and they will be accepted . . .] [11]and while I watched, [the bread was distributed to eighty-four priests . . . from all seven sections of the tables of . . .] [12]the marks [written . . .] [13]the elders among them, and fourteen pr[iests . . .] [14]the priests. Two loaves of bread that were [covered with incense . . . and while] [15]I was watching, one of the two loaves was given to the [high] pr[iest . . . another priest was] [16]with him. The other loaf was given to the second one who was standing opposite [. . .] [17][. . .] While I was watching, there was given to al[l the priests . . .] [18][. . .] one ram of the flock for every one [of them . . .]

The extant text concludes with a prophecy of the kingdoms to come, leading up to the final apocalyptic showdown between the Gentile nations and Israel, in which Israel finally triumphs. The rebuilding of the temple would not be complete unless Israel as a whole had returned to its former glory.

4Q554 Frag. 3 Col. 3 [14][. . . shall rise up] [15]in place of it, and the kingdom of P[ersia . . . and then shall rise up] [16]the Kittim in place of it. All these kingdoms shall appear one after another [. . .] [17]many others, and they will put with them [. . .] [18]with them Edom and Moab and the

Ammonites [. . .] [19]of the whole land of Babylon, which not [. . .] [20]and they shall do evil to your descendants until the time of [. . .] [21]in all [the peoples] the kingdom of [. . .] [22]and among them Gentiles sha[ll d]o [. . .]

—E.M.C.

144. A Text About the Maccabees?

4Q556

This fragment falls into the genre of history written as prophecy, as does, for instance, *A Vision of the Son of God* (text 50). Like that text, it apparently relates the events of the persecution of the Jews by Antiochus Epiphanes. During his reign, according to 1 Maccabees, the inhabitants of Judah were commanded to worship idols and eat swine's flesh (1:47) and their ancestral laws were abolished (1:52–61). The Gentiles complied (1:43), as did many of the Jews. Those who did not obey were forced to eat the flesh of swine (2 Macc. 7; 4 Maccabees), while others rebelled or fled to the wilderness (1 Macc. 2).

The persecution of the Jews by Antiochus.

Frag. 14 [1][. . .] the peoples will obey [2][. . .] which is an idol, and they will dwell [3][. . .] the king of Egypt [4][. . .] lord they [5–6][. . .] by decree not [7][. . .] which are left [8][. . . commanded] to eat the flesh of swine [9][. . .] his kingdom and also [10][. . . they fled] from before the wicked [11][. . .] to the land of desolation [12][. . .] Sinai and that king [. . .]

The faithful will flee or be captured. All has been foretold in prophecy.

Frag. 1 [1][. . .] they will flee [. . .] [2][. . .] to Mount Sinai [. . .] [3][. . . against] the army he will set his face [. . .] [4][. . .] and he will burn with fi[re . . .] the bad fire [. . .] [5][. . .]and before him and will catch [. . .] and he will seize him [. . .] [6][. . .] the new land that he took captive. All that he [. . .] [7][. . .] concerning this the prophet had spoken, who [. . .] [8][. . .] because of the food, for it will be [. . .] [9][. . .] from Joppa to Mount [. . .]

The Maccabean resistance is apparently foretold.

Frag. 3 [2][. . .] and he believed in G[od . . .] [3][. . .] peoples which the book of [. . .] [4][. . .] the [Edomites?] and the Moabites, the Amalek[ites . . .] [5][. . .] we shall destroy them [. . .] [6][. . .] the righteous [. . .] [7][. . .] saying, Behold these [. . .] [8][. . .] is this one [. . .] [9][. . .] "then one shall pursue a th[ousand" (Josh. 23:10) . . .] [10][. . .] they will not leave [. . .]

—E.M.C.

145. A Biblical Chronology

4Q559

Early in the transmission of the biblical books, anonymous scribal copyists began to calculate the chronology of various events about which the Bible gives numerical information. For example, these scholars began to add up the numbers given in Genesis. They soon realized that, as presented in text that had come down to them, these numbers imply that some of Noah's ancestors lived through the Flood. Yet Genesis explicitly says the opposite: none survived other than those on the ark. The scholars solved the problem straightforwardly and efficiently. They simply changed the numbers. The unchanged version of the numbers survives in the text of the Greek version of the Old Testament known as the Septuagint (Gen. 5). For the most part our modern Bibles translate the traditional text and therefore present the changed numbers.

Thus we know that very early on the chronological concerns that motivated the present scroll were present in priestly circles. Anonymous scholars changed the biblical text (though the unchanged form survived as well), and then later other anonymous scholars wrote books in which they tried to solve the chronological problems of one form of the text or the other. Such writings are known as chronographs. The present work is one of the very earliest that has survived and probably dates to the late third century B.C.E. The problems with which our author wrestled were notorious difficulties among ancient scholars, Jewish and Christian. These problems are (1) the length of the Israelites' sojourn in Egypt; (2) the chronology of the wilderness wanderings; and (3) the chronology of the period of the judges. In the case of the first problem, the difficulty was to resolve the apparent conflict between the time given for the sojourn by Genesis 15:13–14 (400 years) and that stated in Exodus 12:40 (430 years). For the wilderness wanderings, the difficulty was to derive any sort of chronology at all. What happened when? The biblical text almost completely lacks time statements for that series of episodes in Exodus and Numbers. In the case of the judges, the main difficulty was to rationalize the implications of a straightforward adding of the time periods given in the book of Judges (410 years). This number presents problems when compared with 1 Kings 6:1, which encompasses all the judges and many other events in a period spanning just 480 years.

The problem of the length of time spent by the Israelites in Egypt. In order to calculate this period, the author considers the chronology of Jacob's life and the ages of the patriarchs when they fathered particular sons.

Col. 1 7[. . . After I]saac [blessed him,] Jac[ob fled] 8[and entered, at the age of fifty-]five, the la[nd of the sons of] the Ea[st.] 9[. . . He s]erved [fo]urteen years for [Leah] 10[and Rachel . . .]

Col. 2 3[. . . Abraham was] nin[ety-nine ye]ars old 4[when he fathered Isaac. Is]aac was [sixty years o]ld [when he fathered] 5[Jacob. Jacob was] sixty-five y[ears old when he fathered Levi.] 6[He gave to Levi the Book of the Words of] Enoch [to preserve and pass on] 7[to his own descendants. Levi was thirty-f]ive when he fa[thered Kohath.] 8[Kohath was twenty-ni]ne when he fathered Am[r]am. Amr[am was] 9[one hundred and twenty-three when he fathered] Aaron. Aaro[n] left Egy[pt] 10[with the priests,] who [totaled] eleven thousand five hundred and thirty-six.

The chronology of certain events during the forty years of wilderness wandering.

Col. 3 2[. . .] From the lan[d of Egypt until] 3[Kor]ah [arose and rebelled was five ye]ars. [Aaron died] 4[and did not cross the Jo]rdan. From Kade[sh until the plains of] 5[Moab was] thirty-f[i]ve [years.]

The period of Joshua and Eleazar the son of Aaron and the subsequent time of the judges.

In Gilgal, [five (?)] ye[ars.] 6[In Shiloh,] twenty years. And after [Eleazar the son of Aaron] died, 7Cushan-rishathaim the king of [Aram-] 8[Naharaim,] ei[g]ht [year]s; Othniel the so[n of Kenaz,] 9for[ty years;] Eglon the king of Moab, [eighteen] ye[ars]; 10[Eh]ud the son of Gera, eighty years; Sham[gar the son of Anath,] **Col. 4** 1[one (?) year; Jabin the king of Canaan, twenty years; Deborah] 2the [prophetess and] Barak the so[n of Abinoam, forty years; Gideon the son] 3[of Joash,] forty [ye]ars; To[la the son of Puah, twenty-three years; Jair] 4the [Gileadite, twenty-two] years [. . .]
—M.O.W.

146. An Exorcism

4Q560

Some years ago Morton Smith wrote a book entitled *Jesus the Magician*. Smith gathered all the evidence of the New Testament and other witnesses to Jesus and tried to show that Jesus was essentially just a magician, a wonder-worker of the sort known from Greco-Roman antiquity who operated partly with illusion and sleight-of-hand and partly with psychological techniques. Smith's book was controversial and ultimately convinced few scholars—yet he had raised important issues for our understanding of the Gospels.

A principal difficulty in assessing the "magical" aspects of the Gospels has been the lack of Jewish magical writings dating to the time and coming from the place where these works were composed. The present work, however, is just such a writing. With this work we hold in our hands a part of the resources of a Jewish magician of the time of Jesus. This formula probably derives from a "recipe book" that contained other, similar formulas as well. Such recipe books are well known from Mesopotamia.

The present formula mentions concerns common to other magical texts: potential problems with childbirth, demons and the diseases that they brought on, sleep or dreams (a common realm of demonic activity—especially nightmares), and perhaps the safety of possessions. Particularly striking is the mention of the Fever-demon, for this same demon appears in the New Testament. Luke 4 tells the story of Peter's mother-in-law, who was sick when Jesus came to visit. Luke 4:39 reports that Jesus healed her and can be translated: "Then he stood over her and rebuked the Fever-demon, and it left her."

The text's reference to a midwife probably reflects a belief similar to that spelled out in other magical texts, which contain prohibitions against certain demons who intend to snatch a child's life by appearing as a midwife, wet nurse, or nanny. The mention of earth and clouds in col. 2 may designate spheres within which the given demons move; alternately, it may be part of an incantation that refers to those areas from which evil spirits are banned.

Col. 1 [2][. . .] the midwife, the punishment of those who bear children, any evil madness or d[emon . . .] [3][. . . I adjure you, all who en]ter into the body: the male Wasting-demon and the female Wasting-demon [4][. . . I adjure you by the name of the Lord, "He Who re]moves iniquity and transgression" (Exod. 34:7), O Fever-demon and Chills-demon and Chest Pain–demon [5][. . . You are forbidden to disturb by night using dreams or

by da]y during sleep, O male Shrine-spirit and female Shrine-spirit, O you demons who breach [6][walls . . . w]icked [. . .] **Col. 2** [2]before h[im . . .] [4]before him and [. . .] [5]And I, O spirit, adjure [you against . . .] [6]I adjure you, O spirit, [that you . . .] [7]On the earth, in clouds [. . .]
—M.O.W.

147. An Aramaic Horoscope

4Q561

A law in medieval Spain stated that if two men were accused of a crime and it was not clear which was guilty, the uglier man should die. The assumption was that character proves itself through outward appearance. This is the same assumption by which the present text operates. Properly speaking, this work is not a horoscope at all, for it contains no mentions of the zodiac or related ideas. This is a physiognomic writing similar to *A Horoscope Written in Code* (text 35). Physiognomy was a "science" whose purpose was to divine individuals' character and destiny by studying their physical appearance. The surviving fragmentary portions of 4Q561 preserve parts of the descriptions and analyses for five individuals. The final column seems to be describing a time of national crisis in the "end time," perhaps associated with the rise of a particular individual whose physical attributes were detailed in portions of the scroll that failed to survive.

Description of the first individual. The reference to this person's shoulder may have to do with bodily symmetry, a concern of the Greco-Roman physiognomic treatises.

Col. 1 (Frags. 10 + 6) [6][Anyone whose . . . is between . . .] and reddish-yellow, [. . .] [7][whose forehead (?)] will b[e] [gl]obular and round, [. . .] [8]his [. . . will b]e [. . .] The hair of his head [. . .] [9][. . .] his shoulder [. . .] [10][. . .] they will be: concerning [his spirit (?) . . .] [11][. . .] but not a great man [. . .]

The second individual. This person possesses the balanced physical qualities of the happy medium. Probably, therefore, the lost portions would have ascribed to him a generally positive spiritual temper.

Col. 2 (Frags. 5 + 1) [6]whose nose is between [long and sh]ort, whose ha[n]ds [7]are bro[a]d, whose thighs [are between] well formed [8]and thick, the sole of whose fee[t will be th]ick but not [9]exce[edingly so, . . .] whose foot [. . .] because [10][. . .] not [11][. . . to] come to an end [. . .]

The third individual. This description is similar to that of the fourth person in text 35, possessing elements of the "Golden Mean," but any reference to concomitant virtue has been lost.

Col. 3 (Frag. 4 Col. 1 + Frags. 7–8) [1][Anyone] whose [ ] is medium and not extreme, whose eyes are [2]neither light nor dark, whose nose is extended [3](and) attractive, whose teeth are even, whose beard [4]will be sparse [but] not ex[tre]mely so, whose limbs [5]are [s]mooth [and a]r[e between] thin and thick: [6][. . .] He will possess a [sp]irit [characterized by (?) . . .] [7][. . . He will suffer (?)] oppression.

A very fragmentary description of a fourth individual.

[8][Anyone whose body] hair [will be] thick [9]and extensive [. . .]

The fifth and final surviving individual description.

Col. 4 (Frag. 4 Col. 2) [1][Anyone whose . . .] will be [. . . whose] voice [. . .] [2]a voice full (?) and st[rong, whose nose is neither short] [3][no]r long [and] is [. . .] [4][and] the hair of whose beard is extremely thi[ck, whose limbs] [5]will be between thick and [thin] [6]and are delicat[e, the fingers of whose hands] [7]are rather thick, whose fingernails are [. . .] [8]Regarding his height and [. . .]

A time of apostasy in Israel, during which a remnant cleaves to a man who may have been described just previously in physiognomic terms. Details of a special sacrifice are part of this picture.

Col. 5 (Frag. 3) [2][and st]rengthening the [an]ointing, the great [. . .] [3]and strengthening first of all [. . .] [4]but they will forsake [. . .] and will go [. . .] [5][a remnant] will be left with him and [. . .] [6]upon him to go after [. . .] [7][fr]om them and strengthening them [. . .] [8][pa]ssing, the taxes of [their] labor [. . .] [9]and you will go [and] will hide in the heart of [. . .] [10][p]ure [and] a pur[e] turtledove [. . .] [11]he [will] find the time [. . .] [12][. . .] rams, and he will see [. . .] [13][. . .] in heaps, and [. . .]
—M.O.W.

148. An Aramaic Text on the Persian Period

4Q562

This text concerns the period of the return from exile in Babylon, where many from Judah had been taken into captivity at the time of Nebuchadnezzar (586 B.C.E.). With the conquest of Nebuchadnezzar's empire by Cyrus and the Persians, the captives were allowed to return to Judah beginning in 538 B.C.E. The present work takes that time of return and life in the Persian period as its setting. The author mentions a prophet—apparently Zechariah—along with priests, captives, and Susa (one of the several capital cities of the Persians).

Discussion of priests disqualified from the priesthood, a major issue of the early Persian period.

Frag. 1 1[. . .] wicked, who by the sword and in war [. . .] 2[. . .] they shall not be ordained to the priesthood [. . .] 3[. . . t]emple [. . .] two [. . .]

The fate of those who plundered Israel.

Frag. 2 1[. . .] that the prophet [Zechariah] said, [. . . 2"One who touches you] is as one who touches the apple of His eye" (Zech. 2:8). Therefore they shall be smitten 3[. . .] there, the place of the cemetery.

Priests, captives, and Susa.

Frag. 3 1[. . .] men from [. . .] 2[. . .] the seventh. (?) Behold, [they] shall gather 3[. . .] that is what we found, that 4[. . .] the priests and all the captives.

Frag. 9 3[. . .] Susa [. . .]

—M.O.W.

149. A Priestly Vision

4Q563

This Aramaic writing is so fragmentary that interpretation is difficult, but what can be made out is tantalizing. The person addressed may be a priest, since the word "service" in the first line is often used of priestly activities in the Temple. Someone is warning this priest about a very dangerous future. Just who is speaking is unclear. Perhaps the priest is experiencing a vision in which he receives this warning from God, or perhaps a prophet has come to him. If the warning is directed to a priest, then the traitorous actions of his relatives and children may be an aspect of future apostasy. Seen in this light, the work may be related to the *Words of Levi* (text 39).

Frag. 1 [3][. . .] you shall be summoned, together with all that you possess. Your service [. . .] [4][. . .] Fear them, because [. . .] [5][. . .] and in the latter part of your life, you shall be betrayed. After you, the bread of your sustenance shall be e[aten by] [6]your relatives. Beware of [your] children, [. . .] and scr[utin]ize them, le[st . . .] [7][ag]ainst you.
—M.O.W.

150. A Sectarian Rule

5Q13

The fragments of this manuscript apparently represent a charter or rule similar in construction to the *Charter of a Jewish Sectarian Association* (text 7). In fact, the writer actually quotes from the *Charter*—or this writing may itself be a strongly variant form of the *Charter.* The numerous other copies of the *Charter* do vary from one another, sometimes profoundly, so one cannot be sure which option is preferable.

A meditation on God's election (?).

Frag. 1 [2][. . .] the God of all [. . .] [3][. . .] He who establishes [. . .] [4][. . .] treasures [. . .] [5][. . .] by themselves, just as [. . .] [6][. . .] You chose from among the he[ave]nly beings and [. . .] [7][. . .]

and You were pleased with Noah [. . .] [8][. . .] of the death and [. . .] [9][. . .] God, to understand the works [of . . .] [10][. . .] the service of [. . .] [11][. . . to make k]nown the hidden [things . . .] [12][. . .] in the year You shall command him to [. . .] [13][. . .] for every Israelite man [. . .] [14][. . .]

A meditation on the history of God's elect.

Frag. 2 [4][. . .] forever [5][. . .] with Abraham [6][. . .] You made [kn]own to Jacob at Bethel [7][. . .] and Levi You [. . .] and You appointed him to bind [8][. . .] You chose [the sons of] Levi to go out [9][. . .] by their spirit before You [10][. . .] and after two [11][. . .] oath against [. . .]

The initiation ceremony preserved here is coincident with 1QS 3:4–5. For the regular observance of the ceremony (l. 4), see 1QS 2:19. (1QS column and line numbers below precede the lines they reference.)

Frag. 4 [1][. . . he shall st]and before the Overseer [. . .] [2][. . . (1QS 3:4) . . .] And ceremonies of atonement cannot restore his innocence, [neither cultic waters his purity. He cannot be sanctified by baptism in seas (3:5) and rivers] [3][nor purified by mere ritual bathing.] Unclean, unclean shall he be [all the] d[ays that he rejects the laws (3:6) of God] [4][. . .] (2:19) These they shall do annually, a[ll the days of Belial's dominion . . .] [5][. . .] to the spirit [. . .]

The examination of the members' works (1QS 5:24).

Frag. 5 [1][. . .] their deeds, their [. . .] [2][. . .] hand of Belial and he shall not [. . .] [3][. . . I]srael, when He establishes [. . .]
—M.G.A.

151. Apocryphal Psalms of David

11Q5–6, 4Q88, 4Q448

Among the more intriguing scrolls to come forth from the caves near Qumran are several copies of the Psalter that differ markedly from the book of Psalms we are accustomed to reading. The differences mainly concern the fifth division of the Psalter (Pss. 107–150), where these scrolls present the poems in an order and often with a wording that diverges from the traditional one. Perhaps more surprising, one finds interspersed among the known psalms additional, unfamiliar ones. A short prose summary paragraph at the end of 11Q5 attributes all these works, familiar and unfamiliar, to the "sweet psalmist of Israel," David.

One of the strange psalms previously known to scholars is from the Greek version of the Old Testament, where it is numbered Psalm 151 (recall that the book of Psalms printed in modern Bibles has only 150 psalms). Two of the other "new" psalms of David survived to our day among the Christians of Syria, denominated as Psalms 154–155. The other "new" psalms are just that—new, unknown before the discovery of the Dead Sea Scrolls.

The language of these compositions is a late form of biblical Hebrew—much later than the time of David—so the claim that David wrote them is spurious. Their attachment to the famous king exemplifies a wider trend in Second Temple Judaism whereby writings of unknown authors were attributed to great luminaries of the past. Thus people believed that many psalmlike works were written by David, whereas various wisdom writings were credited to Solomon, the wisest man in the Bible. Scholars think that these patterns of attribution began early in the years after the return from exile in Babylon. The headings of the biblical psalms were probably written in those years, five or six or centuries after David. A number of these headings relate the psalms they precede to episodes in David's life, events with which, so far as we know, these psalms originally had nothing to do. This process can be checked when one compares the headings of the psalms that have been passed down by various streams of tradition. The headings of the psalms in the Masoretic Text (the traditional Hebrew Bible) do not always agree with those of the Greek Old Testament, nor again with the headings in the Syriac Bible used by the ancient Christians of Syria. The apocryphal Davidic writings translated here give us a window into the fascinating and complex process by which emerged the book of Psalms that we know.

Psalm 151. A poetic account of David's choice as future ruler of Israel, inspired by 1 Samuel 16:1–13.

11Q5 Col. 28 [3]Hallelujah! A psalm of David, son of Jesse. I was smaller
than my brothers, youngest of my father's sons. So he made me a [4]shepherd
for his sheep, a ruler over his goats. My hands fashioned a pipe, my fingers a
lyre, [5]and I glorified the LORD. I said to myself, "The mountains do not
testify [6]to Him, nor do the hills proclaim." So—echo my words, O trees, O
sheep, my deeds! [7]Ah, but who can proclaim, who declare the deeds of the

Lord? God has seen all, [8]heard and attended to everything. He sent his prophet to anoint me, even Samuel, [9]to raise me up. My brothers went forth to meet him: handsome of figure, wondrous of appearance, tall were they of stature, [10]so beautiful their hair—yet the LORD God did not choose them. No, He sent and took me [11]who followed the flock, and anointed me with the holy oil. He set me as prince to His people, ruler over the children of His covenant.

Psalm 151B. This portion was apparently combined with the lines above in the Greek translation of Psalm 151 produced by the Jews of Alexandria, Egypt (the Septuagint). In the Qumran manuscript, however, it is a separate composition.

[13][Dav]id's first mighty d[ee]d after the prophet of God had anointed him. Then I s[a]w the Philistine, [14]throwing out taunts from the [enemy] r[anks . . .]

Psalm 154. This psalm, numbered among Syrian Christians of antiquity as Psalm 154, is a call to worship. A major presence in the psalm is Wisdom, personified as a woman.

*[Lift your voice and glorify God; when the general membership is assembled proclaim His glory. In the multitude of the upright glorify His name, and recount His greatness among the faithful. Bind] **Col. 18** [1]your souls to those who are good, even to the blameless, so to praise the Most High. Assemble together [2]to publish His victory, and be not idle declaring His might—His glory [3]to all the untutored. For to declare the LORD's glory was Wisdom given; to recount [4]His many deeds was she made known to humankind: To make known to the witless His might, [5]to teach the foolish His glory—those far from her gates, [6]those astray from her portals. For the Most High, Lord is He over [7]Jacob, and His majesty o'er all his works. Surely he who glorifies the Most High [8]finds favor as if bringing an offering; as though offering he-goats and calves, [9]as though fattening the altar with myriad burnt offerings; as a sweet savor at the hand of [10]the righteous. From the gates of the righteous is Wisdom's voice heard, from the pious assembly [11]her song. When they eat and are full she is cited, when they drink, bound together [12]as one: their conversation the Law of the Most High, their words but declaring His might. [13]How far from the wicked her word! To

*Portions preceding the first numbered line and most of ll. 16-17 are absent from the Hebrew scroll and are restored from Syriac. Several words in ll. 15-17 have been preserved in another very fragmentary Qumran scroll, 4Q448 (text 114), and that manuscript has been followed for those readings.

know her, from the haughty! Behold, [14]the eyes of the LORD look with compassion on the good. His mercy increases upon them who glorify, (with **4Q448)** [15]from an evil time will He rescue [their] soul. [Bless]ed is the LORD, redeeming the poor from the power of [16]enemies [deliv]ering [the blameless from wicked oppressors. He calls forth a horn out of Ja]cob, [17][from Israel,] a judge [of the peoples;] in Zion [will He desire] His habitation, ch[oosing Jerusalem forever.]

Psalm 155. Like Psalm 154, this psalm survived among Syriac-speaking Christians, but was unknown in Hebrew until discovered at Qumran. This poem is a partial acrostic—l. 5 begins with the second letter of the Hebrew alphabet, l. 7 with the third letter, then (roughly) each line following with the subsequent letters.

***Col. 24** [3]O LORD, I cry out to You, hearken to me. I spread my hands toward [4]Your holy dwelling, give ear and grant my request; [5]do not withhold my boon. Enlighten my soul, cast it not down; let it not be forsaken before the [6]wicked. May the Judge of truth turn back from me the wages of sin; O LORD, [7]judge me not as my sin requires, for none living is justified before You. [8]Grant me, O LORD, to understand Your Law, and teach me Your statutes, [9]that many may hear of Your deeds, and peoples extol Your glory. [10]Remember me, do not forget me; cast me not into hardship beyond bearing. [11]Remove afar off the sins of my youth, and let not my sins be remembered against me. [12]Cleanse me, O LORD, from evil's affliction and let it not again return. Let its [13]roots within me dry up, its le[av]es find no sustenance within. LORD, You are glory itself, [14]wherefore is my plea fulfilled in Your presence. To whom else might I cry to have it granted? [15]To men? [Their] strength has ebbed—my trust, O LORD, is bef[o]re You. [16]I cried out, "O LORD!" and He answered, [He healed] my broken heart. I grew drowsy and [17]slept; I dreamt, then [awoke.] [You, O LO]RD, [did support me,] [18][the stricken of heart; for I cried, "O LORD, my deliverer!" Now shall I see their shame; but hidden in You, I will not be ashamed. Redeem Israel, Your faithful, O LORD; even the House of Jacob, Your chosen.]

A prayer seeking forgiveness of sin and deliverance from the power of Satan. This psalm, known in two copies from Cave 11, had otherwise perished in antiquity. About five lines are missing from the beginning, and another line or so has been lost at the end. Sheol, mentioned in l. 10, was the domain of the afterlife.

*Portions following l. 17 are lost from 11Q5 and are restored from the Syriac.

11Q6 Frags. 4–5[1][Poor] and weak am I, for [. . .] **11Q5 Col. 19 (with 11Q6 Frags. 4–5)** [1]Indeed, no worm gives You thanks, nor any weevil recounts Your loving-kindness. [2]"The living, the living, they thank You" (Isa. 38:19), they of uncertain step give You praise when You make them [3]know Your mercy, when You teach them Your righteousness. For the soul of all the living is in Your [4]hand, You alone breathe life into flesh. Render to us, O LORD, [5]by Your goodness; according to Your boundless compassion, Your myriad righteous acts. The LORD [6]hears the voice of those who love His name, of His loving-kindness He deprives them not. [7]Blessed be the LORD, worker of righteousness, who crowns the pious [8]with mercy and compassion. My soul clamors to praise Your name, to praise [9]Your loving-kindness with a joyous cry—to tell of Your faithfulness; of praise due You there is no measure. I was in death's [10]thrall through my sins; my iniquities had sold me to Sheol—but You saved me, [11]O LORD, according to Your boundless compassion, Your myriad righteous acts. I, too, have loved [12]Your name and sought shelter in Your shadow. When I recall Your might, I take [13]heart and throw myself on Your mercy. Forgive, O LORD, my sins, [14]cleanse me from my iniquities! Favor me with a constant and knowing spirit and let me not be shamed [15]by ruin. Let Satan have no dominion over me, nor an unclean spirit; let neither pain nor the will [16]to evil rule in me. Surely You, O LORD, are my praise; in You I place my hope [17]all the day. My brothers rejoice with me, and my father's house, amazed at Your favor! [18][. . .] I shall be glad in You forever.

An address to Zion in the style of biblical passages such as Isaiah 54:1–8. Zion is in the prayers of those who love her, who remind God of all that the prophets have promised about the city. This is another acrostic poem.

Col. 22 (with 4Q88 Cols. 7–8) [1]I remember you for a blessing, O Zion, with all my might [2]do I love you. May your memory be blessed forever! Great is your hope, O Zion: peace and the [3]victory you await shall come. Age to age shall you be indwelled, generations of the pious will [4]adorn you: they who long for the day of your victory, to rejoice in your bounteous [5]glory. At your glorious bosom they will suckle, in your majestic streets rattle their bangles. The faithful acts of your prophets [6]shall you recall, being glorified by the works of your pious. Purge wrongdoing from your midst, lying and [7]iniquity be cut off from you. Your children shall rejoice within you, your loved ones join themselves to you. [8]How they have hoped for your victory! How your blameless have mourned you! Hope for you shall not perish, [9]O Zion, nor shall your prospect be forgotten. Who, being righteous, has ever perished? Who has escaped [10]in his sin? Man is tested as to his way, each rewarded according to his works. All around your enemies are cut off, [11]O Zion, all who hate you are scattered. How sweet is the waft of your praise, O Zion, [12]over all the earth! Again and again shall I remember you for blessing; I will bless you with all my heart. [13]May you lay hold of righteousness everlasting, may you receive the blessings of the Glorified. Embrace the vision [14]spoken of you, O Zion, the dreams of prophets sought for you! Grow high, spread wide, O Zion; [15]praise the Most High, your redeemer—while my soul rejoices in your glory.

A hymn to God the Creator. Lines 14–15 are a rearrangement of Jeremiah 10: 12–13 and Psalm 135:7. Line 13, in turn, is quoted in modified form in A Sermon on the Flood *1:1–3 (text 87).*

Col. 26 [9]Great and holy is the LORD, a Holy of Holies for generation after generation. At His fore [10]marches majesty, at His rear, the tumult of many waters. Loving-kindness and truth surround His face, truth, [11]justice and righteousness uphold His throne. Darkness He divides from light, preparing the dawn with the knowledge of [12]His heart. When all His angels saw, they rejoiced in song—for He had shown them what they knew not: [13]decking out the mountains with food, fine sustenance for all who live. Blessed be He who [14]by His might created the earth, who by His wisdom established the world. By His understanding He stretched forth the heavens and brought out [15][the wind] from [His] trea[sure stores.] He created [lightning for the ra]in and [from] the end of [the earth] made vapor[s] to rise.

This prose composition describes the literary activity of King David. Not only is he considered the author of the book of Psalms—including the apocryphal psalms above—but he is credited with many other works as well. The claim for David's prolific writing seems intended to compete with similar claims made for Solomon in 1 Kings 5:12. Note the 364 songs of David for the daily sacrifice: this number equates with the number of days in the Qumran calendar, thus associating the greatest king of Israel with the "right side" in the polemical debate over the proper calendar. For the "songs for charming the demon-possessed with music" mentioned in l. 10, compare Songs to Disperse Demons *(text 153).*

Col. 27 [2]Now David the son of Jesse was wise and shone like the light of the sun, a scribe [3]and man of discernment, blameless in all his ways before God and humankind. The LORD gave [4]him a brilliant and discerning spirit, so that he wrote: psalms, three thousand six hundred; [5]songs to sing before the altar accompanying the daily [6]perpetual burnt offering for all the days of the year, three hundred and sixty-four; [7]for the Sabbath offerings, fifty-two songs; and for the new moon offerings, [8]all the festival days, and the Day of Atonement, thirty songs.

[9]The total of all the songs that he composed was four hundred and forty-six, not including [10]four songs for charming the demon-possessed with music. The sum total of everything, psalms and songs, was four thousand and fifty.

[11]All these he composed through prophecy given him by the Most High. —M.O.W.

152. An Aramaic Translation of the Book of Job

11Q10

In the last century or two before the fall of the Jerusalem Temple in 70 C.E., it began to be the custom among some Jews to translate orally the weekly readings of Scripture, rendering the sometimes incomprehensible ancient Hebrew into Aramaic, the language that most people then spoke. We do not know when such oral translations began to be written down (if indeed they ever were) or how otherwise the first written Aramaic translations, or *targums,* began to appear. In fact the Qumran texts give us our earliest direct information on these questions. They suggest that at first the biblical portions selected for written translation may have been those that were especially significant or those whose Hebrew was most difficult for ordinary people to understand. The manuscripts include one Aramaic translation of a portion of Leviticus (4Q156; Lev. 16:12–15, 18–21) and two translations of the book of Job. Leviticus 16 concerns the Day of Atonement and the scapegoat ceremony, thus treating the most important festival of the holy year, while the Hebrew of Job is unquestionably the most difficult of the entire Bible. Of the two translations of Job, the one from Cave 4 (4Q157) is extremely fragmentary, retaining only scattered words from Job 3:5–6; 4:17–5:4. The other copy, from Cave 11, is much more extensive. About 15 percent of the original scroll survives, covering Job 17:14–42:12. This is the work presented here.

For the most part, the translation of Job presented by this targum is literal and straightforward. In only a few places does the scroll suggest a Hebrew original different from what has been preserved by the traditional Hebrew text. Still, the translator not infrequently *understood* the identical Hebrew text that we see differently from modern scholars. His treatment is interesting and sometimes arguably valid, offering new ways of seeing the problems of the book. The final few verses of the book from col. 38 of the manuscript (Job 42:10–12) may serve to illustrate the approach of *Aramaic Job* and how it differs from modern scholarly understanding of the Hebrew book: "(So Eliphaz the Temanite and Bildad) [1][the Shuhite and Zophar the Naamathite went and] did [what they had been told by] [2]God. And G[o]d listened to the voice of Job and forgave [3]them their sins because of him. Then God turned back to Job in compassion [4]and gave him twice what he once had possessed. There came to [5]Job all his friends, brethren and those who had known him, and they ate bread [6]with him in his house. They consoled him for all the evil that [7]God had brought upon him, and each man gave him one sheep [8]and one gold ring. [9]So God blessed J[ob's] latt[er days, and h]e [had] [10][fourteen thousand] sh[eep . . .]"

Three points stand out: (1) The Hebrew text corresponding to ll. 3–4 says something quite different: "And the Lord restored the fortunes of Job when he had prayed for his friends." Here the translator was strongly interpretive, positively affirming that Job had been right all along to resist his friends' calls to repent of sin that he could not identify and did not believe he committed. (2) In l. 5 the Hebrew text reads "brothers and sisters," not, as our translator rendered, "friends and brethren." The targum has removed all reference to women eating with Job. (3) The Hebrew word translated into Aramaic as "sheep" in l. 7 can also mean "money" and is so rendered by modern translations of Job.

The portions that remain from Job's speech (Job 16–17) in the second round of speeches, replying to Eliphaz's second speech (which appears in Job 15:1–35; chapter and verse numbers from Job below precede the lines they reference.)

Col. 1 [1][(17:14) . . . wo]rm. (17:15) What then [. . .] [2][. . .] (17:16) Will y[ou go down] with me to the underworld?

Bildad's second speech (18:1–21).

[3][Or] shall [we] lie down [together in the dust? . . .] [4][. . .] (18:1) Bildad the Shuhite [answe]red [and said . . .] [5][. . . (18:2) When] will you put a stop to [your] words? [. . .] [6][. . . (18:3) . . .] are we like [li]vestock? [. . .] [7][(18:4) . . .] Is it at [your] com[mand . . .] [8][. . .] from [its] pla[ce? . . .]

Job replies to Bildad (19:1–29).

Col. 2 [1](19:11) His anger [has grow]n against me and he [considers me . . . (19:12) Together] [2]come his robbers and beat down [. . . (19:13) My brothers] [3]have moved far off, and those who know me [. . . (19:15)

Those who dwell] [4]in my house, my maidservants, as a stranger [. . .] [5](19:16) I called to my servant, but he did not an[swer . . .] [6](19:17) I humbled my spirit to my wife [. . . (19:18) Even] [7]wicked people afflict [me . . . (19:19) They despise me,] [8]all the men of [. . .]

Col. 3 [1][. . .] evil. [. . .] [2][. . .]

Zophar speaks in the second round (20:1–29).

[3][(20:1) Then Zophar the Naamathite answered and said to Jo]b, (20:2) Therefore my heart [. . .] [4][. . .] (20:3) I hear the [. . .] of my insult, and the spirit of [. . .] [5][. . . (20:4) . . . Surely] you kn[ow this] from of old, from the time that [. . .] [6][. . .] the [earth]? (20:5) For the joy of the wick[ed] [7][. . .] passes away quickly? [(20:6) Even if] [8][his pride goes up to heaven, and] his [no]se [reaches] the clouds [. . .]

Job replies to Zophar (21:1–34).

Col. 4 [1][. . . (21:2) . . .] to me to bring [. . . (21:3) . . . and then] [2]you will mock my intelligence. [(21:4) . . .] [3]Behold, then, [is not my spirit] im[patient? (21:5) . . .] [4]Place your hands on [your mouths. (21:6) . . .] [5]And astonishment has taken hold of me. (21:7) H[ow is it . . .] [6]they have increased their possessions? (21:8) [Their] seed [. . .] [7]before their eyes. (21:9) Their houses [. . . no punishment from] [8]God is upon them. [(21:10) . . .] [9]Those who are pregnant de[liver . . .]

Col. 5 [1][(21:20) . . .] His eyes [shall see] his downfall, and from the wr[ath of the Lord he will drink.] [2][(21:21) For what] interest has God in his house and [. . .] [3][the numbe]r of his months is cut off. (21:22) Is it G[od you will teach] [4][knowledge? But] He will judge the proud.* (21:24) [His] limbs [5][. . .] his bones. (21:25) This one dies with a [bitter] sou[l . . .] [6][goodness he ne]ver tasted. (21:26) Together on [. . .] [7][. . . o]ver them. (21:27) Behold, I know [. . .] [8][. . . th]at you have devised. [. . .]

Eliphaz launches the third round of speeches (22:1–30).

Col. 6 [1][. . . (22:3) . . . to G]od [2][. . .] your way? [3][(22:4) . . . he] enters with you [4][. . . (22:5) . . . th]ere is no [5][. . . (22:6) . . .] your brothers without cause [6][. . . (22:7) . . . to the] thirsty [you] did not [. . .] [7][. . . br]ead. (22:8) And you said [. . .] [8][. . .] his [f]ace [. . .]

*The verse 21:23 is omitted in the Aramaic text.

Col. 7 [1](22:16) who died with[out . . .] [2](22:17) They say to G[od . . .] [3][What can] God do for us? [(22:18) . . .] [4]but the counsel of the wic[ked . . . (22:19) . . .] [5]and they laugh [. . .] [6](22:20) How not [. . .] [7](22:21) Understand [now . . .] [8](22:22) Receive [. . .] [9][. . .]

Job replies to Eliphaz (23:1–24:25).

Col. 7A [1][. . .] (23:1) Job answered and sai[d] [2][(23:2) Even today] because of my speaking which [3][. . .] my [gr]oaning. (23:3) Would that I knew and could fi[nd Him.] [4][I would come to] the place of His dwelling. (23:4) I would speak before [Him] [5][and my mouth] would I fill with rebuke. (23:5) I would know [6][. . .] I would understand what He would say to me. [7][(23:6) . . . he would] enter with me. Would that [. . .] [8][. . .] (23:7) Behold, truth and judgment [. . .] [9][. . .] (23:8) If forwa[rd . . .]

Col. 8 [1](24:12) From their cities [. . .] [2]cries out. God [. . . 24:13) . . .] [3]before him for his fire. [. . . they did not abide] [4]in His paths. [(24:14) . . . He slays the poor] [5]and needy and at ni[ght . . . (24:15) . . . He awaits] [6]darkness say[ing . . .] [7]and he will commit sin. (24:16) [He] d[igs . . .] [8]in [their] evil[doing. (24:17) . . . For morning] [9]is to them [as darkness . . .]

Col. 9 [1][. . . (24:24) they] droop, like cynodon grass they shrivel o[r . . .] [2][(25:25) Wh]o then will answer me a word, or will ma[ke . . .]

Bildad's third speech (25:1–6).

[3][. . .] (25:1) Bild[ad the Shuhite] answered [and said:] [4][(25:2) For do]minion and greatness are with God, he ma[kes peace] [5][in] the [he]ight. (25:3) Is there trust for [. . .] [6][. . .] or upon whom does it not arise? [(25:4) . . . with] [7]God? Or what will be just [. . . (25:5 . . . is not] [8]innocent, and the stars are not [. . . (25:6) . . . man that is] [9][a maggot, and a s]on of man, a wor[m?]

Job in reply to Bildad (26:1–14).

[10][(26:1) Job answered and sai]d: (26:2) Have [you] hel[ped . . .]

Col. 10 [1][(26:10) . . .] on the [ed]ges of the boundary [2][. . . (26:11) . . . sh]ake, and are astonished from [3][. . . (26:12) . . .] the sea, and by His knowledge He slew [4][. . . (26:13) . . . brigh]tened, His hand pierced the fleeing sea serpent. [5][(26:14) . . .] His [ways.] Only a breath of a word do we he[ar.] [6][. . . who] can understand?

Job's conclusion (27:1–23).

7–8[(27:1) Job continued to speak] and said: (27:2) As God lives [. . .] 9[. . .] my soul. (27:3) If however long [. . .] 10[. . . in] my nostrils. (27:4) If [my lips] sp[eak . . .]

Col. 11 1[. . . (27:11) . . . in the h]and of God, and the work of 2[the Almighty . . . (27:12) A]ll of you have seen it; why 3[then . . . (27:13) . . . of] wicked men 4[. . . from] before Him they shall bear it. (27:14) If 5[. . . they shall not] be delivered [from the sw]ord, and they will not be filled 6[with bread. (27:15) . . .] And his widows shall not 7[weep. (27:16) . . . he gathers] coins, like mud he multiplies 8[clothing. (27:17) . . . and] his [mo]n[ey] the honest man shall distribute. 9[(27:18) . . .] like the hut 10[. . . (27:19) . . . l]ies down, but is not taken 11[. . . (27:20)] Harmful things [overtake him] like water [. . .]

An interlude (28:1–28).

Col. 12 1(28:4) foot [. . . (28:5) . . .] 2changed [. . . (28:6) Pl]aces of 3sapphire [. . . (28:7) . . .] 4no [. . . (28:8)] Un]trodden by 5jackals [. . . (28:9) . . .] his [hand] 6upro[ots . . . (28:10) . . . ch]annels 7he te[ars . . . (28:11) . . . he] keeps back 8and [. . . (28:12?) . . .] 9[. . . (28:13) . . . me]n.

Col. 13 1(28:20) [Where is the] place of cunning? (28:21) F[or . . . from] 2the birds of the sky [it] is hid[den. (28:22) . . .] 3With our ears we have heard ne[ws of it. (28:23) . . .] 4in it, for He [. . . (28:24) . . .] 5to the ends of the earth [. . .] 6(28:25) When He makes [a weight] for the wind [. . .] 7by measure. (28:26) When [He] makes [a law for the rain, and a path for the clouds] 8so swift, (28:27) then [. . .] 9(28:28) And He said to the sons of [men . . .] 10and turning away [. . .]

In Job 29 a new character, Elihu, enters the book and has an exchange with Job (29:1–37:24). After Job speaks describing what has happened to him, Elihu offers his views in four speeches. Job begins by describing his former situation of wealth and happiness (29:1–25).

Col. 14 1[(29:7) . . . In] the mornings in the gates of the city, in [the] square [. . .] 2(29:8) Young men saw me and hid; and grown men [. . .] 3(29:9) Princes fell silent from speaking, putting a hand [to their mouth.] 4(29:10) The voice of officials disappeared, [their tongue] stuck to the palate. 5(29:11) When the ear heard, it praised me; when the eye s[aw . . .] 6(29:12) [F]or I delivered the poor man from the [hand of . . .] 7[w]ho had none to help them. (29:13) The blessing of the l[ost . . .] [8][in the mou]th of the widow I became a prayer. [(29:14) . . .] [9][cloth]ed me, and like a tunic I wore [. . . (29:15) . . .] [10][. . . and] feet to the lame [. . . (29:16) . . .] [11][. . .] I knew not [. . .]

Col. 15 [1][. . .] (29:24) I would smile at them, and they would not [believe it . . .] [2][. . .] (29:25) I chose my way and became h[ead . . .] [3][. . .] at the head of his army and like a man who [comforts the mourning.]

Job's present humiliation (30:1–31).

[4][(30:1) And now] those younger than I laugh at me in the days [. . . those] [5]whose fat]hers [I would refuse] to have with the dogs of [my] fl[ock!] [6](30:2) [Their . . .] was no pleasure to me, and by [their] burdens [. . .] [7][(30:3) . . . in] hunger they would graze the grass of the s[teppe . . .] [8][. . .] and evil, (30:4) who ate [. . .] [9][the roots of broom tre]es for the[ir] food [. . .]

Col. 16 [1][. . . (30:13) To] my [des]truction they come, and savior there is none [2][for them. (30:14) And no]w with force my ulcers come; [3][in place of . . .] evil I am bowed down. (30:15) I am bowed down [4][. . . like] the wind my welfare and greatness [are gone]; and like a cloud [5]my [deliverance has passed from me.] (30:16) And now [my soul] is poured out upon me; [6]days of defeat [take hold of me], they surround me [7][. . . (30:17) At night] my bones are fevered, and [my] tendons [8][have no rest. (30:18) With great] strength they clutch [my] garm[ent]; [9][like the collar of my tunic] they [sur]round me. (30:19) They have cast me down [to the mud,] [10][. . . (30:20) . . . un]to you [. . .]

Col. 17 [1][. . . (30:26) . . .] there came [2][evil . . .] [3][. . .] grow strong [. . . (30:27) My bowels roi]led and were not [4][silent;] days of trou[ble out]ran me. [(30:28) I mourned and] went about [5][without the sun (?).] I arose [. . . and] cried out. [6][(30:29) . . . to os]triches. [7][(30:30) . . .] from [8][the heat. (30:31) . . .] my [. . .]

Job's ultimate challenge (31:1–40).

[9][(31:1) . . .] not [. . .]

Col. 18 [1](31:8) will ea[t . . . (31:9) . . . se]duced was [2]my heart by a wo[man . . .] I was h[unting(?).] [3](31:10) Let her grind for [. . . (31:11) For t]his is provocation [4]and that is sin [. . . (31:12) . . . it] b[urns] to [5]Abaddon [. . .] (31:13) If I was ever impatient [6]in the judgment of [my] servant [. . .] (31:14) What shall I do [7]when [God] ari[ses . . .] (31:15) For [8][my] Maker [. . .] one. (31:16) If [9]I with[hold . . .] I made to cease.

Col. 19 [1](31:26) shining, and [the] m[oon . . .] (31:27) my [hea]rt, [2]and my hand has kissed [my] mo[uth, (31:28) . . .] I was [fal]se [3]to God abov[e. (31:29) . . .] I [re]joiced [4]at his harm [. . . (31:29, addition) . . .] [5]my curse, and he hears [. . .] in my anger, [6]and I seized [. . . (31:30) to commi]t sin [7]my mouth to se[ek . . . (31:31) . . . m]en of [8]my house, Wh[o . . . (31:32) . . .] [9]did not l[odge . . .]

Col. 20 [1](31:40) Instead of wheat [. . .] [2]stinkweed. This end[s . . .]

A short introduction to the Elihu speeches (32:1–5).

[(32:1) . . .] These [three men ceased] [3]to give [an answer . . .] [4]Job was righte[ous . . .] [5][. . .] [6](32:2) Then [Elihu son of Barachel the Buzite] grew angry [. . .] [7]descendants of the Rumit[es . . .] [8](32:3) And also ag[ainst . . .] [9]wor[ds . . .]

Elihu's first speech (32:6–33:33).

Col. 21 [1](32:10) I too [will declare] my words. (32:11) For I expected [. . .] [2]you would cease, while you search out the end of [. . . (31:12) . . .] [3]and, behold, there was none among you [to rebuke] J[ob . . .] [4]his words. (31:13) Perhaps you will say [. . .] [5]Therefore God has found us guilty and not m[an. (31:14) . . .] [6]words, and likewise he will not answer him [. . . (31:15) . . .] [7]they became silent, and I kept from them [my words. (31:16) . . .] [8][and] they stood still and would speak no more. [(31:17) . . .] [9][and] I too will declare my words [. . .]

Col. 22 [1][I too.] (33:7) If fear of me does not af[fright you . . . will not] [2][be] heavy. (33:8) Indeed you have spoken in my ears, and the so[und . . .] [3][(33:9) Righteo]us am I, and without sin, and pure [. . .] [4](33:10) If He had found sins, He would have seized me li[ke . . .] [5](33:11) [He] would put my feet in the stocks and lock up a[ll . . .] [6](33:12) For God is greater than man. [(33:13) . . . Against Him] [7]you speak boastfully, for in all [His] w[ords . . .] [8](33:14) [F]or one time God speaks [. . .] [9](33:15) [In] dreams, in delusions of [the] night [. . .] [10][when] he [slum]bers on his bed. [(33:16) . . .]

Col. 23 [1](33:24) Then let him say, Deliver him from des[truction . . . Let no flame of] [2]fire torment him and let [his bones] be filled [with marrow. (33:25) . . .] from [3]youth, and return to [the] days of young man[hood. (33:26) . . .] he hears him [4]and sees his face with healing [. . .]. (33:27) And according to the work of [5]his hands he will repay him, and he will say [. . .] and not [6]according to my way was I repaid. (33:28) He deliv[ered . . . my soul] [7]shall see by (His) light. (33:29) Behold, a[ll

. . .] a man, [8]two times, three times, (33:30) to br[ing back . . . in the ligh]t of [9]life. (33:31) Listen to this [. . . I will sp]eak. [10][(33:32) If] there are w[ords . . .]

Elihu's second speech (34:1–37).

Col. 24 [1](34:6) from sin. (34:7) Who [. . .] sins, (34:8) who joins up [2]with those who act in deceit [. . . wicke]d. (34:9) For he said, What [3]difference is there for a man [. . .] after God.

[4](34:10) Now, men of [. . .] far be it from God to lie [5]or for [the] L[ord] to cause harm. [(34:11) . . . of] a man he will repay him. [6][. . .] (34:12) Now, is it true that God [7]would lie, or the Lord [. . .] (34:13) He made the earth [8]and ordered the wor[ld. . . . (34:14) . . .] his [brea]th ceases upon him, [9](34:15) then dies [all flesh . . . in the dust] they will lie down. [10][(34:16) . . .] my [w]ords. (34:17) Is it by lies [. . .]

Col. 25 [1][. . . (34:24) . . . p]rinces without end and raises up o[thers] [2][. . . (34:25) . . . He kno]ws their deeds (34:26) and casts them into a pla[ce of] [3][(34:27) . . .] His [wa]y, and had no understanding of all His paths, [4](34:28) to [bring upon Him the outcry of] the poor, and He hears the complaint of the afflicted. [5][(34:29) . . . When He hide]s His face, who can make Him return, whether people [6][. . . (34:30) . . .] wicked men are ensnared. [7][(34:31) . . .] for Him I will wait. (34:32) By Himself [8][. . .] I will not do again. (34:33) For [. . .] [9][. . . you will ch]oose, and not I [. . .] [10][(34:34) . . . w]ords and [the] ma[n . . .]

Elihu's third speech (35:1–16).

Col. 26 [1](35:6) [in] you, and in the multitude of your iniquities what will you [do to Him? (35:7) If] you are [right]eous, what [2]will you give Him, or what will He receive from your hand? [(35:8) For a man like] yourself is your sin, [3]and your righteousness is for a human being. (35:9) Because of many [oppressions] they shout, they cry out [4]from before many. (35:10) But [they] do not say, [Where is] God [5]who made us and who distributes to us [. . .] for our strength [6]in the night, (35:11) who separated us from the bea[sts of the earth and] makes us wiser [than] the birds? [7](35:12) There they cry out, but He does not [answer, because of the p]ride of [8][the e]vil ones. (35:13) For will [God] he[ar] vanity? [And the Lord will not] listen to [emp]tiness. [9](35:14) If you say [. . .] [10][. . .] for Him. (35:15) In[deed . . .]

Elihu's fourth speech (36:1–37:24).

Col. 27 [1](36:7) for kings who sit up[on their thrones, and all] his loved ones will be lifted up in safety. [2](36:8) And also with those bound in [chains,] held in the cords of poverty, [3](36:9) and he declares to them thei[r] deeds [and] their [iniquities], for they have magnified themselves. (36:10) And he uncovers [4]their ears for instruction, and s[aid to them,] If they repent of their evil, [5](36:11) if they listen and obe[y, they will finish] their days in happiness, and their years [6]in glory and pleasure. [(36:12) And if they do not lis]ten, they will fall by the sword [7]and perish from kn[owledge. (36:13) . . .] their [he]art to anger [8]upon them [. . . (36:14) . . .] their [c]ities by slayers [9](36:15) But he delivers [the] p[oor . . .] of their ears. [10][. . .]

Col. 28 [1](36:23) [You have] done [wrong? (36:24) Re]member, for great are his deeds that [2]they have se[en. (36:25) And] all men behold him, and the sons of men [3]from afar search [for him.] (36:26) Behold, God is great, and His days [4]are many; [we do not k]now the number of his years, which are without end. (36:27) For [5][He numbers] the clouds [of water;] and the storms of rain pass by. (36:28) And His clouds bring down [6]d[rops of water on] many people. (36:29) If from the cover of [7]cl[ouds . . .] from shade. (36:30) And he spreads out li[ght] [8][. . .] he covers. (36:31) For by them he judges [the] p[eoples]. [9][. . .] (36:32) At his command [. . .] [10][. . .] (36:33) It speaks about [him . . .]

Col. 29 [1](37:10) on the surface of water. (37:11) Also by them he clears cloud[s] away, and from the cloud [2]fire comes out. (37:12) And he speaks, they listen to him, and go to their tasks; [3]to all that he has created he gives commands on the face of the earth, (37:13) whether for pestilence, [4]or the land, or famine and want, or any sinful thing, it shall occur [5]upon the earth. (37:14) Hear this, Job; stand and behold the mighty works of God. [6](37:15) [Do you] know what God has placed upon them, to [make] the cloud gleam with light? [7](37:16) [Do you] know how to clothe the cloud in might, [so] that your clothing [8][. . .] for it is he who has [the] knowledge.* [(37:18) Can you, with him,] forge the mist, [9][strong as a] beaten [mirr]or? (37:19) He knows [. . .]

The Elihu speeches finish without a reply, and Job now enters a dialog with God (38:1–42:6). Two rounds of speeches follow; the Lord speaks first (38:1–40:2).

Col. 30 [1](38:3) Now bind up your loins like a man [and I will ques]tion you, and you will give me an answer. [2](38:4) Where were you when I made the earth? Tell me, if you have wisdom. [3](38:5) Who set its measurement, if

*The verse 37:17 is omitted in the Aramaic text.

you know? Who stretched the measuring line over it? (38:6) Or [4]what were its foundations fixed upon? Or who erected its stony towers? (38:7) When [5]the stars of morning shine together, and all the angels of God cry out together, [6](38:8) will you fence in the sea with doors, when it gushes from the womb of the abyss [7]to come forth? (38:9) When I make clouds its [gar]ment and mists its swaddling clothes, (38:10) will you make [8]boundaries for it, a law [for the sea, bol]ts and [ga]tes? (38:11) Did you say, This far [9]and no farther [. . . your w]aves? (38:12) Have you ever in your days appointed [10][. . . (38:13) . . .] edge[s of the] earth [. . .]

Col. 31 [1](38:23) wh[ich I have kept back for] the time of di[stre]ss, for the day of battle and rebellion. [(38:24) . . . The frost,] [2]how does it emerge? Will you blow wind before it on the earth? (38:25) Who made [3]a time for the rain, or a path for swift clouds, (38:26) to make it fall on desert [4]land where no man is, (38:27) to satisfy a land thorny and forsaken, [5]and to bring forth sprouts of grass? (38:28) Does the rain have a father, or who [6]gave birth to the [cl]ouds of dew? (38:29) And from whose belly does the frost come forth? And the oases [. . .] [7]wh[o bore] it? (38:30) Like a st[one] the waters ice over from it; and the surface of [. . .] [8][(38:31) . . .] Pleiades, or can you [open] the gate of the Giant? [9][(38:32) . . .] will you give rest to [. . .] with her children? [(38:33) . . .] [10][. . .] the earth? [(38:34) . . .] [11][. . .]

Col. 32 [1](39:1) the mountain goats, and the labor pains of [. . . (39:2) Can you numbe]r their [m]onths [2]as they pass, do you know the time of their birth? (39:3) They bear their young and expel them; [3]will you send away their labor pains? (39:4) They toughen their young and they leave; having left, they do not return [4]to them. (39:5) Who has the let the wild ass go free? And the chains of the onager, who [5]has loosened them? (39:6)—for whom I made the steppe his home, and his dwelling place is in the salt land. [6](39:7) He laughs at the harsh noise of the city, the urging of the driver he does not [7]hear. (39:8) He searches the mountains for [his] pasture, [and] every kind of vegetation [8]he pursues. (39:9) Does [the] wild ox want [to] serve you, o[r] will he sleep next to [9]your manger? (39:10) Will you bind [the wild ox by] his neck, and will he plo[w] the plain [10]behind you? And [. . . (39:11) Will] you rely on [him, for] great [. . .]

Col. 33 [1][. . .] (39:20) Can you disturb him in strength [. . .] [2]In his snort(?) is terror and fear. (39:21) And he digs in the plain, and runs, and rejoices, [3]and with strength he goes forth to face the sword. (39:22) He laughs at fear, and does not [4]tremble; and he does not turn away from the sword. (39:23) Upon him hangs the quiver, [5]blade and lance, the sharp sword,★

★The verse 39:24 is omitted in the Aramaic text.

(39:25) and at the sound of the trumpet he says, Aha! And from [6]afar he sniffs battle; at the clash of weapons and the cry of rebellion [7]he rejoices. (39:26) Is it by your wisdom that the hawk whirls away, and spreads [8]his wings to the winds? (39:27) Is it at your command that the eagle flies high [9]or the hawk elevates [his] nest? (39:28) [On] the rock he dwells and nests [. . .] [10][. . .] (38:29) from th[ere he] picks out(?) food [. . .]

Job replies in a very few words to God's first speech (40:3–5).

Col. 34 [1](40:5) I will add [no more . . .]

God speaks again (40:6–41:34).

[2](40:6) God answered Job from [the] w[ind] and cloud and said to him, (40:7) Gird up [3]now your loins like a man; I will question you, and you will give me an answer. (40:8) Will you indeed [4]take away judgment and condemn me so that you may be in the right? (40:9) Or [5]do you have an arm like God, or can you thunder in a voice like his? [6](40:10) Now remove pride and arrogance of spirit, and put on splendor and glory and honor. [7](40:11) Now remove your angry wrath, and see every proud man and bring him low. (40:12) And every [8]prideful spirit you must break, and extinguish [the] w[icked] [in] their [place.] (40:13) Hide [9]them in the dust toge[ther;] cover their [faces] with ash. [10][(40:14) . . .] bring (?)

Col. 35 [1][. . . (40:23) . . . Though] [2]the Jordan [overflow] its bank, he trusts that G[od?] will contain it. [3](40:24) When he lifts up his eyes, can one hold him back? Can one make his nose flow as with a hook? (40:25) Can you pull out [4]the sea serpent with a hook or pierce his tongue with a cord? (40:26) Can you put [5]a muzzle on his snout, or pierce his cheek with a thorn? (40:27) Will he speak [6]peacefully to you or will he speak with you as one who asks you for mercy? (40:28) Will he make [7]a covenant with you, and will you lead him away as a servant forever? (40:29) Will you laugh [8]at him as at a bird? Will you tie him up with a string for your daughters? (40:30) Will [. . .] [9][. . .] and will they divide him up in the land of [Canaan?] [10][(40:31) . . .] of fish [. . .]

Col. 36 [1](41:7) its back [. . . (41:8) One] [2]cleaves to the next and n[o] space [co]mes between them. (41:9) Each [3]grasps the other and they are not separated. (41:10) Its sneezing ignites [4]fire; between his eyes it is like the dawn(?). (41:11) From his mouth lightning [5]comes out, rushing like tongues of fire. (41:12) From his nostrils smoke comes out, [6]as from a kettle heated and stoked with coals. (41:13) His breath belches coals, and sparks [7]come out of his mouth. (41:14) Strength lodges in his neck and before him [8]runs virility. (41:15) The folds of his flesh stick together, poured out [on him] [9]like iron. (41:16) And [his] he[art . . .] like stone and [. . .] [10][(41:17) . . .] fe[ar . . .] bro[ken] [11][. . .]

Col. 37 [1][. . . (41:26) . . .] [2]and he reigns over all that creeps.

Job's reply, conceding that he has no case against God after all (42:1–6).

[3](42:1) Job answered and said before God: (42:2) I know that [4]You can do all things, and no power or wisdom is missing from You. [5](40:5) One thing I said, and I will not repeat it; two things, but I will not [6]add to them. (42:4) Hear now, and I will speak; I will question You, [7]and You answer me. (42:5) With the hearing of the ear I heard of You; but now with my eyes [8]I see You. (42:6) Therefore I am poured out and astonished; and I will become dust [9]and ashes.

The outcome of the story, beginning with God's verdict (42:7–9) and ending with Job's restoration (42:10–17).

Col. 38 [1][(42:9) (So Eliphaz the Temanite and Bildad) the Shuhite and Zophar the Naamathite went and] did [what they had been told by] [2]God. And G[o]d listened to the voice of Job and forgave [3]them their sins because of him. (42:10) Then God turned back to Job in compassion [4]and gave him twice what he once had possessed. (42:11) There came to [5]Job all his friends, brethren, and those who had known him, and they ate bread [6]with him in his house. They consoled him for all the evil that [7]God had brought upon him, and each man gave him one sheep [8]and one gold ring. [9](42:12) So God blessed J[ob's] latt[er days, and h]e [had] [10][fourteen thousand] sh[eep . . .]

—E.M.C./M.O.W.

153. Songs to Disperse Demons

11Q11

As is clear from many of the scrolls, the land and sky of the first centuries B.C.E. and C.E. were, at least in imagination, populated not only by angels but also by demons. Although the legions of the devil would be defeated in the end, in the meantime their power was considerable, and certain measures were needed to dispel their influence. One example is *An Exorcism* (text 146); others may be found here. Instead of as straightforward exorcisms, these demonic defenses are composed as psalms and assigned to biblical characters. Unlike *An Exorcism,* which may have been intended to be worn on the person as an amulet, these texts were meant to be recited.

The God of creation, who separated light from darkness, is invoked for protection against the powers of darkness.

Col. 2 1–2[. . . A Psalm of] Solomon. He call[ed . . .] 3[. . . the spi]rits and the demons [. . .] 4[. . .] these are [the de]mons and the pri[nce of Maste]mah 5[. . . I]sr[ael . . .] 6–7[. . .] with me [. . .] healing 8[. . . the righteous] leans on Your name and calls [. . .] 9[. . . He says to Is]rael, Be strong 10[. . . who made] the heavens 11[and the earth . . .] who has separated [light 12from darkness . . .]

God's power in creation is again entreated.

Col. 3 1[. . .] the abyss [. . .] 2and the earth [. . .] the earth, who m[ade the host of heaven for seasons] 3and for sig[ns . . . in the] earth, He is the LORD [. . .] 4He made the [. . . He] adjures all [his] a[ngels] 5[a]nd all the see[d . . .] which st[a]nd before [Him . . .] 6[. . .] the earth [. . .] 7[. . . every] sin, and concerning all t[hese . . .] they know 8[. . .] which are not [. . .] if not 9[. . .] from before the LORD [. . .] to slay the soul of 10[. . .] the LORD, and let him be afraid [. . .] this great [spell:] 11"One of you [will pursue] a thou[sand" (Josh. 23:10) . . .] served the LORD [. . .] 12[. . .] great [. . .]

Another psalm spell calling on angelic powers to combat the demonic.

Col. 4 1Great is [. . . I] adjure [you . . .] 2and the great [*x*] against [you . . .] the mighty [angel . . .] 3all the earth [. . .] the heavens and [. . .] 4May the LORD smite you [with a mighty blow] in order to destroy you [. . .] 5and by His fierce wrath [may He send] against you a mighty angel [. . .] 6[. . .] which [. . . no] mer[cy] for you, who [. . .] 7[. . .] against all these which [shall be sent forever] into the great abyss 8[. . . to] lowest [Hades], and who [. . . there] you shall lie, and darkness 9[. . .] very much [. . .] in the earth 10[. . .] forever [. . .] with the curses of des[truction . . .] 11[. . .] the fierce wrath of [the LORD . . .] darkness [. . .] 12[. . .] affliction [. . .] your portion [. . .]

A summary statement on the nature of the preceding psalm.

Col. 5 [1][. . .] [2]which [. . .] and those possessed by [demons . . .] [3]those crushed [by Belial . . . on Isra]el, peace [eternal . . .]

An incantation attributed to David, to be uttered against a demonic attacker. Here the chief weapon is mockery. Note the reference to the demon's horns.

[4]A Psalm of David, a[gainst . . .] in the name of the LOR[D . . .] [5]unto the hea[vens . . .] he will come to you at ni[ght, and] you will say to him, [6]Who are you? [Withdraw from] humanity and from the ho[ly] race! For your face is a face of [7][nothing], and your horns are horns of dre[am]. You are darkness, not light, [8][wicked]ness, not righteousness [. . .] the Prince of the Host, the LORD [. . .] [9][in Had]es most deep, [enclosed in doors] of bronze [. . .] [10][. . .] light and not [. . . never again to see] the sun that [11][shines on the] righteous [. . .] and then you shall say [. . .] [12][. . . the rig]hteous to come [. . .] to do harm to him [. . .] [13][. . . tr]uth from [. . . righ]teousness to [. . .]

Col. 6 contains the text of Psalm 91, a psalm that continued to be used throughout the centuries in magical exorcisms in both Judaism and Christianity.

—E.M.C.

154. The Coming of Melchizedek

11Q13

The biblical jubilee year was the fiftieth year, the year following the succession of seven sabbatical years. Whereas a sabbatical year was one in which the land had to lie fallow and rest (analogous to the Sabbath at the end of the week), in the jubilee year all land that had been alienated from its original owners was supposed to return to them. All Hebrew slaves were to be set free. The jubilee year began on the Day of Atonement and was signaled by the blowing of trumpets throughout the land and the proclamation of universal liberty.

The author of the present intriguing mélange of biblical citations has selected many of the Bible's verses that relate to the jubilee year and created a work in which those portions receive their "true" interpretation—one by no means obvious to casual readers of the Bible. He understands the jubilee-year remission of debts as referring not merely to prosaic matters of money, but to the forgiveness of sin. The author declares that the agent of this salvation is to be none other than Melchizedek, a mysterious figure referenced only twice in the Bible, in Genesis 14 and Psalm 110. For our author, Melchizedek is an enormously exalted divine being to whom are applied names generally reserved for God alone: the Hebrew names *el* and *elohim*. In the author's citation of Isaiah 61:2, which speaks of "the year of the LORD's favor," Melchizedek is substituted even for this most holy name of Israel's God. Yet more remarkably, Melchizedek is said to atone for the sins of the righteous and to execute judgment upon the wicked—actions usually associated with God himself. By the power of Melchizedek, dominion on earth shall pass from Satan (here called Belial) to the righteous Sons of Light.

This latter group constitutes those who are predestined to belong to the party of Melchizedek, "the congregation of the sons of righteousness." These people heed the message of a second figure described in this writing as "the messenger." The messenger, also designated "Anointed of the Spirit" (Hebrew *messiah*), is conceived of as coming with a message from God, a message explicating the course of history (that is, a declaration of when the End shall come) and teaching about God's truths. This figure dies, an event that may correspond somehow with the text's references to "jubilee periods." In many of the scrolls, jubilee periods are not only times of liberation as described in the Bible, but also ways of keeping track of time. The present text apparently envisions a scheme in which the coming of the Last Days is calculated by means of these jubilee periods.

Much about this remarkable text remains mysterious, and considerable further research will be needed to achieve a truer understanding of its ideas. The figure of Melchizedek as portrayed here is strikingly reminiscent of the New Testament reference to a heavenly figure of that name, a high priest described as follows: "without father, without mother, without genealogy, having neither beginning of days nor end of life, but resembling the Son of God, he remains a priest forever" (Heb. 7:3). Clearly Melchizedek was a focus of powerful salvific imagery among various Jewish groups in the period of the scrolls.

The figure of Melchizedek, the heavenly savior of those predestined to belong to him.

Col. 2 [2][. . .] And concerning what Scripture says, "In [this] year of jubilee [you shall return, every one of you, to your property" (Lev. 25:13) and what is also written, "And this] [3]is the [ma]nner of [the remission:] every creditor shall remit the claim that is held [against a neighbor, not exacting it of a neighbor who is a member of the community, because God's] remission [has been proclaimed" (Deut. 15:2):] [4][the interpretation] is that it applies [to the L]ast Days and concerns the captives, just as [Isaiah said: "To proclaim the jubilee to the captives" (Isa. 61:1). . . .] and [5]whose teachers have been hidden and kept secr[et], even from the inheritance of Melchizedek, f[or . . .] and they are the inherit[ance of Melchize]dek, who [6]will return them to what is rightfully theirs. He will proclaim to them the jubilee, thereby releasing th[em from the debt of a]ll their sins.

This word [will thus co]me [7]in the first week of the jubilee period that follows ni[ne j]ubilee periods. Then the "D[ay of Atone]ment" shall follow at the e[nd of] the tenth [ju]bilee period, [8]when he shall atone for all the Sons of [Light] and the peopl[e who are pre]destined to Mel[chi]zedek. [. . .] upo[n the]m [. . .] For [9]this is the time decreed for "the year of Melchiz[edek]'s favor" (Isa. 61:2, modified) and for [his] hos[ts, together] with the holy ones of God, for a kingdom of judgment, just as it is written [10]concerning him in the Songs of David, "A godlike being has taken his place in the coun[cil of God;] in the midst of the divine beings he holds judgment" (Ps. 82:1). Scripture also s[ays] about him, "Over [it] [11]take your seat in the highest heaven; A divine being will judge the peoples" (Ps. 7:7–8).

Concerning what scripture s[ays, "How long will y]ou judge unjustly, and sh[ow] partiality to the wick[e]d? [S]el[ah" (Ps. 82:2),] [12]the interpretation applies to Belial and the spirits predestined to him, becau[se all of them have rebe]lled, turn[ing] from God's precepts [and so becoming utterly wicked.] [13]Therefore Melchizedek will thoroughly prosecute the vengeance required by Go[d's] statutes. [In that day he will de]liv[er them from the power] of Belial, and from the power of all the sp[irits predestined to him.] [14]Allied with him will be all the ["righteous] divine beings" (Isa. 61:3). [Th]is is that wh[ich . . . al]l the divine beings.

The figure of the messenger, an Anointed One who comes with a message from God but is "cut off."

This vi[sitation] [15]is the Day of [Salvation] that He has decreed [. . . through Isai]ah the prophet [concerning all the captives,] inasmuch as Scripture sa[ys, "How] beautiful [16]upon the mountains are the fee[t of] the messeng[er] who [an]nounces peace, who brings [good] news, [who announces salvat]ion, who [sa]ys to Zion, 'Your [di]vine being [reigns' " (Isa. 52:7).] [17]This scripture's interpretation: "the mountains" [are] the prophet[s,] they w[ho were sent to proclaim God's truth and to] proph[esy] to all I[srael.] [18]And "the messenger" is the Anointed of the Spir[it,] of whom Dan[iel] spoke, ["After the sixty-two weeks, an Anointed One shall be cut off" (Dan. 9:26). The "messenger who brings] [19]good news, who announ[ces salvation"] is the one of whom it is wri[tt]en, ["to proclaim the year of the Lord's favor, the day of vengeance of our God;] [20]to comfo[rt all who mourn" (Isa. 61:2). This scripture's interpretation:] he is to inst[r]uct them about all the periods of history for eter[nity . . . and in the statutes of] [21][the] truth. [. . .] [22][. . . dominion] that passes from Belial and ret[urns to the Sons of Light . . .] [23][. . .] by the judgment of God, just as it is written concerning him, ["who says to Zi]on 'Your divine being reigns' " (Isa. 52:7). ["Zi]on" is [24][the congregation of all the sons of righteousness, who] uphold the covenant and turn from walking [in the way] of the people. "Your di[vi]ne being" is [25][Melchizedek, who will del]iv[er them from the po]wer of Belial.

Concerning what Scripture says, "Then you shall have the trumpet [sounded loud in] all the land [of . . ." (Lev. 25:9, modified).]

—M.O.W.

155. The Temple Scroll

11Q19–21, 4Q524, 4Q365a

Of all the scrolls to emerge from the caves of Qumran, the primary copy of the *Temple Scroll* (11Q19) takes pride of place as the longest: it unwinds to a full twenty-eight feet. Yet its preserved length is far less remarkable than the scroll's implicit claims. The author has compiled here a new law for life in the land, a "new Deuteronomy" intended to guide Israel during the Last Days. In compiling this law, he extracts many portions from the "old law," the first five books of the Bible (especially from Deuteronomy), while deliberately omitting the name of Moses whenever he quotes biblical portions that contain the name. This omission is reinforced by changes in the verbs, and the total effect is electric: Moses speaks in the first person. The *Temple Scroll* is thereby made to seem a direct revelation from God—Moses' own notes, as it were, which some other person subsequently rendered in the form known to us from the Bible. That rendering has now been superseded, our author says; here is the original and final message from Sinai. This work, according to many scholars, is a claim to present a previously hidden writing from the hand of Moses. According to this view, the *Temple Scroll* is an apocryphal Moses book, one of about a dozen that appear among the Dead Sea Scrolls.

But there is another, equally viable way to understand the contents of the work: as a revelation to a "new Moses," one that naturally reprised many of the original materials as of eternal value, yet added new law for the new age. Many people were awaiting a new Moses figure in the Second Temple era, believing that the Scriptures prophesied his rise. The basis for the belief was Deuteronomy 18:15, where Moses says, "The LORD your God will raise up for you a prophet like me from among your own people." We see this expectation reflected in the Gospel of John, for example, in a question posed to John the Baptist: "Who are you? . . . Are you the prophet?" (John 1:19–21).

The *Temple Scroll* is possibly to be connected with the shadowy figure known as the Teacher of Righteousness (see the *Damascus Document,* text 1, and the *Commentary on Habakkuk,* text 2). Some of his claims about himself fit the new Moses model (see the *Thanksgiving Hymns,* text 12). If the Teacher did not himself compose the work, disciples may have done so after his death and in his spirit. At several junctures the *Temple Scroll* echoes peculiar legal doctrines linked with the Teacher by writings such as the *Damascus Document* (text 1) and the portions of the *Thanksgiving Hymns* (text 12) that seem to come from his hand.

The *Temple Scroll* mandates the construction of a vast temple and surrounding complex. The architectural details square with neither the biblical description of Solomon's Temple nor any other known Israelite or Jewish temple plan. The author depicts a gold-plated temple surrounded by three progressively larger squares, a complex far larger even than that of the famed Temple built by Herod. In fact, its size equals that of the entire city of Jerusalem as it then existed. Moreover, to construct the temple commanded by the scroll would require apocalyptic adjustments to the landscape: the Kidron Valley to the east of Jerusalem would need millions of tons of rock and soil fill, and comparable amounts of both would have to be quarried to level the western side of the city. The huge size of this complex as well as numerous particular details of the architecture point to some connection between the *Temple Scroll* and the New Jerusalem described in *A Vision of the New Jerusalem* (text 143).

The scroll includes a festival calendar that mandates hitherto unknown festivals, sacrifices, and festal regulations. In outline the calendar is the Qumran calendar known from many of the calendrical writings, but the new festivals do not always appear in those other works.

Although the author evidently intended to create a new Deuteronomy, he did not simply reproduce quotations from that book and related biblical portions following the biblical order of presentation. Rather, he organized the material by the principle of concentric circles of holiness. These circles begin with a central ring surrounding the Holy of Holies in the temple and ripple outward to embrace the entire land. Thus, at the beginning of the scroll details concern the architecture for the sanctuary, but by the end we are reading laws governing outlying cities and the land as a whole. On this principle the author inserted the festival calendar, for example, at the juncture where he was portraying the circle surrounding the altar and inner portions of the innermost court. The calendar would especially govern the activities that took place within that circle. Dual constraints guided this "circular" reasoning: an overriding concern for ritual purity and the belief that a new law for life in the land should be based on the existing biblical equivalent, which begins at Deuteronomy 12.

Precisely because of this second constraint, a comparison of the contents of the *Temple Scroll* with the laws of Deuteronomy is useful, for it brings our author's new ideas into focus. Oddly, it is often what he does not say that most clearly expresses his views. For example, the author has eliminated from his law all passages of Deuteronomy that concern, directly or by implication, either divorce or polygamy. These things would not exist in his utopian Israel and so needed no regulation. He also added new laws making niece marriage illegal. (The *Damascus Document* manifests concerns for precisely these same aspects of marriage.) Another striking series of omissions occurs wherever Deuteronomy mentions foreigners or sojourners. The *Temple Scroll* omits every such passage. Because the author conceives of an Israel that excludes all nonconverted foreigners from life in the land, his new law dispenses with the pertinent regulations. This radical antipathy to Gentiles appears in a number of the Dead Sea Scrolls and seems to stem at least in part from a belief that Gentiles were intrinsically impure.

The translation renders 11Q19, with the overlapping fragments of 11Q20–21, 4Q524, and 4Q365a guiding restorations at various junctures.

A general statement about entry into the land God is about to give the people. This portion is a pastiche weaving together Exodus 34:10–16 and Deuteronomy 7:25–26.

Col. 2 [1][. . . For it is an awesome thing that I] am about to do [with you.] [2][See, I will drive out before you] the A[morites, the Canaanites,] [3][the Hittites, the Girgashite]s, the Pe[rizzites, the Hivites, and] [4][the Jebusites. Take ca]re not to make a coven[ant with the inhabitants of the land] [5][into which you] will enter, or they will become a sna[re among you.] [6]You shall tear down their [alta]rs, [their] pillars [you shall break, and] [7][th]eir [sacred poles] you shall cut down. The images of [their] go[ds you shall burn] [8][with fire.] Do not covet the silver or the gold becau[se you could be ensnared by it; certainly it is abhorrent] [9][to Me.] Do [not] take any of it and do not bri[ng an abhorrent thing into] [10][your house] or, like it, [you will] be set aside for destruction. You are utterly to detest and ab[hor it,] [11][for] it is set apart for destruction. You shall worship no [other] god, [for] [12][your God] is a jealous God. Be careful not to make [a covenant with the inhabitants] [13][of the land,] [13][for when they whore] after [their] gods [and] sacrifice to [them, they will invite] [14][you and you will eat of their sacrifices. You will ta]ke [their daughters for your sons,] [15][and when their daughters whore after the]ir [gods, they will] make [your sons also into whores . . .]

Cols. 3–11:8 are very fragmentary. They describe the architecture of the temple and preparation of the temple furnishings. At 11:9 begins a calendar specifying the year's festal occasions and the sacrificial requirements for each. The calendar continues through the subsequent columns until col. 30 and generally weaves together Numbers 28–29, portions from Leviticus, and many nonbiblical details. Col. 12 and the early lines of col. 13 are still not well deciphered. At 13:10 begins text specifying the perpetual offering and Sabbath offerings. According to the Talmud, a hin was a liquid measure equal to the contents of seventy-two eggs. The ephah was a dry measure whose equivalent varied over time.

Col. 11 [9][And you shall offer sacrifices upon the altar of burnt offering for all the LORD's festivals;] on the Sabbaths and at the beginning of [10][the months, and on the first of the fir]st [month], and on the Feast of Unleavened Bread, and on the day of the Waving of the Omer, [11][and on the Feast of the Second Passover and on the Feast of Weeks, that is, of the Feast] of Firstfruits for Wheat, [12][and on the Feast of Wine . . .] and on the Feast of New Oil, and on the six days of [13][the] Wood [Offering,] and on [the Day of Remembrance and on the Day of Atonement and on the Feas]t of Booths and on the assembly [14][of all the people that gathers in] the inner court [. . .]

Col. 13 [10][This is what you shall offer on the altar:] t[wo] yearling [lambs] [11]without defect [every day as a perpetual offering. One lamb shall be offered in the morning, together with its cereal offering, one-te]nth of an ephah [12]of choice flour, mixed [with one-fourth of a hin of beaten oil;] thus for the lambs and the he-[goat, as a perpetual burnt offering for a pleasing odor, an offering by fire] [13]to the LORD. Its drink offering shall be one fou[rth of a hin] of wine [. . .]

[17]On the Sa[bbath] days you shall offer two [yearling male lambs without blemish . . .]

Sacrifices for the first day of the month.

[At the beginning of your months you shall offer a burnt offering to the LORD:] **Col. 14** [1]one [ram, seven male lambs a year old without blemish, and a he-goat as a sin offering;] [2]and a [gra]in offering mix[ed with three-tenths of an ephah of choice flour], [3]with [ha]lf a hin [of oil and wine as a drink offering, half a hin per bull; and two-tenths of an ephah of choice flour] [4][mix]ed with one-third of [a hin of oil, and wine for a drink offering—one third of a hin—for the ram;] [5][and for] the lamb one-tenth [of an ephah of choice flour mixed with a fourth of a hin of oil, with a wine offering of one-fourth of] [6]a hin, for every lamb, [for the seven lambs and for the he-goat, a pleasing] [7]odor to the LORD at the beg[inning of your months.

This is the burnt offering for each month] [8]for the months of the year. [It is a burnt offering] to the LORD.

Sacrifices for the New Year of the first month. This festival is not found in the Bible.

[9]On the first day of the [firs]t month [falls the beginning of months; for you it is the beginning of the months] [10]of the year. [You are to do] no work. [You shall offer a he-goat for a sin offering,] [11]which must be offered separately from the other sacrifices to aton[e for you. In addition, you are to sacrifice one young bull,] [12]one ram, seven [unblemished] yearling lambs, [and] a he-goat as a si[n o]ffering, [13]not including the regular burnt offering of the first day of the month; [together with a grain offering of three-tenths of an ephah of choice flour m]ixed [14]with one-half of a hin of oil, and wine for a drink offering, on[e-half of a hin for the bull, and] two- [15]tenths of an ephah of choice flour as a grain offering, mixed [with oil, one-third of a hin;] and wine for a drink offering, [16]one-th[ird] of a hin for the one ram, and for the lambs and he-goat [one]-tenth of an ephah [17][of choice] flour as a grain offering, [mi]xed with oil, one-fourth of a hin; [and wine for a drink offering, one fourth of] [18]a hin for the one [ram,] for the seven lambs, and for the he[-goat.]

[. . .] **Col. 15 (**with **11Q20 Col. 1)** [1][eve]ry day [. . . lambs] [2]a year old, seven; and one male [goat for a sin offering, along with the requisite grain offerings and drink offerings . . .] [3]according to this ordinance.

Description of an annual seven-day ceremony for the ordination of the priests. Though these rites are derived by analogy with the biblical description of Aaron's one-time ordination, this annual ceremony is not found in the Bible.

For the Ordination Ceremony: one ram for every [day,] [3a][and] baskets of bread for all the ra[ms of the ordination ceremony, one basket for] each [4][ram.] They are to divide all the rams and baskets for the seven [days, each] [5]day having [its] portion. They are to offer to the LORD [6]as a burnt offering from the ram, along with [the fat that covers the entrails and] the two [7]kidneys with [the] fat that is on [them, and the fat that is on] [8]the loins, and the fat tail near the spine, and the appendage of the liver. [9]Its grain offering and drink offering shall follow the usual reg[ulation. They shall take one unleavened cake from the] basket and one cake [10]of bread with oil and [one] wafer, [and place all of them on top of the fats] [11]together with the offering of the right thigh. Then the officiants shall wave the [12]rams and the baskets of bread as a wave offering before the LORD. It is a burnt offering, [13]an offering by fire, a pleasing odor before the LORD.

[They are to burn everything on the altar] over [14]the burnt offering to atone for themselves, each of the seven days of [the ordination ceremony.]

If a new high priest is about to take office, then a special ceremony of ordination takes place at the time of the general ordination of the priests. Again, this ceremony does not appear in the Bible.

[15]If a high priest is about [to take office before the LORD, having] been ordained [16]to we[a]r the priestly garments in place of his father, let them offer two [bulls], [17][one for] all the peo[ple] and one for the priests. He shall offer [18][the pr]iests' first. The elders of the pri[ests] shall lay [their hands on] **Col. 16** [01]its [he]ad, and after them the high [pri]est and all the [other priests. They shall slaughter] [02]the bull; then the elders of the priests shall take some of the bull's blood [and, using their fingers, put it on the horns of the altar. The remainder] [03]of the blood they are to pour around the four corners of the [altar's] ledge [. . .]

[2][Let the elders] take some of its blood and put it [on the high priest's right] thumb [and on] [3]the ti[p] of his right ear. They shall sprinkle [some of the blood and] some of the oil [on his garments.] [4]He shall then be holy to the LORD all of his days. [He is not to . . .] [5]nor defile himself, for he is now hol[y to the LORD his God.]

[6][Then he may sacrifice upon the al]tar and burn th[e first bull's fat], [7][all the] fat on the entrails and th[e appendage of the liver and the two] [8]kidneys, and the fat on the[m], and th[e fat that is on] [9]the loins, along with its grain offering and drink off[ering, following the usual regulation.] He shall bur[n them upon the altar;] [10]it shall be a [bu]rnt offering, an offering by fire, a pleasing odor be[fore the LORD.]

[The flesh of the bull, however,] [11]together with its skin and offal, they shall burn outside the [city of the sanctuary], [12]in a place separated out for the sin offerings. Only there shall they bu[rn it, with its head and legs] [13]and all its entrails. They are to burn it there in its entirety, apart from the fat; for it is a sin off[ering of the priest.]

[14]Then he shall take the second bull, the one for the people, and atone with it [for all the people] [15]who are assembled, using its blood and fat. Just as he did with the firs[t] bull, [so shall he do] [16]with the assembly's bull. Using his finger, he is to put some of its blood on the horns of the [altar. Then] [17]he shall sprinkle the rest of its blood o[n the fo]ur corners of the altar's ledge. [Its fat,] [18][gr]ain offering, and dr[ink] offering he must bu[r]n upon the altar; it is the assembly's sin offering.

Col. 17 [1][. . . the] priests; and they shall place cro[wns upon their heads . . .] [2][. . .] Then they shall rejoice, for atonement has been made for them. [3][. . .] This day shall [be a holy convocation] for them. [These are eternal statutes] [4][for generation after generation,] wherever they may dwell. They are to rejoice and be very [glad . . .]

Commands for the Passover, celebrated on the evening of the fourteenth day of the first month.

[6][On the fo]urteenth day of the first month, [at twilight, let them keep] [7][the Passover to the LORD.] They shall sacrifice the Passover offering prior to the evening offering. [Every male] [8]aged twenty years and up shall prepare it. Then they are to eat it at night, [9]in the courtyards of [the] temple. Afterwards they shall arise early in the morning and return home.

Commands for the Feast of Unleavened Bread, seven days beginning on the fifteenth of the first month.

[10]On the fifteenth of this month a ho[ly] convocation is to take place. [11]You are to do no work on it; it is a pilgrimage feast of unleavened bread, seven days [12]for the LORD. For each of th[ese] seven days you are to offer [13]a burnt offering to the LORD, comprising two bulls, a ram, and seven unblemished yearling lambs, [14]together with a single he-goat—a sin offering—and the requisite grain and drink offerings. [15]You shall [follow] the [us]ual regulations for the bulls, the ram, the [la]mbs, and the goat. Then, on the seventh day, [16][a solemn assembly] to the [LO]RD shall be held; on that day you are to do no work.

Fragmentary commands for the waving of the barley sheaf (the Waving of the Omer) on the twenty sixth of the first month.

Col. 18 [1][. . . lambs a ye]ar old, four [2][. . .] for this ram [. . .] [3][. . . They shall hold a sacred convocation] on this day, and [. . .] [4][. . . a male] goat for a sin offering to [atone] [5][for all the people assembled, its grain offering and dr]ink offering following the usual regulation: a tenth of an ephah of choice flour [6][m]ixed with [oil, one-fourth of a hin, and] wine for a drink offering, one-fourth of a hin. [7][. . . He shall atone] for all the people assembled, for all [their] sin, [8][and they shall be forgiven. Generation after generation,] these shall be eternal [sta]tutes for them, [9][wherever they may dwe]ll. After that they are to sacrifice the ram, once [10][a ye]ar, on the day of waving the sheaf.

Regulations for the festival of the Firstfruits of Wheat, beginning on the fifteenth of the third month. This is a biblical feast, but the method of calculating its date was a matter of dispute at the time of the scroll.

You shall count [11]seven full weeks from the day on which you bring the sheaf [12][of the wave offering. You are to co]unt until the day after the seventh Sabbath : count [13][fifty] days. Then you shall bring a new grain offering to the LORD from wherever you dwell, [14][loaves] of bread, fresh baked with leaven—firstfruits to the LORD, bread made with wheat. There must [b]e two [15][loaves of bread, with two-tenths] of an ephah of choice flour in each loaf. [16][The heads of the tr]ibe[s shall bring them,] and they are to offer [. . .]

Col. 19 [1][. . . after the burnt offering of the mor]ning [. . .] [2][. . . At the first quarter] of the day they shall offer the burnt off[ering of the Firstfruits.] [3][They are to sacrifice a bull], twel[ve goats, and seven yearling lambs] [4][wi]thout blemish, together with their grain offering and [their dri]nk offering following the usual regulations, and [the priests] shall wave [5][them as a wave offering over the bread of the] Firstfruits. They shall belong to the priests, and they shall eat them [6]in the [inner] cour[t] along with the bread of the Firstfruits. Afterward, [7][all the peo]ple [shall eat] new bread made with fresh, ripe ears of grain. [That] day is to be [8][a holy convocation, and these statutes are ete]rnal, for generation after generation. They shall do no work [9][on it.] This is a [pilgrimage Feast of W]eeks, a feast of firstfruits established as a memorial forev[er].

Stipulations for the festival of the Firstfruits of Wine, beginning on the third day of the fifth month. This festival appears nowhere in the Bible.

[11]You shall count beginning from the day when you bring the new grain offering to the LOR[D—] [12]the bread of the firstfruits—seven weeks, seven full weeks, [13]until the day after the seventh Sabbath. You are to count fifty days, [14]then [sa]crifice new wine as a drink offering: four hin from all the tribes of Israel, [15]one-third of a hin from each tribe. In addition to the wine, they are to offer on that day [16]twelve rams to the LORD. All the commanders of the thousands of Israel [. . .]

Col. 20 [01][. . . with their drink offering up]on it, together with their grain offering, following the usual regulations: two-[tenths of an ephah of choice flour mixed with oil,] [02][one-third of a h]in of oil per ram, in addition to this drink offering. [03][Then they shall sacrifice as a burnt offering two bulls, a ram, and] seven yearling [male lamb]s, together with a he-[04][goat for a sin offering, to atone for all the people as]sembled. [05][. . . and] the[ir grain offering] and drink offering following the usual regulations for bulls and rams [06][and sheep and he-goats. It is an offering by fire, a pleasing odor] to the LORD. They are to sacrifice at the first quarter of the day [. . .] [1][and] the rams and the drink offering. Then they are to sacrifice as [pea]ce offerings [. . .] [2][. . .] and fourteen yearling lambs [together with their grain offering and drink offering] [3][following the usual regulations for goats and] for [sheep]. They shall offer them after the burnt offering, [and sprinkle their blood upon] [4][the base of the altar]. They shall burn [their fat] upon the altar, [all the] [5][fat surrounding the entrails], and all the fat that is attached to the entrails, [6]and [the appendage of the liver.] He shall remove the kidneys, and all the fat [that is] on [them] [7][and on the loins, and] the fat tail near the spine, and bu[rn] [8][the entirety on the altar,] along with the requisite grain offering and drink offering. It is an offering by fire, a pl[ea]sing odor [9][before the LORD.]

Any grain offering that is accompanied by a drink offering is to be offered following [the usual regulations.] [10]From [eve]ry grain offering [th]at is accompanied by frankincense, or else offered dry, they are to take a handful—the [11][memor]ial portion—and burn it on the altar. The remainder shall be eaten in the [12][in]n[er] court. The priests are to e[a]t it [without leav]en; it must not be eaten leavened. It must be eaten on that very day; [13][that is,] the sun must [not se]t on [it.] You are to put salt on all your offerings, never relaxing [14]the covenant to use salt, forever.

Then they shall make an offering to the LORD, [15][a w]ave offering from [the ra]ms and the male lambs: the right thigh, the breast, [16][the cheeks, the stoma]ch, and the foreleg extending as far as the shoulder bone. They are to wave them as a wave offering. **Col. 21** [02][The priests' portions] are to be the thigh that is waved and the breast [03][that is waved, as the best part; they shall also assign the foreleg]s, the cheeks, and the stomachs as priestly portions, [04][as an eternal statute, owed them by the children of Isra]el. The shoulder, what remains from the foreleg up, [05][belongs to the Levites; this is theirs from the people] as a perpetual statute; it belongs to them and to their descendants. [06][Afterward they shall bring portions to the children of Israel;] the commanders of thousands [shall be given some] of the rams and some of the [1][lambs. One ram [2]and one sheep shall belong to Aaron and] his sons; one ram and one lamb to the Levites; and to each tribe they are to give one [ram] and one lamb, that is, to all the tri[bes, the twe]lve [3]tribes of Israel. Then they shall eat them in the outer [court] before the LORD, and [the pries]ts shall drink [4]some of the new wine. They shall drink there first, then the Levites second, [5][and after them all the children of Is]rael: the commanders of divisions in first position; [6][after them . . .]; then the whole people, gre[at] and small, [7]may begin to drink the new wine and to eat grapes from the vines, whether ripe or unripe, for [8][on] this [da]y they will make atonement for the wine. So the children of Israel are to rejoice bef[ore] the LORD, [9]this being an eternal [statute,] generation after generation, wherever they may dwell. They shall rejoice this d[ay] [10]in the festival of [new wine] to pour out a fermented drink offering, new wine upon the altar of the LORD, an annual rite.

Stipulations for the festival of the Firstfruits of New Oil. This festival was to occur on the twenty-second day of the sixth month, and, once again, it does not appear in the Bible.

[12]Y[ou] shall count from that day seven weeks—seven times seven days, forty-nine [13]days, seven complete weeks—until the day after [14]the seventh Sabbath : count out fifty days. Then offer new oil from the places where [15]the [tr]ibes of the ch[ildren of Is]rael dwell, half a hin from each tribe, newly extracted oil. [16][They are to offer the firstfruits of the] oil on the altar of burnt offering, as firstfruits before the LORD [. . .]

Col. 22 (with **11Q20 Cols. 5–6**) [03][. . . tw]o [bulls,] two rams [03][and a he-goat as a sin offering], by which [to ato]ne for the entire congregation before [04][the LORD . . .] with one-half a hin of this new oil. [05][. . . following the us]ual regulations. It is a burnt offering, an offering by fire, a [pleasing] odor [06][to the LORD. Using] this oil [1]they shall light the lamps [. . .]

[2][. . .] The commanders of thousands, together with the leaders of [the divisions], [3][fourteen rams and] fourteen [la]mbs, with their requisite grain offering and drink offering, [4][according to the usual regulat]ion for the la[mbs] and the rams. Then the Levites are to slaughter th[ese rams and lambs], [5][and] the priests, the sons of Aaron, [are to spri]nkle their blood [all around on the altar, . . .] [6]and they shall burn [the flesh and] the fat on the altar of [burnt offering] according to the usual re[gulations]. [7]They shall burn [their grain offering] and drink offering on top of the fat[s. Now this flesh is an offering by fire, a] pleasing [odor] [8][to] the LORD.

Next they shall present to the LORD an offering from the rams and lambs: [9]the right thigh, the breast of the wave offering, and, as the best part, [the foreleg.] [10]The cheeks and the stomach shall belong to the priests as their portion, following the usual regulations. The Levites are to receive [11]the shoulder.

Afterward, the portions shall be brought out to the children of Israel, who are to give the priests [12]one ram and one lamb, the Levites the same, and each tribe [13]the same. They shall eat them before the LORD on that very day in the outer court. [14]This is an eternal statute, for generation after generation, as an annual rite. After [15]they have eaten, they are to anoint themselves with the new oil and eat olives, for on that day they shall have atoned [16]for [a]ll [the o]il of the land before the LORD, as an annual rite once a year. The children of Israel shall rejoice **Col. 23** [01][before the LORD wherever they may live; this is an eternal statute for generation after generation.]

The Festival of Wood Offering. Although the Bible requires Israel to provide wood for the sacrifices offered on the altar, no formalized procedure for doing so appears in its pages. The scroll presents a weeklong festival for this purpose, beginning the day after the Festival of New Oil. The reference to the "the fourth of the day" in l. 8 means approximately three hours after sunrise (one-fourth of the way through the daylight hours).

[02][And after the Fe]stival of New Wine [03][the twe]lve [tribes of the children of Israel] are to contribute [04]wood for the alt[ar]. Those contributing on the fir[st] day are to be [05]the tribes of [Levi] and Judah; on the [second day, Benjamin and the sons of] [1][Joseph; on the third day, Reu]ben and Simeon; on the fourth day, Issachar [2][and Zebulun; on the fifth day, Gad and] Asher; on the [sixth] d[ay, Dan] and Naphtali. [3][Along with] the wood, [they are to offer] as a burnt offering to the LO[RD] [4][. . . and] two he-goats as [a sin offering, whereby to atone] [5][for the children of Israel, along with the] requisite [grain offering] and drink offering, following the us[ual regulations. Each tribe shall bring] as a burn[t offering] [6]one bull, one ram, and [one] la[mb born that year], [7][without blemish, tr]ibe by tribe, the twelve sons of Jaco[b.] [8][They shall sacrifice them at the fourth of the da]y upon the altar, after the per[petual] burnt offering [and its drink offering.]

[9]The high priest is to o[ff]er the [Levites'] burnt offering [10]first, then the burnt offering of the tribe of Judah. W[hen he] [11]is ready to begin making offerings, the he-goat shall be slaughtered in his presence as the first thing. He is to raise [12]its blood to the altar in a bowl, and, using his finger, pu[t some] of the blood on the four horns of the altar [13]of burnt offering, and on the four corners of the altar's ledge. Then he shall pour the rest of the blood on the foundat[ion] [14]of the altar's ledge, all around. Subsequently he shall burn its fat on the altar: the fat covering the [15]entrails and that above the entrails. He shall remove the appendage of the liver and the kidneys, [16]as well as the fat on them and on the loins. He is to burn [17]the entirety on the altar, along with its grain offering and drink offering, as an offering by fire, a pleasing odor to the LORD [. . .]

Col. 24 [. . .] the head [and the suet] [2][. . . the two foreleg]s and the sh[oulder] [3][. . . and] the breast, with the [right] [4][thigh. They are to wash the entrails and the t]wo legs [with water] and of[fer] [5][all these things on the altar, a burnt offering to the LORD, together with] its grain offering and drink offering [of wine.] [6][. . . of] a hin he shall pour out [up]on the flesh, as a [pleasing] odor, [an offering by fire] [7][to the LORD. Th]us shall be done with each and every bull, ram, and [lamb. The lamb and] [8]its limbs shall be ke[pt] apart; the gr[ain] offering and drink offering shall rest on top of it. These are [ete]rnal statutes, [9]for generation after generation before the LORD.

[10]After this burnt offering he shall offer that of the tribe of Judah separately. Just as [11]he has performed the burnt offering of the Levites, so shall he perform that of the sons of Judah, after the Levites. [12]Then on the second day he shall offer the burnt offering of Benjamin first, and afterwards [13]that of the sons of Joseph as one, Ephraim and Manasseh. On the third day he is to offer [14]Reuben's burnt offering separately, and that of Simeon separately. On the fourth day [15]he shall offer the burnt offering of Issachar, then that of Zebulun, separately. On the fifth day [16]he shall offer Gad's burnt offering, then Asher's, separately. Finally, on the sixth day **Col. 25** [01][he shall offer Dan's burnt offering, then Naphtali's, separately.]

The stipulations for the Day of Memorial, on the first day of the seventh month.

[2]And in the [seventh] mo[nth, on the first day of] [3][the month, you shall observe a day of rest, a mem]orial proclaimed by trumpets, a [holy] con[vocation.] [4][This day shall be a day of rejoicing be]fore the LORD. Thus [you are to] sac[rifice a burnt offering] [5][to the LORD: one bull,] one ram, and sev[en perfect] yearling [male lamb]s, [along with a he-goat] [6][as a sin offering], accompanied by their grain offerings and drink offerings following the usual regulations—[a pleasing odor before] [7][the LORD. These are in addition to] the perpetual [burn]t offering [and the burn]t offering for the first day of the month. Only after offering those [are you to perform] this [8][burnt offering,] at the third part of the day. These are eternal statutes, for generation after generation [wherever you may dwell.] [9]You are to rejoice on this day, doing no wo[rk] whatsoever. This day is to be [10]a day of rest for you.

Commands for the Day of Atonement, falling on the tenth day of the seventh month. By the time of the Temple Scroll, *Azazel had come to be a name for Satan.*

On the tenth of this month [11]is the Day of Atonement. You are to humble yourselves on it; in fact, anyone who does not [12]humble himself on this very day shall be cut off from his people. You are to offer a burnt offering to the LORD on it: [13]one bull, one ram, and seven yearling male lambs, together with a he- [14]goat as a sin offering—quite apart from the sin offering of atonement—accompanied by their grain offering and drink offering, [15]following the usual regulations regarding the bull, the ram, the lambs, and the goat.

As for the sin offering of atonement, you are to sacrifice [16]two rams as a burnt offering. The high priest shall offer one for himself and his father's house, [and one for the people . . .] **Col. 26** [3][. . . Then] the [high pri]est [shall cast lots for] [4][the two goats,] o[ne] lot [designated "The LORD" and the other "Azazel."] [5]He is to slaughter the goat [upon whom] fall[s the lot designated "The LORD," and receive] [6]its blood in the golden bowl that he ho[lds. He is to d]o with [its] blo[od as he di]d with that [7]of the bull he sacrificed for himself, making atonement with it for all the people assembled. Its fat, grain offering, [8]and drink offering he shall burn upon the altar of burnt offering, whereas its flesh, skin, and offal [9]are to be burned near that of his bull. This is the sin offering for the assembly, wherewith he shall atone for all the people assembled, [10]and they shall be forgiven.

Then he shall wash the blood of the sin offering from his hands and feet and approach [11]the living goat. He is to confess over its head all the iniquities of the children of Israel, as well as [12]all their guilt and sins, thus putting them upon the goat's head. Then he shall send him away [13]to Azazel in the wilderness led by a man prepared for the moment. The goat shall carry away all the iniquities **Col. 27** [01][. . .] the blood [. . .] [02]an offering by fire, a pleasing odor before the LO[RD]. [1][. . . Thus shall the high priest atone] [2]for all the children of Israel, and they shall be forgiven.

[3]Afterwards he is to offer the bull, [r]am, and [lambs following the us]ual regulations [4]on the altar of burnt offering, and the [bur]nt offering will be acceptable on behalf of the children of Israel. These are perpetual statutes, [5]for generation after generation. Once each year they shall observe this day as a memorial. [6]They shall do no work whatsoever on it, because it is a Sabbath of solemn rest. Any man [7]who does work on it or who does not humble himself will be cut off from [8]his people. This day is to be a Sabbath of solemn rest, a holy convocation, [9]so you are to consecrate it as a memorial wherever you may dwell. You are not to do any [10]work.

Commands for the Feast of Tabernacles, a weeklong festival beginning on the fifteenth day of the seventh month. Most of the commands for the first day and everything for the days following the fourth have been lost.

On the fifteenth day of this month **Col. 28** [01][. . . a grain offering, choice flour mixed with oil, one-fourth of] a hin, and a drink offering, [one-fourth]

02[of a hin of wine for each lamb. Thu]s shall they do for the fo[urteen] 1[lambs and for the he-goat, quite apart from the regular burnt] offering, together with [its] grain offering [and drink offering on] 2the altar. This is an offering by fire, a [pleasing] od[or to the LORD. And on the] 3second [day], he shall sacrifice twelve bulls, [two rams, four-] 4teen [male lambs], and one he-goat [as a si]n offering, together with their [gr]ain offering [and drink] offering, 5following the usual regulations for bulls, ram[s], sheep [and] the goat. This is an offering by fire, 6a pleasing odor to the LORD.

On the third day 7he shall sacrifice eleven [b]ulls, two rams, fourteen male lambs, 8and a he-goat as a sin offering, together with their grain offering and drink offering, following the usual regulations for bulls, 9rams, lambs, and the goat. On the fourth day 10he is to sacrifice ten bulls, two rams, fourteen yearling male lambs, 11and a he-goat as a sin offering, together with their grain offering and drink offering as usual for bulls [. . .]

A summary statement for the festival calendar. This portion is a crucial clue to the purpose and intentions of the Temple Scroll. *Apparently the temple for which the scroll provides the architectural plan is not eternal, but will be replaced at the "Day of Creation" by a temple created by God himself.*

Col. 29 2These [are the regulations that you must follow for all of your festivals,] 3with each one's burnt offerings, [grain offerings, and drink offerings], in the temple upon which I shall [cause] My 4name [to dwell. Further, these are] the burnt offerings—[each] on the requisite [day] as stipulated by the law of this ordinance—5required of the children of Israel for always (not including freewill offerings that they may choose to sacrifice), 6together with their vow offerings and all the gifts that they are to bring to find favor with Me.

7And find favor they shall; they shall be My people, and I will be theirs, forever. I shall dwell 8with them for all eternity. I shall sanctify My [te]mple with My glory, 9for I will cause My glory to dwell upon it until the Day of Creation, when I Myself will create My temple; 10I will establish it for Myself for everlasting in fulfillment of the covenant that I made with Jacob at Bethel, **Col. 30** 01[Isaac at Gerar, and Abraham at Haran . . .]

Now begins a lengthy section of the scroll detailing the architecture of the temple complex. Virtually nothing of this description derives from the Bible as we know it, though some portions come from a rewritten Bible (see 4Q365 [text 84] above; it is also possible that frag. 23 of text 84 is actually a copy of the Temple Scroll*). The description begins in the innermost court and works outward. The first structure* *described is a staircase tower, apparently to be used to reach the roof of the temple. Precisely why that would be necessary is unclear; perhaps calendrical observations would be made from that height, or perhaps priests would reach poles down to clean the Holy of Holies without actually entering it. Only the high priest was ever to enter the Holy of Holies, and then only on the Day of Atonement.*

[3][. . .] And you are to make [4]stairs on bo[th sides of the ga]tes of the temple that you are to build so that My [name may] [5][rest upon it]. You are to [m]ake a staircase tower north of the sanctuary, a square structure [6]measuring twenty cubits from one corner to another, for each of its four corners. It shall be a distance of seven cubits [7]to the northwest of the sanctuary wall. You shall make its wall four cubits [8]thick, rising straight from thi[s outworking], in like manner as the sanctuary. The interior measurement from angle to angle is to be [9]twelve cu[bits], with a square column set in the middle, four cubits wide [10]in every direction. The width of the stairs winding upwards around it is to be four [cu]bits [. . .] **Col. 31** [4][. . .] the priest assistant to the high priest [5][. . . the hi]gh [priest].

[6]In the roof chamber of [this] ho[use you must make a ga]te opening to the roof of the sanctuary. A walkway shall lead [7]from this gate to the outworking of the sanctuary, by means of which one can enter the roof chamber of the sanctuary. [8]You are to overlay this entire staircase tower with gold: its walls, gates, and roof, inside [9]and out, its column and stairs. You must do everything just as I am telling you.

The second structure described in the inner court is to house the laver (where the priests washed before and after sacrificing) and related accoutrements. At the end are the tatters of regulations concerning the clothes worn by officiating priests as they rotated into and out of service in the Temple.

[10]You shall make a square house for the laver to the southeast of the sanctuary, twenty-one [11]cubits on a side, fifty cubits distant from the altar. The wall is to be three cubits thick and its height [12]twenty cubits. You must make [thr]ee gates for it, on the east, north, [13]and west, four cubits wide and seven high.

Col. 32 [8][. . .] You are to make nic[hes] on the inner face of the wall of this [9]house, and inside them [. . .] one cubit wide. The niches shall be [10]four cubits above the ground and overlaid with gold. There the priests shall store [11]the clothes in which they [com]e, above the house of the lave[r], [12]when they arrive to serve.

You shall build an aqueduct around the laver near the altar of burnt offering, [13]running un[d]er the laver, with a hole descending into the ground into which [14]the water will pour and go down until it disappears into the earth. None may [15]touch the water because some of the blood from burnt offerings is mixed with it. **Col. 33** [1–5][. . .] [6][they will be com]ing to the laver and exiting in them to [the outer court; they are not] [7]to sanctify the gate with the holy clothes in which they [serve].

A plan for the house storing temple utensils.

[8]You are to build a house east of the house of the laver, the same size as the latter. [9]The wall must be seven cubits distant from that of the house of the laver. The [wh]ole structure and roof shall be the same as those of the laver's house. [10]It must have two gates, one on the north and the other on the south, opposite each other, measuring the same as those of the laver's house. [11]All the inner walls of this house are to have cupboards built in, recessed into the wall. [12]They shall be two cubits wide and two deep and four cubits high. [13]They are to have doors. These shall house the altar's utensils: basins, flagons, fire pans, [14]and silver ladles, with which entrails and [15]limbs are lifted to the altar. When they finish sacrificing, [. . .]

A description of the slaughterhouse, probably located on the north side of the sanctuary. The architectural specifics are badly preserved; most of what can be read concerns the praxis of slaughtering the animals using a system of chains and rings.

Col. 34 [1][. . . plat]ed with a bron[ze] tablet [. . .] [2][. . .] and between one pillar and ano[ther . . .] [3][. . .] that is between the pillars [. . .] [4][. . . setting] the bulls in place between the whee[ls . . .] [5][. . . opening the whe]els and closing the wheels, and [. . .] [6]fastening the bulls' horns to the rings and [. . .] in the rings.

[7]Then they shall slaughter them and gather [all the blood] in bowls [8]to sprinkle on the foundation of the altar, all around. After that they are to open [9]the wheels and flay the bulls' skins from their flesh; next, they shall cut them up [10]into pieces, salting the pieces and washing [11]the entrails and legs, then salting those as well. Afterward they may burn them [12]in the fire upon the altar, bull by bull accompanied by its pieces, its grain offering of choice flour on top of it [13]and the wine of its drink offering alongside (some having been poured on top of it). The priests, the sons of Aaron, are to burn the entirety [14]upon the altar as an offering by fire, a pleasing odor before the LORD.

[15]You are also to design chains hanging down from the ceiling atop the twelve pillars [. . .]

At this point in the architectural description the author inserts a list of those forbidden to approach the precincts or take part in the ceremonies he is describing. Death was to be the penalty for infringement.

Col. 35 [1][to the Hol]y of Holi[es . . .] [2][. . . it]. Any man who has not [. . . It shall be] [3][a holy anointing]. Any man who has not [. . . h]oly [4][must be anoin]ted with it. Any [Israelite man who shall bring it but] is not [5]a priest must be put to d[ea]th. Any man who is [a pr]iest, [a son of Aar]on, who brings [6]it but is not wearing the [holy] vest[ments, or who] has not been ordained [7]to minister, must also be put to death. They are not to profan[e the tem]ple of their God; they must bear [8]the penalty of guilty iniquity and die. You must sanctify the precinct of the altar, the sanctuary, the laver, [9]and the colonnade, so that it is utterly holy forever and ever.

Description of a colonnade, or stoa, for the sin and guilt offerings.

[10]You shall make a place west of the sanctuary. The entire precinct is to be a stoa of many columns [11]for the sin offerings and guilt offerings. There are to be separate sections for the sin offering of the priests and for the he-goats, on the one hand, [12]and for the sin and guilt offerings of the people, on the other. They are not to mix with one another [13]at all. No, their sections are to be separate from each other, so that [14]the priests do not err with any sin offering of the people or with any of their goats for guilt offerings. That would result in [15]guilty sin.

As to birds for the altar: one must prepare turtledoves [. . .]

The command to build the inner court. This court, which would surround the sanctuary and the buildings already described, was the innermost of three courts. The initial details have not survived; the first intelligible lines are describing the four gates of the court.

Col. 36 [2][. . .] gates[. . .] [3][. . .] From the [northeast] angle [4]t[o the corn]er of the gat[e is to be one hundred twenty cubits.] Each gatehouse shall be forty cubits wide; [5]all its dimensions shall have [this same measurement. Its] wall shall be seven cubits [thi]ck. [6]The height [up to the raf]ters of [its] ceiling is to be [forty-]five [cubits.] [The wid]th of [its] side [chambers] is to be [7]twenty-six cubits from angle to angle. The ga[t]es through which they will enter [8]and exit are each to be four[te]en cubits wide and [9]twenty-eight cubits high, measured from threshold to lintel. The height [10]of the ceiling structure above the lintel is to be fourteen cubits.

Each gate shall be roofed over with an entablature [11]of cedar wood overlaid with pure gold. Its doors are also to be overlaid with pure gold.

[12]From the corner of the gate to the southeast angle of the court is to be one hundred [13]twenty cubits. The same measurement shall apply with respect to all the gates and angles of [14]the inner court. The gatehouses shall intrude into the courtyard [*x* cubits . . .]

The inner court could be entered only by priests. This court is where they would eat their sacrificial portions while serving in the temple. Here the author describes some of the priestly structures to be built and the activities that were to take place there.

Col. 37 [2][. . .] new [wine] from the gardens every ye[ar . . .] [3]You are to construct [a colonnade] within the four [4]walls of [the] inner [cou]rtyard, connected to the border around the [al]tar, where [they shall eat] [5]the sacrifices of the peace offerings brought by the children of Israel. Ab[ov]e the colonnade [6][. . .] corners of the lower colonnade shall be made of gold [. . .] [7]the stairs alongside the [walls] of the gates, on both [sides] of each gate.

[8]Inside the [in]ner cou[rt] you are to design a qu[ar]ter with s[e]ats for the priests, with tables [9]placed before the seats. The quarter is to be in the inner stoa, next to the court's outer wall. [10]Also, places are to be made for the priests' sacrifices, firstfruits, and tithes, [11]as well as the peace offerings that they will sacrifice. The peace offerings sacrificed by [12]the children of Israel must never mix with those of the priests.

[13]In each of the four corners of the court you shall make the priests a place for the [ca]ldr[o]ns [14]in which they will boil their sacrifices. The sin offerings **Col. 38** [01]the priests [shall boil] in the northeast corner, then eat [them . . .] [5][. . . to] the sons of Israel.

On each day of the firstfruits [for agriculture] [6]they shall bring south of the western gate [every fruit of th]eir [land,] figs, [7]pomegranates, [and] other edible fruit of the tree.

[To the south of th]is [gate] they shall consume the grain offerings [8]upon which frankincense is sprinkled. To the west of the [nor]thern g[ate] they shall consume the grain offering for jealousy. [9]To the east of this gate [they shall eat] every grain offering, as well as every sin offering that the children of [10]Israel shall sacrifice. They shall eat the sin offerings there—namely, the turtledoves and the young pigeons.

The command to build a middle court surrounding the inner court and instruction on who may and may not enter it. The gerah of l. 9 was a small coin or its equal in metal by weight.

[12]You shall build a second [co]urt surrounding the inner court at a distance of one hundred cubits. [13]The length of its eastern wall shall be four hundred eighty cubits, the same dimension applying to all [14]its walls: south, west, and north. Its wall is to be four cubits thick and [15]twenty-eight cubits high. Chambers must be built into the outside surface of the wall, distant from each other three **Col. 39** [01]and one-half cubits [. . .] [1–3][. . .] [4][. . . Entering] this courtyard shall be all [5]the congregation of [Israel, together with any] fourth-generation proselyte [born among you], ages [6]twenty [and up. And when they enter] to prostrate themselves before me, all the congregation of the sons of [7]Israel, no woman shall enter it, nor any young man before the day [8]on which he fulfills the law [and pays] his atoneme[nt money] to the LORD: one half-shekel. This is an eternal law, [9]a memorial wherever they may dwell. (The shekel shall equate to twenty gerah.) [10]When they collect a man's half-shekel, I [shall be satisf]ied; afterward he may enter—anyone [11]twenty years ol[d] and up.

The twelve gates of the middle court, named after the sons of Jacob. Here Jacob is called "Israel," the name he received after wrestling with God.

The names of the gates for this court shall be according to the na[mes] of [12]Is[r]ael's sons: Simeon, Levi, and Judah on the east; Reuben, Joseph, and Benjamin on the south; [13]Issachar, Zebulun, and Gad on the west; Dan, Naphtali, and Asher on the north.

The measurement between the gates shall be as follows: [14]from the northeastern corner to Simeon's gate, ninety-nine cubits. The gate itself shall be [15]twenty-eight cubits wide. From Simeon's gate to that of Levi, ninety-nine [16]cubits, the gate itself being twenty-eight cubits wide. From Levi's gate to that of Judah [. . .]

The command to build a third, outermost court, with dimensions, structures, and who may enter.

Col. 40 [5][. . .] You shall build a thi[r]d court, [surrounding the middle] [6][court. Entry is permitted to all Israel, their sons and] daughters, and, as to proselytes, the children who are born in Israel [7][up to the third generation.] It shall surround the middle court at a distance of six hundred cubits. [8]The wall shall be about one thousand six [hundred] cubits long from corner to corner, the same dimension applying to all its sides: [9]east, south, west, and no[rt]h. The wall is to be seven cubits thick and forty-nine cubits [10]high. Chambers must be [b]uilt into the outside surface of the wall between the gates, along the foundation [11]and up to the wall's cornice. It shall have three gates in the east, three in the south, three [12]in the west, and three in the north. The gatehouses are to be fifty cubits wide and seventy cubits [13]high. From gate to gate shall [measure] three hundred sixty cubits. From the northeast corner to the [14]gate of Simeon shall likewise be three hundred sixty cubits; from the gate of Simeon to that of Levi [15]shall be the same measure, and so from Levi's gate to that of Judah, three [hundred] sixty **Col. 41** [01][cubits . . .]

[1][. . . and from Benjamin's gate to the we]ster[n corner] [2][shall be three hundred sixty cubits; and likewise from] this [corner] [3]to the ga[te of Issachar shall measure three hundred sixty] cubits; from the gate of [4]Issachar [to that of Zebulun shall be three] hundred [sixty] cubits; [5]from Zebulun's to Gad's, three hundred sixt[y] [6]cubits; and from Gad's [to the northwest corner,] three hundred sixty [7]cubits. From this corner to [8]the gate of Dan shall be three hundred sixty cubits, and the same from Dan's gate to [9]Naphtali's: three hundred sixty cubits; and from Naphtali's gate [10]to that of Asher, three hundred sixty cubits. From the gate of [11]Asher to the northeast corner is to be three hundred sixty cubits.

[12]The gatehouses shall project outward from the court's wall seven cubits, [13]and inward thirty-six cubits. [14]The width of the entrances is to be fourteen cubits, while their height shall be [15]twenty-eight up to the lintel. They must be roofed over [16]with beams of cedar and gilded with gold. Their doors must be overlaid [17]with pure gold.

Facing inward between the gates you shall make chambers, **Col. 42** [01][rooms and stoas.] [02]The rooms shall be ten cubits wide and twenty cubits long; [03]their height shall be four[teen cubits. They shall be roofed over with] cedar [04][beams] and their walls shall be two cubits thick. Opposite this chamber, the wi[dth of the outward-facing chamber is to be ten cubits, and its length] [05]twenty cubits. The wall shall be two cubits thick, [the height fourteen cubits. It is to be roofed over with beams] [1]of cedar, with a door three cubits wide.[. . .] [2][. . .] up to the lintel. [. . .] [3][. . . one measurement] for all the chambers, rooms, [4]and stoas: [they are all to be] ten cubits [wi]de. So, between one gate [5]and the next [there are to be eigh]teen chambers, the corresponding rooms, [6]eight[een in number, and the corresponding stoas.]

[7]You are to build a stairhouse near the walls of the gatehouse, inside [8]each stoa, in which stairs spiral upward to the second and third stories of the stoas [9]and thence to the roof. Second- and third-story chambers must be built, their dimensions, rooms, and stoas [10]corresponding to those of the first story.

On the roof of the third story [11]you are to construct columns, crowned with beams attaching column to column. [12]This will be a place for booths, with columns eight cubits high. Booths [13]will be built around them annually on the Feast of Booths to serve the elders of [14]the congregation, the leaders: the heads of clans among the children of Israel, [15]and the commanders of thousands and hundreds. They shall climb up [16]and sit there until the festival's burnt offering is sacrificed—that is, the one [17]for the Feast of Booths—each and every year.

Between one gate and the next they shall [. . .]

Here the author discusses an important activity that was to take place in the third courtyard: the consumption of the second tithe, which was eaten not by the priests, but by the laypeople who offered it to God. The author stipulates who must bring the tithe, when it may be eaten, and how to dispose of unused portions. This column is closely related to Jubilees *32:10–15; note also the Copper Scroll 1:9–12 (text 16) for a reference to second tithe.*

Col. 43 [1][. . .] the si[x working days] [2][. . .] on the Sabbath days and on the day[s of the new moon] [3][and on the days of the Festival of Unleavened Bread] and on the days of the firstfruits of grain, wi[ne,] [4]and [oil, and during the days for offering the] wood: on these days the second tithe may be eaten.

But none of it may be left over [5]from one year to the next. Rather, they shall consume it as follows: [6]beginning with the pilgrimage feast for the Firstfruits of Wheat, the grain may be eaten [7]until the second year's Firstfruits. So for the wine: from the day [8]of the Feast of New Wine until the second year at the Feast of [9]New Wine. Likewise, the oil: from the day of its festival until the second year [10]at the festival, the day of offering New Oil on the altar.

Everything that [11]remains after the corresponding second year's festival begins is to be sanctified and burned in fire. It may not be eaten anymore, [12]for it has been consecrated.

Those who live three or more days' journey distant from the temple [13]must bring all they are able to bring with them. If they cannot [14]transport it, they may sell the item for money and bring the money. Then they can use it to buy grain, [15]wine, oil, cattle, or sheep.

They shall consume the tithe on festival days; they are not [16]to eat any of it on working days when they are unclean. It is holy; [17]therefore it may be eaten on holy days but not on work days.

Allocation of rooms, chambers, and booths in the third court to priestly and Levitical families, and to the children of Israel generally, tribe by tribe.

Col. 44 [1][. . .] dwelling [. . .] [2][. . .] that is in the midst of the city toward the ea[st . . .] [3]You shall apportion [all] the [chambers from the gate of] [4][Simeo]n to the gate of Judah to the priests, [the sons of Aaron]. [5]These entire sections immediately to the north and south of Levi's gate shall belong to your brothers, the sons of Aaron: you shall appor[tion] them [6]one hundred eight chambers with their rooms, as well as two booths [7]up above them on the roof.

From the gate of Judah south to the corner the sons of Judah [8]shall receive fifty-four chambers with corresponding rooms, and the booth(s) [9]set up above them. From the gate of Simeon north to the corner [10]the sons of Simeon shall receive their chambers and corresponding rooms, together with their booths.

From the angle adjoining the sons of Judah [11]as far as the gate of Reuben the sons of Reuben shall receive [12]fifty-two chambers and corresponding rooms, and their booths. From the gate of [13]Reuben to the gate of Joseph shall belong to the sons of Joseph, that is, Ephraim and Manasseh. [14]From the gate of Joseph to the gate of Benjamin shall belong to the sons of Kohath, subdivision of the Levites. [15]From the gate of Benjamin to the western corner shall belong to the sons of Benjamin. From this corner [16]to the gate of Issachar shall belong to the sons of Issachar; and from the gate of [Issachar . . .]

The changing of the divisions of priests and Levites. Divisions would serve in the temple for one week. On the eighth day, counting from the time when the first group began to serve, a second course would arrive to replace it. They would enter and exit through the gate of Levi.

Col. 45 [1]they shall be arriving [. . .] [2][two hundred and] seventy chambers [. . .] and their vessels [. . .] [3]And when the [new] division enters [on the right,] the old one shall exit to the left. When the incoming division enters [4]the old shall depart My city; they are not to intermingle, neither they nor [their] vessels. Let each division co[me] [5]to its own area and encamp. On the eighth day one comes and the other leaves. The incoming division shall purify [6]the chambers, one after another, [at] the time that the old division exits. There must be no [7]intermingling.

Laws on entry into the temple and temple city. These laws are derived from the Bible in most cases, but are often combined and rewritten to create new meanings. The author's concern is to safeguard the purity of the holy environs.

No m[an] who has a nocturnal emission is to enter [8]any part of My temple until three [com]plete days have passed. He must launder his clothes and bathe [9]on the first day; on the third he must again launder and bathe; then, after the sun has set, [10]he may enter the temple. They are not to enter My temple while unclean, for that would defile it.

[11]If a man has intercourse with his wife, he may not enter any part of the temple [12]city (where I shall make My name to dwell) for three days.

No blind man [13]may enter it as long as he lives, lest the city in whose midst I dwell [14]be defiled. For I, the LORD, shall dwell among the children of Israel forever and ever.

[15]Any man who wishes to purify himself from a genital emission must count seven days as a cleansing period. On the seventh [16]day he must launder his clothes and bathe his entire body in running water. Afterwards he may enter the temple [17]city.

None unclean because of touching a dead body is to enter the city until purified.

No leper [18]or person afflicted with a skin disease is to enter the city until purified. When he has become pure, he may sacrifice **Col. 46** [01][his sin offering. On the eighth day he may approach pure food in the temple city; b]ut he may not enter the temple, [02][nor may he eat holy food. When the sun sets on the eighth day] he may eat [some holy food, and may enter] the temple.

Structures on the wall of the third court and outside it.

[1][. . . No] unclean bird is to fly [2]over [My] temp[le, so you must make spikes on the court's wall and on] the roofs of the gates [3]belonging to the outer court. No [unclean bird may] ever be inside My temple, forev[er], [4]all the days that I [dwe]ll among them.

[5]You are to build a terrace surrounding the outer court, extending [6]fourteen cubits out from the court as measured from the entrances to the gates. You shall make [7]twelve steps by which the children of Israel will ascend to it [8]when entering My temple courts.

[9]You are also to build a dry moat around the temple courts, one hundred cubits wide, in order [10]to separate the holy temple from the city, so that they will not enter My temple without thought [11]and defile it. They must sanctify and reverence My temple, [12]for I dwell in their midst.

Structures outside the city: the outhouse and quarantine areas.

[13]You are to build them a precinct for latrines outside the city. They shall go out there, [14]on the northwest of the city: roofed outhouses with pits inside, [15]into which the excrement will descend so as not to be visible. The outhouses must be [16]three thousand cubits from any part of the city.

You shall also make [17]three places to the east of the city, separated from one another, where [18]those with a skin disease, a genital flux, or a [nocturnal] emission shall go, **Col. 47** [02]distant fr[om the city three thousand cubits]. [03]And all [their] ci[ties are to be pure . . .] [04]matter and sk[in] disease . . . [2][so they will be only] the head and not the tai[l]. [3][Thus] their cities [are to b]e pure, so that [I may cause my name to] dw[ell among] them forever.

Commands regarding entry into the temple city of clean and unclean animal skins. The long and detailed discussion of animal skins indicates that it was a topic of polemics in the author's day.

The city [4]that I shall sanctify by establishing My name and temp[le] there must be holy and pure [5]from anything that is in any way unclean, by which one might be defiled. Everything inside it must be [6]pure, and everything that enters it must be pure: wine, oil, edibles, [7]and any foodstuff upon which liquid is poured—all must be pure.

No skin of a clean animal that has been slaughtered [8]in other cities is to enter My city. Certainly in other cities they may use [9]them for their work, whatever the need may be, but such skins are not to be brought into My city. [10]The reason: their degree of purity corresponds with that of the animals' flesh. Therefore you are not to defile the city [11]that I sanctify, where I have established My name and temple. No, they must use skins of animals sacrificed [12]in the temple of My temple city, where they bring their wine, oil, and [13]edibles. They must not defile My temple with the skins of improper [14]offerings that they have slaughtered elsewhere in the land. Nor are you to consecrate a skin from [15]another city for use in My city; for the skins are only as pure as the flesh from which they come. If [16]you have sacrificed the animal in My temple, the skin is pure for use in My temple; but if you have slaughtered the animal in another city, it is pure [17]only for use in other cities. In sum, all pure foods sent to the temple must be brought in skins originating in the temple. You must not defile [18]either My temple or My city with improper skins, for I dwell in its midst.

Laws concerning animals that may and may not be eaten, including dead animals. The author combines portions of Leviticus and Deuteronomy to fashion his commands. The fragmentary lines at the beginning of the column evidently concern animals that were banned from being raised in Jerusalem.

Col. 48 [02]to enter my city [. . .] [03]you are not to raise chickens [. . .] [04]in any part of the sanctuary [. . .][1](You may not eat) [the cormorant, the stork, any ki]nd of [heron,] the hoop[oe, nor the bat. Any wi]nged insect [that walks about on [2]four feet is detestable to you.]

[3][The following are the] winged [insects] you may eat: the locust according to its kind, the ba[ld] locust according to its kind, the cricket [4]according to its kind, and the grasshopper according to its kind. Also, among the winged insects that go about on four feet you may eat those [5]that have jointed legs above their feet, which both leap on the ground and fly with wings.

[6]You are not to eat the carcass of any winged thing or animal, but you may sell it to a foreigner. You must not eat any abominable thing, [7]for you are a holy people to the LORD your God.

Forbidden mourning and burial practices.

You are children [8]belonging to the LORD your God; therefore you are not to gash yourselves, nor to shave your forelocks [9]on behalf of the dead. You must not incise your flesh or tattoo yourselves for the dead, [10]for you are a people holy to the LORD your God.

Thus you shall not defile [11]your land. You are not to do as the nations do: they bury [12]their dead everywhere, even inside their homes. Rather, you must set apart [13]places in your land where you will bury your dead. For every four [14]cities you must designate one burial ground.

The command to quarantine lepers and others throughout the land.

In each and every city you shall make places for those suffering from a skin disease, [15]whether leprosy or affliction or scab, so that they do not enter your cities and defile them.

Also, you must make places for men suffering from a genital emission [16]and for women during menstruation and after giving birth. Thus they will not defile your houses [17]with their menstrual uncleanness.

As for persons suffering from a skin disease, whether old leprosy or scab, let the priest declare them unclean. **Col. 49** [2]You are to [confine] them for se[ven days, and to cleanse them from sin by offering] [3][two bird]s, and treating them with cedar wood, hyssop, and [a scarlet] co[rd. Thus you are not to defile] [4]your cities with leprous affliction, so that they become unclean.

Uncleanness of a house in which a person dies.

[5]When a person dies in your cities, the house in which the person died becomes unclean [6]for seven days. Everything that is in the house and everyone

who enters the house is likewise unclean [7]for seven days. Any foodstuff upon which wa[t]er is poured becomes unclean: every part of such food [8]is unclean. Earthen vessels become unclean, together with their contents, for every clean man. [9]Open vessels and all the moistened food [10]that they contain become unclean for every Israelite.

[11]On the day on which they remove the dead person, they must cleanse the house from every [12]defiling smirch of oil, wine, and water moisture. Its floor, walls, and doors must be scraped, [13]and its locks, doorposts, thresholds, and lintels washed with water. On the day [14]on which the body leaves, the house must be purified, as well as its implements: mills, mortars, [15]and everything made of wood, iron, and bronze—all implements capable of purification. [16]Clothes, sacks, and skins must be washed.

Every person who was in the house [17]and everyone who entered it must bathe in water and launder his clothes on the first day. [18]On the third day they shall be sprinkled with the water that cleanses from impurity, and they shall bathe and launder their clothing [19]and wash the implements in the house. Then on the seventh day [20]they shall be sprinkled a second time, bathe, and wash their clothing and implements. When evening comes they will be purified [21]of the dead, and may touch their pure things.

As for anyone who was not defiled by [the dead person . . .] **Col. 50** [2]for [they shall sprinkle] the purifying water [on them and they will be cleansed from m]ingling with the dead. [As regards any] [3]who are impure, they are not [to touch] their [pure things] again until they are sprinkled a sec[ond] time [4]on the seventh day and become fully pur[e] at sunset.

Laws regarding a corpse found in an open field.

Any [5]man in an open field who touches the bone of a dead person, or touches a body slain by the sword, [6]or any dead body or its blood, or a grave—let him purify himself by the procedure of the ordinance already described. [7]If he does not purify himself according to the ordinance of this law, he remains unclean. [8]His impurity abides with him, and anyone who touches him must launder his clothes and bathe, becoming pure [9]that evening.

The woman with a dead fetus.

[10]If a woman is pregnant and her child dies in her womb, she is unclean all the days [11]that it is dead inside her, just like a grave. Every house that she enters becomes unclean, [12]and its implements as well, for seven days. Anyone who touches the house is unclean until evening.

But if [13]someone went inside the house with her, he is unclean for seven days. He must launder his clothes [14]and bathe on the first day. On the third day he must be sprinkled, launder his clothes, and bathe. [15]Then on the seventh day he must be sprinkled a second time, launder his clothes, and bathe. When the sun sets, [16]he becomes clean.

You shall treat all the implements, clothes, skins, and [17]things made of goat hair as described already in the ordinance of this law. But all [18]earthen vessels must be broken, for they have become unclean and cannot be made pure again, [19]ever.

Procedures for anyone touching the body of a creeping thing.

[20]You are to regard as unclean anything that creeps upon the ground: the weasel, the mouse, every type of lizard, [21]the gecko, the sand gecko, the great lizard, and the chameleon. Anyone who touches one of them when they are dead **Col. 51** [01][shall be unclean until evening. He must launder his] [02]clothes [. . .] [1][As for everything that co]mes out of them, [if a man touches it, he becomes unclean], for they are unclean. [2]You are [not] to defile yourselves with the[m. But anyone who does touch] a dead [creeping thing] becomes impure [3]until evening. He shall launder his clothes and bathe [and,] when the sun [sets,] he becomes pure.

[4]Anyone who carries one of their bones or any part of their carcass, whether skin, flesh, or nail, must launder [5]his clothes and bathe. Then, after the sun sets, he becomes pure.

An emphatic statement on the necessity of purity. Although this portion is not a quotation from the Bible, note the reference to "this mountain." Either the author is writing in the name of Moses or he imagines himself a new Moses, even down to the detail of where revelation occurs.

You are to warn [6]the children of Israel about every sort of impurity. They are not to defile themselves with the things about which [7]I speak with you on this mountain. They shall not defile themselves, for I am the LORD who dwells [8]in the midst of the children of Israel. You are to sanctify them, so that they become holy. They must not make themselves [9]detestable by anything that I have defined as unclean; no, they are to be [10]holy.

Commands for judges and officials, drawn from passages in Deuteronomy.

[11]You shall appoint judges and officials in all your towns, who will judge the people [12]righteously. They must be impartial in judgment. They are not to take bribes or [13]pervert justice. Most certainly bribery perverts justice,

subverts the testimony of the righteous man, blinds [14]the eyes of the wise, causes great guilt, and defiles the courthouse with iniquitous [15]sin. You shall pursue justice and justice alone, so that you may live, entering and inheriting [16]the land that I am about to give you as an inheritance forever.

Any man [17]who does accept a bribe and perverts righteous judgment must be put to death. You shall not fear him; [18]put him to death.

Commands about idolatry. Asheroth were sacred trees; stelae were stones set upright.

[19]You shall not do in your land as the nations do. They sacrifice here, there, and [20]everywhere; they plant Asheroth, erect sacred stelae, [21]set up carved stones to worship, and build themselves [. . .] **Col. 52** [1][. . .] You are not to plant [any tree as an Asherah next] [2][to My altar that you are to build.] Neither are you to erect a sacred stela, [which I hate, nor] make [any ca]rved [3][st]one to worship anywhere in your land.

The use of animals for sacrifice, slaughter and work.

You shall not [4]sacrifice to Me any ox or sheep that has a serious bodily defect, for they are abominable [5]to Me. Neither are you to sacrifice to Me any ox, sheep, or goat that is pregnant, for they are abominable to Me. [6]You must not sacrifice any ox or sheep, mother and young, both on the same day; nor shall you kill any mother bird [7]with its fledglings.

Every firstborn male among your cattle and sheep [8]you must consecrate to Me. You shall do no work with the firstborn of your oxen, nor shear the firstborn [9]of your sheep. You are to eat those before Me annually in the place that I shall choose. But if one has [10]any bodily defect, or is lame or blind—if it has any serious bodily defect at all, you are not to sacrifice it to Me. [11]You may eat it in your towns, pure and impure among you alike, as though it were a gazelle or a wild ram. Only do not eat the blood. [12]You shall pour that out on the ground like water and cover it up with earth.

Do not muzzle an ox while it plows, [13]and do not plow with an ox and a donkey together. You must not slaughter any clean ox, sheep, or goat [14]in any of your towns within a three-day journey of My temple. Instead you must sacrifice it [15]in My temple, making of it a burnt offering or a peace offering. Then you shall eat [16]and rejoice before Me in the place that I will choose to establish My name.

Any clean [17]animal that has a bodily defect you may eat in your towns, provided you are at least four miles distant from [18]My temple. You are not to slaughter it near My temple, for its flesh is improper. [19]You must not eat the meat of an ox, sheep, or goat within My city (which I shall sanctify [20]by establishing My name in its midst) if it has not been brought to My temple. It must be sacrificed there; [21]then they will sprinkle its blood on the foundation of the altar of burnt offering, and burn its fat [. . .]

Eating clean animals in the cities of the land; bringing offerings to the chosen place.

Col. 53 [07][. . . When I enlarge your territory] [1][as I have promised you, if the place where I shall choose to establish My name is too fa]r, [2][and you think, "I would like to eat meat," indeed,] you crave m[eat—you may] eat [as much] me[at as you want.] [3][You may ki]ll any of your flock or herd with which I have blessed you [4]and eat it in your towns, the clean and the unclean among you alike, as though it were a gazelle [5]or wild ram. Only restrain yourself from eating the blood. You must pour it on the ground like water and cover it [6]with earth, for the blood is the life. You are not to eat the life with the blood, so that [7]it may go well with you and your children after you forever. You must do what I regard as right and good, [8]for I am the LORD your God.

[9]You must take up devoted gifts and all your voluntary offerings and go to the place where I shall establish [10]My name. There you shall sacrifice them before Me, as you have consecrated them or vowed to do.

Laws concerning oaths and vows. For the most part these vows concern a promise made to God, but they can involve human interaction as well.

[11]When you make a vow, do not delay fulfilling it, for I will certainly require it of you [12]and it would become a sin counted against you. But if you refrain from vowing, no sin will count against you. [13]Be careful about what passes your lips, for what you have voluntarily sworn to do must be done [14]as you have vowed. Anyone who makes a vow to Me or who swears [15]an oath, thereby binding himself, cannot break his promise. He must do everything that has [16]passed his lips.

Any woman who makes a vow to Me or who binds herself with an oath [17]while living with her father in her youth—when her father hears of her vow or [18]binding oath, if he says nothing to her, then [19]all her vows shall stand, and every binding oath shall be in force. But if [20]her father forbids her on the day when he hears of all her vows and binding oaths, [21]then they do not stand. I will forgive her, because her father forbade her [. . .]

Col. 54 [1][when her husband] hea[rd of them. But if he nullifies them after] the da[y] on which [he] hea[rd them, then her] hus[band must bear] [2]her sin, [for he has voided them. Any vow] or bi[nding] oath [to afflict herself] [3]must be upheld or voided by her husband on the day when he hears of them. I shall forgive [he]r.

[4]As for any vow made by a widow or divorced woman, everything that she binds herself by [5]shall stand, just as it passed her lips.

You must be careful to do [6]everything that I have commanded you today. You are neither to add to them [7]nor subtract from them.

The false prophet.

[8]If a prophet or interpreter of dreams arises among you and promises you an omen or [9]portent, and then the omen or portent that he has promised actually happens—if he says, [10]"Let us go and serve other gods" that you have not known, you must not [11]obey that prophet or dream interpreter. For [12]I am testing you to know whether you really love the LORD, [13]the God of your fathers, with all your heart and soul. You shall follow [14]the LORD your God and serve Him; you shall fear Him and obey Him [15]and cleave to Him. That prophet or dream interpreter must be put to death. He has spoken rebellion [16]against the LORD your God, who brought you out of Egypt (I redeemed you [17]from the house of bondage), turning you astray from the way in which I have commanded you to walk. Thus you shall purge [18]the evil one from your midst.

[19]If your brother, the son of your father or your mother, or your son or daughter, [20]or the wife of your bosom, or your best friend entices you secretly, saying, [21]"Let us go serve other gods," whom neither you have known **Col. 55** [01][nor] your [ance]stors, any of the gods [of the surrounding peoples, whether near or far] [02][from] you, from one end of the land to [the other, you are neither to yield nor listen to that person, nor show] [03][pi]ty to him, neither compassion. [You shall not protect him, but assuredly kill him; your hand must be] [04][the] first to execute him, then afterwards the hand [of all the people. Stone him to death, because] [05][he sought to] turn you away [from the LORD your God, who brought you out of the land of Egypt, from a house of servitude.] [06][As a result all Israel shall hear and be afraid, and never again do] [1][such an evil thing] among you.

The city led into idolatry.

[2]If you hear concerning on[e of your cities that] I am giving you to in[dwell] [3]that [wor]thless men have gone out from your midst and that they are influencing all the [in]habitants [4]of their city, saying "Let us go and serve gods" that you have not known, [5]then you must inquire, search, and investigate thoroughly. If indeed the rumor proves true and factual—[6]this abomi-

nation has been done in Israel—you must put all the inhabitants [7]of that city to the sword. Destroy the city utterly, together with every person and [8]all its cattle. Gather all its spoil into [9]the city square and burn both the city and its spoil as a whole burnt offering to the LORD [10]your God. It shall become a ruin heap forever, never to be rebuilt. No devoted thing [11]shall cling to your hand, so that I may turn from My anger and be [12]merciful. Indeed, I shall be compassionate and multiply you just as I promised your fathers, [13]provided you obey Me by keeping all My commandments that I hereby command you [14]this day, and do what the LORD your God considers right and good.

Individual idol worshipers.

[15]If there shall be found among you, in one of your towns that [16]I am giving you, a man or woman who does what I consider evil, [17]transgressing My covenant in going to serve other gods, worshiping them—[18]whether sun, moon, or any of the host of heaven—and you are told about it [19]or hear such a rumor, then you must search and investigate thoroughly. If indeed [20]the rumor proves true and factual—this abomination has been done in Israel—then you are to bring [21]that man or woman out and stone him [to death . . .]

The authority of the priestly Law.

Col. 56 [1][o]r ju[dges then in office] and inquire of them [2]concerning the matter that has brought you up. They will pro[nounce] to you the laws, [3]and you must act according to the law that they proclaim to you, in keeping with the decision [4]that they render you from the book of the Law. They shall pronounce to you the truth [5]in the place where I shall choose to establish My name. You must be careful to do [6]everything they teach you, according to the decision that they render you. [7]You are to depart from the law that they declare to you neither to the right [8]nor the left.

Any man who does not obey, but acts rebelliously, [9]heeding neither the priest who stands there to minister to Me, nor the [10]judge, must die. Thus you shall purge the evil one from Israel. All [11]the people will hear of it and be afraid, and none shall again rebel in Israel.

The beginning of the "Law of the King." This law continues through col. 59. Portions in col. 56 are drawn from Deuteronomy 17 (with modifications), but subsequent columns are a new creation. Though they incorporate many biblical phrases and seek to interpret the relevant biblical laws, cols. 57–59 represent a Jewish analog to Hellenistic tractates on ideal kingship.

[12]When you come to the land that I am about to give you to inherit and indwell, [13]and you say to yourself, "I shall appoint a king over me like all the nations round about," [14]you may indeed appoint yourself a king—one whom I shall choose. From among your brethren you shall appoint a king. [15]You must not put a foreigner over you, he who is not one of your brethren.

The king is not [16]to multiply horses for himself, nor shall he return the people to Egypt to wage war and thereby [17]increase for himself horses, silver, and gold. I have said to you, "You shall never [18]again return that way." Further, he must not multiply wives for himself, lest [19]they turn his heart from following Me. Again, he must not unduly increase gold and silver for himself.

[20]When he first takes the throne of his kingdom, this law [21]must be written out for him in a book while the priests look on [. . .]

Duties and functions of the king with regard to the army, the commanders, the royal bodyguard, the royal council, the queen, and acting as judge.

Col. 57 [1]This is the law [that the king shall produce at the direction of] the priests. [2]On the day when he is crowned as king, [a ce]nsus shall be taken of those from [3]twenty to sixty years old, according to their divisions. He shall appoint [4]at their head commanders of thousands, hundreds, fifties, [5]and tens throughout all their cities.

He shall select from them one thousand men [6]from each tribe to stay with him: twelve thousand warriors [7]who shall never leave him alone, lest he be captured by the nations. All those [8]chosen must be truthful men, God-fearing, [9]despising unjust gain, mighty warriors. They shall stay with him always, [10]day and night, in order to protect him from any sort of sin [11]and from a foreign nation, lest he be captured.

Twelve [12]princes of his people shall be with him, and also twelve selected priests and twelve selected [13]Levites. They are to deliberate with him on matters of justice [14]and Law, and he must not become too proud for them or do anything [15]on counsel other than theirs.

He may not take a wife [16]from any of the nations. Rather, he must take himself a wife from his father's house [17]—that is, from his father's family. He is not to take another wife in addition to her; no, [18]she alone shall be with him as long as she lives. If she dies, then he may take [19]himself another wife from his father's house, that is, his family.

He must not pervert judgment [20]or take a bribe to pervert righteous judgment. Nor is he to desire [21]any field, vineyard, wealth, or house, or any precious thing in Israel, so as to steal [. . .]

The king as war leader: enemy raids and formidable armies, the battle in danger of being lost, division of the booty, rules for combat, and the command to seek God's oracle before battle. The oracle was sought using the Urim and Thummim, two stones kept in the breastplate of the high priest. By asking yes or no questions and drawing one or the other unseen stone out from the pouch, one received God's guidance.

Col. 58 [3]At the time that the king hears of any nation or army trying to steal something that belongs [4]to Israel, he must send for the commanders of thousands and hundreds stationed in the cities [5]of Israel. They will dispatch one-tenth of the army to go out with him to battle against [6]their enemies, and with him they shall go.

But if a mighty army comes to the land of Israel, they shall send [7]with him one-fifth of the warriors. If a king with chariots, cavalry, and a mighty army comes, [8]they shall send with him one-third of the warriors. Two-thirds must guard [9]their cities and border, lest an enemy band penetrate to the midst of their land.

[10]If, however, the battle is going against him, they must send him half of the army, the men of [11]war; but the other half of the army cannot be separated from their cities.

If they defeat [12]their enemies, crushing them and putting them to the sword, and carry off their plunder, they are to give [13]the king one-tenth of it. The priests shall receive one part per thousand and the Levites one percent [14]of the total. The rest is to be divided equally between the warriors who fought the battle and their comrades [15]who remained behind in their cities.

If the king goes out to wage war [16]against his enemies and as much as one-fifth of the army accompanies him, warriors, all the valorous [17]heroes, then they must guard themselves against all manner of impurity, indecency, iniquity, and shame.

[18]He must not go to battle prior to coming to the high priest to inquire of him about the judgment of the Urim [19]and Thummim. The king will go out to battle and return guided by the priest—the king and all the Israelites [20]with him. He must not go out by his own decision prior to inquiring of the judgment of the Urim [21]and Thummim. Then he shall succeed in all his ways because he went out by the judgment that [. . .]

The curse to fall upon the people and the king if he is disobedient to God.

Col. 59 [2]and they will disperse them to many lands and they will become ther[e] a horror, a byword and a mockery, under a heavy yoke [3]and in want of every necessity. There they shall serve gods made by human hands from wood, stone, silver, [4]and gold. Moreover, their cities shall become a wasteland, ruins invoking derisive hissing. Their enemies [5]shall devastate them time and again, while, in the lands of their foes, they moan [6]and cry out because of the heavy yoke. They will call, but I will not listen; they will cry out, but I will not answer [7]them because of their evil deeds. Rather will I hide My face from them, so that they become food, [8]booty, and plunder. None shall deliver them for their evil, in which they broke their covenant with Me [9]and refused My law, becoming utterly guilty.

Afterward they will return [10]to Me with all their heart and all their soul, obeying all the words of this Law. [11]Then I will deliver them from the power of their enemies and redeem them from being ground under foot by those who despise them. I will bring them [12]to the land of their fathers. So I will redeem them and multiply them, rejoicing over them, [13]and I will be their God and they My people.

But the king [14]whose heart and eyes whorishly depart from My commandments shall never have a descendant sitting on the throne of [15]his fathers. Indeed, I shall forever cut off his seed from ruling Israel.

[16]If, however, he walks in My precepts, observing My commandments, and does [17]what I regard as upright and good, then he shall never fail to have one of his sons sitting on the throne of the kingdom [18]of Israel, forever. I shall be with him, I shall deliver him from his enemies and the power [19]of those who would seek his life. I shall set all his enemies before him so he can rule them [20]as he wishes—they shall not rule him. I shall set him at the top, not the bottom; at the head, [21]not the tail. He will long endure over his kingdom, he and his sons after him.

Portions rightly due the priests and Levites.

Col. 60 [2](To the priests belong: . . .) and all Israelite wave offerings, all the firstborn males of the Israelites' [cattle], every tit[he] [3]of their animals, all the holy offerings that are consecrated to Me, all the holy [4]fruit offerings set apart for rejoicing, the tax on birds, wild animals, and fish—one part in a thousand of [5]what people get by hunting or catch in a net—and the tax on booty and plunder.

[6]To the Levites belong: the tithe of the grain, the wine, and the oil that [7]is consecrated to Me, the shoulder of the animal given for a sacrifice, the tax on

[8]booty and plunder, the tax on the catch of birds, wild animals, and fish—one percent, [9]and the tithe on wild pigeons and honey, one part in fifty.

Also, the priests are to receive [10]one percent of the catch of wild pigeons; for it is they whom I have chosen of all your tribes [11]to stand before Me, to minister and pronounce blessings in My name, each one and his sons always.

Rights of the rustic Levite.

[12]If a Levite comes from any of your towns throughout all Israel, where [13]he lives, if he comes eagerly to the place where I will choose to establish My name, [14]he may minister just like all his fellow Levites who stand there before Me. They shall get equal shares [15]to eat, not including what each gets through inheritance.

Prohibition of heathen divination.

[16]When you come to the land that I am about to give you, you are not to learn to imitate [17]the abhorrent practices of those nations. There must not be found among you any who forces his son or daughter to [18]walk through fire, or who practices divination, or any soothsayer, augur, sorcerer, spellbinder, warlock, [19]medium, or necromancer. Most certainly these are abhorrent to Me, all who practice [20]such things; indeed, it is because of these abhorrent practices that I am dispossessing them in favor of you. [21]You must be blameless with the LORD your God. For these nations, who [. . .]

The false prophet.

Col. 61 [1](The prophet who presumes) to de[clare something] in [My na]me that I have not commanded [him to] declare, or who [speaks in the name of ot]her go[ds] [2]that prophet must be put to death.

You may say to yourselves, "How shall we recognize that [3]which the LORD has not spoken?" When a prophet speaks in the name of the LORD but the prophecy is not fulfilled [4]and does not come to pass, that is a prophecy I have not spoken. The prophet spoke rebelliously; do not fear [5]him.

The false witness and other rules of evidence.

[6]No single witness shall prevail against a man accused of any wrongdoing or sin. A case may be made only on the testimony of two [7]or three witnesses.

If a malicious witness comes forward against a man to accuse [8]him of a crime, then both men in the dispute must stand before Me—that is, before the priests, Levites, and [9]judges who are then in office. The judges shall conduct an inquiry. If it turns out that the witness has falsely accused [10]his comrade, then you shall do to him what he had schemed to do to his comrade. Thus you will purge the evil one from your midst. [11]The rest shall hear of it and be afraid to do that sort of thing among you again. You are not [12]to take pity on him: it shall be life for life, eye for eye, tooth for tooth, hand for hand, foot for foot.

Rules for going to war.

When [13]you go out to battle against your enemies and you see cavalry and chariotry and an army mightier than yours, do not be afraid [14]of them. For I am with you, He who brought you up from the land of Egypt. When you draw near to battle, [15]the priest shall come forward and speak to the army, saying to them, "Hear, O Israel! You are drawing near [. . ."]

Col. 62 [1][. . . "Let him go back to his house, lest he die in battle and] [2]another man ma[rry her."] The judg[es] shall further [3]speak to the troops and say, "What man is there who is fearful and fainthearted? Let him return to [4]his house, lest he make the hearts of his comrades melt like his own." When the judges finish [5]speaking to the army, commanders are to be commissioned over the troops.

When [6]you approach a city for battle, offer it terms of peace. If it accedes [7]to the terms and opens its gates to you, then all the people found therein shall [8]serve you in forced labor. But if it does not accept the terms and offers battle against you, [9]you shall besiege it. Then, when I give it into your power, you are to put all its men to the sword while taking [10]the women, children, cattle, and all that is in the city, all its booty, as plunder [11]for yourselves. You shall enjoy the booty that I will give you from your enemies. In such fashion you shall treat [12]the cities that are very far away, those not among the cities of these nations.

[13]But in the cities of the peoples that I am giving you for an inheritance, you shall let live [14]nothing that breathes. No, you shall utterly exterminate the Hittites, the Amorites, the Canaanites, [15]the Hivites, the Jebusites, the Girgashites and the Perizzites as I have commanded you, lest they [16]teach you to do all the abhorrent practices that they have done for their gods [. . .]

Expiation for an unknown murderer and the nearest town's responsibility for the victim.

Col. 63 [1](The elders of the town nearest the body shall take a heifer) that has never been worked, [never been yoked. The elders] of that town shall bring [2]the heifer do[wn] to a valley with running water, one neither sown nor plowed, and there break the heifer's neck.

[3]Then the priests, the sons of Levi, shall come forward (for I have chosen them to minister to Me and to bless in My name, [4]and by their decision shall every dispute and assault be settled) and all the elders of that town nearest the dead person's body [5]shall wash their hands over the head of the heifer whose neck was broken in the valley. They shall affirm, "Our hands [6]did not shed this blood, nor did our eyes see it shed. Exonerate Your people Israel, whom You have redeemed, [7]O LORD, and let not the guilt of innocent blood remain among Your people Israel." Then they shall be exonerated for the blood.

In this manner you shall purge [8]bloodguilt from Israel; you must do what the LORD your God considers upright and good.

The beautiful woman taken captive in war. The stipulations about touching pure things and eating peace offerings in ll. 14–15 are extrabiblical additions to Deuteronomy 21:13.

[10]When you go out to battle against your enemies and I give them into your power, and you take captives [11]and see among the captives a beautiful woman whom you desire and want to marry, [12]bring her to your house. Shave her head, cut her nails, and remove [13]the garments she wore as a captive. She shall remain in your house and mourn her father and mother for [14]a month. After that you can go to her and become her husband, and she your wife. Yet she must not touch your pure things for [15]seven years, nor eat peace offerings until seven years have passed; afterward, she may eat [. . .]

The rebellious (presumably teenage) child.

Col. 64 [2]If a man has a stubbornly rebellious child, who does not obey his father or mother, [3]and does not listen when they discipline him, let his father and mother take hold of him and bring him to [4]the elders of his city at the gate of the place where he lives. Let them say to the elders of the city, "This child of ours is stubbornly [5]rebellious, does not obey us, and is a drunken glutton." Then all the men of his city shall stone him [6]to death. So shall you purge the evil one from your midst, and all the children of Israel will hear and be afraid.

The crimes requiring the most shameful death. This portion greatly modifies the text of Deuteronomy 21:22–23.

[7]If a man is a traitor against his people and gives them up to a foreign nation, so doing evil to his people, [8]you are to hang him on a tree until dead. On the testimony of two or three witnesses [9]he will be put to death, and they themselves shall hang him on the tree.

If a man is convicted of a capital crime and flees [10]to the nations, cursing his people and the children of Israel, you are to hang him, also, upon a tree [11]until dead.

But you must not let their bodies remain on the tree overnight; you shall most certainly bury them that very day. Indeed, [12]anyone hung on a tree is accursed of God and men, but you are not to defile the land that I am [13]about to give you as an inheritance.

Lost livestock. Note the continuing emphasis in the scroll on the community members' responsibility to one another.

You are not to see your neighbor's ox, sheep or donkey [14]going astray and ignore it. Most certainly you must return it to your neighbor. But if your neighbor is not near [15]you, or you do not know who he is, then take the animal to your house, where it shall remain until claimed [. . .]

Prohibition on taking a hen with her young. It was permissible to take the eggs after chasing away the hen, but to kill the hen as well was wrong.

Col. 65 [2]If you happ[en] upon a bird's nest, in a tree or on the ground, [3]with fledglings or eggs inside and the hen sitting upon them, [4]you must not take both the hen and the young. Most certainly you will chase the hen away; then you may take [5]the young, that it may go well for you and you may live a long time.

Command to build a parapet with any new house.

When you build a new house, [6]you must build a parapet on the roof, so that you do not bring bloodguilt upon your house if someone should fall from the roof.

The questionable virgin. After the wedding night it was traditional to expose the bloodied bedsheet as proof that the bride had been a virgin. The bride's family was to keep the sheet as insurance against false accusations.

[7]If any man takes a wife and consummates the marriage, but then spurns the woman and makes charges against her, [8]so giving her a bad reputation, saying "I married this woman, but when I had intercourse [9]with her I did not find her a virgin," then the young woman's father or mother shall bring [10]the evidence of her virginity to the elders at the gate. The young woman's father shall say [11]to the elders, "I gave my daughter to this man as a wife, but now he spurns her, and he has made [12]charges against her, claiming 'I did not find your daughter a virgin.' Yet this is the evidence of [13]my daughter's virginity." Then the sheet shall be spread before the elders of that city.

Afterward the elders [14]of that city are to take that man and discipline him, as well as fining him one hundred shekels of silver, which [15]shall be given to the young woman's father. For the man brought a bad reputation upon a virgin of Israel; and [. . .]

Laws governing different situations of rape. These laws are drawn from Deuteronomy 22:24–29 and Exodus 22:15, but the parenthetical phrase in l. 9, "one who by statute is a possible marriage partner for him," does not occur in the Bible. This addition actually changes the meaning of the biblical text and points to the existence of a body of laws regarding marriage, of which those in 66:11–17 are a selection.

Col. 66 [07][If it should happen that a young woman,] [08][a virgin betrothed for marriage to one man, is encountered by another man in the city and he rapes her,] [1][then they shall both be brought to the elders] of that city, to the ga[te of their place,] [2]and stoned until dead: the woman, on the grounds that she did not cry out for help [3]in the city, and the man, on the grounds that he violated his neighbor's woman. So you will purge [4]the evil one from your midst.

But if the man encountered the woman in a distant field out of sight [5]of the city, and he overpowered her and raped her, then only the man who raped her shall be put to death. [6]To the woman you shall do nothing, for she has committed no sin worthy of death; this case is like that of a man [7]attacked by his neighbor who kills in self-defense. For he encountered her in a field; the betrothed woman cried out for help, [8]but there was none to save her.

If a man seduces a [9]virgin who is not betrothed (one who by statute is a possible marriage partner for him) and he has intercourse with her [10]and is discovered, then the man must give the woman's father fifty shekels of silver, and she [11]will become his wife. Since he has violated her, he cannot divorce her as long as he lives.

Prohibitions against illicit and incestuous marriages. The ban on niece marriage does not appear in the Bible and is probably an attack on Pharisaic practice; it is condemned in the Damascus Document *(text 1) as well. Rabbinic literature praises niece marriage, and this form of endogamy probably goes back to the ancestors of the rabbinic movement, the Pharisees.*

No man is to marry [12]his father's ex-wife, for that would violate his father's rights. No man is to marry [13]his brother's ex-wife, for that would violate his brother's rights, even if the brother shares only the same father or only the same mother. Surely that would be unclean.

[14]No man may marry his stepsister, whether his stepfather's daughter or his stepmother's daughter; that is abhorrent. No man may [15]marry his aunt, whether paternal or maternal; that is immoral. No man [16]is to marry [17]his brother's daughter or his sister's daughter; that is abhorrent. No man may marry [. . .]

—M.O.W.

III

Indices

Bibliography

Collections of Photographs

Eisenman, R. H., and J. M. Robinson, *A Facsimile Edition of the Dead Sea Scrolls.* 2 vols. Washington, DC: Biblical Archaeology Society, 1991.

Lim, T., in consultation with P. Alexander. *The Dead Sea Scrolls: Electronic Reference Library.* Oxford: Oxford University Press; Leiden: Brill, 1997.

Tov, E., with the collaboration of S. J. Pfann. *The Dead Sea Scrolls on Microfiche: A Comprehensive Facsimile Edition of the Texts from the Judaean Desert.* Leiden: Brill, 1993.

Trever, J. C. *Scrolls from Qumran Cave 1.* Jerusalem: Albright Institute of Archaeological Research and Shrine of the Book, 1974.

Textual Editions

Abegg, M. G., Jr. *Qumran Sectarian Manuscripts: Qumran Texts with Grammatical Tags.* Altamonte Springs, FL: OakTree Software, 2001.

Allegro, J. M. *The Treasure of the Copper Scroll.* London: Routledge and Kegan Paul, 1960.

———. *The Treasure of the Copper Scroll.* 2d rev. ed. Garden City, NY: Doubleday, 1964.

———. "An Unpublished Fragment of Essene Halakah (4QOrdinances)." *Journal of Semitic Studies* 6 (1961): 71–73.

Allegro, J. M., with the collaboration of A. A. Anderson. *Qumrân Cave 4, I (4Q158–4Q186).* DJD 5. Oxford: Clarendon, 1968.

Alexander, P. S., and G. Vermes. *Qumran Cave 4: XIX.* DJD 26. Oxford: Clarendon, 1998.

Attridge, H. W., et al. *Qumran Cave 4, VIII: Parabiblical Texts, Part 1.* DJD 13. Oxford: Clarendon, 1994.

Avigad, N., and Y. Yadin. *A Genesis Apocryphon.* Jerusalem: Magnes, 1956.

Baillet, M. *Qumrân Grotte 4, III (4Q482–4Q520).* DJD 7. Oxford: Clarendon, 1982.

Baillet, M., J. T. Milik, and R. de Vaux. *Les 'Petites Grottes' de Qumrân: Exploration de la falaise, Les Grottes 2Q, 3Q, 5Q, 6Q, à 10Q, Le Rouleau de cuivre.* DJD 3. Oxford: Clarendon, 1962.

Barthélemy, D., and J. T. Milik. *Qumran Cave I.* DJD 1. Oxford: Clarendon, 1955.

Baumgarten, J. M. "4QHalakaha 5, the Law of Hadash, and the Pentecontad Calendar." *Journal of Jewish Studies* 27 (1976): 36–46.

———. "The 4Q Zadokite Fragments on Skin Disease." *Journal of Jewish Studies* 61 (1990): 153–58.

———. "Purification After Childbirth and the Sacred Garden in 4Q265 and Jubilees." In *New Qumran Texts and Studies: Proceedings of the First Meeting of the International Organization for Qumran Studies, Paris 1992.* STDJ 15. Edited by G. J. Brooke. Leiden/New York: Brill, 1994. Pp. 3–10.

———. *Qumran Cave 4 XIII: The Damascus Document (4Q266–273).* DJD 18. Oxford: Clarendon, 1996.

———. "The Red Cow Purification Rites in Qumran Texts." *Journal of Jewish Studies* 46 (1995): 112–19.

Baumgarten, J. M., T. Elgvin, E. Eshel, E. Larson, M. Lehmann, S. Pfann, and L. Schiffman. *Qumran Cave 4: XXV, Halakhic Texts.* DJD 35. Oxford: Clarendon, 1999.

Beyer, K. *Die aramäischen Texte vom Toten Meer.* Göttingen: Vandenhoeck & Ruprecht, 1984.

———. *Die aramäischen Texte vom Toten Meer: Ergänzungsband.* Göttingen: Vandenhoeck & Ruprecht, 1994.

Brooke, G. J. *Exegesis at Qumran.* Sheffield: JSOT Press, 1985.

Brooke, G. J., J. Collins, T. Elgvin, P. Flint, J. Greenfield, E. Larson, C. Newsom, É. Puech, L. H. Schiffman, M. Stone, and J. Trebolle Barrera. *Qumran Cave 4 XVII: Parabiblical Texts Part 3.* DJD 22. Oxford: Clarendon, 1996.

Broshi, M., and A. Yardeni, "On Temple Servants and False Prophets." *Tarbiz* 42 (1992): 50–52 (Hebrew).

Broshi, M., E. Eshel, J. Fitzmyer, E. Larson, C. Newsom, L. Schiffman, M. Smith, M. Stone, J. Strugnell, and A. Yardeni. *Qumran Cave 4 XIV: Parabiblical Texts Part II.* DJD 19. Oxford: Clarendon, 1995.

Burrows, M. *The Dead Sea Scrolls of St. Mark's Monastery.* Vol. 2, Fasc. 2, *Plates and Transcription of the Manual of Discipline.* New Haven, CT: American Schools of Oriental Research, 1951.

Charlesworth, J. H., et al. *The Dead Sea Scrolls: Hebrew, Aramaic, and Greek Texts with English Translations.* Vol. 1, *Rule of the Community and Related Documents.* Tübingen: Mohr, 1994.

Charlesworth, J., N. Cohen, H. M. Cotton, E. Eshel, H. Eshel, P. Flint, H. Misgav, M. Morgenstern, C. Murphy, M. Segal, A. Yardeni, and B. Zissu. *Miscellaneous Texts from the Judaean Desert.* DJD 38. Oxford: Clarendon, 2000.

Chazon, E., T. Elgvin, E. Eshel, D. Falk, B. Nitzan, E. Qimron, E. Schuller, D. Seely, E. Tigchelaar, and M. Weinfeld. *Qumran Cave 4: XX, Poetical and Liturgical Texts, Part 2.* DJD 29. Oxford: Clarendon, 1999.

Cross, F. M. "Fragments of the Prayer of Nabonidus." *Israel Exploration Journal* 34 (1984): 260–64.

Dimant, D. "An Apocryphon of Jeremiah from Cave 4 (4Q385B = 4Q385 16)." In *New Qumran Texts and Studies: Proceedings of the First Meeting of the International Organization for Qumran Studies, Paris 1992.* STDJ 15. Edited by G. J. Brooke. Leiden/New York: Brill, 1994. Pp. 11–30.

———. "New Light from Qumran on the Jewish Pseudepigrapha — 4Q390." In J. T. Barrera and L. V. Montaner, eds., *Proceedings of the International Congress on the Dead Sea Scrolls, Madrid, 18–21 March 1991.* Leiden: Brill, 1992. Pp. 405–48.

———. *Qumran Cave 4 XXI: Parabiblical Texts Part 4: Pseudo-Prophetic Texts.* DJD 30. Oxford: Clarendon, 2001.

Dimant, D., and J. Strugnell. "4Q Second Ezekiel." *Revue de Qumran* 13 (1988): 45–58.

———. "The Merkabah Vision in Second Ezekiel (4Q385 4)." *Revue de Qumran* 14 (1991): 331–48.

Eisenman, R. H., and M. O. Wise. *The Dead Sea Scrolls Uncovered.* London: Element, 1992.

Elgvin, T. "Admonition Texts from Qumran Cave 4." In *Methods of Investigation of the Dead Sea Scrolls and the Khirbet Qumran Site: Present Realities and Future Prospects, Annals of the New York Academy of Sciences* 722. Edited by M. O. Wise, N. Golb, J. J. Collins, and D. G. Pardee. New York: New York Academy of Sciences, 1994. Pp. 179–96.

———. "The Genesis Section of 4Q422 (4QParaGenExod)." *Dead Sea Discoveries* 1 (1994): 180–96.

Elgvin, T., M. Kister, T. Lim, B. Nitzan, S. Pfann, E. Qimron, L. Schiffman, and A. Steudel, in consultation with J. Fitzmyer, S. J. *Qumran Cave 4 XV: Sapiential Texts, Part 1.* DJD 20. Oxford: Clarendon, 1997.

Eshel, E. "4Q477: The Rebukes by the Overseer." *Journal of Jewish Studies* 45 (1994): 111–22.

Eshel, E., and H. Eshel. "4Q471 Fragment 1 and Ma'amadot in the War Scroll." In J. T. Barrera and L. V. Montaner, eds., *Proceedings of the International Congress on the Dead Sea Scrolls, Madrid, 18–21 March 1991.* Leiden: Brill, 1992. Pp. 611–20.

Eshel, E., H. Eshel, C. Newsom, B. Nitzan, E. Schuller, and A. Yardeni. *Qumran Cave 4: VI, Poetical and Liturgical Texts, Part 1.* DJD 11. Oxford: Clarendon, 1998.

Eshel, E., H. Eshel, and A. Yardeni, "A Qumran Composition Containing Part of Ps. 154 and a Prayer for the Welfare of King Jonathan and His Kingdom." *Israel Exploration Journal* 42 (1992): 199–229.

Eshel, E., and M. Kister. "A Polemical Qumran Fragment." *Journal of Jewish Studies* 43 (1992): 277–81.

Evans, C. A. "A Note on the 'Firstborn Son' of 4Q369." *Dead Sea Discoveries* 2 (1995): 185–201.

Falk, D. "4Q393: A Communal Confession." *Journal of Jewish Studies* 45 (1994): 184–207.

Fitzmyer, J. A. "The Aramaic 'Elect of God' Text from Qumran Cave 4." *Essays on the Semitic Background of the New Testament.* Missoula, MT: Scholars Press, 1974. Pp. 127–60.

———. *The Genesis Apocryphon of Qumran Cave 1.* 2d ed. Rome: Biblical Institute Press, 1971.

Fitzmyer, J. A., and D. J. Harrington. *A Manual of Palestinian Aramaic Texts.* Rome: Biblical Institute Press, 1978.

García-Martínez, F. "11QTemple[b]: A Preliminary Publication." In J. T. Barrera and L. V. Montaner, eds., *Proceedings of the International Congress on the Dead Sea Scrolls, Madrid, 18–21 March, 1991.* Leiden: Brill, 1992.

———. "4Q Mess ar and the Book of Noah." *Qumran and Apocalyptic: Studies on the Aramaic Texts from Qumran.* Leiden: Brill, 1992. Pp. 1–44.

———. *Qumran Cave 11.* DJD 23. Oxford: Clarendon, 1998.

Greenfield, J. C., and E. Qimron. "The Genesis Apocryphon Col. XII." *Abr-Nahrain Supplement* 3 (1992): 70–77.

Gropp, D. M., M. Bernstein, M. Brady, J. Charlesworth, P. Flint, H. Misgav, S. Pfann, E. Schuller, E. J. C. Tigchelaar, and J. VanderKam. *Wadi Daliyeh II: The Samaria Papyri from Wadi Daliyeh and Qumran Cave 4 XXVIII: Miscellanea, Part 2.* DJD 28. Oxford: Clarendon, 2001.

Larson, E. "4Q470 and the Angelic Rehabilitation of King Zedekiah." *Dead Sea Discoveries* 1 (1994): 210–28.

Larson, E., L. H. Schiffman, and J. Strugnell. "4Q470, Preliminary Publication of a Fragment Mentioning Zedekiah." *Revue de Qumran* 16 (1994): 335–50.
Lefkovits, J. K. "The Copper Scroll — 3Q15: A New Reading, Translation, and Commentary." Ph.D. dissertation, New York University, 1993.
Licht, J. *Megillat Ha-Serakhim.* Jerusalem: Mosad Bialik, 1965.
Luria, B. Z. *Megillat Ha-Nehoshet Mimidbar Yehudah.* Jerusalem: Kiryath Sepher, 1963.
Milik, J. T. *The Books of Enoch.* Oxford: Clarendon, 1976.
———. "Écrits préesséniens de Qumrân: d'Hénoch à Amran." In M. Delcor, ed., *Qumrân: sa piété, sa thélogie et son milieu.* Paris-Gembloux: Leuven University Press, 1978. Pp. 91–106.
———. "Milki-sedeq et Milki-resha dans les anciens écrits juifs et chrétiens." *Journal of Jewish Studies* 23 (1972): 95–144.
———. "Les modèles araméens du livre d'Esther dans la grotte 4 de Qumrân." *Revue de Qumran* 15 (1992): 321–406.
———. " 'Prière de Nabonide' et autres écrits d'un cycle de Daniel: Fragments araméens de Qumrân 4." *Revue Biblique* 63 (1956): 407–15.
Newsom, C. A. "4Q370: An Admonition Based on the Flood," *Revue de Qumran* 13 (1988): 23–44.
———. "4Q374: A Discourse on the Exodus/Conquest Tradition." In D. Dimant and U. Rappaport, eds., *The Dead Sea Scrolls: Forty Years of Research.* Leiden: Brill, 1992. Pp. 40–52.
———. "The 'Psalms of Joshua' from Qumran Cave 4." *Journal of Jewish Studies* 39 (1988): 56–73.
———. *Songs of the Sabbath Sacrifice: A Critical Edition.* Atlanta: Scholars Press, 1985.
Nitzan, B. "4QBerakhot (4Q286–290): A Preliminary Report." In *New Qumran Texts and Studies: Proceedings of the First Meeting of the International Organization for Qumran Studies, Paris 1992.* STDJ 15. Edited by G. J. Brooke. Leiden/New York: Brill, 1994. Pp. 53–71.
Penney, D. L., and M. O. Wise. "By the Power of Beelzebub: An Aramaic Incantation Formula from Qumran." *Journal of Biblical Literature* 113 (1994): 627–50.
Pfann, S., P. Alexander, M. Broshi, E. Chazon, H. Cotton, F. M. Cross, T. Elgvin, D. Ernst, E. Eshel, H. Eshel, J. Fitzmyer, F. García-Martínez, J. C. Greenfield, M. Kister, A. Lange, E. Larson, A. Lemaire, T. Lim, J. Naveh, D. Pike, M. Sokoloff, H. Stegemann, A. Steudel, M. Stone, L. Stuckenbruck, S. Talmon, S. Tanzer, E. Tigchelaar, E. Tov, G. Vermes, and A. Yardeni. *Qumran Cave 4 XXVI: Cryptic Texts and Miscellanea, Part 1.* DJD 36. Oxford: Clarendon, 2000.
Ploeg, J. P. M. van der. "Fragments d'un manuscrit de psaumes de Qumrân (11QPsb)." *Revue Biblique* 74 (1967): 408–12.
———. "Les Manuscrits de la Grotte XI de Qumrân." *Revue de Qumran* 12 (1985–87): 3–16.
———. "Un petit rouleau de psaumes apocryphes (11QPsApa)." In G. Jeremias, et al., eds., *Tradition und Glaube: Das frühe Christentum in seiner Umwelt: Festgabe für Karl Georg Kuhn zum 65. Geburtstag.* Göttingen: Vandenhoeck & Ruprecht, 1971. Pp. 128–39.
Ploeg, J. P. M. van der, and A. S. van der Woude. *Le targum de Job de la Grotte XI de Qumrân.* Leiden: Brill, 1971.
Puech, É. "4Q Apocalypse Messianique (4Q521)." *Revue de Qumran* 15 (1992): 475–522.
———. "Fragment d'une apocalypse en arameen (4Q246 = pseudo-Dan^{d}) et le 'Royaume de Dieu.' " *Revue Biblique* 99 (1992): 98–131.
———. "Fragments d'un apocryphe de Lévi et le personnage eschatologique. 4QTestLévi$^{c-d(?)}$ et 4QAj^{a}." In J. T. Barrera and L. V. Montaner, eds., *Proceedings of the In-*

ternational Congress on the Dead Sea Scrolls, Madrid, 18–21 March, 1991. Leiden: Brill, 1992. Pp. 449–501.

———. "Un hymne essénien en partie retrouvé et les Béatitudes." *Revue de Qumran* 13 (1988): 59–88.

———. "Notes sur le manuscript de 11QMelkisedeq." *Revue de Qumran* 12 (1987): 483–513.

———. "La pierre de Sion et l'autel des holocaustes d'apres un manuscrit hebreu de la grotte 4 (4Q522)." *Revue Biblique* 99 (1992): 676–96.

———. *Qumrân Grotte 4: XVIII.* DJD 25. Oxford: Clarendon, 1998.

———. *Qumrân Grotte 4: XXII, Textes Araméens, Premiére Partie.* DJD 31. Oxford: Clarendon, 2001.

———. "Le Testament de Qahat en araméen de la grotte 4 (4QTQah)." *Revue de Qumran* 15 (1991): 23–54.

Qimron, E. "Times for Praising God: A Fragment of a Scroll from Qumran (4Q409)." *Jewish Quarterly Revue* 80 (1990): 341–47.

Qimron, E., and J. Strugnell. *Qumran Cave 4, V: Miqsat Ma'ase Ha-Torah.* DJD 10. Oxford, 1994.

Sanders, J. A. *The Psalms Scroll of Qumran Cave 11 (11QPsa).* DJD 4. Oxford: Clarendon, 1965.

Schiffman, L. H. "4Q Mysteries: A Preliminary Translation." *Eleventh World Congress of Jewish Studies, Div. A.* Jerusalem: World Union of Jewish Studies, 1994. Pp. 199–206.

———. "4QMysteries^{a}: A Preliminary Edition and Translation." In Z. Zevit, S. Gitin, and M. Sokoloff, eds., *Solving Riddles and Untying Knots: Biblical, Epigraphic, and Semitic Studies in Honor of Jonas C. Greenfield.* Winona Lake, IN: Eisenbrauns, 1995. Pp. 207–55.

Schuller, E. M. "4Q372 1: A Text About Joseph." *Revue de Qumran* 14 (1989–90): 349–76.

———. "A Hymn from a Cave Four *Hodayot* Manuscript: 4Q427 7 i + ii." *Journal of Biblical Literature* 112 (1993): 605–28.

———. *Non-Canonical Psalms from Qumran: A Pseudepigraphic Collection.* Atlanta: Scholars Press, 1986.

———. "A Preliminary Study of 4Q373 and Some Related (?) Fragments." In J. T. Barrera and L. V. Montaner, eds., *Proceedings of the International Congress on the Dead Sea Scrolls, Madrid, 18–21 March, 1991.* Leiden: Brill, 1992. Pp. 515–30.

Smith, M. H. "4Q462 (Narrative), Fragment 1: A Preliminary Edition." *Revue de Qumran* 15 (1991): 55–77.

Starcky, J. "Psaumes apocryphes de la grotte 4 de Qumrân (4QPs^{f}VII-X)." *Revue Biblique* 73 (1966): 353–71.

Steudel, A. *Der Midrasch zur Eschatologie aus der Qumrangemeinde (4QMidrEschat^{a,b}).* Leiden: Brill, 1994.

Stone, M. E., and E. Eshel. "An Exposition on the Patriarchs (4Q464) and Two Other Documents (4Q464^{a} and 4Q464^{b})." *Le Muséon* 105 (1992): 243–64.

Stone, M. E., and J. C. Greenfield. "The First Manuscript of the Aramaic Levi Document from Qumran (4QLevi^{a} aram)." *Le Museon* 107 (1994): 257–81.

———. "The Prayer of Levi." *Journal of Biblical Literature* 112 (1993): 247–66.

———. "The Second Manuscript of the Aramaic Levi Document from Qumran (4QLevi^{b} aram)." *Le Muséon* 109 (1996): 1–15.

———. "The Third and Fourth Manuscripts of *Aramaic Levi Document* from Qumran (4QLevi^{c} Aram and 4QLevi^{d} Aram)." *Le Muséon* 109 (1996): 245–59.

Strugnell, J. "Moses-Pseudepigrapha at Qumran: 4Q375, 4Q376, and Similar Works." In L. Schiffman, ed., *Archaeology and History in the Dead Sea Scrolls: The New York University Conference in Memory of Yigael Yadin.* Sheffield: JSOT Press, 1990. Pp. 187–220.

Strugnell, J., D. Harrington, and T. Elgvin. *Qumran Cave 4: XXIV, Sapiential Texts, Part 2.* DJD 34. Oxford: Clarendon, 1999.

Sukenik, E. L. *The Dead Sea Scrolls of the Hebrew University.* Edited by N. Avigad and Y. Yadin. Jerusalem: Magnes, 1955.

Talmon, S., and I. Knohl. "A Calendrical Scroll from a Qumran Cave: Mishmarot B[a] 4Q321." In *Pomegranates and Golden Bells: Studies in Biblical, Jewish, and Near Eastern Ritual, Law, and Literature in Honor of Jacob Milgrom.* Edited by D. N. Freedman et al. Winona Lake, IN: Eisenbrauns, 1995. Pp. 267–301.

Talmon, S., J. Ben-Dov, U. Glessmer. *Qumran Cave 4 XVI: Calendrical Texts.* DJD 21. Oxford: Clarendon, 2001.

Tov, E. "The Exodus Section of 4Q422." *Dead Sea Discoveries* 1 (1994): 197–209.

Tov, E. , with contributions by M. G. Abegg, Jr., A. Lange, U. Mittmann-Richert, S. J. Pfann, E. J. C. Tigchelaar, E. Ulrich, and B. Webster. *The Texts from the Judaean Desert: Indices and an Introduction to the Discoveries in the Judaean Desert Series.* DJD 39. Oxford: Clarendon, 2002.

Trever, J. C. "Completion of the Publication of Some Fragments from Qumran Cave I." *Revue de Qumran* 5 (1965): 323–44.

Wacholder, B. Z., and M. G. Abegg, Jr. "The Fragmentary Remains of 11QTorah (Temple Scroll)." *Hebrew Union College Annual* 62 (1991): 1–116.

———. *A Preliminary Edition of the Unpublished Dead Sea Scrolls.* Fasc. 1–3. Washington, DC: Biblical Archaeology Society, 1991–95.

Wilmot, D. J. "The Copper Scroll: An Economic Document from First Century Palestine." Ph.D. dissertation, University of Chicago, n.d.

Wise, M. O. "An Annalistic Calendar from Qumran." In *Methods of Investigation of the Dead Sea Scrolls and the Khirbet Qumran Site: Present Realities and Future Prospects, Annals of the New York Academy of Sciences* 722. Edited by M. O. Wise, N. Golb, J. J. Collins, and D. G. Pardee. New York: New York Academy of Sciences, 1994. Pp. 389–408.

———. "Observations on New Calendrical Texts from Qumran." In *"Thunder in Gemini" and Other Essays on the History, Language, and Literature of Second Temple Palestine.* JSPS 15. Sheffield: JSOT Press, 1994. Pp. 222–39.

———. "*Primo Annales Fuere:* An Annalistic Calendar from Qumran." In *"Thunder in Gemini" and Other Essays on the History, Language, and Literature of Second Temple Palestine.* JSPS 15. Sheffield: JSOT Press, 1994. Pp. 186–221.

———. "Second Thoughts on *duq* and the Qumran Synchronistic Calendars." In *Pursuing the Text: Studies in Honor of Ben Zion Wacholder.* Edited by J. Reeves and J. Kampen. Sheffield: Sheffield Academic Press, 1994. Pp. 98–120.

———. "Thunder in Gemini: An Aramaic Brontologion (4Q318) from Qumran." In *"Thunder in Gemini" and Other Essays on the History, Language, and Literature of Second Temple Palestine.* JSPS 15. Sheffield: JSOT Press, 1994. Pp. 13–50.

———. "To Know the Times and the Seasons: A Study of the Aramaic Chronograph 4Q559." Forthcoming in *JSP.*

Wolters, A. *The Copper Scroll: Overview, Text and Translation.* Sheffield: Sheffield Academic Press, 1996.

Woude, A. S. van der. "Ein neuer Segensspruch aus Qumran (11QBer)." In *Bibel und Qumran: Beiträge zur Erforschung der Beziehungen zwischen Bibel und Qumranwissenschaft: Hans Bardtke zum* 22.8.1966. Edited by S. Wagner. Leipzig: Evangelische Haupt-Bibelgesellschaft zu Berlin, 1968. Pp. 253–58.

———. "Melchisedek als himmlische Erlösergestalt in den neugefundenen eschatologischen Midraschim aus Qumran Höhle XI." *Oudtestamentische Studiën* 14 (1965): 354–73.

Yadin, Y. *The Temple Scroll*. 3 vols. and supplementary plates. Jerusalem: Israel Exploration Society, 1983.

Translations

Carmignac, J., and P. Guilbert, eds. *Les Textes de Qumran*. Vol. 1. Paris: Letouzey et Ané, 1961.

Charles, R. H. "Translation of Aramaic and Greek Fragments of an Original Source of the Testament of Levi and the Book of Jubilees." *Apocrypha and Pseudepigrapha of the Old Testament* 2: 364–67. Oxford: Clarendon, 1913.

Cothenet, E. "Le Document de Damas." In J. Carmignac, ed., *Les Textes de Qumran*. Paris, 1963. Pp. 131–204.

Dupont-Sommer, A. *The Essene Writings from Qumran*. Translated by G. Vermes. Reprint, Gloucester, MA: Peter Smith, 1973.

García-Martínez, F. *The Dead Sea Scrolls Translated: The Qumran Texts in English*. Translated by W. G. E. Watson. Leiden: Brill, 1994.

García-Martínez, F., and E. J. C. Tigchelaar. *The Dead Sea Scrolls Study Edition*. 2 vols. 2d ed. Leiden: Brill; Grand Rapids, MI: Eerdmans, 2000.

Gaster, T. H. *The Dead Sea Scriptures*. 3d ed. Garden City, NY: Anchor Press, Doubleday, 1976.

Parry, D. W., and E. Tov, eds. *The Dead Sea Scrolls Reader*. 6 vols. Leiden: Brill, 2003–5.

Rabin, Ch. *The Zadokite Documents*. Oxford: Clarendon, 1954.

Vermes, G. *The Complete Dead Sea Scrolls in English*. London: Penguin, 1997.

———. *The Dead Sea Scrolls in English*. Rev. and ext. 4th ed. London: Penguin, 1995.

Other Studies

Abegg, M. G., Jr. "4Q471: A Case of Mistaken Identity?" In *Pursuing the Text: Studies in Honor of Ben Zion Wacholder*. Edited by J. Reeves and J. Kampen. Sheffield: Sheffield Academic Press, 1994. Pp. 135–47.

———. "4QMMT, Paul, and 'Works of the Law." In *The Bible at Qumran: Text, Shape, and Interpretation*. Edited by P. Flint. Grand Rapids, MI: Eerdmans, 2001. Pp. 203–16.

———. "Messianic Hope and 4Q285 — A Reassessment." *Journal of Biblical Literature* 113 (1994): 81–91.

———. "1QSb and the Elusive High Priest." In *Emanuel: Studies in Hebrew Bible, Septuagint, and Dead Sea Scrolls in Honor of Emanuel Tov*. Edited by S. M. Paul, R. A. Kraft, L. H. Schiffman, and W. W. Fields. Leiden/Boston: Brill, 2003. Pp. 3–16.

Alexander, P. S. "A Note on the Syntax of 4Q448." *Journal of Jewish Studies* 44 (1993): 301–2.

Allison, D. C. "4Q403 frag. 1, col. 1, 38–46 and the Revelation to John." *Revue de Qumran* 12 (1985–87): 409–14.

Avigad, N. "The Palaeography of the Dead Sea Scrolls and Related Documents." In *Scripta Hierosolymitana IV: Aspects of the Dead Sea Scrolls*. Edited by Ch. Rabin and Y. Yadin. Jerusalem: Magnes, 1958. Pp. 56–87.

Baumgarten, J. M. "The Cave 4 Versions of the Qumran Penal Code." *Journal of Jewish Studies* 43 (1992): 268–76.

———. "4Q503 (Daily Prayers) and the Lunar Calendar." *Revue de Qumran* 12 (1985–87): 399–407.

———. "Halakhic Polemics in New Fragments from Qumran Cave 4." In *Biblical Archaeology Today.* Jerusalem: Israel Exploration Society, 1984. Pp. 390–99.

Beckwith, R. "The Modern Attempt to Reconcile the Qumran Calendar with the True Solar Year." *Revue de Qumran* 7 (1969–71): 379–96.

Bernstein, M. J. "4Q252: From Rewritten Bible to Biblical Commentary." *Journal of Jewish Studies* 45 (1994): 1–27.

Bockmuehl, M. "A 'Slain Messiah' in 4Q Serekh Milhamah (4Q285)?" *Tyndale Bulletin* 43 (1992): 155–69.

Brooke, G. J. "The Deuteronomic Character of 4Q252." In *Pursuing the Text: Studies in Honor of Ben Zion Wacholder.* Edited by J. Reeves and J. Kampen. Sheffield: Sheffield Academic Press, 1994. Pp. 121–35.

———. "The Genre of 4Q252: From Poetry to Pesher." *Dead Sea Discoveries* 1 (1994): 160–79.

———. "Psalms 105 and 106 at Qumran." *Revue de Qumran* 14 (1990): 267–92.

———. "The Wisdom of Matthew's Beatitudes (4QBeat and Mt 5:3–12)." *Scripture Bulletin* 19 (1989): 35–41.

Carmignac, J. "Les horoscopes de Qumran." *Revue de Qumran* 5 (1964–66): 199–206.

———. *La Règle de la Guerre.* Paris: Letouzey et Ané, 1958.

Charlesworth, J. "The Temple Scroll (11Q19, 11QT[a]), Columns 16 and 17: More Consonants Revealed." In *Emanuel: Studies in Hebrew Bible, Septuagint, and Dead Sea Scrolls in Honor of Emanuel Tov.* Edited by S. M. Paul, R. A. Kraft, L. H. Schiffman, and W. W. Fields. Leiden/Boston: Brill, 2003. Pp. 71–83.

Chazon, E. "Prayers from Qumran and Their Historical Implications." *Dead Sea Discoveries* 1 (1994): 265–84.

Chyutin, M. *The New Jerusalem Scroll from Qumran.* JSP Supplement Series No. 25. Sheffield: Sheffield Academic Press, 1997.

Clemens, D. "A Study of 4Q370." Seminar paper, University of Chicago, 1989.

Collins, J. J. *The Scepter and the Star: The Messiahs of Dead Sea Scrolls and Other Ancient Literature.* Anchor Bible Reference Library. New York: Doubleday, 1995.

Collins, J. J., and D. Dimant. "A Thrice-Told Hymn: A Response to Eileen Schuller." *Jewish Quarterly Revue* 85 (1994): 151–55.

Cook, E. M. "4Q246." *Bulletin of Biblical Research* 5 (1995): 43–66.

———. "Remarks on the Testament of Kohath from Qumran Cave 4." *Journal of Jewish Studies* 44 (1993): 205–19.

Cross, F. M. "The Development of the Jewish Scripts." In *The Bible and the Ancient Near East: Essays in Honor of William Foxwell Albright.* Edited by G. E. Wright. Garden City, NY: Doubleday, 1965. Pp. 133–202.

Davies, P. R. " 'Age of Wickedness' or 'End of Days'?: Qumran Scholarship in Prospect." *Hebrew Studies* 34 (1993): 7–19.

———. *1QM, the War Scroll from Qumran: Its Structure and History.* Biblica and Orient 32. Rome: Biblical Institute Press, 1977.

Delcor, M. "Recherches sur un horoscope en langue hébraîque provenant de Qumran." *Revue de Qumran* 5 (1964–66): 521–42.

De Vaux, R. *Archaeology and the Dead Sea Scrolls.* Rev. ed. London: British Academy, 1973.

Dimant, D. "The 'Pesher on the Periods' (4Q180 and 4Q181)." *Israel Oriental Studies* 9 (1979): 77–102.

———. "Qumran Sectarian Literature." In *Jewish Writings of the Second Temple Period.* Edited by M. E. Stone. Philadelphia: Fortress, 1984. Pp. 483–550.

Donceel-Voûte, P. " 'Coenaculum' — La salle à l'étage du locus 30 à Khirbet Qumran sur la Mer Morte." *Banquets d'Orient, Res Orientales,* vol. 4. Leuven: Peeters, 1992. Pp. 61–84.

Doudna, G. *4QPesher Nahum: A Critical Edition.* Sheffield: Sheffield Academic Press, 2001.

Dupont-Sommer, A. "Deux documents horoscopiques esséniens découverts a Qoumrân, près de la Mer Morte." *CRAIBL* (1965): 239–46.

Elliger, K. *Studien zum Habakuk-Kommentar vom Toten Meer.* Tübingen: Mohr, 1953.

Eshel, E. "The Identification of the 'Speaker' of the Self-Glorification Hymn." In *The Provo International Conference on the Dead Sea Scrolls: New Texts, Reformulated Issues, and Technological Innovations.* Edited by D.W. Parry and E. C. Ulrich. Leiden: Brill, 1999. Pp. 631–33.

Fine, J. "Aramaic E: 4Q563." Seminar paper, University of Chicago, 1994.

Fitzmyer, J. A. *The Genesis Apocryphon of Qumran Cave 1 (1Q20): A Commentary.* 3d ed. Rome: Pontifical Biblical Institute, 2004.

Francis, F. "Humility and Angelic Worship in Col. 2:18." *Studia Theologica* 16 (1963): 109–34.

García-Martínez, F. "4QPseudo Daniel Aramaic and the Pseudo-Danielic Literature." *Qumran and Apocalyptic: Studies on the Aramaic Texts from Qumran.* Leiden: Brill, 1992.

Glessmer, U. "Investigation of the Otot-text (4Q319) and Questions About Methodology." In *Methods of Investigation of the Dead Sea Scrolls and the Khirbet Qumran Site: Present Realities and Future Prospects, Annals of the New York Academy of Sciences* 722. Edited by M. O. Wise, N. Golb, J. J. Collins, and D. G. Pardee. New York: New York Academy of Sciences, 1994. Pp. 429–40.

———. "Der 364-Tage Kalender und die Sabbatstruktur seiner Schaltungen in ihrer Bedeutung für den Kult." In *Ernten, was man sät: Festschrift für Klaus Koch zu seinem 65. Geburtstag.* Edited by D. R. Daniels. Neukirchen-Vluyn: Neukirchener Verlag des Erziehungsvereins, 1991. Pp. 379–98.

Golb, N. *Who Wrote the Dead Sea Scrolls?* New York: Scribner, 1994.

Gordis, R. "A Document in Code from Qumran — Some Observations." *Journal of Jewish Studies* 11 (1966): 37–39.

Gordon, R. P. "The Interpretation of 'Lebanon' and 4Q285." *Journal of Jewish Studies* 43 (1992): 92–94.

Hendel, R. S. "4Q252 and the Flood Chronology of Genesis 7–8: A Text-Critical Solution." *Dead Sea Discoveries* 2 (1995): 72–79.

Hollander, H.W., and M. de Jonge. *The Testaments of the Twelve Patriarchs: A Commentary.* Leiden: Brill, 1985.

Holm-Nielsen, S. *Hodayot: Psalms from Qumran.* Aarhus: Universitetsforlaget, 1960.

Horgan, M. P. *Pesharim: Qumran Interpretations of Biblical Books.* CBQMS 8. Washington, DC: Catholic Biblical Association, 1979.

Huggins, R.V. "A Canonical 'Book of Periods' at Qumran." *Revue de Qumran* 15 (1992): 421–36.

Hultgard, A. *L'eschatologie des Testaments des Douze Patriarches.* Uppsala: Alquist & Wiksell, 1982.

Jacobson, H. "4Q252, Addenda." *Journal of Jewish Studies* 44 (1993): 118–20.

Kister, M., and E. Qimron. "Observations on 4QSecond Ezekiel." *Revue de Qumran* 15 (1992): 595–602.

Kittel, B. P. *The Hymns of Qumran.* Edited by D. Knight. SBL Dissertation Series 50. Chico, CA: Scholars Press, 1981.

Klein, D. "4Q562: An Aramaic Text from Qumran." Seminar paper, University of Chicago, 1994.

Klinghardt, M. "The Manual of Discipline in the Light of Statutes of Hellenistic Associations." In *Methods of Investigation of the Dead Sea Scrolls and the Khirbet Qumran Site:*

Present Realities and Future Prospects, Annals of the New York Academy of Sciences 722. Edited by M. O. Wise, N. Golb, J. J. Collins, and D. G. Pardee. New York: New York Academy of Sciences, 1994. Pp. 251–70.

Knibb, M. A. "A Note on 4Q372 and 4Q390." In *The Scriptures and the Scrolls: Studies in Honour of A. S. van der Woude on the Occasion of his 65th Birthday.* Edited by F. García-Martínez, A. Hilhorst, and C. J. Labuschangne. Leiden: E. J. Brill, 1992. Pp. 164–78.

Kugel, J. L. "Levi's Elevation to the Priesthood in Second Temple Writings." *Harvard Theological Review* 86 (1993): 1–64.

Kugler, R. *From Patriarch to Priest: The Levi-Priestly Tradition from Aramaic Levi to Testament of Levi.* SBLEJL 9. Atlanta: Scholars Press, 1996.

Lange, A. *Weisheit und Prädestination: Weisheitliche Urordnung und Prädestination in den Textfunden von Qumran.* STDJ 18. Leiden: Brill, 1995.

Licht, J. *Megillat Ha-Hodayot.* Jerusalem: Bialik Institute, 1957 (Hebrew).

———. "Thighs as a Sign of Election." *Tarbiz* 35 (1965/66): 18–26 (Hebrew).

Lim, T. H. "The Chronology of the Flood Story in a Qumran Text (4Q252)." *Journal of Jewish Studies* 43 (1992): 288–98.

———. "Notes on 4Q252 fr. 1, cols. i-ii." *Journal of Jewish Studies* 44 (1993): 121–26.

Liver, J. "The Half-Shekel Offering in Biblical and Postbiblical Literature." *Harvard Theological Review* 56 (1963): 173–98.

Maier, J. *The Temple Scroll.* Sheffield: JSOT Press, 1985.

McCarter, P. K. "The Copper Scroll as an Accumulation of Religious Offerings." In *Methods of Investigation of the Dead Sea Scrolls and the Khirbet Qumran Site: Present Realities and Future Prospects, Annals of the New York Academy of Sciences* 722. Edited by M. O. Wise, N. Golb, J. J. Collins, and D. G. Pardee. New York: New York Academy of Sciences, 1994. Pp. 133–48.

Milik, J. T. "The Dead Sea Scrolls Fragment of the Book of Enoch." *Biblica* 32 (1951): 393–400.

———. Review of *The Manual of Discipline* by P. Wernberg-Møller. *Revue Biblique* 67 (1960): 410–16.

Morgenstern, M., E. Qimron, and D. Sivan, "The Hitherto Unpublished Columns of the Genesis Apocryphon," *Abr-Nahrain* 33 (1995): 30–54.

Nebe, G. W. "Das hebraische Testament Naphtali (4Q215)." *Zeitschrift für die alttestamentliche Wissenschaft* 30 (1994): 315–22.

Nitzan, B. "Benedictions and Instructions from Qumran for the Eschatological Community (11QBer, 4Q285)." *Revue de Qumran* 16 (1993): 77–90.

———. "Hymns from Qumran — 4Q510–4Q511." In *The Dead Sea Scrolls: Forty Years of Research.* Edited by D. Dimant and U. Rappaport. Leiden: Brill; Jerusalem: Magnes, 1992. Pp. 53–62.

———. *Megillat Pesher Habakkuk mi-megillot midbar Yehudah (1QpHab).* Jerusalem: Mosad Bialik, 1986 (Hebrew).

Pardee, D. "A Restudy of the Commentary on Psalm 37 from Qumran Cave 4." *Revue de Qumran* 8 (1973): 163–94.

Patrich, J. "Khirbet Qumran in Light of New Archaeological Explorations in the Qumran Caves." In *Methods of Investigation of the Dead Sea Scrolls and the Khirbet Qumran Site: Present Realities and Future Prospects, Annals of the New York Academy of Sciences* 722. Edited by M. O. Wise, N. Golb, J. J. Collins, and D. G. Pardee. New York: New York Academy of Sciences, 1994. Pp. 73–96.

Pixner, B. "Unravelling the Copper Scroll Code: A Study of the Topography of 3Q15." *Revue de Qumran* 11 (1983): 323–58.

Puech, É. "4Q525 et les péricopes des Béatitudes en Ben Sira et Matthieu." *Revue Biblique* 98 (1991): 80–106.

———. "Préséance sacerdotale et Messie — Roi dans la Règle de la Congrégation (1QSa ii 11–22)." *Revue de Qumran* 16 (1994): 351–66.

———. "Quelques aspects de la restauration du Rouleau des Hymnes (1QH)." *Journal of Jewish Studies* 39 (1988): 38–55.

Puech, É., and F. García-Martínez. "Remarques sur la colonne XXXVIII de 11 Q tg Job." *Revue de Qumran* 9 (1978): 401–7.

Qimron, E. "Observations on the Reading of 'A Text About Joseph.'" *Revue de Qumran* 15 (1991–92): 603–4.

———. "On the List of False Prophets from Qumran." *Tarbiz* 63 (1994): 273–75 (Hebrew).

———. "Review of *Songs of the Sabbath Sacrifices: A Critical Edition* by C. Newsom." *Harvard Theological Review* 79 (1986): 349–71.

———. *The Temple Scroll: A Critical Edition with Extensive Reconstructions.* Jerusalem: Ben Gurion University of the Negev Press, Israel Exploration Society, 1996.

———. "The Text of CDC." In M. Broshi, ed., *The Damascus Document Reconsidered.* Jerusalem: Israel Exploration Society, 1994. Pp. 9–49.

———. "Toward a New Edition of the Genesis Apocryphon." *Journal for the Study of the Pseudepigrapha* 10 (1992): 11–18.

Richardson, H. N. "Some Notes on 1QSa." *Journal of Biblical Literature* 76 (1957): 108–22.

Sachau, C. E., ed. *The Chronology of Ancient Nations: An English Version of the Arabic Text of the Athar-ul-Bakiya of Albiruni.* London: Allen, 1879.

Schiffman, L. H. *The Eschatological Community of the Dead Sea Scrolls.* Atlanta: Scholars Press, 1989.

———. "Miqsat Ma'aseh Ha-Torah and the Temple Scroll." *Revue de Qumran* 14 (1991): 435–58.

———. "New Halakhic Texts from Qumran." *Hebrew Studies* 34 (1993): 21–33.

———. "Pharisaic and Sadducean Halakhah in Light of the Dead Sea Scrolls." *Dead Sea Discoveries* 1 (1994): 285–99.

———. *Reclaiming the Dead Sea Scrolls.* New York: Ktav, 1994.

———. *Sectarian Law in the Dead Sea Scrolls: Courts, Testimony, and the Penal Code.* Brown Judaic Studies 33. Chico, CA: Scholars Press, 1983.

Schuller, E. M. "Prayer, Hymnic, and Liturgical Texts from Qumran." In *The Community of the Renewed Covenant: The Notre Dame Symposium on the Dead Sea Scrolls.* Edited by E. Ulrich and J. VanderKam. Notre Dame, IN: University of Notre Dame Press, 1994. Pp. 153–71.

———. "Some Observations on Blessings of God in Texts from Qumran." In *Of Scribes and Scrolls: Studies on the Hebrew Bible, Intertestamental Judaism, and Christian Origins.* Edited by H. W. Attridge, J. J. Collins, and T. H. Tobin, S. J. Lanham, MD: University Press of America, 1990. Pp. 133–43.

Smith, M. H. "Ascent to the Heavens and Deification in 4QMa." In *Archaeology and History in the Dead Sea Scrolls: The New York University Conference in Memory of Yigael Yadin.* Edited by L. H. Schiffman. Sheffield: Sheffield Academic Press, 1990. Pp. 181–88.

Stone, M., and J. Greenfield. "Remarks on the Aramaic Testament of Levi." *Revue Biblique* 86 (1979): 214–30.

Strugnell, J. "Notes en marge du volume v des 'Discoveries in the Judaean Desert of Jordan.'" *Revue de Qumran* 7 (1970): 163–276.

Talmon, S. "Yom Hakippurim in the Habakkuk Scroll." *Biblica* 32 (1951): 549–63.

Tcherikover, V. *Hellenistic Civilization and the Jews.* New York: Atheneum, 1982.

VanderKam, J. "The Granddaughters and Grandsons of Noah." *Revue de Qumran* 16 (1994): 457–62.

Vermes, G. "The Oxford Forum for Qumran Research Seminar on the Rule of War from Cave 4 (4Q285)." *Journal of Jewish Studies* 43 (1992): 85–90.

———. "Preliminary Remarks on Unpublished Fragments of the Community Rule from Qumran Cave 4." *Journal of Jewish Studies* 42 (1991): 250–55.

———. "Qumran Forum Miscellanea I." *Journal of Jewish Studies* 43 (1992): 299–305.

———. "The So-Called King Jonathan Fragment (4Q448)." *Journal of Jewish Studies* 44 (1993): 294–300.

Wechsler, M. G., "Two Para-biblical Novellae from Qumran Cave 4: A re-evaluation of 4Q550." *Dead Sea Discoveries* 7 (2000): 130–72.

Weinert, F. D. "4Q159: Legislation for an Essene Community Outside of Qumran?" *Journal for the Study of Judaism* 5 (1974): 179–207.

Weinfeld, M. *The Organizational Pattern and the Penal Code of the Qumran Sect.* Göttingen: Vandenhoeck & Ruprecht, 1986.

Wernberg-Møller, P. *The Manual of Discipline.* Leiden: Brill, 1957.

Wise, M. O. *A Critical Study of the Temple Scroll from Qumran Cave 11.* Chicago: Oriental Institute, 1990.

———. "Dating the Teacher of Righteousness and the Floruit of His Movement." *Journal of Biblical Literature* 122 (2003): 53–87.

———. "4Q245 (psDan^{c}ar) and the High-Priesthood of Judas Maccabaeus." *Dead Sea Discoveries.* Forthcoming.

———. "A New Manuscript Join in the 'Festival of Wood Offering' (Temple Scroll XXIII)." *Journal of Near Eastern Studies* 47 (1988): 113–21.

———. "That Which Has Been Is That Which Shall Be: 4Q Florilegium and the miqdash adam." In *"Thunder in Gemini" and Other Essays on the History, Language, and Literature of Second Temple Palestine.* JSPS 15. Sheffield: JSOT Press, 1994. Pp. 152–85.

Wolters, A. "The Fifth Cache of the Copper Scroll: 'The Plastered Cistern of Manos.'" *Revue de Qumran* 13 (1988): 167–76.

———. "Literary Analysis and the Copper Scroll." In Z. J. Kapera, ed., *Intertestamental Essays in Honour of Josef Tadeusz Milik.* Kracow: Enigma Press, 1992. Pp. 239–52.

———. "Textual Notes on the Copper Scroll." Forthcoming.

Yadin, Y. "A Note on 4Q159 (Ordinances)." *Israel Expedition Journal* 18 (1968): 250–52.

———. *The Scroll of the War of the Sons of Light Against the Sons of Darkness.* Translated by Ch. Rabin. London: Oxford University Press, 1962.

Yardeni, A. "Remarks on the Priestly Blessing on Two Ancient Amulets from Jerusalem." *Vetus Testamentum* 41 (1991): 176–85.

Index of Manuscripts

Index of References

I. Hebrew Bible

Genesis

Exodus

Leviticus

Numbers

Deuteronomy

Joshua

Judges

Proverbs

Isaiah

Jeremiah

Lamentations

Ezekiel

II. Apocrypha/Pseudepigrapha

Jubilees

1 Maccabees

III. New Testament